Date Due

EL Exmo. e Illmo. S. D. Pedro de Moya de Contreras Arzobispo de México que en 1585 fue nombrado Visitador gral, goberno en Calidad de Virrey de 17 de Octe. de 1584. hasta el año de 1585.

PEDRO DE MOYA Y CONTRERAS

Archbishop of Mexico, Visitor-General, Inquisitor-General, and Viceroy, 1584, 1585. The combining in one person of the highest civil and ecclesiastical offices exemplifies the close union of Church and State in the Colonial régime.

CHURCH AND STATE IN LATIN AMERICA

A HISTORY OF POLITICO-ECCLESIASTICAL RELATIONS

By

J. LLOYD MECHAM, Ph.D.

PROFESSOR OF GOVERNMENT
THE UNIVERSITY OF TEXAS

CHAPEL HILL
THE UNIVERSITY OF NORTH CAROLINA PRESS
1934

PRINTED IN THE UNITED STATES OF AMERICA BY EDWARDS & BROUGHTON
COMPANY, RALEIGH, N. C.; BOUND BY L. H. JENKINS, INC., RICHMOND, VA.

To My Mother
LUCÍA PRECIADO MECHAM
IN LOVING GRATITUDE

Render to Caesar the things that are Caesar's, and to God the things that are God's.—JESUS.

Our era recognizes that religion is the work of the conscience and past eras believed that religion is the work of the state.— EMILIO CASTELAR.

PREFACE

The Latin-American nations, preponderatingly Roman Catholic in population, and, prior to the winning of independence, having lived for centuries under a common politico-religious régime, have espoused strikingly dissimilar ecclesiastical policies. In those republics one encounters the independent Church, the established Church, and the Church burdened under oppressive State control. The present study is an inquiry into the historical evolution of the political position of the Roman Catholic Church in Latin America. This analysis of the origins and development of the somewhat anomalous present-day legal status of the predominant faith in those countries is designed to give the answer to the question so often heard in the United States when the religious conflict in Mexico was raging: What about the Catholic Church in the other Latin-American countries?

The religious disorders in Mexico were not exceptional, for the Catholic Church suffered vicissitudes in many other countries of Central and South America. Anti-clericalism is a widespread movement, and in analyzing its causes and manifestations one can arrive at a clearer conception of the Mexican situation. Because of its greater importance and interest to the American public, the religious question in Mexico has been given a more lengthy and detailed treatment.

This is not a Church history. It is rather a discussion of politico-ecclesiastical relationships. Facts and events illustrative of this are mentioned; all others are intentionally omitted. Failure to include important incidents in the ecclesiastical histories of the various countries can probably be justified therefore, as not being pertinent to the subject under discussion. Nor was this book written to prove a thesis. It seeks only to shed a little additional light on the meaning of Latin-American anti-clericalism. The subject is of the author's own choosing; and in the preparation and publication of this book he received no support from any individual, institution, or organization. He has endeavored to present this subject objectively; yet when occasion demanded he has not avoided voicing personal judgment. The conclusions and opinions, which are intended to be impartial, are based upon careful study and evaluation of the facts. It is hoped that a critical examination of the work will not reveal bias.

The author acknowledges with gratitude valuable aid and suggestions which he received from Dr. Carlos E. Castañeda, Librarian of the Latin-American Collection in the University of Texas Library, and Dr. J. Fred Rippy of Duke University. He appreciates also, the courtesy of the editors of *The Catholic Historical Review* and *The Hispanic American Historical Review* in allowing him to make use of his own articles published in these periodicals. Finally, the author wishes to express the greatest indebtedness to his wife, Mabel Olive Mecham, for her invaluable aid in composition, typing and proof-reading.

J. LLOYD MECHAM.

Austin, Texas

TABLE OF CONTENTS

LIST OF ILLUSTRATIONS

CHAPTER I

CHURCH AND STATE DURING THE SPANISH RÉGIME IN AMERICA

Even as the antecedents of many of the political institutions of the Latin-American nations extend far back into the colonial period, so also distinctive features of the present-day civil status of the Roman Catholic Church in those countries originated under the colonial régime. During the Spanish domination the ecclesiastical power was coetaneous with the colonial system and was deeply rooted. This affiliation of the civil and religious authorities was known as the royal patronage of the Indies, or *real patronato de las Indias*. No adequate comprehension of the difficult Church problem which confronted the nascent republics when embarking upon their independent careers, and which, furthermore, still disturbs some of them, is possible without an understanding of the nature of the relationship which existed between the Spanish crown and the Catholic Church in America.

From an early period there existed two schools of thought on the subject of the *real patronato de las Indias*. They might be called the "regalists" and the "canonists," or "ultramontanists." Briefly, the regalists believed that royal patronage was laical in origin and therefore inherent in temporal sovereignty. The canonists contended that patronage was originally not laical but spiritual, and was founded solely on pontifical concessions which were rescindable but non-transferable. An eminent proponent of this latter theory says: "The pontifical concession of the *patronato de Indias* to the kings of Spain was a simple, juridic, unilateral act produced *motu proprio*. There were no concordats, contracts, or decrees, but only direct concession from the Holy See."[1] This conflict of interpretations became a subject of far more than mere academic interest when the Spanish colonies in America put

---

[1] Faustino J. Legón, *Doctrina y Ejercicio del Patronato Nacional* (Buenos Aires, 1920), p. 186.

off the control of the mother country. Then the paramount question became: Do the republics inherit the patronal rights previously exercised by the Spanish crown? The regalists said Yes! The canonists said No! Innumerable treatises have been written to support the two divergent viewpoints, yet no generally accepted conclusion has been reached, and it is highly improbable that any is possible. It is not without significance that the papacy has never deviated from its position that *patronato de Indias* was not inherent in sovereignty and consequently could not be inherited by the infant republics. Furthermore, several of the new states at different periods in their histories have tacitly, through the negotiation of concordats, recognized the papal claim. Keeping in mind, therefore, this very complex problem, certain features of which will be discussed in the next chapter, we shall now address ourselves to the task of explaining the nature of ecclesiastical patronage in Spain and the Indies.

Patronage is commonly regarded as the power to nominate or present a cleric for installation in a vacant benefice. The right of canonical institution to major benefices belongs to the pope; in the case of minor benefices it belongs to a bishop or to other prelates. Presentation, in reality, is only a part of ecclesiastical patronage, for the latter includes the following: (1) the right of presentation; (2) honorary rights; (3) utilitarian rights; and (4) obligations. The most important of these is the first i.e., presentation or nomination to an ecclesiastical dignity. When a vacancy occurs in a benefice the patron proposes the name of a suitable candidate to the ecclesiastical authority empowered with the right of collation. The right of nomination is the very essence of patronage. The honorary rights include such distinctions as the granting of precedence to the patron and his family in various religious ceremonies, the according of seats of honor to them, special prayers said in their behalf, and the distinction of being buried beneath the high altar. Utilitarian privileges are found in the moral obligation of the favored religious establishment of coming to the financial aid of the patron should he ever be in straits. Moreover, utilitarian rights often included the concession to the patron of first fruits, tithes, and other incomes from the benefice. Certain obligations devolve upon the patron. He must watch over his benefice and be ever ready to defend it against attack. Patronal obligations of this character were a matter of serious moment in the days of the feudal régime. The patron's interest in caring for the welfare of his benefice gave him no authority to interfere in the administration of its property or the discharge of its spiritual duties.

According to Ribadeneyra,[2] who was an outstanding exponent of regalism during the colonial period, royal patronage was laical. Patronage, he said, derived its nature not from its source but from its possessor. Therefore, when a laic possessed it, it was temporal. He contended further that it need not necessarily be an apostolic concession, for from the earliest days of Christianity the founders enjoyed the natural right of patronage over churches established by them. The first pontifical document in which this right of nomination or presentation was called the "right of patronage" was a decree of Pope Nicholas II in the sixth century.[3] The mere fact that there is no record of the papacy ever declaring the founder of a benefice incapable of enjoying the rights of patronage seems to indicate that this right was acquired by the mere act of founding or endowing. The popes, said Ribadeneyra, by their concessions added nothing to a natural right; indeed, the title bestowed by the pope was in fact superfluous for there was no necessity of confirming, as a reward, the temporal founders in a privilege which they were entitled to in simple justice. When Pedro of Aragon renounced the royal patronage and placed it in the hands of Innocent III, the Aragonese resisted, claiming that this right did not belong to the royal person but to the nation. This incident illustrates that the people in the medieval period believed that patronage was inherent in sovereignty.[4]

The above views are vigorously denied by the canonists—particularly the claim that the mere act of founding a church brings

---

[2] Antonio Joaquín de Ribadeneyra, *Manual Compendio de el Regio Patronato Indiano* (Madrid, 1755), pp. 70-72. In addition to Ribadeneyra, Pedro Frasso (*De Regio Patronato,* Madrid, 1677) and Juan de Solórzano y Pereyra (*Política Indiana,* Madrid, 1776) were the foremost lay defenders of *regalismo.*

[3] Matías Gómez Zamora, *Regio Patronato Español é Indiano* (Madrid, 1897), p. 10.

[4] Lucas Ayarragaray, *La Iglesia en América y la Dominación Española* (Buenos Aires, 1920), p. 171.

to the founder willy-nilly the right of patronage. The fount and source of the duties and privileges known as patronage, they contend, is the Holy See, which, having supreme jurisdiction over the Church, can do anything it desires for the advancement of its vital interests. In consequence the Apostolic Father has been accustomed to reward, *motu proprio* (of his own free will), the performance of a certain class of good works, like the founding of temples and the establishment of pious works, by bestowing the patronal concessions. The common designation of patronage in papal decretals as *ius spirituali annexum* indicates that the rights of the patron pertain to the spiritual order. Although patronage is generally called a right, says Zamora, it is more exactly a *concession*. The efficient cause of this concession is the ecclesiastical authority; the final cause, the gratitude of the Church and the desire to encourage religion and the cult. In sum, the canonists contend that patronage is a purely spiritual matter, a simple apostolic tolerance revocable at the will of the grantor, notwithstanding the fact that sovereigns have exercised it like an inherent part of their secular sovereignty.[5]

Thus, with respect to the essential nature of patronage in general, there are two divergent views. It has been suggested that a compromise might be effected by acknowledging that patronage derives its validity from both spiritual and temporal sources. It is civil, says an authority, because it exists before the ecclesiastical power recognizes it or gives its free consent, but it is likewise canonical because it is dependent on explicit sanction by the supreme authority of the Church.[6] No attempt will be made, at least at this stage of the discussion, to settle the issue. This must wait upon a description of the nature of the *real patronato Español* and the *real patronato de Indias*.

In Spain during the first six centuries after the disappearance of the immediate successors of the Apostles, it was the customary practice for the bishops to be designated by both the clergy and

---

[5] Zamora, *op. cit.*, p. 143; Joaquín Rodríguez Bravo, *Estudios Constitucionales* (Santiago de Chile, 1888), p. 21; Juan Manuel Estrada, *La Iglesia y el Estado* (Buenos Aires, 1929), pp. 68-74.

[6] Cesáreo Chacaltana, *Patronato Nacional Argentino* (Buenos Aires, 1885), p. 62.

the people.[7] Until the time of Constantine the Great, this practice was necessary because of the obvious circumstances which did not allow to the greater number of Christian groups frank communion with the successors of St. Peter, in whom was vested theoretically the exclusive right of naming and confirming bishops. With the assurance of protection and the establishment of a hierarchy of bishops and ecclesiastical provinces, the pope, who enjoyed the plenitude of power over all benefices which only he could create, in order to stimulate interest in the new religion and filial attachment to its functionaries, encouraged the practice of entrusting the elections of prelates to the clergy and the people of the city where the vacant see was located. Pope Leo I declared that "a bishop should not be given to a people who did not want him." For that reason he deemed it best to leave the election of bishops to the people and the clergy. During the first six centuries in Spain there were numerous instances of elections by clergy and the people, but none of royal nomination. There were also numerous cases of direct action of the pontiff in the creation of dioceses and in the institution of bishops. Prior to the invasion of the Arian Goths, therefore, the bishops of Spain were elected by the clergy in the presence of the people, and later under the aegis of the princes. During this period the relations with Rome were most intimate. The direct intervention of the populace in the designation of bishops frequently degenerated into strife. These riots gave the temporal lords pretext to intervene in protecting the canonical elections. At first their intervention was limited and legitimate; later the lords began to exercise greater influence in the elections, especially after the ruin of the Western Empire, and eventually they arrogated to themselves a dominant influence in the naming of prelates.[8]

---

[7] Regarding the intervention of the people in the elections some canonists claim that the suffrage of the people, presided over by the clergy, is required by divine right. They cite as evidence the election of the seven deacons (Acts 6:3). Others answer that this doctrine does not agree with historical facts, for in most cases the Apostles acted directly and by themselves. (Legón, *op. cit.*, p. 68.) For an account of the early episcopal elections see Ernest Renan, *Histoire des Origens du Christianisme* (Paris, n.d.), VI, 93 ff., and Joaquín Aguirre, *Curso de Disciplina Eclesiástica General* (Madrid, 1871), III, *passim*.

[8] Rafael Altamira y Crevea, *Historia de España y de la Civilización Española* (Barcelona, 1913-1914), I, 123; Legón, *op. cit.*, p. 69; Zamora, *op. cit.*, p. 166;

In the Arian Church the influence of the crown was most pronounced. Consequently, when the Arian heresy came to an end under Reccard the old practices of the Arian Gothic kings in ecclesiastical matters were continued. They exercised the prerogative of both universal patronage and a quasi-absolute government over the churches of the kingdom. Not only did they intervene in all the elections to ecclesiastical benefices, but they convoked national and provincial councils, established new episcopacies, and outlined the limits of the same. As can be readily imagined, the relations between Spain and Rome during this period were not intimate, although the Spanish Church, after the abolition of the Arian heresy, always recognized the pope as head.[9] Indeed, the intimacies of the first period before the Gothic invasion were not restored until the time of Hildebrand the Great.

With the invasion of the Moors the exercise of the patronage was suspended until the reconquest began to gain headway. Then, when the ancient sees were liberated, the princes appointed bishops to occupy them. In general the Castilian kings followed the Visigothic tradition in their ecclesiastical relations. They founded and restored episcopal sees, elected and deposed bishops with just cause, convened councils, and judged ecclesiastical *pleitos* or causes. The right of the king to elect bishops was exercised sometimes directly, sometimes indirectly by permitting the cathedral chapter to elect, but in the event of the latter procedure the king had to confirm the election, otherwise it was considered invalid.[10]

Thanks to the efforts of Gregory VII and the other Cluniac reformers, steps were taken in the twelfth century to make the authority of the pope felt in Spain in the election of bishops and in matters of discipline. Owing to the fact that the Spanish monarchies were weak and decentralized, and that the ecclesiastical holdings had not been feudalized to the extent that they were in northern Europe, Spain was spared the disorders of the German

---

T. Ayuso, "El privilegio de los reyes de España en la presentación de obispos," in *Razón y Fé* (Madrid, 1904), II, 469.

[9] Zamora, *op. cit.,* pp. 179-180; Ribadeneyra, *op. cit.,* pp. 43-44. For a description of the royal control over the Arian Church, see Legón, *op. cit.,* pp. 121-122, and Aloysius K. Ziegler, *Church and State in Visigothic Spain* (Washington, D. C., 1930).

[10] Ribadeneyra, *op. cit.,* pp. 44-45; Altamira, *op. cit.,* I, 438-439.

investiture conflict.[11] Remarkably enough, the kings of Castile co-
operated with the papacy in abolishing their old privileges over
the Church. They did not capitulate absolutely, however, for they
insisted that the acts of the pope, to have effect in Spain, must
receive the royal assent. Thus, as a result of Cluniac influence
and the policy of Gregory VII, the Spanish Church became dependent on the papacy and it was freed from the interference of
the civil power in ecclesiastical business. Thereafter the pope maintained in Spain legates and representatives who presided at general councils and intervened in Church questions. Gregory IX
decreed that bishops in Castile were to be elected by majority
vote of the cathedral chapter, and the right of confirmation was
to be vested in the metropolitan. The disorders at the elections
finally made it necessary for the pope, in the fourteenth century,
to rule that confirmation of bishops belonged to the Roman pontiff.
The question of episcopal nomination was settled sooner and more
radically in Aragon than in Castile. Jaime II agreed, over the
protests of the cathedral chapters, to entrust the elections to the
pope himself.[12] Thus in Spain by the fourteenth century, the right
of universal patronage was lodged in the Holy See where according to canonists it originally resided, after having been exercised
respectively by the people, the clergy, and the temporal rulers.

Particular patronage continued to flourish in Spain after universal patronage came to an end. Its essential nature needs to be

---

[11] The great controversy between Gregory VII and the German emperors
Henry IV and Henry V centered about the imperial practice of granting to
bishops and abbots, besides their titles, the possessions which constituted their
benefices and the political rights which they were to exercise. Investiture meant
that on the death of a bishop or abbot, the king was accustomed to select a successor and bestow on him the ring and staff, symbolic of his office, with these
words: "Accept this church." Gregory VII determined to destroy all lay pretentions to the administration of the Church, and so, in 1075, withdrew from the
king the right of disposing of bishoprics in future and relieved all lay persons
of the investiture of churches. The resultant conflict was finally settled by the
Concordat of Worms, 1122. The decision at Worms was a compromise, for a
distinction was made between the ecclesiastical and secular elements in the
appointment of bishops and abbots. The emperor renounced investiture with
ring and staff and allowed all churches liberty of election and free consecration.
The Pope conceded to the lay authority the right of investing with the sceptre,
signifying the granting of the temporalities.

[12] Altamira, op. cit., I, 124, 439; Zamora, op. cit., p. 245.

described to obviate confusion. From an early date in the history of the Christian Church it became the custom to make concessions to the founders of religious establishments. At first these privileges were conceded only to ecclesiastics. The first recorded instance was a conciliar decree of 441 which provided that bishops who founded churches in foreign dioceses with their own property or that of their diocese should enjoy the right of electing the ecclesiastics of the new churches. When patronage was conceded to laymen it was only honorary at first. For example, the patron's name or coat of arms was displayed on the church in a prominent place. Later the founder acquired the right of presentation. Originally the words "patron" and "rights of patronage" were not used, but "founders" or "builders." In the time of Justinian the rights of patronage were purely personal, that is, non-transmittable. The transmission to heirs was a later step, but when it occurred cannot be determined exactly. According to early authorities the real reason for the introduction of the right of patronage was not only to excite the faithful to found and construct churches, but also to express the gratitude of the Church to the founders.[13]

Some writers place the date of the Spanish origins of the practice at 655 when the Synod of Toledo granted to laymen the right of presentation to each church erected by them. The reconquest of ancient sees from the Moors and the establishment of new ecclesiastical districts in the conquered territory gave impetus to the development of particular patronage. Gregory VII in 1073 recognized conquest as the title to patronage, following the example of his predecessor, Alexander II, who had conceded to the kings of Aragon and their successors the right of presentation to the churches retaken from the Moors or those newly erected in the reconquered territory. These concessions of the Holy See were regarded as recompense for the incessant zeal which the kings of Spain displayed in the wars of the Moorish Crusade. Instead of working against this type of lay privilege, Gregory VII condemned the opposition and resistance of the ecclesiastics of Aragon to the grants made by Alexander II. Since the resistance continued, Pope Urban II in 1095 confirmed the grant of patronage over all places conquered from the Moors and over newly founded churches

---

[13] Legón, *op. cit.,* pp. 77-79.

excepting episcopal churches. The king was also conceded first fruits and tithes of these foundations. The Fourth Lateran Council declared, "It is not just to destroy the legitimate rights of patrons."[14] From the time of Alfonso I of Castile to the conquest of Granada the Spanish monarchs exercised the privilege of particular patronage.

Some authors attempt to find in the reconquest the real origin of royal patronage. Canon law does not recognize the reconquest as sufficient title for acquiring the patronage. If it was exercised in Spain its foundation had to be based in some special concession or some pontifical privilege. When France reacquired Roussillon in the seventeenth century the Holy See refused to recognize the right of patronage in the form enjoyed while the province was in the possession of Spain. The same principle applied when the Catholic people conquered regions inhabited by the infidel, save that they converted the mosques into churches, endowed them, and in that case acquired the patronage by foundation.

During the last two centuries of the reconquest the question of the election of bishops continued to be an element of dispute between pope and king. The general practice of the thirteenth century was that the cathedral chapters nominated the bishops, the king approved, and the metropolitan confirmed. But by virtue of papal action in the next century, the right of confirmation was taken from the metropolitan by the pope. The kings, however, did not cease to intervene in elections. Alfonso X of Castile reasserted in royal decrees of 1328 and 1348 that it was an ancient custom in Spain for the Castilian kings to give consent to capitular elections of bishops and prelates. He based his claim on three factors: (1) the kings reconquered the territory from the Moors, extended Christianity, and converted mosques into churches; (2) they founded new churches; and (3) they endowed other churches. Successors of Alfonso made like declarations, always being very careful to assure to the Church new facilities for carrying on its august mission. Thus, while they prescribed ways of filling offices, the kings of Castile ordered that all pontifical dispositions should be faithfully complied with in the kingdom, and ecclesiastical lands and persons were accorded special *fueros* or privileges.

[14] Ayarragaray, *op. cit.*, pp. 152, 159-160; Zamora, *op. cit.*, pp. 17-18, 194, 220.

Several notable papal documents of the middle fifteenth century considerably extended the royal control over the Church in Spain. Pope Eugene IV by a concordat, in 1444, conferred upon the king of Aragon the privilege of appointing to lesser benefices. In 1448 Pope Nicholas V conceded to the king of Castile the right of nomination to the greater dignities in fifty-one ecclesiastical benefices in Castile and León. In the same year the Grand Master of the Order of Santiago was given the right of nominating to thirty ecclesiastical benefices. In 1455 Pope Calixtus III confirmed the royal right of presentation in Guipúzcoa and Vizcaya. Furthermore the pope agreed that, in electing archbishops, bishops, and abbots for benefices in Castile and Aragon he would elect only persons suitable and acceptable to the king. The kings interpreted this privilege broadly, implying that it was necessary to present candidates to them in order that they might pass upon their suitability.[15]

By the time of Ferdinand and Isabella the Spanish sovereigns possessed in the traditions of the Gothic Church, in the religious character of the Moorish wars, and in numerous pontifical concessions, a juridic base upon which to establish their patronage over many churches. But it was particular and not universal patronage, and it was not easy to extend the royal authority over all the sees and prebends of the kingdom. The Catholic Kings in their efforts to consolidate the monarchy resolved to prevent at all cost the election of bishops in Rome. They insisted, at least, on their right of being informed and of approving the elections. When Pope Sixtus IV in 1482, without reference to the Spanish crown, appointed a foreigner to the bishopric of Cuenca, Ferdinand and Isabella protested that this was contrary to an earlier law (1476), which prohibited such a practice. When they threatened to convoke a general council to reform the Church and make it more harmonious with the interests of the state, the pope yielded and conceded to the Catholic Kings the right to supplicate in favor of candidates whom they considered qualified. Notwithstanding the pope's promise the case of Cuenca was repeated in Seville in 1485. As a consequence of this difficulty, the Conde de Tendilla, the Spanish envoy at Rome, secured from Pope Innocent VIII a notable

---

[15] Ayarragaray, *op. cit.,* pp. 151-152, 160; Altamira, *op. cit.,* II, 90.

concession to the Spanish demands. In a bull published in 1486 the pope granted to the Catholic Kings the right of universal patronage over all the benefices whether conquered or founded later within the Kingdom of Granada. Furthermore the crown was conceded the perpetual *diezmos*, or tithes, which the converted Moors had to pay to the Church. In 1494 Alexander VI confirmed the above bull and granted the crown one-third of all the tithes collected not only in Granada but even throughout the monarchy.[16] The pope declared that he was motivated in making these grants because of the religious zeal of the Catholic Kings and their conquest of Granada from the Crescent. According to Zamora the bull of Innocent VIII in 1486 was the first pontifical grant of universal patronage in Spain.[17]

The famous bulls of Alexander VI and Julius II which granted patronal rights in the Indies did not affect the Spanish kingdom proper. The next step to be noted in the development of the *real patronato Español* was the grant of Adrian VI in 1523. At that time the pope conceded to the Spanish king the right of patronage over all the consistoral benefices in Spain. It was specifically declared that the patronage thus conceded was "of the same nature, vigor, force, and privilege as that which appertained to the kings by virtue of foundation or endowment." Clement VII in March, 1530, extended the patronage to all the cathedral churches. In 1536 these grants were confirmed by Paul III in consideration of the services of Charles V in the siege of Tunis and the saving of Christians at that place. When Portugal was under the crown of Spain (1580-1640), Pope Urban VIII extended the *real patronato Español* to Portugal and the Algarves.[18]

The nature and scope of the *real patronato Español* was extremely complicated. Since it was based on traditional practices and numerous grants, its complex character is understandable. Furthermore, the effectiveness of its enforcement varied in accordance with the strength or weakness of the Spanish sovereigns. The situation became acute when the first of the Bourbon kings, Philip

---

[16] P. Leturia, "El Origen Histórico del Patronato de Indias," in *Razón y Fé*, Vol. 78, pp. 25-26.

[17] Zamora, *op. cit.*, p. 285.

[18] *Ibid.*, p. 249; Ayarragaray, *op. cit.*, p. 165.

V, brought to Spain new ideas regarding the prerogatives of the crown and the centralization of power within it. In the Concordat of 1737 a weak attempt was made to define the legal relationships of Church and State. It remained for Pope Benedict XIV and Ferdinand VI to agree, in the Concordat of 1753, on the exact nature of the Spanish patronage. The concordat was the means of reëstablishing the traditional friendly relations between Rome and Madrid, and it continued to regulate the relations of Church and State in Spain until 1851.[19]

The pope, in the concordat, recognized the right of patronage in the Spanish crown without any limitation other than the reservation to himself of the privilege of election to fifty-two enumerated benefices in Spain. There was put into writing what was meant by *real patronato Español* concerning which there had been much doubt and controversy. But since there was no question about the *real patronato de Indias,* because of the specific pontifical concessions, the concordat expressly excluded the Church in America from the scope of its terms, as follows: "there having been no controversy concerning the nomination by the Catholic Kings of archbishops, bishops, and vacant benefices in the Indies."[20] Thus the control of the crown over the Church in the Indies was sanctioned and reconfirmed by this concordat. Thenceforward, however, there was vested and recognized in the Spanish kings the right of universal patronage over all benefices of the kingdom with the exception of those reserved to the pope.

The union of altar and throne was much more intimate in America than in Spain. Indeed, it is difficult to conceive of a more absolute jurisdiction than that which the kings of Spain exercised over all the ecclesiastical affairs of the Indies. The control of the Church by the crown and its representatives in America was regarded as the most valuable of the regal attributes. Ribadeneyra describes the *real patronato de Indias* as "la piedra más rica, la más preciosa Margarita de su real diadema."[21] The patronage of

---

[19] Zamora, *op. cit.,* p. 285.

[20] Dalmacio Vélez Sarsfield, *Relaciones del Estado con la Iglesia en la Antigua América Española* (Buenos Aires, 1889), p. 42. For the text of the concordat of 1753, see *Nueva Recopilación* (Madrid, 1775), I, 45-65.

[21] Ribadeneyra, *op. cit.,* pp. 3-4.

the Indies existed both independent of and supplementary to that of Spain. It was based largely (in the estimation of the canonists, *absolutely*) on the following pontifical documents: (1) the bull of Alexander VI, May 4, 1493, which conceded to the Catholic Kings the dominion of the Indies and the exclusive privilege of Christianizing the natives; (2) the bull of Alexander VI, November 16, 1501, which granted to the Spanish crown the tithes and first fruits of the churches of the Indies; and (3) the bull of Julius II, July 28, 1508, which gave to the kings of Spain the right of universal patronage over the Catholic Church in the Indies. The circumstances under which these bulls were granted and the general nature of their content will be examined.

When Columbus reported the discovery of the Indies to Ferdinand and Isabella, the Catholic Kings appealed to the pope to grant them title to the newly discovered lands. In presenting their petition they insisted that their most ardent aim was to extend the dominion of the Roman Catholic faith. With respect to Queen Isabella this may be accepted as the truth, for in her letter of instructions to Columbus (Barcelona, May 29, 1493), she declared as her first care the conversion of the natives of the new lands. Since the papacy enjoyed such great moral and political authority, the temporal rulers sought its aid to prevent other Christian princes from wresting their conquests from them. Portugal at that time was actively engaged in exploration, and it would have been easy for serious conflict to arise between the two Iberian crowns. Thus Ferdinand and Isabella sought the papal confirmation, not so much to legitimize their possession of the new lands as to avoid differences with Portugal. They felt that this could be best accomplished by papal intervention. Moreover, since the task of Christianization, which the Spanish rulers were anxious to assume, constituted a real "apostleship," it was natural and necessary that it should be done under the authority of the successor to the Prince of the Apostles.[22]

The pope, because of the great distance which separated Rome from America, as well as the lack of means to equip expeditions,

---

[22] Leturia, *op. cit.*, pp. 28-29; Antonio María Fabié, *Ensayo Histórico de la Legislación Española* (Madrid, 1896), p. 19.

was, obviously, unable to Christianize the Indies and establish there an ecclesiastical régime independent of the temporal power. The sovereigns of Spain, on the other hand, were the only ones capable of undertaking the establishment of the transatlantic Church. Thus, in proof of his impotence, and to give impetus to the proselyting zeal of the Spanish kings, Pope Alexander VI acquiesced in their requests. By the bull *inter caetera*, May 4, 1493, there was conceded to the Catholic Kings title to the lands discovered or to be discovered to the west of a line drawn from pole to pole and distant one hundred leagues west of the Azores and Cape Verde Islands. A condition attached to the papal grant was the assumption by the Catholic Kings of the obligation to prosecute missionary work in the new lands.[23]

Some writers detect in the exclusive privilege granted to the kings of Spain to select and control the sending of missionaries to America, a grant of the right of ecclesiastical patronage. This interpretation sounds logical, for indeed, the exclusive right of evangelization was as absolute a delegation of authority as it was in the power of the pope to bestow. According to Ribadeneyra this bull granted the Spanish kings authority to exercise jurisdiction in all matters relating to ecclesiastical government in the Indies, "with full and complete power to act of their own free wills in all that seems to them to be most convenient for the spiritual government."[24] By the bull *inter caetera* the Spanish sovereigns were created a species of apostolic vicars with authority over spiritual matters in America.

On May 4, 1493, Alexander VI published another bull known as *eximae devotionis*. To the Catholic Kings he granted "all of the concessions, privileges, exemptions, rights, liberties, immunities, and indults" that had been granted by other pontiffs to the kings of Portugal in their overseas possessions. The most notable of these bulls was that of Pope Calixtus in 1456, which conceded the right of presentation. In addition, the same bull granted to the Order of Christ complete spiritual jurisdiction from Cape Bojador "over

[23] Francisco Javier Hernáez, *Colección de Bulas, Breves, y otros Documentos relativos á la Iglesia de América y Filipinas* (Brussels, 1879), I, 12-14.

[24] Ribadeneyra, *op. cit.*, pp. 58-60.

all Guinea unto the East Indies."[25] Pope Alexander declared that his purpose in bestowing the great privilege upon the Spanish sovereigns was to recognize and reward their Christian zeal in liberating Granada from the Moors, and in sending Columbus to distant lands to discover more people who might be won to the Catholic fold. It is possible that Alexander's nationality, he being an Aragonese of illustrious family, may have influenced him to favor the Spanish monarchs.

On November 16, 1501, Pope Alexander VI published another bull, also called *eximae devotionis* but to be distinguished from that of 1493. This bull most canonists regard as the third great pontifical concession of the *patronato de Indias*. The text of the bull was as follows:

Alexander, bishop, servant of the servants of God: to the Catholic sovereigns of Spain—Ferdinand the king, dearest son in Christ, and to Elizabeth (Isabella) the queen, dearest daughter in Christ, health and Apostolic blessing. The sincerity of your devotion and the unswerving faith with which you honor us and the Roman Church, merit, and not unworthily, that your wishes, especially those relating to the spread of the Catholic faith, and the overthrow of infidel and barbarous nations, should be freely and promptly granted. Indeed, on your behalf, a petition recently laid before us sets forth that, compelled by pious devotion for the spread of the Catholic faith, you greatly desire—inasmuch as quite recently, and not without great expense and effort on your part, you began and from day to day continue to do more toward the capture and recovery of the islands and regions aforesaid, it will be incumbent upon you to incur heavy expenses and undergo great perils, it is expedient for the conservation and maintenance of the said islands, after their capture and recovery by you, and for the defraying of the expenses necessary for the conservation and maintenance of the same,—you should be empowered to exact and levy tithes on the inhabitants of the aforesaid islands and dwellers therein for the time being. On this account we have been humbly petitioned on your behalf to deign through our apostolic graciousness to make in the premises suitable provision for you and your state. Therefore yearning most eagerly for the spread and increase of that same faith particularly in our own days, we commend in the Lord your loving and praise-

---

[25] Hernáez, *op. cit.*, I, 15-16. The validity of this bull has been contested because of its use, in 1456, of the name "East Indies." (Leturia, *op. cit.*, pp. 28-29.)

worthy purpose, and being favorably disposed thereto we hereby through our apostolic power in virtue of these presents do as a special favor grant to you and your successors for the time being that in the aforesaid islands after their capture and recovery, (as observed) you may receive a tithe from the inhabitants thereof and the dwellers therein for the time being, and levy the same freely and lawfully, providing after dioceses shall there be established (whereon we charge your consciences as well as your successors'), you first from your own and their estate shall really and effectively devise a sufficient revenue for the establishment of churches in those islands through you and your aforsaid successors, whereby the incumbents of the same and their administrators may support themselves suitably, carry on the necessary work of those churches for the time being, as well as celebrate rightly the divine worship of Almighty God, and fulfill all diocesan requirements.   The Lateran Council, other apostolic constitutions and ordinances or other decrees, to the contrary notwithstanding. Let no one then infringe this our grant, nor dare with rashness to contravene its provisions. But should any one presume to set it at naught, let him recognize that he has thereby incurred the displeasure of Almighty God, and of the Blessed Apostles Peter and Paul. Given at Rome at St. Peter's, in the year of the incarnation of our Lord one thousand five hundred and one, the sixteenth day of November, the tenth year of our Pontificate.[26]

The bull of 1501 increased the patronal privileges of the Spanish monarchs by granting them the use of the tithes in America. In return for the grant the crown assumed the obligation of defraying from the royal treasury all the expenses incidental to the maintenance and propagation of the faith. In this concession can be detected another phase of the patronage, the utilitarian right, to be specific. The pope declared that the occasion of this great concession was to compensate the crown for the heavy expenses incurred by the temporal and spiritual conquest. This pontifical disposition bestowed a special character on the patronage of the Spanish kings over the Church in America which was even more comprehensive than that of Granada. In Spain the Church was supported by tithes and special rents; in America these revenues went to the crown and the Church was, in theory at least, supported by royal appropriations and regular endowments.

---

[26] N. A. N. Cleven, *Readings in Hispanic American History* (New York, 1927), pp. 248-249. For text in Spanish, see Zamora, *op. cit.*, pp. 299-301.

Although the royal authority over the Church in America was extensive, because of the bulls of 1493 and 1501, nevertheless Julius II was reluctant to recognize the patronal rights contained in the bulls of his predecessor, Alexander VI. King Ferdinand, on the other hand, entertained little doubt that the rights of patronage had been conferred, although not explicitly expressed. The question came to an issue in 1504 following Queen Isabella's request that an archbishopric and two bishoprics be created in the island of Española. Julius II on November 15, 1504, acquiesced in sanctioning the foundation of the sees, but he did not mention the rights of presentation and the royal claim to the tithes. This meant that the ecclesiastical rents belonged to the future prelates of the sees to administer just the same as they did in the dioceses of Spain. The bull was a patent and unwarranted violation of established policy, and can be explained only as an attempted stroke at independence by Julius II.

Ferdinand, who firmly believed in the patronal concessions of the earlier bulls, was not the type of king to acquiesce in such a policy. When the bull was received it was withheld and the sees in Española were not allowed to be founded. Ferdinand, who was a regent of Castile, now that Isabella was dead, wrote to Francisco de Rojas, the Spanish ambassador in Rome, the following instructions: "I order you to look into the bulls that were issued for the creation and provision of an archbishop and bishop in Española; in them there is not conceded to us the patronage of the said archbishop and bishop, nor of the *dignidades* and canons, prebends, and benefices with curate and without curate, which ought to be erected in the said isle of Española. It is necessary that His Holiness concede the said patronage perpetually to me and the kings who succeed to the kingdoms of Castile and Aragon, since no mention was made of it in the aforesaid bulls, as was the case of these (bulls) of the kingdom of Granada."[27]

The demands of Ferdinand were later incorporated in three petitions to the pope. He asked that, (1) there be express grant of the right of patronage for the erection and provision of all ecclesiastical benefices; (2) those appointed to benefices should

---

[27] Leturia, *op. cit.*, pp. 31-32.

2

not receive more than that part of the tithes which was appor-
tioned to them by the king; and (3) the king should have the
power to determine the territorial limits of the dioceses. Ferdinand
demanded that these rights be made to apply to all the Indies,
and that the pope act immediately. The pontiff, however, would
not be hastened, and nothing was done until 1508, when Ferdinand
returned to the regency of Castile after the death of Philip I. He
then declared with his customary vigor that he would not permit
the erection of new sees in America until the right of royal patronage was recognized; that is, until the concessions of Alexander VI
were confirmed.[28]

Eventually Julius II capitulated, and by the bull *universalis
ecclesiae*, July 28, 1508, he conceded universal patronage in the
Indies to the Spanish crown. Whether it be true that this bull
granted for the first time the *real patronato de Indias*, or whether
it merely recognized and reconfirmed rights bestowed in earlier
bulls, it is nevertheless generally regarded as the principal documentary evidence of the legal right of the Spanish sovereigns to
exercise jurisdiction over the Catholic Church in America.[29] Because of its prime importance, therefore, it is presented here
in extenso:

Julius, bishop, servant of the servants of God. We, presiding by
divine choice, although unworthily, over the government of the Universal Church, do concede voluntarily to the Catholic kings principally
those things that augment their honor and glory, and contribute effectively to the benefit and security of their dominions. Since our beloved
son in Christ, Ferdinand, illustrious king of Aragon, and also of Sicily,
and Isabella, of cherished memory, Queen of Castile and León, after
having expelled the Moors from Spain, crossed the ocean and planted
the Cross in unknown lands, and subjugated many islands and places,
and among these being one very rich and extremely populous named
New Spain, thereby fulfilling to the extent of their ability the saying
in omnem terram exivit sonus eorum—Therefore, we, in order that it
(New Spain) might be purged of false and pernicious rites, and the
true religion be planted there, have acceded to the most urgent requests

---

[28] *Ibid.*, p. 32.

[29] Ayarragaray (*op. cit.*, p. 162), in commenting on the importance of this
bull, writes eloquently of "the magnitude of its conception and the loftiness of
its language."

of the king and queen, and do hereby erect for the greater glory of the name of Christ, a metropolitan church in Ayguacen, and two cathedrals in Maguen and Bayunen, and if the converts imbued by the new faith should attempt to found any church or pious place, they should do so in such a way as not to injure the new religion or the temporal dominions of the king.

In view of the fact that the said Ferdinand, who is also at present governor-general of the kingdoms of Castile and León, and our most cherished daughter in Christ, Juana, queen of the same kingdoms and daughter of the aforementioned Ferdinand, wish that no church, monastery, or pious place be erected or founded either in the islands and lands already possessed, or in those subsequently acquired, without their express consent and that of their successors; and considering that since it is convenient to those kings that the persons who preside over churches and monasteries be faithful and acceptable to them, they desire that they be conceded the right of patronage and of the presentation of qualified persons for both the metropolitan and cathedral churches already erected, or to be erected in the future, and for all the other ecclesiastical benefices inside of a year of their vacancy, and also for inferior benefices; and in case the *ordinario* should refuse without legitimate cause to grant the one presented with canonical institution inside of ten days, any other bishop, at the request of the king should grant it. We, appreciating that these privileges increase the honor, beauty and security of those islands, and also of the said kingdoms, whose kings are always devout and faithful to the Apostolic See, and heeding the reiterated demands made on us by King Ferdinand and Queen Juana, after mature deliberation with our brothers the cardinals of the Holy Roman Church, and with their advice, by these presents we concede with apostolic authority, other constitutions, ordinances, and laws to the contrary notwithstanding, to the said Ferdinand and Juana, and to the future kings of Castile and León, that nobody without their consent can construct or build in the above mentioned islands, now possessed or to be possessed, large churches; and we concede the right of patronage and of presenting qualified persons to cathedral churches, monasteries, *dignidades,* collegiates, and other ecclesiastical benefices and pious places in this manner: respecting benefices that are instituted in the consistory, the presentation is to be made to us, or our successors, within one year after the vacancy occurs; and respecting the other benefices, presentation will be made to the respective *ordinarios,* and if these refuse without cause to give institution inside of ten days, any bishop in those lands, on the petition of King Ferdinand or of Queen Juana, or the king ruling at that time, can bestow, under those conditions, free and legal canonical institution on the person presented. Nobody should deign to infringe on or act contrary to this concession, and if any one attempts to do so, let him know that he will incur the indignation of God Almighty and of the blessed apostles Peter and Paul. Given in Rome, etc., July 28, 1508.[30]

Since the concession of patronage was linked, in the bull of 1508, with the creation of the ecclesiastical province of Española, fear was felt in Spain that Ferdinand's demands for universal patronage had been ignored. In 1510 the Council of Castile seriously considered demanding an amendment to the bull. But it was decided to be unnecessary when it was pointed out that the identical purpose of extending the territorial scope of the grant could be accomplished, if, in establishing new sees, there was an express papal recognition of patronage and presentation for each one. Due to the rapid decline of population in Española, the bishops for the three sees were never appointed. The king, on the contrary, asked the pope to suppress the dioceses and create only one bishopric in Española and another in Porto Rico, both to be dependent on the Archbishop of Seville. This was done by the bull *Romanus Pontifex* in August, 1511. An examination of this bull, or any one of the subsequent bulls of erection, will show that all were drawn up according to standard form and modeled after that of 1508.[31]

The most extreme canonists contend that the sole title of *real patronato de Indias* was the pontifical concession contained in the bull *universalis ecclesiae*. They regard it as the organic charter of the royal right of patronage in America. Less ardent protagonists of the idea that patronage is purely spiritual in origin, without relinquishing the contention that the privilege is based on pontifical grant, feel that these concessions were conveyed in three papal bulls rather than in one. By virtue of the bulls of 1493 and 1501 the Spanish sovereigns would have exercised the absolute canonical patronage even though the bull of 1508 had never been issued. As has already been noted, Pope Alexander VI forged three strong links in the chain of the *patronato de Indias*; they were: (1) the concession of the evangelical mission to the crown with the obligation in conscience of responding to it; (2) the granting of the exclusive right to found churches and benefices as a conse-

---

[30] Hernáez, *op. cit.,* I, 24-26.
[31] Solórzano, *op. cit.,* Lib. IV, Cap. IV, No. 11.

quence and reward of that mission; and (3) the concession of the tithes as a reward for those foundations.

Ferdinand believed that the crown enjoyed the right of patronage over the churches which it founded in America even before the privilege was formally conceded by the pope in 1508. However, it is to be noted that Ferdinand based his claims on positive historical sources, i.e., earlier pontifical concessions, and not on customary practices. In support of this assertion it is noteworthy that the Spanish sovereigns had been accustomed to petition the pope for certain "concessions." Answering their supplications the pope "conceded" with apostolic authority what had been requested of him. The bull of 1508, for example, did not "recognize" patronage as already existing by virtue of its inherency in sovereignty, but it explicitly "conceded" it. A clause in the original Latin reads: "Ad magnam instantiam quam super hoc fecerunt ac faciuent . . . auctoritate apostolica tenore praesentium *concedimus*." Thus, in the natal period of the *real patronato de Indias*, the crown consistently declined to base its rights upon anything other than the papal bulls. It remained for regalism of a later period to claim patronage to be a legal right which originated simultaneously with the establishment of Spanish dominion over the Indies. Philip II was of this opinion as evidenced by his instructions concerning ecclesiastical patronage, addressed to the viceroy of New Spain on June 1, 1574: "As you know, the right of ecclesiastical patronage belongs to us throughout the realm of the Indies—both because of having discovered and acquired that new world, and erected there and endowed the churches and monasteries at our cost, or at the cost of our ancestors, the Catholic Kings; and because it was conceded to us by bulls of the most holy pontiffs, conceded of their own accord."[32] Thus, according to Philip, there was a threefold basis of the *real patronato de Indias:* (1) the establishment of dominion through discovery and conquest; (2) the founding and endowing of churches; and (3) the papal grants. It is to be presumed that, in Philip's opinion, any one of these sufficed as legal justification for the exercise of the royal patronage.

In spite of the extensiveness of the papal grant of 1508, it will

---

[32] Cleven, *op. cit.,* p. 250.

be observed that that bull contained nothing about the royal claims
to the tithes and the demarcation of the dioceses—two of the three
points contained in the petitions of Ferdinand. Regarding the
privilege of outlining dioceses it does not appear that Ferdinand
renewed his demands. This right was conferred on the Spanish
crown by pontifical concession in 1543. With respect to the tithes,
however, he registered a vigorous protest, as can well be imagined,
considering the practical-mindedness of this king. As a result, two
bulls were issued, one on April 8, 1510, and the other on August
13, 1511, reconfirming the royal rights to the tithes.[33] The *real
patronato de Indias* was won and preserved by the tenacious and
absorbing policy of King Ferdinand. Had a weaker king occupied
the Spanish throne in 1508 it is entirely conceivable that he would
have been content to enjoy no greater privileges over the Church
in America than he enjoyed in Spain. Therefore, it can be said
that, to a large extent, the *real patronato de Indias* was the work
of Ferdinand the Catholic.

Father Mariano Cuevas, S.J., Mexican ecclesiastical historian,
and arch-opponent of the politico-religious alliance of the colonial
period, while accepting the bull of 1508 as the juridic base of the
patronato de Indias by virtue of its acceptance by the papacy for
so many years, doubts the authenticity of the bull. He suspects
that it never existed because the original copy is not extant at
the present day, and because it was never entered in either the
Corpus Juris Canonici or the *Bulario Magno*. While granting that
the bull may have existed, Father Cuevas is firm in his denial of
the integrity of its text. His conclusion is based upon the appearance of the name "Novam Hispaniam" (i.e. New Spain) in the
papal document which was dated eleven years before New Spain,
or Mexico, was discovered. If the bull was not forged in its entirety, thinks the learned Jesuit, at least, in the process of copy-
ing, ardent regalists interpolated the name New Spain in order
that the patronage conceded in the Antilles might be extended to
the mainland.[34]

There is evidence that the bull of 1508 actually existed. In
1510 the Council of Castile considered an amendment to the

---

[33] Leturia, *op. cit.*, pp. 33-34.

[34] Mariano Cuevas, *Historia de la Iglesia en México* (Mexico, 1928), II, 47-48.

"bull of patronazgo," obviously the bull of 1508. In 1580 a *cédula* of Philip II consigned the bull to the Archivo de Simancas. In 1639, according to Solórzano, the original of the bull was kept in the *Archivo del Consejo de Indias*. When the archives were transferred to Seville in the eighteenth century, the bull disappeared. The manuscript now in the Archivo General de Indias, *Estante* I, *Cajón* I, *Legajo* I, No. 8, is only a copy. Considering the above facts there appears to be some evidence that the bull actually existed. Finally, Father Cuevas' claim that its non-entry in either the *Corpus Juris Canonici* or the *Bulario Magno* implied its non-existence, is weakened by the fact that many other well known bulls were not entered in those compilations. The insinuation that the name "Novam Hispaniam" was inserted is likewise untenable. Consideration of the historical events leading up to the publication of the bull of 1508 indicates that the pope had in mind the island of Española (Hispaniola) when making the grant. Furthermore, it was not unnatural to apply the name New Spain to Española, since it was the first colony of old Spain overseas. Finally, there was no need of the regalists adding the name New Spain, for it was evident from succeeding bulls that the future New Spain was included in the grants. Why, when the regalists were making changes, did they not add Peru and New Granada?[35]

The rapidity with which the Spanish crown developed a policy of control and administration of the patronage was remarkable. By the end of the reign of Philip II the civil control of the Church was thoroughly consolidated. Subsequent history added nothing to its essential nature, except perhaps to strengthen and expand even more the royal control. For that reason it is not necessary to enumerate the many papal bulls of erection which were issued throughout the colonial period. They extended the scope but not the nature of the royal control. Of some importance, however, in the history of the patronage in the Indies were the bulls of Benedict XIV, issued in 1753. The first (January 11) confirmed the rights of the Spanish kings as then exercised in the Indies, and the second (June 9) declared that the royal patronage was

---

[35] Hernáez, *op. cit.,* I, 26; Leturia, *op. cit.,* p. 33.

acquired "by foundation and endowment, by privilege and apostolic concession, and by other legitimate title." This bull has been frequently cited by regalists as confirmation of their claims.[36]

The ecclesiastical patronage of all Spanish America belonged exclusively to the royal crown, which was always most zealous of the conservation and inviolability of such an ample right. The zeal of the crown in protecting its rights is admirably set forth in a *cédula* of Philip II to the viceroy of New Spain:

The King. To our viceroy of Nueva España, or the person or persons who shall, for the time being, be exercising the government of that country: As you know, the right of the ecclesiastical patronage belongs to us throughout the realm of the Indias—both because of having discovered and acquired that new world, and erected there and endowed the churches and monasteries at our own cost, or at the cost of our ancestors, the Catholic Sovereigns; and because it was conceded to us by bulls of the most holy pontiffs, conceded of their own accord. For its conservation, and that of the right which we have to it, we order and command that the said right of patronage be always preserved for us and our royal crown, singly and *in solidum,* throughout all the realm of the Indias, without any derogation therefrom, either in whole or in part; and that we shall not concede the right of patronage by any favor or reward that we or the kings our successors may confer.

Further, no person or persons, or ecclesiastical or secular communities, or church or monastery, shall be able to exercise the right of patronage by custom, privilege, or any other title, unless it be the person who shall exercise it in our name, and with our authority and power; and no person, whether secular or ecclesiastical, and no order, convent, or religious community, of whatever state, condition, rank and preëminence he or they may be, shall for any occasion and cause whatever, judicially or extra-judicially, dare to meddle in any matter touching my royal patronage, to injure us in it—to appoint to any church, benefice, or ecclesiastical office, or to be accepted if he shall have been appointed—in all the realm of the Indias, without our presentation, or that of the person to whom we commit it by law or by letters-patent. He who shall do the contrary, if he be a secular person, shall incur the loss of the concessions that shall have been made to him by us in all the realm of the Indias, shall be unable to hold and obtain others, and shall be exiled perpetually from all our kingdoms and seigniories, and if he shall be an ecclesiastical person, he

---

[36] *Dictamen sobre Provisión de Benefices Eclesiásticos* (Mexico, 1824), p. 8.

shall be considered as a foreigner, and exiled from all our kingdoms, and shall not be able to hold or obtain any benefice or ecclesiastical office, and shall incur the other penalties established against such by laws of these my kingdoms. And our viceroys, audiencias, and royal justices shall proceed with all severity against those who thus shall infringe or violate our right of patronage; and they shall proceed officially, either at the petition of our fiscals, or at that of any party who demands it; and in the execution of it great diligence shall be exercised.[37]

In the above and numerous other decrees the right of royal patronage was held to be indivisible and imprescriptible. The sovereign did not lose it through lack of exercise and no one could acquire it through use or custom. No person or persons, ecclesiastical or secular, were to use the patronage except under the crown's authority and severe penalties were provided for infringements of the royal privilege. Royal officials, particularly viceroys, *oidores*, and governors were cautioned to watch over the rights and preëminences of the patronage and to issue the necessary orders. The prelates also were ordered to preserve the patronage, and, in doubtful matters, they were to advise the Council of the Indies. The archbishops and bishops had to vow, before entering their offices, fealty and obedience to the crown and observance of the royal patronage.[38]

So jealously did the king guard his patronal rights that the bull of Clement VII in 1532, which granted the right of patronage to Hernando Cortés in the marquisate of Oaxaca, was retained by Charles V. A royal *cédula*, December 19, 1593, addressed to the archbishop of Mexico, reprimanded him for difficulties placed in the way of the viceroy in the exercise of the patronage. In Peru at an early period the archbishop and other prelates had usurped the patronage. In consequence Viceroy Francisco de Toledo restored the royal prerogative in spite of the strenuous opposition of the clergy. The ecclesiastical invasion was only temporarily stopped, for in 1604 Viceroy Velasco advised his successor that he would have a perpetual warfare in Peru con-

---

[37] Cleven, *op. cit.*, pp. 250-251.

[38] *Recopilación de Leyes de los Reynos de las Indias* (Madrid, 1756, 2 ed.), Lib. 1, Tit. 6, Leyes, 1, 35, 45, 47. (Hereafter referred to as *Recop. de Leyes*.)

cerning the royal patronage.[39] In Charcas in the middle of the
seventeenth century occurred a case which illustrates how jealously the Spanish crown was attached to its ecclesiastical rights.
A lawyer argued before the audiencia of Charcas that the royal
patronage only gave extra judicial protection to the churches of
the Indies and that the crown did not acquire thereby the right to
hear ecclesiastical cases. The royal fiscal claimed that this argument was false, scandalous, contrary to the royal rights and to
the nature, prerogatives, and dignity of the patronage. The
lawyer was fined one hundred ducats, and was forbidden to practice for four years. The king, when notified of this decision, approved it. The royal attitude toward the patronage might be
summed up as in a *cédula* to the bishop of Cuba (July 23, 1639),
"As you know, or ought to know, the said patronage is a thing
which I cherish greatly, and which I cannot and ought not
[to] permit to be injured."[40]

Although the patronage was held to be imprescriptible, nevertheless it could be delegated by the Spanish kings. Due to the
distance between Spain and America, it was impossible for the
king to exercise the patronal rights personally. Therefore he entrusted this power to his viceroys, audiencias, and governors.
This delegation of powers was approved by the papacy, for Boni-
face VIII said that one could not expect the impossible. The laws
of the Indies bestowed complete power on the viceroys, presidents,
oidores, and governors in America to discharge the rights and
preëminences of the royal patronage and to oblige all ecclesiastical authorities to conform to their orders with respect to it.
By virtue of his position as vice-patron, the viceroy had manifold
duties arising from his relations with the ecclesiastical organizations. It was generally through his intermediation, or independent
action, that the right of presentation was exercised, that the
clergy, secular and regular, were controlled, churches established,
councils held, and education, hospitals and institutions of charity
were administered. "Marquina [viceroy of New Spain] declared
that the authority of the viceroy was made evident by his functions as vice-patron, which caused him to be distinguished even

---

[39] Lillian Estelle Fisher, *Viceregal Administration in the Spanish-American
Colonies* (Berkeley, 1926), p. 207.   [40] Sarsfield, *op. cit.,* p. 46.

by the ecclesiastics, who were always objects of veneration among the populace. The ceremonies whereby he was honored gave him a certain dignity of his own which surpassed that of the highest functionary." When the presidents of the audiencias exercised the privileges of the royal patronage it was always understood that they were subordinate to the viceroy. Governors in turn were generally considered as subordinate to the audiencias and viceroy. After the intendancies were established, the intendants were given a few of the patronal rights to relieve the viceroy of these duties in the provinces. By Article 6 of the *Ordenanza de Intendentes* the right of patronage in the viceroyalty of La Plata resided in the viceroy and the governors-intendants of the provinces. By the *cédula* of May 9, 1795, which modified the intendancy system, the intendants were allowed to retain the vice-patronage in their capacity as sub-delegates of the viceroys and presidents.[41]

Dating from the bull *inter caetera* of 1493 the Spanish crown exercised the exclusive right of licensing ecclesiastics to come to the Indies. Coincident with this power was that of controlling their movements once they were in America. Licenses were issued by the Council of the Indies and complete data relating to the age, birthplace, and the like, of the applicants were recorded. These licenses had to be scrutinized by the officials of the *Casa de Contratación* before they would allow embarkation. Expenses of transportation were paid from the royal treasury. When ecclesiastics came to America they did not go where they pleased, but where the viceroy and governor directed them. Religious who came to America without license were sent back to Spain. Whenever settlements lacked a sufficient number of ecclesiastics, the civil authorities did not hestitate to call on the regular orders for friars. If a religious wished to leave the Indies, the permission of the pope himself did not suffice; the cleric had to get the consent of the king. Even the viceroys were not allowed to grant licenses for parish priests to return to Spain. After 1589 an exception was made in favor of those friars who had been in America for at least ten years.[42]

---

[41] Fisher, *op. cit.*, pp. 182-184; *Recop. de Leyes*, 1-6-26, 47.

[42] Diego de Encinas, *Provisiones, Cédulas, Capítulos de Ordenanzas*, etc. (Madrid, 1596), I, 107, 122; *Recop. de Leyes*, 1-13-2, 1-14-19.

In the same manner as the Supreme Pontiff was impotent in controlling the movements of ecclesiastics to and from America, so also was he legally restrained from founding churches or other pious establishments without royal permission. For the erection of cathedrals it was necessary that the pope issue an express bull, but these bulls of erection were, without exception, solicited by the crown and made to conform to royal desires and the laws of the Indies. The usual procedure in securing permission to erect a church, convent, or pious work was somewhat as follows: An *información*, or petition accompanied by supporting documents, was drawn up setting forth the object and necessity of the desired church. This, accompanied by the opinion of the diocesan prelate, was sent to the viceroy or president of the audiencia. Then, with that officer's opinion attached, the documents were sent to the Council of the Indies, which, if it decided favorably, issued the license for the erection of the church. Due to the fact that the vice-patrons gave permission too readily for the building of convents, a *cédula* was issued on March 19, 1593, which ordered them not to grant licenses for such buildings without first securing the king's permission. This law was reaffirmed on June 14, 1616, and the viceroys were severely reprimanded for disregarding it. So insistent was the king that no ecclesiastical establishment be erected without proper license that he empowered the viceroys to demolish all religious structures which had been erected without proper authorization. This order was put into effect, too, as evidenced by numerous examples. For instance, in 1608 the viceroy Montesclaros of Peru was ordered to destroy the convent of the Mercedarians, which the Count of Monterey had illegally permitted to be established. License was even necessary for the organization of *cofradías*, or religious brotherhoods, although the object might only be spiritual and pious. If any person should build or endow a church, the king, according to the laws of the Indies, would be the patron of it. However, the crown only exercised the patronage over the cathedral churches and parishes, and did not extend it to the lesser churches. A law of the Indies permitted private persons to found with their own money, monasteries, hospitals, hermitages, churches, and other pious works, and to exercise the patronage over them.[43]

When the Spanish king acquired the use of the tithes in 1501, he at the same time assumed the obligation of assisting in all the expenses connected with the building of churches. The ordinary practice was that one-third of the cost was paid from the royal treasury, and two-thirds were paid by the encomenderos and the Indians. "In fact the Indians really bore the entire burden for the construction of churches, since they provided the manual labor, and, by working on the encomiendas, enabled the encomenderos to pay their share. They paid tribute to the king from which the portion donated by the royal treasury was taken." When a church needed repairs a petition was sent to the viceroy who submitted it to his council, which decided the amount of money that ought to be contributed from the royal treasury.[44]

Although the crown enjoyed the use of the tithes by virtue of the bull of 1501, it rarely availed itself of the grant, but donated to bishops, clergy, hospitals, etc., the greater part of what was due to it from this source. The tithes of each diocese were ordinarily divided into four parts; one part went to the bishop, and one part to the chapter. The remaining half was divided into nine parts called *novenos*. One and one-half went to the corporate body of the church which administered the temporalities; four were given to the lower clergy; one and one-half *noveno* went to the hospitals; and the remaining two-ninths to the king. All but the two royal *novenos* were variable. Generally these two were spent on churches, although the king had the right to use them for temporal matters. Whenever the tithes were not sufficient to pay the clerics the established amount due them, the balance was always forthcoming from the royal treasury. Numerous *cédulas* were directed to royal officials ordering this to be done. The royal treasury officials had charge of collecting the tithes, and it was the duty of the viceroy to see that no person escaped who was required to pay. The military orders tried to claim exemption but the king refused it. The Jesuits offered the greatest opposition.

---

[43] Fisher, *op. cit.*, pp. 186-187; Encinas, *op. cit.*, I, 145-147.

[44] Fisher, *op. cit.*, p. 187, n. 17.

They alleged that their order enjoyed pontifical privileges which exempted the members from payment. The question was still in controversy at the time of the expulsion. It should be noted, however, that the expulsion of the Jesuits was in no way connected with *real patronato*. Other revenues to the State from ecclesiastical sources were: the income from the sale of bulls of the Holy Crusade, subsidies donated by the papacy, and the *mesadas* and ecclesiastical half-annates, or salary taxes.[45]

If there was one point in public ecclesiastical law on which the crown would not give way to Rome, it was the determining of the territorial limits of dioceses and parishes. Since the boundaries of bishoprics coincided with the political territorial divisions, the power of determining the former had to be subordinated to the temporal authority. Furthermore, the pope being far away and not cognizant of local conditions, could not weigh all the considerations necessary for the creation of bishoprics. Only the political government of the territory was in position to know its population and resources. Sarsfield mentions that in the bull of erection for the cathedral of Tucumán, the pope believed Tucumán to be an island. [46]

The royal right of controlling the territorial extent of dioceses was based on the bull of 1508 and subsequent bulls of erection. For example: Clement VII in the bull *sacri apostolatus ministerio* which provided for the erection of a cathedral church in Mexico, and conceded the royal patronage over it, left to the decision, disposition, and order of Charles V, everything relating to the erection of the said church, *even to the establishment of the limits of the diocese.* There are four laws covering this matter in the *Recopilación de Indias.* The first declared that only the king had the power to outline and divide bishoprics. The second reaffirmed that it was the king who had the power to divide bishoprics, even by acts posterior to the erection of cathedrals. The third laid down a rule for the Council of the Indies to the effect that ecclesiastical districts should be made to conform as far as possible to the political divisions; for example, archbishoprics and provinces of the regulars to conform to the district of the audiencia; bishop-

---

[45] Cleven, *op. cit.,* p. 247, n.l; Encinas, *op. cit.,* I, 179-201, 108-111; Solórzano, *op. cit.,* Lib. IV, Cap. IV, Nos. 26-29.

[46] Sarsfield, *op. cit.,* p. 115.

rics to the *gobernaciones* or *alcaldías mayores;* parishes and curacies to *corregimientos* and *alcaldías ordinarias.* The fourth law concerned the curacies: "We grant license and permission to the diocesan prelates of our Indies to, when there is necessity, divide, unite, or suppress curate benefices, provided that they have previously informed our vice-patrons in order that they may jointly issue the orders they regard as necessary." Thus the ecclesiastical power only took part in the delimiting of curacies, and even then it had to act with the temporal powers. With respect to the outlining of the greater and more important districts like the bishoprics and provinces, the king acted alone in his royal council.[47]

The essence of the *real patronato de Indias* was of course the right of presentation. The origins of the privilege have already been discussed. The manner of its operation in America will now be described. Whenever a higher ecclesiastical office like an archbishopric, bishopric, or canonicate was to be filled, the candidate had to be presented by the king. The king's nominations for archbishops and bishops were presented to the Holy Father for canonical installation; the candidates for the lesser benefices were presented to the archbishop or bishop of the particular diocese.

Presentation to the lesser ecclesiastical positions in the Indies was entrusted to the vice-patrons. A law of April 4, 1609, gave the power of appointment to parishes and *doctrinas* entirely to the viceroys. With respect to these latter benefices, it was ordered that they should be filled in the following manner:

When a benefice (whether a sinecure or a curacy), or the administration of any hospital or a sacristy or church wardenship, or the stewardship of a hospital, or any other benefice or ecclesiastical office, shall become vacant, or when it has to be filled for the first time: the prelate shall order a written proclamation to be posted in the cathedral church, or in the church, hospital, or monastery where such benefice or office is to be filled, with the suitable limit, so that those who desire to compete for it may enter the lists. From all those who thus compete, and from all the others whom the prelate shall believe to be suitable persons for such office or benefice, after having examined them and after having informed himself concerning their morals and ability, he shall choose two persons from them—those whom, in the sight of God and his conscience, he shall judge most

---

[47] *Recop. de Leyes,* 1-2-8, 1-7-3, 1-6-40, 2-2-7.

suitable for such office or benefice. The nomination of the two thus named shall be presented to our viceroy or to the president of our royal Audiencia; or to the person who, in our name, shall exercise the superior government of the province where such benefice or office shall become vacant and must be filled, so that he may select one from the two appointees. He shall send that selection to the prelate, so that the latter in accordance with it, and by virtue of the presentation, may grant the appointment, collation, and canonical installation—by way of commission and not by perpetual title, but removable at will by the person who shall have presented them in our name, together with the prelate. And should there be no more than one person who desires to compete for such benefice or office, or the prelate shall not find more than one person whom he desires to receive the nomination to it, he shall send the name to our viceroy, president, or governor, as above stated, so that the latter may present him. Then by virtue of such presentation, the prelate shall make the appointment in the form above directed. But it is our desire and will that when the presentation shall be made by us, and we shall expressly state in our presentation that the collation and canonical installation shall be by title and not by commission, those presented by us be always preferred to those presented by our viceroy, presidents, or governors, in the form above mentioned.

And in the repartimientos and villages of Indians, and in other places where there shall be no benefice or any regulations for electing one, or any form of appointing a secular or religious to administer sacraments and teach the doctrine, providing it in the form above directed, the prelate—after posting a proclamation, so that if there shall be any ecclesiastical or religious person, or any other of good morals and education who may go to teach the doctrine at such village—from those who shall compete, or from other persons whom he shall deem most suitable and fitting, shall elect two, after informing himself of their competency and good character. He shall send the nomination to our viceroy, president, or governor who shall reside in the province, so that the latter may present one of the two thus nominated by the prelate. If there shall be no more than one, by virtue of that presentation the prelate shall appoint him to the mission, giving him installation, as he has to teach the doctrine. He shall order to be given to such person the emoluments that are to be given to ministers or missions, and shall order the encomenderos and other persons, under the penalities and censures that he shall deem suitable, not to annoy or disturb such person in the exercise of his duty and the teaching of the Christian doctrine; on the contrary, they shall give him all protection and aid for it. That appointment shall be made removable at the will of the person who shall have appointed him in our name, and that of the prelate.[48]

The crown was insistent that there should be no delay in filling vacancies. In the greater consistoral benefices one year was allowed, due to the fact that confirmation had to be bestowed by the papacy. The prelates and viceroy were ordered to notify the king of prebendaries and vacant benefices, of worthy candidates and what considerations ought to be observed in the matter of presentation. Parochial benefices and *doctrinas* could not be vacant longer than four months. In 1540 the viceroy was ordered to make new appointments when ecclesiastics were absent from their positions for more than a year. In 1574 only eight months were permitted in case of legitimate cause.[49]

The discretion of the vice-patron in the exercise of his rights of presentation was greatly circumscribed by measures designed to maintain purity of appointments. The laws commanded the viceroys always to favor the most learned and worthy candidates. Those who set the best examples by their lives were to be given preference. No cleric could hold more than one benefice. Foreigners were not to be considered for appointments unless they bore letters of naturalization. No one should be admitted to a *doctrina* who did not understand the Indian language. Furthermore, a *doctrina* was not to be presented to any relative of an encomendero. In case the governors did not present worthy religious, they were to be presented by the viceroy.[50]

The presentation having been made in due form, the canonical institution followed. As has been noted, the pope installed archbishops and bishops, and the prelate of the particular diocese conferred the other ecclesiastical benefices. It was often the practice that the prelate presented by the king would assume his office before receiving papal confirmation. Without waiting upon papal action, due to the ordinary delay because of the great distance from Rome, the king would order the ecclesiastical chapter of the vacant see to turn over the office to the bishop-elect.

---

[48] Cleven, *op. cit.*, pp. 253-255; *Recop. de Leyes*, 1-6-3, 4, 7, 15.

[49] *Recop. de Leyes*, 1-6-19, 55, 48.

[50] *Recop. de Leyes*, 1-6-20, 27, 29, 30, 31, 33; Encinas, *op. cit.*, I, 97-99.

3

Although the chapters complied without opposing the least objection, nevertheless Rome never acquiesced in the practice. Before the prelates could assume their dioceses they had to exhibit to the viceroy their credentials of election and evidence of having taken the regular oath of fealty to the crown. The act of conferring the office was regulated in the following manner: "After the original warrant of our presentation has been presented, appointment and canonical installation shall be made without any delay; and order will be given to assign to him the emoluments, unless there is some legitimate objection against the person presented, and one which can be proved. If there is no legitimate objection, or if any such be alleged that shall not be proved, and the prelate should delay the appointment, installation, and possession, he shall be obliged to pay to such person the emoluments and income, costs, and interests, that shall have been incurred by him." The prelate was supposed to institute within ten days. If he failed to act by that time, the act of institution could be performed by another prelate. If the candidate did not present himself to exercise his office within the fixed period, he forfeited the position. Those provided with benefices by the king could only be removed by royal order. The holders of lesser benefices could be removed by the prelates or superiors with the permission of the vice-patron. The royal audiencias were not to hear causes of priests removed from office in conformity with the laws of the patronage.[51]

The privileged position of the clergy in the enjoyment of its own courts was known as the *fuero eclesiástico.* This exemption from the control of the ordinary tribunals was no distinctive feature of the *real patronato de Indias,* but rather was borrowed from customary Spanish practice dating back to the fourth or fifth century. These courts, organized by dioceses, were ordinarily of three kinds: *provisorato* for Spaniards, *provisorato* for Indians, and *juzgado de testamentos, capellanías, y obras pías* (court for wills, chapels, and pious works). The powers of the last court were later curtailed by the civil probate of wills of

---

[51] *Recop. de Leyes,* 1-6-23, 24, 36, 38, 39; Solórzano, *op. cit.,* Lib. IV, Cap. VII; Cleven, *op. cit.,* pp. 252-253.

clergymen. In 1789 the cases of *capellanías* and *obras pías* were also made cognizable in secular courts.[52]

The ecclesiastical courts had no jurisdiction over cases either civil or criminal concerning persons not Catholics. They could not inflict corporal punishment, or sentence Indians to hard labor or impose fines on them. In later times the jurisdiction of the ecclesiastical courts was reduced. By royal decree of October 25, 1795, the common courts were allowed to take cognizance of grave offenses committed by ecclesiastics. Questions of jurisdiction between the ecclesiastical and civil courts were decided by the viceroy. In Europe the papal court in Rome was accustomed to hear appeals from the decisions of the ecclesiastical courts. Such a practise was not thought to be desirable in America, for it was feared that the inevitable delay would breed scandal. Therefore, by a bull of Gregory XIII (February 28, 1578) it was provided that all ecclesiastical cases should be definitely decided in America. After obtaining the brief, Philip II did not publish it, and it remained inoperative during his lifetime because he had scruples regarding the termination of pontifical jurisdiction in such matters. Consequently appeals continued to be carried to the pope until 1606. In that year and in 1722 and 1731, royal orders provided for the enforcement of the provisions of the bull of 1578.[53]

Litigation arising out of the royal patronage, or *causas de patronato*, was not cognizable in the ecclesiastical courts. A *cédula* of 1540, directed to the president and *oidores* of the Audiencia of Mexico, fixed the jurisdiction of patronal causes in the said audiencia and expressly prohibited the ecclesiastical courts from hearing such cases. The ordinary procedure was first to have recourse to the vice-patron. If the cause originated in the territory of an intendancy, the governor-intendant was first appealed to as delegate of the vice-patron. From the decision of the vice-patron appeal could then be taken to the audiencia. Disputes between bishops, curates, canons, and dignitaries concerning benefices and canonical capacity to fill them were regarded as

---

[52] H. H. Bancroft, *History of Mexico* (San Francisco, 1883), III, 188.

[53] *Recop. de Leyes,* 1-9-10; Solórzano, *op. cit.,* Lib. IV, Cap. 9, Nos. 1-6.

patronal causes or *pleitos de patronato,* and not matters for the ecclesiastical courts. In conclusion, all cases concerning the limits of bishoprics, canonical impediments to the filling of benefices, conflicts between the beneficiaries themselves over their rights and prerogatives, *pleitos* between ecclesiastical chapters and the bishops or archbishops concerning the administration of the Church, as well as all causes between curates over their respective offices, and, in general, all cases which in any way touched the *real patronato,* were attended by civil authorities and heard in civil tribunals, even though it often appeared that the subjects involved were purely spiritual in nature.[54]

In the control of church councils and synods convened in the Indies, the Spanish crown also intervened to an exceptional degree. Although the matters considered in the councils more often referred to dogma, cult, and discipline, nevertheless the laws of the Indies required royal permission for the holding of councils. Provincial church councils, as provided by the papal brief of December 6, 1610, were to be held in the Indies every twelve years, but only thirteen were actually held during the colonial period. An early law provided that the king should be consulted and his consent secured before a council could be convened. Later the archbishops of America were allowed to summon provincial councils merely with the approval of the viceroy or captain-general, without having to appeal to the king. The vice-patron attended these meetings in person and saw that the rights of patronage were not violated. In the provincial councils only the bishops could vote. The canons, superiors of religious orders, and the presbyters could attend but not vote. The matters discussed in the provincial councils related to morality and good conduct of the clergy, the enforcement of the decrees of the Council of Trent, and the good treatment and instruction of the Indians. The decisions of the councils were sent to the king for his approval. After the royal assent had been secured, the findings were sent to the pope who ordered them published in the provinces

---

[54] *Ibid.,* III, 687-688; Lucas Alamán, *Historia de México* (Mexico, 1849), I, 68; *Recop. de Leyes,* 1-9-10, 2-15-34, 35; Solórzano, *op. cit.,* Lib. IV, Cap. IX, Nos. 1-6; Sarsfield, *op. cit.,* pp. 51, 54; Bernard Moses, *The Spanish Dependencies in South America* (New York, 1914), II, 221-222.

where the councils had been held. Thus, no measure enacted by a council could be executed without the royal approval.[55]

The Spanish sovereigns also ordered observance of a law of the Council of Trent which provided that the bishops should each year summon a synod of the prelates and clerics of their dioceses. The measures passed by the synods had to be submitted to the vice-patron, so that he could determine whether the royal rights of patronage had been observed. If he felt that the royal sovereignty had been invaded he sent the synodal constitution to the Council of the Indies. Upon receiving temporal approval the bishops published the measures that had been passed by the synod.[56]

The same motive which impelled the Spanish kings to control the councils and synods, actuated them in asserting control over the admission into America of papal bulls, briefs, rescripts, and other pontifical documents. The reason for this was in brief the fear that the pope would trespass the limits of his divine office and legislate in purely temporal matters with a consequent invasion of the royal prerogative. This right, like that of controlling the councils, was based on ancient Spanish custom and later-day legal sanction. In following these precedents the laws of the Indies ordered the civil and ecclesiastical authorities in America not to obey briefs and pontifical bulls which did not have the approval of the Council of the Indies. A *cédula* of Philip IV in 1643 repeated the commands of his predecessors that papal bulls should be examined first in the Council of the Indies. As an additional precaution, it was ordered in 1777 that bulls, briefs, and rescripts, even though provided with the Council's exequatur, were not to be circulated without the permission of the vice-patron. Viceroys, audiencias, and governors in America were ordered to send back to the Council of the Indies all papal documents that had not been approved by it. Either the pope was very careful not to invade the royal prerogative, or the crown was liberal in its examination of papal bulls, for, according to Ribadeneyra, only six bulls were retained by the Council of the Indies. There were

---

[55] Moses, *Spanish Dependencies*, II, 222-223; Fisher, *op. cit.*, pp. 218-219; Encinas, *op. cit.*, I, 137-138; *Recop. de Leyes*, 1-8-6.

[56] *Recop. de Leyes*, 1-8-6; 2-15-147; Encinas, I, 136-137.

numerous cases, however, of the viceroys stopping circulation of bulls or briefs which did not have the permission of the Council.[57]

So opposed was the crown to direct correspondence between the Church in Europe and in America, that when the papal nuncio at Madrid, without permission, published in 1642 the proclamation of a jubilee by Clement X, the act was condemned by the king. The papal legates and nuncios resided near the Spanish court, but they were not allowed to go to America. As far as America was concerned these papal representatives did not exist except in negative laws which refused them the power and jurisdiction exercised in Spain. In America all of the apostolic jurisdiction was regarded as being delegated to the metropolitans.[58]

The royal patronage embraced the regular orders quite as comprehensively as it did the secular clergy. The law of 1574 specified that the religious orders should observe and maintain the right of patronage in the following manner:

We also will and order that the religious orders observe and maintain the right of patronage in the following form:

First: No general, commissary-general, visitor, provincial, or any other superior of the religious orders, shall go to the realm of the Indias, without first showing in our royal Council of the Indias the powers that he bears and giving us relation of them; and without the Council giving him our decree and permission so that he may go, and a warrant so that our viceroys, audiencias, justices, and our other vassals may admit and receive him to the exercise of his office, and give him all protection and aid in it.

Any provincial, visitor, prior, guardian, or other high official, who may be elected and nominated in the realm of the Indias, shall, before being admitted to exercise his office, inform our viceroy, president, audiencia, or governor who shall have in charge the supreme government of such province, and shall show him his patent of nomination and election, so that the latter may give him the protection and aid necessary for the exercise and use of his office.

The provincials of all the orders who are established in the Indias, each one of them shall always keep a list ready of all the monasteries and chief residences (maintained there by his orders) and of the members (resident in each) that fall in his province, and of all the

---

[57] Bancroft, *Mexico,* III, 685-686; Ribadeneyra, *op. cit.,* pp. 226-229; *Recop. de Leyes,* 1-7-55, 1-9-2, 5.

[58] Alamán, *op. cit.,* I, 36-37; Sarsfield, *op. cit.,* p. 94.

religious in the province—noting each one of them by name, with a report of his age and qualifications, and the office or ministry in which each one is occupied. He shall give that annually to our viceroy, audiencia, or governor, or the person who shall have charge of the supreme government in the province, adding to or removing from the list the religious who shall be superfluous and those who shall be needed. Our viceroy, audiencia, or governor, shall keep those general lists which shall thus be given, for himself, and in order that he may inform us by report of the religious that there are, and those of whom there is need of provision, by each fleet sent out.

The provincials of the orders, each one of them, shall make a list of all the religious who are occupied in teaching the Christian doctrine to the Indians, and the administration of sacraments, and the offices of curas in the villages of the chief monasteries. They shall give such list once a year to our viceroy, audiencia, or governor, who shall give it to the diocesan prelate, so that he may know and understand what persons are occupied in the administration of sacraments and the office of curas and the ecclesiastical jurisdiction, and who are in charge of the souls for whom he is responsible; and in order that what is or must be provided may be apparent to him, and from whom he has to acquire account of the said souls, and to whom he must commit what is to be done for the welfare of those souls.

Whenever the provincials have to provide any religious for instruction or for the administration of the sacraments, or remove any who shall have been appointed, they shall give notice thereof to our viceroy, president, audiencia, or governor, who shall exercise the supreme government of the province, and to the prelate; and they shall not remove any one who shall have been appointed, until another shall have been appointed in his place, observing the above order.[59]

The houses of religious orders were under the supervision of the Council of the Indies, which was assisted in these matters by a commissioner-general. The provincial or custodian of the regulars was named by their particular general, but the latter had to notify the commissioner-general in Spain who communicated with the Council of the Indies. Without the permission of the Council the nomination was void. The creation or suppression of provinces, the founding of new convents, the sending of visitors-general to America, and like matters were all controlled by the Council of the Indies. The ordinary procedure necessary for the founding of a new mission or seminary was somewhat as follows:

---

[59] Cleven, *op. cit.*, pp. 255-256; *Recop. de Leyes*, 1-6-49.

The province seeking permission appointed a commissioner, who personally or through his superiors, presented the request to the bishop, the audiencia, and the viceroy. All of these were required to prepare exhaustive reports. The commissioner armed with the necessary permits of the viceroy and his superior, then went to Spain and laid the matter before the commissioner-general of the Indies. The latter presented it with all the necessary documents to the Council of the Indies.

In promoting the greater spiritual and material prosperity of the Church in the Indies, the Spanish kings were even more zealous than in safeguarding their patronage. Every effort was exerted to insure morality and purity of faith and dogma. In presenting to benefices the viceroys were always charged to favor those prelates distinguished for virtue and learning. The punishment of irregularities and the settlement of religious differences was a frequent and oftimes annoying task of the vice-patron. Whenever bishops or superiors became negligent in their manner of living it was the duty of the viceroy to adopt effective measures to compel them to obey. Also the vice-patron was ordered to help the prelates reform subordinates and oblige them to live according to their rules. Archbishops and bishops were often reminded to conform to the decree of the Council of Trent, which required frequent visitations of their respective archdioceses and dioceses. The viceroys were given absolute power to expel rebellious ecclesiastics from their viceroyalties. There are numerous examples of actual cases of expulsion of friars by viceroys. Whenever it was necessary to reprimand an ecclesiastic, the law suggested that it be done secretly, for fear that publicity might have a bad influence upon the Indians.[60]

The dreaded institution of the Inquisition, which was extended to the New World to promote the extension of the Catholic faith and to eradicate heresy, was undoubtedly the most powerful means at the disposal of the crown to maintain purity of faith and dogma. Basing his action upon the bull of Pope Sixtus IV in 1478, which authorized the Catholic Kings to appoint inquisitors who were to have jurisdiction over heretics, Philip II in

---

[60] Encinas, *op. cit.,* I, 117-118; Fisher, *op. cit.,* pp. 197, 206-207, 211.

1569 announced his decision to establish inquisitorial tribunals in Spanish America. The first tribunal was erected in Peru. Two inquisitors named by the crown were installed in Lima in 1570. In 1571 two inquisitors were installed in Mexico. Prior to this time temporary representatives of the Holy Office had been sent to America.

The jurisdiction of the Holy Office extended over Catholics accused of heresy and schism. Foreigners and Protestants who were unfortunate enough to be shipwrecked in America and fall into the hands of the Spaniards were also subjected to it. The Inquisition was specifically charged with vigilance against intrusions of Moors, Jews, and "New Christians," or converts. The Indians were humanely excused out of tender consideration for their immaturity. In the later days of the colonial period the Inquisition came to be used more and more for political ends. In particular it was used to keep liberal ideas out of America by placing a strict surveillance over the importation of books. Not only were books of an heretical nature prohibited, but the works of the eighteenth century political philosophers were proscribed.

The Inquisition was entirely under the control of the king in the *Consejo de la Suprema y General Inquisición;* it had long before established its independence of the papacy. The inquisitors were appointed by the king, and were responsible to him alone. The viceroy took an oath to aid the Holy Office and to guard its privileges and immunities. Likewise he was charged with reporting any invasion of the patronage by the judges of the Inquisition. In minor cases of conflict between the tribunal and the secular courts, an adjustment was generally worked out in a conference of the senior *oidor* and the ranking inquisitor. In the event of no compromise, the viceroy made the decision. In serious differences between the viceroys and inquisitors the matters were referred to a committee of two members of the Council of the Indies, and two members of the General Council of the Inquisition in Spain. Charles III, however, gave the viceroy the final word in all questions relating to disputed jurisdiction of the Inquisition. Also, the inquisitors had to secure the consent of the viceroy before any of its edicts could be published. The alliance between the Inquisition and the civil government is evidenced by the fact that it was the latter power which executed the decisions of the tribunal. Not only did the civil authorities inflict corporal punishment when the inquisitors decreed it, but it collected and administered the fines that were imposed by the tribunal. This same close relationship of the political and inquisitorial can be illustrated by citing the kinds of offices held simultaneously by two famous Mexican viceroys. Moya y Contreras, the first inquisitor-general of New Spain, was also archbishop and viceroy. Palafox was inquisitor-general, visitor-general, bishop of Puebla, and viceroy.[61]

Since education, hospitals, and charitable institutions were largely under the control of the Church, these subjects became important divisions of the *real patronato de Indias.* Although these are important matters, and worthy of extended discussion, it will serve the present purpose to mention merely the all-pervading supervision and control of the king over these institutions. The intervention of the crown and its agents in the fostering of educational and charitable works was second only to its zeal in propagating the faith. In fact one often was inseparable from the other. The relation of the viceroy as vice-patron over the above mentioned matters has been adequately summarized in the following words: "The viceroy was likewise vice-patron over institutions of learning. He conferred fellowships and professorships in the colleges under the royal patronage, but left their administration entirely to the prelates. Some of the viceroys were enthusiastic patrons of education, culture, and science long before their English and French neighbors made any attempts to found schools. The rules of the patronage applied to hospitals and institutions of charity, as well as to schools; therefore the viceroy acted as superintendent over them."[62]

Due to the fact that the essential features of the Church-State relations were developed at an early date, the following brief description of the *real patronato de Indias* is applicable to any time during the colonial period:

---

[61] The above summary description of the Inquisition is based on H. C. Lea, *The Inquisition in the Spanish Dependencies* (New York, 1908).

[62] Fisher, *op. cit.,* pp. 249-250.

"By virtue of it (Bull of Julius II, *Universalis Ecclesiae*), of other concessions obtained later, and somewhat by custom and corruption, the kings of Spain came to acquire such a hand in the ecclesiastical government of America, that with the exception of the purely spiritual, they exercised an authority which appeared to be pontifical. Without his permission no churches, monasteries or hospitals could be erected; nor even could a bishopric or parish be founded. Clerics and religious could not go to America without express license. The kings named bishops and without awaiting confirmation they sent them to administer their dioceses. They determined the limits of bishoprics and changed them as they wished. They had the right of presentation or nomination to all benefices or employments, even to that of sacristan, if they wished. They reprimanded severely, calling to Spain or exiling any ecclesiastic, including bishops, who repeatedly acted contrary to orders of the governors, pretending not to hear the voice of the king. They administered and collected the *diezmos,* deciding who ought to pay and how, without making use of bulls and exemptions. They fixed the rents of the benefices and increased them or decreased them as they judged to be convenient. They heard many ecclesiastic causes, and with the *recursos de fuerza* they paralyzed the action of the tribunals or prelates of the church. Finally, no disposition of the Holy Pontiff could be executed without the approval or *pase* of the king. In our primitive ecclesiastical history, for a bull, brief, or rescript from Rome, there were to be counted a hundred *cédulas,* provisions, or *cartas acordadas* of the king or of the council. . . . To the king, not directly to the pope, the bishops presented their doubts, and we are surprised to see that those relating to baptism are sent to the council. Always the civil power interposes itself between our Church and the Supreme Pastor."[63]

The real patronato de Indias, when compared with the *patronato de España,* was certainly an extraordinary patronage. Never before or since did a sovereign with the consent of the pope so completely control the Catholic Church within his dominions. This jurisdiction, as has been noted, was not confined to ecclesiastical persons and temporalities, but even encroached upon the sphere of purely spiritual matters. For this reason it can be contended with considerable truth that the king was more than a patron in America; he exercised quasi-pontifical authority. However excep-

---

[63] Joaquín García Icazbalceta, *Biografía de don Fr. Juan de Zumárraga* (Mexico, 1881), p. 127.

tional were the powers of the crown in ecclesiastical matters, there is little doubt that the royal aid and supervision was of inestimable advantage to the Church in America. If the patronage implied the planting, protection, and promotion of the Catholic faith and the conversion of the Indians in the newly-discovered lands by endowing churches and missions, certainly the crown discharged its trust with success. The great number of churches, monasteries, convents, and missions, as well as the hospitals and charitable institutions that were established in the New World, were all tangible evidences of the faithful discharge by the Spanish sovereigns of their holy trust as patrons.

The king was amply compensated for the obligations and responsibilities he assumed with reference to the Church. Since Catholicism was indissolubly linked with legal authority, the Church was quite as effective an instrument in the conquest and domination as was the army. It was one of the principal agents of the civil power in America for over three centuries. The clerics, being beholden to the king for great and numerous favors, served him without the slightest inclination to rebel. They felt more closely attached to him than to the pope; they were more regalist than papalist. Given the almost absolute domination exercised by them over the minds of their ignorant flocks, the inestimable value to the crown of its control over the clergy can be appreciated.[64]

Undoubtedly the blind obedience and almost fanatical reverence of the colonials for their "most Catholic Sovereigns" were largely the result of clerical promptings. This was most ample compensation for the cares and expenses of propagating the faith.

---

[64] "The strain of religious enthusiasm could be evoked when necessary by almost any skillful ecclesiastic. Also the fact that every good Catholic attended the confessional once a year, and frequently oftener, gave to the priest the whip hand in many a difficult situation." (Wilfred Hardy Callcott, *Church and State in Mexico, 1822-1857*, Durham, 1926, p. 11.)

CHAPTER II

THE CATHOLIC CHURCH AND THE SPANISH-AMERICAN REVOLUTION

The achievement of independence by Spain's colonies in America disturbed the centuries-old politico-ecclesiastical status. The attitude assumed by the pope, the prelates, and the clergy towards the independence movement and the religious policies adopted by the revolutionaries are subjects of vital importance in this transitional period since they exercised far-reaching influences on the determination of later Church and State relationships.

Conditions within the Church of colonial Spanish-America on the eve of the outbreak of the revolt might have constituted justifiable reasons for added dissatisfaction with Spanish rule.[1] But it is an undeniable fact that religious discontent was not one of the major causes of the wars for independence. This chapter, devoted to the Catholic Church in the Revolution, is prefaced with a description of certain unsatisfactory conditions within the colonial Church, not because of their immediate bearing on the Revolution itself, but because the outcome of the revolt emphasized the necessity of finding a solution for these problems.

The most serious matter was the supremacy of the Church in the economic sphere. The vast wealth of the colonial clergy was notorious, and was represented not only in ecclesiastical buildings and their ornate furnishings, but also in revenue-producing lands and capital loaned at interest on property of individuals. In Peru on the eve of independence there was scarcely an estate of any size which did not belong in whole or in part to the clerics. In Lima, out of 2,806 houses, 1,135 belonged to religious com-

---

[1] The abuses of the ecclesiastical government of the colonies as contributing cause of the wars for independence, are discussed by Miguel Luís Amunátegui, *Los Precursores de la Independencia de Chile* (Santiago, 1870), I, 147-202.

munities, secular ecclesiastics, or pious endowments.[2] Juan and Ulloa in their famous *Noticias Secretas* also remark on the wealth of the clergy in Quito and Peru.[3] A traveler describing Lima in the middle of the eighteenth century wrote, "There are but few who do not pay rent to the Church, either for their houses or their farms."[4]

In New Spain the Church was even more strongly entrenched, economically, if such a thing were possible. On the authority of Lucas Alamán, a staunch defender of the Catholic Church, the property of the Mexican Church in the last days of the colonial period, consisted of one-half of the total value of all productive real estate in New Spain.[5] In 1790, out of 3,387 houses in Mexico City, 1,935 belonged to the Church. Of course, the right of mortmain possessed by it facilitated the gradual but never ending increase in the size of its properties, for land acquired could never be alienated. "The greater became the Church holdings, and they were usually of the best land in a given community, the less land was left for the laity to own, and the fewer were the chances that the very small incipient middle class would get a foothold."[6]

A recent writer on Mexico comments on the wealth of the colonial Church as follows: "The clergy was an economically privileged class from the beginning. The members of it received large grants of land from the crown. Many monasteries, cathedrals and individual prelates were given *encomiendas*—which had more or less the same history as those conferred upon laymen. For the erection of churches, monasteries and residences the royal treasury furnished half the money, the *encomenderos* or the Spanish population in general furnished the other half, and the Indians did the work without remuneration. Ecclesiastical capital was free from taxation—legally in the early days, virtually, al-

---

[2] Sebastian Lorente, *Historia del Peru bajo los Bourbones* (Lima, 1871), pp. 270-271.

[3] Don Jorge Juan y Don Antonio de Ulloa, *Noticias Secretas de América* (London, 1826), pp. 523-525.

[4] *A True and Particular Relation of the Dreadful Earthquake* (London, 1748), pp. 279-280, quoted in Bernard Moses, *Spain's Declining Power in South America* (Berkeley, 1919), p. 301.

[5] Alamán, *Historia de Méjico*, I, 67.

[6] Callcott, *Church and State in Mexico*, p. 14.

ways. The clergy were entitled to collect tithes and first fruits of all agricultural products, to receive fees, dowries, gifts, bequests, alms, and perpetual trust funds. From the outset they had an economic advantage over even the richest *encomenderos*, who had to build their own houses and provide their own working capital, and had not the sources of income that the clergy had. So, with the immense prestige of the Church behind them, it is not surprising that the clergy dominated the colonial era economically and politically."[7]

The considerable sums derived from various sources, like tithes, fees, proceeds from the sales of bulls, gifts, and bequests were generally invested in real estate and real estate mortgages. "As money came easily to the ecclesiastics and as the Church fulminated against usury, they were indulgent creditors. They lent at six, five, and even four per cent, and allowed the debt to run on from generation to generation, provided interest payments were prompt. Real estate mortgages, as a rule, were nominally for a period of ten years, yet the mortgagor felt perfectly sure that he would not be called upon for the principal at the end of the period, if he kept up the interest, but usually he was at liberty to pay the whole debt when he pleased. Some mortgages, however, were 'irredeemable' by agreement. The clergy preferred this form, naturally, as it gave them a perpetual investment without further effort on their part. Mortgaged property was bought and sold freely without consulting the creditor, but could not be divided. Since borrowing was so easy, it is no wonder that landowners continued to invest all capital that came into their possession in this substantial and tax-free form of wealth and to depend upon the never-failing source for their working capital."[8]

Early in the colonial period the crown became convinced of the advisability of restricting the ownership of land by the Church. Viceroy Mendoza was directed to dispose of public land but prevent its falling into mortmain. In 1576 a decree forbade religious orders from acquiring any more property. A decree of 1796 imposed a tax of fifteen per cent on all property sold to the

---

[7] Helen Phipps, *Some Aspects of the Agrarian Question in Mexico* (University of Texas Bulletin, No. 2515), p. 45.

[8] *Ibid.*, pp. 56-57.

Church. The expulsion of the Jesuits in 1767 afforded the crown an excellent opportunity to recover vast estates held in mortmain. In 1804, by a royal decree, all real estate belonging to benevolent institutions, most of which was controlled by the clergy, was taken over by the State. This confiscation included sums invested as loans on properties. Abad y Queipo, bishop-elect of Michoacán, who drew up a memorial in opposition to the decree, pointed out that the withdrawal of the vast loans of the Church would paralyze agriculture and business. The united opposition of the clergy and the great landowners finally accomplished the defeat of the measure.[9]

Within the ranks of the clergy there was an amazing disparity in economic condition. Whereas many prelates enjoyed incomes of from 200,000 to 650,000 pesos, nine-tenths of the clergy did not receive more than 150 to 300 pesos annually. Alexander von Humboldt commented with surprise on this "inequality of income of the clergy, a part of which lives in utmost misery, a step from some individuals, who enjoy incomes superior to that of many sovereigns of Germany."[10]

There was also great disparity among the clergy as to morality. Unfriendly critics of the Catholic Church seem to delight in relating in detail the worldliness, acquisitiveness, love of ease and luxuries, and loose morals of the clerics. It is true that there was grave immorality among the clergy, especially the regulars, and it was on a sufficiently large scale to warrant remark.[11] Even Alamán admits this. But to stress this side of ecclesiastical life and activity in the Spanish colonies to the exclusion of any mention of the real constructive and lasting achievements of the Church in the transplanting of European civilization to America is to distort history. Pages are devoted to particular and isolated instances of the violation of the vow of celibacy by prelates and monks, but nothing is said of the devotion and self-abnegation of

---

[9] Alamán, op. cit., I, 137.

[10] Alexander von Humboldt, Ensayo Político sobre la Nueva-España (Paris, 1821), I, 247; José María Mora, Obras Sueltas (Paris, 1837), I, 112.

[11] Juan and Ulloa devoted a chapter in their famous secret report of investigations in Peru to the subject of clerical immorality. Their evidence has been accepted as incontrovertible. It is interesting to note that they gave the Jesuits a clean bill of health. (Noticias Secretas, Chap. VIII.)

the vast majority of friars and priests who labored for the faith
among the Spaniards in the cities, the castes in the rural districts, and the neophytes along the far-flung frontiers. It is
charged that the clergy were heartless exploiters of the Indians,
but there is no mention of the fact that the Church was the Indians'
staunchest defender from first to last. There are lengthy descriptions of the great wealth of the Church, but no admission that
all educational and charitable facilities, in so far as they existed
(and they were not inconsiderable), were supported by that institution. All this is represented as history.[12] So conspicuous was
the work of the Catholic Church in the missionary field, in education, the charities, and the arts, that failure to recognize its constructive achievements would be most unjust.

That the Spanish colonials, high and low, were superficially
instructed in the mysteries of religion is another story, and, unfortunately, true. To what extent the clergy were responsible for
this situation it is difficult to say. As regards the Indians and
the castes, who can claim that they were promising material for
conversion? Given their undeveloped, primitive minds, and their
bewilderment on being thrust suddenly into a social state to which
they could not adapt themselves for hundreds of years, what could
be expected of the missionaries? The Catholic Church with its
imagery and ceremonials was best adapted to appeal to the savages, and realizing this, the friars quite naturally made good
use of pomp and display. If the result was a thin veneer of Christianity, that at least was an achievement. The missionaries were
deserving of more credit for what they accomplished than condemnation for what they failed to do. And, as for the whites,
those of European origin, their religious shallowness must have
been the result of the failure of the clergy to distinguish between
their mentality and that of the Indians. The priests carefully
avoided making any appeal to mature and self-reliant intellects.
All were treated like children; their emotions were aroused by
the use of lavish ceremonials, display, and imagery. What wonder,

---

[12] Mr. Ernest Gruening, for example, in his recent book on Mexico (*Mexico
and Its Heritage*, New York, 1928, pp. 171-183), in his chapter on the
colonial Church has much to say about the wealth of the Church, but absolutely nothing about its work in education and the charities.

4

then, that the colonials, white and colored, came to believe that
the essence of the faith was its trappings? There was much profane pomp with little piety.[13] Theirs was superficial faith, blind
belief with little understanding. And there was no disposition on
the part of the clergy to make them understand so long as they
believed. Unreasoning obedience to Church and king was inculcated
by the clergy, who studiously avoided analysis of the foundations of this dual obedience.

Although the Church was drawn into the vortex of the Revolution, religion itself, superficial as it was, did not constitute a
cause of the revolt from Spanish authority. Substantiation of the
truth of this assertion is not difficult to find. The fact that the
lower clergy generally supported the Revolution, whereas the
higher ecclesiastics remained loyal to the Spanish cause is significant. It meant that the clericals participated in the movement
for social, political, and economic, but not for religious reasons.
A dominant cause for dissatisfaction with Spanish rule was the
monopolizing of the highest positions, political, military, and
ecclesiastical, by the Spanish-born, or *Gachupines.* The Amer-
ican-born whites, or creoles, resented Spanish favoritism and this
resentment was as bitterly harbored by the parish priest as by
the sergeant in the army or the *regidor* in the municipality.
Among the clergy there existed the rivalry of birth. There were
actually entire religious communities made up of *Gachupines* or
of creoles. The great economic inequality existent in the colonial
clergy has already been alluded to. The cry of Father Hidalgo
typified the spirit of creole revolt; "Down with bad government!
Death to the *Gachupines!* Long live religion! Long live our most
holy Virgin of Guadalupe!" In this cry was proclaimed the revolt against political, social, and economic abuses. No opposition
to the Church was expressed; rather, adherence was proclaimed;
but the invocation of the Indians' Virgin did portend a nationalization of the faith.

Not only was religion not a cause of the Revolution, but rebellion against the Church at that time was unthinkable. The
colonials, for the greater part, professed a very different attitude towards religion from that felt for the State. The Church

---

[13] Alamán, *op. cit.,* I, 65.

had impressed itself upon the minds of the people and had convinced them that only by its ministrations was it possible to secure the blessings of eternal salvation. So great was the power of the clergy and its influence over the ignorant inhabitants of the colonies, that the French minister Vergennes believed this alone would make secession of the Spanish colonies impossible.[14] And well it might had the whole weight of the clergy, high and low, been thrown into the balance on the side of the Spanish king. But, strangely enough, leadership was assumed by the clergy on both sides in the struggle, and at times the war was carried on almost wholly by them.

If religion was not a contributing factor to the outbreak of the Revolution, it nevertheless was dragged into the fray and made to serve personal interests. "Who would believe," asked Father Hidalgo, "that the shamelessness of the Spaniards would go so far as to profane the most sacred things in order to perpetuate their intolerable domination . . . to make use of excommunications against the very spirit of the Church, to launch them when there is no religious issue whatever involved"?[15] "Religion," wrote Lucas Alamán, "served as the instrument of one and the other party, and the people did not know whom to believe, hearing its respectable name invoked in favor of the two causes."[16] For example, when Hidalgo, as a political move to secure the support of the Indians, proclaimed the Virgin of Guadalupe as the patroness of the revolt, Viceroy Venegas, to excite the religious fanaticism of the other social classes, proclaimed the *Virgen de los Remedios* "generala" of the royalist troops. Thus we have a war of the Virgins. This instance was neither the first nor the last in Mexican history in which religious prejudices were excited to serve political ends.

Perhaps nothing could evidence more emphatically the virtual non-existence of the religious issue in the Spanish-American Revolution than declarations by revolutionary leaders of loyalty to

---

[14] Bernard Moses, *The Intellectual Background of the Revolution in South America, 1810-1824* (New York, 1926), p. 69.

[15] Genaro García, ed., *El Clero de México y la Guerra de Independencia* (Mexico, 1906), pp. 45-47.

[16] Alamán, *op. cit.*, II, 31.

Catholicism and the inclusion in the first organic laws of clauses providing for the continuance of that religion as a privileged faith. Francisco de Miranda, "the precursor of the Revolution," in submitting a plan of government to the *cabildo* of Caracas in 1808, advocated Roman Catholicism as the national religion. The status of the Church, including its tithes, he advised, should be preserved. Since he was saturated with the liberal doctrines of the French Revolution, it is but natural that he should have advocated religious toleration "as a principle of natural right."[17]

Father Hidalgo, in the *Grito de Dolores*, as has been shown, declared adherence to the faith. Notwithstanding his denunciation by the Church as an "heretic, apostate, and follower of Martin Luther," he was always a fervent Catholic. In his manifesto of December 15, 1810, he declared that it was his intention to establish a representative congress of the Mexican people, and the principal object of that congress was to maintain the Catholic religion. Ignacio Rayón declared on October 23, 1810, in the name of the *generalísimo* (Hidalgo): "the object of the plan of independence is nothing other than the maintenance of the Holy Religion and its dogma, the conservation of liberty, and the alleviation of the people."[18]

José María Morelos, a curate like Hidalgo, was a Roman Catholic from first to last. To the Congress of Chilpanzingo he declared himself to be in favor of the Roman Catholic religion without the toleration of any other faith. His advice was accepted and incorporated into both the declaration of independence (November 6, 1813), and the Constitution of Apatzingan (October 22, 1814).

Mariano Moreno, secretary of the Buenos Aires *junta*, and so-called "soul of the Revolution of 1810," although steeped in the philosophy of Rousseau (he translated the *Social Contract*), was nevertheless fanatical in his religious opinions. His reverence for the doctrines of the Church and appreciation of her divine

---

[17] William Spence Robertson, *History of the Latin-American Nations* (New York, 1925), pp. 35-55.

[18] Vicente Riva Palacio, ed., *México á Través de Los Siglos* (Barcelona, 1889), III, 95.

mission, constrained him to oppose any alteration in the position of Catholicism as the national faith.

San Martín, "the Protector," and Belgrano, the Argentinian military hero, advocated Roman Catholicism as the state religion. General Belgrano was a Catholic who imposed rigid religious practices on his army. He understood the value of the influence of the clergy and sought their aid. Although he was accused of being a hypocrite and of making an ostentatious display of religious practices to deceive the people, he may nevertheless have been a sincere Christian. On April 6, 1814, Belgrano wrote a remarkable letter to San Martín advising him to keep alive in his army a religious sentiment. He said that it was a war not only of arms but of opinions. "Do not cease to implore Nuestra Señora de los Mercedes," he wrote, "and name her *generala* of the rebel armies. Give scapularies to the troops. Act like a Christian general [i.e., a Roman Catholic]. Watch your language. Say nothing disrespectful about religion." San Martín followed the advice of Belgrano. In the center of the camp a portable altar was erected on which the chaplains attached to the army celebrated mass on Sundays and feast days. San Martín's ideas on the subject of the Church are best expressed in his *Estatuto Provisorio* of 1821, proclaimed for the temporary governance of Peru. The Roman Catholic faith was declared to be the religion of the State and the government recognized as one of its prime duties the maintenance and protection of that Church, by all possible means. Whoever attacked its dogmas or principles, in public or private, was to be severely punished.[19]

Simón Bolívar was an exception among the great leaders of Latin-American independence, for he advocated separation of Church and State. Nominally a Catholic himself, the "Liberator," like Miranda, had drunk deeply of the teachings of the French philosophers and religion at best rested but lightly upon him, until the last few years of his life. Notwithstanding his liberal

---

[19] Agustín Piaggio, *Influencia del Clero en Independencia Argentina, 1810-1820* (Madrid, 1912), pp. 67-69, 101; L. F. Villarán, *La Constitución Peruana* (Lima, 1899), p. 78; G. H. Stuart, *The Governmental System of Peru* (Washington, 1925), p. 4.

religious views and his unflagging efforts to have them incorporated into the organic laws of Venezuela and New Granada, Bolívar recognized the political importance of clerical support of the Revolution. No one realized better than he the strength of the hold exercised by the Church over the masses of both high and low degree. He therefore was careful not to antagonize the clergy and put aside personal opinion for the sake of the general good.[20] For example, seeing that separation of Church and State was unacceptable, he hastened to propose that a diplomatic mission be sent to Rome to conclude a concordat with the papacy. His relations with Bishops Lasso and Jiménez reveal Bolívar as a man who would not allow his personal opinions to override practical considerations in formulating a religious policy for Colombia. The Liberator's handling of the religious problem mark him as a great statesman. As indicated by the above survey, no prominent leader of the Revolution, "good" Catholic or not, was an enemy of the Church.

In the early days of the revolt the political practice in Latin America was to offer to Catholicism respect for its old privileges and exclusions. In the opinion of the great Argentinian constitutionalist Alberdi, this was a tactical concession upon which the success of the Revolution depended, and was comparable to the same discretion of the revolutionaries in protesting that they were fighting for the rights of Ferdinand VII.[21] It seems, however, that the analogy was poor, for the religious course adopted was a matter of both conscience and policy, whereas the political course was one of policy alone. In the writing of the religious clause of our own constitution, for example, the framers made no bid for originality; they merely guaranteed the *continuance* of religious liberty and freedom of conscience. The Latin Americans, also, chose to perpetuate what they were accustomed to, i.e., the official cult which they had inherited from Spain.

An examination of the first organic laws adopted by the nascent republics of Latin America shows that they maintained the Roman

---

[20] José Gil Fortoul, *Historia Constitucional de Venezuela* (Berlin, 1907), I, 160, note 2; Carlos A. Villanueva, *La Santa Alianza* (Paris, n. d.), p. 202.

[21] J. B. Alberdi, *Bases y Puntos de Partida para la Organización Política de la República Argentina* (Buenos Aires, 1914), p. 111.

Catholic religion as the privileged faith. The first Argentinian constitutions contained this significant religious seal. The *Estatuto Provisional* of 1815 declared Roman Catholicism to be the religion of the State. A notable feature of this instrument of government was that it sanctioned religious toleration. The *Reglamento* of 1817 reproduced the religious declarations of the *Estatuto Provisional*. The Constitution of 1819 declared, "The government owes to religion the most efficacious and powerful protection, and all the inhabitants are bound to respect it, whatever might be their private opinions." Ecclesiastical dignitaries were placed in the category of State officials.[22]

The different constitutions of Chile from 1811 to 1818 contained provisions proclaiming the Roman Catholic religion to be that of the State, and excluded all others. The Constitution of 1818 declared that the protection, conservation, purity, and inviolability of the Catholic religion ought to be one of the chief duties of the State, "which will never permit any other public religion or doctrine contrary to that of Jesus Christ." The organic law of 1823 prohibited even the private exercise of the other religions.[23] As for Peru the features of San Martín's *Estatuto Provisorio* have already been mentioned. Only by a narrow margin was religious toleration excluded from Peru's next constitution, that of 1822.

In Mexico, the Congress of Chilpanzingo when proclaiming Mexican independence on November 6, 1813, declared that, in casting off the Spanish control, the Mexican people would be free "to celebrate concordats with the Holy Pointiff for the governance of the Catholic Church, in order that no other religion shall be recognized." In the Constitution of Apatzingan a great deal of space was devoted to the subject of Catholicism as the sole tolerated religion of the nation. Heresy and apostasy constituted offenses for which naturalized citizens could lose their citizenship. In the electoral system, the parish was the primary voting unit;

---

[22] Agustín de Vedia, *Constitución Argentina* (Buenos Aires, 1907), pp. 41, 49; Legón, *Patronato Nacional,* p. 249.

[23] Alcibiades Roldán, *Elementos de Derecho Constitucional de Chile* (Santiago, 1917), p. 221; Justo Arosemena, *Estudios Constitucionales sobre los Gobiernos de la América Latina* (Paris, 1888), I, 105.

the electors there chosen by the voters were obliged to pass into the principal church "where a solemn mass to the Holy Ghost will be [was] celebrated and an address appropriate to the circumstances delivered by the priest or some other ecclesiastic." When the electors had named a representative for Congress, they were again to attend church for a solemn *Te Deum.* The *Plan de Iguala,* announced February 24, 1821, provided as one of its three guarantees the security of the Church. Only the Roman Catholic religion was to be tolerated in Mexico, and the members of the regular and secular clergy throughout the country were to be protected in all their rights and properties. In other words the ecclesiastical *fueros* were guaranteed.[24]

The Venezuelan declaration of independence of July 5, 1811, contained the following confession of faith: "Taking the Supreme Being as witness to the justice of our actions and the rectitude of our intentions, imploring this Divine and Heavenly aid, and protesting before Him, in the moment of our birth to that dignity which His Providence restores to us, our desire to live and die free, and maintaining the Holy Catholic and Apostolic Religion of Jesus Christ as the first of our duties." In the Constitution of 1811, the Roman faith was declared to be the religion of the State. Although the majority of the delegates were members of the school of Rousseauan philosophy, they consented to the religious article so as not to alienate the good will of the national clergy. The oath of allegiance to the Republic was as follows: "I swear to defend with my body and all my strength the States of the Venezuelan Confederation, and to conserve and maintain pure and sound the Roman Catholic Apostolic faith, one and exclusive, and to defend the mystery of the Immaculate Conception of the Virgin our Mother." Without exception the numerous revolutionary charters of government in Venezuela and New Granada were featured by clauses declaring Roman Catholicism to be the religion of the State.[25]

Not only did the revolutionary governments swear continued

---

[24] José M. Gamboa, *Leyes Constitucionales de México Durante el Siglo XIX* (Mexico, 1901), pp. 235-273, 282-283.

[25] Gil Fortoul, *op. cit.,* I, 160, 175, 177; P. Pedro Leturia, *La Acción Diplomática de Bolívar ante Pío VII, 1820-1823* (Madrid, 1925), p. 74.

allegiance to the Roman faith, but, with equal unanimity, they proposed to exercise the patronage that once belonged to the kings of Spain. The problem of *patronato nacional* occupied a more important position in the revolutionary history of Argentina than elsewhere because the patronal authority of the Spanish king was never restored after the original outbreak in 1810. Mariano Moreno, secretary of the *junta*, in a set of rules drawn up for the guidance of that body declared, "The objects of the *patronato* are cared for by the *junta* in the same way as by the viceroys." The *junta* in substituting itself for the viceroy presumed to assume the jurisdiction that belonged to that official as vice-patron.[26] The colonial laws on patronage were recognized just as were Spanish laws in other matters. The *junta* not only exercised the old patronage, but with wise foresight, it proposed to extend these rights if non-communication between the ecclesiastical authorities in the colonies and the home country made it necessary.

A deposition of the bishop of Córdova created a problem touching on the right of the *junta* to exercise the patronage and appoint to benefices. The question was submitted by Saavedra and Moreno, president and secretary respectively of the *junta*, to two Córdovan ecclesiastics: Dean Gregorio Funes, and Dr. Juan Luís de Aquirre y Texada. The reports of both clerics were impregnated with vigorous regalism; in brief, they were strongly of the opinion that royal patronage inhered in sovereignty, and consequently the *junta* as the legitimate sovereign, could exercise the one-time regal patronal rights. The opinion of Funes is worth quoting: "The Spanish kings acquired their notable prerogative by their liberalities toward the Church, but these liberalities were not made with their own patrimonial goods, but with the public funds of the State, whose faithful administration prohibited them from any other use than the common good; thus they owed the right of patronage to the expenditures from the public treasury; it came to be an extension of the rights of sovereignty, which were consolidated in the crown but not in the persons who possessed or administered the regal authority."[27]

---

[26] Chacaltana, *Patronato Nacional Argentino,* p. 64; Legón, *op. cit.,* p. 229.
[27] Piaggio, *op. cit.,* p. 330; Legón, *op. cit.,* pp. 234-240.

Until June 4, 1813, the revolutionary government of La Plata posed as the vice-patron, upon the legal fiction that it was ruling in the name of Ferdinand VII. On that date, however, the *patronato de Indias* was formally terminated by the constituent assembly, which body proceeded to make rules for the filling of ecclesiastical vacancies. By the *Estatuto* of 1815 the Supreme Director was delegated authority to make appointments to vacant benefices. Finally, the inherence of the patronage in the State was specifically stated in a resolution of the Congress of Tucumán (1817), in the *Reglamento Provisorio* of 1817, and in the Constitution of 1819. Needless to say, none of the radical pretentions of the rebel government to exercise the patronage, were recognized in Madrid or Rome.[28]

In Venezuela, Archbishop Coll y Prat, on July 6, 1811, proclaimed the end of the Spanish patronage. The constitution which was framed soon after vested in the government rights over the Church which had previously belonged to the Spanish crown. However, to conciliate the Archbishop and recalcitrant clergy, the government entered into negotiations with the former concerning appointments "until contact could be established with Rome." But the Republic was overthrown before an agreement could be reached. In New Granada, the Constitution of Cundinamarca, March 30, 1811, while providing for the establishment of *patronato nacional,* declared that for the secure continuance of the patronage it would be necessary to appeal to the Holy See. After the Congress of Angostura had provided for the assumption of the right of patronage by Colombia, a provisional law was passed, which declared that until a concordat could be arranged with the Vatican to settle the matter of the patronage, the vice-presidents of Venezuela and New Granada should pass upon those nominated for ecclesiastical offices below that of bishop.[29] This inclination to seek pontifical confirmation of the patronage has been interpreted by Father Leturia as meaning recognition on the part of the republics that the patronage was

---

[28] *Ibid.,* pp. 247-250, 492.

[29] P. Leturia, "Alusiones en la Cámara Argentina al Origen Histórico del Patronato de Indias," in *Razón y Fé,* V, 78, p. 332; Leturia, *Acción Diplomática,* pp. 143-144.

not inherent in their newly-won sovereignty. This is not necessarily true, for one can firmly believe in the legitimacy of his
rights, and at the same time seek to have others recognize them.

It was inevitable, since the Spanish monarchs had emphasized
for three centuries *real patronato* "as a traditional symbol, a
ritualistic principle of power, incarnate in monarchy and in the
historical entity of Spain," that the revolting colonials should
regard it as an inherent, secular right, inseparable from sovereignty. What was more natural than that they, as the heirs
of the prerogatives of the Spanish monarchy in America, should
exercise national patronage over the Church? It has been suggested, and the explanation is plausible, that the new republics
assumed control over the Church to curb its power and prevent
as far as possible the interference of the ecclesiastics in the political affairs of the states. This policy was rendered doubly necessary since the higher Church dignitaries were Spanish sympa-
thizers who frowned on the Revolution.

The support given the revolutionary cause by clericals was no
inconsiderable factor in the eventual winning of independence.
The nature and extent of their assistance, rendered under radically different conditions, is adequately exemplified in the revolutionary histories of Argentina and Mexico.

In Argentina, as in other parts of America, a considerable
portion of the creole clergy, both regular and secular, not only
favored independence but worked for it. One of the leaders of
the "Revolt of May 25th" was a Dominican friar, Ignacio Grela.
It is said that he did more than anyone else to maintain order.
In a petition presented to the *cabildo* on the above date appeared
the names of seventeen religious of different orders. An observer
spoke of seeing, in the interior, more than three thousand Indians
in arms under the direction of curates. Perhaps the most famous
of all the clerical supporters of independence was Dean Gregorio
Funes of Córdova. It was largely due to his efforts that the
counter-revolutionary activities centering in Córdova were defeated.[30] Says Levene, "To its honor the Hispanic-American clergy
were enrolled in the revolutionary ranks embracing the cause of
emancipation. In the province of La Plata not only could numer-

---

[30] Piaggio, *op. cit.*, pp. 21, 48-54.

ous priests be mentioned who figured in the Revolution, but a legion of them did quiet work in favor of the revolutionary cause. These were the parish priests who after mass read to the people articles declaring principles and ideals of the Revolution."[31]

Not only did the clergy preach support of the Revolution in La Plata, but they aided it with money. "The War of Independence," says Piaggio, "was waged in large part with the money which the clergy gave personally." The influence of clerics in popular assemblies was equal to that of any other class. In the *Junta de Gobierno*, named on May 21, 1810 by the *Cabildo Abierto*, the presbyter Dr. Sola occupied a seat. A *vocal*, or member of the *Junta* of May 25 was the curate Manuel Alberti. In the Assembly of 1813 were twelve ecclesiastics. The "reporter" of this assembly was Father Cayetano Rodríguez. This same religious, as secretary of the Congress of Tucumán, was the principal author of the famous declaration of independence promulgated by that congress. Of the twenty-nine signers of the declaration, sixteen were curates. In the same congress, it was a curate, Justo de Oro, who was most responsible for the defeat of the monarchial project presented by Belgrano.[32]

In Mexico, in addition to Hidalgo and Morelos, "More than one hundred parish priests, including the leaders, Matamoros and Mercado, and some fifty members of the religious brotherhoods, took the field.[33] Their presence in the revolutionary ranks testified to the social ingredients of the movement, and refuted the allegations of its 'heretical' character. More in contact with the masses than the higher clergy, many of them risen from the ranks of the dispossessed, they knew and felt keenly the oppressions and discriminations of the colonial system. Like their leaders many of them died on the battle-fields or before the firing squad."[34]

---

[31] Ricardo Levene, *Lecciones de Historia Argentina* (Buenos Aires, 1919), II, 273.

[32] Piaggio, *op. cit.,* pp. 19, 24, 108, 213, 233; For additional information on the contribution of the clergy of Argentina to the winning of independence, see Adolfo P. Carranza (ed.), *El Clero Argentino de 1810 á 1830* (Buenos Aires, 1907, 2 v.), and J. Francisco V. Silva, *El Libertador Bolívar y el Deán Funes* (Madrid, n.d.), pp. 106-114.

[33] A list of the members of the secular and regular clergy who fought for independence in Mexico is given in Riva Palacio (*op. cit.,* III, Doc. 11, in the Appendix). [34] Gruening, *op. cit.,* pp. 187-188.

So active were the Mexican clergy in the Revolution that Lucas Alamán credits them with sustaining it almost alone. He says, "The clergy and disorder were precisely what sustained the Revolution; without the first there would have been a lack of chiefs; without the second there would have been no followers."[35]

After fulminating with the bitterest venom for ten years against the "heresy of rebellion," the higher clergy, and therefore the Mexican Church itself, suddenly threw its support in favor of independence. The reason for the *volte-face* was fear for the clerical interests in Mexico because of the startling anti-clerical reforms adopted by the Spanish Cortes of 1820. The detested Constitution of Cádiz with its democratic features and curtailment of clerical immunities had been reëstablished; the Inquisition was abolished; liberty of the press was guaranteed; the *fuero eclesiástico* was abolished; religious orders were suppressed, and church tithes were seized. These ecclesiastical reforms of the Cortes produced a greater discontent in Mexico than in Spain, because, according to Alamán, those offended by the measures were the most influential and most elevated. Consequently, "religion no longer 'condemned rebellion' when it was in the clerical interest. Forgotten were the solemn oaths of loyalty to king and constitution, and the ever-pledged support of constituted authority. Bishop Pérez of Puebla, who shortly before had held that the people's love for their king should become a 'rational delirium,' and their fidelity 'a dominant passion,' was the ecclesiastic leader of the new movement. The clergy conceived the plan, selected its military leader, supplied funds, furnished the printing press to disseminate the new idea, and worked actively in persuading the royalist soldiers to desert their banners. *Te Deums* in every temple celebrated the new order which seated an emperor on the Mexican throne with

---

[35] Alamán, *op. cit.*, III, 213. Because Genaro García disagreed with the popular opinion as expressed by Alamán that the lower clergy were very partisan toward the War for Independence, he published a set of documents (*El Clero de México y la Guerra de Independencia*, Mexico, 1906) to demonstrate that the lower clergy, except on rare occasions were unconditionally allied with the Spanish monarchy, and that the insurgents, far from giving evidence of religious fanaticism, were distinguished by lack of religious scruples. This publication does not disprove, however, that not a few curates, although a small minority, were sympathetic toward the insurgent cause.

unusual pomp and glitter, established 'exclusion and intolerance of any religion but the Catholic, Apostolic, and Roman,' and ranked blasphemy with 'atrocious murder' as the only unpardonable crimes."[36] The part played by the higher clergy of Mexico in the achievement of independence deserves for them not the title of "patriot," such as belongs to Hidalgo and Morelos, but that of "traitor." There is no blacker page than this in the history of the Catholic Church in America.[37]

Opposed to the disorganized minority of the lower clergy which supported the Revolution was the great Catholic hierarchy of Spanish America which exerted its might against the disavowal of the legitimate authority of the Spanish king. That the Church should combat rebellion was obvious, for in America it was closely identified with the monarchy. If the crown was beholden to the Church for the implanting of Spanish civilization in the New World, and the inculcation in the colonials of a spirit of obedience to the king, the Church on the other hand was obligated to the crown for protection, and for the innumerable privileges, exemptions, and grants which had enabled it to become great and wealthy. The American Church, therefore, would have been not only ingrate, but short-sighted, to abandon its ancient champion and benefactor and tempt fate by making a change.

In Mexico the revolutionary outbreak initiated by Father Miguel Hidalgo and continued by Morelos, another curate, and by other patriots, was "received by the higher clergy with a bolt of lightning in their hands, and maledictions on their lips."[38] This, nothwithstanding the fact that Hidalgo declared that one of the principal objects of the congress he intended to summon was to maintain the Catholic religion. There is no doubt that the Church was more aroused against the *rebellion*, than against the supposed heresy of those rebelling. This is evidenced by statements and actions of ecclesiastical dignitaries and of institutions like the Inquisition.

Bishop-elect Manuel Abad y Queipo of Michoacán issued a proclamation which declared that the curate Hidalgo "a pastor

---

[36] Gruening, *op. cit.*, pp. 188-189.

[37] For the support of the clergy to the Revolution in New Granada, see José Manuel Groot, *Historia Eclesiástica y Civil de Nueva Granada* (Bogotá, 1889), III, 244-245, 269, IV, 35.   [38] Riva Palacio, *op. cit.*, III, 127.

of souls, a priest of Jesus Christ, a minister of the God of Peace, had raised a standard of rebellion and seduced a number of innocent people." It is to be noted that he was accused of rebellion, not against the Church, but against political authority; and because he had disturbed the peace and broken faith with Ferdinand VII he was excommunicated. Since Hidalgo was not under the jurisdiction of the Bishop of Michoacán, he denied the validity of the edict of excommunication. Furthermore, he contended that, since Abad y Queipo had been nominated by the Spanish Regency, which had no authority over the patronage in America, and since the nomination had not been confirmed by the pope, he therefore was holding his office illegally and could not exercise its powers.[39] Archbishop Lizana, however, published an edict in which he declared that the ban published by Abad y Quiepo was valid and emanated from competent authority, and the faithful were obliged under penalties to observe it. A few days later the Archbishop issued a pastoral in which he condemned the principles of the Revolution. The curate Hidalgo was branded as an heretic and the faithful were commanded to "flee from him who teaches doctrines contrary to the Holy Faith."[40] The venom of Abad y Queipo is revealed in the following denunciation of the patriots: "The Count of Buffon and other naturalists contend that animals of the Old World, transferred to the New, have degenerated. Experience proves this false, for those that live in good climes and fields are as big and robust in this continent as the best of the species in the old continent. But if all the children and descendants of the Spaniards transplanted to the New World were like the curate Hidalgo and his principal accomplices, then it could be affirmed in all truth that the Spanish race had degenerated in the tropics, losing all the good and acquiring all the evil that can be found in the human species."[41]

---

[39] A few years later, Abad y Queipo wrote an exposition (*Breve Exposición sobre el Real Patronato,* Madrid, 1820), to prove that his nomination by the Spanish Regency was definitive. The lack of pontifical confirmation possessed no value, he said. His argument contains a strange mixture of regalistic and ultramontane doctrine.

[40] Alamán, *op. cit.,* I, 390; Riva Palacio, *op. cit.,* III, 130-131.

[41] *Colección de Documentos para la Historia de la Guerra de Independencia de México de 1808 á 1821* (Mexico, 1877), IV, 439.

The death of Archbishop Lizana early in 1811 made way for the nomination by the Regency of Antonio Bergosa y Jordán, Bishop of Oaxaca, as successor to the archiepiscopal see. Of all the Mexican ecclesiastics, Bergosa was perhaps the most outspoken in his condemnation of the Revolution. He celebrated with a great and solemn festival the restoration of Ferdinand VII. "It would be impossible," said Alamán, "to repeat it with equal grandeur." Notwithstanding the belligerent *Españolismo* of Bergosa and Abad y Queipo, both prelates were rewarded by Ferdinand for their untiring support of his cause by being removed from their respective sees. Since the king did not wish to confirm acts of the provisional government during his absence, and since he regarded the naming of prelates as a royal prerogative which could not be exercised by the Regency, the appointees of that government were removed. Abad y Queipo returned to Spain, and Bergosa to his see at Oaxaca. Canon Pedro Font was appointed by Ferdinand Archbishop of Mexico. Although not as vitriolic as Abad y Queipo and Bergosa, the other bishops of Mexico joined the chorus of denunciation. On March 28, 1811, the metropolitan chapter of Mexico issued the following, "When the future generations read with horror about the enormous crimes, the abominable projects, the incalculable evils of which on New Spain a single perfidious priest, ignorant and belonging to Satan, has been the author, they will see with the greatest pleasure the clergy of Mexico, especially all the parish priests, reproving such an iniquitous revolution, abominating the detestable means that were adopted for it, cursing the authors of so many and such horrible crimes, deploring the sins committed, preaching peace and subordination, and restraining in a thousand ways the torrent of misfortune that was about to submerge the most happy people in the world."[42]

In the following year the same archiepiscopal chapter exhorted the curates who were partisans of the Revolution, to comply with the duties of their ministry and "abstain from mixing in questions foreign to their profession." Thereby exhibiting a refreshing disregard for their own extra-ecclesiastical interference. In remarking about the censures and excommunications issued by

---

[42] García, *op. cit.*, p. 112.

the higher clergy upon the rebels, Lucas Alamán says, "The arms of religion began at that moment to be weakened, and it cannot be doubted that employing them on this occasion as auxiliaries in political matters was one of the principal causes which contributed to lessen their effectiveness."[43]

In this ardent crusade the Inquisition took an active part. This was not to be wondered at for the Holy Office had been used for political purposes since its establishment in America. During the revolt at Valladolid in 1808 it issued an edict to the following effect: "The sovereign pontiffs, among them Clement XI, having entrusted to the Holy Office of the Inquisition of Spain, the duty of watching over the fidelity which all their vassals owe to their Catholic Majesties, and at the same time regarding it as their duty to strengthen the throne of our august monarch Ferdinand VII, establish it as a rule . . . that the king received his power and authority from God, and that you ought to believe it as divine faith."[44] Thus the Inquisition, to aid the Spanish cause in America, did not hesitate to brand as heresy the very principle of popular sovereignty which was being invoked by the Spaniards in the struggle against the French.

The weight of the Holy Office was brought to bear upon the rebellious curates Hidalgo and Morelos. On October 13, 1810, a report was published concerning the former in which violent accusations were made against his Catholicism. It was charged "that Hidalgo was a partisan of French liberty, a libertine, a formal heretic, a Judaiser, a Lutheran, a Calvinist, a rebel, a schismatic, and a suspected atheist." Three days later the Inquisition issued an edict concerning Hidalgo. In that proclamation certain denunciations which had been quietly reposing in the inquisitorial archives were published as damning evidence. Hidalgo was accused of denying that God chastised with temporal punishments. He was accused of speaking disdainfully of the Popes and of intimating that a certain Pope who had been canonized ought to be in hell. He was accused of accepting the doctrines of Luther in regard to the eucharist and auricular confession. With apparent inconsistency, he was accused of denying

---

[43] Alamán, *op. cit.*, I, 392.

[44] J. Pérez Lugo, *La Cuestión Religiosa en México* (Mexico, 1927), p. 15.

5

the authenticity of certain portions of the Bible. Further, it was alleged that Hidalgo had described fornication as a natural and innocent act, and that he had made a compact with a woman to foster that crime. It was stated that Hidalgo had declared war on God, his holy religion, and the fatherland. Upon pain of excommunication, the accused priest was summoned to appear before the inquisitorial tribunal in Mexico City within thirty days. It was proclaimed that, if he failed to appear, his trial would proceed *in absentia*. The edict concluded by announcing that all persons who supported the revolution, who received revolutionary proclamations, who maintained relations with Hidalgo, who failed to denounce him, or who promulgated revolutionary ideas, would be punished by a heavy fine, by excommunication, and by the other punishments provided by canon law and papal bulls."[45] Because of his political activities and pretended heresies Father Hidalgo was unfrocked and turned over to the civil authorities for execution.

No sooner was the Constitution of Apatzingan adopted than the Inquisition rushed to the aid of the civil authorities in attacking it. Although that instrument of government declared Roman Catholicism to be the State religion to the exclusion of all others, it was condemned because it sought to legalize the rebellion. In this instance the Holy Office resorted to no subterfuge— it was acting openly in a political capacity.

When Morelos was captured toward the end of 1815 he was thrown into a cell of the Inquisition in Mexico City. The Holy Office declared him to be "heretic, propagator of heresy, pursuer and disturber of the ecclesiastical hierarchy, profaner of the holy sacraments, schismatic, lascivious, hypocrite, irreconcilable enemy of Christianity, and traitor to God, king, and pope." After a two days' trial, "the most expeditious in the annals of the Holy Office," according to H. C. Lea, the tribunal condemned Morelos to degradation and execution. Morelos was the last heretic sentenced to death by the Inquisition in Mexico.

Father Mariano Cuevas, ecclesiastical historian, declares that

---

[45] William Spence Robertson, *Rise of the Spanish-American Republics* (New York, 1918), pp. 90-91.

the Church was in no way responsible for the activities of the Inquisition in Mexico as narrated above. "That tribunal," he says, "after 1808 did not have in Mexico a personnel which could function validly or licitly; its excommunications were null and they and all the acts of the judges were outside the responsibilities of the Church." Grounds for the above assertion he finds in the following: On December 4, 1808, Napoleon decreed the suppression of the Holy Office in Spain, and the decree was enforced by Joseph Bonaparte. Since the Mexican Inquisition was subordinate to that of Spain, it legally ceased to exist with the suppression of the parent body. The tribunal which condemned Hidalgo, therefore, was a spurious body. The Cortes of Spain declared in 1813 that the Inquisition was incompatible with the Constitution of 1812, and so abolished it. But Ferdinand restored it in 1814 in Spain and in America. What then about the legality of the body which condemned Morelos in November, 1815? Father Cuevas asserts that this also was a "fictitious Inquisition," for he thinks that the conduct of the *auto de fé* by Viceroy Calleja and the Inquisitor General was uncanonical.[46] Whatever may have been the validity of the acts of the Inquisition in Mexico, it is nevertheless true that the high ecclesiastics in that tribunal adopted the same attitude toward the Revolution as that of their brother prelates in the secular and regular clergy.[47]

Not with bans and fulminations alone were the high clergy content to fight the Revolution. The most considerable material contribution of the Church to the royalist cause was its financial assistance. Church bells were gladly donated to the civil authorities to be melted into cannon. Whereas the Spaniards themselves showed little will to make contributions, the clergy dug deep into their treasures. Finally, some of the most belligerent curates actually bore arms in the royalist armies. Bishop Cabañas of Guadalajara organized a regiment of friars, clerics, and sacristans called "Los Cruzados." It drilled daily in the streets of

---

[46] Cuevas, *La Iglesia en México,* V, 62.

[47] For the Holy Office and the Revolution, see José Toribio Medina, *Historia del Tribunal del Santo Oficio de la Inquisición en México* (Santiago, 1905), pp. 471-499.

Guadalajara to the sound of the great cathedral bell. Such was the character of ecclesiastical opposition to the Revolution in Mexico.[48] It is doubtful if, in any other part of Spanish America, the clergy were more strongly entrenched and were able to afford the Spanish authorities more valuable assistance.

In the La Plata country clerical opposition to independence was in evidence during only the first stage of the Revolution. Bishops Lué of Buenos Aires, Orellana of Córdova, and Videla del Pino of Salta, being strongly royalist, although the last-named was a creole, were opposed to the establishment of the *Junta Gubernativa* in May, 1810. The general clergy on the other hand, supported the *junta*. In the *Cabildo Abierto* of May 22, 1810, the prelate of Buenos Aires questioned the legality of both the autonomous and provisional governments. He however submitted to the *junta* which was set up to govern in the name of Ferdinand VII. Until the time of his death in 1812 all the acts of Bishop Lué fell under the suspicious vigilance of the patriot government. For example, when he asked permission to make a pastoral visit of his diocese, the *junta* refused to grant him a passport. He was told that it was best that he should not leave his see, for his presence would be beneficial in calming agitation. In reality it was feared that he would provoke trouble in the Banda Oriental. After the death of Bishop Lué the cathedral chapter elected Diego Zavaleta as ecclesiastical governor. The election was approved by the government which had assumed patronal rights over the Church.[49]

Bishop Orellana of Córdova was more tenacious and stubborn than Lué and consquently his fate was more tragic. He joined the counter-revolution headed by ex-viceroy Liniers, and following the victory of the Porteño forces, he was captured and narrowly escaped being executed with Liniers. On August 7, 1810, the *junta* declared the see of Córdova vacant, and Orellana was exiled. The cathedral chapter was ordered to turn over the episcopal authority to Rafael Ardreú, bishop *in partibus*. This action precipitated a veritable schism in Córdova, for the chapter was evenly divided between regalists and ultramontanists. Some con-

---

[48] García, *op. cit.,* pp. 242, 256; Pérez Lugo, *op. cit.,* p. 14.
[49] Legón, *op. cit.,* pp. 463-470; Leturia, *Acción Diplomática,* p. 43.

sidered the diocese to be headless, and others held that the lawful bishop, Orellana, was merely absent.[50]

The diocesan of Salta, Nicolás Videla del Pino, was able to maintain control of his see until 1812. In that year, during the campaign of the royalist Goyeneche against Belgrano, the Bishop was discovered to be in communication with the royalists. As a result, he was exiled to Buenos Aires by Belgrano. He was ordered first to turn over his authority to the ecclesiastical governor, the canon Zabala. Videla del Pino presented his case to the Assembly of 1813, and to the Congress of Tucumán, but without avail, and although he officiated on the anniversary of independence, he was not allowed to return to his bishopric. With his demise in 1819, there expired the last of the legal bishops of La Plata. The patronal authority of the Spanish king was definitely terminated in 1810, yet Ferdinand steadfastly refused to recognize the independence of La Plata. Consequently he declined to nominate bishops for the Republic, and after 1819, all of the sees were vacant.[51]

In addition to the above named prelates, the Capuchins of Buenos Aires were staunch supporters of the royalist cause. When they were discovered to be in communication with the enemy, the abbeys in Buenos Aires were ordered abolished by a decree of the government. Because of the early removal of royalist clericals, and the substitution of patriot prelates, the Church exerted the least influence against the Revolution in La Plata than in any other part of Spanish America.

The Revolution in Chile afforded the same opportunity to royalist and Spanish clergy to combat independence. There is no doubt that many of the clergy, particularly the Spanish, were not sympathetic. Just as the supporters of the revolt used the pulpit to advance their cause, so the royalists used the pulpit to combat it. For example, when General Pareja occupied Concepción, Biship Villodres preached in the name of God against the patriots, while Bishop Andre y Guerrero, in the name of God, preached to the army of General Carrera in support of the war and against the soldiers of the king. During the royalist reaction

---

[50] Leturia, *op. cit.*, pp. 43-44.

[51] Piaggio, *op. cit.*, p. 129; Legón, *op. cit.*, p. 466.

(1814-1816) José Santiago Rodríguez was consecrated bishop of Santiago. He, a member of the aristocracy and unable to conceive of another order of things, was an ardent partisan of the king, and called the patriots "perfidious insurgents and infamous traitors." He celebrated the triumph of the royalists at Rancagua and helped to establish the hated tyranny. He also aided in the organization of the clergy into a fanatically reactionary faction violently opposed to the Revolution. As late as 1817 the clergy of Chile were hostile to the cause of independence, "with the exception of a few who wished to imitate Judas in his treason." In the conservative society of Chile the influence of the clergy was considerable. Joel Poinsett reported that, after the overthrow of Spanish rule the rural priests were the real rulers in the country district. After the patriot triumph at Chacabuco, the Chilean government ordered the expulsion of Bishop Rodríguez. He retired to Mendoza and remained there until O'Higgins allowed him to return to Chile.[52]

Clerical opponents of the Venezuelan Republic of 1811 were given their big opportunity when the great earthquake of 1812 occurred. Until that time Archbishop Coll y Prat of Caracas and his clergy viewed the republican maneuvers of Miranda, Bolívar, and their companions with ill-concealed distrust. The earthquake of March 26, 1812, which destroyed the rebel centers but spared the royalist cities, was interpreted by the Archbishop as providential punishment. The clergy attributed the earthquake to the ire of Heaven, and friars preached to the terrified multitudes that "the earthquake was the punishment of God irritated against the upstarts who had refused to recognize the most virtuous of monarchs, Ferdinand VII, the annointed of the Lord." The republican government attempted to combat the clerical propaganda by issuing a proclamation to the Venezuelan people declaring that the earthquake was to be regarded either as a common manifestation of nature, or else, it might be regarded as a divine act to punish vicious morals, and was not to be connected with political reforms.

[52] Francisco V. Vergara, *Historia de Chile* (Valparaiso, 1898), pp. 252-253; Luís Galdames, *Historia de Chile: La Evolución Constitucional, 1810-1925* (Santiago, 1926), I, 13-26.

Throughout the early period of the revolution in Venezuela, Archbishop Coll y Prat acted with the most astute opportunism. After counselling the obedience of his clergy to the Republic, and thereby escaping the ban of expulsion which was being contemplated against him, he welcomed the royalist troops of Monteverde into Caracas on October 15, 1812, with open arms. When in the following year, Bolívar triumphed temporarily, the prelate feigned to be a patriot once more, and issued an edict, in which he ordered the clergy to recognize independence, and obey the laws of the Republic.[53]

Yet, when the course of the Revolution appeared to lead directly to independence, a reasonable regard for their temporalities induced many high ecclesiastics to manifest sympathy for the party which was destined to exercise power in the new State. These clerics, fearing the vengeance of the patriots when independence should be established, decided wisely to ward off this danger by joining the independentists. This explains then, why, in certain colonies and contrary to the general rule, prelates espoused the revolutionary cause.

The Catholic Church had its critics among the revolutionaries, it is true, but it is incorrect to regard their motives as entirely irreligious. Their adverse criticism was directed almost exclusively at the Inquisition and the wealth of the Church; that is, non-religious adjuncts of the Church which seriously menaced the freedom of the State and the liberty of the individual. The most severely criticised ecclesiastical institution was the Inquisition. The *Junta* of Caracas suppressed the Holy Office in 1810. An Argentinian patriot, Monteagudo, in attacking the tribunal charged the Church with "raising the standard of the Cross in order to assassinate men with impunity; to introduce discord among them; to deprive them of their rights; and to snatch from them the wealth which they possess in the soil of the country." On March 24, 1813, the General Constituent Assembly of Buenos Aires abolished the Inquisition and ordered it to turn over to the ordinary ecclesiastics its old function of watching over the purity of the faith.[54] There was no defending the degenerate Holy Office

[53] Gil Fortoul, *op. cit.,* I, 182-184.
[54] Chacaltana, *op. cit.,* p. 66.

of the early nineteenth century, and when the Cortes of Cádiz declared the abolition of the tribunal, in 1813, its decision was received with acclaim by all Catholics who had not abandoned themselves to morbid fanaticism. Following the restoration of Ferdinand VII, however, the Inquisition was reëstablished throughout the Spanish dominions with the exception of La Plata, where the revolutionaries retained control. The new lease on life accorded the Inquisition in America proved to be of short duration, for when Spanish authority was discarded definitely in the various colonies, its most detestable politico-ecclesiastical ally was abolished for all time. The abolition of the tribunal was a positive good, for: "It had spread a blight over the intellectual life of the colonists; it had smothered the spirit of inquiry; it had silenced the voice of reason; and under its malign influence Christian charity disappeared. . . . It is to the credit of the political reformers that they saw in the complete destruction of the Inquisition the first essential step towards individual liberty and social progress."[55] It would be preposterous to characterize the patriotic reform which accomplished the dissolution of the Inquisition in America as an irreligious action. It would be ridiculous also, to agree with certain narrow-minded clericals that the acts of the Assembly of 1813 in Buenos Aires were irreligious. Some of these clerical reforms were: prohibition of the use of cold water in baptisms; prohibition of burials within churches; free baptisms of the children of castes; abolition of the Inquisition; and denial of the right to occupy benefices to Spanish ecclesiastics, not citizens. Nor is it proper to attribute anti-religious motives to the attack upon the wealth of the Church. The voices raised in opposition to the accumulation of vast propertied interests by the Church were not numerous, and, moreover, they generally fell upon unsympathetic ears. But the conviction that the dominant economic position of the ecclesiastical organization curbed individual opportunity and jeopardized political freedom was well-founded. These reforms were not based on irreligion. It is impossible to ascertain to what extent Freemasonry, which was introduced into Latin America in the early years of the nineteenth

---

[55] Moses, *op. cit.*, pp. 71-72. For the decadence of the Holy Office and its extinction, see Medina, *op. cit.*, pp. 445-470.

century, was an antagonist of the Catholic organization. Yet there is little doubt that the Church, because of the inculcation of liberal ideas by the Masons, attributed to them a radical anti-religious program which was in the main fictitious.[56]

The foregoing survey of the Church in the wars for Spanish American independence leads one to the conclusion that throughout the struggle there was manifested undiminished allegiance to the Catholic Church. Religion did not play a positive part in causing the revolt. Yet the Church was destined to undergo, as a result of the Revolution, profound changes in its political status.

---

[56] Representative of the fanatical opposition of the Church to Masonry was a little pamphlet entitled *Intento de la Masonría,* which summarized the alleged purposes of the order: "We are agreed then that when the sectarians [Masons in this case] preach the secularization of the source of sovereignty, that of the family, through civil marriage, when they deny the necessity of Christian baptism, when they attempt to secure possession of education, when they separate Christians from the sacraments and religious practices, when they change the appearance of towns by destroying temples and monasteries, excloistering religious communities, silencing the bells, prohibiting religious and priestly garb, secularizing charity, profaning Christian festivals, introducing death without sacraments, civil burial and [control of] cemeteries, when they despoil the Church, weave restrictions against the Holy See, elaborate constitutions and laws, open lay schools, organize masonic associations, etc., etc., in regard to all this we say: they do nothing less than fight without quarter against the reign of Christianity on earth." (Quoted in Callcott, *op. cit.*, p. 38, note 26.)

CHAPTER III

PAPAL RELATIONS DURING THE STRUGGLE FOR INDEPENDENCE

The revolt and emancipation of Spanish America created problems both perplexing and embarrassing to the papacy in its relations with Spain and that country's seceding colonies. These problems were political and religious in nature, arising from both the temporal and the spiritual character of the papal office. The principal political question which confronted the Vatican was: Should the Holy See recognize the independence of the Spanish-American republics? Because of his attachment to the Metternichean System the pope was not inclined to listen to American pleas for recognition, and consequently it was not difficult for him, as a temporal prince, to find an answer to this political question. A more serious question belonging to the ecclesiastical category, which was forced upon Rome by the Spanish-American Revolution, was: How long should the patronage of the Spanish king over the American Church be observed, and, after its termination, what was to be the nature of the control to be substituted in America for it? It was mainly because of his position as visible head of the Catholic Church that the Spanish American wars for independence created problems of extreme delicacy for the Holy Father.

The non-communication of the Church in America with Rome, due to the breakdown of Spanish authority, and the consequent alarming decline of the Catholic hierarchy in America, caused the American rebels to appeal to Rome, if not for political, at least for religious recognition. What constituted "religious recognition" was a troublesome question. The Spanish king contended that any official contact between the papacy and the colonies would be interpreted as political recognition, in fact if not in theory, and therefore injurious to Spanish interests. Furthermore, His Catholic Majesty contended that any direct intercourse between the pope and American prelates would constitute an invasion of the ancient right of *real patronato de Indias*. The pope, however, when finally constrained because of the deplorable ecclesiastical state in America to reëstablish the hierarchy, defined his action to the king of Spain as being purely ecclesiastical and having no political significance. As for his violation of the *real patronato*, he promised that if Spain's political authority were ever reëstablished in America, her old patronal rights would be restored. To the Spanish Americans, on the other hand, the pope announced that the patronage had reverted to the papacy, its original source. The American governments, however, took sharp issue with the Holy Father, for they were advancing claims as heirs of the king of Spain in America. Thus, essentially religious, in addition to political, considerations controlled papal policy towards Spain and her erstwhile overseas possessions.

In the controversy with the republics of Spanish America, the papacy, anxious to reassert its legitimate authority over the Church, consistently espoused the ultramontane theory, that is, that the *patronato de Indias* was originally a concession, therefore not inherent in sovereignty, and consequently not inheritable by the republics. The latter quite as logically championed the regalistic theory, for they sincerely believed that their independence could not be guaranteed if they were not in control of the Church; and Spain, because of the forlorn hope that it would be the means of eventually restoring Spanish political authority in America, tenaciously clung to the royal patronage, threatening dire consequences if the pope dared to disregard it.

At an early date in the Revolution, the rebel governments recognized the importance of approaching Rome to secure papal confirmation of national patronage, or *patronato nacional*. Legislation which established the Catholic Church as the State-Church was generally accompanied or followed by provisions for the assumption of the old royal patronage by the new governments. For example, the first constitution of Venezuela (1811) provided that the conduct of relations with the Holy See belonged to the government and declared that direct communication between the episcopacy and the Holy Pontiff was illegal.[1] In New Granada authority was granted by the federal act of 1811 to negotiate

---

[1] Gil Fortoul, *Historia Constitucional de Venezuela,* I, 160.

with the pope for the continuation of the patronage. The article read: "To avoid a schism and its dire consequences, as soon as possible the proper authority shall attempt by diplomatic negotiations, to establish direct correspondence with the Holy See for the purpose of negotiating a concordat and a confirmation of the patronage which the government exercises over the churches in these dominions." In 1813 the federal Congress of Tunja in New Granada again sanctioned by law the opening of diplomatic relations with the pope to settle the matter of the patronage. In La Plata provision for the establishment of State control of the patronage was contained in the *Estatuto* of 1813, in a resolution of the Congress of Tucumán in 1817, in the *Reglamento Provisorio* of 1817, and in the Constitution of 1819.[2]

The real reason for the desire of the rebel leaders to enter into an agreement with Rome was their fear that the discontent of the Catholic people with the isolation of the Church would endanger independence. Yet, notwithstanding their anxiety to enter into diplomatic relations with the Holy See, many years passed before their hopes were realized. From 1810 to 1814, even if the American governments had been more stable, they would still have found it well nigh impossible to treat with the pope, for Pius VII was held a virtual prisoner by Napoleon at Fontainebleau. It is thought that a meeting occurred between Pope Pius VII and Manuel Palacio Fajardo, agent of New Granada, in April, 1813. Fajardo had been sent to France to solicit Napoleon's aid. The Emperor, then preparing for the Leipzig campaign, was in no position to aid the rebels, but he suggested that Fajardo attempt to interest Pius VII in the cause of creole autonomy. Napoleon could see no objection to papal confirmation of prelates nominated by the republican governments. Whether Fajardo actually had an audience with the pope is not certain, but it is clear that he made an appeal for papal recognition. Nothing was accomplished, for Pius VII was unwilling to act, believing that any action on his part before the unquestioned establishment of Spanish-American independence would be premature.[3]

---

[2] Ayarragaray, *La Iglesia en América,* p. 234; Legón, *Patronato Nacional Argentino,* p. 492.   [3] Leturia, *La Acción Diplomática,* pp. 76-79.

After 1814 and until 1818 the royalist reaction in America destroyed all rebel organizations capable of diplomatic action save in autonomous La Plata. It was in that region then that the only attempt, and this a feeble one, was made during these years to negotiate with Rome. Although several of the Spanish-American episcopal sees had become vacant during the first phase of the Revolution (1810-1814), they were all, with the exception of La Plata, refilled by Ferdinand VII whose nominations were confirmed by the pope. The provision of the vacant sees in La Plata constituted a serious problem which increased in intensity with the continued non-communication with Rome. The problem was considered by the Congress of Tucumán in 1816, and 30,000 *escudos* were appropriated to defray the expenses of an envoy who was to proceed first to France to implore the support of Louis XVIII in securing a Bourbon prince for a throne in the Argentine. Then, with the aid of France, the agent was to go to Rome to urge papal provision for the vacant sees. Dr. Valentín Gómez, chosen for the mission, arrived in France in November, 1818. Failing to interest the French king in the monarchical scheme and realizing that without French support he could accomplish nothing in Rome, he did not attempt to present his petition to the pope.

Prior to 1820 the pope would not listen benevolently to the overseas separatists, for it was natural and necessary that he respect Spanish rights in America. Spanish authority was rather generally reëstablished by 1820 and preparations were made to send an army against the one remaining rebellious province, La Plata. Considering the fact that all the powers, not even excepting the United States, had refrained from recognition, it would have been imprudent and faithless for the pope to violate legitimacy by ignoring the royal rights of patronage. He therefore was quite willing to listen to Ferdinand's request that he publish a brief exhorting the obedience of American subjects through the intercession of the colonial prelates. On January 30, 1816, Pius VII issued an encyclical to the archbishops and bishops of America, urging them to win over their flocks to obedience to the Spanish king. It read: "You can easily accomplish the suppression of disorders and sedition if each one of you is willing to expose zealously the dangers and grave evils of defections, and expound the noble and exceptional qualities and virtues of our dear son, and your king, Ferdinand, Catholic king of Spain, to whom nothing is more important than religion and the happiness of his subjects; and finally, if you cite the illustrious example, which should never perish, of the Spanish people who did not hesitate to sacrifice goods and life in showing their adherence to religion and fidelity to king."[4]

In 1817 the Cardinal-Secretary of State announced that he would receive no communication from the rebel governments in America. The occasion for this statement was the filing of a protest by the Spanish ambassador in Rome urging the Holy Father not to confirm the action of the Congress of Tucumán which had proclaimed Santa Rosa of Lima as patroness of their independence.[5] Finally, the most conclusive evidence of papal support of Spanish rights was the willingness of the pope during the years 1814-1820 to confirm the persons presented to him by the king of Spain for the vacant sees of Santiago de Chile, Charcas, Arequipa, Mérida, Popayán, Bogotá, México, and Puebla.

After 1820, however, the papacy was not deaf to American entreaties, and papal support of Spanish policy was no longer unqualified. Between 1820 and 1822 Pope Pius VII recognized that the spiritual interests of America could not be hidden in the legitimist formula and that the ecclesiastical problems required tactful and benevolent treatment. This change of attitude was due to two causes: the achievement, or practical achievement, of Hispanic-American independence and the liberal Spanish revolt of 1820.

The capture of Lima by San Martín, Bolívar's victory at Carabobo, and the Treaty of Córdova between Iturbide and O'Donojú, convinced the pope that the colonies were irrevocably lost to Spain and that the exercise of the *real patronato* was impossible. Continued non-communication with Rome meant paralysis of the ecclesiastical organization in Spanish America. Unless

---

[4] "La Encíclica 'Etsi Longissimo' de 30 de Enero de 1816," in Leturia, *op. cit.*, pp. 281-282; Legón, *op. cit.*, pp. 249-250.

[5] Ayarragaray, *op. cit.*, pp. 175-176.

he listened to American pleas the pope would be confronted with the very unpleasant prospect of a serious schism, or the breakup of the Catholic Church in America, with resultant indifference and "exposure to Methodists, Presbyterians, and even sun worshippers," as Cardinal Consalvi told Leo XII.[6] The Holy Father was faced with a dilemma. It was his duty to see that the faithful in America were provided with adequate spiritual leaders. To supply them by means of Spanish presentation would be regarded as an insult in America. Yet, the reverse, i.e., recognition of national patronage or even the ignoring of the royal patronage, would be regarded by Spain as political recognition of the new states and justification for a break.

At the precise moment when Rome altered its attitude because the loss of the Spanish colonies appeared to be a certainty, the Liberal Constitutional government in Spain, set up as a result of the Revolt of 1820, proceeded to antagonize the pope and impel him along the new road. The anti-clerical measures of the Madrid government, which culminated in the expulsion of the nuncio from Madrid in January, 1823, filled the pope with apprehension for the Church not only in Spain but also in America. He began to question why he should now lend his moral support to a government, which, if its authority were reëstablished in America, would cause irreparable damage to the Church in the New World. In fine, the unsympathetic attitude of the Liberals toward the ancient privileges of the Church in Spain made the pope lukewarm in his championship of the old ecclesiastical rights of the Spanish government in America.

The Spanish Cortes, anti-clerical and liberal though it may have been, was essentially nationalistic and therefore just as determined as Ferdinand had been not to recognize Spanish-American independence. On February 22, 1822, the Spanish ministry issued a circular to the European governments supplicating them not to put obstacles in the way of the reëstablishment of Spanish rights in America "which had never been renounced." The pope, when given the circular, was asked to promise in writing not to recognize American independence before Spain did. Pius VII refused to comply with the request and declared his

[6] Leturia, *op. cit.*, pp. 12, 39.

adherence to the principle of neutrality. Such a declaration was indeed a departure from the old policy, for, as has been seen, the pope was willing to issue an encyclical in 1816 urging the American clergy to support the Spanish cause. A renewed demand by the Madrid government in June, 1822, elicited the response that the pope "could be severely censured, and with good reason, if he supported in writing, because of political reasons, a policy which would prolong transcendental spiritual ills."[7] In view of the fact that the pope, only two years later, when absolutism was reëstablished in Spain, was willing to issue another encyclical urging the American clergy to support Ferdinand VII, one cannot avoid the conclusion that the Holy Father was not averse to using his office for political purposes if the government he supported adhered to political principles in harmony with his own. Yet, it cannot be denied that throughout this period no matter whether the Spanish government was liberal or absolutist, the papacy was sincerely endeavoring to find a way to heal the spiritual ills of America.

The period 1820-1823 was the psychological time for the rebel governments to approach Rome and present their cases. During those years, Pius VII was in a receptive mood, and undoubtedly, if the Spanish-Americans had been fully aware of their opportunity and had hastened to take advantage of it, they would have been able to secure real concessions from him. Unfortunately the American governments generally were slow in acting, or, if prompt action was taken, the ecclesiastical business was entrusted to political agents who neglected or totally ignored their spiritual instructions. When special ecclesiastical missions with definite instructions were finally sent to Rome, absolutism had been reëstablished in Spain, and the propitious moment had passed.

As early as 1819, Simón Bolívar considered seriously the problem of negotiating an agreement with Rome which would give to Colombia the right of patronage as exercised by the Spanish kings in the colonies. Due to his influence, the Congress of Angostura (1819) decided to entrust to a political mission ordered to England, the additional duty of securing from Pius VII the preconization of bishops for vacant sees. Fernando Peñalver and José Ver-

---

[7] *Ibid.*, pp. 185-187.

gara were entrusted with the politico-religious mission. Their instructions, issued by the Congress on July 7, 1819, ordered them to negotiate with the pope "as head of the Catholic Church, and not as the temporal lord of the Legations." They were to tell the Holy Father that the people of New Granada and Venezuela were loyal Catholics who refused to believe that the oppressive and tyrannical Spanish government was being supported against them by the successor of St. Peter. Finally, they were to prepare the way for the negotiation of a concordat. On January 3, 1820, the Congress passed a provisional law which provided that until a concordat could be arranged the vice-president should approve those nominated for the lower ecclesiastical offices.[8]

Peñalver and Vergara arrived in London on September 20, 1819. The refusal of Castlereagh to meet them meant failure as far as the political objective of the mission was concerned. Peñalver determined to return to Venezuela to report on the situation, but before embarking he and Vergara disposed of their ecclesiastical business by forwarding a memorial to the pope through the nuncio at Paris. This was a statement of ecclesiastical conditions in America, and it concluded with a petition that the pope confirm as bishops those persons proposed by the American governments. Cardinal Consalvi, the papal Secretary of State, refused to consider the proposal that the pope confirm proprietary bishops for America, for that would have amounted to recognition, which was not to be considered. It is to be remembered that at that time not a single foreign government had bestowed recognition on the rebel states, and it was therefore unwise to ask Rome to take that step.[9]

Francisco Antonio Zea was the next agent sent to Europe by Bolívar (June, 1820). His instructions, drawn up by the Liberator himself, dealt primarily with political matters, but he was also charged to negotiate with the pope for a nuncio or extraordinary delegate with ample powers to examine the real state of affairs in America and propose a remedy. It was unfortunate that Zea did not take advantage of the favorable situation created

[8] Villanueva, *La Santa Alianza*, p. 202; Leturia, *op. cit.*, pp. 91-92.

[9] Ayarragaray, *op. cit.*, pp. 209-210; "Texto original latino del informe de Peñalver y Vergara," in Leturia, *op. cit.*, pp. 294-297.

by the Liberal Revolt in 1820, to go to Rome and negotiate directly with the pope. But he was principally concerned with the larger question of independence and had no time to devote to the religious problems entrusted to him. Finally on April 8, 1822, Zea addressed to the pope through the nuncio at Paris a note demanding immediate recognition of the Colombian government. The note was couched in such intemperate and tactless language that the *Journal des Debats,* in commenting on it, said, "Mr. Zea, brilliant botanist, is still somewhat of a novice at diplomacy." The nuncio on the advice of the representatives of the Holy Allies in Paris returned the note to Zea with the explanation that he had no authority to send it to Rome. Cardinal Consalvi, in writing to the nuncio concerning the incident, said that, while he did not disapprove of the nuncio's action, it should be remembered that since Colombia was a Catholic country the position of the Holy See was very difficult, and it must treat the Americans with some consideration. "I do not intend by this," he said, "that we should adopt a conduct different from that of all the other countries and ministries in Europe, but I only remark that the double character of the office of the Holy Father—political and spiritual—places him, on the religious side, in a more delicate and embarrassed position than that of all other sovereigns, because of the injury which anger aroused by a rebuff could cause religion."[10]

It is contended by Lucas Ayarragaray that Zea, as well as Peñalver and Vergara, did not go to Rome, because, due to the protests of the Spanish government, the pope refused to grant them permission. This was possibly the truth, for, from 1814 to 1833, the chief obstacle to the establishment of direct relations between Spanish America and Rome was the Spanish embassy in the Eternal City. Antonio Vargas y Laguna, the Spanish ambassador since 1814, was called the "Marquis de Constancia" because of his personal loyalty to absolutism and legitimacy, and his never failing efforts to combat the representation of the American governments in the Roman Curia. Narrow, intransigent, fanatical, he organized a veritable camarilla against the American agents. When constitutional government was established in

---

[10] Leturia, *op. cit.,* pp. 104-106.

Madrid, Vargas refused to support it, and was removed from his post on May 21, 1820. José Aparicio, who succeeded as chargé of the embassy until the return of Vargas in 1824, was equally tireless in his efforts to prevent American agents from gaining an audience with the pope.[11]

Two high ecclesiastics of Colombia, Bishops Lasso de la Vega of Mérida and Jiménez of Popayán, coöperated with Bolívar in attempting to secure papal intervention. Both bishops were appointees of Ferdinand VII and were loyal to the Spanish cause up to the time of the establishment of constitutional government in Spain. The bishop of Mérida was the first to abandon his allegiance to Spain and embrace the republican cause. On the occasion of the installation of the Congress of Cúcuta (1821), he published a pastoral encouraging the people to obedience to the national representative authority. General Santander said of him, "The bishop is more patriotic than Bolívar." The Liberator himself wrote of Lasso, "He is a holy man full of eminent qualities, who abhors the Liberals of Spain even more than the patriots, because they have declared against the ecclesiastical institutions, whereas we protect them." When Lasso told Bolívar that he would have no difficulty communicating with Rome, the Liberator urged him to do so. Consequently, on October 20, 1821, the Bishop wrote a letter to Pius VII, in which he justified American independence, presented a picture of ecclesiastical conditions in Colombia, and touched upon certain grave problems confronting the Church. The letter, which was significant as being the first one written by an American bishop in support of emancipation, was unaccountably delayed, and was not received by the pontiff until September, 1822. The pope, now inclining to a free America, welcomed the letter and replied immediately. He refrained from discussing politics, saying that he was anxious to avoid being enmeshed in the political question, but desired to remedy the re-

---

[11] Because of the refusal of the pope to accept as Spanish ambassador the Jansenist Joaquín Lorenzo Villanueva, the liberal government of Madrid expelled the papal nuncio and reduced Aparicio, in charge of the post at Rome, to a mere agent. When the absolutist régime was reëstablished in Spain, Aparicio left Rome hurriedly. Yet he returned in 1827 as *Chargé*, and, in 1834, he became ambassador for Queen Christina. (Ayarragaray, *op. cit.*, pp. 208-209.)

ligious situation and requested more information. He wished to be above party and confine his interest to the spiritual well-being of America.

The pope's reply was received with great acclaim in America (Bishop Lasso had it published broadcast), for his adoption of a neutral attitude was interpreted to mean that he was not opposed to American independence. This was assuredly a far cry from the encyclical of 1816. Lasso's second letter, with the detailed information requested by the pope, was despatched March 19, 1823. In this letter he said of the Colombian government: "I have no hesitation in affirming that its dispositions with respect to religion are most favorable and satisfactory." He suggested as a temporary remedy for the spiritual ills of Colombia, the appointment of auxiliary bishops for the vacant sees. Lasso's report was accompanied by a letter from Vice-President Santander to the pope. Pius VII died before an answer could be prepared to Lasso's letter, but his successor, Leo XII, wrote the Bishop on November 19, 1823. The new pontiff promised to study the problem carefully, and decide "soon" on a policy. In the meantime, he suggested that they appeal to Muzi, the apostolic vicar then being sent to Chile, for he had been given the powers necessary to handle such a situation. The failure of Muzi's mission in Chile prevented his doing anything for Colombia.[12]

Bishop Jiménez of Popayán also wrote the pope (April 19, 1823), beseeching him to stay the disintegration of the Church in America. Bishop Jiménez, an obstinate royalist, had been on the point of abandoning his diocese and returning to Spain, when a remarkable letter written to him by Bolívar induced him to remain with his flock and recognize the Republic. The Liberator stated as his conviction that politics were one thing and religion another, and if the Bishop left his post he would be abandoning his divinely appointed mission, not for religious, but for political reasons. "I wish to believe," he wrote, "that you are swayed by firm and powerful reasons to consider abandoning your gentle lambs of Popayán. But I do not believe that you can be deaf to

[12] Leturia, op. cit., pp. 130-139, 247-253, 271-276; "S. Bolívar al Ill. señor Obispo de Mérida, Guayaquil, 14 de junio de 1823," in Vicente Lecuna (ed.), Cartas del Libertador (Caracas, 1929-1930), III, 206.

the cries of those afflicted sheep, and to the voice of the government of Colombia which entreats you to be one of the leaders on the road to Heaven. Think of the great number of faithful Christians and tender innocents prevented from receiving the sacrament of confirmation because of your absence; how many students of divinity will be unable to receive the august character of minister of Christ, because you will not consecrate their vocation at the altar, and in the profession of holy truth. You know that the people of Colombia need priests and that the war has deprived them of divine aid because of the scarcity of priests. The responsibility of a possible disintegration of the Church in America falls squarely upon those who could maintain unity of the Catholic Church." Bolívar's arguments, seemingly, were unanswerable, for the Bishop decided to remain in Colombia and justified his decision by citing the anti-religious revolt of 1820 in Spain and the actual emancipation of Colombia, in fact, if not in law. The long-delayed reply of Leo XII (June 5, 1824) to the letter of Bishop Jiménez, contained only words of praise for his loyalty to the papacy in remaining in America. Thus no change was effected in the diplomatic or political orders by the letters of the two bishops of Colombia.[13]

When Santander was installed in Bogotá as vice-president of Great Colombia he determined to use the powers granted him by the Congress of Cúcuta to enter into negotiations with the papacy. He began by avoiding the errors of prior missions like those of Peñalver, Vergara, and Zea, of entrusting the agent with mixed political and ecclesiastical business. José Echeverría, who was at that time in Spain, was appointed minister plenipotentiary to Rome (July 12, 1822). He was instructed to work for the recognition of Colombian independence and national patronage. The mission did not materialize, for in September, 1822, Echeverría died in Dieppe while preparing to go to Rome. Agustín Gutiérrez Moreno, then in Chile, was appointed by General Santander to succeed Echeverría, but he was unable to accept, and Dr. Ignacio Sánchez de Tejada, then living in London, was appointed in June, 1823, as Colombian minister to the

---

[13] Leturia, *op. cit.*, 130-278.

Holy See.[14] Before Tejada could reach his post important events in Madrid and Rome had transpired, with consequent alteration of papal policy. The psychological moment for rapprochement between Rome and America had passed. Before entering upon a narration of Tejada's mission it is necessary to discuss the efforts of La Plata and Chile to enter into an understanding with the Holy See.

Since non-communication between La Plata and Rome had been of longer duration than that of any other part of Spanish America, the ecclesiastical situation by 1820 was consequently most distressing in the Platine provinces. The inability of the revolutionary government to secure papal consecration of bishops led inevitably to the consideration of radical plans to meet the emergency. One was to ignore the pope and consecrate bishops without his consent. Since this plan would amount to the establishment of a national church, it scandalized the loyal adherents of papal supremacy, particularly a Franciscan friar named Pedro Pacheco, a teacher of philosophy at the University of Córdova, and a staunch supporter of independence. The friar was a curious personality; he was suspected of being a royalist by the revolutionaries, and of being a revolutionary by the royalists. As a matter of fact, he was an active agent of the revolutionary cause. Pacheco after visiting Spain and Italy, suddenly appeared in Buenos Aires declaring that the pope and the king of Spain had appointed him bishop of Salta. When asked to show his papers he refused and left for Rio de Janerio with the intention of being consecrated there. The willingness of the friar to accept nomination at the hands of the king of Spain was severely condemned by the government of Buenos Aires, for it was felt that such an action would compromise their independence. Dean Funes, the most prominent of the Argentinian ecclesiastics, also condemned Pacheco, for he felt that the king of Spain had no power to nominate bishops in that country, and to receive an appointment from him was tantamount to treason.[15]

Pacheco did not go to Rio de Janerio but sailed for Rome

---

[14] Pedro A. Zubieta, *Apuntaciones sobre las Primeras Misiones Diplomáticas de Colombia* (Bogotá, 1924), pp. 575-576.

[15] Legón, *op. cit.*, p. 481; Leturia, *op. cit.*, pp. 45-46, 58.

instead. He arrived in the Eternal City, via Gibraltar, on September 3, 1821. The object of his personally appointed mission to the pope has been a subject of mystery to historians. His enemies declared that he "fled from Argentina overcome with the mania of being consecrated bishop of Salta." His defenders declared that he "undertook the long and perilous journey to inform the Holy Father of the condition of the Church and to implore his aid in finding a remedy." Perhaps Pacheco's real purpose was to be consecrated bishop of Salta and by this act renew the extinguished hierarchy in Argentina.[16]

Although the objects of the friar's mission were nebulous, he caused the Spanish government serious concern. The Spanish Minister of State ordered Chargé Aparicio to learn if Pacheco was instructed to work for the recognition of the independence of La Plata. Aparicio thereupon conducted a most artful campaign against him. Notwithstanding Spanish opposition, the friar was received twice in secret audience by Pius VII, but he was not presented at the Vatican as a political agent either for or against Spanish-American independence. He presented several memorials to Cardinal Consalvi in which were described the irreligious spirit of the Argentinian revolt, the persecution and extinction of bishoprics, and the failure of the attempted approach to Rome by the mission of Valentín Gómez. He came to Rome, he said, to ask aid to save the Church in its present crisis. Pacheco proposed a remedy for the problem; it was to send to La Plata an apostolic vicar with archiepiscopal dignity and provided with ample powers. Also, two or three bishops *in partibus* should be sent.[17]

---

[16] Leturia, *op. cit.*, p. 59.

[17] Both residential and titular bishops receive on consecration, the episcopal power; they are really bishops. The difference is this: the residential bishops are ordinary and immediate administrators of a diocese of which they take possession. The titular bishops do not take possession of any diocese; it is the custom to grant them nevertheless the archiepiscopal or episcopal title of primitive or extinct dioceses or those fallen into the hands of the infidel (*in partibus infidelium*). The pope employs the titular bishops in the government of the Church either as nuncios, extraordinary administrators of constituted dioceses, coadjutors or auxiliaries of proprietary bishops, and ecclesiastical governors of territory not constituted a diocese. The *patronato de Indias* did not cover these offices and thus the creation of titular bishops

Pacheco's proposal was both sound and practical. To send to Argentina a nuncio with diplomatic character would be premature and would involve political recognition. On the other hand, a vicar or apostolic delegate without diplomatic character could not arouse Spanish protests for the nomination of bishops *in partibus* had never been a matter subject to the patronage, and objection to the naming of proprietary bishops would thereby be avoided. Thus the spiritual necessities of America would be served without precipitating a break with Spain. The pope declined to act on Pacheco's proposal, for he undoubtedly realized that the government of Buenos Aires would refuse to accept an apostolic delegate considering the manner in which his appointment had been petitioned.

Yet, the very plan that was suggested by Pacheco was adopted by Pius VII, in 1823, with reference to Chile. In Chile, as in other parts of Spanish America, the episcopacy was thoroughly disorganized because of the revolution. Bishop José Rodríguez Zorrilla of Santiago had been deprived of his ecclesiastical authority and exiled by order of the Dictator. In 1821 he was allowed to return to Chile, but not to resume his office. This circumstance made Catholic reorganization of Chile a difficult matter. Dictator O'Higgins decided, with the advice of the governor of the bishopric, the presbyter, José Ignacio Cienfuegos, who was a liberal creole ecclesiastic and ardent supporter of independence, to send an official delegation to Rome. Cienfuegos himself was appointed chief of the mission. His instructions, drawn up by O'Higgins, were partly as follows: "Declare our filial and religious obedience to the Holy See, protesting our faith, belief, union and communion with the head of the Church. Request of him an apostolic nuncio who may be either a citizen of this country or any other when His Holiness may wish to appoint; petition a declaration conceding to the Chilean nation the patronage granted the kings of Spain by Julius II; request the erection of cathedrals in Cochimbo, Talca, and Chiloé, in addition to Osorno and Valdívia, and that this capital (Santiago) be made a metropolitan see; ask of him that, at least in the interim,

---

as delegates, apostolic vicars, or auxiliary bishops was the most sensible provisional solution of the matter of the patronage.

he send to Chile auxiliary bishops to take the places of the proprietary bishops."[18]

Cienfuegos, accompanied by five companions, sailed from Valparaiso, January 25, 1822, and arrived in Genoa on June 19. He immediately wrote the Cardinal-Secretary announcing that the Chilean government had sent him to swear obedience to the pope and to report to him on the spiritual necessities of his people. When the Spanish Chargé Aparicio requested that Cienfuegos be refused entry into Rome, Cardinal Consalvi replied (July 6, 1822), "Having been informed that Archdeacon Cienfuegos came to Rome to explain to the pope the spiritual necessities of his people, the Holy Father believed that as common father of the faithful he could not refuse to listen to whatever news they brought from America touching on the state of religion, although without entering into any political relations that could offend the rights of the legitimate sovereign. Not long ago there came to Rome from Buenos Aires an ecclesiastic [Fray Pedro Pacheco] to lay before His Holiness the necessities of those faithful, and His Holiness, because of his apostolic ministry listened to him, without injuring in this way any of the rights of His Catholic Majesty. Thus the Holy Father and his government will absolutely abstain from recognizing and treating Cienfuegos as a minister of the Chilean government."[19]

On August 6, Cienfuegos was granted an audience with the pope. After he described the necessities of the Chilean Church, he suggested as a temporary measure that an apostolic vicar be sent to Chile. This suggestion was submitted to a congregation of six cardinals. Among these was Della Genga, the later Leo XII. The pope in the meantime approached Madrid with a proposal that, if Spain would permit the naming of proprietary bishops in America, the Holy See would bind itself not to recognize Spanish-American independence for at least thirty years. The Spanish government would not listen to the proposal. After a lengthy discussion in the congregation, the proposal of Cienfuegos was approved in April, 1823, by the cardinals, and

---

[18] Luís Galdames, *Estudio de la Historia de Chile* (Santiago, 1911), p. 309; Leturia, *op. cit.*, p. 178.

[19] Leturia, *op. cit.*, pp. 188-189.

Mgr. Ostini was named Vicar Apostolic of Chile. But since he was unable to accept, Mgr. Juan Muzi was appointed. Muzi was consecrated Archbishop of Filipos *in partibus infidelium* and Vicar Apostolic. Because of the insistence of Friar Pacheco, who was then in Rome, that La Plata was in even greater need of a vicar apostolic than Chile, the congregation enlarged Muzi's jurisdiction to include all of America. He was empowered to consecrate titular bishops, and to repair as soon as possible the injuries caused by the struggle over investiture. He was advised to be cautious in the exercise of his powers and to abstain from the use of his authority in any colony where Spanish authority existed, or where there was a probability of its being reëstablished.[20]

As was to be expected, Spain protested the pope's appointment of a vicar apostolic. Pius VII justified his decision by declaring that his action was made necessary because of his pastoral obligations, and that it was merely a provisional action which would not disparage Spain's rights in any way. Cardinal Consalvi reiterated on several occasions that Muzi's mission had no political meaning and would in no way injure the *real patronato*.

Apostolic Vicar Muzi, accompanied by his secretary José Sallusti, and the canon, Conti Mastai (the later Pius IX)[21] sailed from Genoa on October 4, 1823. The death of Pius VII, which occurred shortly after Muzi's departure did not interrupt the mission. The Apostolic Vicar received confirmatory papers from the new pope, Leo XII, shortly after his arrival in Buenos Aires. The papal delegate was given an enthusiastic reception by the populace of Buenos Aires, and General San Martín visited him twice to welcome him. The authorities, however, were very reserved in presenting themselves, and they even prohibited Muzi from exercising his ministry. When the provisor of the vacant bishopric, Señor Zavalleta, requested instructions on the attitude he should assume toward the pontifical representative, Rivadavia replied that he "did not recognize any character in that individual."

---

[20] José Sallusti, *Historia de las Misiones Apostólicas de Monseñor Juan Muzi en el Estado de Chile* (Santiago, 1906), pp. 7-8.

[21] For an account of the rôle played in the mission by the later Pius IX, see J. J. Shea, *The Life of Pope Pius IX* (New York, 1877), pp. 32-40.

The newspapers adopted an antagonistic attitude toward the Vicar and accused him of being the envoy of the Holy Alliance. Furthermore his sale of vast quantities of bulls and relics which he had brought over with him was criticised as being mercenary. Using the pretext that the presence of Muzi threatened a revolt, Rivadavia ordered him to leave the country immediately.[22] Thus ended in rancor and disappointment the attempt of Cardinal Consalvi to bring Argentina back into the fold.

The Apostolic Vicar arrived in Santiago de Chile in March, 1824. He was received with enthusiasm by the populace, and with pomp and veneration as the nuncio of the pope by General Ramón Freire, who had succeeded O'Higgins as dictator of Chile. Muzi delivered to Director Freire a letter addressed to him by Leo XII. This letter was notable as being the first one written by the pope to a political chieftain in America. In March, 1824, the Vicar Apostolic was voted a monthly subsistence of five hundred pesos by the Chilean Congress.[23] On July 13, 1824, Simón Bolívar wrote from Peru complimenting Muzi on his arrival in America. He expressed hope that arrangements could be made for the conclusion of a concordat with Colombia.[24]

Muzi's mission to Chile resulted in disastrous failure when the Apostolic Vicar ran afoul of the *patronato nacional*. The papal representative resolutely refused to accept the government's nominees for ecclesiastical positions. For this conflict Cienfuegos was partly responsible, since he, when the mission had been approved by Pius VII, wrote O'Higgins telling him that the Chilean government had been conceded the right of presentation to benefices and the administration of the tithes, and that the Vicar was to consecrate those persons nominated for vacant episcopacies by the government. All this practically amounted, he said, to a recognition of Chilean independence. This was untrue and was flatly contradicted by the new Cardinal-Secretary, Della Somaglia. Cienfuegos, therefore, led the Chilean government to

---

[22] *Ibid.*, pp. 227-228; Legón, *op. cit.*, p. 490.

[23] Ricardo Anguita (ed.), *Leyes promulgadas en Chile desde 1810 hasta el 1° de Junio de 1913* (Santiago, 1913), I, 150.

[24] "José Sánchez Carrion al Illmo. Señor don Juan Muzi, Arzobispo Filipense, Vicario Apostólico en la República de Chile, Huanuco, 13 de Julio de 1824," in *Cartas del Libertador*, IV, 114; Sallusti, *op. cit.*, p. 237.

believe that the right of national patronage had been confirmed. Muzi, on the other hand, could not acknowledge the right of the Chilean government to make ecclesiastical appointments. The difficulty of his position was increased because in Chile, as in Buenos Aires, he was regarded as being an agent of the Holy Alliance. Muzi, recognizing the impossibility of conciliating the irreconcilable, asked for his passports.[25]

The Vicar sailed from Valparaiso for Montevideo via Cape Horn, on October 30, 1824. While in the capital of the Banda Oriental he published an apostolic letter in which he defended his actions.[26] He sailed from Montevideo for Europe, and arrived in Rome on June 18, 1825. The fundamental cause of the failure of the mission was misunderstanding for which Cienfuegos was responsible, and the Chileans' lack of confidence in the Vatican because of its acts in support of conservative and royalist tendencies. The intervention of the Holy Father, far from being beneficial in the dioceses of La Plata and Chile, left a very bad impression and an antagonistic attitude toward the papacy. On the other hand the mission of Muzi was significant because it was the beginning of a *modus vivendi* with the American governments. In spite of Spanish protests a relationship of a kind was established between Rome and America. Later events proved this to be the logical stepping stone to recognition.

In 1824, the history of Papal-American relations assumed a different character. The change was due to the accession of a new pope, Leo XII, the restoration of Ferdinand VII to his absolute authority, the appearance of Mexico as a prominent supplicant at the Vatican, and the presence in Rome of the first great American diplomat, Ignacio de Tejada of Colombia.

---

[25] Sallusti, *op. cit.*, p. 146; Galdames, op. cit., pp. 317-318. According to Riva Palacio (*op. cit.*, IV, 151) Muzi was sent to America to combat the independence movement, but when he started to work for Ferdinand VII he was dismissed from Chile. There is no foundation for this assertion.

[26] The minister of Chile to London, Mariano Egaña, told the Mexican agent, Vázquez, that the treatment of Muzi by Chile was a national disgrace. The actions of the Vicar, said Egaña, had been correct and disinterested, and his intentions the most honorable; he did not in the least fail to perform his duty. If he refused to consecrate two candidates proposed to him by the government he had excellent reasons for refusal. (Antonio de la Peña y Reyes, *León XII y Los Países Hispano-Americanos,* Mexico, 1924, p. 67.)

When Leo XII ascended the throne of Peter, the aged Cardinal Consalvi, although no longer Cardinal-Secretary, summarized for the new pontiff his handling of the delicate ecclesiastical relations with Hispanic-America. He said, "What position ought we to take towards the Catholics in South America? Last year I treated the Spanish Cortes with forbearance with a view to obtaining, in case they should remain in power for a lengthy period, the right of appointing bishops to the vacant sees in distant lands. The legitimate Spanish monarch has no authority over these provinces, each of which is like a kingdom. I have allowed Spain more than fifteen years in which to work for the establishment of its sovereignty, but whether it is due to ingratitude or to infirmity, Spain has used our silence as a weapon against the rebels. If Spain had granted us permission to appoint bishops in Colombia, Mexico, and wherever we demanded it, we would have granted the legitimate monarch a respite of thirty years in which to get firmly into the saddle; but the time might easily come when Spain, without having regained its power, would say to us: 'I must resign my sovereignty; save your dogmas as well as you can.' It would then be too late for Rome. If we had waited so long, our apostolic vicar might have found the country filled with Methodists, Presbyterians, and even sun-worshippers. I have therefore maintained friendly relations between Rome and those who so violently and with such a well-founded hope of success have refused obedience to the *juntas* and to Ferdinand VII."[27]

Ferdinand VII, having resumed the full enjoyment of his absolute power, thanks to the Holy Allies, and France in particular, was anxious to be restored to his authority in America as well. His one remaining hope in America was the clergy who had always loyally supported the royal cause. He hoped that they, being convinced of the evils of republican government which was in direct opposition to their own interests, would decide to organize their forces to destroy the new political system. Ambassador Vargas, who had been restored to the Roman embassy, was ordered to request Leo XII to issue an encyclical to the prelates

---

[27] Artaud de Montor, *Histoire du Pape León XII* (Paris, 1843), I, 166 ff.

of America exhorting them to preach obedience to the legitimate
authority of the Spanish king. A subtle argument used by Vargas
to influence Cardinal Somaglia was somewhat as follows: the
Americans were opposed to the establishment of legitimate
government; this could be equally applied to apostolic authority;
the only way to keep them in the Roman faith was to oblige their
submission to the legitimate political authority; otherwise, the
result would be serious schism, or, at least, indifference on the
subject of religion.[28]

On September 24, 1824, the pope issued his celebrated encyclical to the archbishops and bishops of America, asking them to
support the cause of "our very dear son Ferdinand, Catholic
King of Spain, whose sublime and solid virtues cause him to place
before the splendor of his greatness the luster of religion and
the happiness of his subjects."[29] The publication of this document, first in the *Gaceta de Madrid* (February 1, 1825), and
then in the *Gaceta Extraordinaria de México* (July 6, 1825),
created a sensation throughout the length and breadth of
America. American confidence, won by Pius VII after years of
effort, was lost at a stroke. The suspicion that Leo XII was in
league with the Holy Allies was now confirmed. A positive result
produced by the encyclical was that of strengthening the Americans in their determination to protect their independence. An intense love of the national state was professed by all classes, including the ecclesiastics. According to Riva Palacio, "The encyclical, since it praised the virtues (?) of Ferdinand VII, and
advocated a return to the colonial system (i.e. slavery), alienated
many loyal Catholics in America."[30] In view of the fact that
it was recognized by all, save Ferdinand VII, that the colonies
were irrevocably lost, the action of the pope in issuing the encyclical is unintelligible. Indeed, because of the very absurdity of the
action, the encyclical has been declared by some to be apocryphal.
They point to the singular circumstances under which it first
appeared, i.e., in the *Gaceta de Madrid*, six months after the
date of its purported signature by the pope. Yet, to refute all

---

[28] Ayarragaray, *op. cit.,* pp. 185, 234-235.

[29] Peña y Reyes, *op. cit.,* p. iii.

[30] Riva Palacio, *op. cit.,* IV, 139.

this, the Cardinal-Secretary when questioned, did not deny the authenticity of the encyclical.[31] But whatever the reason for its issuance, its publication certainly did not facilitate the establishment of a working agreement between Rome and America. The evident subservience of the Roman pontiff to the king of Spain gave encouragement to the groups in Spanish America that were aiming at the establishment of national churches.

Within a year, however, the attitude of the pope changed and he agreed to receive American agents charged with negotiating on ecclesiastical matters. But he was still unwilling to treat on political subjects. The person most responsible for the modification of papal policy was Ignacio de Tejada, the Colombian representative at Rome. Tejada stands out among the several American agents who were sent to Rome as the most capable and the most successful. Undoubtedly the prestige of Great Colombia, the best organized government in South America, with the great Liberator at its head, tended to lend considerable support to Tejada. Nevertheless, his ability, discretion, energy, patience, and perseverance were qualities which contributed in even greater measure to the success of his long mission in Rome. He became the veritable head of the different American agencies accredited to the pope, and on numerous occasions he was entrusted with the business of the other republics. Indeed, he came to be regarded as the *agente privado* of all America before the pope. Tejada, like the majority of diplomatic agents sent to Rome, was a cleric. It was thought that ecclesiastics would have a better chance of success, for if the Spanish ambassador protested their missions, they could claim that they were concerned only with spiritual matters and that they did not come to Caesar but to the vicar of Christ. Tejada was instructed to negotiate for: the immediate provision of all vacant bishoprics; authority to bishops to secularize the regulars; appointment by the pope of a legate authorized to negotiate a concordat which would allow the primate of Colombia to erect or divide dioceses in accordance with the needs of

---

[31] See Ayarragaray, *op. cit.*, pp. 184-188, 199-203, for proof of the authenticity of the encyclical. See also, Peña y Reyes, *op. cit.*, p. 49, Cuevas, *op. cit.*, V, 165-170, and Joaquín Ramírez Cabañas, *Las Relaciones entre México y el Vaticano* (Mexico, 1928), pp. 14-22.

the population, and to confer canonical institution on the bishops presented by the government; and, the confirmation in the government of Great Colombia of the patronage which the kings of Spain had exercised.[32]

Tejada arrived in Rome in September, 1824, and took up his residence in an obscure pension near the Plaza de Popolo. Although Ambassador Vargas, who was now reinstated in his old post in Rome, was unsuccessful in his efforts to prevent Tejada's entry, he continued to intrigue against the American agent. Twice the Colombian's residence was entered by the spies of the Spanish Ambassador. Notwithstanding the protests of Vargas, who was supported by the Austrian ambassador, Tejada was received privately by the Cardinal-Secretary of State, Della Somaglia. His mission, he declared, was not political, but merely spiritual. He only came to enlighten the pope on the state of the Church in Colombia, where, after fourteen years of non-communication with the papacy, all but two of the episcopal sees were vacant. These two bishops, he said, had to administer to three million people scattered over a country as large as France and Spain combined. He also described the menace of Protestantism in Colombia. The English, Dutch, Swiss, and other Protestants were coming to America in great numbers, and the Bible Society of England was scattering its doctrine and missions in profusion. He concluded by expressing the confidence of the people of Colombia that their petitions would be speedily granted since they only asked for a satisfactory settlement of matters in the purely spiritual order. Cardinal Somaglia listened attentively but would not commit himself beyond promising that the matter would be studied. He counseled Tejada not to pose as a diplomatic or public character for he would not be received as one. Furthermore, it was the pope's desire, he said, that the Colombian retire to Bologna to avoid the criticism of the Spanish Ambassador. Tejada acceded, saying that he was still hopeful for the success of his mission. Vargas, however, was dissatisfied with Tejada's residence in Bologna, and as a result of his continued protestations, the Colombian agent was ordered, in Novem-

---

[32] Zubieta, *op. cit.*, p. 580.

ber, 1824, to leave the Papal States. He then took up his residence in Florence. The expulsion of her minister was regarded by Colombia as an affront, and Tejada was ordered to abandon his mission if the papacy did not raise the ban against him. The agent, however, understood that success depended on patience, and he was content to bide his time. His perseverance was rewarded, for within a year he was allowed to take up his residence in Civita, Vecchia, and in the following year, 1826, he was invited to return to Rome as "Diputado para los negocios eclesiásticos de Colombia en Roma."[33]

Rome's new policy, to receive American representatives as ecclesiastical delegates, but on the express condition that this action did not imply political recognition, was adopted as an immediate reaction to the news that Mexico was sending a notable mission to the papacy headed by the presbyter Francisco Pablo Vázquez.

After 1824 the problem of the Mexican Church was added to that of Colombia, Argentina, and Chile, to plague the Holy Father. Although Mexican independence had been achieved in 1821 and patronage was declared terminated by the Regency, the rapid political changes accompanying the rise and fall of the Empire prevented the despatch of a mission to Rome. The necessity of appealing to the Vatican for a restoration of ecclesiastical relations was apparent to all from the beginning, and with the passage of time the need of a solution became more pressing because Mexico was feeling the disastrous effects of non-communication with Rome. By 1825 the metropolitan and five suffragan sees were vacant. The only bishops were those of Puebla, Oaxaca, and Yucatán, and, by 1829, when Antonio Pérez, Bishop of Puebla, died, Mexico had not a single bishop. There was also an alarming decline in the number of secular clergy.[34]

After the establishment of the Republic, the Congress turned to a consideration of the ecclesiastical situation. The debates

---

[33] *Ibid.*, pp. 567-581; Ayarragaray, *op. cit.*, p. 228; Gil Fortoul, *op. cit.*, I, 381.

[34] Lorenzo de Zavala, *Ensayo Histórico de las Revoluciones de México* (Mexico, 1845), II, 170; Cabañas, *op. cit.*, pp. LXI-LXV.

over patronage, concordats, and like subjects were so protracted
that the government decided to lose no more valuable time but
to send an agent to Rome at once. Therefore, while the Congress
was still debating on the nature of the envoy's instructions,
Francisco Vázquez departed for Europe. He arrived in England
on July 25, 1825.[35] News that Mexico was sending a mission
to Rome interested Leo XII greatly, for the condition of the
Church in Mexico, particularly the alleged Protestant propaganda
from the United States, troubled the pope. He was inclined to
admit Vázquez to Rome and grant him an audience. But the
Spanish ambassador presented the usual protests. The assurance
of Cardinal Somaglia that Rome did not intend to recognize any
legation from a rebellious colony of Spain, but was only disposed
to receive the Mexicans in his capacity as head of the Church,
had no effect upon Spain. "The Spanish government," reported
the papal nuncio in Madrid to the Cardinal-Secretary, "in spite
of its absolute impotence, is determined to continue the unequal
struggle which it has been prosecuting for so long with its rebellious colonies. It conforms in this with the national character
not to accept any workable or intelligent proposal; and consequently proceeds to lose the little influence that it retains. . . .
For this fatal obstinacy the Holy Alliance bears responsibility
since its representatives in Madrid and in Paris do not cease to
encourage Spain to defend at all cost her rights in America,
and prevent the triumph of the rebel demagogues."[36]

The pope then sought the good offices of France to aid him
in breaking down the opposition of Ferdinand VII. The French
government accepted, seeing in this an opportunity to play the
rôle of protector of the Catholic Church in Spanish America,
which could be used to counteract the commercial influence of
England over the new nations. Consequently a conference attended
by the papal nuncio, the ambassadors of Russia and Austria,

---

[35] *Ibid.*, I, 292-293. Father Cuevas (*op. cit.*, V, 157-158) discusses the mission of a secret agent who was sent to Rome soon after the overthrow of
Iturbide. This man, Father José María Marchena, was instructed to learn
what the Roman Curia thought of Mexican independence, and whether it was
willing to enter into a concordat with the republic. Marchena, quite irresponsible and incompetent, was, of course, unable to accomplish anything. Cuevas
believes he caused more harm than good.   [36] Leturia, *op. cit.*, p. 7.

the minister of Prussia, and the French minister Baron de Damás, met in Paris on October 7, 1825. The nuncio explained the situation created by the Mexican mission and requested the members of the Holy Alliance to persuade the Spanish king to cease his opposition. The conference advised the pope to receive the Mexican envoys only as delegates in purely spiritual matters, and they agreed to invite their representatives at Madrid to convert Ferdinand VII to their point of view. But when approached the Spanish sovereign refused positively to heed the advice of the Holy Allies. He flatly declined to consent to the reception of the Mexican delegates on the ground that permission would be contrary to the interests of Spain and of legitimacy. In commenting on Spanish intransigence the papal nuncio at Madrid wrote, "The obstacles put in the way of the ecclesiastical authority in America should be enough to drive out of those lands all principles of canonical jurisprudence, and to introduce in Spain a species of Anglican supremacy." Notwithstanding the objections of Spain, Leo XII was not to be deterred. Tejada and Vázquez were both invited to come to Rome, but only as ecclesiastical agents. The Colombian representative consented. Vázquez, unfortunately, since the *sine qua non* of his instructions was that he be received as a diplomatic envoy, had to refuse. The papal nuncio in Paris tried in vain to convince the Mexican Minister of Foreign Affairs, Señor Camacho, of the impossibility of the Holy See receiving Vázquez in a diplomatic character. "Señor Tejada, the Colombian agent," he said, "does not bear any title except that of deputy for the ecclesiastical business of Colombia, and he is content with this. Why should Mexico wish for more with things in their present state?"[37] Personally Vázquez was inclined to favor a compromise, and in a letter to Ramos Arizpe, the Mexican Minister of State, he wrote that he was convinced that Rome was kindly disposed toward the Colonies and inclined to do anything short of recognition. The pope was really desirous of meeting their spiritual necessities but without compromising himself with the Spanish government. As for political recognition, it was certain that Rome would wait upon the European powers.[38]

---

[37] Villanueva, *op. cit.*, pp. 27, n. 47, 204-207.
[38] Peña y Reyes, *op. cit.*, pp. 52-59, 65-69.

The result was that Vázquez did not go to Rome; at least not until 1830.

Leo XII did not stop with receiving ecclesiastical agents from the Spanish-American republics. He decided to disregard the ancient right of royal patronage, and in the celebrated consistory of May 21, 1827, he preconized candidates presented by the government of Colombia, as proprietary bishops for six vacant seats in Colombia. The following were confirmed at that time: Fernando Caicedo y Flórez as archbishop of Bogotá, Ignacio Méndez as archbishop of Caracas, Félix Calixto Miranda as bishop of Cuenca, José María Estévez as bishop of Santa Marta, Manuel Santos Escobar as bishop of Quito, and Mariano Garnica as bishop of Antioquia. In a letter to the pope Bolívar expressed great pleasure that the ecclesiastical vacancies had been filled. He also announced that the government of Great Colombia had assumed the right of patronage.[39] This act deprived *real patronato* of that which constituted its chief value, i.e., the privilege of royal presentation. It is not surprising then that Ferdinand VII regarded the pope's action in preconizing bishops without royal presentation as a non-recognition of the Spanish patronage. The act was condemned as giving aid and comfort to the rebels, for since the independence movement centered about the native ecclesiastics, said Ferdinand, the new bishops would be the most bitter enemies of the Spanish régime. In other words the pope's action made independence more certain. Ferdinand VII demanded that in the future, the pope wait upon him for nominations. The assurance of the nuncio in Madrid that the bulls of confirmation sent to the Colombian bishops did not contain any expression which could be construed by the government of Colombia as granting it the right of presentation did not satisfy Ferdinand. Nor was he moved by a personal letter written to him, on July 4, 1827, by Leo XII, which contained assurances that the pope did not intend to depart from his policy to refuse political recognition to the new states in America. "But when we were solicited," wrote Leo XII, "for purely spiritual purposes to

---

[39] "S. Bolívar á Su Santidad el Papa León XII, Bogotá, 7 de Noviembre de 1828," in *Cartas del Libertador*, VIII, 105-106; Jesús María Henao y Gerardo Arrubla, *Historia de Colombia* (Bogotá, 1912), II, 428.

remedy an unhappy religious situation which threatened to destroy the Church completely, after announcing that we would perform this election of our own free will (*de motu proprio*), how could we refuse to give spiritual aid and render an account to God? . . . If we had questioned your Majesty on these candidates, we would surely have run the risk of having the Americans refuse them."[40]

The next move of Leo XII was to send a new nuncio to Madrid to seek an understanding with Ferdinand. The king, although not aiming at an actual termination of relations with the Vatican, ordered the nuncio stopped at Irún and refused to allow him to enter Spain. The breach between Rome and Madrid was soon healed when Ferdinand's anger cooled and he wrote the pope a conciliatory letter. His conduct, he said, was dictated by necessity and not by choice. But since he was anxious to give proof of his affection for the Holy Father, he was sending an ambassador to Rome to settle the difficulty. Don Pedro Gómez Labrador, a councillor of state of wide experience, was appointed ambassador to Rome on this difficult mission. Labrador, mentally and temperamentally very much like Vargas, entered into his negotiations with the Holy See by demanding in a high-handed manner that the patronal rights of his sovereign be recognized to the limit. Furthermore, since there was a widespread belief that the bulls of investiture of the Colombian bishops had been issued after presentation by Bolívar, he requested that the pope publish in the newspapers a notice to the effect that "in the nomination of bishops, he did not act on the proposal of any rebel chief." The Cardinal-Secretary finally consented and inserted a short notice in the papers to this effect. But when Labrador tried to prevent the pope from receiving agents from America he was met with refusal. Also, when the ambassador proposed that the pope should observe previous presentation by the Spanish king "since His Catholic Majesty had not renounced the prerogatives of sovereignty as founder of the Church in the rebellious colonies," Cardinal Somaglia countered with the statement that "the privileges conceded by

[40] Ayarragaray, *op. cit.*, pp. 259-268; Villanueva, *op. cit.*, pp. 208-209; Zubieta, *op. cit.*, p. 581.

the Holy See to the Catholic Sovereigns cease to have value when they would be injurious to the Church."[41]

In the midst of the negotiations the pope announced that he planned at the next consistory to be held in September, 1828, to preconize more bishops for America. To avoid a new conflict with Spain he proposed to name only titular bishops, "concerning whose nomination the patronal monarch has confessed he has no rights," he said. Still Labrador protested, and then Leo XII, with great emotion, exclaimed that he would give his blood for the king, but that he could never give him his soul. The September consistory had to be postponed, but on December 22, 1828, the pope preconized several apostolic vicars with episcopal character, among these being Dean Cienfuegos of Santiago, Chile, and Friar Justo Santa María de Oro of Cuyo.[42]

Leo XII died on March 31, 1829, and was succeeded in the Vatican by Pius VIII. The new pope was firm in his refusal to recognize national patronage. He refused to consecrate bishops, not only for Colombia, but for Mexico and the other American states. The reason advanced for his refusal was that, as regarded Mexico, the internal disorders presaged the extinction of the national state, and, as for Great Colombia, the disintegration of the federal state was imminent. The efforts of Pius VIII to harmonize his policy with that of the Spanish king were met with the usual rebuff. The pope, therefore, in spite of his natural reserve, had to yield to the pressure of facts. The impending ruin of the Church in America and the demoralization of the clergy, for now there was scarcely a bishop in all America, compelled the pope to consider measures to remedy the evils. Therefore, in spite of his favorable attitude toward Spain, he notified the Spanish ambassador of his intention to consecrate bishops for America at the Christmas consistory (1830). Labrador was thoroughly discouraged and wrote his government that in his judgment it was useless to object further.[43]

It was about this time (1830) that the Mexican envoy, Francisco Vázquez, finally entered Rome. Because of the pope's

[41] Ayarragaray, op. cit., pp. 269-271, 278-281.

[42] Legón, op. cit., p. 492.

[43] Ayarragaray, op. cit., pp. 288-290; Zubieta, op. cit., p. 588.

refusal to treat him as the diplomatic representative of an independent nation, Vázquez had been detained for three years in Brussels, Paris, and London. In the summer of 1830, accompanied by a numerous retinue, Vázquez went to Rome to present a virtual ultimatum to the pope. He was instructed by his government to negotiate a concordat in which the *conditio sine qua non* was the nomination of proprietary bishops. In the name of his government he was to declare that in the future Mexico would not receive apostolic vicars, but only proprietary bishops. Vázquez presented a list of persons whom the Mexican government wished to have confirmed in the vacant sees. When the Cardinal-Secretary attempted to induce Vázquez to accept as a temporary measure the naming of titular bishops, he flatly refused to negotiate, saying that he was bound by a limited and express mandate. In the lively discussion which ensued, the Mexican was bold enough to insinuate that the pope's freedom of action was limited because of Spanish opposition. This the Cardinal denied, and declared that to name proprietary bishops in the midst of so much turbulence in America would be a dangerous policy. The lack of stability, he contended, was the reason for the pope's refusal to recognize independence.[44]

Death saved Pius VIII from the radical action of confirming proprietary bishops for America. Gregory XVI, who was elected to the see of Peter on February 2, 1831, was the pope who first recognized the independence of the Spanish-American republics. When Gregory became pope, the atmosphere in the Vatican was charged with a bitter resentment for the Spanish king because of his intransigence. Since the restoration of Spanish power in America was now an absolute impossibility, the high ecclesiastics advised the pope to restore normal ecclesiastical relations with America. Gregory heeded the advice and lost no time in adopting a definite policy. The new course was stated in the bull "Sollicitudo Ecclesiarum" (August, 1831), which referred

---

[44] Ayarragaray, *op. cit.*, pp. 294–295. Zavala's (*op. cit.*, II, 172–173) account of Vázquez's mission disagrees with the above. According to Zavala, Vázquez consented to go to Rome as a simple ecclesiastic. There, without mentioning the Mexican government, he requested that the pope *motu proprio* (that is, without consideration of national rights) appoint bishops for America. The action of Vázquez, says Zavala, was an insult to the Mexican nation.

particularly to the Portuguese situation,[45] but which could be extended to all Spanish America. In this bull the pope declared his intention to exercise freely his rights and his spiritual functions. If he treated of ecclesiastical affairs with temporal governments, it was not to be regarded as political recognition, but only recognition of the existence of the said government for the carrying on of ecclesiastical affairs. Finally, he declared his intention to establish relations with *de facto* governments when they gave indication of stability. When the Spanish ambassador inquired if, as one would deduce from the bull, the pope intended to recognize the Spanish-American republics, he was put off with the reply, "Almost none of the new states can present circumstances similar to those of Portugal. Thus the Spanish ambassador can imply that the moment is not so imminent when the Holy See would recognize any of them."[46] Notwithstanding this explanation, it was well understood that papal recognition of America was not far distant.

Beginning with the consistory of 1831, Gregory XVI proceeded boldly to preconize proprietary bishops for America. In Mexico seven sees were filled: Puebla, Chiapas, Linares, Guadalajara, Durango, Michoacán, and Monterey. Francisco Vázquez was consecrated by the pope Bishop of Puebla, and he in turn consecrated the other Mexican bishops. More Mexican sees were filled in 1834 and in 1836. By 1838 only the archdiocese of Mexico and the see of Oaxaca were vacant due to the voluntary exile of their prelates. The archiepiscopal see of Mexico was not filled until 1840.[47]

In 1832 titular bishops for vacant sees in Argentina and Chile were appointed by the pope. It was not until the next year, 1833, that Tejada, now the agent for New Granada only, since

---

[45] Dom Miguel, son of John VI and brother of Pedro I of Brazil, after the death of his father and during the minority of his niece, María da Gloria, was regent. Supported by absolutists he tried to retain the throne for himself. A struggle ensued in which both factions tried to secure from the pope the provision of bishops for vacant sees. Finally Gregory XVI decided to preconize the candidates presented by Dom Miguel. To explain his policy he issued the bull. (Ayarragaray, *op. cit.*, p. 306.)

[46] *Ibid.*, pp. 304-310; Zubieta, *op. cit.*, pp. 589-591.

[47] Riva Palacio, *op. cit.*, IV, pp. 29, 284, 454.

the dissolution of Great Colombia, secured the preconization of bishops for Antioquia, Santa Marta, and Popayán, and for an archbishop for Bogotá. In none of these cases did the pope formally recognize the right of presentation in the American governments, although he was often willing to accept names suggested to him.

In an encyclical to the bishops of America Gregory XVI expressly ordered them to refuse to recognize patronage, and in the oaths of obedience demanded of the bishops, the same denial was implied.[48] It is noteworthy that to the present day the papacy has never recognized patronage as being an inherent right in sovereignty.

It might be thought that Gregory XVI would not recognize the political independence of the Spanish-American republics without first arriving at a settlement regarding the patronage. He, however, prudently made the act a political one only, leaving the problem of national patronage for later study and solution. He realized that if recognition waited upon a settlement of the religious issue, it might never come. The death of Ferdinand VII in 1833 facilitated a solution of the problem. Out of consideration for Ferdinand himself, who chose to regard recognition as a very personal affront, the pope had refrained from political action. With that obstacle now removed, and the Spanish government distraught by civil strife, the opportune moment had arrived for decisive action. On November 26, 1835, Gregory XVI formally recognized the independence of the Republic of New Granada. On December 14, 1835, Ignacio Tejada's long years of patient, tactful diplomacy were rewarded when he was received in papal audience as the *chargé* of the Republic of New Granada. When the pope manifested a desire to send a nuncio to New Granada, Tejada was instructed to oppose this because the Holy Father wanted the Republic to bear the expenses and because it was feared that the papal representative would exercise an ultramontane influence which would be danger-

---

[48] Zubieta, *op. cit.*, p. 598. Pope Pius IX, in allocution *numquam fore* (December 15, 1856) energetically denied the legitimacy of national patronage as a right inherited from the kings of Spain. Also, the right of secular presentation was condemned as an error in the *Syllabus*. (Zamora, *Patronato Español é Indiano*, pp. 245-246.)

ous to the infant State. Tejada, however, was not able to halt the pope, for, on May 18, 1836, Mgr. Baluffi was named inter-nuncio extraordinary to New Granada. He was the first nuncio accredited to a Spanish-American republic.[49]

The recognition of New Granada marked the end of the American problem as far as political recognition and Spanish opposition were concerned. Thereafter the pope's dealings with Spanish America were direct and unhampered by considerations for Spanish susceptibilities. When Rome became satisfied as to the political stability of the new governments set up in America, and as to their friendliness toward the principle of papal supremacy, recognition was bestowed. The problem of the patronage, however, remained to complicate and strain Papal-American relations for many years to come.

---

[49] "Ignacio Tejada á Santander, Roma, 18 de Diciembre de 1835," in *Archivo Santander* (Bogotá, 1924-1925), XXI, 372-373; Zubieta, *op. cit.,* pp. 597-598.

CHAPTER IV

CHURCH AND STATE IN VENEZUELA

I

GREAT COLOMBIA

For nearly a decade after the achievement of independence the political fortunes of Venezuela, Colombia, and Ecuador were merged in a single republic, Great Colombia. This remarkable State, the handiwork of Simón Bolívar, had its genesis in the Congress of Angostura, which had been convened by the Liberator following the inauguration of his third, and eventually successful, attempt to liberate the Spanish colonies of northern South America. On August 15, 1819, the legislators of Angostura, representing Venezuela and New Granada, signed a provisional constitution which embodied with slight change, a constitutional project submitted by Bolívar. Neither in the project nor in the adopted instrument was there any reference to religion. Bolívar was of the opinion, and the constituents evidently concurred, that the constitutional guarantee of civil liberty comprehended religious liberty and should not be a subject of special legislation because it belonged exclusively to individual conscience.[1]

It was the purpose of Bolívar to weld New Granada and Venezuela into a single State, and in recognition of this objective a few representatives from New Granada were admitted into the Congress of Angostura even at a time when most of the viceroyalty was still under Spanish control. This control was effectively and permanently broken by the Liberator's great victory at Boyacá (August 7, 1819). An immediate political result of this victory was the formal union of the former Viceroyalty of New Granada

---

[1] The most novel feature of Bolívar's project, that having to do with the organization of the "Moral Power," a great institution of censorship and supervision of education and public morality, was rejected by the Congress. For the text of the Moral Power, see "El Poder Moral Propuesto por Bolívar en Angostura," in Gil Fortoul, *op. cit.,* pp. 545-551.

and the Captaincy-General of Venezuela into a State called "Great
Colombia." The act of December 17, 1819, which constituted the
republic, provided that a congress should meet at Rosario de Cúcuta
to draw up a constitution.[2] In evidence of the fact that the Colombian clergy favored independence and union with Venezuela, the
ecclesiastical *cabildo* of Bogotá shortly after the battle of Boyacá,
paid to the government a considerable part of the tithes, despite
its poverty.[3]

While Bolívar was winning a decisive victory at Carabobo (June
24, 1821), which assured the independence from Spain of northern
South America, a constituent congress composed of representatives from New Granada and Venezuela convened at Cúcuta. The
Constitution of Angostura, which, as we have seen, contained no
article on religion, was used by the constituents as the basis for
their deliberations. Some of them wished to insert an article
making Catholicism the religion of the State, but the majority
opposed, and, after a noisy scene, the constitution was approved
without any reference, in its body, to an official religion or even
to religious toleration.[4] This was in accordance with the wishes
of Bolívar, for, as the Liberator explained to an American in
1824, "When the Constitution of Colombia was drawn up, knowing that tolerance of any religion other than the Catholic would
not be permitted, I was careful that nothing should be said (in
the constitution) about religion, so that, since there was no clause
which prescribed the form of cult, aliens could adore God as they
pleased. The people of Colombia were not yet prepared for any
change in the matter of religion. The priests exercised a great
influence over the ignorant masses. Religious liberty ought to be
the consequence of free institutions and a system of general edu-

---

[2] Daniel F. O'Leary, *Bolívar y la Emancipación de Sur-América* (Madrid,
1915), II, p. 24; "S. Bolívar al Excmo. señor Vicepresidente de Cundinamarca,
Angostura, 20 de diciembre de 1819," in *Cartas de Bolívar,* II, 125.

[3] Henao y Arrubla, *Historia de Colombia,* II, 425.

[4] "Constitución de la República de Colombia, Rosario de Cúcuta, 1821," in
Manuel Antonio Pombo y José Joaquín Guerra, *Constituciones de Colombia*
(Bogotá, 1911), I, 717-759. The representatives of the Department of Venezuela were most antagonistic toward the Church. Mary Watters, "The Present Status of the Church in Venezuela," in *The Hispanic American Historical Review,* XIII, No. 1 (Feb. 1933), p. 24.

cation."[5] As is noted elsewhere, the same argument here expressed by Bolívar prompted him to omit any reference to religion in his model constitution for the Republic of Bolivia. But, contrary to the action of the Congress of Cúcuta, the Bolivians refused to accept Bolívar's religious policy.

It is not true, as is commonly asserted, that the Constitution of Cúcuta contained no reference whatsoever to religion. The preamble read: "In the name of God, Author and Legislator of the Universe." But more important was the prologue or introductory statement. In presenting the constitution to the people the framers wrote: "That which your representatives have always had in view, and that which has been the object of their most serious meditations, is that these laws should conform entirely to the maxims and dogmas of the Roman Catholic Apostolic religion which all of us profess and which we glory in professing. It has been the religion of our fathers, and it is and will be the religion of the State; its ministers are the only ones who enjoy the free exercise of their functions, and the government authorizes necessary contributions for the Sacred Cult."[6] The fact that the Catholic religion was not established, in the body of the constitution, itself, as the State religion, was due not to atheistic or Masonic opposition to the principle, but only to the inexperience of the constitution makers. It was taken for granted that the old religious status would continue (as witness the preamble quoted above), and that it would be regulated by ordinary legislation.

The legislative Congress of Cúcuta was very active, as a matter of fact, in determining by special laws the ecclesiastical jurisdiction. A law of August 22, 1821, abolished the Inquisition and appropriated its property for the public treasury. It provided that archbishops and bishops "reassume the ecclesiastical and purely spiritual jurisdiction, of which they had been deprived by the establishment of the Inquisition, hear causes of faith according to the canons and common ecclesiastical law, and impose on the guilty penalties established by the power of the Church." To remove obstacles to foreign immigration, the law added, "The hearing of such causes of faith will affect only the Roman Cath-

---

[5] Gil Fortoul, *Historia Constitucional de Venezuela*, I, 318.

[6] Pombo y Guerra, *op. cit.*, p. 720.

olics born in Colombia, their children, and those who, having come from other countries, have been inscribed in the parochial registers as Catholics. Aliens or their dependents cannot be molested in their beliefs, providing they do not show disrespect for the Catholic faith." Likewise, by the same law, full episcopal jurisdiction was guaranteed over purely spiritual matters, but all causes relating to the external discipline of the Church, like the prohibition of books, were left to the civil power. It was also provided that Colombian bishops were to be limited to the native-born.[7] Since the constitution guaranteed the privilege of writing, printing, thought, and opinion, the Congress in consequence, on September 14, 1821, legislated on the subject. After prohibiting the publication of sacred books without license of the ecclesiastical ordinary, the law classified as punishable writings those contrary to the dogmas of the Roman Catholic faith. Vice President Santander interpreted this law very liberally, for he authorized the publication of the works of Voltaire, Rousseau, and Diderot, which had been on the Index.[8]

In sponsoring a law which declared that the supreme government was the protector of the Catholic Church in Colombia, Bolívar revealed himself as a truly great statesman. Although he opposed the establishment of a State-Church, on the other hand he opposed absolute separation such as obtains in the United States. Since the Catholic Church was not only dominant, but universal, in Colombia, he felt that the government was morally bound to protect it and maintain it in all its purity. To do otherwise would make it remiss in its duty to advance the moral and spiritual well-being of Colombians. Thus we see Bolívar, personally a freethinker, *as president* attend mass regularly on Sunday, endow convents and other ecclesiastical institutions with public funds, honor bishops officially, and seek contact with the Holy See.[9]

General Santander, the head of the Colombian government on the numerous occasions when Bolívar was campaigning in Quito, Peru, and Charcas, was more insistent than the Liberator that the State should dominate the Church. He demanded that re-

---

[7] *Ibid.,* I, 319; Leturia, *La Acción Diplomática,* pp. 137-138.

[8] A. Berthe, *García Moreno, Président de L'Equateur* (Paris, 1887), p. 37.

[9] Gil Fortoul, *op. cit.,* I, 435.

strictions be placed upon the political activities of the clerics; by such means, he argued, not only would the security of republican principles be enhanced, but the status of religion would be improved. Santander, a prominent Mason, has been accused of encouraging Masonic anti-Catholic propaganda.[10] This assertion is subject to some doubt, yet it is true that Santander's extreme regalistic attitude evoked the severe criticism of Bolívar.[11]

Although the Congress of Cúcuta tried to avoid the patronal problem, that difficult and delicate question could not be successfully side-tracked. When the republican army occupied Popayán, in 1819, Bishop Salvador Jiménez de Encina, a Spaniard abandoned his diocese and threatened to excommunicate anyone who should attempt to assume his office. The republican authorities, accustomed as they were to royal interference in such a situation, felt constrained to intervene. The chapter was ordered to name a diocesan governor. This was done, and the capitular action was ratified by the government (April, 1821). By convincing Bishop Jiménez that republican principles were not contrary to the Church, Bolívar induced him to return to his diocese. By decree of July 28, 1823, the bishop was restored to his post.[12] Thus it is seen that the Congress without constitutional delegation of power or prior legislative action, proceeded on the assumption that it had inherited the patronal authority.

The question of the tithes also brought up the problem of patronage. On September 15, 1821, Bishop Lasso de la Vega of Mérida addressed a memorial to Vice President Santander on the subject of the tithes. He declared that since the tithes had been granted by Pope Alexander VI to the kings of Spain, it was evident that, with the founding of the republic, they reverted to the Church and belonged to her alone. Santander replied that the republican government had inherited the sovereignty of the Spanish kings, and all that belonged to it, particularly the tithes. As for bestowing the tithes upon the Church, Santander said, "Your

---

[10] Berthe, *op. cit.*, p. 36.

[11] "S. Bolívar á S. E. el General F. de P. Santander, Potosí, 21 de octubre de 1825," in *Cartas del Libertador,* V, 135-144.

[12] "S. Bolívar al Illmo. señor don Salvador Jiménez, Obispo de Popayán, Popayán, 31 de enero de 1822," in *Cartas del Libertador,* III, 17; Gil Fortoul, *op. cit.,* I, 319-20.

worship [Lasso] ought to be well informed that the government
of the republic has not failed and will not fail to do so . . . because
it is the duty of all government to support its cult and its
ministers."[13]

Bishop Lasso was puzzled by the reply of the Vice President,
for he did not understand how a government, which had just refused to recognize Catholicism as the religion of the State, could
declare itself to be in possession of the patronal rights. Congress,
nevertheless, declared adherence to the principle that the existing
laws remained in force "until a concordat can [could] be celebrated with the Apostolic See on this grave problem." Therefore
the government convoked an ecclesiastical *junta* in Bogotá to
agree on the essential principles of a concordat. In the *junta*,
which did not meet until March, 1823, the opinion of Bishop
Lasso prevailed; that is, that the patronage had come to an end.[14]

The Congress was not disposed to accept the decision of the
junta, for the Chamber, on August 4, 1823, approved a measure
declaring the inherency of patronage in national sovereignty.
But the Senate delayed and the session ended without action. The
next Congress, however, passed a law (July 28, 1824) declaring
that the right of patronage, which had been exercised by the
Spanish kings, belonged to the State. Because of the importance
of this law, its principal features are presented below:

The Senate and Chamber of Representatives of the Republic of
Colombia in Congress assembled:
Decree:

Article 1.   The Republic of Colombia ought to continue in the
exercise of the right of patronage which the kings of Spain had over
the metropolitan churches, cathedrals, and parishes in this part of
America.
Article 2.   This right is a duty of the Republic of Colombia and
of its government, and it demands that the Apostolic See do not
change or alter it; and the Executive Power under this principle will
celebrate with His Holiness a concordat which will assure for all

---

[13] Leturia, *op. cit.*, p. 146.

[14] *Ibid.*, pp. 146-147; José Manuel Restrepo, *Historia de Colombia* (Bogotá,
1848), III, 412; Juan Pablo Restrepo, *La Iglesia y el Estado en Colombia*
(London, 1881), pp. 140-143.

time, and irrevocably, this prerogative of the Republic and avoid conflicts and claims for the future.

Article 3. The right of patronage and protection are exercised, first, by the Congress; second, by the Executive Power with the Senate; third, by the Executive Power alone; fourth, by the intendants; and fifth, by the governors.

The High Court of the Republic, and the Superior Courts will hear cases that arise out of this matter.

The law proceeds to give in considerable detail the patronal powers and duties of the Congress, executive power, intendants, governors, High Court, and Superior Courts. These are presented in summary as follows:

Article 4.   The Congress is empowered to:

1.   Erect new dioceses or reorganize old ones, to designate their territorial limits, and assign funds to be employed in the building and repairing of metropolitan and episcopal churches.

2.   Permit, or even summon, national or provincial councils or synods.

3.   Permit or refuse the founding of new monasteries and hospitals, and to suppress those existing if deemed advisable, and to assume control of their property.

4.   Draw up tariffs of parochial fees.

5.   Regulate the administration of the tithes.

6.   Grant or refuse the exequatur to bulls and briefs.

7.   Enact legislation deemed necessary for the vigorous maintenance of exterior discipline of the Church, and for the conservation and exercise of the ecclesiastical patronage.

8.   Nominate those to be presented to His Holiness for the archiepiscopal and episcopal sees.

9.   Enact legislation for the establishment, rule, and support of the missions for the Indians.

Article 6.   The Executive is empowered to:

1.   Present to the pope for his approval the actions of Congress on the erection of new dioceses and the alteration of old ones.

2.   Present to the pope the nominees of Congress for the archiepiscopal and episcopal positions.

8

3. Present to the prelates and chapters for the dignities and canons, nominees selected jointly with the Senate.

4. Grant or refuse consent to the nominees of the prelates and chapters for provisors and capitular vicars.

5. Guard against the introduction of any novelty in the exterior discipline of the Church, and see that the ecclesiastics do not usurp the patronage of the State.

6. Grant the exequatur to briefs on matters of grace.

7. Watch over the proper supervision of the dioceses by the prelates.

8. Issue administrative decrees regulating the laws of Congress to protect religion, the public cult, and its ministers.

Article 7. The intendants are empowered to:

1. Name and present to the respective prelates the curates of the diocese included within the department.

2. Erect and fix the limits of new parishes.

3. Take care that the national patronage is observed and report on same to the Executive Power.

4. See that ecclesiastics do not usurp the civil jurisdiction.

5. Keep the Executive Power informed regarding clerics worthy of advancement.

Article 8. The governors are empowered to:

1. Name the *mayordomos de fábrica* of the cathedral and parish churches of their provinces, and to make them render an account of their management according to law.

2. Name, on the proposal of the respective municipalities, the syndics, *mayordomos*, and administrators of the hospitals of their provinces.

3. Permit or refuse the founding of chapels and churches, but not cathedrals, parochial churches, or monasteries.

4. Watch over the observance of the patronage.

5. Visit hospitals and remedy abuses in them; propose to the Executive Power, through the intendants, the reforms that should be introduced to improve those establishments.

6. Supervise *cofradías*.

7. Inform the intendants regarding the need of establishing new parishes.

8. Inform the intendants regarding ecclesiastics worthy of promotion.

Article 9. The High Court of Justice has jurisdiction over the following subjects:

1. Disloyalty of the archbishop and bishop to the republic, and violation on their part of the national patronage.

2. Controversies between two or more dioceses concerning their territorial limits.

3. Controversies arising out of concordats.

Article 10. The Superior Courts have jurisdiction over the following subjects:

1. Disloyalty to the republic, or usurpation of the patronage, by the other ecclesiastics.

2. Conflict over jurisdiction between civil and ecclesiastical courts.

The remaining articles of the *Ley de Patronato* regulate very minutely the manner of filling ecclesiastical vacancies, from the highest to the lowest. This law, substantially unchanged, is in force in Venezuela today.[15]

Papal confirmation, by concordat, of Colombia's pretentions to the patronage had been the ideal of the government from the inception of the republic. Peñalver and Vergara, in 1819, and Francisco Zea, in 1820, were instructed among other things to negotiate with the Holy See a formal recognition of the national patronage. The failure of the ecclesiastical *junta* of 1823 to approve the principle of the inherency of patronage in national sovereignty did not prevent the government, when Dr. Ignacio Tejada was appointed Colombian minister to Rome, from specifically instructing him to negotiate a concordat which would recognize the claims of the nation over ecclesiastical matters. In fairness to the Colombian government, it should be mentioned that its prime concern in despatching envoys to Rome was not to

---

[15] *Ley de Patronato Eclesiástico* (Caracas, 1911), pp. 4-25.

secure papal recognition of national claims, but papal consent to the restoration of the hierarchy and clerical establishment in Colombia. It was most concerned, in short, with the promotion of the spiritual welfare of the people who were sadly in need of clerics, both high and low. This deplorable situation is testified to by Mgr. J. Mazio in a *relación* written at the end of 1823: "In the other dioceses of the new Republic of Colombia, very many suffer, in addition, the still greater misfortune of being deprived of their pastors, whether by emigration or by death. Among them, counting Venezuela (Caracas), Cuenca, Santa Marta, Guayana, Cartagena, Quito, and the archbishopric of Santa Fé de Bogotá, there remain only Popayán, Panamá, and Mérida which enjoy the presence of their own bishops."[16] The conversion of Bishop Lasso de la Vega of Mérida and Bishop Salvador Jiménez de Encisco of Popayán, both royalists, to the revolutionary cause, and their efforts to induce the papacy to supply the episcopal vacancies in Colombia have been fully discussed elsewhere.

Despite obstacles and delays that would have taxed to the breaking point the endurance of the most patient of men, Tejada persisted in his efforts to secure favorable action by the Holy See on the demands of Colombia. Finally the tact and patience of Colombia's envoy were partially rewarded in that most of the difficulties regarding papal relations were settled, but the pope was adamant in his opposition to recognition of national patronage. Colombia's first diplomatic victory in Rome occurred in 1825 when Mgr. José Buenaventura Arias was appointed Auxiliary Bishop of Mérida. He was the candidate presented by Bishop Lasso de la Vega. In 1827 Pope Leo XII confirmed in the other vacant sees the candidates presented by the government. These were Fernando Caicedo y Flórez as Archbishop of Bogotá, Ramón Ignacio Méndez as Archbishop of Caracas, Félix Calixto Miranda as Bishop of Cuenca, José María Estévez as Bishop of Santa Marta, Manuel Santos Escobar as Bishop of Quito, and Mariano Garnica as Bishop of Antioquia. In August, 1829, Mariano de Talavera y Garcés was consecrated Bishop of Guayana. The year before he had been preconized Bishop of Tricala *in partibus*

---

[16] Leturia, *op. cit.*, p. 112, note 10.

infidelium and Vicar Apostolic of the diocese of Guayana which had at that time but one parish priest.[17]

On November 5, 1828, Bolívar wrote to Pope Leo XII expressing gratitude for the nomination by His Holiness of the first bishops of Colombian nationality, "in the absence now of the royal patronage." Bolívar was inclined to regard the law of patronage of 1824 as an idle gesture if pontifical confirmation were not secured. Therefore, he discretely explained the law to the pope, and concluded with the hope that His Holiness would finally confirm it.[18]

The desire of the Holy See to meet the demands of Colombia, short of entering into a concordat, was demonstrated by the filling of the vacant episcopacy of Mérida. When the see of Quito became vacant, the pope acceded to the petition of the government for the transfer to Quito of Lasso de la Vega, then Bishop of Mérida de Maracaibo. To fill the vacancy in Mérida, the pope thereupon named Auxiliary Bishop Arias. But the government had not solicited his appointment and expressed surprise that the pope on his own authority should act thus in opposition to the law of patronage. When Tejada conveyed to the Vatican the protest of his government, he was told that the pope thought it legitimate to fill the vacancy *motu proprio* and in the exercise of the plenitude of his powers for the better service of the Church. As for Bishop Arias, Tejada was also told since he had been auxiliary to Lasso de la Vega he was fully informed and competent to administer the diocese, and furthermore, being a bishop *in partibus*, he only lacked the right of jurisdiction which the brief conceded him. Tejada, however, was not satisfied with the pope's explanation and pointed out that according to the Council of Trent, the ecclesiastical chapters named vicars for vacancies. The result was that the pope called on the chapter of Mérida to approve Arias' name.[19] This was not papal acquiescence in Co-

---

[17] Henao y Arrubla, *op. cit.,* p. 428; Zubieta, *Misiones Diplomáticas de Colombia,* p. 581.

[18] "S. Bolívar á Su Santidad el Papa León XII, Bogotá, 7 de noviembre de 1828," in *Cartas del Libertador,* VIII, 105-106; José D. Monsalve, *El Ideal Político del Libertador Simón Bolívar* (Madrid, 1917), II, 398-400.

[19] Zubieta, *op. cit.,* pp. 582-584.

lombian ecclesiastical pretentions by any means, but the incident does illustrate the anxiety of Rome to conciliate the republican government.

A subject of particular interest to the Colombian government, in the exercise of its patronal prerogative, was the reform of the regular orders. In Colombia, as in other parts of Spanish America, the most numerous and flagrant instances of lax discipline and immoral practices among ecclesiastics were to be found in the establishments of the regulars. Since a contributing cause of this unfortunate situation was the large number of houses with a greatly depreciated membership, the Congress of Cúcuta on August 6, 1821, suppressed convents of regulars that did not have at least eight religious. The property of the suppressed convents was confiscated and applied to education and charity. Another law (March 4, 1826) prohibited the admission into convents of novices under the age of twenty-five years. On July 10, 1827, a decree was published excepting convents actually being conducted as schools and hospitals from the force of the law of 1821.

The political vicissitudes of Great Colombia convinced the Liberator more and more through the passing years that greater dependence had to be reposed in the Church as a stabilizing force. We find him actually, in his last years, becoming somewhat of a pro-clerical. The failure of the constituent congress of Ocaña (June 10, 1828), due to the opposition of the Santanderistas, forced Bolívar, much against his will, to assume dictatorial power. Having suspended the constitutional régime he proceeded to strengthen the position of the Church by special decree. As he wrote General Páez, he proposed to inaugurate a reform régime "on the solid basis of religion."[20] By decree of July 11 he suspended the law of March 4, 1826, which prohibited the admission into convents of novices under the age of twenty-five years. The purpose of the Liberator was to provide more clergy to work in the missions. He also suspended the laws of August 6, 1821, and April 7, 1826, which suppressed the small regular establishments. Another decree restored in the army the positions of vicars

---

[20] "S. Bolívar á S. E. el General J. A. Páez, Bogotá, 30 de junio de 1828," in *Cartas del Libertador*, VII, 338.

general and chaplains.[21] In support of religion as one of the greatest forces that can be opposed to anarchy, the Liberator recommended to General Páez friendly relations with the Archbishop of Caracas. To the Archbishop, on the other hand, Bolívar stressed the urgency of necessary reforms.[22]

On August 27, 1828, Bolívar resorted to the novel expedient of constitutionalizing the dictatorship by issuing an "organic decree of the dictatorship." In article 25, he established, for the first time, the Catholic religion on an official basis. The article read, "The government supports and protects the Roman Catholic Apostolic religion as the religion of Colombians." One of the functions of the Council of State (article 10) was, "to nominate persons for the positions of archbishop, bishop, *dignidades*, canons, *raciones*, *y media raciones* of the metropolitan and cathedral churches."[23] In his decree of the dictatorship, Bolívar filled in certain gaps, so far as religion was concerned, left by the Constitution of Cúcuta.

After an unsuccessful attempt upon his life (September 25, 1828), the Liberator swung even farther to the side of the proclericals. Attributing the conspiracy to the Masonic adherents of Santander, Bolívar prohibited secret societies of all kinds. All who met in secret societies were to be judged as conspirators. Moreover he attributed the conspiracy to the radical philosophy and political science being taught in the schools and colleges. Consequently he reorganized the general plan of studies, giving it a pronounced religious character in the hope that "the precepts of holy religion will abate the sophisms of the impious." Subjects prescribed for the primary schools were: reading, writing, arithmetic, dogma, morals, and the social rights and duties of man. The college curriculum comprised, the Castilian language, Latin, rhetoric, philosophy, mathematics, civil and canon law, dogmatic theology, and the rights of people. Resorting to the methods of the Inquisition, Bolívar ordered deleted from the texts of Jeremy

---

[21] Gil Fortoul, *op. cit.,* I, 434.

[22] "S. Bolívar al Exmo. Señor General J. A. Páez, Bogotá, 23 de agosto de 1828," and "S. Bolívar al señor Cristóbal Mendoza, Bogotá, 22 de agosto de 1828," in *Cartas del Libertador,* III, 28-30.

[23] Pombo y Guerra, *op. cit.,* pp. 812-814.

Bentham those parts opposed to religion, morals, and public order. Schools for girls were ordered established in convents for women, a college in each provincial capital, and an elementary school in each parish of one hundred inhabitants.[24]

Bolivar's reactionary decrees of 1828 favoring the Church aroused anti-clericalism in Venezuela which was much more pronounced than in Colombia. Páez wrote the Liberator: "We have worked much to destroy the horrors of fanaticism and the influence of the priests on the people; in Venezuela they now rarely meddle with public matters in their ministry . . . I judge that when you tell me the government is to support religion, it will be with all the delicacy that the enlightenment of an age which prefers, in my opinion, liberty of thought to civil liberty, demands."[24a]

When Bolívar resigned his dictatorial power to the constituent congress of Bogotá (January, 1830), he said, "Permit me that as my last act I recommend that you protect the holy religion which we profess; the profuse fountain of the benedictions of heaven."[25] This was the Liberator's last public act in support of the faith. Was Bolívar a Catholic? From the foregoing there should be little doubt that he was. Yet writes a notable Venezuelan authority, "Scarcely a Christian, or perhaps purely a deist, impregnated with the French philosophy of the eighteenth century against Catholic dogma, he always defended liberty of conscience, and of cults, with the exception, in the nature of a parenthesis, of the political reaction of 1828. That he confessed in his last hours, proves only that now the spirit of the Liberator was no more than its shadow."[26] Just as the growing anarchy in Colombia undermined Bolívar's faith in the republic and inclined him to monarchy, so also the license of free-thinking convinced him of the necessity of returning to religious authority. As early as 1825 he was convinced of this for he wrote his sister that he was prepared to protect religion to the death. [27] There is little doubt

---

[24] Gil Fortoul, *op. cit.*, I, 322, 434, 443-444.

[24a] Simon B. O'Leary, *Memorias del General O'Leary*, II, 149-150, quoted by Watters, *op. cit.*, pp. 25-26.

[25] Pombo y Guerra, *op. cit.*, p. 818.

[26] Gil Fortoul, *op. cit.*, I, 495, note 1.

[27] "S. Bolívar á la Señora María Antonia Bolívar, Potosí, 27 de octubre de 1825," in *Cartas del Libertador*, V, 147.

that the political experiences of the Liberator converted him to Catholicism.

The constituent congress of Bogotá, to which Bolívar resigned his authority, faithfully performed its duty in drawing up an instrument of government in spite of the opposition of Venezuela and Ecuador. Under the presidency of Marshal Sucre, and the vice presidency of José María Estévez, Bishop of Santa Marta, the new constitution was signed April 29, 1830. The Roman Catholic religion was recognized as that of Colombia, and it was declared that "it is the duty of the government, in the exercise of the patronage of the Colombian Church, to protect it and not to tolerate the public exercise of any other." With respect to appointment to ecclesiastical dignities the Senate was to draw up a *terna* from which the president should select the names to be proposed to the pope.[28]

Despite the mediatory efforts of Sucre and Bishop Estévez, the Venezuelan adherents of General Páez refused to accept the new constitution. Instead, Páez issued a decree ordering a Venezuelan congress to be held in Valencia on April 30. On May 31, 1830, General Juan Flores convoked a constituent congress for Ecuador to meet at Riobamba on August 10. Thus Venezuela and Ecuador seceded from Great Colombia, and the unified republic for which Bolívar had struggled so valiantly collapsed only a few days before his death (December 17, 1830).

II

VENEZUELA

Following Venezuelan secession from the Republic of Great Colombia, a constituent assembly convened at Valencia, in May, 1830, to recreate a separate and independent state of Venezuela. The party in control of the Congress had championed, since 1821, the federal principle and had opposed the unitary constitution of Cúcuta. The "Conservative Oligarchy," as this majority group was called, supported a liberal religious policy, and therefore, following the example of the constitutions inspired by Bolívar, in-

---

[28] "Constitución de la República de Colombia, Bogotá, 1830," in Pombo y Guerra, *op. cit.*, pp. 829-868.

serted no special article on the subject of religious liberty in the constitution which was promulgated in September, 1830. The proponents of a State-Church had submitted to the Congress, but without success, the following article: "In Venezuela, the Catholic, Apostolic, Roman religion, which is the one which, happily, has always existed, and which all the inhabitants profess, is the religion of the State. Tolerance of cults will be freely permitted, and nobody will be persecuted for his religious opinions; consequently strangers who wish to establish themselves in Venezuela, adopting it as their new country, will enjoy this right, conforming to the laws passed by the constituent congress." In imitation also of the Colombian régime, the constituent congress, by resolution, on October 14, 1830, declared that the right of patronage belonged to the nation, and incorporated the *Ley de Patronato* of 1824 into its legislation.[29]

In the course of its national history Venezuela has enacted twenty constitutions, but it has never to the present day altered the essential features of the Law of the Patronage. It has been characterized as "a classic of Venezuelan jurisprudence."

The acts of the Congress created bitter opposition in the ranks of the militarists and the clericals. The former, led by José Gregorio Monagas, proclaiming a program of Colombian federation, military *fueros*, and Roman Catholicism as the exclusive religion of the State, staged a futile revolt in 1831. Thereafter the resistance of the militarists proved to be less menacing. The clerical opposition was confined largely to the refusal of the prelates to swear an oath of unqualified obedience to the constitution, because of its failure to recognize explicitly Catholicism as the State religion. The government had ordered all citizens to assemble on a given day in the churches where a mass was to be celebrated and an oath of obedience sworn to the constitution. Archbishop Méndez protested the act of the government in going "outside of its civil powers to concern itself even with the liturgy of the Church," but declared he would overlook the "defect of power" to order the various acts performed.[30]

[29] Gil Fortoul, *op. cit.,* II, 34; *Catholic Encyclopedia,* XI, 330.

[30] Gil Fortoul, *op. cit.,* II, 35-36, 144. Archbishop Méndez, uncle of Bolívar's faithful secretary, Briceño Méndez, was beholden to the Liberator for his eleva-

A few days later the Archbishop enumerated the articles and omissions of the constitution that alarmed his conscience. He deplored the failure of the Congress to include an article relating to religion. He said also that the article dividing the territory into provinces, cantons, and parishes needed clarification as to whether it meant civil or ecclesiastical parishes. He protested free speech to senators and representatives if extended to religious subjects. The control of Congress over education, he contended, should not include the seminaries; the constitutional guarantee of doing all which is not prohibited by law ought to comprise also the divine and ecclesiastical law; and liberty of thought ought not to apply to religion, its dogmas, morals, or discipline. Méndez then communicated to the government the following oath which he was willing to take: "In the opinion that the Roman Catholic religion will continue to be the only one in Venezuela, and on condition that the Republic will negotiate and conclude a concordat with the Holy See . . . and excepting always the liberty, independence, and discipline of the Church—I swear, by the Holy Gospel, to obey, sustain, and defend the constitution sanctioned by the constituent congress of the State of Venezuela on September 22, 1830."

The Council of State refused, quite obviously, to sanction a conditional oath, and the Archbishop was notified that if he persisted in his opposition he would be removed from office and banished. But the prelate remained obstinate, and was exiled to Curaçao on November 21, 1831. At the same time, and for the same reason, the bishops of Mérida and Guayana were banished also. While at Curaçao Archbishop Méndez was in communication with General Santander, to whom he complained of irreligion, immorality, and radical activities of the "Jacobins" in Venezuela.[31] Exile

---

tion to the archiepiscopal see. Vice-Admiral Fleming wrote about the prelate (November 29, 1829, La Guaira): "The Archbishop is a mediocre man, ignorant, uneducated and dissolute, who has spent most of his life among the *llaneros* whose manners he has adopted. Like them he has many natural children, and I have seen him dispute and quarrel at a gambling table." (Gil Fortoul, *op. cit.*, II, 36-37). The high character and ability of the Archbishop is vigorously defended by Miss Watters. (*Op. cit.*, p. 30, note 22.)

[31] "El Arzobispo de Caracas á Santander, Curazao, enero 23 de 1832," and "El Arzobispo de Caracas á Santander, Curazao, marzo 24 de 1832," in *Archivo Santander*, XIX, 181, 278.

cooled the ardor of the prelates, and when they agreed to take the oath, they were allowed to return to Venezuela (April, 1832).[32]

Not only did the government of the "Oligarchy" force the submission of the prelates, but it adopted drastic ecclesiastical reform measures. By act of Congress (February 18, 1834) freedom of all religious sects was decreed. This action was intended primarily to encourage foreign non-Catholic immigration. In that same year there was founded in Caracas the first Protestant church—an English chapel. The Protestants were also allowed to maintain a cemetery. The impost of the tithes was suppressed on April 16, 1833, and it was decreed that the Catholic Church and its ministers should be paid from the public treasury; the ecclesiastical budget was to be drawn up annually with the approval of Congress.[33] In 1836 the government ordered established in the capital of each province, a main office, and in each canton a sub-office of the civil registry for births, marriages, and deaths. This law, which would have deprived the clerics of one of their most influential functions, remained a dead letter for many years to come. Since the Venezuelan prelates had increased the number of feast days out of all reason and to the great economic detriment of the country, the government asked the pope, in 1836, to reduce them to a reasonable number. On June 20, 1837, Pope Gregory XVI published a brief fixing the number of feast days. Although the list was still too long, the Congress finally agreed to grant the *pase*. To the number of fiestas were to be added, of course, the several national holidays. In 1837 a law was passed revoking the act of the government of Great Colombia in 1828 which legalized the existence of several monasteries despite the law of suppression. The few remaining monasteries in Venezuela consequently were suppressed, and their property devoted to the purposes of public education. After 1837 there were in Venezuela only convents for nuns. These were suppressed in 1874.[34]

The Oligarchy was, furthermore, a vigilant guardian of the

[32] Rafael María Baralt y Ramón Díaz, *Resumen de la Historia de Venezuela* (Curaçao, 1887), III, 403.

[33] "A. Fortique á Santander, Paris, 9 de mayo de 1834," in *Archivo Santander*, XX, 341; Gustavo Arboleda, *Historia Contemporanea de Colombia* (Bogotá, 1918), I, 192; Gil Fortoul, II, 34; *Catholic Ency.*, XV, 331.

[34] Gil Fortoul, *op. cit.*, II, 34-35.

national prerogative of the patronage. Indeed, this very watchfulness has been declared to have been the means of saving the republic from clerical reactions such as occurred in other States. On March 21, 1833, in reply to a petition of the hierarchy that the *Ley de Patronato* of 1824 be suspended or reformed, the Congress declared it to be in force and ordered its observance "to avoid inconveniences to the civil authority in the exercise of its rights, and to the government as patron and protector of the Church of Venezuela."[35] In the face of the oft-repeated policy of the Republic to maintain complete the right of patronage inherited from Spain, Archbishop Méndez refused canonical institution to prebendaries presented by the government. Moreover, in opposition to the law which suppressed the tithes, he threatened in a pastoral, to excommunicate all Christians who did not pay the tithes. Because of his opposition he was banished again in 1836.[36] He went to Curaçao where he lived for three years, and then to New Granada where he died in 1839. He was succeeded as Archbishop of Caracas by Ignacio Fernandez Peña.

On May 13, 1841, the Congress decreed that the exequatur of the government granted to bulls of institution issued to any Venezuelan prelate by the Supreme Pontiff should contain a clause stating that the *pase* was to be conceded only when the rights and prerogatives of the nation were preserved in their entirety. Also that the *pase* should be granted only after the archbishop and bishop named in the bull of institution, should swear the following oath: "I, ———, Archbishop or Bishop of ———, swear that never will I consider the oath of obedience to the constitution, the laws, and the government of the republic, which I swore to prior to my presentation to His Holiness, directly or indirectly annulled nor in any part diminished by the oath of obedience to the Apostolic See which I must take at the time of my consecration; nor by any later act under any motive. So help me God."[37]

Also in exercise of its patronal duties the government, in 1843, under the presidency of General Carlos Soublette, on observing

[35] *Ley de Patronato*, pp. 3-4.
[36] "J. F. Blanco á Santander, Caracas, 20 de octubre de 1836," in *Archivo Santander*, XXII, 344-345; Baralt y Díaz, *op. cit.*, III, 421.
[37] *Ley de Patronato*, p. 28.

the lamentable scarcity of curates, endowed several parishes, and introduced about one hundred Spanish priests. The Liberal opposition criticised this action as being unwarranted and outside of the patronal obligations. Their accusation of ignorance and immorality against the Spanish priests was undoubtedly exaggerated because they opposed the policy of introducing foreign clerics. In 1845 a law was passed prohibiting, without permit of the national government, the entry of foreign priests into Venezuela.[38]

The Conservative Oligarchy, triumphant in Venezuela after the dissolution of Great Colombia, retained control of the government until 1847. The policies of the dominant faction were enlightened, progressive, and moderate. Páez, Vargas, and Soublette gave Venezuela a relatively peaceful and auspicious start along the road of political and economic development. Their religious policy was firm yet tolerant, and was devoid of that harshness and tactlessness, which, in other countries, crystallized fanatical opposition and reaction. In the conflicts with Archbishop Méndez, the government exerted itself to avoid conflict, but so stubborn was the prelate that a reasonable understanding was impossible. With the realization that Venezuelan development was dependent on immigration, acts were passed to make the country more inviting to non-Catholics. Yet, it is illogical to conclude from these acts that the government was disposed to separate Church and State. Quite to the contrary, the Conservatives were intent on maintaining the patronal control, and in rendering the Church a more effective instrument to perform its divine mission.

The election of José Tadeo Monagas inaugurated the Liberal Oligarchic régime in Venezuelan history. Elected as a Conservative, Monagas soon deserted the "Godos," as the Conservatives were called, and allied himself with Antonio Leocadio Guzmán, leader of the Liberals. In February, 1849, Guzmán, as Minister of Interior and Justice, ordered the governors of the provinces to issue more peremptory orders not to admit into any port foreign priests who should arrive without the permission of the national government. In August, 1848, a similar prohibition had already been directed at the Jesuits. Guzmán, while recognizing the need of increasing the national clergy, would not consent to the immi-

---

[38] Gil Fortoul, *op. cit.*, II, 34-35, 276.

gration of foreign clerics. He also sponsored measures, which, however, were not enforced, to regulate the appointment of priests and the administration of parishes. He proposed the creation of a *junta* to be named annually by the parish voters, which with the priest was to prepare the budget for the parish. The *junta* also was to select candidates for vacant curacies to be presented to the diocesan prelate. Guzmán also recommended as a stimulus to immigration suspension of the law which provided that the marriage ceremony could only be celebrated by Catholic priests. He advocated a prior civil ceremony. Guzmán's liberalism found little support in the program of Monagas, which was strictly personalistic. Consequently it was not long before the Liberal leader was ousted from the government. [39]

The Monagas brothers, José Tadeo and José Gregorio, alternated in control of the presidential office from 1848 to 1858. Although not as pro-clerical as at the time of the revolt of 1831, they were on the whole friendly to the Catholic Church. In 1852 the government ordered established in all the national colleges chairs in ecclesiastical sciences. In 1853 a moderate increase was made in ecclesiastical appropriations. An impost of one-half per cent on imports was provided for the construction and repair of churches. In 1857 an ephemeral constitution sponsored by President José Tadeo was promulgated. This fundamental law contained a clause declaring that the State protected the Roman Catholic religion, and that the government would always sustain its ministers and the cult. Contrary to his demand of 1831, Monagas did not demand Catholicism as an exclusive religion.

When José Tadeo Monagas was overthrown in 1858 by a Conservative-Liberal coalition, his constitution of 1857 was also scrapped. In December, 1858, a new frame of government with federalistic features was promulgated. In this instrument there was a reversion to the old practice of remaining silent on the subject of religion. Yet it seemed to be understood that the laws providing for liberty of cults and the payment of ecclesiastical appropriations as a consequence of the right of patronage, were still in force. There was no change wrought in the political status of the Church other than that if a subsequent congress desired,

[39] Gil Fortoul, *op. cit.*, II, 34-35, 275-278.

it could separate Church and State by simple legislation.[40]

The establishment of federalism, instead of solving Venezuela's difficulties, merely constituted the pretext for another, and even more bloody, civil war. There soon emerged, temporarily, out of the conflict, General Páez as dictator. In this, his final tenure of power, Páez revealed himself quite unmistakably as a pro-clerical. In the hope of having the pope recognize by concordat those patronal prerogatives claimed and maintained up to that time by all parties, Conservative as well as Liberal, on May 6, 1862, President Páez conferred credentials as a plenipotentiary on the Archbishop of Caracas, Silvestre Guevara y Lira. [41] The Archbishop, although a man of considerable political experience, was inclined to conciliation and peace; he was, it was said, *dulce y fácil* (sweet and easy). Therefore, although he was instructed to negotiate a concordat, "without losing sight of our law of patronage," he brought back to Caracas, in September, 1862, a document which convinced many that he had lost complete sight of the national claims. "In Rome," his critics declared, "he put his religious conscience before that of the State; he was the representative of the Church, and not of the Republic."

The concordat which was signed in Rome on July 26, 1862,[42] and which aroused a perfect furore of opposition in Venezuela, is worthy of careful examination because it exhibits so well a settlement acceptable to the papacy. Article 1 provided: "The Catholic religion will continue to be that of the republic, and the government will recognize the duty of defending and conserving it effectively with all the rights and prerogatives that belong to it by the ordination of God and the canonical sanction." The religion of the republic, however, never existed so broadly as stated. Also, the proposed article did not provide for religious

---

[40] Gil Fortoul, *op. cit.*, II, 353; Arosemena, *op. cit.*, II, 141-142.

[41] Guevara y Lira was consecrated archbishop in 1853, having been named by the National Congress on the recommendation of President José Gregorio Monagas, who was his relative. He had considerable experience in politics, having served in the Senate and in the Council of State. (Gil Fortoul, *op. cit.*, II, 493.)

[42] "Concordato fra Pio IXe la Republica di Venezuela, 26 luglio 1862," in *Raccolta di Concordati Su Materie Ecclesiastiche Tra la Santa Sede e Le Autorita Civil* (Rome, 1919), pp. 971-983.

toleration, yet liberty of cults had been expressly recognized in 1834.

Regarding public instruction the concordat provided that it should conform entirely to Catholic doctrine, and that bishops should have free direction and inspection of faculties of theology, canon law, and other ecclesiastical subjects. Also, the bishops should be given the right of inspection to see that nothing contrary to Catholicism was taught. Since this would have given the prelates the right to censor books and writings of all kinds, the concordat, therefore, would have violated liberty of thought guaranteed by the constitution.

In consideration of the government's agreement to pay specified sums for the support of the cult and its ministers, the Holy See agreed to tolerate the law of 1833 which abolished the tithes. Until 1833, the ecclesiastical income had been based on the tithes. The Congress regarding this impost as excessive and contrary to public prosperity, passed a law which abolished the tithes, and provided for the support of the cult by annual congressional appropriations. The evident intention of the papacy was to make the clergy economically independent of the Congress by itemizing fixed incomes for the clerics. The total annual appropriation amounted to 32,250 pesos.

The concordat provided that, in exchange for the obligations which the government contracted, the Holy See would concede the right of presentation. It specified the mode of procedure in selecting and making nominations, i.e., the president of the republic should propose to the pope candidates for vacancies in archiepiscopal and episcopal sees and dignities, and the pope would then give canonical institution in the accustomed form, it being agreed that the person proposed could not assume office or participate in affairs of his church until after he had received the bull of institution. The pope, in turn, agreed not to erect new dioceses except with the government's approval.

The Council of State advised ratification of the concordat, and President Páez signed it on March 6, 1863. That Páez and his councillors should have approved such a reactionary concordat can be explained only as a frantic eleventh hour effort to ward off disaster by courting the support of the clericals. A

9

few days later, however, Páez was ousted from the government
by the federalists and the National Assembly rejected the concordat. The new congress established under the Constitution of
March 28, 1864, advised President Falcón to reopen negotiations
with Rome "to put the concordat in harmony with the national
laws and the spirit and letter of the new constitution, which, like
earlier ones, guarantees religious liberty and freedom of the
press." Lucio Pulido was sent to Rome in June, 1864, to negotiate,
but his mission was a failure. Thus by a narrow margin Venezuela escaped falling under a clerical blight.[43]

Within ten years after the fall of Páez, and the menace of
clerical supremacy, another and more powerful dictator had arisen
in Venezuela, and unfortunately for the Catholic Church, he pursued a religious policy antithetical to that of his predecessor. Out
of the welter and turmoil of internecine warfare which followed
the formation of the Venezuelan Confederation, emerged Antonio
Guzmán Blanco, Liberal-Federal leader, president, dictator, and
dominator of Venezuelan politics for almost two decades. Guzmán
Blanco was of the same opinion as his father, Antonio Guzmán,
that the political power of the Catholic Church had to be curbed.
Since the clerics were the supporters of the Conservatives, or
"Godos," arch-enemies of the Liberals, they were regarded as
serious obstacles in the path of Guzmán Blanco's ambition. In
his wars upon the Godos, he was constantly confronted with the
necessity of dealing with opposition clerics. In one of his dispatches
he complained of the church in Valencia being the general head-
quarters of the "oligarchic reaction," and asked that the archbishop be requested to appoint a liberal priest in Valencia "to
avoid conflict between Church and State."[44] In commenting on
clerical opposition to the federal cause, Guzmán Blanco wrote: "I
desire harmony with the Church, but if the clergy persist, so unwarrantedly, in provoking a conflict, I shall suppress them. To
do otherwise would make us remiss in our duties to the Revolution,

---

[43] Lisandro Alvarado, *Historia de la Revolución Federal en Venezuela*
(Caracas, 1909), pp. 526-527; *Cath. Ency.*, XV, 331.

[44] "Guzmán Blanco á Ciudadanos General Primer Designado y Ministro
del Gobierno Nacional, Cuartel General en Valencia, 19 de setiembre de
1870," in *Memorandum del General Guzmán Blanco* (Caracas, 1876), p. 76.

the Liberal cause, and to the Republic. We can never consent
that the words of clergy, in the press or in the tribune, shall be
the echo of reaction. Not only should we stop those who write
against the legitimacy of the government, but we should request
the Archbishop to remove all curates who are notoriously counter-
revolutionary. I am going to arrest in Caracas (certain named
curates)."[45]

Archbishop Guevara y Lira, unfortunately for harmony between the powers, was also anti-Liberal and resented the demands
of the Liberals that priests be appointed and removed to suit
party convenience. The Archbishop's ultramontanism had been
exhibited in his negotiations for a concordat in 1862. Furthermore,
after the new civil code had been issued in 1867, Archbishop
Guevara showed himself a vigorous defender of Catholicism in protesting against certain features in the code which he believed to
be out of harmony with the laws of the Church.[46] It was inevitable
that the Archbishop and Guzmán Blanco should have clashed. Consequently, when the dictator ordered *Te Deums* sung in the churches
in celebration of the Liberal victory, the prelate objected and
suggested that a thanksgiving mass would be more appropriate
if deferred until the general amnesty offered by the president
should be put into effect.[47] The suggested postponement was not
acceptable to the acting chief executive in Caracas, and somewhat against the wishes of Guzmán Blanco the Archbishop was
banished to the island of Trinidad. When Guzmán Blanco returned
to Caracas he attempted to effect a reconciliation with the prelate
but to no effect, since Guevara y Lira was obdurate in his opposition to the Liberals. From Trinidad he fomented plots against the
government through his faithful clerical agents. Since the situation had become intolerable, the Congress, on June 3, 1873, decreed the vacancy of the archiepiscopal see, for Guevara y Lira
was still technically the incumbent. Dr. J. M. Arroyo was elected

---

[45] "Guzmán Blanco á Ciudadano General Primer Designado y Ministros
del Gobierno Nacional, Cuartel General in Puerto Cabello, 26 de agosto de
1870," in *Mem. del G. Blanco,* pp. 56-57.

[46] Arosemena, *op. cit.,* II, 182-183.

[47] "Guzmán Blanco á Ciudadano General Encargado de la Presidencia,
Cuartel General en Puerto Cabello, 22 de setiembre de 1870," in *Mem. del
G. Blanco,* p. 81; *Cath. Ency.,* XV, 331.

archbishop a few months later, but after he accepted and took an oath of obedience to the government, he resigned when notified that the pope disapproved. In 1875 the difficulty was terminated when Guevara y Lira abdicated the see at the suggestion of Pius IX and through the mediation of Mgr. Rocca Cocchia, the apostolic delegate. The nomination of José Ponte to the see was promptly confirmed by the pope.[48]

The clash between Archbishop Guevara y Lira and Guzmán Blanco served to break down the flood-gates which restrained the dictator's resentment for clerical influence. In 1873 he inaugurated one of the most complete and devastating attacks ever directed against the Catholic Church in Latin America. The initial act deprived the clergy of control over the civil registry; or, to be more exact, the law of 1836 was ordered enforced. The recording of births, marriages, and deaths in the parish books without a corresponding entry in the public register was prohibited. It was hoped that this would diminish clerical influence over domestic relations. Cemeteries were taken from the control of the clergy and were opened to Jews and heretics. At the same time, the civil rite of marriage was declared to be the only legal form. The civil ceremony was given precedence over the religious, and many technicalities were introduced to render the latter difficult. The attempt of the dictator to legalize the marriage of those in holy orders was prevented by an outraged public conscience. In 1874 the Congress, appealing to the law of patronage, abolished all convents, monasteries, colleges, and other religious institutions. Monastic and church property was confiscated for the benefit of the government. The Church was stripped of all it held of value. The customary ecclesiastical revenues were abolished and appropriations for the Church were suspended. Public education was declared to be lay, gratuitous, and obligatory; consequently, parish schools were abolished notwithstanding the fact that existing educational facilities were sadly deficient. Even ecclesiastical seminaries were suppressed, and priests were to be educated in the national university where the doctrine of infallibility

---

[48] Arosemena, *op. cit.*, II, 186-87; "Guzmán Blanco á Ciudadanos Ministros del Despacho, Valencia, 25 de febrero de 1871," in *Mem. del G. Blanco*, p. 126.

was repudiated.[49] In the hope of seeing Protestantism take root and prosper in Venezuela, Guzmán Blanco offered one of the confiscated churches to the Protestants, but as there was no organization to accept the offer, it was withdrawn.[50]

In spite of the radical reform measures imposed on Venezuela by the fiat of Guzmán Blanco, Church and State, in theory at least, continued to be united. In the Constitution of May 23, 1874, religious liberty was guaranteed, but "only the Roman Catholic Apostolic religion can [could] exercise the public cult outside of churches."[51] The Catholic Church was accorded, therefore, a privileged position which was denied to other cults. In further evidence of a continuation of a connection between Church and State, the constitution provided (Art. 98) that the right of exercising the ecclesiastical patronage belonged to the nation, and that the nature of its exercise was to be determined by law.[52]

A bold but futile attempt was made by Guzmán Blanco, at the time of his controversy with Archbishop Guevara y Lira, to nationalize the Venezuelan Church. The refusal of Guevara to resign and of the pope to compel his resignation induced Guzmán Blanco to suggest to Congress the termination of papal control over the Venezuelan Church. The President, a grand master of the Masonic Order, had long been desirous of establishing a national church independent of the papacy. His message, suggesting this radical step, was as follows: "I have taken upon myself the responsibility of declaring the Church of Venezuela independent of the Roman Episcopate, and ask that you further order that parish priests shall be elected by the people, the bishops by the rectors of the parish, and the archbishops by Congress, thereby returning to the custom of the primitive Church founded by Jesus Christ and his apostles. Such a law will not only solve the clerical question, but will be moreover a good example for the Christian Church of republican America, obstructed in her march towards liberty,

---

[49] William E. Curtis, *Venezuela* (n.p., n.d.), pp. 204-208; Gil Fortoul, *op. cit.*, II, 501; *Cath. Ency.*, XV, 331; Watters, *op. cit.*, pp. 34-35.

[50] W. R. Wheeler and W. E. Browning, *Modern Missions on the Spanish Main* (Philadelphia, 1925), p. 286.

[51] Art. 14, Sec. 13, Arosemena, *op. cit.*, II, 108.

[52] Arosemena, *op. cit.*, II, 121.

order, and progress by the retrograde policy of the Roman Church; and the civilized world will see in this act the most characteristic and palpable sign of advance in the regeneration of Venezuela."

The servile Congress replied to the dictator: "Faithful to our duties, faithful to our convictions, and faithful to the holy dogma of the religion of Jesus Christ, of that great Being who conserved the world's freedom with his blood, we do not hesitate to emancipate the Church of Venezuela from that episcopacy which pretends, as an infallible and omnipotent power, to absorb from Rome the vitality of a free people, the beliefs of our conscience, and the noble aspirations and destinies which pertain to us as component parts of the great human family. Congress offers and will give Your Excellency all the aid you seek to preserve the honor and the prerogative of our nation, and hereby announce, with patriotic pleasure, that it has already begun to elaborate the law which Your Excellency asks it to frame."[53]

The resultant legislation, however, did not embody the ideas of the president, for it aimed, in substance, to prohibit entry into Venezuela of foreign ecclesiastical prelates and abrogated the laws of patronage. In short, the Congress proposed to disestablish the Roman Church without substituting anything in its place, certainly not a national church such as Guzmán Blanco suggested. Fortunately, the law was not promulgated, since the controversy over the archiepiscopal see was satisfactorily settled. After that the government desisted in its attack on the Church, but it did not abrogate the laws which had been enacted. With due consideration to this fact, relatively harmonious relations existed between Church and State during the remaining years of Guzmán Blanco's dictatorship (1876-1888). On the occasion of his return from France in 1886, where he had gone on one of his numerous diplomatic missions, the clergy greeted him in Caracas with a *Te Deum* in the cathedral. The archbishop felicitated the president, and he in response said, "I am convinced by faith, opinion, study, and experience, that the secret of harmony between Church and State is found in each of the powers, civil and ecclesiastical, moving in its own orbit, like the sun, Jupiter, Saturn. . . . To

[53] Arosemena, *op. cit.,* II, 180-186; Curtis, *op. cit.,* pp. 205-206.

work to maintain harmony is now, more than ever, my greatest ambition."[54]

During his last tenure of power, Guzmán Blanco evidenced a conciliatory attitude toward the Church by sponsoring the introduction into Venezuela, from France, of the Sisters of Charity of St. Joseph of Tarbes. They were entrusted with the direction of the hospitals, and also of education for girls. After the overthrow of Guzmán Blanco in 1888, the rapprochement between Church and State continued to grow. In spite of special laws to the contrary, various religious orders were allowed to return to Venezuela. In 1891, the government invited the Capuchins to undertake missionary work among the savages of the Orinoco. In 1894 the Selesians were invited to aid in education. In 1899 and in 1903 the Augustinians and the Dominicans returned. By law of September 28, 1900, the ecclesiastical seminaries were ordered reëstablished.[55]

The return of the Church to a normal status after the reforms of Guzmán Blanco was a slow and tedious process. Many of the laws of "the Illustrious American" were continued in force because a spirit of antagonism toward the Church was pronounced for many years among the legislators of the country. The laws of liberty of cults, the civil register, civil marriage, secularized cemeteries, prohibition of entry into Venezuela of foreign ecclesiastics of any cult, prohibition of religious ceremonies outside of church buildings, and prohibition of all regular orders were still kept on the statute books, but as has been noted, they were not all enforced. Under President Cipriano Castro the Civil Code was reformed by introducing a divorce law. On the other hand the Roman Catholic Apostolic religion was declared once more, in the Constitution of 1904, to be the national religion, and the State contributed to its support. Likewise the State reasserted its control over the ecclesiastical patronage and declared the Law of 1824 to be in force once more. In the Constitution of 1904, for example, Article 124 read: "Since the nation is in possession of the right

---

[54] Francisco González Guinán, *Historia del Gobierno de la Aclamación* (Caracas, 1899), p. 31.

[55] *Cath. Ency.*, XV, 331; Watters, *op. cit.*, pp. 37-38.

of ecclesiastical patronage, it will exercise it conforming to the Law of July 28, 1824."[56]

During the long dictatorship of Juan Vicente Gómez (1909—) the relations of Church and State in Venezuela have been maintained under the most complete cordiality and in conformity with the law of ecclesiastical patronage.[57] Although many of the anticlerical measures of Guzmán Blanco still remained technically in force, President Gómez was inclined to be lenient and saw that they were not drastically applied. Many religious orders, for example, reëntered Venezuela in spite of the existence of special laws against them. This did not signify, on the other hand, that Gómez was a less zealous protector of patronal rights, for quite to the contrary, he extended the scope of patronage to non-Catholic cults. By decree of October 24, 1911, it was declared: "(1) The exercise of all cults tolerated in the Republic will be regulated by the *Ley de Patronato* of 1824; (2) where the *Ley de Patronato* refers to the see of the Catholic Church, or to the pontiff, it is understood as referring, to all effects of this decree, to the superior ecclesiastical authority of each non-Catholic cult legally established in this country." In pursuance of this decree, the Minister of Interior Relations notified all officials to enforce the observance of the *Ley de Patronato*, and in particular those provisions of the law that reserved to the national congress the right to establish missions, and to the executive the right to regulate and designate where missions ought to be established, and to prohibit the entry into the country of foreigners dedicated to the service of some cult. Therefore, those missionaries who had not observed the laws were to be deprived of their posts.[58] It is suspected that Gómez issued this decree in answer to clerical protest against foreign missionary activity. It was an effective way to attack Protestantism and at the same time adhere to the letter of the law of toleration. As can be readily appreciated, Protestantism stood small chance of propagation in Venezuela so long as the law prohibiting the entry into the republic of "foreigners dedicated especially to the service of any cult or religion" remained in force.

[56] N. Veloz Goiticoa, *Venezuela* (Caracas, 1919), pp. 75-78.

[57] J. A. Gonzalo Salas to J. L. Mecham, Caracas, October 17, 1927.

[58] *Ley de Patronato*, p. 48.

The present constitution of Venezuela, promulgated in 1925, contains but two articles touching on the religious question. The first (Art. 32, No. 14) guarantees to Venezuelans religious liberty under the supreme inspection of all cults by the federal executive according to law, and reserving the rights of ecclesiastical patronage. The nation is declared (Art. 52) to be in possession of the exercise of the ecclesiastical patronage conforming to the law of July 28, 1824.[59] Thus, according to the law of patronage, the government designates Church officials for various ecclesiastical offices, the appointments are made by Congress and are confirmed by the papacy. The government in recognition also of its patronal obligations, makes appropriations for the support of the Catholic Church; these appropriations being gradually increased in recent years. In 1930 the appropriation was 442,568 bolivars, or approximately $90,000.[60] The official budget gives an itemized list of the salaries paid by the government to functionaries of the Church. In addition, rather important contributions to the Church are made from government funds by official decrees issued from time to time. Venezuela has a diplomatic representative with the rank of minister plenipotentiary accredited to the Vatican. The papal nuncio is the dean of the diplomatic corps in Caracas.[61] Ecclesiastical matters are entrusted to the care of the Ministry of the Interior. This minister is the special guardian, one might say, of the national right of patronage.[62] The political relationship which exists in Venezuela between Church and State, is, therefore, very intimate, and although the constitution purposely avoids the designation, the Catholic Church is the State-Church of Venezuela.[63]

---

[59] *Constitución de los Estados Unidos de Venezuela sancionada por El Congreso Nacional en 1925* (Caracas, 1925).

[60] Watters, *op. cit.*, p. 40.

[61] *El Libro Amarillo de los Estados Unidos de Venezuela presentado al Congreso Nacional en sus sesiones de 1930 por el Ministro de Relaciones Exteriores* (Caracas, 1930), pp. 208-209, 211, 356-357.

[62] For a controversy over the patronal right of determining the territorial limits of ecclesiastical jurisdictions, see *Memoria que Presente el Ministro de Relaciones Interiores al Congreso Nacional en 1909* (Caracas, 1909), II, 272 ff.

[63] H. M. Wolcott, American Consul, to J. L. Mecham, Caracas, November 22, 1927.

During the dictatorship of Guzmán Blanco the Church was despoiled of much of its property and left in pecuniary straits. For some time the clergy were compelled to live on poor offerings. Furthermore the right of the Church to acquire property through donations and bequests was denied. Persons in holy orders, moreover, were forbidden to receive anything under testamentary disposition or by gift outside of the eighth civil degree of relationship. After the advent of Juan Vicente Gómez, some of these restrictions were removed. There are today no legal impediments placed upon the power of the Church to receive entailments, bequests, and the like. The Church has been able thereby to build up large and valuable holdings of urban and country realty. With an increased income it has been able to embark upon a more energetic program of social action.[64]

Under the law Catholic schools are required to observe all regulations affecting public instruction, but actually no supervision is exercised over them by the State. These schools, which bear a numerical ratio of one to ten to the public schools, are supported by tuition fees. The fees, of course, vary greatly according to the grade of instruction given, location of the schools, and circumstances of the pupils' parents. The Protestant schools in Venezuela are very few in number; for example, there are only two in Caracas, whereas there are in that place ten prominent Catholic schools. The greatest opportunity for the success of Protestant missions, that is in education, is being sadly neglected.[65] The public school system of Venezuela is obligatory and gratuitous, but as a matter of fact, this means nothing, for, like the public educational systems of all Latin America, it is thoroughly inadequate to meet the national needs. There are few lay teachers and no adequate physical equipment. Indeed, it is said that, with one exception, Venezuela has never erected a building for the purposes of instruction. The exception is the Military Academy— the West Point of Venezuela.[66] The work of the private institutions, therefore, is indispensable. The school law of Venezuela is liberal toward the Catholic faith in that tenets of that religion

---

[64] Ibid.

[65] Wheeler and Browning, op. cit., p. 302.

[66] Ibid., op. cit., p. 296.

are a part of the curriculum of the public schools in which a limited number of male ecclesiastics is employed.[67] The inadequacy of educational facilities in Venezuela, public and private, is evidenced by the fact that eighty-five per cent is a conservative estimate of illiteracy in that country.

The control of the civil register has not been returned to the Church, nor is there any likelihood that it will be restored. Furthermore, civil marriage continues to be the only legal form. It is usually followed, it is true, by the religious ceremony, but the civil certificate must be produced before the priest can legally perform the ceremony. No charge is made for the performance of the civil rites when they take place inside a government building, but when they take place in a private home, a charge of Bs. 60 ($12.00) is made. For the performance of the religious ceremony, there is also theoretically no charge, but for the publication of the banns (which the devout consider essential) a charge of Bs. 20 is made. The exorbitant fee charged by the clergy has prevented thousands of unions from being blessed by the Church. Since the civil ceremony cannot be substituted for the sacrament of matrimony, the poor, ignorant, and superstitious men and women dispense with the lay rites and live in open concubinage. In 1912 the Civil Register showed that there were 23,937 legitimate births and 51,955 illegitimate births. Of 75,312 mothers, 51,580 were listed as unmarried. The popularity of free love unions in Venezuela is not to be attributed solely to exorbitant clerical fees, for, says one writer, "Frequently it is the woman who objects to being legally bound, averring that she has a stronger position when simply cohabiting with the man than if he could claim any legal rights as a husband." There is no social degradation attached to this form of concubinage.[68]

The Catholic Church of Venezuela is handicapped, as it is in other Latin-American countries, because of the caliber of its priesthood. The clergy is recruited from men of low intellectual ability thoroughly incompetent to formulate or direct a method by

---

[67] *Instrucción Pública en Venezuela* (Caracas, 1922), pp. XX-XXVIII; *Gaceta Oficial* (Caracas, June 17, 1924), p. 7.

[68] Charles E. Akers, *A History of South America, 1854-1904* (London, 1912), pp. 637-638; Wheeler and Browning, *op. cit.*, p. 272; Watters, *op. cit.*, pp. 41-42.

which the people's social and spiritual welfare might be improved.[69] The ignorance of the lowest classes is so dense that superstition plays a great part in their lives, and it is not difficult for the priesthood to instill into their minds outward respect for religious forms and dread of direful consequences to follow disobedience to priestly injunctions. But the people of the better classes, particularly the men, scorn the medieval arguments and threats of the clergy, and incline to free thought in matters of religion. These men, and they are the ones who direct the political destinies of Venezuela, must be called back to the flock of the faithful, but this is a task beyond the competence of the clergy of Venezuela today. The clerical personnel must be thoroughly revamped; there is a crying need for better blood, and particularly better minds. Although the Catholic Church in Venezuela has recovered many of its old prerogatives temporarily lost during the period of Guzmán Blanco, it has never recovered its spiritual power and life. "The Church has ho power in Venezuela," says a native critic, "political, moral, or spiritual. It is degenerate and we have no use for it and no confidence in it. We have no religion."[70] The increase in the number of free-thinkers and the continued waning respect for the clergy and the Church, will result, unless these tendencies are checked, in despoiling the Catholic Church of the remaining privileges which it enjoys in the Republic of Venezuela.

---

[69] *Revista de Instrucción Pública* (Caracas, Febrero de 1910), p. 20.

[70] Wheeler and Browning, *op. cit.*, p. 288.

CHAPTER V

THE RELIGIOUS PROBLEM IN THE CONSTITUTIONAL HISTORY OF COLOMBIA

In Colombia, to a far more marked degree than in Venezuela, the struggle of the parties for power revolved about the religious issue. From the independence period to the present day religious policy has ever been a prominent feature of party programs, and the recurrent alterations of the political order have always been attended by radical changes in ecclesiastical polity. No doubt the origin of this unfortunate tendency can be traced back to colonial times when the royal officials of New Granada and the prelates were accustomed to strive for political control, the latter generally being the victors. At any rate the Catholic Church has been more tenacious in its hold upon national and civil life in Colombia than in any other Latin-American country.

The Conservatives governed Colombia, then called New Granada, most of the period, from the time of the dissolution of Great Colombia in 1830 until 1849. They, like the Conservative Oligarchy in Chile, represented the permanent interests and effective powers of the country, the landowners, clericals, and the military. An essential part of their program of organization and stabilization was protection of Catholicism. When the State of New Granada was created (November 17, 1831) after the fall of Great Colombia, Roman Catholicism was declared to be the religion of the republic, the public worship of any other faith was not to be tolerated, and the government assumed the exercise of the patronage. This was in conformity with the religious provisions of the Constitution of 1830 of Great Colombia which was adopted temporarily (December 15, 1831) until a new constitution should be framed and promulgated.[1] In the convention which proclaimed the State of New Granada, two prelates, Bishop Sotomayor of Cartagena and Bishop Estévez of Santa Marta, played prominent

---

[1] Pombo y Guerra, *Constituciones de Colombia,* II, 882.

rôles. At the head of the provisional government was Archbishop Caicedo y Flórez of Bogotá.[2]

In February, 1832, a new constitution for the republic of New Granada was promulgated. The loyalty of the constituents to the Catholic faith was clearly evidenced in their introduction to the constitution. It read in part as follows: "In it (the constitution) has been established . . . the rigorous duty of New Granada to protect the Roman Catholic Apostolic religion; this divine and only true religion, precious cause of the good which the people of New Granada inherit from their fathers . . . will be preserved pure and intact."[3] Consequently Article 15 read, "It is the duty of the government to protect the Granadinos in the exercise of the Roman Catholic Apostolic religion."[4]

Under the new constitution General Francisco de Paula Santander was elected president, and Joaquín Mosquera was elected vice president. Since Santander was in New York at the time and did not return to assume his office until the fall of 1832, Mosquera exercised the temporary headship of the government. Mosquera was a member of one of the most influential families of the republic and was a devoted Catholic. He retained the cabinet of Archbishop Caicedo, and, in agreement with the new constitution, designated for the Council of State, the Archbishop, Bishop Sotomayor, and Fr. Manuel Benito Revollo, a canon.[5] The new republic was inaugurated by warm friends and official members of the Roman Catholic Church.

In October, 1832, General Santander took over the reins of government, and Vice President Mosquera retired to his home in Popayán. Soon a conflict occurred between Mosquera and Bishop Jiménez of Popayán, which showed that the republican government was quite as insistent as had been the king of Spain in assert-

---

[2] "Francisco Soto á Santander, Bogotá, 29 de diciembre de 1831," in *Archivo Santander*, XIX, 139-144; Arboleda, *Historia Contemporanea de Colombia*, I, 46.

[3] "Constitución del Estado de la Nueva Granada Dada Por La Convención Constituyente en el año de 1832, Bogotá, 1832," in Pombo y Guerra, *op. cit.*, II, 888.

[4] "Florentino González á Santander, Bogotá, 31 de diciembre de 1831," in *Archivo Santander*, XIX, 144-146.

[5] Arboleda, *op. cit.*, I, 47.

ing control over the prelates. Mosquera, anxious to develop compulsory, popular education, took steps to establish in Popayán, with governmental aid, schools where they were needed. Bishop Jiménez manifested hostility toward the plan, and eventually he and the Vice President were quite emphatically at odds. In a moment of peevishness the Bishop requested his passports of Santander, that he might leave the country. Although Santander was friendly toward the Church, he was insistent that tight reins of control be kept on the prelates. Consequently he called the Bishop's bluff and offered him his passports, upon which Bishop Jiménez, pretending that the demands of his flock that he remain were too insistent to be refused, altered his decision to leave the country. Indeed, he even altered his attitude to the extent of lending financial support to Mosquera's educational plan.[6]

The Granadine government entertained pretentions to a patronage more ample than that enjoyed by the king of Spain. The Law of Patronage of 1824 was regarded as continuing in full force, and many actions were taken which presumed the existence of that right, although it had never been recognized by the papacy. By decree of May 3, 1833, for example, Santander created in Casanare an auxiliary bishop of the metropolitan see of Bogotá, and Fr. José Antonio Cháves was nominated for the position. He was canonically instituted soon after as bishop *in partibus*. In April, 1834, the Congress met to elect an archbishop of Bogotá, and bishops of Cartagena and Panamá. Manuel José Mosquera, a brother of the vice president, and only thirty-four years old, was elected archbishop. Bishop Estévez of Leuca was elected bishop of Cartagena, and Juan José Cabarcas was elected bishop of Panamá. Thus the government of New Granada exercised the patronal right of presentation.[7] It undertook, moveover, to exercise the rights of *pase* or exequatur over pontifical communications. In the constitutional convention of 1832 the desirability of reducing the number of religious festival days was discussed.[8]

---

[6] "Joaquín Mosquera á Santander, Popayán, 24 de setiembre de 1833" and "Joaquín Mosquera á Santander, Popayán, 5 de noviembre de 1833," in *Archivo Santander*, XX, 193, 221; Arboleda, *op. cit.*, I, 186-190.

[7] Arboleda, *op. cit.*, 181, 216-218.

[8] "M. M. Nuñez á Santander, Cartagena, 25 de enero de 1832," in *Archivo Santander*, XIX, 191.

It was decided not to constitutionalize the reform, but instead the pope was requested to publish a brief providing for a reduction of feast days. On March 28, 1835, the *pase* was given to the pontifical brief, and a few days later it was ordered executed in New Granada by legislative act.[9] Another brief on reform of the regular orders was issued by the pope in 1835. To restore discipline in the regular orders, the pope delegated to the archbishop the duties of visiting and reforming. This brief, however, was not given the governmental *pase* until May 8, 1840, and then, with the following reservation, "the *pase* is conceded without prejudice to the sovereignty and prerogatives of the nation."[10] The acme of control over the patronage was reached in 1841, when a law of May 18 of that year provided that the police should keep watch over prelates, priests, and chapters, to see that they "introduced no novelty in external discipline, or usurped the patronage or sovereign prerogatives of the republic."[11]

In addition to scrupulous and unduly severe defence of the patronal rights by the government of Santander, certain actions were branded as anti-Catholic. Such, for example, was the law of April 16, 1836, which established the supremacy of civil tribunals over the ecclesiastical in many matters commonly regarded as belonging exclusively to the religious and spiritual order. This was a severe blow at the ecclesiastical *fuero*, or right to maintain separate and independent courts. "The priest," said Santander, "is not removed from the jurisdiction of the civil laws and the temporal authorities in all things that have relation to society."[12] In 1835 Santander sponsored a law granting land in cemeteries for non-Catholics. When accused of being anti-Catholic because of this tolerant action, Santander said, "I love my religion because I live happily in it, and know that outside of the Catholic Church there is no eternal salvation."[13] That Santander was a

---

[9] Restrepo, *La Iglesia y el Estado en Colombia,* p. 163; Arboleda, *op. cit.,* p. 252.

[10] Restrepo, *La Iglesia y el Estado,* p. 164; "Ignacio Tejada á Santander, Roma, 27 de junio de 1835," in *Archivo Santander,* XXI, 265.

[11] Restrepo, *op. cit.,* p. 166.

[12] "F. de P. Santander á José M. Botero, Bogotá, 9 de agosto de 1835," in *Archivo Santander,* XXI, 316; Restrepo, *op. cit.,* p. 165.

[13] Santander á José M. Botero," in *Archivo Santander,* XXI, 313.

friend of the Church was further evidenced by his suppression, in 1833, of a radical periodical, "El Cachaco de Bogotá," which was fighting for liberty of cults and suppression of all religious orders.[14] Yet, the religious policy of Santander was so displeasing to the clerics that many of them joined with the discontented "Bolivianos" who constituted the opposition.

The ecclesiastical policy of New Granada was not so unsatisfactory to Pope Gregory XVI but that he agreed to recognize the independence of the republic on November 26, 1835. This event, as has been indicated elsewhere, was due in large measure to the untiring efforts of Ignacio Tejada, who had been sent to Rome as the representative of Great Colombia, and who was retained at his post as the Chargé of New Granada. In receiving Tejada in public audience, the act which constituted recognition, the pontiff said that he "experienced a particular pleasure in being able to recognize a government which gave so many proofs of stability, no less than its adhesion to the Catholic religion, and of its constant veneration of the Holy See."[15]

New Granada enjoys the distinction of being the first Spanish-American republic to be recognized politically by the Holy See. Recognition was attended by a complete restoration of the hierarchy in the republic. The following prelates were preconized by the pope: José Antonio Cháves as Auxiliary Bishop of the archdiocese of Bogotá, Juan de Cruz Gómez Plata as Bishop of Antioquia, Luís José Serrano as Bishop of Santa Marta, Antonio Barbano as Bishop of Popayán, and Manuel José Mosquera as Archbishop of Bogotá. When the pope indicated his intention of sending an official representative to Bogotá, Tejada was instructed to oppose the plan for it was feared that a representative of the pope would exercise an ultramontane influence and render difficult the operation of the patronage and the inauguration of reforms. His Holiness was not to be deterred, however, for in May, 1836, Mgr. Cayetano Baluffi was sent to New Granada as internuncio extraordinary. He arrived in Bogotá on January 16, 1837, and was recognized as the diplomatic representative of the pope, but he was

---

[14] Arboleda, *op. cit.*, p. 192.

[15] "Ignacio Tejada á Santander, Roma, 27 de noviembre (and) 18 de diciembre de 1835," in *Archivo Santander*, XXI, 372-373.

10

not permitted to exercise functions relative to ecclesiastical government and discipline. Thus inflexible were the Granadinos in the exercise of the right of patronage.[16] By law of June 12, 1840, the executive power was given the right to accord the *pase* to briefs and papal acts granting powers and instructions to envoys or internuncios to act in New Granada. After the passage of this law Baluffi was recognized in his religious functions.[17]

Santander's successor in the presidency, José Ignacio de Márquez (1837-1841), was also a good Catholic but he refused to allow this to influence him in enforcing the laws. For example, when serious pressure was brought to bear on him to exclude the works of Jeremy Bentham from the schools, he pointed out that they had been sanctioned by law as texts, and he refused to suspend their use. [18] Furthermore, in August, 1837, President Márquez issued a circular to the governors demanding that the law of March 4, 1826, regarding admission of novitiates be observed. It will be recalled that this law established twenty-five years as the minimum age at which novices could be admitted into convents. Flagrant and widespread disregard of the prohibition occasioned the presidential instruction. The actions noted seemed to lend color to the charge of the opposition "Santanderistas," that Márquez was a "liberal."[19]

The most serious ecclesiastical problem which confronted President Márquez was the case of the convents of Pasto. To explain the problem it is necessary to recapitulate the legislative history concerning religious establishments. The Congress of Cúcuta in 1821 suppressed convents having less than eight religious, and applied the property to public instruction. In 1826 this law was ratified with certain amplifications. In 1828, however, Bolívar revoked the preceding laws. But after the establishment of the State of New Granada in 1832, by law of January 13, the decree of Bolívar was nullified, and the laws of suppression were restored. But later in the same year the convents of the province of Pasto

---

[16] Zubieta, *Misiones Diplomáticas de Colombia*, pp. 595-597; "J. de D. Aranzazu á Santander, Rionegro, 20 de octubre de 1836," in *Archivo Santander*, XXII, 350-352.

[17] Arboleda, *op. cit.*, I, 385; Restrepo, *op. cit.*, p. 166.

[18] Arboleda, *op. cit.*, I, 311.

[19] *Ibid.*, pp. 310-311.

were granted exemption from the law of suppression, because of the recognition of local missionary needs. By law of May 11, 1835, the properties of the convents suppressed by the laws of 1821, 1826, and 1832, but which had not been applied to educational uses and support, were to be applied to provincial income. Furthermore, all convent properties had to be registered and no sale could be made without governmental approval.[20]

By act of Congress, June 5, 1839, the exemption enjoyed by Pasto with respect to the small or "minor convents" was removed. It was provided that the property of certain convents which were almost deserted, should be applied to the support of missions and education. Although the measure had been sponsored by the bishop of Popayán, a cry went up that this was an attempt to destroy religion. Urged by local members of the clergy, the people of Pasto arose in rebellion. That the hierarchy did not condone the revolt is shown by the pastoral of Archbishop Mosquera (July 17, 1839), "In no case can we justify revolutionary acts under the pretext of religion." The provincial authorities, unable to put down the revolt by arms, signed a humiliating capitulation. President Márquez refused to recognize the capitulation, and determined to enforce the law. General Pedro A. Herrán was appointed to restore order. This he accomplished, although he had to use force, to the indignation of the Santanderistas.[21] Consequently the Pasto incident was cited as additional evidence of the anti-Catholic or "liberal" policy of the President.

General Pedro Alcántara Herrán, the man who suppressed the Pasto rebellion, was elected in 1842 to succeed President Márquez. During his administration clerical influence increased considerably. The new Constitution of 1843, more conservative than that of 1832, stated in even more emphatic terms the close union which existed between Church and State. In the preamble "the name of God the Father, Son and Holy Ghost," was invoked, instead of, as in the charter of 1832, "God, author and Supreme Legislator of the Universe." In addition to the provision (Article 15) that "it is also the duty of the government to protect the exercise of the Roman Catholic Apostolic religion for the Granadinos," there

---

[20] Restrepo, *op. cit.*, pp. 259-261.
[21] Henao y Arrubla, *Historia de Colombia,* II, 487-493.

was added (Article 16), "The Roman Catholic Apostolic religion is the only cult which the Republic supports and maintains."[22] In further evidence of the increasing support given by the government to the Catholic faith, the Jesuits were allowed to return to New Granada to assume educational and missionary activities. The Jesuits arrived in 1844, the first to tread the soil of New Granada since their expulsion in 1767.[23]

In 1845 General Tomás Mosquera was elected president with the aid of the clergy, the militarists, and a Conservative majority. Although a Conservative, President Mosquera (1845-1849) manifested liberal leanings; he abolished the tithes and diminished the fiscal protection to the Church. Yet, on the other hand, he extended the jurisdiction of the Jesuits in the missionary field, for he realized the exceptional importance of the missions in assuring to the government control of the interior.[24] When Mosquera's candidate for the presidency was defeated in 1849, the long Conservative rule came to an end, and there was inaugurated a radical régime under which the Church suffered grievously. Under the Conservatives the status accorded the Church was not what the ultramontanes desired, but notwithstanding the extreme *regalismo* of Santander and Márquez, Catholicism found constant protection and support in the Conservative presidents. Its status was a happy one compared to that of the period of the Liberal supremacy.

The Liberal party, victorious in 1849, and remaining in the ascendancy with only short interruptions until 1880, promoted a vast "democratic" program in which the Church was the principal sufferer. The first act of President José Hilario López, which ended the long peace between Church and State, was the order of May 21, 1850, which allowed the Jesuits but forty-eight hours to leave the country. The hardships of the expulsion duplicated the events of 1767. Some of the Jesuits went to Jamaica, and others found refuge in Ecuador. Shortly after (June 20) the sanctity of matrimony was attacked by the legalization of divorce. Strongly influenced by the '48 socialistic ideas, President López and his

---

[22] "Constitución Política de la República de la Nueva Granada, Reformada por el Congreso en sus sesiones de 1842 y 1843, Bogotá, 1843," in Pombo y Guerra, *op. cit.,* pp. 957-1002.

[23] Henao y Arrubla, *op. cit.,* II, 506.   [24] *Ibid.,* p. 529.

Liberal adherents in the Congress pursued their anti-ecclesiastical policy. In 1851 laws were passed annulling the tithes and setting a fixed income for the clergy, abolishing the right of asylum in Catholic churches, giving to *cabildos* the right to nominate parish curates, and extinguishing all *fueros* or ecclesiastical privilege of separate courts. The Supreme Court of the nation was given jurisdiction over cases concerning prelates regarding not only common crimes but "the improper exercise of their functions." This was an invasion of the ecclesiastical right for it delegated to the ordinary courts subjects of exclusive ecclesiastical control. In short, the civil courts were given ecclesiastical power superior to that of the prelates.[25]

In March, 1852, the state further arrogated to itself exclusively ecclesiastical rights by incorporating the conciliar seminary of the archdiocese with the national college of San Bartolomé. This act took away from the Church the right to educate its own priests. Archbishop Mosquera protested in vain.[26] In February, 1852, the government sent a circular to the prelates, asking if they did not deem it necessary and advisable to consent to the establishment of absolute separation of Church and State. The prelates, of course, refused to recognize any good in the proposal. The Archbishop stated emphatically that the union of the spiritual and temporal powers was the natural state.[27]

Notwithstanding the objections of the prelates, President López appeared before Congress as an advocate of separation. He said, "I have meditated profoundly on this troublesome matter, and I have finally decided to indicate to you the convenience of sanctioning the complete independence of the Church. The Constitution is opposed, it is true, to the adoption of this idea, but it can be amended during the coming year, and in the meantime certain dispositions in this matter can be advanced."[28] As will be indicated shortly, the suggestion of the president was enacted into constitutional law the next year.

The radical act of actual separation was not necessary to

---

[25] Restrepo, *op. cit.*, pp. 220-221; 510-511; Pombo y Guerra, *op. cit.*, II, 1008-1010.

[26] Restrepo, *op. cit.*, p. 346.

[27] *Ibid.*, p. 172.

[28] Pombo y Guerra, *op. cit.*, II, 1011.

bring about a break with the hierarchy. Archbishop Mosquera had written several vigorous protests against the anti-Catholic laws passed by the Congress, and several other prelates joined him in his protests. Finally, because of the vigor of the metropolitan's opposition, a process was brought against him in the Senate. He was charged with "exciting and provoking disobedience to public authority," and "representing as contrary to religion or precepts of evangelical morality, the legal operation of governmental authority." The prelate was found guilty, although it is difficult to see in what respects he erred, and he was exiled from the country. In September, 1852, he went to New York, and from there he proceeded to Europe. He was called to Rome by Pius IX, who approved his actions. He died in Marseilles, December 10, 1853. Archbishop Mosquera was unquestionably one of the outstanding prelates of Latin America, and his loss to New Granada, not alone to the Church of that republic, was irreparable. The bishops of Pamplona, Santa Marta, and Cartagena, who also protested against the anti-clerical laws, were exiled. With them were included quite a number of priests.[29]

In the presidential election of 1853, the Conservatives offered no candidate and refrained from voting. Two factions of the Liberal party offered candidates. The Radicals or *Golgotas*, composed of young intelligentsia who desired to destroy all influence of the clergy not only in politics but in "the tribunal of conscience" as well, nominated General Tomás Herrera. The *Democráticos* or *Draconianos*, supported General José Mariá Obando. The election (April 1, 1853) resulted in the victory of Obando. Herrera consequently became president of the Senate.[30]

One of the first acts of the new administration was to promulgate a new constitution which guaranteed to all Granadinos (Article 5) "the free profession, public or private, of their religion, providing it does not disturb the public peace, offend pure morals, nor impede the exercise of any other cult." It further

---

[29] Pombo y Guerra, *op. cit.*, II, 1010; Restrepo, *op. cit.*, pp. 222-225; 231-240.

[30] Pombo y Guerra, *op. cit.*, pp. 1011-1012; Henao y Arrubla, *op. cit.*, p. 542.

provided (Article 10) that there should be no forced contribution for the support of any cult.[31] With the limitations imposed by the Constitution of 1843 removed, the Congress proceeded (June 15, 1853) to separate Church and State. This was the first act of separation in Latin-American history. According to the law, "From September first, next, all intervention of the civil, national, and municipal authorities will cease in the election and presentation of all persons whatsoever for the provision of ecclesiastical benefices, and in all and any matters relating to the exercise of the Catholic cult or any other professed by the people of New Granada." The ownership of churches was declared to be vested in the resident Catholics of the parishes, and that of cathedrals in the resident Catholics of the dioceses.[32] The act of separation should have inaugurated an era of liberty for the Church, but instead it meant close surveillance verging on servitude.

Other anti-clerical acts passed during the short administration of Obando (1853-1854) were: marriage made an obligatory civil ceremony, and the cemeteries secularized and placed under the control of the municipal authorities. Since the powers were separated it was deemed no longer necessary to maintain representation at Rome.[33]

A better understanding between Church and State became noticeable after 1855. By law of May 14 of that year, churches and congregations were given juridic personality to hold property. In the next year the repugnant divorce law was abrogated, and the law of civil marriage was tempered somewhat by providing that the religious ceremony would be accepted as valid for civil effects if the contracting parties repaired to a notary or judge immediately after the religious ceremony for the purpose of registration.[34]

In May, 1858, to the rapidly accumulating list of Colombian constitutions another one was added. This supreme charter established a Granadine Confederation. Religious liberty was guaran-

---

[31] "Constitución Política de la Nueva Granada Expedida por el Congreso, Bogotá, 1853," in Pombo y Guerra, *op. cit.*, II, 1017-1042.

[32] Restrepo, *op. cit.*, p. 191, 264.

[33] Pombo y Guerra, *op. cit.*, II, 1011; Henao y Arrubla, *op. cit.*, p. 545.

[34] Restrepo, *op. cit.*, pp. 379, 511.

teed (Article 56).[35] Since the prohibition in the constitution of 1853 against the entry of Jesuits into the country was no longer in force, President Ospina allowed them to return and put the College of San Bartolomé under their direction. Other measures of the government conciliatory toward the Catholic Church served to reëstablish a considerable measure of tranquillity. But it proved to be merely the calm before the storm—the most devastating storm ever experienced by the Catholic Church in Colombia.

In 1860, General Tomás Mosquera, who had been a leader of the Conservatives, joined with the Liberals for personal reasons and became one of the most radical opponents of the Church. After a successful conflict with the army of the Confederation, Mosquera gained control of the government in July, 1861. In an effort to retain power and rule above the law, he instituted radical politico-religious reforms. In short he declared a "Kulturkampf." Because of clerical opposition, more potential than actual, the dictator decreed (July 20, 1861) that no cleric could exercise his religious functions without the authorization of the president of the republic or governor of a state. This patent denial of the independent existence of the Church, as legally established by the law of Separation, was based on extravagant claims of the governmental right of *tuición* or protection. On July 26 once more the Jesuits were ordered out of the country, "as a police measure."[36] On September 9 a law of disamortization was passed. Property held in the dead hands of religious corporations or communities was to revert to the nation. Only buildings needed for the direct use of the cult were exempt from the decree. The government derived from disamortized property, during the years 1861-1879, $12,707,694. Most of the Church property fell into the hands of a few individuals, and thus one of the objects of the law, i.e., the creation of a large number of small landowners, was defeated. This was identical with the results of disamortization in Mexico.[37] On November 3, all convents, monasteries, and religious houses were sup-

[35] "Constitución Política para La Confederación Granadina. Sancionada el día 22 de mayo de 1858, Bogotá, 1858," in Pombo y Guerra, *op. cit.*, II, 1059-1091.

[36] Henao y Arrubla, *op. cit.*, pp. 570-571; Restrepo, *op. cit.*, p. 380, 570; Pombo y Guerra, *op. cit.*, II, 1097.

[37] Restrepo, *op. cit.*, p. 416.

pressed. By later legislation it was provided that each nun should be paid by the government 240 pesos annually. To each male religious was to be paid from 180 to 480 pesos, according to the number of years they had been in orders in 1861.[38]

It was not to be expected that the Archbishop and other prelates would supinely acquiesce in the despoliation of the Church. On the contrary, Archbishop Antonio Herrán registered such a vigorous protest that he was charged with sedition and desire to overthrow the supreme authority of the State. Consequently, by decree of November 3, 1861, he was ordered imprisoned "until the executive power determines his term of confinement or expulsion." He was eventually confined for some time at a place on the Atlantic seacoast. Other prelates also suffered either imprisonment or exile.[39]

In disregard of the legal status of separation of the temporal and religious powers, President Mosquera interpreted the governmental right of *tuición* or protection to imply intervention in the internal affairs of the Church. "It is the duty of the government," he said, "by the right of *tuición*, which the Republic exercises, to protect the Colombians in the exercise of their religious cult, and to avoid conflicts which arise from the intervention of ecclesiastics in political subjects." Consequently the dictator decreed that no minister of any cult could exercise his ministry without having previously taken an oath to obey the constitution and the laws of the republic. Those who refused to obey were to be exiled.[40]

When his power was sufficiently consolidated Mosquera convoked a convention to reform the constitution. An amnesty was granted to political prisoners, but it is noteworthy that it did not apply to clerics. The constitutional convention, in the control of the Liberals, drew up a federal constitution in which, as was to be expected, Catholicism fared worse than ever. The preamble was significant; it read, "In the name and by the authority of the people of the United States of Colombia." The name of God

---

[38] Henao y Arrubla, *op. cit.*, pp. 570-571; Restrepo, *op. cit.*, p. 381; Pombo y Guerra, *op. cit.*, II, 1098.

[39] Restrepo, *op. cit.*, pp. 576-581.

[40] *Ibid.*, pp. 582, 592.

was not mentioned. The free profession, public or private, of any religion was guaranteed (Article 15), but, as Rafael Núñez said, "Religious liberty was guaranteed, but not for Catholics."[41] It was Article 23, which provided that "to support national sovereignty and maintain public security and tranquility, the national government or that of the states, may exercise the right of supreme inspection over religious cults," which was contorted to deny the privilege of religious liberty.[42] Since under the constitution Colombia was supposed to be a federal State, most subjects relating to religion were left to the states. But as a matter of fact there was considerable uniformity in policy, due to the all-pervading influence of the federal government.

In 1866 Mosquera was "reëlected" president, and soon after he became dictator. Then, because of the opposition he was encountering in a political way from certain Catholic prelates, he returned to a violent persecution of the Catholic religion. The archbishop of Bogotá, and the bishops of Pasto and Santa Marta were imprisoned or exiled. This was the final furious effort of the dictator to create radical support for his personal rule.[43] He failed and was exiled (1867).

Liberal control still persisted in Colombia for the next thirteen years. The party, however, abandoned much of its original extremeness, and, after 1870, no longer desired the complete separation of Church and State. But the Conservatives, who had become a clerical party, were constantly on the watch to frustrate any attempt to harm the Church further. The election to the presidency of Aquileo Parra, a Liberal, was evidently regarded as a threat to the Church, for the Conservatives in the State of Cauca took up arms against the federal government. During the years 1876-1877 a civil war raged. The Liberals prevailed, and, in May, 1877, a drastic law was passed imposing severe penalties for clerical opposition to the government. Also the civil authorities were given extensive powers of inspection in matters of cult.[44]

---

[41] Rafael Núñez, *La Reforma Política en Colombia* (Bogotá, 1886), p. 241.

[42] "Constitución de los Estados Unidos de Colombia. Sancionada por la Convención Nacional el 8 de mayo de 1863, Bogotá, 1867," in Pombo y Guerra, *op. cit.*, II, 1127-1164; Restrepo, *op. cit.*, p. 588.

[43] Pombo y Guerra, *op. cit.*, II, 1173; Restrepo, *op. cit.*, p. 600.

[44] Restrepo, *op. cit.*, pp. 601-602.

This was the final assault made by the Liberals upon the Catholic citadel, for their supremacy terminated when they made the serious mistake of electing Dr. Rafael Núñez to the presidency. During the long years of Liberal ascendancy (1849-1880) numerous ecclesiastical reform measures, many of which were frankly anti-clerical in character, had been enacted. Some of these were revoked or altered, but nevertheless in 1880, on the eve of the era of Rafael Núñez, the legal status of Catholicism was unique for a Catholic country of that period. Church and State were separated; the ecclesiastical *fueros* were abolished; the government recognized no civil compulsion in the payment of tithes; ecclesiastical property, with the exception of the actual Church buildings and residences of the clergy, had been appropriated by the government; the religious orders were abolished; cemeteries were secularized; marriage was declared to be an obligatory civil ceremony; and in the exercise of the right of "inspection of cults" the government controlled purely spiritual matters. Such was the unhappy state of the Catholic Church in Colombia in 1880.

The Church found a savior and champion in President Rafael Núñez. Elected to the presidency as a Liberal, in 1880, Núñez, who had once been a socialistic radical, learned from governmental experience that excessive liberalism had disorganized the country. He became convinced that the cause of Colombia's travail was vain idealism, and consequently he espoused conservative, realistic policies which he hoped would bring peace and progress. The Liberal turned Conservative; but it was not until after his reëlection to the presidency in 1884 that Dr. Núñez formally inaugurated his conservative program. Restoration of the power and influence of the Catholic Church in Colombia was a cardinal feature of the new policy, as will become abundantly evident by what follows.

In 1885 President Núñez convened a national council of states to frame a new constitution. The document, which was promulgated in August, 1886, was strongly centralistic and pro-clerical. The preamble proclaimed God as the supreme fountain of all authority. Roman Catholicism was to be respected as an essential factor of the social order. The constitution declared, however: "It is understood that the Catholic Church is not and shall not be official, and shall preserve its own independence." This independence was guaranteed further in Article 53: "The Catholic Church will be free to administer its interior affairs and to exercise acts of spiritual authority and ecclesiastical jurisdiction without necessity of authorization of the civil power. And as a juridic person represented in each diocese by the respective legitimate prelate, it can also exercise civil acts by its own law which the present constitution recognizes." The exercise of all cults not contrary to Christian morality was guaranteed, as well as freedom of the individual from molestation on account of religious opinions. Finally, the government was authorized by Article 56 to celebrate a concordat with the Holy See for the purpose of settling pending questions and defining and establishing relations between the civil and ecclesiastical powers.[45]

In proposing the scrapping of the Constitution of 1863 and the drafting of a new one, Núñez suggested, among other things, that the main object of the educational system should be the inculcation of Christian doctrine. He therefore ordered the teaching of religion in the public schools. He protected religion like Portales of Chile, said García Calderón, in order to give a disorganized nation the firm unity of a law.[46] "Fanaticism," wrote Rafael Núñez, "is not religion any more than demagogy is liberty; but between religion and morality there is an indissoluble bond." Although he was a strong believer in the moralizing office of the Church, Núñez did not fail to recognize its past abuses.[47] The Constitution of 1888, which continues to be the fundamental law under which Colombians are governed today, was significant religiously in that it recognized the primacy of the Catholic Church, and symbolized the triumph of the clerical party.

The clerical reaction was climaxed by the negotiation, as authorized by the constitution, of a concordat with the papacy, which was signed on December 31, 1887, and sanctioned by Congress in 1888. This concordat, which is declared by the Archbishop

---

[45] "The Constitution of Colombia," in J. I. Rodríguez, *American Constitutions* (Washington, 1906), II, 318-379.

[46] Francisco García Calderón, *Latin America, Its Rise and Progress* (London, 1913), p. 210.

[47] Núñez, *op. cit.*, pp. 539-541.

of Cartagena to be "one of the best in the world,"[48] and by an eminent ecclesiastical historian to be "a model of mutual relations between Church and State,"[49] has been in force in the Republic of Colombia from 1888 to the present day. Since this treaty has been acceptable to ecclesiastics the full text is presented here in order that the reader may appreciate what the Church regards as the most satisfactory agreement possible, for the pope does not consider concordats to be wholly desirable, since in an ideal Catholic society they would not be necessary:

In the name of the most holy and indivisible Trinity, His Holiness the Supreme Pontiff Leo XIII and the President of the Republic of Colombia, His Excellency Señor Rafael Núñez, name as plenipotentiaries respectively:

His Holiness, the most eminent Signor Mariano Rampolla del Tindaro, cardinal presbyter of the Holy Roman Church of Santa Cecilia, and his Secretary of State, and

The President of the Republic, his excellency Señor Joaquín Fernando Vélez, Envoy Extraordinary and Minister Plenipotentiary before the Holy See:

Who, after presenting their respective credentials, have agreed to the following:

Article 1. The Roman Catholic Apostolic religion is the religion of Colombia, the public powers recognize it as an essential element of the social order, and they are bound to protect and enforce respect for it and its ministers, leaving to it at the same time the full enjoyment of its rights and prerogatives.

Article 2. The Catholic Church will enjoy complete liberty and independence of the civil power, and consequently there shall be no intervention of this power in the free exercise of its spiritual authority and ecclesiastical jurisdiction, its government and administration conforming to its own laws.

Article 3. Canonical legislation is independent of the civil law, and forms no part of it, but it will be solemnly respected by the authorities of the Republic.

Article 4. The State recognizes in the Church, represented by its legitimate hierarchial authority, true and proper juridical personality, and capacity to enjoy and exercise the rights that appertain to it.

Article 5. The Church has the right to acquire by legal title, and possess and administer freely movable and immovable property in

---

[48] Archbishop of Cartagena to J. L. Mecham, Cartagena, November 7, 1927.
[49] Zamora, *Patronato Español é Indiano*, p. 90.

the manner established by the common law, and its properties and foundations will be no less inviolable than those of citizens of the Republic.

Article 6.   Ecclesiastical properties can be taxed in the same manner and to the same extent as private property; however, buildings destined for the use of the cult, conciliar seminaries, and episcopal and cural residences, can never be burdened with contributions nor occupied or used for other purposes.

Article 7.   The members of the secular and regular clergy cannot be obliged to perform public duties incompatible with their ministry and profession, and furthermore, they will always be exempt from military service.

Article 8.   The government is obliged to incorporate in its laws of criminal procedure provisions to safeguard the sacerdotal dignity, wherever, for any reason, a minister of the Church figures in a process.

Article 9.   The diocesan and parochial ordinaries can collect from the faithful emoluments and ecclesiastical rents canonically and equitably established and based in either immemorial custom in each diocese, or the performance of religious services; and, in order that the acts and obligations thus originating create civil effect, and that the temporal authority shall lend its aid, the ordinaries will act in agreement with the government.

Article 10.   There can be freely constituted and established in Colombia religious orders and associations of both sexes, always provided that their canonical foundation is authorized by the competent ecclesiastical authority. These will be governed by their own constitutions; and, in order to enjoy juridic personality and be under the protection of the laws, they shall submit to the civil power the canonical authorization granted by the respective superior ecclesiastical authority.

Article 11.   The Holy See will accord its aid and coöperation to the government in establishing in Colombia religious institutions dedicated particularly to the exercise of charity, missions, education of the young, instruction in general, and other works of public utility and beneficence.

Article 12.   In the universities, colleges, schools, and other centers of learning, education and public instruction will be organized and directed in conformity with the dogmas and morals of the Catholic religion.   Religious instruction will be obligatory in such centers, and the pious practices of the Catholic religion will be observed in them.

Article 13.   Consequently, in said centers of learning, the respective diocesan ordinaries, by themselves, or by special delegates, will exercise the right, respecting religion and morals, of inspection and revision of textbooks. The archbishop of Bogotá will designate the books that ought to serve as texts for religion and morals in the universities; and to the end of assuring uniformity of instruction in the indicated matters, this prelate, in agreement with the other diocesan ordinaries, will select the texts for the other schools of official instruction.[50] The government will prevent, in the conduct of literary and scientific courses, and, in general, in all branches of instruction, the propagation of ideas contrary to Catholic dogma and to the respect and veneration due the Church.

Article 14. In the event that the instruction in religion and morals, in spite of the orders and preventive measures of the government, do not conform to Catholic doctrine, the respective diocesan ordinary can restrain such professors or masters of faculty from the teaching of such subjects.

Article 15. The right of making nominations to vacant arch-bishoprics and bishoprics belongs to the Holy See. The Holy Father, nevertheless, as proof of special deference, and with the intention of preserving harmonious relations between Church and State, agrees that, in the filling of archiepiscopal and episcopal sees, the wishes of the President of the Republic take precedence. Consequently, for each vacancy he will recommend directly to the Holy See the ecclesiastics who in his opinion possess the necessary gifts and qualifications for the episcopal dignity. The Holy See, on its part, before making nominations will always announce the names of the candidates it wishes to promote so that it may learn whether the President has reasons of a civil or political character to consider the said candidates as *personas non grata*. Diocesan vacancies will be filled as soon as possible, and will not last longer than six months.

Article 16. The Holy See can establish new dioceses and alter the territorial limits of those existing today when it regards this as useful and necessary for spiritual welfare, consulting the government previously and receiving any opinions from it that are just and convenient.

Article 17. The marriage ceremony celebrated according to the provisions of the Council of Trent applies to all who profess the Roman Catholic Religion and is necessary for the creation of civil effects appertaining to the persons and property of the contracting parties and their descendants. The act of the ceremony will be witnessed by the functionary determined by law for the sole object

---

[50] For example, on the title page of Carlos Alberto Lleras Acosta, *Instrucción Cívica* (Bogotá, 1926) which is used in the public schools as a textbook, appears the following: "Approved by the ecclesiastical censor Félix Restrepo, S. J. Permission to print given by the Archbishop of Bogotá."

of verifying the entry of the marriage in the civil register, providing it is not a marriage in *articulo mortis,* in which case such supplementary proof may be dispensed with if it is not practical to satisfy this formality. It is the duty of the contracting parties to fulfil the requirements relative to the intervention of the civil functionary of the register, the duty of the parish priest being limited to notifying them of the obligation which the civil law imposes on them.[51]

Article 18.   Concerning marriages celebrated any time in conformity with the provisions of the Council of Trent, and which ought to have the desired civil effect, those of ecclesiastical origin should be admitted preferentially as supplementary proof.

Article 19.   Causes affecting the bond of matrimony and the cohabitation of husband and wife, as well as those relating to the validity of betrothals, will be under the exclusive jurisdiction of the ecclesiastical authorities. The civil effects of matrimony will be regulated by the civil powers.

Article 20.   The armies of the Republic will enjoy the exemptions and favors known as military privileges, which will be determined by the Holy Father in a separate act.

Article 21.   After the divine offices, the following prayer will be recited in all the churches of the Republic: *Domine Salvam fac Praesidencius et supremas eius auctoritates.*

Article 22.   The government of the Republic recognizes in perpetuity in the nature of a consolidated debt, the value of redeemed mortgages in its treasury and of disentailed properties belonging to churches, *cofradías, patronatos,* chapels, and institutions of instruction and beneficence controlled by the Church, which have been at a certain time, entered into the public debt of the nation. This recognized debt will pay without diminution the annual liquid interest of 4½ per cent, payable semi-annually.

Article 23.   The income from *patronatos,* chapels, *cofradías,* and

---

[51] Regarding marriages between non-Catholics (mixed marriages had to be canonical) a law was passed in 1927 to the following effect: "The first part of Article 18 of the Concordat is not applicable when the two individuals who contract matrimony declare that they are formally separated from the Catholic Church, providing always that those who make such declaration have not received holy orders, nor any religious who have taken solemn vows, these being in all cases subject to the principles of the canon law." Those desiring the civil ceremony declare in writing to a municipal justice that they wish to marry, and they state the time that they have been separated from the Catholic Church. Such declaration is inserted in the notice which is published and communicated by the justice to the respective ecclesiastical ordinary. The marriage takes place a month after the declaration. (Ministro de Gobierno to J. L. Mecham, Bogotá, December 12, 1927).

other particular foundations will be recognized and paid directly to whoever, according to the foundations, has the right of receiving it, or to their legally constituted proxies. The payment will be made without diminution, as in the preceding article, and will start after the next year of 1888. In the event of some of the indicated entities being extinguished by prior agreement between the competent ecclesiastical authorities and the government, the income will be applied to pious and beneficent uses without violating in any way the will of the founders.

Article 24. The Holy See, in recognition of the condition of the national treasury of Colombia, and of the utility which the Church derives from the convention, grants to the Republic the following concessions: (a) the disentailed property belonging in its major part to convents and religious associations already extinguished and not included in the preceding article, is not to be recognized as part of the capital amount: and (b) it is granted exemption from obligations for rents or interests due, or for any other cause, on disentailed ecclesiastical properties up to December 31, 1887.

Article 25. In return for this concession the government of Colombia pledges itself to assign in perpetuity an annual liquid sum, which, at present, is fixed at 100,000 pesos Colombian, and which will be increased when the treasury situation improves; this money will be proportionately assigned and within limits agreed on by the two supreme powers, for the support of the dioceses, chapters, seminaries, missions, and other proper works of the civilizing action of the Church.

Article 26. The surviving members of the extinguished religious communities will continue to enjoy the income which the preceding provisions have assigned to them for their maintenance and other necessities.

Article 27. If, regarding this (preceding) point, there are doubts or difficulties, the government will confer with the competent ecclesiastical authority with the object of establishing procedure.

Article 28. The government will turn over to the religious entities the disentailed properties belonging to them, which have no assigned use, and in the event that the owner does not appear or has no mission to perform, there will be applied the returns of the sale of such property or its administration to analogous beneficences and pious works according to the most pressing necessities of each diocese following the advice of the competent authority.

Article 29. The Holy See, with the object of contributing to the public tranquillity, declares, on its part, that the persons in Colombia, who, during the past vicissitudes have purchased disentailed property or redeemed mortgages in the national treasury according to the provision of the civil laws in force at that time, will not be molested at any time or in any manner by the ecclesiastical authorities; this dispensation extends not only to those executing such acts, but to those who have taken part in them as first buyers or as legitimate successors, and those who have redeemed mortgages. They will enjoy securely and peacefully possession in these properties, emoluments, and returns; (the Holy See) requiring, nevertheless, that similar abusive alienations will not be repeated in the future.

Article 30. The government of the Republic will regulate with the respective diocesan ordinaries all matters concerning the cemeteries, endeavoring to reconcile the legitimate exigencies of civil and sanitary character with the veneration due these sacred places and the ecclesiastical prescriptions; and in case of discord this matter will be the subject of a special agreement between the Holy See and the government of Colombia.

Article 31. Agreements between the Holy See and the government of Colombia for the encouragement of Catholic missions among the barbarian tribes will require no additional approval on the part of Congress.

Article 32. By the present agreement all laws, orders, and decrees, of any description, promulgated at any time, which contradict or oppose this convention, which, when signed, will have the force of law of the State, are derogated and abrogated.

Article 33. The ratification and exchange of the present convention will take place within six months of the date of signature, and sooner if possible.

In pledge of which the indicated plenipotentiaries place their signature and seal on this convention.

Done in Rome on December 31, 1887.

(Signed) Cardinal Rampolla.
Joaquín F. Vélez.[52]

The relations between the Colombian government and the Holy See are regulated, in addition to the Concordat of 1888, by some important supplementary conventions. On July 20, 1892, Cardinal Rampolla and Joaquín Vélez signed a *convención adicional* to the Concordat concerning the *fuero eclesiástico*, cemeteries, and the civil register. Regarding the *fuero eclesiástico*, it was agreed that: (1) civil causes of ecclesiastics and causes relating to property and temporal rights of churches and ecclesiastical

[52] *Raccolta di Concordati,* pp. 1051-1061; The concordat is also found in Antonio José Uribe, *Anales Diplomáticos y Consulares de Colombia* (Bogotá, 1920), VI, pp. 330-335.

foundations should be heard in civil tribunals; (2) criminal causes concerning ecclesiastics in crimes foreign to religion should also be heard in the lay courts, but these trials should not be public; (3) sentences against ecclesiastics providing for the death penalty or opprobrious punishment should not be executed until the president of the Republic reviewed the case; (4) ecclesiastics should not be sentenced to labor on public works; and (5) in the arrest, detention, and punishment of ecclesiastics all possible respect should be paid to their sacred character.

On the subject of cemeteries, the convention supplemented Article 30 of the Concordat as follows: (1) all cemeteries of the Republic, with the exception of those belonging to private individuals, should be entrusted to the ecclesiastical authority, who would administer and regulate them independently of the civil authority; (2) an exception was made to allow the government to continue its financial support of certain large cemeteries in some of the cities. With respect to these, administration was to continue in the civil authority, but the Church reserved the right of supervision; (3) cemeteries for non-Catholics were to be created with municipal funds; and (4) the Church recognized the government's right to enforce sanitary and public regulations with respect to the cemeteries.

As to the civil register the convention provided that the ecclesiastics entrusted with the records of births, marriages, and deaths should submit authentic copies to the government every six months, but these copies were not to serve as evidence except in the event of loss of the parochial books.[53]

On August 4, 1898, another supplementary convention was signed by representatives of the Holy See and the Colombian government amending Article 25 of the Concordat. It was agreed that the government should appropriate annually, for ten years, the sum of $112,000, to be distributed as follows: to the dioceses, $12,000; to the cathedrals and chapters, $24,000; to the seminaries, $48,000; to the missions, $25,000, and to other purposes, $3,000. In 1908 and 1918, at the expiration of the decennial periods, supplementary conventions reduced the annual appropriation to $82,000. In October, 1928, President Méndez and the

---

[53] *Raccolta di Concordati,* pp. 1061-1069.

Apostolic Nuncio negotiated a further extension of the agreement. This appropriation is regarded as compensation for the injuries caused by confiscation of Church property during the administration of Mosquera.[54]

A convention concerning the missions was negotiated in 1902. This treaty provided for the administrative organization of the mission work and delimitation of fields of activity. The government obligated itself to appropriate annually $75,000 for the support of the missions. To the mission authorities was entrusted the direction of public primary schools within the mission districts. The government, in addition, agreed to grant to the missions, out of the public domain, lands for cultivation and pasturage.[55] In commenting on governmental interest in the missions, President Nel Ospina said, "The government supports the missions with the aid of the Church, for they are not only powerful instruments of civilization and culture, but they are also a means of making effective the national action in unknown and far-off regions."[56] In 1928 an accord was entered into between Colombia and the Holy See for the purpose of organizing the religious service of the army. By this agreement the "castrensial jurisdiction" was established.[57]

The terms of the Concordat provide that instruction in the universities, colleges, schools, and other centers of instruction shall be "in conformity with the dogmas and morals of the Catholic religion." Religious instruction is made obligatory in all public schools, and the right is reserved to the prelates to designate textbooks on morals and religion. Other texts are often included. For example, in a geography text approved by the ecclesiastical authorities appears the following remarks on religion:

"Religion is that body of beliefs which men profess in regard to God, and worship is the visible obeisance accorded divinity. . . .

---

[54] *Anales Diplomáticos y Consulares,* VI, pp. 406-409, 497, 563; Ministro de Hacienda y Crédito Público to J. L. Mecham, Bogotá, November 17, 1927; *Mensaje Presidencial al Congreso Nacional en las Sesiones Ordinarias de 1929* (Bogotá, 1929), p. 28.

[55] *Anales Diplomáticos y Consulares,* pp. 432-436.

[56] *Mensaje de Presidente de la República de Colombia al Congreso Nacional en las Sesiones de 1926* (Bogotá, 1926), p. 74.

[57] *Mensaje Presidencial de 1929,* p. 28.

Christianity, which is dominant particularly in Europe and America, is the religion founded by our Lord Jesus Christ, and it is professed by the most civilized peoples of the earth. It is divided into a Church, Catholicism, which is the repository of truth, and two schisms, the Greek Schism of the Orient, and Protestantism. The only true religion, Catholicism, preserves without change dogma and discipline, and the Pope is recognized as the visible head of the Church which has the greatest number of professors, 230,000,000, and it has extended and continues to expand throughout the world. Protestantism, which separated from the Catholic Church in the sixteenth century, refuses obedience to the Pope, and acknowledges no human authority in the interpretation of the Holy Scripture. At first Protestantism was divided into two sects, Lutheran and Zwinglian, or Calvinist, and later into many more which are daily being converted to Catholicism."[58]

The right of clerical inspection is also exercised over professors and teachers, who, on complaint of the ecclesiastical authorities, may be dismissed. No diploma of *bachiller* which entitles the holder to admission to the professional courses in any one of the five universities of the country will be granted without completion of the prescribed courses in religion taught by Catholics. This requirement effectively bars graduates of non-Catholic schools from admission to the universities. The Church sees to it that no instruction is given in any grade which does not conform to its own rigorous censorship. Furthermore, in protecting the purity of the faith, the Church has placed on the *Index Librorum Prohibitorum* all writers who in any degree vary from its established doctrine. It is indeed true that "Colombia remains one of the few strongholds of the spirit of obscurantism that distinguished the Middle Ages."[59]

The State recognizes a superior interest of parents and the Church in the field of education. A Minister of Public Education made the following statement: "Education, even that which is primary, is a special and proper duty of the parents, and, although the State ought, by natural right, to help parents carry out that

---

[58] Ángel M. Díaz Lemos, *Compendio de Geografía de la República de Colombia* (Barcelona, 1907), p. 32.

[59] Wheeler and Browning, *Modern Missions,* pp. 229-230.

duty, it has no right to interfere in the government of the family.
. . . In this respect all writers of moral philosophy are in accord.
Parents are more interested than anyone else in the instruction
of their children, as is also the Church of Jesus Christ . . . and
the repugnance which both have always shown toward obligatory
instruction is well known."[60] This being an expression of the
official attitude toward education, it is not surprising that public
instruction is sadly deficient. In Colombia, as in most of Latin
America, higher education is favored at the expense of the lower
grades. The religious orders, particularly the Jesuits, control
advanced instruction. Although the government proclaims a brave
and ambitious program of free, but not compulsory, primary education for children between the years of seven and fifteen, little is
done to put it into effect.[61] Trained teachers are lacking and buildings are scarce, for very few occupied by schools have been erected
for that specific purpose. Generally convents and monasteries are
utilized. The public secondary schools, which exist exclusively
for boys because of the clerical opposition to higher education for
women, enrolled in 1924 only 17,000 pupils in the whole nation.[62]
In Colombia the estimated illiteracy is about 90 per cent.

In revolt against the narrow, intolerant, unscientific type of
education supported by the government under the supervision of
the clerics, the Liberals have undertaken to establish, in Liberal
centers like Sagamosa, Honda, and Bucaramanga, schools of
their own, heading up in a Liberal University founded in Bogotá
in 1922. It was hoped that the Liberal University would afford an
escape from the religious test which the Catholic Church imposes
on all candidates for the professions. Since the Liberal revolt is
largely iconoclastic and has no definite moral ideal in view, there
is danger that, when the fetters forged by the dominant Church
are broken, the students will go to the opposite extreme and abandon
all religion.[63]

The government of Colombia, since December 14, 1835, when
Ignacio Sánchez de Tejada was officially received as the *chargé*

---

[60] Quoted in *Ibid.*, pp. 238-239.

[61] "Decreto No. 57," in *Diario Oficial*, 19 de enero de 1928, p. 87.

[62] Mary W. Williams, *The People and Politics of Latin America* (Boston,
1930), p. 518.

[63] Wheeler and Browning, *op. cit.*, p. 126.

d'affaires, with the exception of a short break during the Liberal régime, has maintained a diplomatic representative before the Holy See. In 1927, the rank of this representative was raised to that of ambassador. A papal nuncio, on the other hand, is accredited to the government of Bogotá. In Colombia there is no separate department of ecclesiastical affairs, these subjects being distributed among the various departments, particularly the Ministry of Foreign Affairs.

The relations between Church and State in Colombia since the days of President Rafael Núñez and the negotiation of the Concordat, have been entirely cordial. The Catholic Church is given by the Concordat complete ecclesiastical freedom and a guarantee of governmental protection as the State-Church. So satisfactory is the status to the clergy that it is unlikely they will make their position the basis of further internal strife. In the camp of the Liberals, however, there has been manifested intense opposition, marked by several unsuccessful insurrections, to the reversed *kulturkampf* sponsored by the Conservatives. The revolution of 1899-1902, for example, was waged almost exclusively on theological grounds. The political parties remain aligned today as they were in the struggle that culminated in the Constitution and the Concordat. The main principles of the platform of the Liberals are, (1) genuine liberty and freedom of speech and of institutions for all; (2) development of primary education, especially in the rural districts; and (3), separation of Church and State. The Liberals, who are increasing greatly in numbers and influence, are strongly opposed to the Concordat, and are in favor of annulling or thoroughly changing it.[64]

The Church, throughout the period since Núñez, played and still plays, a most influential rôle in politics. It favors the conservation of the established order and opposes innovations, especially those of a politico-religious type. "Doubtless the Liberals have grounds for their objection to the influence the clergy have wielded in the past," wrote Akers in 1904, "and the part they play today in the National destinies; but too often the movements ostensibly set afoot for a more progressive policy in the public administration have degenerated into attempts to obtain con-

---

[64] Wheeler and Browning, *op. cit.,* p. 129.

trol of the government for the personal ends of ambitious political adventurers who are far from seeking reforms for the general welfare; and while the principles of the Liberals may be worthy of support the instruments chosen for their execution are too often faulty. Under these circumstances the conservatives, aided by Church influence, have maintained their position as the dominant faction in spite of the strenuous efforts of their political adversaries."[65]

The priestly influence is immense in Colombia in matters far outside the scope of the religious. Not only do the clergy exercise a widespread influence over both the upper and lower classes in the affairs of everyday life, but they exercise great power in directing the votes of the ignorant and superstitious in political matters. In the presidential elections of 1930 Archbishop Perdomo issued a circular recommending support of the Conservative candidate. But, notwithstanding ecclesiastical opposition, Enrique Olaya Herrera, the Liberal nominee, was the victor at the polls.[66] However, in its legitimate sphere the Church is remiss in its duties, for, contends a critic, "The opportunity offered to the priesthood to educate and civilize is of a most wide description, but little taken advantage of; for, as in many other South American countries, the priesthood is recruited from the lower strata of the community, and the men have neither tradition nor ambitious desire to spur them on to the work of regeneration so urgently required. . . . Foreign priests from Spain and Italy, of whom there are many in Colombia, make no determined effort either to bring about any strong reaction against the low moral standard everywhere apparent."[67] The above statement, however, should not be taken as a disparagement of the fine work of the Jesuits in education. These highly trained and indefatigable workers were entrusted, in 1910, by contract with the Ministry of Public Instruction, with control over important branches of higher education. In 1927, by governmental decree and decision of the Council of State, a virtual monopoly of secondary education by the Jesuits was broken.[68]

There seems to be some disagreement of opinion as to the exist-

---

[65] Akers, *op. cit.,* p. 593.

[66] *Current History,* March, 1930, p. 1206.   [67] Akers, *op. cit.,* p. 610.

[68] *La Prensa* (New York), January 10, May 14, and May 20, 1928.

ence or absence of religious toleration in Colombia, even as many of us might dissent from the constitutional assertion that the Catholic Church in Colombia is not an established church. The Constitution, it is true, guarantees liberty of conscience and the free exercise of cults, but it is the understanding of the Ministry of Gobierno that "these articles establish toleration but not liberty of cults." It has interpreted the law to mean that the non-Catholic religious propaganda must take place in private places and not in public.[69] It is futile therefore to contend that equality of cults and absolute toleration of all forms of worship is observed in Colombia.

Whether or not the Constitution deals in a liberal spirit with non-Catholic religions, the fact remains that the Catholic Church, which is a power to be reckoned with to say the least, regards with intense jealousy any attempt of other religious sects to establish places of worship within the country. Catholicism being so deeply rooted, there is little scope for other denominations, particularly for missionary work. The Presbyterian Church of the United States is the only Protestant sect represented in the missionary field of Colombia. The Presbyterian Board of Foreign Missions sent its first missionary to New Granada in 1856 at the request of the Liberal government. The efforts of the Protestants, though laudable, are meager, for only a few years ago there were but thirty missionaries in the field, that is, one missionary to 200,000 Colombians. Justification for Protestant missionary effort in an essentially Catholic country like Colombia is found in the fact that "the Catholic Church is doing nothing effective in social service, or in raising the parishioners' standards of living."[70] Furthermore, large sections of the country are without priests, and, as has been indicated above, educational work is practically non-existent. It is in education particularly where the Protestants can do the greatest good, but so far they have barely scratched the surface. Yet their puny efforts have elicited vigorous opposition and protests from the Catholic prelates and priests.[71]

---

[69] Ministro de Gobierno to J. L. Mecham.

[70] Wheeler and Browning, *op. cit.*, p. 99.

[71] For the pastoral of the Archbishop of Medellín in condemnation of Protestant missionary work, see *Ibid.*, pp. 151-152; see also, pp. 128-129.

All who have any knowledge of the past history and present tendencies in Colombia. agree that the religious question is not definitely settled in that republic. Since the clergy regard the status as established by the Concordat to be a model one, for that very reason it is destined to be subjected to constant attack by the elements that refuse to accept the clerical viewpoint. The writer cannot refrain from observing that, as concerns the Church, the situation is too good to last, for sooner or later the enemies of the Concordat will be swept into power and the inevitable reform of ecclesiastical legislation will follow.

CHAPTER VI

THE VICISSITUDES OF ROMAN CATHOLICISM
IN ECUADOR

The aversion of the Latin American to compromise, or to the adoption of half-way measures in meeting problems, is clearly illustrated by the vicissitudes of the Catholic Church in the Republic of Ecuador. There, as in Colombia, religious policy has always been a prominent feature of political campaigns, and, as the factions, generally calling themselves "Conservatives" and "Liberals" alternated in the control of the government, the political status of the Church has been changed within extreme and unreasonable limits. It is difficult to imagine a greater divergence in policies than between those advocated and translated into fact by García Moreno and Eloy Alfaro. Yet these systems, as widely separated as the poles, were foisted on the people of Ecuador because, presumably, the leaders knew better than the people what they wanted and what was good for them. The history of the Catholic Church in Ecuador is interesting primarily because of the marked ebb and flow of its fortunes.

"Intolerance of cults distinct from the Catholic has been consecrated (in Ecuador), thus departing from the accepted policy of New Granada and Venezuela, and adhering to the current ideas in Peru and Bolivia." Thus wrote a political commentator in 1888 when analyzing religious policy in Ecuador.[1] This description, inapplicable to Ecuador since 1900, was nevertheless true for most of the nineteenth century. When Ecuador separated from Great Colombia, she established, in the Constitution of September 11, 1830, Roman Catholicism as the religion of the State to the exclusion of any other faith.[2] General Juan José Flores, compatriot of Bolívar, and first president of Ecuador, although charged with

---

[1] Arosemena, *Estudios Constitucionales,* I, 539.
[2] Annibal Velloso Rebello, "García Moreno," in *Revista do Instituto Historico e Geographico Brasileiro* (Rio de Janeiro, 1920), CXLI, 126.

being an atheist,[3] supported Catholicism during his first administration (1830-1834) as the sole State religion. His internal policy
was characterized by preference for the military and the clergy,
but as a matter of fact President Flores, selfish and dictatorial
by nature, had little respect for the Church. He supported it if it
in turn consented to be subjected and reinforced his authority.

Vicente Rocafuerte, the successor of Flores to the presidency,
was the official champion of the Liberals, a great intellect, and
a good Catholic withal.[4] Regarded as the greatest of Ecuador's
reformers, one of Rocafuerte's first acts as president was to have
a new constitution drafted in the interest of greater liberalism.
Remarking on the need of constitutional reform he said, "The
Constitution of 1830, which should be reformed or annulled, as
is convenient, presents rare anomalies. Beside the declarations
of sovereignty of the people, the creation of a legislative body,
the distribution of powers, liberty of the press, and other similar
subjects, which are pure democracy, are intolerance of cults other
than the Roman Catholic, the recognition of *fueros*, the pupilage
of the natives, and the *status quo* of the ecclesiastical and monastic
establishments which had been consecrated by our colonial laws."[5]
In dilating on the subject of constitutional reform, President
Rocafuerte made the following pertinent remarks concerning religion: "There can be no public income without productive labor,
no productive labor without intelligence and good customs, no
intelligence and customs without religion, from which it can be
deduced that all the worldly treasures have their noble origin in
Heaven itself. . . . The reform of the clergy, the purity of their
customs, the dignity of the cult, the education of the priests,
abolition of certain abuses, the extinction of so many feast days
which retard the increase of public wealth, should engage the
attention of the legislators . . . ; religious reform should always
precede the political."[6]

In spite of the recommendations of the President the constitu-

---

[3] *Ibid.*, p. 137.

[4] *Ibid.*

[5] "El Jefe Supremo á la Convención," in Francisco Ignacio Salazár, *Actas
de la Convención Nacional del Ecuador, Año de 1835* (Quito, 1891), p.
CCXXXV.

[6] *Ibid.*, p. CCXXXVIII.

ents did not liberalize the religious clauses of the Constitution of 1835. Roman Catholicism was declared to be the religion of the republic to the exclusion of any other, and the government was specifically obligated to protect it. Since Rocafuerte felt that the religious conservatism of the great majority of Ecuadoreans hampered progress, he attempted to secularize public education. A step in this direction was the taking of the College of San Fernando from the Dominicans and combining it with the University. Also, manifesting leanings toward religious freedom, he tried to introduce Protestantism into Ecuador. But the inherent conservatism and religious attachment of the people against which Rocafuerte struggled proved to be too strong for him. For example, when a Quaker was allowed to enter Quito, and was put in charge of a school, the people were outraged and speedily drove him from the country.[7]

Whatever of a liberalizing nature had been implanted in Ecuador during the presidency of Vicente Rocafuerte, was lost during the reaction of Flores' second and third terms of office (1839-1845). Ambitious and opportunistic, Flores secured the adoption of a new constitution in 1843 which lengthened the presidential term to eight years. With an air of orthodoxy the religious clause of the Constitution read, "The religion of the State is the Roman Catholic Apostolic"; but, as a bid for Liberal support it read further, "to the exclusion of the public exercise of any other cult." The freedom of private worship of non-Catholic cults aroused violent opposition, particularly in Quito and Cuenca, "where reigned a medieval fanaticism which proscribed independent thought and religious independence."[8] The clergy refused to take the oath to the constitution and accused Flores of being in league with the Masons of New Granada. When the Liberals finally mustered enough strength to revolt against the corrupt and despotic rule of Flores the clerics joined them with cries of "Viva la Religión," and "Abajo la Constitución."[9] Flores was unable to with-

[7] Berthe, *García Moreno*, pp. 80, 103; "J. M. Obando á Santander, Pasto, 8 de julio de 1835," in *Archivo Santander*, XXI, 275.

[8] Rebello, *op. cit.*, pp. 137-138; Berthe, *op. cit.*, p. 106.

[9] Berthe, *op. cit.*, pp. 106-108; Pedro Fermin Cevallos, *Historia del Ecuador* (Guayaquil, 1886-1889), V, 534.

stand the diverse forces of an outraged public conscience, and so, in 1845, he was driven into exile.

After the overthrow of Flores, Ecuador was plunged into veritable anarchy, from which condition it was not rescued until Gabriel García Moreno assumed the control of government in 1860. This most remarkable man in the history of Ecuador, and, for that matter, in the history of Latin America, was a scion of one of the most aristocratic families of pure Castilian blood in Ecuador. Trained in the law at the University of Quito, he became well known as a publicist and writer. In the political and religious war which accomplished the overthrow of Flores, he was one of the principal actors, thereby evidencing at that early date in his career his devotion to the Roman Catholic Church. Because of the Liberal ascendancy there was no political place for García Moreno in Ecuador; consequently he went to Europe. After six months spent in the Old World, in 1850, he recrossed the sea firmly convinced by the excesses of liberalism that "Jesus Christ was the only Savior of the people, and that the State without religion was irremediably destined to the sabre of the autocrat or the poinard of the anarchist."[10] He felt that the Church should be used to restrain the nation and give it the moral discipline it so badly needed.

Following his return from Europe García Moreno was instrumental in securing for the Jesuits, who had been expelled from New Granada, admission to Ecuador (1951). By law of March, 1851, the Jesuits were restored their old properties which had not been alienated. A great festival marked the opening, after eighty-three years, of the Church of Jesus in Quito. The government of New Granada protested vigorously against the admission of the Jesuits into Ecuador. The diplomatic agent of New Granada accredited to the government in Quito was guilty of the questionable diplomatic action of publishing a venomous pamphlet against the Holy Company. García Moreno assumed the rôle of defender of the Jesuits. His "Defensa de los Jesuitas" is a remarkably restrained, dignified, and scholarly treatise on the work and objects of the Society of Jesus.[11] The able support of García Moreno

---

[10] Berthe, *op. cit.*, p. 143.
[11] Rebello, *op. cit.*, pp. 151-152; Berthe, *op. cit.*, pp. 146-149.

was of no avail, however, for, in 1852, the expulsion of the Jesuits was decreed.[12] Then the author of the celebrated "Defensa de los Jesuitas," wrote as a complement to that work a "Farewell to the Jesuits."

The attack by García Moreno, in satirical verse, on the dictatorial government of the pseudo-Liberal José Urbina brought upon him the decree of expulsion from Ecuador (1855). His experience as an exile in Europe added to his political and religious conservatism, and when he returned to his native country in 1857, he founded a political party, the National Union, to advance his reform program. After resorting to the use of arms, in traditional Ecuadorean style, to gain possession of the government, García Moreno established his authority in Quito in 1860. The next fifteen years in the Republic of the Equator was truly the "age of García Moreno." As dictator he forced acceptance by his country of his peculiar ideas on the subject of politico-ecclesiastical relationships. In brief he aimed at establishing a religious despotism in which the clergy should be supreme and the civil authority secondary thereto. The Ecuadorean State under García Moreno represented the nearest approach to a theocracy in the western world.

"The Church," said García Moreno, "should always march side by side with the civil power under conditions of real independence."[13] Therefore the Constitution of 1861, which reflected the political philosophy of the President, made a special effort to secure an exclusive position for the Catholic Church.[14] García Moreno represented all the forces of social conservatism under the tutelage of the Church. He believed that the Roman Catholic religion was the only national tradition in the republic, the only creative agent and instrument of unity. Faith and order were, in his estimation, inseparably linked, but the Church could only function successfully if it were free of all official tutelage. Therefore he negotiated a concordat with the papacy which authorized exceptional privileges for the Church.

Late in 1861 Ignacio Ordoñez, Archdeacon of Cuenca, was sent

---

[12] Berthe, *op. cit.,* p. 159.

[13] Rebello, *op. cit.,* p. 179.

[14] Berthe, *op. cit.,* p. 297.

on mission to France to secure religious of both sexes for the primary schools. From France he was ordered to proceed to Rome to negotiate a concordat. In his instructions to Ordoñez, the President wrote, "I wish complete liberty for the church, and comprehensive reform of the secular and regular clergy." After six months of discussion the Concordat was signed, September 26, 1862, by Cardinal Antonelli and Ignacio Ordoñez. Pope Pius IX sent an apostolic delegate to Quito to exchange ratifications. García Moreno expressed satisfaction with all terms of the Concordat, but was disappointed to note that it contained nothing regarding the reform of the clergy which he had solicited. He therefore sent Ordoñez back to Rome with instructions that the Concordat would be ratified only on condition that the pope agreed to the reform. The pope finally acquiesced, and decided to send an apostolic delegate to Ecuador with full powers to institute reform measures. All obstacles having been removed, the Concordat was promulgated in Ecuador on April 22, 1863. In Quito a pontifical mass celebrated the event.[15]

The Concordat entered into by Pius IX and García Moreno conveyed to the Church in Ecuador greater privileges than it had enjoyed under the Spanish régime. Since this instrument is universally regarded as one of the most notable of modern times, the text is presented as follows:

Concordat between Pius IX and the Republic of Ecuador.

September 26, 1862.

In the name of the most holy and indivisible Trinity, His Holiness the Supreme Pontiff Pius IX and the President of the Republic of Ecuador name as their respective plenipotentiaries.

His Holiness, his eminence the Sig. Jacobo Antonelli, Cardinal of the Holy Roman Church, Deacon of Santa Agata de Suburra and Secretary of State and Foreign Relations.

And His Excellency the President of the Republic, the most excellent Señor Don Ignacio Ordoñez, Archdeacon of the Cathedral Church of Cuenca in the same republic and Minister Plenipotentiary near the Holy See.

Who, after having exchanged their respective plenary powers, agree on the following articles:

---

[15] *Ibid.*, pp. 318-324.

Article 1. The Roman Catholic Apostolic religion will continue to be the only religion of the Republic of Ecuador, and it [the State] will always protect all the rights and prerogatives which it ought to enjoy according to the laws of God and canonical dispositions. Consequently there will never be permitted in Ecuador a dissident cult or any society condemned by the Church.

Article 2. In each one of the present dioceses, and in those which will be erected later, there will be a diocesan seminary whose direction, régime, and administration belong freely and exclusively to the diocesan ordinaries according to the dispositions of the Council of Trent and of the canonical laws. Rectors, professors, and others employed in the instruction and direction of said establishments will be freely nominated and removed by the ordinaries.

Article 3. The instruction of the youth in the Universities, colleges, faculties, and public and private schools will in all things conform to the doctrine of the Catholic religion. The bishops will have the exclusive right to designate texts for instruction in ecclesiastical sciences as well as in moral and religious instruction. In addition the bishops and the ordinaries will exercise freely the right to prohibit books contrary to religion and good customs, and to see that the government adopts proper measures to prevent the importation or dissemination of said books in the Republic.

Article 4. The bishops, in accordance with the duties of their pastoral ministry, will take care that there shall be no instruction contrary to the Catholic religion and proper customs. With this aim no one can instruct in any public or private institution in the subjects of theology, catechism, or religious doctrine without having obtained the authorization of the diocesan prelate, who can revoke the permit if he deems it opportune. For the examinations (of teachers) in the primary institutions the diocesan will always name an assistant to examine in religious and moral instruction. He cannot assume the discharge of this duty without the consent of the said diocesan.

Article 5. Since by divine right the primacy of honor and jurisdiction in the Universal Church belongs to the Roman Pontiff, all bishops, as well as clergy and the faithful will have free communication with the Holy See. Consequently no secular authority can place obstacles in the way of the full and free exercise of this right of communication by obliging the bishops, clergy and people to submit to the government as an intermediary in their communications with the Roman See, or by subjecting bulls, briefs, and rescripts to the exequatur of the government.

Article 6. The ecclesiastical ordinaries of the Republic can govern their dioceses with full liberty, convoke and celebrate provincial

12

and diocesan councils, and exercise the rights which belong to them by virtue of their sacred ministry and current canonical provisions approved by the Holy See, without being interfered with in the performance of their duties. Thus the government of Ecuador will dispense with its patronal power, and will assist the bishops when solicited, particularly when they are confronted with the evil works of those people who seek to pervert the spirit of the faithful and corrupt their customs.

Article 7. Appeals to the civil power (*recursos de fuerza*) are abolished, and sentences pronounced by the ordinary ecclesiastical judges can only be appealed to the superior ecclesiastical tribunals or to the Holy See, according to the discipline established by the brief *Exposcit* of the Supreme Pontiff Gregory XIII, and likewise by canonical prescriptions. Matrimonial causes in particular must conform to the prescriptions of the constitution *Dei Miseratione* of Pope Benedict XIV. . . . The ecclesiastical judges will pronounce their judgments, without submitting them to the prior opinion of the secular assessors, to whom nevertheless they can go for advice when they deem it opportune. The ecclesiastics who are lawyers can discharge the office of assessor in this kind of judgment.

Article 8. All ecclesiastical causes and especially those relating to faith, the sacraments (which includes matrimonial causes), customs, holy functions, sacred rights and duties whether by reason of persons or subject, excepting the major causes reserved for the Holy Pontiff . . . will be heard in the ecclesiastical tribunals. The same will be tried as civil causes of ecclesiastics, and other matters included in the penal code of the Republic will be tried as crimes. To all ecclesiastical judgments the civil authorities will lend aid and protection, so that the judges can enforce the execution of penalties and sentences pronounced by them.

Article 9. The Holy See consents that persons as well as ecclesiastical properties shall be subject to the public imposts on a par with persons and properties of other citizens. The civil authority should enter into an agreement with the ecclesiastical to obtain the corresponding authorization whenever coaction is necessary. Excepted from said imposts are seminaries, properties and things immediately destined for the cult, and charitable institutions.

Article 10. Out of respect for the majesty of God who is the King of Kings and Lord of Lords, the immunity of churches will be respected in so far as public security and the exigencies of justice permit. In such event the Holy See consents that the ecclesiastical authority, the parish priests, and prelates of the regular houses, permit the extraction of refugees on the request of the civil authorities.

Article 11. Since the income from the tithes is devoted to the support of the divine cult and its ministers, the government of Ecuador is obliged to maintain Catholic instruction in the Republic, and His Holiness consents that the government continue to receive a third part of the tithes. For the collection and administration of the tithes the two authorities, civil and ecclesiastical, will enter into an agreement.

Article 12.   By virtue of the right of patronage which the Supreme Pontiff concedes to the President of Ecuador, the latter can propose for archbishops and bishops clerics, qualified in the sense of the sacred canons. Thus, immediately after an episcopal vacancy appears, the archbishop will ask the other bishops for their votes for the filling of the vacancy; if the vacancy happens to be that of the archbishop, the senior bishop will order the votes, and will present a list of three candidates to the President who will select one of these, and will propose it to the Supreme Pontiff so that he might confer canonical institution in the form prescribed by the sacred canons. In case the bishops fail to make the presentation within six months, for any cause whatever, the President of Ecuador may do it himself, and if he does not act within three months, the right of election is reserved to the Holy See, just as if it had been solicited. To facilitate this action, the government, or the ecclesiastical authority in the event of its failure to act, will notify His Holiness immediately after the designated time has elapsed. But those proposed cannot under any circumstance enter upon the performance of their duties and the administration of churches, without first receiving the bulls of canonical institution. In the erection of new bishoprics the President of the Republic will propose directly for the first time the new bishops to the Holy See.

Article 13.   In the same manner His Holiness concedes to the President of the Republic the right of naming qualified ecclesiastics for prebends, dignities, and canons. . . .

Article 14.   Regarding the provision of parochial benefices, the ordinaries, complying with the prescriptions of the Holy Council of Trent, will send to the government a list of qualified ecclesiastics upon whom the parish can be conferred; and the President will directly by himself, or by means of his delegates in the provinces, elect one of them. . . . If it is necessary to make territorial divisions in the parishes this can be done in agreement with the ordinary and the local civil authority.

Article 15.   When a vacancy occurs in an episcopal church the chapter will freely elect the capitular vicar in the time and form prescribed by the Council of Trent. . . .

Article 16.   The Holy See, in the exercise of its proper jurisdiction, will erect new dioceses and will establish new limits in those now in existence. Considering the too vast extent of the present dioceses in the Republic, as soon as this concordat is ratified, there will be conceded to a special delegate the necessary powers to proceed with the aid of the government and the respective bishops to the territorial delimitation of the dioceses that can be conveniently established, and to fix the grants and income of the church, bishops, chapters, and seminary.

Article 17. The executive decree of May 28, 1836, concerning the redemption of mortgages held in favor of pious causes remains abolished in Ecuador. The Holy See, in view of the benefits derived from the present concordat, and desirous of providing for the public tranquility, in order to remedy the evils caused by the transfer of the mortgages held by the Ecuadorean Church to the national treasury, accedes to the reiterated requests of the President; and hereby decrees and declares that those who, from the year 1836 until the present promoted such transfer, as well as the possessors of the said redeemed funds and those who by any means acquired possession of same, will not be subjected at any time or in any manner, to the slightest molestation on the part of His Holiness or of the Roman Pontiffs his successors.

Article 18. Regarding the obligations contracted by the government with its creditors on account of the transferred mortgages, the Holy See consents that by paying a tenth part to the treasury, both of the transferred capital, as well as of the suppressed rents, the government can be free of all responsibility. As security for the payment of this amount, the government assigns a fourth part of the third which it derives from the tithes, which will be put in the hands of the ordinaries so that they may be divided by them in proportional parts in favor of their legitimate creditors, taking care that the principal will be capitalized in a secure and profitable manner. . . .

Article 19. The Church will enjoy the right to acquire property freely and by any just title, and the properties now in its possession or acquired later, will be guaranteed by law. The administration of ecclesiastical properties belongs to the persons designated by the sacred canons, who alone will examine the accounts and economic regulations. The property of ecclesiastical foundations of any kind, such as hospitals and other charitable institutions, which are not administered by the ecclesiastical authority, will be transferred to it, so that it can immediately make the proper investments. Regarding the old and new ecclesiastical foundations, none can be suppressed or combined without the intervention of the authority of the Holy See, excepting the right which belongs to the bishops according to the Holy Council of Trent.

Article 20. In addition to the orders and religious congregations which now exist in the Republic of Ecuador, the diocesan ordinaries can freely and without exception admit and establish in their respective dioceses new orders or institutes approved by the Church in conformity with the necessities of the people. To facilitate this the government will lend its aid.

Article 21. After the divine offices in all the churches of the Republic of Ecuador, the following prayer will be said: *Domine salvam fac Rempublicam; Domine salvam fac Praesidium ejus.*

Article 22. The government of the Republic of Ecuador is obligated to employ all proper measures for the propagation of the faith and for the conversion of people found in that territory; and in addition, to lend all favor and aid to the establishment and progress of the holy missions, which with laudable purpose, have been undertaken under the authority of the Sacred Congregation of Propaganda.

Article 23. All other things which pertain to ecclesiastical persons and things, and concerning which nothing is provided in the articles of the present concordat, will be directed and administered according to the present canonical discipline of the Church, approved by the Holy See.

Article 24. By virtue of this concordat all contrary laws and decrees published up to the present in any manner and form in Ecuador are revoked; and the same concordat ought always to be considered as a law of the State. Therefore, each one of the contracting parties promises for himself, and for his successors, the faithful observance of all and each one of the articles which it contains. If any difficulty arises at a future date, the Holy Father and the President of Ecuador agree to settle it in an amicable manner.

Article 25. The ratification of the present concordat will take place within a year, or sooner if possible. In pledge of which the undersigned plenipotentiaries sign and seal the present convention with their respective seals.

Given in Rome on September 26, 1862.

Jacobus Cardinal Antonelli.
Ignacio Ordoñez.[16]

By the Concordat Ecuador definitely abandoned to the Holy See national pretentions to the exercise of the ecclesiastical patronage. Although the instrument recognized in the Catholic Church in Ecuador exceptional rights and privileges, it was not unique in this respect by any means. In fact, it was, with a few exceptions, a recapitulation of the concordats entered into by Pope Pius IX

---

[16] *Raccolta di Concordati*, pp. 983-995.

and the republics of Costa Rica and Guatemala, both on October 17, 1852. These concordats were, in a way, models for subsequent Latin-American concordats. They represented the maximum concessions the papacy was willing to make to national claims over the Church.[17] Within and without the Republic of Ecuador great dissatisfaction was expressed toward the Concordat. Liberals and Radicals determined to destroy it and several attempts were made in the Congress to modify it by law, but none of these succeeded because of the dominating influence of the President. Externally, throughout South America the Concordat was denounced as treason to South American independence, for it was claimed that by the agreement, Ecuador was converted into a fief of Rome. President Mosquera of Colombia invited the Ecuadoreans to overthrow their President, and in 1863, he undertook an invasion "to liberate the brother democrats of Ecuador from the theocratic yoke of Professor Moreno." This outside interference tended, however, to strengthen the hold of the dictator who continued to bestow more and more power and privileges upon the Church.[18]

Education, as was stipulated in the Concordat, was placed under the complete control of the clergy. García Moreno, intensely interested in education, had a law passed providing for a public school system, and instruction in the schools was divided up between the religious orders. Because of a dearth of competent native teaching material, foreign teaching orders were introduced, particularly from France. Since García Moreno wished to reorganize higher education on a solid base, he sought the aid of the Jesuits. The Congress consequently authorized the Jesuits to establish institutions of learning in Ecuador, with full and entire liberty to employ their traditional educational methods. The Jesuits, inured to reverses in the school of experience, stipulated in the agreement with the government, which allowed for their return to Ecuador, that "in the event altogether improbable, that the government suppresses the Company of Jesus, the members of the Society will not be deported or dispersed except after the lapse of eight months after the day of suppression. They will enjoy

---

[17] For the concordats of October 7, 1852 with Costa Rica and Guatemala, see *Raccolta di Concordati,* pp. 800-821.

[18] Berthe, *op. cit.,* pp. 376-377, 393.

during this time all the constitutional and legal guarantees to arrange for their voyage and dispose of their property."[19]

The reform of the clergy, demanded by García Moreno as a prerequisite to the ratification of the Concordat, was undertaken in good faith by the pope. The papal delegate assigned to supervise this work was vigorously supported by the President. The regulars, however, presented real difficulties, and much still remained to be done when García Moreno's term of office expired in 1865. In consequence of the Concordat, four new bishoprics were created in Ecuador. They were Cuenca, Loja, Riobamba, and Ibarra.[20]

At the expiration of his four-year term of office García Moreno gave way to another man who was expected to be his puppet. The new president, however, was quickly pushed aside, and during the absence of García Moreno in Europe on a diplomatic mission, the Radicals gained control of the government. For a brief period ensued a bitter anti-clerical reaction. The execution of the Concordat was suspended and the law of patronage was restored. In vain the apostolic delegate protested and the followers of García Moreno charged the government with betrayal. Fortunately for the Church, García Moreno returned to power in January, 1869. Then for the next six years Ecuador was taken further than ever on the road to theocracy.[21]

Since García Moreno wished to increase the powers of the president he summoned a constituent convention "composed of Conservatives and good Catholics." His project for a new constitution was adopted without modification (1869). The new frame of government, which was made to conform to the principles of the *Syllabus*, was as strongly impregnated with theocracy as if it had issued from the Vatican. "The Roman Catholic religion," stipulated Article 1, "is declared to be the religion of the State, to the exclusion of any other, and it remains in possession of its inalienable rights and prerogatives which are invested in it by divine law, and canonical prescriptions; the public powers are obligated to aid and make it respected." Being a Catholic was

---

[19] *Ibid.*, p. 583.

[20] *Ibid.*, pp. 331-333; Rebello, *op. cit.*, p. 185.

[21] Berthe, *op. cit.*, pp. 468-469, 509.

made a requisite for citizenship, and whoever belonged to a sect
condemned by the Church lost his civil rights (Article 3). Since
it was impossible to keep heretics out of the country, García
Moreno hoped that by depriving them of civil rights they would
be discouraged from coming. The Constitution also guaranteed
the right of ecclesiastics to be tried in Church courts in all civil
causes except those of a financial and political character. Ecclesiastical judges in civil cases were to be guided by the civil law.[22]
When García Moreno assumed the presidency under the new Constitution he swore the following oath: "I swear by God Our Lord,
and by the Holy Gospel, to perform faithfully my duty as president of this republic, to profess the Roman Catholic Apostolic
religion; to preserve the integrity and independence of the State;
to observe and enforce the observance of this Constitution and
the laws. If I am successful it is because God is my support
and my defence; if not, then God and the *patria* will be my judges."
Religion and *patria* were the dominant passions in the life of
García Moreno.[23]

The governmental program of García Moreno, following the
adoption of the Constitution of 1869, "read like an episcopal
address." The following statements were uttered by him during
this period: "Civilization, which is built on Catholicism, degen-
erates and debases in measure as it departs from Catholic principles," and, "Religion is the sole bond which is left to us in this
country, divided as it is by the interests of parties, races, and
beliefs." His program was, he said: "the respect and protection
of the Catholic Church, unshakable attachment to the Holy See,
education based on morality and faith, and liberty for all and in
everything, excepting crime and criminals."

The reform of the clergy, the preoccupation of García Moreno
in his first administration, had languished during the Radical
régime because of the abolition of the ecclesiastical tribunals.
After the inauguration of his second term, the President appealed
once more to the pope to send another delegate to resume the
work of reform of the regular orders with the support and co-
operation of the government and the episcopate. Pleased with

[22] Rebello, *op. cit.,* pp. 200-201; Berthe, *op. cit.,* pp. 538-540.
[23] Berthe, *op. cit.,* p. 529.

the zeal of the President, the pope hastened to acquiesce. Under the impulse of García Moreno a number of provincial councils were convened to consider the reform of ecclesiastical discipline. One of the principal achievements of the provincial councils was a complete revamping of seminary curricula and discipline.[24]

The welfare of the faith outside of Ecuador was also a matter of deep concern to García Moreno, for he intervened in the domestic affairs of Colombia when a radical government was assaulting the Church. He eulogized Maximilian as the deliverer of Mexico from the "excesses of a rapacious, immoral, and turbulent demagogy." He protested to Victor Emmanuel against the taking of Rome, and the absorption of the Papal States into the Kingdom of Italy. Congress was induced to make a gift of 52,000 francs to "the Prisoner of the Vatican." Finally, in 1873, in mystic ardor, García Moreno, by official decree, consecrated Ecuador to the Sacred Heart of Jesus.[25]

On August 6, 1875, President García Moreno, a religious fanatic perhaps, but nevertheless a great benefactor of Ecuador, fell in the public square of Quito at the hands of assassins. Since the assassination was thought to be a Masonic plot, the murdered president was decreed by Congress the name of "Regenerator of the *patria* and martyr of Catholic civilization." The Congress also ordered a statue erected with this inscription, "To the most excellent García Moreno, Ecuador's greatest son, died for religion and the *patria*." Catholics throughout the world recognized in the death of García Moreno the loss of a zealous champion of the Church. Pope Pius IX, a prisoner in the Vatican, expressed sincere sorrow over the death of a faithful son of the Church.[26] The Peruvian litterateur and publicist, Francisco García Calderón wrote the following estimate of García Moreno: "Indefatigable, stoical, strong in decision, admirably logical in his life, García Moreno is one of the great individuals of American history. He was not a tyrant like Guzmán Blanco or Porfirio Díaz. For fifteen years, from 1859 to 1874, he completely transformed his little country in accord with a vast plan which only his death prevented

---

[24] *Ibid.*, p. 559.

[25] Garcíá Calderón, *op. cit.*, pp. 218-219; Berthe, *op. cit.*, pp. 672, 684, 691.

[26] Berthe, *op. cit.*, pp. 63, 82, 745-746.

from realization. Mystic in the Spanish manner, he was never satisfied with sterile contemplation; he felt the necessity of action to be an organizer and creator."[27]

After the death of García Moreno, the Congress of Ecuador sent an address to Pope Pius IX, announcing their allegiance to the Catholic principles of the martyred president. The clericals were aggressively anxious to retain as many as possible of the privileges gained during the ascendancy of "the Catholic President." But the old forces of clericalism and conservatism, without the guiding genuis of García Moreno, soon aroused a powerful opposition. The Liberals and Radicals were successful, in 1877, in forcing the deposition and exile of President Borrero, "whose absurd policy," said General Ignacio Veintemilla, leader of the Radicals, "perpetuates institutions incompatible with democratic government."[28] The seizure of the presidency by General Veintemilla ushered in a short but turbulent period of anti-clerical reform.

One of the first acts of the new government was to suspend the Concordat in June, 1877, as being contrary to national sovereignty. The law of patronage was restored. These acts provoked a clerical revolt, and the Bishop of Riobamba went so far as to threaten excommunication of all those who refused to recognize the Concordat. Veintemilla countered with a decree which provided that all rebel prelates would be deprived of their ecclesiastical revenues. After fifteen months of dictatorship, Veintemilla convened a constituent convention to fabricate the ninth of Eucador's constitutions. On the religious question it was suggested that the old article providing: "The Catholic religion is that of the State to the exclusion of all others," be suppressed. But the proposal was defeated on the ground that, "The government protects the actual status which is religious unity." On the other hand an attempt of the moderates to restore the Concordat was defeated. However, in 1882, when Veintemilla's grip was weakening, to conciliate the Conservatives, he received the papal nuncio and declared his intention to defend the Holy Catholic faith. As proof of his sincerity he restored the Concordat. But these

---

[27] Francisco García Calderón, *Democracías Latinas de América,* quoted by Rebello, *op. cit.,* p. 92.

[28] Berthe, *op. cit.,* p. 776.

measures were satisfactory neither to the Conservatives nor the Liberals, for a temporary union of these elements accomplished the overthrow of the dictator.[29]

Again the pendulum swung to the other extreme. Once more the clericals came into power, for President José Camaño, the successor of Veintemilla, formed an intimate alliance with the clergy and the old partisans of García Moreno. On May 2, 1881 a new concordat was negotiated, substantially the same as that of 1862, with the exception that the jurisdiction of the ecclesiastical courts was somewhat restricted.[30] Once more the republic was dedicated to the Sacred Heart of Jesus, and it was decreed that a national temple should be erected and dedicated to the Sacred Heart as a perpetual monument of gratitude to God. The decree had to be ratified by the constituent convention which had just been convened to frame a constitution satisfactory to the Conservatives. The proposal to erect a national temple was approved despite the objections of some members that Quito had too many churches and could spend the money to better advantage on the Indian missions.[31]

On November 18, 1890, a special concordat was negotiated with the papacy. Its purpose was to provide a substitute for the tithes. It was agreed that in lieu of the tithes the Church should receive thirty cents per year on each hundred *sucres* collected on rural lands. This tax was to except holdings of a value not in excess of one hundred *sucres*, buildings used for residence purposes, and cacao plantations. Also, property belonging to the Church was exempt from the tax.[32]

It was stated in a bulletin published by the Bureau of American Republics in 1892, that the relations between Church and State in Ecuador had been settled satisfactorily to both parties. This optimistic declaration was proved within a very short time to be unfounded in fact, for, by 1897, another anti-clerical régime

[29] *Ibid.*, pp. 784-793; Juan Montalvo, *Las Catilinarias* (Paris, 1925), I, 41.
[30] *Raccolta di Concordati*, pp. 1001-1013.
[31] Berthe, *op. cit.*, pp. 794, 797; Pedro Fermin Cevallos, *Resumen de la Historia del Ecuador* (Guayaquil, 1889), p. 27; C. R. Enock, *Ecuador* (London, 1914), p. 82.
[32] *Raccolta di Concordati*, pp. 1079-1085.

was established, which, excepting minor fluctuations of control, is still dominant in the Republic of Ecuador. The Liberals under General Eloy Alfaro, an anti-clerical who hated the somewhat corrupt and retrograde priestcraft which controlled the country, seized the government in 1897 and proceeded to purge Ecuador of clericalism. The reform movement was inaugurated with moderation as evidenced by the fact that the new Constitution of 1897 contained the traditional clause providing that Roman Catholicism should be the State religion to the exclusion of all other forms of religious worship. But, because of a Conservative and clerical movement against his government, President Alfaro was driven to more extreme measures against the Church. A law of patronage enacted September 11, 1899, violated numerous provisions of the Concordat; for example, (1) papal legates should not exercise jurisdiction in the Republic without the consent of the Council of State; (2) bulls and rescripts could not be published without the approval of the president; (3) revenues for the support of the Church should be raised by the State alone; (4) Congress should have the power (a) to create new parishes and determine the number of priests in cathedral churches, (b) elect archbishops and bishops, who must be native-born Ecuadoreans, and whose names should be presented to the Apostolic See by the president, (c) permit the meeting of Church councils; (5) only citizens of Ecuador should have the right to act as curates; and (6) no new religious orders should be established in the Republic.[33] These violations of the terms of the Concordat, unrecognized by the papacy, really terminated that agreement. Since 1900 therefore, there has been no concordat between Ecuador and the Vatican, and diplomatic relations have been discontinued.[34] Though the Catholic Church remained the State religion, it was made dependent on the civil authorities to an extreme degree.

The anti-clerical policy inaugurated by Alfaro was continued by President Plaza Gutiérrez (1901-1905) who effected a veritable social revolution. In 1904 a law was passed guaranteeing religious

---

[33] John Lee, *Religious Liberty in South America* (New York, 1907), pp. 234 ff.

[34] Harold D. Clum, American Consul, to J. L. Mecham, Guayaquil, November 11, 1927.

toleration and protection to ministers of dissident faiths. The establishment of new convents and monasteries was prohibited and rural land held in the dead hands of the Church was nationalized and let to the highest bidders. Another law signed by President Plaza Gutiérrez permitted civil marriage and divorce. According to this measure and subsequent modifications of it absolute divorce must be by mutual consent, but separation can be secured for cruelty, desertion, or adultery. The civil marriage is the only legal form recognized by the government.[35]

The measures of Alfaro and Plaza Gutiérrez have been characterized as "the inevitable reaction from the dogmas and oppression of papistry." But Latin-American people cannot hastily materialize their ideals without serious injury to their social state, and since the great majority of the people belong to the Catholic faith, the excessive zeal of the reformers caused the Conservatives to rush once more to the defense of religion. The Conservatives gained control of the government in 1905, but their triumph was short-lived, for the anti-clerical forces were too strong. Ex-president Alfaro emerged from retirement, and in defense of "democracy and liberal principles of government," not to mention "constitutionality," ousted the Conservative incumbent and seized the reins of government—as "Supreme Dictator."[36]

In 1906 Alfaro proclaimed a new constitution. This instrument, which has only recently (1929) been set aside to make way for another, contained no article referring to the religion of the State, but guaranteed "liberty of conscience in all its aspects and manifestations, provided these be not contrary to morality and public order." By this act, therefore, Church and State were separated in Ecuador. But this separation was not absolute by any means. If it were there would have been no need of a Department of Worship with a cabinet minister at the head to administer the ecclesiastical patronage as defined in the law of 1899.

President Alfaro was desirous of freeing public education from the control of the clergy, and thus is found the following article inserted in the Constitution of 1906: "Education is free from any restrictions except those designated in the laws; but public edu-

[35] *Ibid.*
[36] Enock, *op. cit.,* pp. 85-86.

cation and that borne by municipalities shall be essentially secular and laical. Primary education and education in the arts and trades shall be free, and, in addition, the former is obligatory without prejudice to the rights of parents to give their children whatsoever kind of education they may deem advisable. Neither the State nor the municipalities shall subsidize or aid in any way whatsoever, other educational institutions that are not official or municipal."[37]

The most recent of Ecuador's numerous fundamental charters was promulgated on March 26, 1929. This instrument provides for no marked alteration in the political status of the Catholic Church other than in the field of education. As in the Constitution of 1906, the State recognizes no official religion, but grants freedom of worship to all. Members of the episcopate must be citizens of Ecuador. Civil marriage is obligatory.[38] Since the Constitution of 1906 did not prevent the Church from maintaining an educational system, it took full advantage of this liberty. By 1927 there were numerous primary schools in Ecuador conducted by the Church (estimated at fifteen per cent of the number of public schools) and supported by tuition fees. These schools, it is true, had to conform their courses to the terms of the law of public instruction. In the field of secondary education, the Church enjoyed a near-monopoly. Secondary education was almost entirely in the hands of the religious orders who conducted the *colégios*. There were no Protestant schools in Ecuador.[39] Consequently, because of the hold the Church had regained over education, it was proposed by the Liberals in the Constituent Congress of 1929 that elementary and secondary education be taken out of the hands of the Catholic Church. During the discussion a demonstration took place in the galleries in which many women of the best families of Quito took a part crying, "Long live religion and down with the infidels." In the present Constitution, liberty of instruction is guaranteed, and free from restrictions, but public instruction is required to be secular and laical.[40]

---

[37] *Constitution of the Republic of Ecuador, December 23, 1906* (MS), Article 16.

[38] *Constitución Política de la República del Ecuador* (Quito, 1929).

[39] H. D. Clum to J. L. Mecham.

[40] *Current History*, April, 1929, p. 147; Article 51 of the Constitution.

As the new constitutional law on education will indicate, the Catholic Church in Ecuador is being subjected to a renewed and even more bitter attack. An old law passed by Alfaro in 1906 prohibiting the entry of foreign priests, has recently been resurrected and is being enforced with vigor. President Ayora, in 1927, issued the following decree: (1) In conformity with Article 5 of the Law of Cults, the immigration, individually or collectively, of foreign religious of whatever communion, order, or existing religious congregation is prohibited; (2) the Minister of Interior is authorized to permit, in exceptional cases, the entry of foreign religious to the territory of the republic only for a period not to exceed forty days.[41] The government of President Ayora was energetic in preventing foreign priests from entering the Republic, particularly by way of the Colombian border. The recent anti-clerical legislation and activities in Ecuador are thought to be due to the discovery of clerical plots against the State.

The failure of the Constitution to mention Catholicism as the State religion is not to be taken to mean that there is an absolute separation of Church and State. The government is inextricably involved in ecclesiastical relationships because of its nationalization of Church properties. Title to Church buildings, schools, dwellings, etc., is vested in the State, and they are turned over to the Catholic Church and its ministers for use. We have here, then, government property entrusted, under the most favorable conditions, to the use of a sect. Is this not a species of State favor and support? The religious orders once owned large estates amounting to about $20,000,000 in value. These have been taken by the government, leased to the highest bidders, and, in partial compensation, the members of the orders have been given an income by the government. This income is provided in the annual government estimates. Is this not, in reality, support of the cult by the State? The actual status of the Catholic Church in Ecuador is that of dependence on and control by the State.[42]

Furthermore, the Constitution to the contrary notwithstanding, it is impossible to concede that religious toleration exists *in fact*

---

[41] *La Prensa* (New York), September 25, 1927; *South American Handbook* (1931), p. 338.

[42] H. D. Clum to J. L. Mecham.

in Ecuador. For witness recent attacks on Protestant missionaries by fanatical Indians encouraged by their priests ;[43] and the public indignation aroused by the recent anti-Catholic lectures of Seño-rita de Sarraga, which resulted in her expulsion from the country.[44] Amongst this Indian population the influence of the Roman Catholic religion is paramount, and the idealistic proclamations emanating from Quito are idle, profitless, verbiage. The majority of the people of Ecuador are ignorant and superstitious, and are forcibly impressed by the outward forms of Christianity as preached by the Catholic priesthood. Particularly are they fearful of the penalties which they are taught to expect for direct disobedience to priestly injunctions.

The present Liberal government of Ecuador is making the great, cardinal mistake of preceding administrations, Conservative as well as Liberal, i.e., the prosecution of an extreme or radical policy to illogical limits and absolute refusal to compromise or temporize. The inevitable result will be reaction. There seems to be no end to Ecuador's religious troubles.

[43] *La Prensa* (New York), April 27, 1928.
[44] *Current History*, March, 1930, p. 1207.

CHAPTER VII

THE STATE-CHURCH OF PERU

That the Catholic Church is the State ecclesiastical establishment of Peru admits of no question, for, indeed, the system of interdependence of State and Church is one of the most comprehensive and absolute in Latin America. Furthermore, this ecclesiastical policy has been maintained with little or no change throughout the years. The relations between the government of Peru and the Roman Catholic Church have been both intimate and friendly from independence to the present time. Despite the fact that the Peruvian colonial background (political, economic, and ethnical) was very similar to that of Mexico, it is remarkable that the histories of the Church in the two countries have been so different. In contrast with Mexico's turbulent religious history, relations between Peru and the Vatican, once established in 1835, when the first republican archbishop was appointed, have never been interrupted and a formal *modus vivendi* amounting practically to a concordat has been established between the two authorities; the Peruvian governments have been almost uniformly friendly to the Church; the Church has never been a serious political issue, and, finally, no anti-clerical campaign in Peru has gained much headway. Since some explanation for this remarkable contrast might be found in the religious history of Peru, there is additional justification for undertaking a careful survey of the political fortunes of the Catholic Church in that country.

In Peru, as in other parts of colonial Spanish America, there existed a perfect coöperation between the religious hierarchy and the political autocracy. Since, with the exception of the abortive revolt in Cuzco in 1814, Peru was untouched by the wars for independence until invaded by the armies of San Martín and Bolívar, this alliance continued without impairment until 1821. The Church of Peru as an organized body, indeed, remained loyal to the Spanish cause as long as there was any hope of its success. The

13

hierarchy, while it existed, worked energetically for the old régime, and consequently many of the bishops were forced to abandon their sees in the face of the oncoming patriot armies. Although Archbishop Las Heras of Lima remained at his post after the advent of San Martín and even signed the declaration of independence, he and the Bishop of Huamanga were expelled from the country because of their opposition to the provisional government's action in limiting the freedom which the Church had previously enjoyed.[1]

The severance of Spanish control and the interruption of papal relations contributed to the dismemberment of the hierarchy, and consequently the lower clergy were left very much to their own devices. Most of the clerics, being natives of Peru, and often mestizos, were favorable towards independence, and the absence of hierarchial restraint afforded them an opportunity of which they were prompt to take advantage. Conspicuous among the pro-independence clerics was Luna Pizarro, a native of Arequipa and occupant of high positions in educational institutions and in the cathedral of Lima. A disciple of Bishop Chávez de la Rosa of Arequipa (1789-1815), who was a teacher of political liberalism, Luna Pizarro was strongly imbued with the philosophy of the French Revolution.[2]

On February 12, 1821, General San Martín, shortly after his invasion of Peru, issued a *reglamento provisional*, based on his authority as "Protector" of the country. In this provisional instrument he declared that the right of national patronage was assumed by the independent government of Peru. Later, when the Protector occupied Lima, he issued an *estatuto provisional* for the governance of Peru until a permanent constitution should be adopted. The first section related to the Roman Catholic Church:

The Apostolic Roman Catholic religion is the religion of the State; the government recognizes as one of its first duties that of maintaining and conserving it by all the means that are within the bounds of human prudence. Whoever attacks its doctrines and principles,

---

[1] Pérez Armendaris, Bishop of Cuzco (1809-1819), openly favored the revolutionary movement of 1814 in his diocese. (Francis Merriman Stanger, "Church and State in Peru," in *The Hispanic American Historical Review*, November, 1927, p. 420.)   [2] *Ibid.*

either in public or in private, shall be severely punished in proportion to the scandal he may have caused.

Others who profess the Christian religion but who dissent in some principles from the religion of the State, may obtain permission from the government, with the consent of the Council of State, to make use of the right which may be theirs, provided their conduct is not prejudicial to public order.

No one may hold public office who does not profess the religion of the State.[3]

San Martín, a sincere and ardent communicant of the Catholic faith, favored, as the above article indicates, the Catholic Church as the State religious establishment. But he was not religiously uncompromising, as is evidenced by the fact that he was willing to concede a limited degree of religious freedom. Also, when he learned that certain religious houses supported the royalist régime, he did not hesitate to suppress them, nor to expel the archbishop himself for expressions of opposition.[4] San Martín displayed, during his brief dictatorship in Peru, a pronounced regalistic attitude with respect to the relative positions of Church and State.

In further evidence of San Martín's tolerance, he invited to Peru James Thomson, a Scottish Baptist minister, to undertake the direction of public instruction in the republic. Thomson had done good work setting up the Lancastrian school system in Argentina and Chile, and, in recognition of his services in the latter country he was conferred by special act the status of citizen. It is interesting to note that Thomson was enthusiastically supported in his educational work, and even in the distribution of the Bible, by Catholic priests. The lower clergy of Peru during this period were remarkably liberal and tolerant. In commenting on this tolerance, Thomson wrote several years later, after his departure from Peru, "The writer has traveled during some ten years over a great part of the new states of South America and Mexico, distributing Holy Scriptures in them in the freest and most open fashion without interruption or molestation."[5]

[3] *Ibid.*, p. 421; Juan F. Olivo, *Constituciones del Peru, 1821-1919* (Lima, 1922), p. 15.

[4] Moses, *Background of Revolution in South America*, p. 81.

[5] W. E. Browning, John Ritchie, and K. G. Grubb, *The West Coast Republics of South America* (London, 1930), p. 77.

When, as a result of his famous interview with Simón Bolívar in Guayaquil, San Martín became convinced that no effective co-operation with the latter was possible, he decided to lay down his authority and withdraw from Peru. Accordingly, he convoked the first Peruvian Congress in Lima, and on September 20, 1822, surrendered his power as Protector into its hands. This assemblage of fifty-one delegates was composed of some twenty clerics, including the presiding officer Luna Pizarro. But, remarkably enough, the clerical members were the most liberal group in the Congress.[6]

The Congress proceeded actively to the formulation of a constitution, and in the course of its discussions was confronted with the problem of the legal status of religion in the State. At first it was proposed, and the proposal was supported by most of the clerical delegates, that the constitution should contain the simple clause: "The religion of the nation is the Roman Catholic." This, it was hoped, would leave the way open for religious liberty. Peru, however, was not ready for such a progressive step, for, although the proposal was approved by the Congress, on the following day (November 30, 1822), due to the presentation of a petition signed by a great number of the leading citizens of Lima, there was added to the clause: "with the exclusion of any other."[7] Thus, in the Constitution of 1823 even the qualified toleration granted by the Protector came to an end.

The Constitution of 1823 did not conform with Bolívar's plan for the government of Peru, and although that charter was not legally supplanted until December 9, 1826, it nevertheless was practically a dead letter from the beginning. The Liberator was not able to secure the acceptance of his *constitución vitalicia* until December, 1826, but in the meantime he ruled without constitutional restraint as the "Supreme Political Chief of the Peruvian Nation." During this period he was responsible for administrative regulations and reforms affecting the Church. With the acquiescence of the ecclesiastical authorities he reduced the number

---

[6] Stanger, *op. cit.*, p. 421; P. Pruvonena, *Memorias y Documentos Para la Historia de la Independencia del Peru* (Paris, 1858), p. 115.

[7] Guillermo U. Olaechea, *La Constitución del Peru* (Lima, 1922), p. xxiii; Olivo, *op. cit.*, pp. 27-70.

of convents and dedicated their buildings and income to public use, particularly for hospitals and orphanages. He also designated quotas for the rich convents to pay for the support of the new charitable institutions. The Liberator displayed a particular solicitude for the poverty-stricken Indians, and their onerous payments to the clergy were substantially reduced. To prevent further abuse he fixed a tariff of fees for religious services. He also secured a reduction in the number of religious holidays.[8]

The regular orders seemed to be the particular object of Bolívar's attention since he suspected them of royalist sympathies. Several monasteries were suppressed, and their properties confiscated and devoted to public education and charity. In the future all regulars were to submit to diocesan authority. Eight was established as the minimum number of inmates of a monastery, and minors were prohibited from taking the vows.[9]

The filling of ecclesiastical vacancies and the resumption of relations with Rome were other ecclesiastical problems attacked by the Liberator. By 1826 Bishop José Sebastián Goyeneche of Arequipa was the only bishop in Peru. Indeed, for a period, he was the only bishop from Ecuador to the Straits of Magellan. Since for several years he was the sole authority for the ordination of priests, he was called "The Spiritual Father of America." Bolívar attempted to solve the problem of filling vacancies in the prelacies by electing men who were ostensibly presented to the pope for consecration, but who, since there was no hope of securing papal institution, entered upon their official duties as bishops-elect. This plan was so strenuously opposed by the clergy that it was applied for only a short time. Bolívar was always hopeful that relations between Peru and the Roman Curia could be established and a concordat concluded. Accordingly, when giving instructions to the *Consejo de Gobierno*, preceding his departure for Bolivia, he advised that the diplomatic mission then

---

[8] Daniel F. O'Leary, *Bolívar y la Emancipación de Sud-América* (Madrid, 1915), II, 419.

[9] Stanger, *op. cit.*, p. 423; "Bolívar al Exmo. Señor Presidente del Consejo de Gobierno, D. J. Hipólito Unanué, Cuzco, 22 de julio de 1825," in *Cartas del Libertador*, V, 42.

being sent to Europe be also authorized to negotiate with the Holy See. However, no Peruvian agents ever reached Rome.[10]

The reforms of the Liberator in the ecclesiastical domain did not necessarily manifest an anti-clerical attitude on his part any more than did the reform measures of San Martín. Bolívar was a firm believer in the efficacy of the Church as an aid to the political arm. He was a practical statesman and recognized the Church as a factor to be reckoned with. Accordingly, in his *constitución vitalicia* of 1826, which he proposed for Peru, Catholicism was made the religion of the State, but with no restrictions on other religions. He provided elaborate clauses for the control of the patronage by the national government.

Intense clerical opposition was aroused because of the reforms introduced by the Liberator in ecclesiastical matters. In the pulpit and in the confessional the policy of the government was branded as impious. Then the enemies of independence took advantage of the clerical discontent to intrigue for the royalist cause. In Arequipa, a hot-bed of royalism, the royalist party was headed by Bishop Goyeneche. Since he refused to heed Bolívar's entreaties to desist in his opposition, most of his authority was taken from him, although he was not removed from office. The dean of the cathedral, Dr. Córdoba, was authorized by the government to govern the diocese. This interference on the part of the civil authorities in making ecclesiastical appointments served to accentuate the opposition and Bolívar even lost the support of the National Liberal Party with Luna Pizarro at its head.[11] For religious and political reasons, the *constitución vitalicia* of Bolívar, containing the most liberal provisions on religion to appear in any Peruvian constitution until 1915, was put aside immediately after the retirement of the Liberator from Peru.

The third constitution of Peru (1828), framed after the withdrawal of Bolívar, contained the following article on religion: "The religion of the State is the Apostolic Roman Catholic; the

---

[10] Stanger, *op. cit.*, p. 424; Lcluilu, *La elección Diplomática* n, 112; Sallusti, *Misiones Apostólicas,* p. 402; José Sánchez Carrión al Illmo. Señor don Juan Muzi, Cuartel General en Huanuco, 13 de julio de 1824," in *Cartas del Libertador,* IV, 114.

[11] O'Leary, *op. cit.,* II, 543.

nation protects it by all the means in keeping with the spirit of the Gospel, and will not permit the exercise of any other religion." It is to be observed that the prohibition is extended to the exercise of any dissident cult without distinguishing between public or private ceremonies. The same extreme intolerance was preserved in the next of Peru's numerous constitutions, that of 1834. But in 1839 the severity was lessened by limiting the prohibition to the public exercise of any other cult. This was carried over into the charters of 1856 and 1860, notwithstanding the efforts of President Castilla and the so-called "Liberals" to induce Congress to amend the constitution to allow religious liberty.[12]

In the meantime, that is, in June, 1835, formal religious relations were established with Rome when the pope instituted the first republican archbishop of Peru. In phrasing the bulls of institution, however, the Holy Father carefully avoided both political recognition and the right of national presentation, although the government's nominees were accepted for preconization. These bulls of institution were given the *pase*, but the government attached to them legalizing formulas protesting against any phrasing of the document which failed to recognize the right of national patronage. President Echenique, being hopeful that a concordat would straighten out the difficulties with the Vatican, decided to send to Rome an envoy extraordinary on special mission. Accordingly, in 1853, Dr. Bartolomé Herrera went to Rome with particular instructions on the following two propositions: first, "It is clearly established that the President of the Republic will continue to exercise the patronage like the kings of Spain were accustomed to exercise it. He will not consent, consequently, that the Holy See should reserve any benefice or ecclesiastical dignity"; second, "Bishops-elect can govern their churches before receiving the bulls of institution, and only require presentation and official charge to the chapters of the vacant sees."[13] The mission failed, and, until 1874, papal communications which continued

---

[12] R. M. Taurel, *De La Liberté Religieuse au Pérou* (Paris, 1851), p. 1. The Constitution gave to the Congress the sole right of initiating constitutional amendments; Olivo, *op. cit.*, pp. 149-188.

[13] Chacaltana, *Patronato Nacional Argentino*, p. 103; Stanger, *op. cit.*, p. 426.

to be couched in the same objectionable terms, were accorded the *pase* with the customary reservations.

Although failing to establish religious toleration, Castilla and the Liberals were more successful in their efforts to abolish the *fueros* and the tithes. The former exempted clerics from the jurisdiction of the regular courts, and made the clergy a separate and privileged class, something which was thought incompatible with democracy. The Liberals hoped that this reform would not only terminate the privileged position of the clericals, but would also terminate their influence in politics. Therefore, although the ecclesiastical courts were brought under the jurisdiction of the judicial branch of the civil government in 1852, the *fueros* were abolished outright in the Constitution of 1856, an instrument dictated by the Liberals. The tithes were abolished, and, in 1859, it was provided that the archbishop, bishops, dignitaries, and canons in the service of cathedrals should be paid from the national treasury. Conciliar seminaries, colleges, and hospitals were to be given aid by the government sufficient to make up the deficit caused by the abolition of the tithes.[14] Other more drastic anti-clerical reforms were contemplated by the Liberals, but their program was frustrated by the opposition of the clergy and the Conservatives. In 1860 the latter party came into power and proceeded to amend the constitution to suit its needs. This Conservative, revised edition is known as the Constitution of 1860, and it enjoyed the very long life, for Peruvian constitutions, of sixty years.

The Constitution of 1860 provided not only for the State profession and support of the Catholic religion, but it also contained numerous provisions respecting the exercise of the patronage and the maintenance of relations with the Holy See.[15] With few changes the religious articles of 1860 were incorporated into the present organic law of 1920. Although Article 4 of the former charter declared: "The Nation professes the Roman Catholic Apostolic religion; the State protects it and does not permit the *public* exercise of any other," and although the penal code (March 1, 1863) imposed a penalty of one year's imprisonment upon

---

[14] Villarán, *Const. Peruana*, p. 86.

[15] For the Constitution of 1860, see Rodríguez, *American Constitutions*, II, 254-277.

anyone who publicly celebrated any cult other than the Catholic,[16] there was little interference with personal religious beliefs, and Protestants were even allowed to maintain their own churches. For example, in Bellavista there was attached to a Protestant cemetery, a chapel under the charge of a minister. In Lima there was an Evangelical church which was attended in an official capacity by the Minister of Foreign Relations when a funeral service was celebrated in 1911 in memory of Edward VII.[17] Nevertheless there occurred in 1890 an incident which illustrated how precarious was the position of Evangelical missionaries in Peru. In that year a certain Francisco G. Penzotti, agent of the American Bible Society, was arrested in Callao charged with violating the fourth article of the Constitution. A sensational trial followed, for the clergy were determined to secure a decision favorable to their interpretation of the Constitution. The judges of the lower courts sought evasion and the case finally came to the Supreme Court which handed down a decision favorable to Penzotti. This was regarded by the Protestants as a great victory for religious liberty. At any rate it removed apprehension and missionary enterprise was stimulated. In the next decade as many missionaries visited Peru as during the preceding three-quarters of a century.[18] After the Penzotti case there were some instances of missionaries being impeded in their work, but these were isolated cases.

An English traveler wrote of Peru in 1910: "Under no Latin-American government is there greater freedom for, and license to, alien religions than in Peru. This is the more remarkable since Peruvians still maintain the most complete adhesion to Rome and in spite of the wholly aggressive manner in which certain Protestant missionaries have come to the country to stir up revolt and rebellion among the poor and ignorant Indians against the teaching and influence of the Church."[19]

It is doubtful if the prohibitory clause in the Constitution

---

[16] Eduardo García Calderón, ed., *Constitución, Códigos, y Leyes del Peru* (Lima, 1923), Art. 100, p. 501. Mr. Stanger (*op. cit.*, p. 434) evidently overlooked the Penal Code when he declared, "No law had ever defined offenses or established penalties."

[17] Pedro Dávalos y Lissón, *La Primera Centuria* (Lima, 1919), I, 199.

[18] *The West Coast Republics*, p. 71.

[19] P. F. Martin, *Peru in the Twentieth Century* (London, 1911), p. 131.

would have been suppressed in 1915 had not the Congress become aroused because of a mob attack on a Protestant mission among the Indians. By constitutional amendment, there was struck out of Article 4 the prohibition of the public exercise of any other religious cult. The passage of the law was strongly resisted by the clergy, and even by the president, who refused to proclaim it after its adoption. Accordingly, in a tumultuous session, during which the galleries were crowded by ardent female supporters of the Church, the Congress proclaimed the law.[20]

The present constitution of Peru (promulgated January 18, 1920) retains the amendment of 1915, i.e., "The Nation professes the Roman Catholic Apostolic religion, and the State protects it" (Article 5). In the constituent congress the Committee on the Constitution recommended an article recognizing liberty of thought and conscience and definitely forbidding religious persecution, but after a prolonged debate there was inserted in the bill of rights: "No one may be persecuted for his ideas or his beliefs."[21] The Constitution thus grants full liberty of conscience and religion. There are no religious tests for exercising the suffrage or holding public office. In Peru, unlike many Latin-American countries, clerics can vote and hold office. But this is subject to the following condition: archbishops, bishops, ecclesiastical governors, capitular vicars, and ecclesiastical judges cannot be elected to the Senate or the Deputies within the departments or provinces of their respective dioceses, and curates for provinces to which their parishes belong (Article 76, No. 4). This same provision was to be found in the Constitution of 1860. Regulars, however, cannot vote or hold office, for their political rights are regarded as being merely suspended and subject to recovery upon leaving the cloister.[22]

The Roman Catholic Church, being the only religious body recognized by law, the civil code contains provisions (Articles 83-94) covering the definition of clergymen and religious, the qualifications necessary for the profession; their exemptions from public services (army and jury); the recovery of civil rights

[20] Dávalos y Lissón, op. cit., I, 199; Stanger, op. cit., p. 434.

[21] Stuart, Governmental System of Peru, p. 23.

[22] Archbishop Emilio Lissón to J. L. Mecham, Lima, December 23, 1927.

of religious upon their being secularized, and the like. For example, a cleric is defined as a person dedicated to the divine cult by virtue of major or minor orders. To enjoy the quality of minor orders it is required that one wear the *corona abierta* (clerical tonsure) and a habit of long robes, that he be appointed by the ordinary to the service of some church, and that he study in some public college or seminary. The regulars are forbidden to live outside of their convents without license from their prelates and knowledge of the civil authorities. Persons of both sexes are prohibited, under pain of nullity, from taking religious oaths before arriving at the age of twenty-five years. The *Reglamento de Regulares*, approved by Congressional Resolution of January 12, 1872, governs the religious orders today.[23]

As is to be expected in the case of a country having a State-Church, the crimes against the established religion and its ministers are carefully enumerated in the penal code and heavy penalties are attached. Until 1915 anyone publicly celebrating a non-Catholic cult was subject to a maximum imprisonment of one year. But, as has been noted above, even before 1915 this law was a dead letter, as was also Article 99 of the penal code which read: "An attempt to abolish or change the Roman Catholic religion in Peru will be punished with expatriation of one to three years." More enforceable are the following penalties: profanation of the Eucharist, imprisonment up to three years; obstruction of religious ceremony, imprisonment up to two years; abuse of a priest in a church or public place while officiating, imprisonment up to one year; public blasphemy of God, jail, 14 to 18 days; public blasphemy of the Virgin, saints and dogmas, jail, 8 to 12 days; and, irreverent acts in churches, jail, 2 to 6 days.[24]

Since 1856, when the ecclesiastical *fueros* were abolished, the clergy have enjoyed no special exemption in legal trials; they are tried in public courts, civil or criminal, as the case may be. According to the organic law of the judiciary, the Supreme Court may take original cognizance of cases brought against archbishops and bishops. Therefore, the practice in Peru, as in Argen-

---

[23] García Calderón, *Constitución, Códigos y Leyes*, p. 37.

[24] *Ibid.*, p. 501 (Art. 100), p. 543 (Arts. 101-106).

tina under the Constitution of 1819, is that archbishops and bishops are subject to the jurisdiction of the ordinary courts for common crimes but when delinquent in the exercise of their episcopal functions, they are judged by the Supreme Court.[25]

There is no law in Peru enforcing the observance of holy days, although in Lima a particular ordinance requires stores to be closed on Sundays and holy days. Processions and other public acts of worship may be held without interference on the part of the government.

The efforts of various chief executives of Peru beginning with Bolívar, to secure apostolic recognition of national patronage through the negotiation of a concordat have been noted. The Constitution of 1860, like its predecessors, called for a concordat in the following terms: "In order that there might be established on a solid basis the existing relations of Church and State, and in order that obstacles might be removed that opposed the exact fulfillment of Article 6 regarding the ecclesiastical *fuero*, there should be concluded, in as short a time as possible, a concordat." Consequently the president was given the power of entering into concordats subject to the approval of the Congress.[26]

Although Pius IX refused to confirm Peru's radical pretentions to national patronage in a formal concordat, he was finally induced, in 1874, to grant by papal brief, the right of patronage, but without the concessions and obligations usually contained in a concordat. This bull, which has established a *modus vivendi* still effective today, was as follows:

Pius—Servant of the servants of God:
Among the notable favors which God in his boundless mercy has heaped on the Peruvian nation, the gift of the true Catholic religion, which the Peruvians have wisely cherished exactly as it was announced by the preachers of the Gospel, outshines all others. They have so wisely cultivated it that they have become heroes whom the Church judges worthy of being honored on the altars. This becomes for the said nation a real glory, since it also has never faltered in its duty to support the faith after Peru separated itself from the control of the Catholic kings of Spain. It was declared, in fact, in a solemn

---

[25] Stuart, *op. cit.*, p. 86; Chacaltana, *op. cit.*, pp. 69-70.
[26] Articles 94, No. 18; 59, No. 16; 134.

manner in the Constitution of the Republic, that Peru professes the Catholic religion which it protects, and does not permit the public exercise of other cults.

This solicitude in maintaining Catholic unity has been responsible for other acts of a similar nature by the public authority. Such are: grants to existing dioceses or to newly created ones have been increased or liberally established; subsidies have been granted to the seminaries established for the propagation of the faith; with equal munificence provision has been made for the dissemination of the holy doctrine, that is, parishes have been founded in towns of those who have been converted to the faith; and, finally, considerable money has been expended to embellish or repair churches, to build new ones, and to favor or promote the splendor of the religious cult.

All these things which were known to us, we have been reminded of and told again by our very loved son and illustrious person Pedro Gálvez, delegate of the Republic of Peru near this Apostolic See, for the purpose of obtaining from us a public and solemn testimony of the merits acquired by the said republic respecting the Catholic Church.

For this reason, being desirous of satisfying the wishes which the government of Peru has expressed to us by its representative, and following in this an example of our predecessors who desired to heap favors and grace upon those who have merited well of the Christian cause:

We have resolved, after having sought the advice of some cardinals of the Roman Church, to concede, as we in fact do concede by our apostolic authority, to the president of the Republic of Peru and to his successor *pro tempore,* the enjoyment, in the territory of the republic, of the right of patronage, such as was enjoyed by grace of the Apostolic See, by the Catholic kings of Spain before Peru was separated from their authority.

Nevertheless we impose as a condition and rule upon the concession of this privilege, that the property actually assigned to the clergy by act of gift, as well as to the sacred ministry and to the exercise of the cult in the dioceses of the territory of the Republic, will be preserved integrally and distributed with diligence and fidelity; and also, we impose as a condition that the government of Peru shall continue favoring and protecting the Catholic religion.

In observing these laws and conditions, the president of the Republic of Peru and his successors, will have the right when vacancies occur in the archiepiscopal and episcopal sees to present to the Apostolic See worthy and proper ecclesiastics, in order that canonical institution shall take place according to the rules prescribed by the Church. The presentation of candidates, however, ought to be made, excepting when legitimately prevented, within one year of the time when the vacancy occurs. The candidates, thus presented, will not exercise any right, with respect to episcopal administration, before they have obtained the apostolic letters of institution. . . .

The president of the Republic will also have the right of presenting to the bishop worthy persons to be promoted to the dignities and canoncies *de gratia* . . . also, to present worthy persons for the collation of prebends of cathedral churches . . . if the vacancy has been declared by the ecclesiastical authority.

The said president will also enjoy the right of presentation to canoncies *de oficio* and to parishes, always observing the canonical form of *concurso y del examen;* in exercising this examination the president will elect an ecclesiastic from among the three suggested (the best qualified having been presented to him), to the end that the said ecclesiastic will receive immediately canonical institution from the bishop.

Finally, the presidents of the Republic will enjoy in the churches of Peru the honors that were once enjoyed by the kings of Spain by virtue of the right of patronage conceded by the Holy See.

We desire, order, and establish all these things. . . .

Given in Rome, near St. Peters (March 3, 1874).[27]

Since the terms of the bull were regarded as being incompatible with the prerogatives of national sovereignty, the government of Peru refused to accept it. It was not until Nicolás de Pierola became president, or rather dictator, that the exequatur was granted on January 27, 1880.[28] Since that date the bull has operated as a *modus vivendi* in the place of a concordat, which evidently the Peruvian government is still hopeful of concluding for the Constitution of 1920 delegates to the president power "to enter into concordats with the Holy See in conformity with instructions given by Congress" (Article 121). Peru's responsibility for the failure of repeated attempts to negotiate a concordat has been analyzed as follows: "So long as radical religious reform was unthinkable in Peru, the national control of the patronage was, from the liberal point of view, the most important thing to be guarded. The anti-clerical party was strong enough to secure this control without the giving of any special privilege to the Church, other

---

[27] Olaechea, *op. cit.,* pp. 253-257.

[28] *Ibid.,* pp. 257-258; Chacaltana, *op. cit.,* p. 102.

than the financial support it had always received."[29]

Somewhat in conformity with the papal grant, but not necessarily as a consequence of the same, the present and immediately preceding constitutions of Peru provide that the president may exercise the patronage in accordance with the laws and existing practices. The Congress, moreover, is empowered to make regulations necessary for the exercise of the right of patronage. In the civil code *patronato* is defined as the right of presenting some person for a benefice and of watching over its property. It is national and private. National patronage is exercised by the supreme government. The duties, attributes, and perquisites that appertain to national patronage are determined by special laws.[30] In agreement with the bull of 1874, and conforming to law, in the election of archbishops and bishops the president nominated twice as many as were to be chosen and presented this list to the Congress. The Congress, in joint session, thereupon elected, and the president presented the names of those elected to the pope for his approval. In the same way the president nominated the various dignitaries of the Church chosen by the bishops. In 1926 the Constitution was amended to allow archbishops and bishops to be appointed directly by the Vatican instead of by Congress.[31]

Although the law requires that the president "approve or disapprove conciliar decrees and pontifical bulls, briefs, and rescripts with the consent of Congress, and in contentious matters only after having first been heard by the Supreme Court of Justice," the old *regalia* of the *pase* has fallen into disuse and it is only preserved in the institution of bishops and the demarcation of dioceses. The clergy are accustomed to communicate freely with the Vatican, provided this is done through the archiepiscopal chancellery, notwithstanding that the civil code provides: "To obtain from the Roman Pontiff dispensations, indults, and other favors, it is necessary to appeal to the Supreme Government which will grant authorization and give the proper direction. The indults,

---

[29] Stanger, *op. cit.*, p. 427; *West Coast Republics*, p. 95.

[30] García Calderón, *Constitución, Códigos y Leyes*, p. 149.

[31] *Current History*, October, 1926, p. 125; Stuart *op. cit.*, p. 47.

dispensations, and favors which are consigned in any other way shall not be issued."[32]

As has been noted, Pope Pius IX was induced to recognize the right of patronage in Peru because of the fine Catholic spirit manifested there in supporting the Church. Furthermore, the term of the bull was conditioned on the continuance of financial support. We find therefore, that the government makes an annual appropriation for the salaries of certain dignitaries of the Church. When the tithes were suppressed in 1859, the nation made itself responsible to the Church for the amount the tithes had produced. Consequently, from 1859 to the present date, the general budget has carried annual appropriations for the salaries of the archbishop and bishops.[33] The budget for 1928 contained an appropriation of Lp. 25,250 ($101,000) for the Church. The lesser clergy are paid from fees and contributions, supplemented by income from Church property. There are no subventions by the State. The tariff of parochial fees is approved by the government.

The chief sources of ecclesiastical income, aside from governmental contributions and fees, are income from Church property and gifts. The Catholic Church in colonial Peru, as in New Spain, because of the munificence of the crown, the pious grants of individuals, and the industry of the clergy, reinforced by the principle of mortmain, was by all odds the greatest property holder and the wealthiest institution in the colony. The wealth and economic influence of the Church suffered slight impairment even after the winning of independence. This was true notwithstanding an effort made in 1828 to abolish vinculation of property as well as the giving of it into mortmain.[34] Since the law was not made retroactive, the numerous pious foundations dating from distant colonial times remained untouched.

The Church today has the right of possession of its properties and juridic personality to litigate before the courts with respect to them. There is no legal restriction on its ability to receive bequests, but, until 1901, it was prohibited from receiving inherit-

[32] García Calderón, *Constitución, Códigos y Leyes*, p. 37.

[33] Archbishop Lissón to J. L. Mecham.

[34] This law was incorporated in the civil code, Article 1194. (García Calderón, *Const., Códigos y Leyes*, p. 148.)

ances and real estate. The object of this was to prevent more *property*
property falling into mortmain. But on September 30, 1901, the
law of free-disposition, so-called, was passed, which removed the
prohibition on the Church and religious orders of the right of
disposing of their property without the consent of the government. Since the passage of this law the Church may freely acquire
property, although the provisions of the civil code which relate
to the inheriting of real estate have not been annulled. Thus the
Church in Peru, as a juridic person, can acquire and possess property of all kinds, as well as contract obligations and exercise civil
actions according to the statutes of the country. Churches and
all places of worship are exempt from taxation, but all revenue-
yielding property of the Church pays the same imposts as private
property. It is remarkable that, notwithstanding the vast ecclesiastical holdings in urban and rural real estate, this condition
has not been a matter of popular concern. Unlike Mexico and
other Latin-American countries, Peru has experienced no serious
movement towards wholesale confiscation.[35]

As is to be expected in a country where the Catholic religion
is the favored cult, it enjoys certain privileges in the realm of
education. Although the Church has no authority whatever over *Educ*
public instruction, nevertheless, according to the *Reglamento
General de Instrucción,* it is not only permitted, but is required,
to give instruction in the Catholic faith in the public schools of
primary and intermediate grades. With respect to the general
program of instruction, which applies not only to State schools,
but to private schools as well, the Church has no authority. Ecclesiastics, male and female, are allowed to instruct in non-religious
subjects in the public schools if they have the qualifications.[36]

A limited number of private institutions, mostly of the elementary grade, are maintained by religious orders. They bear
an approximate ratio of one to ten to the public schools. Church
schools, as noted above, are controlled by an official program of
instruction which is common to private and State schools without
any distinction whatever. The Catholic schools receive no subven-

---

[35] Archbishop Lissón to J. L. Mecham; Stanger, *op. cit.,* p. 437.

[36] Archbishop Lissón to J. L. Mecham; For a brief description of the educational system, see *West Coast Republics,* p. 70.

14

tions from the State, but are supported by fees of the students. There are about one hundred Protestant schools in Peru. There are two in Lima and two in Callao. The remainder, of primary grade, are generally for mestizos and Indians in the back country.[37] A distinguished Catholic Peruvian author is unstinting in his praise of the work of Protestant missionaries. He says, "It is remarkable the way the missionaries work in the sierras. Their efforts are interesting whether viewed from the moral or civic side. They direct their activities to correct the immoral customs of the Indians, and what is more useful, they fight alcoholism, the terrible scourge of the indigenous population; a vice which up to now has been tolerated by the curates in all the religious festivals."[38] In June, 1929, a severe blow was delivered the non-Catholic schools in Peru. On that date the Government issued a decree which prohibited the teaching of non-Catholic faiths in schools, public and private. It required that even in Protestant schools, the Roman Catholic teaching should be the only religious instruction given. Thus, education is more fully dominated by the clergy now than at any period since the general government school system was set up. Yet, the Archbishop was dissatisfied with the decree. He would have all schools, not subject to the government and Church control, closed.[39]

Since matrimony is one of the sacraments of the Catholic Church and is regarded as a peculiar subject for regulation, it was natural that its ecclesiastical monopoly should have been sanctioned by law. This, moreover, was merely confirmation of a practice which had been established during centuries of Spanish rule. The civil code prescribes that "marriages in the republic shall be celebrated with the formalities established by the Church in the Council of Trent." The ecclesiastical ceremony is sufficient and legal and needs only to be registered in the civil register of the district governor within eight days. According to a law enacted in 1921, the priest, under penalty of imprisonment, must demand of the contracting parties a civil certificate before per-

---

[37] *Ibid.*, George A. Makinson, American Consul in Charge, to J. L. Mecham, Callao-Lima, January 13, 1928.

[38] Dávalos y Lissón, *op. cit.*, I, 205-206.

[39] *West Coast Republics*, p. 95.

forming the marriage ceremony. The State requires a small clerk's fee for registration. The charges of the Church are determined by the parochial tariff, and fluctuates between two and three *libras*. There is a well-established custom that the officiating priest must be given thirteen pieces of silver or other coin.[40]

The prohibition of marriages outside of the Church, even of non-Catholics, was implied from the constitutional proscription of the public exercise of dissident faiths. Because of the great hardships and manifest injustice of this law upon non-Catholics, there was long agitation for its amendment. Finally civil marriage of non-Catholics was legalized in 1897, when a storm of public protest was aroused because a North American couple were denied legalization of their union. The refusal, or inability, of the president to come to the relief of the Americans, resulted in congressional action. The law of December 23, 1897, relieves persons not of the Catholic religion, from the Church ceremony. They must appear, however, before a judicial court in order that it may be shown that they are entitled to be married under the provisions of the civil code. The ceremony is performed by the alcalde of the provincial council in the district where they are domiciled. Those to whom the Church denies license because of the difference in cults must also conform to this procedure. The clericals strongly resisted the passage of this statute, as they did the toleration law of 1915, and, in this instance likewise, the Congress passed the law over the objections of a reluctant Chief Executive.[41]

The laws of the Church on the indissolubility of the marriage bonds have been given civil sanction. Thus, the civil code recites: "Matrimony legally contracted is indissoluble; it is terminated only by the death of one of the contracting parties"; and, "The ecclesiastical tribunals will hear causes relative to matrimony and divorce, and the secular judges will hear cases of betrothal, support, care of children, *litis expensas*, liquidation and devolu-

---

[40] García Calderón, *Const. Códigos y Leyes*, p. 43; Samuel Guy Inman, *South America Today* (New York, 1921), pp. 71-72; George A. Makinson to J. L. Mecham.

[41] Stanger, *op. cit.*, p. 434; García Calderón, *Const., Códigos y Leyes*, pp. 41-42.

tion of property, crimes concerning adultery, and, in general, all causes concerning the civil effects of matrimony and divorce."[42] It is to be noted that ecclesiastical divorce does not mean the same as legal divorce in America; in Peru it means separation of the persons *manenti vinculo*, that is, it is equivalent to legal separation in this country. Divorce which allows remarriage is never permitted by the Catholic Church; there can only be remarriage after the death of one of the parties, or annulment of the union. Thus, in Peru, legal separation is granted after a hearing in the ecclesiastical tribunal; and, after the verdict, the parties proceed to the civil tribunal for the division of their properties and the liquidation of their conjugal society. Marriage can only be nullified through the regular ecclesiastical procedure, if by reason of canonical disabilities, and by the ordinary courts of justice, if on account of civil impediments.[43]

Another practice in Peru which was sanctioned by centuries of experience under Spanish rule, was the delegation to the Church of control of cemeteries. "The idea that the place and circumstance of burial have directly to do with the happiness of the deceased in the next world has furnished one of the clergy's most effective means of control over the people, by the granting or refusal of interment in ground consecrated by the Church."[44] The clerical control was maintained until 1869 when municipal councils were instructed to provide and maintain lay cemeteries for the burial of non-Catholics. The adoption of these laws was based in a very limited tolerance and also in sanitary considerations because of the religious prejudice against the proper burial of "heretics." Since 1869 there has been further liberalization of practice with the result that the old clerical control of burials has been broken. Although Catholic cemeteries are kept separate from others, they are all under the supervision of benevolent societies which are under the direction of the Bureau of Charities in the Department of Justice, Education, Religion, and Charity. Where there are no benevolent societies, the municipalities control the cemeteries. In small communities, however, the parish priests often administer them, and it rarely occurs that Protestants en-

---

[42] *Ibid.*, p. 41.   [43] Archbishop Lissón to J. L. Mecham.
[44] Stanger, *op. cit.*, p. 432.

counter difficulty in obtaining burial permits. "The infrequency of such instances," says a recent writer, "is due as much to the small number of Protestants as to the development of religious tolerance."[45]

The Section of Worship, in the Department of Justice, Instruction, Worship, and Charity, has charge of matters of patronage relating to the archdiocese of Lima, the dioceses of Trujillo, Chachapayas, Ayacucho, Cuzco, Arequipa, Puno, Heránuco, Hurarez, Cajamarca, the vicarship of Madre de Diós, and the various missions and hospitals controlled by the Church. "Such is the discretion with which our prelates govern the Peruvian Church," says a Peruvian historian, "and so rare the conflicts the *patronato nacional* causes them, that there is almost nothing which the Ministers of Justice have to say of the Church in the annual *memorias* to Congress. There are in these *memorias* twenty-four pages devoted to instruction, as many more to justice, half to charity, and scarcely one or two to the section of the cult."[46] By law of 1857 the prefects of the departments were given supervisory powers over ecclesiastical affairs connected with patronage. They are in the nature of vice-patrons. Peru maintains an embassy at the Vatican, and the pope in turn has accredited to Lima a papal nuncio who is the dean of the diplomatic corps.[47]

The passage of the toleration act of 1915 was followed by increased Protestant missionary activity in Peru. In the decade 1915-1925, 159 missionaries went to Peru to work for the propagation of Protestantism. This was a larger number than had gone to the Land of the Incas in all the preceding hundred years. In 1928 the total number of Protestant missionaries, with their native helpers, totaled 339 or one to 18,133 inhabitants. At the same time there were in Peru 2,595 Roman Catholic clerics, or one to 2,369 inhabitants. Of the Protestants, the Seventh Day Adventists are generally conceded to be doing the best work. But there is no gainsaying the fact that Protestantism has made little headway in Peru.[48]

---

[45] *Ibid.,* p. 433.

[46] Dávalos y Lissón, I, 202. The same is true of the *Memorias* of other countries where there is a union of Church and State.

[47] G. A. Mackinson to J. L. Mecham.   [48] *West Coast Republics,* p. 97.

A more far-reaching and significant result of the passage of the Act of 1915 was the reaction on Catholicism itself. Contrary to the predictions of dire disaster made by clerics in opposing the passage of the bill, it marks the beginning of a real revival of the Catholic Church in Peru. The act served to awaken the hierarchy to a realization that the Church had no real hold on the heart of the people. This awakening led to numerous measures of reform. There was a general tightening up on the part of the Church of the control of the government departments where the religous and educational interests were affected. A Catholic University was founded in Lima in 1917 "to conserve the continuity of education given in the elementary and high schools, and to train up a body of one hundred per cent Catholics." Another significant reform measure was the order of the Archbishop of Lima that ten-minute sermons in the vernacular should be delivered at all Sunday masses. A significant result of the new revival has been that more men are attracted to the Church.[49]

In Peru there is a strong tradition of clerical interference in political matters. This proclivity, which is by no means peculiar to Peru among Latin-American countries, is the result of the practice of the Spanish kings to delegate political duties to the members of the clergy. The crown was accustomed, because of the comprehensive nature of the patronage, to make use of the Church for administrative purposes in the purely civil and political realm. Cases in point were the entrusting of the civil register to the Church, and the proclamation by the clergy of governmental edicts and the counseling of obedience to same. Also, the constant use of ecclesiastics, generally of high rank, in political and administrative positions tended to emphasize the community of interests of the two orders, the civil and ecclesiastical. These practices, or prerogatives, became deeply imbedded in the clerical inner consciousness and their extirpation could not be expected immediately after the winning of independence. The counseling of parishioners as to how they should vote, and the influencing of legislation and governmental offices, are regarded as legitimate and necessary activities on the part of the clergy. The Church

---

[49] *West Coast Republics,* pp. 71-72; *Christian Work in South America,* The Montevideo Congress, 1925 (New York, 1925), I, 263.

in Peru, therefore, is still accustomed to make use of its organization and discipline to apply pressure when and where it chooses,
and it usually works through individuals in strategic positions.

The influence of the Roman Catholic Church in Peru is widespread, and its power is felt in both public and private life. Politically it occupies a stronger position today than it has for several
years past. A well-organized and disciplined institution, the Church
has been recognized by the dictators of Peru as necessary to stable
government. It is significant that the chief executive was unwilling to promulgate the anti-clerical laws passed by Congress
in 1897 and 1915. President Leguía, a strong conservative, and
dictator for many years, bestowed signal favors on the Church,
and a few years ago he modified, in the interests of clerical education, the original draft of the law of public instruction.[50] Yet,
on the other hand, it is a notable fact, that had it not been for
executive evasion of the laws, non-Catholic missionary enterprises
could not have been carried on in Peru.

Clerical domination is, to no small degree, the result of its by
no means negligible control of education. The exclusive privilege
of giving religious instruction in public schools virtually assigns
the youth of the land to be cast in the Catholic mould. A reverence
for the Church and its dogmas, profound respect for its ministers,
and a dread of disobeying its authority, are cardinal aims of
this ecclesiastical instruction. If these aims are attained, and no
one can say that the Church has failed, then the political position
of the cult is given greater security. The medium of education
as a bulwark of Catholic control is effectively reinforced by its
privileged position in other matters, notably those affecting and
regulating the private lives of individuals, such as matrimony.

In regard to domestic life the dominating influence of clerical
authority is most marked. The Catholic women of Peru, as of
other parts of South America, are most ardent, almost fanatical,
supporters of the faith, and subservient followers of clerical instructions and advice. As witness, for example, female demonstrations when the Toleration Act of 1915 was passed by Congress.
While the men are not so imbued with marked religious inclination,
they dread disobeying the authority of the Church. Among the

---

[50] Inman, *op. cit.*, p. 72.

uneducated Indians of the sierras and coastal region, the priest-hood is regarded with superstitious awe and fear. The uncivilized savages of the great Amazonian river valleys pay little attention to priests or creed.[51]

Although the Peruvian Church is menacingly strong politically, and exercises a dominant control over domestic life, it is charged with failure in the performance of its divine mission to inculcate real spirituality among its communicants. Pedro Dávalos y Lissón writes, "Those of us who were born under Divine favor and who still feel warmth in our hearts for the beauties and sweetness of religion, see with deep concern the way that this spiritual world is disappearing."[52] In the cities, says another recognized authority, indifference is extreme; there "religion is a parlor tradition."[53] An Augustinian friar, quoted by Inman, said that there was no such thing in Peru as a truly spiritual life or conviction—the apparent devotion to the Church was nothing more than a mixture of tradition and social convenience.

"The sacred word in the pulpit," says Dávalos y Lissón, "al-though it reaped regular fruit in the missions and in the *ferias de cuaresma*, in general did not move the hearts to contrition. The Christian people were content to hear mass and oblige their chil-dren to confess." Furthermore, he points out, in evidence of de-creased spirituality, few people accompanied the procession of *Santísimo* and even fewer those of the saints. Yet the remembrance of the old destructive earthquakes brought numerous participants to the procession of Señor de los Milagros. Needless to remark, the continued observance of this custom is based in superstition and not piety. In the provinces the cult continues in the same state as in the colonial régime. On the part of the Indians there is the same ignorance, the same superstition. There are numerous cases of "miracles" and consequent patron saints in the sierras where ignorance and fanaticism are common. But, in Lima there are no saints.[54]

The failure of the Catholic Church in Peru to prevent religious

[51] Akers, *op. cit.*, p. 538; G. A. Mackinson to J. L. Mecham.

[52] Inman, *op. cit.*, p. 70.

[53] Francisco García Calderón, *Le Pérou Contemporain* (Paris, 1907), p. 182.

[54] Dávalos y Lissón, I, 202-205.

indifference and to inculcate a spiritual appreciation can be attributed in no small degree to the very unsatisfactory caliber of clerical personnel. Since the modern Church is lacking in the prestige which it enjoyed in the past, it no longer attracts to the priesthood and regular orders the sons of aristocratic Catholic families or even those of modest and middle circumstances. The clerical career, instead of being looked up to with awe and reverence, is scorned today with slighting remarks. The students of the seminaries come from the sierras, from the least desirable physical and social stock. Few faces of distinguished aspect can be seen when the *seminaristas* of Peru are on review. Thus, whereas in prior times the persons of both sexes in the convents and monasteries mounted into the thousands, now in Peru very few wish to serve God in the priesthood. So few are the qualified for the higher ecclesiastical positions that the government often has difficulty in presenting a full *terna* to the Congress for the election of a bishop. Because of the serious scarcity of priests it has been necessary to provide curacies and chaplaincies with foreign priests —mostly Spanish. And although these foreigners were almost always sent with guarantees of rectitude and culture, too many of them sought only to enrich themselves.[55]

The bishops cannot be held to too strict responsibility for the curates, careless of instruction in the catechism and lacking in abnegation and the necessary dedication to social and moral reform. Their hands are tied. The scarcity of priests makes discipline impossible. Certainly removal from office could not be used as a disciplinary measure, for the bishops feel that non-administration of the sacraments would be an even greater evil. Of course the exceptions among the curates are numerous; there are many men who labor and perform good work in the face of many difficulties, but these are in the minority.

The deficient qualities of the clergy must inevitably result in an increasing lack of respect. Although it is true that the clerics still maintain, thanks to the force of a centuries-old custom, a strong hold upon the people, there are evidences appearing of a decreasing respect and influence—as witness a statement by Dávalos

---

[55] *Ibid.,* I, 199-201.

y Lissón: "The attacks which the faithful make on their priests are continual. The loss of a sacred object, the removal of a picture from the church, or the removal from the sacristy of some saint that had a preferred place on the altar, causes violent outbreak on the part of believers, which cause the priests to hide themselves or seek the protection of the civil authorities. Certainly the faith that our country people have in their priests' honor is not very great, since they attack them and treat them like church-robbers, whenever anything disappears from the church."[56]

The separation of Church and State although freely predicted has not been popular in Peru. Indeed, it has not been officially proposed except by the student federation. Yet, there is a definite anti-clerical movement which aims at disestablishment. These modern anti-clericals are not to be confused with the Liberals who were responsible for such religious reform as abolition of *fueros* and tithes, legalization of civil marriage, and religious toleration. The Liberals of the earlier years were nominally Catholics, who protested their loyalty to the Church while they fought its control in politics. The antagonists of the Peruvian Church today are not even nominal Catholics. They are frankly, even boastingly, irreligious; they see no need for either Church or religion.[57] There appears to be small likelihood, if the religious history of Peru, Mexico, and other Latin-American countries means anything, that iconoclastic and skeptical arguments will accomplish a separation of Church and State. The separation will come peacefully and automatically when the State and the Church become convinced that they are both prepared for it and their individual interests will be best served thereby. A hastening of disestablishment and the adoption of drastic and coercive measures could result only in violence and a generally unsatisfactory situation. This has been the cause of Mexico's religious travail. In Peru, on the other hand, all the justifiable reasons for religious reform such as have obtained in Mexico have existed for years.

---

[56] *Ibid.*, I, 203.

[57] The "master" of the skeptical Peruvian youths of today is Manuel González Prada (1848-1918). It is said that the influence of this famous iconoclast in shaping the religious philosophy of Peruvian youths has been greater than that of any other person. (Stanger, *op. cit.*, p. 433.)

Why then the different current of her religious history? An answer to this question must be an expression of opinion, and that of the writer is that Peru has been lacking in the necessary intellectual leadership. The country has not produced the leaders necessary to construct a really honest liberal régime.

CHAPTER VIII

THE ESTABLISHED CULT IN THE MID-CONTINENTAL REPUBLICS OF BOLIVIA AND PARAGUAY

I

BOLIVIA

Alto Peru, Bolivia today, did not break away from Spanish authority until August 6, 1825, following the liberation of Peru at the battle of Ayacucho. Prior to the definitive establishment of her independence, Bolivia, after an ineffective creole revolt in Chuquisaca and La Paz in 1809, was continuously under Spanish control, notwithstanding determined efforts of the patriots of La Plata to liberate the province. An effective force in prolonging the rule of Spain in the Audiencia of Charcas was the Roman Catholic hierarchy which was unswerving in its loyalty. Archbishop Moxó of Chuquisaca and Bishop La Santa of La Paz lent invaluable support to José Goyeneche, the royalist commander, in suppressing separatist and liberal tendencies within the province, and in preventing their introduction from La Plata. Bishop La Santa, in addition to fulminating excommunications, even organized armies against the patriots. Since the population of Alto Peru was nearly ninety per cent Indian, ignorant and superstitiously attached to the Roman Catholic Church, the influence of the Church in the cause of Spain was incalculable. Not all the clergy, however, were affiliated with the Spanish cause, for the leader of the uprising in La Paz was José Medina, a curate. And a guerrilla leader who harassed the loyalists for several years was Muñecas, also a cleric. Furthermore, the unwelcome (although needed) reform measures instituted by Archbishop Moxó, a strict disciplinarian, caused many curates to league against him, and this league served to aid the cause of independence.[1]

---

[1] Alcides Arguedas, *Historia General de Bolivia* (La Paz, 1922), pp. 5-6; José María Camacho, *Compendio de la Historia de Bolivia* (La Paz, 1927), pp. 126-128, 159-160.

There was nothing in the history of Bolivia, either before or during the wars for independence, to indicate religious dissent or desire for a change in the political status of the Catholic Church. The disposition of the subject of religion in the model constitution submitted by the Liberator to the republic which bore his name was, therefore at variance with the popular demands of the new state. At the beginning of 1826, the Liberator sent to Bolivia from Lima his project of a constitution. Bolívar recognized the Church as a factor to be reckoned with, and provided in his constitution for the national control of the ecclesiastical patronage. Thus, to the Senate he delegated power (1) to make *reglamentos eclesiásticos;* (2) to propose in triple lists (*en terna*) to the Chamber of Censors names of those to be presented for archbishops, bishops, dignitaries, canons, and prebends of cathedrals; (3) to make rules for the exercise of the patronage and issue laws on all ecclesiastical subjects which had any relation to the government; and (4) to examine and approve or disapprove conciliar decrees, bulls, briefs, and pontifical rescripts. To the president he gave the power to present to the ecclesiastical government one of the candidates proposed on triple lists by the electoral body for curates or vicars in the provinces. Bolívar carefully avoided any mention, however, in his list of constitutional guarantees or elsewhere in his constitution, of religion, either as to proscription or as to privilege.[2]

In explaining his omission of an article on religion, the Liberator, in a statement to the Bolivian Assembly which accompanied the proposed constitution, said:

"I will mention one article which my conscience has forced me to omit. In a political constitution no religion should be prescribed, because, according to the best doctrines on fundamental laws, these are the guarantees of political and civil rights, and, as religion does not pertain to either of these rights, it is of an indefinable nature in the social order and belongs to the moral and intellectual. Religion governs man in his home, in his office, within himself; it alone has the right to examine his intimate conscience. Laws, on the contrary, look on the surface of things; they do not

---

[2] *Proyecto de Constitución para la República de Bolivia y Discurso del Libertador* (Buenos Aires, 1826), pp. 12-13, 15, 21.

govern except outside the house of the citizen. Applying these considerations, can a State govern the consciences of its subjects, watch over the fulfilment of religious laws, and reward or punish, when the tribunals are in Heaven and when God is the judge? The Inquisition alone would be capable of replacing such courts in this world. Shall the Inquisition return with its fiery torches? Religion is the law of the conscience. All law over it annuls it, for by imposing necessity for duty, there is destroyed the merit of faith which is the basis of religion. The sacred precepts and dogmas are useful, luminous, and of metaphysical evidence; all of us ought to profess them, but this is a moral and not a political duty."[3]

Notwithstanding the eloquent plea of the Liberator for religious toleration and the separation of Church and State, the Bolivian Constituent Assembly added to the constitution the following article: "The Roman Catholic Apostolic religion is the religion of the Republic to the exclusion of all other public cults. The government protects it and insures it respect, recognizing the principle that there is no human power over conscience." The final contradictory statement in the article was evidently the result of a desire on the part of the framers of the constitution to appease Bolívar. At the same time a more compelling force, a desire to satisfy Bolivians and recognize their religious demands, was responsible for the constitutional law of exclusion. Considering the religious background of Bolivia, the break suggested by Bolívar was too precipitous and unwarranted. The Assembly also stipulated in the new constitution that the president must profess the religion of the republic. But the provisions suggested by Bolívar regarding the national control of patronage were left untouched.[4]

The wisdom of the framers of the Constitution of 1826 in providing for a civil-ecclesiastical relationship conformable to the actual demands and limited attainments of the overwhelming majority of the population has been justified by the subsequent history of the cult in Bolivia. The privileged position enjoyed by the Catholic Church has caused very little dissatisfaction of any

---

[3] *Ibid.*, pp. 14-15.

[4] Jenaro Sanjinés, *Las Constituciones de Bolivia* (La Paz, 1906), pp. 2, 13-15, 41, 74.

consequence.[5] Indeed, it has never constituted a problem, and today, after a hundred years of trial, the political status of the Catholic Church is very much what it was in 1826.

In Bolivia's numerous constitutions, which succeeded one another with bewildering rapidity until 1880, when the one in force today was promulgated, the articles relating to the Roman Catholic religion have, with only a few exceptions, been very slightly changed. In 1871 the article prohibiting the public exercise of non-Catholic cults was amended to read "except in the colonies where it is tolerated." The object of the exception was to attract foreign immigration which might be restrained because of the prohibition of the exercise of other cults.[6] In 1905 the same article was amended again to permit the public exercise, throughout the republic, of all cults. Thus religious toleration, legally at least, was not introduced into Bolivia until a recent date. The act of 1905 is called "the Magna Charta of the missions in Bolivia," for few or no Protestant missions existed in Bolivia prior to the enactment of the law.[7]

Not only are liberty of conscience and religious toleration guaranteed, but practically all religious tests for the exercise of political rights have been abolished. There are no restrictions on the exercise of the suffrage, and no religious tests for holding public office, excepting the requisite of taking the oath of office on the Holy Gospels and before a cross. No longer, for example, is it stipulated that the president of the republic must be a Roman Catholic. Although it is true that the law of municipal organization prevents clerics from holding office in the councils, the national constitution does not disqualify an ecclesiastic from being named a senator or deputy if he has the qualifications.[8] As a consequence

---

[5] "Bolivia has been less influenced by religious discussion than other countries [in Latin America]." (Chacaltana, *Patronato Nacional Argentino*, p. 104.)

[6] Sanjinés, *op. cit.*, pp. 19-31.

[7] *The West Coast Republics*, p. 126.

[8] Ley Orgánica de Municipalidades (La Paz, 1915), Article 9; *Bolivia, Constitución Política del Estado y Reglamentos de Debates del Senado y de la Cámara de Diputados* (La Paz, 1926), Article 45; Mgr. Francisco Pierini, Archbishop of La Plata—Sucre, to J. L. Mecham, Sucre, November 17, 1927.

of the constitutional status of the Roman Catholic Church as
the State-Church of Bolivia, that cult enjoys special protection
in the national penal code. Under the subject of Crimes Against
the Religion of the State we find that "All who conspire directly
to establish another religion in Bolivia, or to cause the Republic
to cease professing the Roman Catholic Apostolic religion, are
traitors and will suffer the penalty of death." Severe penalties
are prescribed for blasphemy and acts of desecration.[9]

The president of the republic, through the Ministry of Foreign
Relations and Cult, administers ecclesiastical affairs in so far as
they have been assumed by the government. The contemporary constitution of Bolivia lists among the powers of the president: (1)
exercise of the right of patronage in the churches and over ecclesiastical persons and benefices; (2) nomination of archbishops and
bishops, selecting them from among the names submitted—three
for each place—by the Senate; (3) appointment of canons, prebendaries, and other Church dignitaries, selecting the names from
those suggested by the cathedral chapters; and (4) the grant
or refusal, with the advice of the Senate, of acceptance of the
decrees of councils, or the briefs, bulls, and rescripts of the supreme pontiff (Article 89). Because of these provisions, the system which exists in Bolivia, says a Bolivian prelate, is that of
national patronage, but it is exercised mildly on the part of the
government.[10] For example, in practice the exequatur is only
required on bulls of institution of residential prelates. With respect to all the remaining papal documents full liberty of entry
is accorded. Communication between the Bolivian hierarchy and
the papacy is free and unhampered. Bolivia and the Vatican exchange diplomatic representatives; since 1917 the Holy See has
sent an apostolic nuncio to La Paz. In spite of the fact that the
Bolivian government has not had the stimulus to defend the patronage as have other countries, yet it has been given the same interpretation. In an effort to have the State's interpretation accepted by
the pope, General Santa Cruz was sent to Rome to conclude a

---

[9] Federico Alarcón (ed.), *Código Penal Boliviano* (La Paz, 1902), pp.
38-39.

[10] Mgr. Augusto Sieffert, Bishop of La Paz, to J. L. Mecham, La Paz,
December 29, 1927.

concordat. On May 29, 1851, the Bolivian delegate and the Cardinal-Secretary of State signed an agreement designed to serve as a norm for the relations of Church and State in Bolivia. In this pact the pontiff conceded to the president of Bolivia the patronage or privilege of presenting for any vacancy in archiepiscopal or episcopal churches or for ecclesiastical dignities. The president was also conceded the right to nominate six prebends for each chapter. The pope also agreed that personal causes of ecclesiastics in civil matters should be referred to lay tribunals. All criminal causes, of course, were to be strictly reserved for the ecclesiastical tribunals. Because the pope "arrogantly conceded" patronage, instead of recognizing its inherency in national sovereignty, the Bolivian Congress refused to approve the concordat.[11]

Three times during the history of Bolivia negotiations have been initiated to arrange a concordat with the Vatican, but with no result. "The reason for failure," says Archbishop Pierini of Sucre, "is that the Constitution of Bolivia attributes by itself, to the nation, the right of patronage which can only be conceded by virtue of a concordat."[12] In Bolivia, as in several other Latin-American countries where concordats have not been concluded, the pope has never recognized *patronato nacional*, but tolerates it. A sort of working agreement exists between the Republic and the Vatican, with the latter accepting, but not recognizing the validity of the national pretentions. Thus, "the Church is living," says Bishop Sieffert, "with more or less liberty according to *la manía* [whim] of each government."[13]

According to the Constitution, the State "recognizes and supports" the Catholic religion; also, "real estate belonging to the Church, and property belonging to charitable, educational, and municipal establishments or religious corporations, shall enjoy the same guarantees as are granted to property of private individuals." These suggest an inquiry into the nature of the financial support of the Church, and the legal status and extent of its properties.

The principal sources of ecclesiastical income are donations,

[11] Chacaltana, *op. cit.*, p. 104; *West Coast Republics*, p. 122.

[12] Archbishop Pierini to J. L. Mecham.

[13] Bishop Sieffert to J. L. Mecham.

collections, fees, income from properties held, and governmental subsidy. The chief means of support, says Archbishop Pierini, is the charity of the faithful. This is expressed principally in the regular collections and occasional gifts and endowments both in money and in property. There are no legal restrictions in Bolivia on the right of the Church to receive entailments. The money received from fees is not inconsiderable, and constitutes the chief means of support of those lesser ecclesiastics who do not enjoy a salary paid by the government. In each diocese there is a published tariff of rates called an *arancel,* in which is listed the amounts the faithful ought to pay for the performance of various religious services. For example, in the *Arancel Eclesiástico* for the diocese of La Paz, it is stipulated that the fee for baptisms *de primera,* that is, at the altar and with candles, music, and bells, shall be six *bolivianos;* baptisms *de segunda,* that is, minus the accessories, shall be, for whites, one *boliviano,* and for Indians, one-half *boliviano.*[14] The fees for performing a simple marriage ceremony in church or at home ranges from twelve and fifteen *bolivianos* for Indians and mestizos, to twenty-five for whites. A *matrimonio pomposo,* which includes decorating the Church, costs fifty *bolivianos.* Burial fees are quoted at one to twenty *bolivianos* for infants, and fourteen to thirty-five for adults; the inclusion or omission of items like vigil, mass, and singing accounts for the different rates. The fees for a great variety of special masses range from three *bolivianos* for the most simple mass (*misa rezada sencilla*) to 150 *bolivianos* for an elaborate *misa gregoriana.* In the *arancel* it is stipulated that priests perform services gratuitously for the poor; by way of illustration, the priests are ordered to give the poor free and decent funerals and burials without cost. They are ordered not to make changes in the rates and to keep a careful record of all fees received.[15]

It is impossible to ascertain the extent of real property belonging to the Church in addition to the buildings actually used for religious purposes, but undoubtedly it is quite large. The income from the revenue producing properties which, incidentally, are not

[14] *Arancel Eclesiástico de la Diócesis de La Paz* (La Paz, 1927), pp. 15-16. The *boliviano* is ordinarily worth $0.389 in U. S. currency.

[15] *Ibid.,* pp. 3, 5, 11-15, 25-26.

tax exempt and enjoy no advantage over private property, is an important item in the support of the Church. By law of July 17, 1880, all ecclesiastical buildings belonging to both the secular and regular clergy are exempt from the property tax. Yet in practice this law has not saved the Church from the payment of various municipal imposts. It has legal title and possession of its properties, under the administration of the bishop. He names as his agents the curates of the parishes, whose bookkeeping he audits each year. The regular establishments have their own administrators named by the bishop. To alienate ecclesiastical property it is necessary to secure permission from the *Patronato Nacional*, that is the government.[16]

Finally, the State contributes a small sum for the support of the Church. When the tithes and primacies were supplanted by a land tax in 1880, the Republic recognized the obligation of paying from the rural land tax a subsidy for the support of the cult. For many years the national budget provided for the appropriation of this money, and every year a competence was paid to parish priests. Today, however, these payments have been stricken from the budget, and only prelates and chapters of cathedral churches are made an assignment, some from the national and some from the departmental budgets. Because of this curtailment in the national budget, the ecclesiastical appropriation fell from $76,815 in 1905 to $45,000 in 1926, and $37,000 in 1929. From the small sum which the government now appropriates, the salaries of bishops are paid, and an assignment made to the cathedrals for the expenses of the cult. In 1920 (figures for a later date were not available) there were in Bolivia 570 secular clergy and 510 regulars living in 17 conventual establishments. The national episcopacy consisted of the metropolitan see of La Plata and the episcopal sees of La Paz, Cochabamba, and Santa Cruz.[17]

The law does not recognize any authority of the Church over the public schools, although religious instruction outside of regular hours is permitted. There is no legal prohibition, but very few of the public schools have ecclesiastics on their staffs. It was stipulated by law of February 6, 1900 (Article 3), that "all

[16] Bishop Sieffert to J. L. Mecham.

[17] *Ibid.*, Archbishop Pierini to J. L. Mecham; *West Coast Republics*, p. 122.

establishments of instruction of whatever grade, official, free, civil, or ecclesiastical, special or general, scientific schools as well as disciplinary and economic, are subject to the laws and decrees of the legislative and executive powers." Article 4 adds, "The seminaries will continue under the immediate direction of the diocese, as long as those establishments are confined exclusively to the preparation for the faculty of theology and of no other."[18] Thus, instead of there being ecclesiastical control of public education, there is governmental supervision over Catholic schools. The Ministry of Education exercises supervision over courses, degrees, and hours of study, and prescribes regulations governing all these matters.

In Bolivia, the public schools of primary grade far outnumber the Church schools, because instruction up to the *cursos facultados* is free. In 1926 there were 82,165 pupils in the primary schools and 17,209 in the private institutions. Of the last number, only 3,801 were in religious schools.[19] To illustrate the woefully inadequate governmental support of education, in the 1929 national budget approximately $1,500,000 was appropriated for education and $3,500,000 for military purposes. For the past ten years only 9 per cent of the total budget has been devoted to public education. It is not surprising therefore that the percentage of illiteracy in the nation is estimated to be in excess of eighty-five.[20]

The Catholic schools must be supported by fees and donations, although on occasion the government pays them a small subvention. In the secondary educational field the Church schools are more numerous and are preferred for their superior excellence. Several schools and colleges for young men are conducted by the Jesuits, Franciscans, and Christian Brothers. Most of those for girls are maintained by the Christian Sisters and Daughters of Santa Ana. In Sucre, La Paz, and Cochabamba, there are diocesan seminaries. To the credit of the Catholic prelates in Bolivia, they have recently (1926) called attention to the government's neglect of the problem of Indian education. Of an estimated pop-

---

[18] *Ibid.*

[19] *West Coast Republics,* pp. 120-121; *Christian Work in South America,* I, 243-244.

[20] Margaret A. Marsh, *The Bankers in Bolivia* (New York, 1928), p. 29.

ulation of 2,500,000, 1,000,000 are Indians and practically the total number is to be classified as illiterate. In the interest of the greatly abused and downtrodden Indian the Church has launched a "Pro-Indio Crusade." Remarkably enough, liberal elements like the Student Federation have attacked the crusade because of their anti-clericalism and fear of a general Indian uprising.[21]

The Protestants in Bolivia have confined their educational efforts almost entirely to missionary schools for the Indians. In La Paz and Cochabamba there are Methodist colleges called *El Instituto Americano*. They are supposed to be of a purely educational and non-sectarian nature, but have been accused of engaging in Protestant propaganda. The Protestant schools in Bolivia are very few, says Archbishop Pierini, "because, happily, Protestantism among us, as a religion, is an exotic plant, and this despite the fact that for some years the emissaries of Protestantism have made supreme efforts to establish a foot-hold in this country."[22]

In Bolivia, as in other Latin-American countries, the ancient exclusive control of the Church over the institution of matrimony has been broken. Prior to 1911 the law sanctioned and recognized as binding and exclusive, the formalities regulating matrimony as ruled by the Council of Trent. However, on October 11, 1911, a new law was enacted by the Bolivian Congress to the following effect: "The law only recognizes the civil marriage, after which there can be performed the canonical or religious ceremony, but it will not satisfy the legal requirements of the civil ceremony." In 1920 an exception was made in favor of the Indians, allowing them to fulfil the requirements of civil matrimony by celebrating the canonical. This law was deemed advisable because of the fanatical attachment of the ignorant Indians to the priests, and their inability to regard anything other than the religious ceremony as being binding. In an effort to curb the numerous illegal unions among the Indians, therefore, the civil law was amended as noted. Thus today, the marriage of whites and *cholos* must be civil, and that of Indians may be religious. As has been noted

---

[21] Marsh, *op. cit.*, pp. 28-29; *Christian Work in South America*, I, 126-127.

[22] *Ibid.*; For an account of the feeble efforts of Protestantism in Bolivia, see *West Coast Republics*, pp. 125-136.

above the Church charges for the performance of the marriage ceremony from twelve to twenty-five *bolivianos*. The sum of the various civil fees for the ceremony equals twenty *bolivianos*.[23]

Bolivian law does not recognize absolute divorce permitting remarriage. It only recognizes separation of bodies and goods. All questions arising between husband and wife can be decided only by the ecclesiastical tribunals. In 1926 a law was introduced in the Congress to legalize absolute divorce and to allow remarriage. Public opinion was strongly opposed to the measure, and it was defeated.[24]

Until October 7, 1908, cemeteries in Bolivia were under the direction and government of the ecclesiastics. On that date they were entrusted to municipal authorities and free burials were provided. Outside of La Paz there are no sectarian burial grounds. In commenting on the municipal control of the cemeteries, Bishop Sieffert says, "There has been established the greatest confusion in the administration of the cemeteries, which are perfect images of disorder and lack of care. At the same time there do not exist complete registers of deaths in La Paz."[25]

The contemporary situation of the Catholic Church in Bolivia is a logical consequence of the nature of its membership—the illiterate natives and half-breeds who constitute nearly ninety per cent of the population of the country. Considering its *milieu* the unhealthful condition of Church and religion in the Andean republic is not surprising. The descendants of the Aymaras and Quichuas of Alta Peru are nominally Catholics. They receive the sacrament of baptism; most of them are married by the Church, and they attend all imaginable kinds of ceremonies which occur with an unfortunate rapidity of succession, from an economic and social standpoint. They show outward reverence for Church ritual, but their general ignorance on all subjects beyond their limited domestic life renders it unlikely that they hold any religious convictions. As for precepts of religion and prescriptions of its commandments, they know not a word. There is a great

---

[23] *West Coast Republics*, pp. 126-127.

[24] J. F. McGurk, American Consul, to J. L. Mecham, La Paz, October 6, 1927; Bishop Sieffert to J. L. Mecham.

[25] *Ibid.*

proportion of paganism in their faith, and the Catholic rites are merged in others inherited from the days of the Incas. In commenting on the mixture of primitive and Christian worship which he detected among the Indians of Bolivia, an American scholar says, "The old rites of the Indians are grafted upon a new principle, often with but a change in name and not in symbol. The spirit of the old prayers for abundant rivers and rich harvests breathes through the new devotions, and the quaint melancholy songs of the ancient Quichua or Aymara tribes often follow upon a fiesta in which the rites of the Christian religion are but new form for an old and pathetically simple speech. The rivers and the harvests are the forms in which they understand the Deity. It is hard to teach men new faiths or religious or moral niceties whose first and only prayer has always been for the daily bread fairly wrung from a stubborn earth."[26] "To see and hear the Indians during a religious festival," writes a European visitor in the same vein, "one might well take them for idolators accomplishing the ceremonies of the ancient cult of the sun, followed by a Roman saturnalia, but never for Christians celebrating Easter or the Feast of the Trinity."[27] Another writer says, "The fiestas, which are so prominent in the Indians' life, though ostensibly celebrating a Christian feast or national holiday, are in reality Bacchanalian debauches."[28] Bacchus is frequently mentioned in descriptions of religious festivals. For example, a native reporter writes, "The feast days come, the carnivals, the saints' days. Behind the squalid countenances of all the saints of the calendar, the people worship Bacchus, robust and rotund. Bacchus is the absolute and essential God."[29]

This very ignorance of the Indians strengthens the influence of the clergy, for the priesthood is regarded with awe and is accorded servile obedience. The willingness of the Indians to be exploited has undoubtedly influenced many of the less scrupulous curates to requite the faith and trust of their charges with ex-

[26] Isaiah Bowman, "Regional Population Groups of Atacama," in *Bulletin,* American Geographical Society, XLI, 1909, p. 211.

[27] Paul Walle, *Bolivia* (London, 1914), p. 145.

[28] Marsh, *op. cit.,* p. 31.

[29] *La Patria,* Oruro, July 31, 1919, quoted in *West Coast Republics,* p. 123.

tortionate demands. Serious accusations, exaggerated it is true, but legitimately based, have been brought against the venality and perverted morals of the Bolivian clergy, particularly those curates entrusted with parishes remote from the diocesan capitals. "If an Indian is comfortably off or possesses any property," asserts an unsparing critic, "he is charged double for all religious ceremonies; the burial duty, abolished by law, is still actually paid in the provinces; and is even augmented by 20 to 50 per cent; it is the same with marriages, which are consequently very costly, so that many Indians form free unions, postponing the ceremony until a more propitious occasion."[30] The fees for the performance of the marriage ceremony, as noted above in the *arancel* of the diocese of La Paz are extremely high, and for the Indians often prohibitive. Why the Catholic Church, not only in Bolivia, but in other parts of Latin America, should, through the establishment of impossible fees, actually encourage illicit unions, is a subject impossible of comprehension. In the same connection, it is a cause for wonder that the drunken and immoral orgies that inevitably constitute the aftermath of religious festivals seem to trouble the Bolivian clergy not at all. There seems to be an absolute divorce between religion and morality. The answer perhaps can be found in the ignorance and grossness of the clerics themselves. The rural clergy of Bolivia, like that of Peru, is sadly deficient. Recruited from the half-breeds and Indians, raised amid the most humble surroundings, and given a superficial training, these country priests are impossible moral mentors of their parishioners. In the last twenty years there has been a marked decline in the caliber of candidates for holy orders. The problem confronting the hierarchy in Bolivia is identical with that of Peru—i.e., the difficulty of procuring worthy candidates for service in the Church. Praiseworthy desires of the bishops to replace bad priests are constantly balked by the scarcity of material. The disciplining of delinquents is rendered ineffectual because of this unfortunate situation. Since the moral tone of the existing priesthood is so low, great danger lies ahead for the Catholic Church in Bolivia unless a comprehensive reform is effected in the near future.[31]

---

[30] *Ibid.*, p. 146.   [31] *West Coast Republics,* p. 124.

On at least two occasions the government has undertaken to reform the clergy. Bolivia's first president, the great revolutionary General Antonio José Sucre, observing the relaxation of discipline and the increasing immorality among the clergy, which was even greater in 1826 than in 1808 when Archbishop Moxó attempted his reforms, issued a decree affecting the regular orders. Since there were many convents with as few as two and three inmates, Sucre ordered the abolition and consolidation of numerous religious houses. The property confiscated was applied to public uses, such as schools, colleges, and charitable institutions.[32]

Sucre's reform measures were aimed only at the regular clergy. It was not until 1859 that a more serious situation, the immorality and unsatisfactory training of the secular clergy, was recognized by the government. President José Linares promulgated a decree on November 25, 1859, designed to reform the clergy by striking at the very heart of the problem, that is, inadequate instruction and training in ecclesiastical seminaries. The decree provided that seminaries should be established in the various provinces to give solid instruction to prospective priests.[33] The reforms of Linares were evidently in the right direction, but the present-day prevalence of unsatisfactorily trained curates evidences the need of additional seminary facilities in Bolivia. Whether or not it is the duty of the government to assume this task is a question that we shall not attempt to answer. But, so long as it pretends to be the ecclesiastical patron, it has assumed responsibilities and deficiencies in the ecclesiastical system must be shared by the political authorities.

The strength of the movement which aims at a separation of Church and State in Bolivia does not appear to be great. Certainly there is no historical background, such as one finds in Chile, to warrant the prediction of a separation of Church from State in Bolivia in the near future. It was not until after the War of the Pacific that there was heard for the first time faint murmurs of discontent with the system of a privileged cult. The Conservative and Liberal parties, in the early post-war days, were thor-

---

[32] Vicente Lecuna (ed.), *Documentos Referentes á la Creación de Bolivia* (Caracas, 1924), II, 84-85.

[33] Arguedas, *op. cit.*, p. 190.

oughly revamped, and then for the first time were actually sponsoring distinct and distinctive political principles and policies.
Although the Liberals as a party group took no united stand
on religous questions, the party was accused of being anti-Catholic because free thinkers and others who entertained radical
ideas on religious subjects and policy ordinarily enrolled themselves in the Liberal ranks. The periodicals of the Conservative
party indeed, attacked the Liberals as heretics, and voiced a fear
that Catholicism was menaced by Masonic influence. In an attempt
to refute these charges and defeat the campaign of the Conservative writers the Liberals organized and participated, with candles
in their hands, in religious processions. There is little doubt that
the Liberal party in the decades of the 80's and 90's was a staunch
supporter of the Catholic faith. This was further evidenced by
an incident in 1892. Certain unauthorized elements within the
party were responsible for the publication of what purported
to be the "Program of the Liberal Opposition." In addition to
the non-ecclesiastical planks like universal suffrage, popular election of judges, the jury system, and habeas corpus, the program
pledged separation of Church and State, civil marriage, and
laicization of cemeteries. The party chieftain immediately refuted
the program as being unauthorized and unacceptable to the religious and conservative elements within the Liberal party. He
declared: "The Liberal Party is politically on the most advanced
frontiers of the democratic ideal, but religiously it supports the
belief of our fathers and lives in the beneficent shadow of Catholicism which the Constitution protects."[34]

Since 1892 a campaign, but of no considerable proportions,
has been conducted by the anticlerical elements, the Student Federation and the labor organizations, to force the acceptance of a
constitutional amendment to separate Church and State. In almost
every congressional session such a measure is introduced, and
although it has up to the present date been consistently tabled,
there is no presaging what might be accomplished by a radical
parliamentary *coup d' état*. In the event that separation occurs
within the next decade, it can be fairly asserted that such a change

---

[34] *Ibid.*, pp. 440-441, 499-500.

in religious policy will not represent the will or the needs of the majority of Bolivians.

II

PARAGUAY

The Catholic Church in Paraguay, like the Paraguayans themselves, was the victim of heartless oppression during a large part of the nineteenth century. From the time when the Spanish authority was cast aside in 1811, and the *real patronato*, consequently, was disavowed, until the death of Francisco Solano López in 1870, the Church was in fact not a Roman, but a Paraguayan Catholic Church. Under the dictators Francia and the López, the clergy plumbed the lowest depths of degradation, insult, and servility. The curse of the dictators not only retarded the political and economic development of the republic, but the moral and the spiritual likewise, because of the unnatural channels into which religious endeavor and precepts were forcibly diverted.

Unfortunately the Church itself was indirectly responsible in a small way for the tyrannical rules imposed upon the hapless country. "In the state in which Paraguay was after the revolution," says an American writer of Paraguayan history, "it required neither superior talent nor education to lead the simple people whose ignorance was their inheritance from the Jesuit fathers."[35] The Jesuit plan of training and evangelization resulted, whether they intentionally desired it or not, in keeping the Indians as ignorant as possible of every duty but that of unquestioning, passive obedience.[36] Although the Jesuit control came to an end, in theory, a half century before independence, nevertheless their lessons in complete and abject submission to the clerical will continued to be taught by their successors, the Franciscans. Thus, when the time came for the Paraguayans to assume

---

[35] Charles A. Washburn, *A History of Paraguay* (Boston, 1871), I, 163. Washburn was American Minister to Paraguay during the Paraguayan War. His two volume history of Paraguay, although suffering in balanced judgment according to the modern canons of historical criticism, is nevertheless the best history of the country. His adverse criticism of the Jesuits is too severe and causes one to question his impartiality.

[36] For a sympathetic treatment of the "Jesuit Republic," see R. B. Cunningham Graham, *A Vanished Arcadia* (New York, 1901).

control of their own political destinies, they were the least fit for the task of all the peoples of Spanish America. How natural was it then, that they should bow submissively to the absolute will of a domineering personality.

Dr. José Gaspar Rodríguez Francia, *El Supremo*, seized control of the Paraguayan government soon after its declaration of independence, and for the next thirty years he ruled the inland republic with a despotic fiendishness unparalled in the history of America. Although Christian belief rested lightly upon the conscience of the dictator, he being in reality an infidel notwithstanding the fact that he received a degree of doctor of theology in the University of Córdova; and although he entertained contempt for the gross ignorance and scandalous lives of the lazy and dissolute priests, it was not for these reasons that Francia hated them. It was because the priests exercised great influence over the lower classes, and because a church government with authority independent of the civil power was inconsistent with absolute rule. Since Francia proposed to brook not even a shadow of authority other than his own, the Church, the only institution likely to rival his influence, was forced to bow to his will. To obviate all possibility of danger from that institution, Francia took all its property into his own hands, deprived it of all ceremonials which were wont to impress the populace, caused the priests to become his passive agents by making them report to him, and in the end made himself the head of the Church after the example of Henry VIII of England. When the bishop, because of insults and persecution suffered at the hands of the tyrant, became insane, Francia appointed to the headship of the diocese a creature of his own whom he called a vicar-general. The priests were so persecuted that they scarely ventured to exercise any of their functions except receive death-bed confessions and administer extreme unction. As for confessions, the dictator did not object to people confessing to the priests, but the priests had to confess to him. Naturally all relations with Rome were suspended, for in closing the ports to the ingress of foreigners, Francia made no exception in favor of papal nuncios or agents. However, it was scarcely likely that the

Holy See would countenance the high-handed measures of *El Supremo*.[37]

The treatment of the Church by Francia's successor, Carlos Antonio López, was a slight improvement (it could scarcely have been worse), but still the troubles of the ecclesiastics were not over by any means. In 1844 López gave Paraguay a constitution carefully designed by himself to preserve the supreme authority in his own hands. This constitution contained the customary provisions regarding the nation's right to control the ecclesiastical patronage. For example, the president exercised the patronage of the churches, the livings, and ecclesiastical persons according to the laws; he could name the bishop and the members of the ecclesiastical senate; he could celebrate concordats with the Holy Apostolic See, concede or refuse his approval to the decrees of ecclesiastical councils, and give or deny the exequatur to the pontifical bulls or briefs, without which requisite nobody should enforce them.[38]

In an endeavor to renew relations with the pope, which had been entirely suspended during Francia's time, López made overtures while he was consul, asking for the appointment of a bishop. In accordance with the national pretention to patronage, he recommended for the episcopal office his brother, Basilio López. The nomination was accepted by the pope and thus relations were restored.

Carlos López, however, was the real head of the Paraguayan Church, for Basilio, an eccentric, good-natured individual, thoroughly devoid of ambition or avarice, exercised no authority or power which was not conceded to him by his brother the president. The dictator, like Dr. Francia, had been educated in theology, but in later life was a scoffer at religion, howbeit he observed the outward forms. And although he entertained no greater fondness for the clergy than did *El Supremo*, he found that he could put priests to better use than did Francia. That is, he determined

---

[37] Washburn, *op. cit.*, I, 166-170, 213; W. H. Koebel, *Paraguay* (London, 1917), pp. 174-175.

[38] Washburn, *op. cit.*, I, 467-468.

not to suppress them, but to make them the auxiliaries to his power. He restored parishes throughout the country, and in many cases gave the priests civil authority in addition to their spiritual functions. But, like Francia, he required them to report to him, and the secrets of the confessional all came to his knowledge.[39]

Bishop Basilio López died in 1859, and the pope was requested to appoint another bishop. The Holy Father, however, demanded: first, a restoration of Church property that had been withheld for nearly fifty years, and second, the right of appointing a bishop, not a Paraguayan, who should be responsible to him, and not to the president of the republic. López, naturally, refused to consent to either demand, and resolved, in an extremity, to assume the headship of the Church himself. When the pope threatened to place an interdict over Paraguay, López defended his stand by declaring that divided authority was not compatible with peace and order, and therefore he could not yield. Piux IX finally agreed, in 1860, to invest Bishop Juan Gregorio Urbieta, López' nominee. Bishop Urbieta was an old, infirm, and inoffensive person who never pretended to question the right of the government to render his spiritual functions entirely subordinate to the temporal authority. The actual diocesan administrator was Manuel Antonio Palacios, who was appointed auxiliary bishop in 1862 with the right of succession when a vacancy should occur. Palacios had been recommended by Carlos López at the solicitation of his son Francisco Solano López, presumably because Palacios was an abject, servile flatterer of the dictator's heir apparent.[40]

Francisco Solano López followed the examples of his father and Dr. Francia in refusing to tolerate any authority apart from his own in Paraguay. Since he considered the Church as the most formidable of his potential rivals, he used Bishop Palacios as a willing tool to subordinate the complete ecclesiastical organization to his will. The shameful subservience of the Bishop to the Dictator is reported by a foreign observer, a certain Mr. Thompson: "The Bishop used to go and wait in López' corridor with his hat in his hand. When López came out, the Bishop shuffled up towards him with a deprecating look, and made a deep bow,

---

[39] *Ibid.,* I, 465-467, 477.
[40] *Ibid.,* I, 463; II, 54-55.

to which López would return a nod, without touching his cap."[41]

All the clergy from the Bishop down were converted into an active instrument of espionage, systematized into complete subordination. The greatest service the Bishop and the clergy performed for the tyrant was that of instructing the populace in their duties to a divinely appointed ruler. From the pulpit López was proclaimed as the anointed of the Lord, and it was consequently the duty of the people to devote their lives, labor, and fortunes to him, and to count nothing a sacrifice which he might demand. To question the legitimacy of his acts was both treason and heresy. A catechism, originally prepared by a bishop of Tucumán in 1784, to instruct the people in the principal obligations that the vassal owes to his king and lord as the divinely appointed ruler, was adapted by Palacios, with slight changes, to inspire in the people their proper duty to López.[42]

The responsibility of the Bishop for changing a peace-loving people into fanatically aggressive warriors, is evidenced by a letter which he wrote to López in 1865: "With the desire to excite this spirit (self-abnegation and heroism), and with much success, we are continuing our pastoral labors with all possible care and force, omitting no measure or diligence, using the power and influence of the Holy Religion, whose representation and ministry have been confided to us by God among this chosen portion of the flock of Jesus Christ of our dear country with the end of directing it in the path of justice, good order, and patriotism. It has been with no small difficulty, excellent sir, that we have labored with a people so unwarlike as ours, but happily this difficulty we have now overcome, and made to almost disappear by the words of evangelical truth, and by means of the confessional, in which daily we are engaged confessing hundreds of soldiers, disposing and fortifying them for the struggle and making them to understand with the greatest clearness, that those who give their lives in the combat for their country will be recompensed and eternally rewarded by the Eternal Creator."[43]

Thus, a Catholic prelate was responsible in no small measure

---

[41] Koebel, *op. cit.*, p. 188.

[42] Washburn, *op. cit.*, II, 56.

[43] *Ibid.*, II, 57-58.

for "the tragedy of Paraguay." The decimation of the Paraguayan race, the awful result of blind, fanatical allegiance sworn to an insane ruler, was only made possible because of clerical teaching of religious duty to the "divinely appointed president."

After Paraguay had been liberated by the allied arms from the tyranny of Francisco Solano López, it was necessary to overhaul the government. Unfortunately the tendency of the framers of the new Constitution (promulgated, 1870), was to follow too closely foreign, particularly Argentinian, practices, and accord little attention to the peculiar needs of Paraguay. As one writer states, "If we had to express in a few words the result of a comparison between the two constitutions which Paraguay has had up to now, we would say that the first was too Paraguayan, and the second too Argentinian."[44] Yet, if the Argentinian example was followed in framing the religious clauses of the constitution, regarding which there is no evidence, then, fortunately for Paraguay, the Argentinian policy with respect to the Catholic Church was remakably well adapted to the religious requirements of the Paraguayans. The Constitution of 1870, in fact, involved a very slight departure from the principles theoretically proclaimed and guaranteed in the Constitution or 1844, but it differs from the earlier instrument in that the actual ecclesiastical policy of the government harmonizes with the constitutional requirements.

The Roman Catholic Apostolic religion is declared to be that of the State. Nevertheless toleration is protected in the denial to Congress of the power to forbid the free exercise of any other religion within the territory of the republic, and in the guarantee to all inhabitants of the right of professing freely their cult. And, in order to encourage immigration, of which Paraguay is in great need, the Constitution guarantees to aliens the right to freely profess their religion.[45] This inducement, however, has not attracted Protestants, for the great majority of the few immigrants to Paraguay have been Italians and Argentinians who already professed the Catholic faith. Although Protestant immigration has been negligible, a recent rather notable exception was the Mennonite community. In 1927 the Mennonites abandoned their colony

---

[44] Arosemena, *op. cit.,* I, 291-292.
[45] *Constitution of Paraguay,* Articles 3, 18, 33.

in Canada and settled in Paraguay in the Gran Chaco on a vast tract of land given them by the government. To facilitate the immigration of the Mennonites the Paraguayan Congress granted them a charter containing exemptions which they were not able to secure elsewhere. Since the founding of the Mennonite colony "represents one of the most ideal-impelled migrations on record," the main clauses of the charter deserve to be mentioned. They were:

Article 1.   Members of the community known as Mennonites who come to the country as components of a colonization enterprise, and their descendants, shall enjoy the following rights and privileges:

a. To practice their religion and to worship with absolute liberty without any restriction and consequently, to make affirmation by a simple "Yes" or "No" in courts of justice, instead of by oath; and to be exempt from obligatory service either as combatants or non-combatants, both in times of peace and during war.

b. To establish, maintain, and administer schools and establishments of learning, and to teach and learn their language, which is German, without any restriction.

Article 2.   The sale of alcoholic or intoxicating beverages is prohibited within a zone of five kilometres from the properties belonging to the Mennonite colonies, unless the competent authorities of these colonies request that the government permit such sale and the government accedes to the request.

Article 3.   The following concessions are granted to the Mennonite colonies for a period of ten years from the arrival of the first colonists:

a. The free entry of furniture, machinery, utensils, drugs, seeds, animals, implements, and, in general, of everything that may be necessary for the installation and development of the colonies.

b. Exemption from all classes of national and municipal taxes.

Article 4.   No immigration law, or law of any other character, existing or that may be passed in future, shall impede the entrance of Mennonite immigrants into the country because of age or physical or mental incapacity."[46]

According to the terms of the above contract, several hundred Mennonites established a temporarily successful colony on a tract

---

[46] Quoted in Webster E. Browning, *The River Plate Republics* (London, 1928), pp. 59-61; *La Prensa* (New York), August 5, 1927.

16

of land some 3,000,000 acres in extent on the eastern slope of the Andes and along the Paraguay River. Although the Mennonite enterprise was not missionary in any sense of the term, it was hoped that their presence in Paraguay must eventually influence the customs and religious habits of the Catholic Paraguayans. Unfortunately the Paraguayan-Bolivian conflict in the Gran Chaco has forced the abandonment of the colony.

The president of Paraguay exercises the rights of national patronage. He nominates the bishop of the diocese, said nomination to be made upon presentation of three names by the legislative Senate, or in default thereof, of the national clergy assembled. The president may grant or refuse, with the advice of Congress, the acceptance of the decrees of the councils, and of bulls, briefs, and rescripts of the pope. He is also empowered to sign concordats; however, none has been concluded because of papal refusal to recognize the national patronage. The Vatican acquiesces nevertheless, in the nation's exercise of the patronage. The Minister of Justice, Worship, and Public Instruction aids the president in the inspection of all branches of divine worship in so far as the national patronage is concerned. It is also his duty to negotiate with the apostolic delegates in behalf of the executive.

The Catholic Church, being the State-Church, receives a small and inadequate governmental subsidy. This sum, amounting to approximately only $25,000 per year, certainly does not lay the government open to the charge of lavishing financial favors on the Church, and moreover it is so insignificant that the Church must come to feel in time that its bargain with the State is unprofitable. For support the clergy are dependent almost exclusively upon such sources of income as gifts, bequests, fees, and rents.[47]

The extent of real ecclesiastical holdings in Paraguay is not great, and compared with other South American countries the Church is poor. It has never been able to recover from the despoilations of the dictators. The tenure of Church property is regulated by laws similar to those in force in Argentina. The same may be

<hr/>

[47] According to Browning, *River Plate Republics,* p. 35, the annual appropriation for the Church is 278,400 pesos, and for the army and navy, 14,930,380 pesos.

said of wills, testaments, and charitable bequests, for the Argentine civil code of 1871 was adopted as the law of the country by act of Congress dated August 19, 1876.[48]

Marriage has been declared a civil contract, and although the Roman Catholic and other religious marriage rites are permitted, for the legitimization of children and in matters of inheritances, only the civil ceremony is legally taken into account.[49] Absolute divorce allowing remarriage is not sanctioned by law. When such a project was introduced in 1921, says Mr. Inman, the Church opposed the measure very strenuously, since it represented a dangerous break from authority. Noted ecclesiastical orators were imported from Buenos Aires to assist in the defeat of the law. The cemeteries belong to the State and are open to all irrespective of creed. Any religious group, however, may maintain its own burial grounds.[50]

Public education is free, compulsory, and lay; religious instruction is not allowed in the public schools as a part of the regular curriculum. Most of the public educational work of whatever grade is confined to the cities and towns; consequently the great majority of the children of Paraguay, being full-blooded Indians living in rural communities, are denied all educational facilities. Private primary instruction, in charge of religious as well as secular entities, is on the increase. A few private schools are subsidized by the government. Both Catholic and Protestant missionaries are extending educational facilities to the Indians, but it must be admitted they are lamentably inadequate to cope with their great problem. In so far as facilities for secondary education exist, they are afforded by the religious schools. Although instruction in the private schools is under the general supervision of the government, the administration of the internal affairs of the schools is untrammeled. These schools are free to teach religion as a special subject.[51] In criticism of the system of higher educa-

---

[48] *Catholic Encyclopedia*, XI, 471.
[49] *Anglo-South American Handbook*, p. 506; *River Plate Republics*, p. 35.
[50] Inman, *South America Today*, p. 68; *River Plate Republics*, p. 35.
[51] *La Nueva Enseñanza*, Asunción, November, 1927; *Anglo-South American Handbook*, p. 506; Heloise Brainerd, *Public Instruction in Paraguay* (*Bulletin* No. 10, Education, Pan American Union, Washington, 1928), p. 5; *Christian Work in South America*, I, 259.

tion in Paraguay, President Eusebio Ayala said in 1922, "Our seconary education is lacking on the moral side. Unfortunately those who have the care of souls are more interested in the work of proselytizing than in elevating the mind of our youth to a noble and austere conception of the reality of life."[52] Regarding education in Paraguay, it can be fairly concluded that neither the State nor the private agencies have more than scratched the surface of appalling illiteracy.

The missionary needs and opportunities in Paraguay are great. Of an estimated population of about 1,000,000 people, only one-third are on the parish registers. Thus, 600,000 people are without religious ministration.[53] In all Paraguay there were in 1925, less than 100 priests, and nearly all of them were in the city of Asunción, and one-half of them were engaged in teaching and not preaching. From 1881 to 1911, only sixty clergy were graduated from the Seminario Conciliar, the lone theological school in Paraguay.[54] The only episcopal diocese is that of Asunción, the bishop of which is a suffragen of the archbishop of Buenos Aires. In a region once the stronghold of the Jesuits, the Catholic Church is now relatively weaker in leadership, membership, influence, and enterprise than in any other South American republic.

The failure of Catholicism in Paraguay should be to the advantage of Protestantism, yet with the exception of Ecuador, it is the most neglected of South American republics by the evangelical missionaries.[55] This, despite the efforts of the Paraguayan government itself to aid evangelical missionary work. In 1909 a law was passed to facilitate the establishment of Protestant missions to convert the Indian tribes. By virtue of this act the president of the republic was authorized to grant public lands in parcels

---

[52] *River Plate Republics,* p. 29.

[53] *Christian Work in South America,* I, 116-117; R. Streit, *Atlas Hierarchicus* (Poderborn, 1913), p. 117, says that 360,000 Paraguayans were Catholics at that time.

[54] *Catholic Encyclopedia,* XI, 471; *River Plate Republics,* p. 35.

[55] In 1925 there were only fifty foreign missionaries in the inland republic (*Christian Work in South America,* p. 115); Rev. W. B. Grubb, the pioneer Protestant missionary in Paraguay comments on missionary opportunities as follows: "In vast districts, over wide areas, the (Roman) Church is not even known. Nor have the Indians here any traditions concerning it." (*Ibid.,* p. 116, n. 55.)

not exceeding 7,500 hectares (18,750 acres) to individuals or companies organized for the purpose of converting the Indians. On each of these concessions was to be established a "reduction," with the necessary churches, houses, and schools. The Christianizing and civilizing of the Indians is a paramount consideration with the Paraguayan government, and it has wisely refrained from discriminating against any Christian sect.[56]

This same tendency of avoiding particular favor to the Catholic Church and ecclesiastics is witnessed in the constitutional requirement that the president of the republic shall profess the *Christian* religion. Also, no ecclesiastic is eligible to membership in Congress. In December, 1927, when a cleric, Ernesto Pérez, was elected to the Council, it was reported that he was the first ecclesiastic in Paraguay to occupy a public office.[57]

In Paraguay, as in other Latin-American countries where there is a legal connection between the Church and the State, there is a movement directed toward separation. As in Bolivia the campaign is supported by the young intelligentsia, but as is also true of the sister inland republic the movement does not appear to be strong or destined to achieve success in the near future. It is the policy of the politicians to let the Church alone so long as it does not interfere in matters of State. But changes have been accomplished in other countries with such unexpected suddenness, that it would be foolhardy to declare the improbability of similar action in Paraguay. Like Ecuador, Bolivia, and other countries where the Indian population is in the overwhelming majority, Paraguay is governed by a small group of whites, or those who pose as such. These people are often well-educated and widely traveled, and are inclined, religiously, to be only nominal Catholics, if not actual free-thinkers. There is no assurance, therefore, that the rulers of Paraguay, without reference to the backward, even semi-civilized, conditions, may not suddenly decide to adopt what is called "the modern religious policy," which indeed is a logical one for advanced states, but is perhaps thoroughly inapplicable to a country like Paraguay.

---

[56] Koebel, *op. cit.*, pp. 218-219.

[57] *La Prensa* (New York), December 13, 1927; *Constitution of Paraguay,* Articles 69, 89.

CHAPTER IX

THE RELIGIOUS QUESTION IN CHILE

The most recent separation of Church from State in Latin America occurred in Chile in 1925. The religious question has occupied a most prominent position in the history of that country, and great difficulty has been experienced in finding a satisfactory solution of the problem. But after inaugurating her independent career as one of the most intolerant of the Catholic governments of South America, Chile has become in recent years one of the most liberal nations in matters of religion.

From the outbreak of the struggle for independence until 1833, proclamations, provisional statutes, and organic laws proclaimed the Catholic religion as that of Chileans to the exclusion of all other faiths. In explaining this exclusive policy the great liberal, Balmaceda said, "The revolution of independence was waged by valorous, patriotic men imbued with a love of Chilean nationality; but they were under the influence of Church customs, beliefs, and superstitions even, of the colonial period. It is not strange, then, that in the different constitutions and constitutional projects from 1810 to 1833 they stipulated privileges in favor of the Catholic Church, and frankly refused liberty of conscience."[1] In support of the denial of freedom of worship, Juan de Egaña, a revolutionary patriot, wrote a treatise (1820) on religious liberty entitled, *Memoria política sobre si conviene en Chile la libertad de cultos* (*Political Memorial on the Advisability of Religious Freedom in Chile*). The propositions emphasized by him were: (1) a number of cults within a single State conduces to irreligion; (2) the existence of two or more religions side by side will tend to inevitable conflict which will destroy the State; and (3) religious uniformity is the most effective means of establishing tranquillity

---

[1] Julio Bañados Espinosa, *Balmaceda, su Gobierno, y la Revolución de 1891* (Paris, 1894), pp. 32-33.

in the affairs of the nation.[2] The views of Egaña found general acceptance, not only in post-revolutionary Chile, but throughout Spanish America.

The Constitution of 1818, the first fundamental law designed to guide the course of the infant republic after its independence had been definitely secured, denied freedom of worship to any faith other than the Roman Catholic, which was put under the protection and control of the new government. The article pertinent to this subject read: "The Roman Catholic Apostolic religion is the sole and exclusive faith of the State of Chile. Its protection, conservation, purity, and inviolability will be one of the duties of the chiefs of society who will never permit another public cult or doctrine contrary to that of Jesus Christ."[3] The republic also declared its right to assume the patronal authority once exercised over the Catholic Church in Chile by the kings of Spain. Only Chilean citizens resident in the State could be appointed to ecclesiastical benefices.[4] As has been noted elsewhere, national patronage could only exist when there was a formal or tacit agreement by the papacy. This acquiescence on the part of Rome was not forthcoming for several years. In the meantime the governmental authorities undertook to provide for the emergency. On January 4, 1819, a decree was published providing rules for the better government and control of the mendicant orders during the continuance of non-communication with the Holy See. Rules of conduct were prescribed looking to an improvement of the morals of the regulars.[5] The relations between the government of Dictator Bernardo O'Higgins and the Church dignitaries and clergy were relatively cordial. "But," declares a Chilean historian, "enemies of emancipation as these dignitaries had been, if they tolerated the dictatorship of O'Higgins, they did not accept it in good faith."[6] The majority of the high church officials were native Spaniards, and, as neither Spain nor the papacy had as yet recognized the independence of Chile, it is not surprising that the Spanish

---

[2] Moses, *Background of the Revolution*, pp. 67-68.

[3] Ricardo Anguita (ed.), *Leyes Promulgadas en Chile desde 1810 hasta el 10 de junio de 1913* (Santiago, 1913), I, 53.

[4] *Ibid.*, I, 55.

[5] *Ibid.*, I, 64-65.

[6] Galdames, *Historia de Chile*, p. 309.

clergy were in secret sympathy with the mother country.

The intransigent royalism of the higher ecclesiastics was most pronounced in Bishop Rodríguez Zorrilla of Santiago. Although a creole, he had been nominated for the vacant see of Santiago by Ferdinand VII, and, in 1815, the pope issued a bull for his institution. Bishop Rodríguez, a narrow, dogmatic pedant, was a notorious opponent of the Revolution. In his first episcopal letter he condemned the revolt. To him the rebellion was the greatest of crimes, and he predicted that it would result in opening the door to irreligion. To his clergy he represented the Revolution as an impious schism and its leaders as "impenitent Voltaireans." In legitimate defense, O'Higgins, after failing to quiet the Bishop by gentle means, was forced to exile him to San Luís in the province of Cuyo. Besides Bishop Rodríguez, three other ecclesiastics were expelled from the country. O'Higgins, because of his desire to placate the clericals, and because, as a good son of the Church himself he was confident that it would put no obstacles in his way if it realized that he had no ulterior motives, allowed Bishop Rodríguez to return to Chile in 1821.[7]

Since the other Chilean bishopric, Concepción,[8] was vacant, O'Higgins was confronted with the ticklish problem of filling it. Although the right of national patronage had been asserted in the Constitution, he realized that it would be futile to make nominations until the pope should consent to recognize them. O'Higgins decided, therefore, with the advice of the acting governor of the diocese of Santiago (the patriot canon José Ignacio Cienfuegos), to send an official delegation to Rome to negotiate the restoration of religious relations with the papacy. Cienfuegos was induced by the dictator to head the mission, and was successful, as has been seen, in persuading the pope to agree to a temporary arrangement by sending an apostolic vicar to Chile. The mission of Juan Muzi

---

[7] Ayarragaray, *La Iglesia en América*, pp. 239-241; Leturia, *La Acción Diplomática*, p. 176.

[8] In the colonial period there were two bishoprics in Chile, Santiago and Concepción, suffragens of the Archbishop of Lima. Pope Gregory XVI in 1840 elevated the see of Santiago to archiepiscopal dignity, and created two new dioceses, La Serena and Ancúd. The first bishop of Santiago was Manuel Vicuña. He died, May 3, 1843. (Francisco V. Vergara, *Historia de Chile,* Valparaiso, 1898, p. 254.)

was a failure because of the demand of the Chilean government that national patronage be recognized. This, Rome would not concede.

Notwithstanding the generally cordial feeling that existed between O'Higgins and the Church, on occasion their *entente* became strained. When, for example, the Dictator favored the founding of a theatre in Santiago to stimulate interest in the drama, he was criticized by the clergy who regarded theatrical presentations as immoral. Likewise, when O'Higgins, as a service to the large foreign population of Valparaiso and because of his desire to encourage immigration, even of communicants of other faiths, ordered the establishment in Valparaiso of a cemetery for dissidents, a storm of clerical protest was aroused.[9]

The creation of a quasi-liberal government under the headship of General Ramón Freire, after the deposition of Dictator O'Higgins, was followed by legislative enactments which were branded by the clergy as being anti-clerical. Because of his financial needs, as well as his conviction that the clergy needed reform, Freire suppressed some of the religious houses and confiscated their property. Several of the orders were dispossessed of their convents in order to give James Thomson, agent of the British and Foreign Bible Society, room for his schools established on the Lancastrian plan.[10] The tithes were abolished and regular salaries were fixed for the clergy to be paid by the government. The bishop of Santiago, for example, was paid two thousand *escudos* (gold crowns) a year, in addition to four thousand paid by the diocese.[11] This attack upon the Church was also a direct consequence of the support given by the clergy to the centralistic-conservative forces known as the *Pelucones*, who were opposed to the *Pípolos*, or federal-liberals who were in control of the government almost continuously from 1823 to 1830.

The determination of the Freire administration to assert national patronage, plus its anti-clerical legislative program,

---

[9] Galdames, *op. cit.*, pp. 307-308.

[10] *West Coast Republics*, p. 27.

[11] Sallusti, *Misiones Apostólicas de Monseñor Juan Muzi*, p. 439; According to Galdames (Luís Galdames, *Historia de Chile; La Evolución Constitucional, 1810-1925*, Santiago, 1926, I, 947) the confiscation of the property of the regulars was applied on a small scale and did not continue for long.

doomed to failure the mission of Juan Muzi. The withdrawal of the papal vicar amid conditions which Nicolás Bravo branded as a national disgrace, and Muzi's subsequent defense proclamation, issued at Montevideo, in which he attacked the good faith of the Chilean government, strained the relations between the clericals and the civil authorities almost to the breaking point. Under these conditions Bishop Rodríguez renewed his criticism of the republic. He had the temerity to voice opinions which were guarded fearfully in the devout consciences of many of the old aristocrats. Since the Bishop refused to refrain from his attacks, Freire was forced to remove him from office. Later, on December 22, 1825, Supreme Director Blanco Encalada banished the militant bishop from the territory of the republic. From Valparaiso Rodríguez sailed to Acapulco, where he arrived sick and sad of heart, but regretting that he had not made an even more strenuous fight. He passed the remainder of his days in Spain, supported by a small pension granted him by Ferdinand VII.[12] When Bishop Rodríguez was removed from his see, the cathedral chapter met, and in accordance with custom, nominated as capitular vicar Archdeacon Cienfuegos whose candidature Blanco Encalada had presented. When Cienfuegos resigned, in 1825, another governmental nominee, Canon Diego Antonio Elizondo, was installed in the administration of the diocese. In 1832 the vacancy in the see came to an end when Cienfuegos was appointed titular bishop of Santiago.[13]

During the decade of the 1820's Chile was afflicted with several constitutions. These elaborate, but short-lived, fundamental laws, although differing as to idealistic principles of government, were all in agreement in assigning to Catholicism a favored legal position as a cult. The Constitution of 1822, which was published by O'Higgins in a futile eleventh hour effort to prevent his overthrow, contained the religious articles of the Constitution of 1818, with this addition: "The inhabitants of the territory shall pay it (Roman Catholic Church) the greatest respect and veneration, whatever might be their private opinions. . . . Article 11. All vio-

---

[12] Galdames, *op. cit.,* p. 317; Vergara, *op. cit.,* pp. 253-254; Ayarragaray, *op. cit.,* pp. 241-242, 246.

[13] Ayarragaray, *op. cit.,* pp. 241-244.

lations of the preceding article will be a crime against the fundamental laws of the land."[14]

The Constitution of 1823, which was framed by Juan de Egaña for General Freire, declared the Roman faith to be the religion of the State, and prohibited the public or private exercise of other cults. Citizenship was confined to Roman Catholics. The president was given the right of ecclesiastical presentation and control of the *pase*. Moreover the Constitution provided that each year a senator should undertake an investigation tour of the provinces to examine the status of religious and moral conditions.[15] When enabling legislation was being enacted to enforce the judicial clauses of the Constitution an attempt was made to suppress the ecclesiastical *fuero*. The reform was frustrated, however, as being too impolitic.[16] High lights in the ensuing near-anarchic political situation in Chile were: (1) the derogation of the Constitution of 1823 by General Freire in January, 1825; (2) the declaration of federalism in 1826; (3) the assuming by Freire, in 1827, of the position of *jefe político y militar* (a dictatorship); and (4) the promulgation of a most liberal constitution in 1828.[17] During these chaotic times there was no abatement in the exercise of the patronage. In 1827 Freire decreed that he would name to the lesser benefices only those nominated to him by the ecclesiastical *cabildos*. Time was also found to undertake a further reform of the regulars. In 1826 properties belonging to some of the regular communities were confiscated and sold. The realization from the sales was devoted "to the support of the cult and the number of regulars deemed convenient." This reform therefore had as its prime motive curtailment of the number of the too-numerous regulars.[18] The Constitution of 1828 was more liberal religiously than the preceding instruments in that it sanctioned the private worship of dissidents, and declared that no one could be persecuted or molested for his private opinions. The executive power was given the control of the *pase*, the power to

---

[14] "Constitución Política de 1822," Art. 11, in Anguita, *op. cit.*, I, 102-113.

[15] "Constitución Política de 1823," in Anguita, *op. cit.*, I, 126-143.

[16] Galdames, *Evolución Constitucional*, I, 947.

[17] Anguita, *op. cit.*, I, 165, 168, 174.

[18] *Ibid.*, I, 171, 177.

negotiate concordats, and the exercise of the patronage with this limitation, i.e., bishops could not be presented without the consent of the Deputies.[19] A retrogressive step was taken in 1828, when a law concerning abuses of the liberty of the press was enacted. By this act all published attacks on the dogma of the Roman Catholic Church were defined as blasphemy and punishable as same.[20]

Not until 1833 did political and social conditions become composed in Chile. The preceding decade was indeed a period of trial and tribulation, yet it is important to note that throughout the political vicissitudes of Chile little was done by legislation or governmental action to destroy or curtail the rights of particular interests. The Church emerged practically unscathed in fortune and privilege.[21]

The Constitution of 1833, which represented a thorough remodeling of that of 1828 after the decisive victory of the Conservatives at the battle of Lircai, was in force in Chile until 1925, a longer period than enjoyed by any other Latin-American constitution. No attempt was made in that notable document to reduce the severity of Chile's religious policy. This was not to be expected, in truth, since the staunchest allies of the clericals were in control of the government. The constitutional provisions relating to the Church and religion, were the following: (1) the religion of the republic was Roman Catholic, and the public exercise of any other faith was prohibited; (2) the president in taking his oath of office was to swear to observe and protect the Catholic religion; (3) the president was empowered (a) to nominate, subject to approval by the Senate, archbishops, bishops, canons, and prebends of cathedrals, selecting from lists of three names for each office prepared by the Council of State, (b) to exercise the right of patronage with respect to churches, benefices, and ecclesiastical persons, (c) to grant or refuse, with the consent of the Council of State, admission to decrees of councils, papal bulls, briefs, and rescripts; and (d) to maintain diplomatic relations with the Vatican and conclude concordats with it; and (4) the Council of State, of

---

[19] "Constitución Política de 1828," in *Ibid.,* I, 180-189.

[20] *Ibid.,* I, 193.

[21] Galdames, *Evolución Constitucional,* I, 947.

which a Church dignitary must be a member, was to have cognizance over all matters of ecclesiastical patronage that might be subject to litigation.[22] According to the above constitutional provisions, therefore, the customary procedure of filling a vacant archbishopric or bishopric in Chile was the following: The Council of State named three ecclesiastics who met the requirements of the office as determined by the Council of Trent. The triple list was then sent to the president who selected one name and submitted it to the Senate. Approved by the Senate it went to the Holy See for preconization. In Argentina it was the Senate which drew up the triple list.

Article 5 of the Constitution of 1833 which read: "The religion of the Republic of Chile is Roman Catholic to the exclusion of the public exercise of any other faith," in the opinion of Balmaceda confirmed religious despotism and slavery of conscience.[23] But says Galdames, "The Constitution of 1833 corresponded perfectly to the social condition of that time. Thus, the establishment of the Catholic religion as that of the State was simply due to the fact that all were Catholics."[24] It is true indeed that the prohibition of the public exercise of dissident faiths in Chile was due to the effect of the historical traditions of the country, and the collective thought that the one true faith was the Catholic.[25]

The constitutional exclusion of the public exercise of other cults was never completely enforced. The first Anglican chaplain as-

---

[22] "Constitución Política de 1833," in Anguita, *op. cit.*, I, 214-226.

[23] Espinosa, *op. cit.*, p. 33.

[24] Galdames, *op. cit.*, p. 333.

[25] Dr. Jorge Huneeus, the notable Chilean writer on constitutional and legal subjects, in commenting (*Obras de Don Jorge Huneeus,* Santiago, 1890, I, 68) on Article 5, declared that literally interpreted, it was intended as a recognition of the existing religious status, and should have read, for purposes of clarity, that the Roman Catholic religion was the religion of the majority of Chileans. But, says Huneeus, constitutions do not have as their purpose the recognition of status; and therefore, being superfluous, Article 5 should have been suppressed for it was certainly not the intention of the framers of the constitution to impose on the State a determined religion. This is artful and subtle reasoning, which, nevertheless, reflects no credit on Huneeus. The framers of the Constitution of 1833 certainly *did* intend to impose on the State a determined religion, and a cursory examination of the conditions under which the constitution was framed will substantiate this contention.

signed to Chile reached Valparaiso in 1837 and remained there
two years. In 1847, Rev. David Trumbull organized a Protestant
Union church in Valparaiso, and in 1856 this congregation erected
its own building, the first Protestant church edifice to be erected
on the west coast of South America.[26] Soon afterward a second
church was built. Services were held regularly and openly and
the authorities did not interfere. The constitutional phrase "public exercise" was generally regarded as not prohibiting religious
worship of non-Catholics *inside* buildings. This interpretation,
fortified by thirty years of practice, was incorporated into law
in 1865, when the so-called *Ley Interpretativa* was passed by
the Congress. This law declared that the prohibition, in Article 5,
of the public exercise of dissident faiths did not refer to religious
services indoors. Not only were Protestants permitted to conduct
services inside private buildings belonging to them, but they were
permitted to establish and support schools for the instruction
of their children in the doctrines of their respective religions.[27]
As a result of the *Ley Interpretativa* of 1865, which legalized
religious toleration, numerous Protestant churches were erected
throughout the country. Yet it must be admitted that the establishment in fact of liberty of cults in Chile, was realized only by
violation of constitutional principle.[28]

In 1836 legislation was enacted which created two new bishop-

---

[26] *West Coast Republics,* pp. 28-29.

[27] The text of the famous Ley Interpretativa was the following:

Interpretative Law of Article 5,
Santiago de Chile, July 27, 1865.

The National Congress has discussed and approved the following project
of law:

Article 1.   It is declared that by Article 5 of the Constitution those who
do not profess the Roman Catholic Apostolic religion are permitted to
practice their cult inside private buildings.

Article 2.   Dissidents are permitted to establish and support private
schools for the instruction of their children in the doctrine of their religion.

Approved and sanctioned by the Council of State and promulgated as law.

Juan Joaquín Pérez,
Federico Errázuriz.

(*Constitución y Leyes Políticas de la República de Chile Vigente en 1881,*
Santiago, 1881, p. 48.)

[28] José Guillermo Guerra, *La Constitución de 1925* (Santiago, 1929), p. 39.

rics, Coquimbo and Chiloé. These with the bishopric of Concepción were made suffragans of the new archiepiscopal see of Santiago. The *dotación* or grant to the bishops was 4,000 pesos per year, and to the archbishop, 12,000 pesos per year.[29] In 1842 the University of Chile was recreated by law. It comprised five faculties, one of which was in theology.[30] In 1846 another law on abuses of the liberty of the press was published which prescribed heavy penalties of fine and imprisonment for published attacks upon the religion of the State.[31] The above facts, somewhat isolated it is true, are presented to evidence the satisfactory status enjoyed by the Church under the régime of the Conservative Oligarchy. Yet the clericals were not allowed free rein to their ambitious pretentions as evidenced by the following facts. The *Ley sobre Matrimonio de Disidentes* (1844) freed non-Catholics from the obligation of celebrating nuptials according to the Catholic rites. The *Ley sobre el Patronato Civil* conceded to the executive authority of the government the right of watching over curates to see that they fulfilled their duties. The *Ley sobre Profesión Religiosa* required twenty-five years as the minimum age for receiving major orders.[32] These acts caused considerable discussion and dissension in the clerical ranks and disrupted the long standing harmonious relations that existed between the Church and the temporal authorities. So opposed was Archbishop Eyzaguirre to the "aggressions of the government," that he resigned in 1845, after having held his position for but two years. His successor, Rafael Valdivieso, continued to resist the so-called "regalistic prerogatives" for the balance of the term of President Bulnes (1841-1851).

Protestant ideas were being widely disseminated during this period and there began to develop an element which was unfriendly to the religion of the State. This culminated in the founding in Santiago of a periodical, *El Mercurio*, dedicated to religious toleration. The leading lights of Chilean letters, Bilbao and Las-

[29] Anguita, *op. cit.,* I, 262, 392.

[30] *Ibid.,* I, 395.

[31] *Ibid.,* I, 478.

[32] Galdames, *op. cit.,* pp. 376-377; Anguita, *op. cit.,* I, 436-437; Guerra, *op. cit.,* pp. 38-39.

tarria, also began at this time to attack the Conservative order and its various props, particularly the clergy. The Church was stimulated to action, and under the protection of the Archbishop, *La Revista Católica* was founded in 1843 to check the subversive teachings that "threatened to corrupt the intellectual youth of Chile." The Jesuits, who had recently been permitted to return to Chile, lent the Archbishop their able assistance. It appears, however, that notwithstanding clerical resistance, the domination of the Church and the religious spirit of Chileans were gradually waning. For instance, no longer was "Ave María Purísima" added to the cries of the hours or weather conditions by the *serenos*, or night-watchmen. Also, the practice of dipping the banners of the batallions when a priest passed with the host in the procession of the *Corpus*, was abolished. These changes were trivial, but they indicated in which direction public opinion was shifting.[33]

During the first term of President Montt (1851-1856), cordial relations existed between the spiritual and temporal orders. The governmental budget for the State cult was increased annually after 1853, and the condition of the Church continued to improve. In 1853 the republic pledged itself to support the Church out of the national treasury. The tithes, which were still collected even after the reforms of Freire, were abolished. The Archbishop of Santiago was authorized by the pope to agree to this arrangement.[34] In the civil code, promulgated on January 1, 1857, the State confirmed strict religious exclusion by entrusting the register to the clergy. On the subject of matrimony the code contained the following provisions: (1) marriage between Catholic persons shall be celebrated with the solemnities established by the Church and shall comply with ecclesiastical authority; (2) those who profess a different religion and wish to contract marriage can do so by having the ceremony performed by a priest in the presence of two witnesses; and (3) marriage is dissolved only by the death of one of the parties.[35] It was during the second term of President Montt (1857-1861), when a younger and more liberal element gained control of the government, that there developed a growing

[33] *Ibid.,* p. 376.

[34] Bravo, *Estudios Constitucionales,* p. 26, note 1.

[35] Galdames, *Historia de Chile,* p. 334; Anguita, *op. cit.,* I.

coolness between Church and State. The particular incident which terminated the old-time harmony was rather insignificant. Two canons who were expelled from the cathedral chapter because of lack of respect for their superiors appealed to the Supreme Court which revoked the sentence of the chapter. The archbishop protested vigorously, alleging unwarranted interference on the part of the civil authorities. A protracted discussion between the metropolitan and the Minister of Cult was terminated by the submission of the canons, through the mediation of the government, to the will of the Church. The incident, although closed, left bitter memories which rankled in the breasts of clericals and non-clericals alike, and any future harmonious understanding became impossible. Although the clergy and the old aristocracy opposed the so-called irreligious government and its liberal tendencies, they were forced to give way before a changing order in Chile. The bigotry and intransigence of an earlier time was being replaced by a temperate tolerance. Therefore, in spite of frenzied clerical opposition, the *Ley Interpretativa* legalizing religious freedom was passed. The *Ley* was not a constitutional amendment, but only a congressional law. Therefore, since it appeared to many to run counter to the constitutional proscription of religious freedom, an attempt was made to guarantee the liberty of cults by constitutional amendment. The effort was defeated. A second attempt was made in 1874. At that time a constitutional amendment suppressing Article 4 and changing Article 10 to include "religious freedom," was adopted by the Congress, but since it failed of ratification by the next Congress it did not become an amendment to the constitution.[36]

During the administration of President Errázuriz (1871-1876) the control of the government passed out of the hands of the old Conservative party and into the control of the Liberals and Radicals who were frankly opposed to the pretentions of the Catholic Church. At the beginning of Errázuriz's administration the government was composed of a Conservative-Liberal coalition. The futility of such a combination soon became apparent when dissension arose over the educational program. The Conservative

---

[36] Alcibiades Roldán, *Elementos de Derecho Constitucional de Chile* (Santiago, 1917), p. 222; Guerra, *op. cit.,* p. 42.

17

members of the coalition government disapproved the measure
sponsored by the Liberals which granted preference to the natural
sciences in the State schools. This they declared to be prejudicial
to religion and dangerous to private morals. In opposition to
the Liberal proposal that the University be granted a monopoly
of professional degrees, the Conservatives, headed by Abdon Cifuentes, the Minister of Public Instruction, hastened to the support
of the small colleges, particularly the religious. In 1872, Cifuentes
issued an edict denying to professors of State schools the right to
examine students of private schools, as provided by law. Because
of this act the Minister was removed from the cabinet. Next
year a decree was issued which declared that religious instruction
was not obligatory in State colleges, but was available for students
whose parents demanded it. The so-called "theological questions"
were the rock upon which the coalition government foundered
in 1873. These questions were: (1) suppression of the *fuero eclesiástico;* (2) secularization of cemeteries;[37] (3) civil marriage;
and (4) separation of Church and State. An irreconcilable difference of opinion in the cabinet precipitated a crisis which resulted in the dissolution of the coalition and the ousting of the
Conservatives. Although the Liberal-Radical bloc was triumphant,
it was not able or willing to enact far-reaching clerical reform.
Nevertheless the *fuero eclesiástico* was abolished for all civil and
criminal causes, and the penal code, promulgated in 1874, enumerated penalties for priests, without distinction to cults, who
preached doctrines subversive of public order and contrary to
the Constitution and the laws of the republic. Regarding the use
and control of cemeteries, it was provided that Protestants might
be buried in designated portions of Catholic cemeteries. Finally,
the tithes were abolished and were replaced by a tax. Nothing
was done at this time about civil marriage and the separation of
Church and State.[38]

The clergy, naturally, offered violent opposition to the reform
measures. "The political struggle," says Galdames, "became a

---

[37] Old colonial decrees regulating the control of cemeteries were still in
force. The clergy could refuse to bury persons who had died without fulfilling the precepts of Catholicism.

[38] Galdames, *op. cit.,* pp. 410-413; Bravo, *op. cit.,* p. 64.

religious fight and the Conservative party became a clerical or
ultramontane party."[39] The fight was led by the aged Archbishop
of Santiago, Rafael Valentín Valdivieso, who even proceeded to
the limit of excommunicating those who had supported the laws.
His fulminations and bans were not sufficient, however, to alter
the course of the government. The Archbishop, an energetic defender of the prerogatives of the Church, never ceased to protest
the exercise of *patronato* by the government. The election of a
successor to Archbishop Valdivieso, who died in 1878 after having
been primate for thirty years, led to the renewal of an even more
determined governmental assault upon the exclusive privileges
and prerogatives of the Catholic Church. President Pinto (1876-
1881), a Liberal, in endeavoring to insure the establishment of
harmonious relations between the government and the Church,
proposed as candidate for the see of Santiago, Francisco de Paula
Taforo, canon of the cathedral of Santiago and a man of pronounced liberal leanings. Due to the objections of the Chilean clergy
the pope refused to install the government's nominee, and thus
there was created a conflict over the right to exercise the national
patronage.[40] Notwithstanding protracted negotiations, both the
Vatican and the Chilean government were obdurate, and in the
meantime the archiepiscopal see remained vacant. Finally, in response to a request of President Santa María (1881-1886), an
apostolic delegate was sent to Chile. Mgr. Celestino del Frate, the
pope's envoy, after a careful study of the problem, became convinced that it was inadvisable to confirm Taforo's nomination, and
counseled the pope against it. President Santa María then decided
that the time for a break with the Vatican had arrived and gave
the Apostolic Delegate his passports. Before withdrawing from
Chile Del Frate publicly announced that the pretense to national
patronage by Chile was without foundation or sanction. Although
this statement was made in a tactless manner, nevertheless it was
literally true. There had never been a concordat between Chile
and the papacy. The *entente* was not one of law, but only of convenience. "The failure of the negotiations," writes a constitutionalist authority, "made the Chilean regalists realize that patronage

---

[39] Galdames, *Historia de Chile,* p. 412.
[40] *Ibid.,* pp. 436-437; Espinosa, *op. cit.,* pp. 35-36; Bravo, *op. cit.,* pp. 64-65.

was not an inherent right of the national sovereignty, because the political power lacked adequate means to enforce it; and the Roman Curia, in spite of threats and violence, possessed sufficient strength to resist the exercise of this pretended right when it saw the peace of the Church compromised. Nevertheless, there emerged from the conflict profound modifications of the union of Church and State, proceeding on the road to its complete liquidation."[41]

The pretext sought by Santa María to inaugurate the reforms demanded by the *partidos de libertad* was furnished by the unfortunate outcome of Del Frate's mission. The dismissal of the Apostolic Delegate was followed by the passage of notable ecclesiastical reform laws. On June 1, 1883, the president in his message to Congress, declared that the time had arrived for the realization of the oldest and dearest aspirations of the liberal thinkers of Chile; i.e., common cemeteries, civil matrimony, civil register, and liberty of conscience. The Congress, composed almost exclusively of Liberals, Radicals, and Nationalists, was thoroughly in accord with the administration's program. More influential than the President himself in the passage of the reform laws was the Minister of Interior, José Manuel Balmaceda. Balmaceda had studied for the priesthood in the Seminario de Santiago, but constant reading of philosophical and scientific works had shaken his faith, and he sought refuge first in agriculture and later in politics. As a member of the Congress in 1874 he supported the constitutional amendment to disestablish the Church. As Minister of Interior in the cabinet of President Santa María, José Balmaceda was the man most responsible for the *reformas teológicas*. He regarded the power of the Church as an iron despotism which seized a person at birth and controlled his most serious acts up to and even after death. "The Church marches, in a sense, against the liberal current of the century," he said. "The existence of an enlightened and cultivated people is not possible if they are not assured liberty of labor, material and intellectual property, civil liberty in the constitution of the family . . . and finally liberty of conscience."[42] He proposed to check the invading pre-

---

[41] *Ibid.,* p. 65.
[42] Espinosa, *op. cit.,* pp. 35, 47-48.

LEADING ACTORS IN THE CHURCH-STATE DRAMA IN LATIN AMERICA

Top left: Benito Juárez, great liberal President of Mexico, 1858-1872; author of anticlerical measures known as the Laws of Reform. *Top right:* Gabriel García Moreno, President of Ecuador, 1861-1865, 1869-1875; Latin America's greatest lay champion of clerical pretentions. *Bottom left:* Antonio Guzmán Blanco, President and Dictator of Venezuela, 1870-1889; the nemesis of the Catholic church in Venezuela. *Bottom right:* José Manuel Balmaceda, President of Chile, 1886-1891, who as Minister of State, stripped the church of special privileges, 1883-1884.

tentions of the Church against the independence of the State, the individual, and civil society. He did not delude himself into believing that the solution of the problem of Church-State relationships was simple, for he realized that it required laborious and prudent governmental action. Galdames describes Balmaceda as "liberal, reformista, pensador, laico, casi ateo."[43]

The first of the *leyes reformas teológicas*, the *Ley de Cemeterios Laicos*, released the cemeteries from the control of the Church and provided for their free use by all religious communions. The law was passed by a large majority. The capitular vicar of Santiago condemned it and prohibited the exercise of the cult within the State cemeteries and chapels annexed thereto. The government replied by closing Catholic cemeteries and prohibiting burials within churches. On January 16, 1884, the law of civil marriage was passed, which legalized and made compulsory the civil ceremony conducted by the official in charge of the civil register. Although marriages without the participation of Catholic priests were now valid, those desiring the religious ceremony either before or after the civil act were at liberty to have it performed. According to the new legislation questions of divorce and nullity belonged to the civil jurisdiction, and not to the ecclesiastical courts as in the past. Divorce, however, was declared to be only suspension and not dissolution of the married state.[44] Thus the Church was deprived of its old prerogative of legally constituting the family, and very naturally the passage of the civil marriage law caused the clergy to cry to high heaven. They protested, threatened, and even went to the extreme of attempting to prevent the marriage of anyone who voted for the measure. So much opposition was aroused by the clergy against this "sacrilegious law" that the country seemed to be on the verge of revolution.[45]

On July 17, 1884, the Law of the Civil Register was enacted.[46] The records of births, marriages, and deaths had been kept by the parish priests, not to aid the State in the discharge of admin-

---

[43] Galdames, *op. cit.,* p. 439.

[44] Eulojio Rojas Mery (ed.), *Códigos de Chile* (Santiago, 1893), pp. 577-583; Anguita, *op. cit.,* II, 592-595; Luís F. Borja, *Estudios sobre el Codigo Civil Chileno* (Paris, 1901-1908), III, 50.

[45] Espinosa, *op. cit.,* pp. 38-44.

[46] Mery, *Codigos de Chile,* pp. 584-592; Anguita, *op. cit.,* II, 606-609.

istration, but because the Church thought this was the logical complement of its right to preside over the most solemn events in the lives of the people. The keeping of the register, claimed the Liberals, was not a religious but essentially an administrative act and should be entrusted to the civil authorities. Furthermore, because of the great importance of these documentary proofs in matters of litigation, inheritance for example, the custody of the records should constitute a public service where responsibility could not be affected by religious ideas, and where they would be administered with greater efficiency, for rarely indeed were the parochial registers free of omissions and errors.[47] For these reasons, then, the Church was deprived of its administration of the records of vital statistics.

Liberty of conscience was another important item in the program of the Liberal administration. The *Ley Interpretativa* of 1865, although professing to guarantee religious liberty, was nevertheless unconstitutional, and, as has been noted above an unsuccessful attempt was made in 1874 to provide for religious toleration by constitutional amendment. In November, 1884, the Congress again approved the suppression of Article 5, but the succeeding Congress allowed the required period of time to pass without ratifying the reform. But notwithstanding the failure of the amendment religious freedom had been recognized and continued to be recognized in Chile.[48] By way of pertinent illustration: in 1885 the government granted an unusually liberal charter to a Protestant group, whereby "Those who profess the Reformed Church religion according to the doctrines of Holy Scriptures, may promote primary and secondary instruction according to

---

[47] *Ibid.,* p. 42. Maladministration of the civil register was not uncommon during the colonial period for witness the plaint of a viceroy: "Experience has shown that the clergy do not give this register and these lists complete, but (with a pious falsehood) certify that some have died—in which they are in collusion with the governors and principal Indians—pocketing the tribute themselves and benefitting to the prejudice of the royal treasury." ("Instrucción Para el Virrey . . . Marqués de Amarillas," in *Instrucciones Reservadas que los Virreyes de Nueva España Dejaron á sus Sucesores,* Mexico, 1867, p. 81).

[48] Guerra, *op. cit.,* p. 42; Anguita, *op. cit.,* II, 632-633.

modern methods and practice, and propagate the worship of their belief obedient to the law of the land."[49]

The hardest battle was fought over the question of the separation of Church and State. Three possible systems of Church-State relationships were championed: (1) the union of Church and State without patronage and without liberty of cults (the ideal of the Church) ; (2) the union of Church and State, the patronage, and freedom of cults (the proposal of the administration) ; and (3) absolute separation of Church and State, and the reduction of the Church to the status of a simple institution of private law (championed by the Radicals). When he was a deputy in 1874, Balmaceda had supported a measure designed to separate Church and State, but which reserved to the Church a status in public law and supported it by a State subsidy. Nevertheless, for politic reasons, he and President Santa María supported plan number two above. They realized that the storm aroused because of the religious laws was carrying the country to the brink of revolution, and it would be foolhardy to invite additional trouble. Immense pro-clerical parades, pilgrimages, and meetings proclaimed revolt, and priests from the pulpits added fuel to the fire. In the interest of expediency, the union of Church and State was not abolished, but, said Balmaceda, "Between the partisans of definite and immediate separation of Church and State, and the partisans of gradual and progressive separation, there is no difference of doctrine. There's only a difference in procedure. We will advance step by step with perfect security and we propose to arrive at the same goal."[50] The *reformas teológicas*, although not embodied in legislation in their entirety, seriously weakened the Chilean Church; in a formal encounter it had been defeated and humiliated; its prestige was shaken and thereafter it was placed on the defensive.

When Balmaceda succeeded his old chief to the presidency in 1886, he tried, in the interest of peace and harmony, to conciliate the clericals by settling in accord with their views the old question

[49] *West Coast Republics,* p. 29.

[50] Espinosa, *op. cit.,* p. 48.

of the vacant archbishopric. Accordingly, relations were reëstablished with the Vatican and Mariano Casanova was preconized Archbishop of Santiago (1887). The restoration of contact with the papacy inaugurated a quarter century or more of satisfactory Church-State relations. Archbishop Casanova and his successor, in 1911, Juan Ignacio González Eyzaguirre, were both able and tactful men, zealous of the rights of the Church, but wise in avoiding violent conflicts such as had embittered relations under Archbishop Valdivieso. In 1895 Archbishop Casanova summoned a diocesan synod which thoroughly reorganized the internal régime of the Church. In 1905 he convened a solemn Eucharistic Congress. A Catholic University in Santiago and numerous schools and colleges connected with conciliar seminaries were founded. And finally, an appeal was made to workmen to attach themselves to Catholic socialist associations which were under the direction of priests. Protestantism was making little headway in Chile. Almost all Protestants were foreigners, English, Americans, and Germans.[51] As a result of its intensive propaganda campaign, the Catholic Church in Chile enjoyed a remarkable renaissance. Its prestige and influence were supported and advanced in no small way by its great wealth. So vast were the holdings of the Church and so great its income that it was seldom necessary for the government to appropriate more than a million dollars annually for its support.[52]

In its struggle for rehabilitation, the Church was consistently supported by the Conservative party which regarded it as the staunchest champion of order and authority. The Conservatives, in league with some Liberals, withstood successfully the attempt of the Radical party in 1906 to bring about complete separation of Church and State. The question of education was always conducive to conflict in the Congress. There were numerous schools of all grades conducted by the Church within the republic. In them, of course, religious instruction was an essential part of the curriculum. Concerning this there was no argument. In the public schools, however, religious instruction was compulsory.

---

[51] In 1900, out of a total foreign population of 72,000, 16,000 were Protestants. (Akers, *South America*, p. 493.)

[52] *Ibid.*, pp. 417-418; Galdames, *op. cit.*, pp. 440, 492, 495.

The Conservatives thought that the State should concern itself with education as little as possible, leaving this matter to private individuals and institutions. The Radicals, on the other hand, contended that the State should be the only educator, and its instruction ought to be free, obligatory, and laical. It was impossible, obviously, to reconcile such extreme viewpoints.

The Treaty of Ancón, which ended the War of the Pacific, contributed in addition to the well known territorial problem between Chile and Peru, a serious religious difficulty which reached a crisis in 1910. The ecclesiastical conflict originated in the omission of any clause in the Treaty of Ancón to regulate for the future the ecclesiastical jurisdiction of the territory which changed hands. Although deprived of political jurisdiction over the provinces, Peru attempted to retain moral control through the clergy who were under the diocesan authority of Arequipa. The clergy, violently patriotic, responded nobly, and kept their flocks permanently attached to the Peruvian cause. The diocese of Arequipa embraced not only the provinces of Tacna and Arica, but Tarapacá as well. It was in the latter province where the religious difficulty appeared first. When Tarapacá was occupied by Chile during the war most of the Peruvian priests withdrew and it became the duty of the Chilean government to fill the vacancies. Since military chaplains could not administer to the spiritual needs of people not a part of the army, the pope was persuaded, April 6, 1882, to make an exception to the law by granting parochial jurisdiction over Tarapacá to a military chaplain. Shortly after, the apostolic vicarates of Tarapacá and Antofagasta were created under Chilean control, although certain parishes in Tarapacá continued under Peruvian control and independent of the apostolic vicar. On November 16, 1892, the Vicar Apostolic Fuenzalida wrote to the Chilean Minister of Foreign Relations, Cult, and Colonization, pointing out the gravity of the anomalous situation. He claimed that by the terms of the papal act which created the vicarate apostolic of Tarapacá, its jurisdiction was intended to include all the province. Since Tarapacá was definitely annexed to Chile, he felt that the ecclesiastical authority should depend exclusively upon that country. The Bishop of Arequipa flatly refused to relinquish control of the parishes.

He declared that the right to divide bishoprics belonged exclusively to the pope; and he added that the Treaty of Ancón was one of force and therefore not binding.

As for the provinces of Tacna and Arica, there the ecclesiastical control of the Peruvian Church was complete, and for several years the Chilean government seemed to be unconcerned. During the decade 1887-1897 several missions were sent by Chile to the Vatican, but nothing was ever said about the religious situation in Tacna. After 1900, however, the matter became too prominent to be disregarded. The Bishop of Arequipa refused to grant licenses to Chilean priests, and Peruvian priests refused to officiate at Chilean festivals. Also, and most serious, the Peruvian clergy were redoubling their efforts to incite greater resistance to the Chileans. A crisis became inevitable when the Chilean government determined to Chileanize the provinces, and, in 1901, appointed Mariano Bascuñán director of the campaign. Acting on a suggestion of Bascuñán, Chile asked the Bishop of Arequipa to appoint none but foreign priests, neither Peruvian nor Chilean, to the parishes of Tacna. The Bishop not only refused, but attempted to remove the few foreign priests in the provinces and replace them with Peruvians. Then, also on the advice of Bascuñán, Chile appealed, May 15, 1908, to the pope to create an apostolic vicarate for Tacna dependent only on Rome and governed by a foreign functionary, neither Peruvian nor Chilean. The pope, striving to avoid any semblance of political intervention, refused to act.

Since it was recognized by Chile that the dispute could not be settled by the pope, she decided to resort to direct and severe measures with Peru and abandon useless discussions. Consequently, on February 17, 1910, an order was issued expelling all Peruvian priests from Tacna and Arica. As a result all religious services in the provinces were suspended and diplomatic relations between Peru and Chile were broken off. The religious crisis compelled the pope to abandon his attitude of non-interference, and, on April 15, 1910, he agreed to name, in conjunction with the Chilean government, a military vicar general for the two provinces. The vicar, in turn, was to name and remove chaplains. Rafael Edwards Salas was appointed, February 9, 1911, first military vicar general. He bore the rank of a brigardier general, the dignity of a bishop, and received a salary of eight thousand *pesos*. The Bishop of Arequipa, supported naturally by public opinion in Peru, opposed the papal action in the provinces, but to no avail. In 1915 the pope elevated the military vicar general to the position of bishop auxiliary of the diocese of Santiago, and thus the parishes were restored to their normal ecclesiastical status. Such was the outcome of the vexed Tacna-Arica religious problem. When Church and State were separated in Chile in 1925, the clergy of the provinces were freed of governmental control, as were the clergy of the rest of the republic. The return of Tacna to Peru, under the agreement of 1929, means evidently, that the Church in that province will be absorbed into the Church-State system which exists in the Republic of Peru.[53]

Separation of Church and State was a cherished political ideal of advanced thinkers in Chile. Many times in the history of the republic they had attempted to abolish what they regarded as an antiquated civil-ecclesiastical union. Their efforts resulted invariably in failure; yet, with the passage of time the prospects of ultimate success became brighter. Several factors contributed to the eventual peaceful and eminently satisfactory dissolution of the Church-State bonds.

After, and even before, the World War, a great change in religious attitude came over Chileans. Writing in 1911, Galdames said, "There is to be noted in the entire country a marked religious evolution. It is not that the people are separating from the Church, for at least three-quarters of the population continue to be sincere Catholics. Nor is it due to hostility of Protestantism. The free-thinkers do not constitute an organized nucleus against the Church. It is simple tolerance and religious indifference."[54] In evidence of this increased tolerance, Chileans no longer regarded it as a stamp of honor for a believer to abominate another cult than his own, and in judging an individual, no longer was it the practice as of old, to inquire into his religious beliefs. As for increased religious indifference, one needs but mention the astonishing scarcity of men at mass and the general laxity in the

---

[53] The above account is based on José Luis Fermandoiz, *El Conflicto Eclesiástico de Tacna* (Santiago, 1923).

[54] Galdames, *Historia de Chile*, p. 493.

observance of fasting and confession. Chileans were becoming mentally prepared for the separation. This applied to the thinker as well as to the religious laggard. The former, with his developing tolerance, was becoming convinced that neither Church nor State could gain anything through a continuance of the union. As for the latter, he was no longer a serious factor, except that he could not be relied upon by the Church to support it in a struggle.

Another event which contributed immediately to dissolution was the victory of the Radical and Democratic parties at the polls in 1920. In the elections of that year the candidate of the dominant political Oligarchy, supported by the Conservatives and a large section of the Liberals, was defeated by Señor Arturo Alessandri, who became Chile's first "middle-class president." Now that the Radicals were in power it was a foregone conclusion that they would make another attempt to abolish the union between the Church and State. It was not unexpected, therefore, when President Alessandri proposed to the Congress, June 1, 1923, the advisability of amending the fundamental law to free the Church of all governmental connections. He wished the State, he said, to be the neutral and impartial protector of the rights of all. It was not proper therefore that a particular cult should be privileged above others. Moreover it was injurious to the Church, for it became inextricably involved in politics. On the dangers of this position, President Alessandri quoted Bishop Valdivieso (April 30, 1859), "When ministers become affiliated with political groups, they compromise the sacred interests of their charge. The future of the Church, the most precious interests of religion, are then tied up to the fortunes of a party."[55]

There was a slight murmur on the part of the hierarchy at first, but once convinced that the movement was sincere and had no ulterior motives, the clergy, led by the octogenarian primate Mgr. Edwards Errázuriz, agreed that both Church and State would profit by the disestablishment.[56] The ecclesiastical and governmental officials therefore entered into a friendly, business-like agreement, the former promising no resistance to separation, the

---

[55] *Mensaje Leido por S. E. el Presidente de la República* (Santiago, June 1, 1923), pp. 28-31.

[56] *The Chicago Tribune*, August 24, 1929.

latter guaranteeing to the Church title to its vast properties, the right to conduct its own schools, and financial aid over a brief transitional period. Consequently there was little or no opposition to the incorporation in the new constitution of Chile, which was promulgated on September 18, 1925, of a clause which definitely terminated the ancient system of a State-Church. This step was made possible, not only because of the ascendancy of the Radical opponents of the patronal system, but also because the other elements of society, even including the clergy, realized, either that this was a logical and beneficial action, or else that it would be futile to attempt opposition. Chile has thus earned the enviable distinction of being one of the few Latin-American nations that has solved this delicate problem, not only without bloodshed, but in a spirit of good fellowship and hearty coöperation on both sides. "The dissolution was not accomplished," said one of the constituents, "by repudiation, but by divorce through mutual consent."[57]

The new constitution contains the following provisions touching on religion:

Article 10. The Constitution insures to all the inhabitants of the Republic:

Practice of all beliefs, liberty of conscience and the free exercise of all religions that may not be contrary to morality, good usage and public order. Therefore, the respective religious bodies have the right to erect and maintain houses of worship and accessory property under the conditions of security and hygiene as fixed by the laws and regulations.

The churches, creeds, and religious institutions of any ritual shall have those rights in respect to their property as the law now in force may stipulate or recognize; but they will be subject, under the guarantees of this constitution, to common law in the exercise of ownership of their future acquired property.

Churches and accessory property intended for the service of any religious sect are exempt from taxation.[58]

---

[57] Guerra, *op. cit.,* p. 49.

[58] *The Constitution of Chile* (Pan American Union, Washington, 1925); For the religious question in the convention see *Ministerio del Interior Actas Oficiales de las Sesiones celebrados por la Comisión y Subcomisiones encargadas del estudio del Proyecto de Nueva Constitución Política de la República* (Santiago, 1925), pp. 397, 471.

The first of the transitory provisions of the Constitution declares abolished all laws concerning the interrelations of Church and State, appointment to ecclesiastical positions, presentation to benefices, authorization of papal communications, and related subjects. Also, it was provided that, to facilitate the transition of the Catholic Church from a protected organization into an independent entity, the government should appropriate it the sum of 2,500,000 pesos annually for a period of five years. Brazil, in pronouncing separation, granted the Church a subvention for one year. But Chile, more generous, made the period five years, and it appears it may be indefinitely extended.[59]

In commenting on the act of separation, President Alessandri said, "There has been established the principle of liberty and conscience in respectful form without wounding the sensibilities of anyone, and thus there has been consecrated the principle of absolute separation of the temporal and spiritual orders."[60] On September 20, 1925, in referring to the termination of the union of Church and State, Mgr. Errázuriz, the venerable Archbishop of Santiago, said in his pastoral: "It is just to note that the authorities of Chile, in establishing this separation, have not been actuated by the spirit of persecution which characterizes other countries where Catholicism has been attacked. By the sacrifice of separation, the Church acquires, at least, the liberty which divine law accords it; and, finally, the State is separated from the Church; but the Church is not separated from the State, and will always be ready to serve it."[61]

The actual régime of religious cults in Chile is that of separation from the State. Liberty of conscience and freedom of worship are guaranteed so long as they are not opposed to morals, good customs, and public order. There are no religious tests for the exercise of the suffrage or for holding public office. The only tie between the Catholic Church and the government is the annual subsidy which was supposed to terminate in 1929. When it is discontinued, separation will be complete. Yet in recognition of the

---

[59] Guerra, *op. cit.,* 50.

[60] Arturo Alessandri, *Reformas Constitucionales* (Santiago, 1925), p. 56.

[61] *Informativo Postal N. 38,* Ministerio de Relaciones Exteriores, Republica de Chile (to J. L. Mecham).

fact that the great majority of the Chileans are counted as Catholics, Chile continues to accredit a diplomatic representative to the Vatican, and the Vatican in turn accredits an apostolic nuncio to Santiago.[62] The department of government in Chile which looks after ecclesiastical affairs is the Ministry of Foreign Relations. Having renounced all patronal claims the government obviously has no present rights in the election of ecclesiastical officers, and the Chilean clergy are free to communicate at will with the Vatican.

Title to the vast ecclesiastical holdings valued at millions of dollars was handed over to the Church without any restrictions whatever. It was recognized as independent possessor and administrator of its revenue producing properties, as well as approximately 1300 churches, 250 monasteries and convents, scores of primary and secondary schools, over a dozen seminaries, about a hundred hospitals, and the Universities of Santiago and Valparaiso, the former being almost as large and influential academically as the University of Chile. The Church property which is used exclusively for religious purposes is tax exempt. This, of course, applies to all cults. When the property is devoted to commercial purposes, however, and incidentally the Catholic Church is one of the largest landowners in Chile, it is assessed the same tax as that of private individuals. No restrictions are placed upon the Church to receive entailments, bequests and the like. The chief sources of income are revenues from properties, and donations and subscriptions of the faithful. The people have taken up the chief burden of supporting the Church by voluntary contribution without a protest.[63]

Under the new Constitution the Church exercises no control over public education. On the other hand it is not prevented from maintaining a complete educational system, under a limited governmental supervision, from the primary grades to the university. In the public schools there are classes in religion, but these are elective. There are in Chile, out of a total of 4200 schools and colleges, 600 private schools, and of the latter, 500 are maintained

---

[62] Consul-General of Chile to J. L. Mecham, New York, May 21, 1927; Ralph H. Ackerman, American Commercial Attaché, to J. L. Mecham, Santiago, December 3, 1927.

[63] *Chicago Tribune,* August 24, 1929; R. H. Ackerman to J. L. Mecham.

by the Catholic Church. The majority of the remaining private schools, about 60, are supported by Protestant sects. The Catholic schools, primary as well as secondary, usually require no tuition fees and are maintained by money from members of the Church and from the bishopric subsidies. Only a few receive funds from the government. Members of the priesthood are not allowed to teach in public schools.[64]

The *teológicas reformas* of Santa María relating to matrimony and the control of cemeteries are still in force in Chile. The only legal form of marriage is the civil marriage according to the law of 1884. The religious ceremony may be performed when desired, but for several years it has been the law that the civil rites must be celebrated first.[65] Everyone goes through the form of civil marriage obediently, but no Catholic considers himself married until after the ceremony has been performed by the Church. The priests coöperate with the government and refuse to marry a couple until the civil marriage certificate is produced. Chile does not permit divorce. There may be legal separation, but this does not allow for remarriage. Only when civil nullity has been proclaimed may individuals again marry.

There are public, or general, and private cemeteries in Chile. The general cemeteries, of which there are several in Santiago, are under the charge of the Charity Council under the direction of the Minister of Interior. Funds for their maintenance are derived from rents or sales of plots, and from governmental and public subscriptions. In Santiago there are Catholic and Protestant cemeteries. There are likewise private cemeteries scattered throughout Chile. The public has exercised the right since 1884 of electing cemeteries for their deceased. Since that date the Cath-

---

[64] *Current History,* May, 1927, p. 312; R. H. Ackerman to J. L. Mecham; *Christian Work in South America,* I, 249-254; *Mensaje Leido por S. E. el Vicepresidente de la República* (Carlos Ibañez) *en la apertura del Congreso Nacional el 21 de Mayo de 1927* (Santiago, 1927), p. 13.

[65] The marriage of President Ibañez was an exception to this rule. After the religious ceremony, which occurred in a church in the presence of a notable assemblage, the bridal couple did not present themselves until several hours later before the civil officials for the performance of the civil ceremony. (*La Prensa,* New York, December 4, 1927.)

olic Church has been forced to abandon its one-time right of exclusive jurisdiction over interments.[66]

Chile is evidently working out a satisfactory solution of the problem of ecclesiastical relations. Although the Catholic Church is still a powerful force in the body politic, it is no longer the troublesome political factor of the past; there is today neither a clerical nor an anti-clerical party in the republic. As the political activities of the clergy decreased their moral influence increased. Suspicion and opposition have given place to reverence and support. The clergy of Chile, well-educated, widely traveled, alert, and broad-minded, rank high among Latin-American ecclesiastics. Most of the prelates have been recruited from the hundred or more families of the aristocracy which has ruled Chile in the past. Clerical influence in recent years has been of a correspondingly high order and a remarkable religious revival has resulted. Separation it seems has stimulated an increased dependence on the spiritual mentors. Attendance at mass has actually increased in recent years. On all holy days public offices and business houses close as before the separation. Religious processions through the streets are as popular as before. On the Feast of the Virgin of Carmen, the patron saint of the Chilean military forces, the army and navy turn out en masse to carry an image of their patron saint through the principal streets.[67] The Rev. Webster E. Browning, a prominent and trustworthy Evangelical worker in South America, comments (1930) on the present status of the Catholic Church in Chile:

"The Roman Church, in spite of its boast that it is *semper eadem*, trims its sails to meet altered circumstances, and it is quietly adapting itself to the new conditions. The old spirit of intolerance is no longer so evident, though it still exists among some of the clergy; a better class of men are entering the priesthood; there are fewer foreign priests; education is encouraged and fostered by the Church; social conditions are studied by the ecclesiastical authorities and efforts made to better them, and authorized editions of the Gospels have been circulated in order to offset the

---

[66] R. H. Ackerman to J. L. Mecham. [67] *Chicago Tribune*, August 24, 1929.

18

influence of those sold by the Bible societies. A recent order of the Archbishop obliges all priests under seventy years of age to read a portion of the Gospels, in the language of the country, in every mass celebrated by them."[68]

Surely the history of the Catholic Church in Chile since 1925 refutes the time-worn argument that separation of Church and State would inaugurate an era of irreligion resulting eventually in the destruction of the Church.

[68] *West Coast Republics*, p. 43.

CHAPTER X

THE STATE-CHURCH IN ARGENTINA

In the Argentine Republic there has been steady adherence to
a religious policy determined in the earliest days of the struggle
for independence. The most successful of the Spanish colonies
in maintaining without interruption their political independence
after the home authority was discarded in 1810, the provinces of
La Plata made no attempt to reduce the Church from the high
position it enjoyed in the colonial system. The Constitution of
April 22, 1819, the first formal one of the Argentine Nation, then
known as the United Provinces of La Plata, sanctioned the traditional principle of the religion of the State. "The government
owes to religion," it declared, "the most efficacious and powerful
protection, and the inhabitants of all the territory respect it,
whatever might be their private opinions."[1] The right to exercise
the patronal privilege of presentation was affirmed. It provided that
the executive should select from triple lists of names (*ternas*)
prepared by the Senate, nominees for vacant archiepiscopal and
episcopal sees. Nominations for other benefices and dignities were
vested in the executive alone. To the Church was accorded the
privilege of permanent representation in the Senate, in the persons of a bishop and three lesser ecclesiastics. On the other hand,
archbishops and bishops were placed on a par with the highest civil
functionaries, such as ministers of state, and, like them, were subject to accusation in the Senate by the Chamber of Representatives, "for the crimes of treason, collusion, misappropriation of
the public funds, violation of the Constitution" and other crimes.
In subjecting ecclesiastics to trial before the Senate, the privilege of the ecclesiastical *fuero* was denied. In order that there
should be no doubt as to the intent of the Constitution to consider
prelates supported by the State as public employees, it required

---

[1] Vedia, *Constitución Argentina,* p. 100.

that "no political, civil, military, or *ecclesiastical employee* can [could] continue in his office without taking oath to observe and support the Constitution."[2] A notable feature of this, as well as of other constitutions of La Plata, was that it guaranteed liberty of conscience. In the constituent assembly which framed the Constitution of 1819 were nine clerics, and the presiding officer of the convention was the distinguished liberal canon Dr. Gregorio Funes.[3]

The kaleidoscopic political changes in La Plata did not permit the application of the new constitution, for there ensued a ten-year period of near-anarchy during which the only semblance of order appeared in the province of Buenos Aires under the governorship of Martín Rodríguez. The Church had been, since 1810, independent of papal control; and when the hierarchy became extinct, the clergy, free of all restraint, fell into corrupt ways. By 1820 the situation became intolerable and it was necessary for Bernardino Rivadavia, principal minister of Governor Rodríguez, and one of Latin America's greatest statesmen, to include the Church in his reform program. "It would be puerile," says an Argentinian authority, "to stop and discourse on doctrinaire questions, when all who have investigated the events know the truth: the immediate object of the reform was to correct the habits of an undisciplined and licentious clergy. . . . The corruption of the monastic orders was great, and their reform was hoped for and desired by Catholics themselves."[4] Under the guidance of Rivadavia the Congress passed an ecclesiastical reform law on December 21, 1822. It abolished the tithes and the ecclesiastical *fuero*. Rules of discipline were prescribed for religious orders, the membership of ecclesiastical houses was limited to a minimum of sixteen and a maximum of thirty, and no one was allowed to enter orders until he was twenty-five years old. Some regular orders, like the Bethlehemites, were suppressed and their property confiscated by the State. The goods and rents of houses not suppressed

---

[2] Chacaltana, *Patronato Nacional Argentino,* p. 70.

[3] Piaggio, *El Clero en Argentina,* p. 240; Silva, *Bolívar y Dean Funes,* pp. 106-114.

[4] José Ingenieros, *La Evolución de las Ideas Argentinas* (Buenos Aires, 1920), I, 440-441.

were administered by the prelates, but in conformity with the law which required an annual accounting of the administration to the government. Also, cathedral churches and all buildings, lands, and other properties not appertaining to the immediate service of the cult were put under the exclusive control of the government. By decrees of January 4 and 17, 1823, provision was made to support the Church from the public treasury and control the construction of churches in the province. In short, these laws consolidated the preëxisting régime of a national Church, partially reformed the regulars, and improved the civil organization of the secular Church.[5]

It was during the ascendancy of Rivadavia that Vicar Apostolic Mgr. Juan Muzi arrived in Buenos Aires. The political functionaries, regarding Muzi as a diplomatic agent not accredited to the government of La Plata, refused to allow him to perform any official act prior to papal recognition of Argentine independence, and ordered him to leave the country. Following his arrival in Santiago, Chile, on March 6, 1824, Muzi issued a pastoral to Chileans, and, indirectly, to all Americans. He pointed out the necessity of maintaining relations with Rome and combatting those who with "the false and specious name of reformers treat like a purely human work the divine constitution of the Church and of its supreme head, pretending to form a National Church separated from the Universal Church and its head."[6] There is little doubt that the Apostolic Vicar was alluding to the reforms of Rivadavia. When Muzi stopped at Montevideo, on his return to Italy, he secretly named Mariano Medrano apostolic delegate with all the rights and powers enjoyed by a capitular vicar in a vacant episcopal see. Medrano had distinguished himself, as will be noted shortly, by opposing the ecclesiastical reform.[7]

The reforms of Rivadavia, which strongly smacked of doctrinaire regalism, and which, although well-intentioned, were in many

[5] *Ibid.,* I, 492-495; Mariano de Vedia y Mitre, *De Rivadavia á Rosas,* Buenos Aires, 1930, pp. 51-52; For a temperate discussion of the ill-advised reform policy of Rivadavia, see José Manuel Estrada, *La Iglesia y el Estado* (Buenos Aires, 1929), pp. 35-37.

[6] Legón, *Patronato Nacional,* p. 491.

[7] Ingenieros, *op. cit.,* II, 518.

cases anti-canonical, aroused a storm of protest on the part of the so-called *apostólicos* or ultramontanes. The officers of the government were called "the libertines of Buenos Aires," and were charged with license, aspostacy, and impiety. Some of the more fanatical of the *apostólicos*, under the leadership of a certain Gregorio Tagle, with the cry of "religión ó muerte" on their lips, even resorted to violence. Dr. Mariano Medrano, provisor of the bishopric of Buenos Aires, *en sede vacante*, objected strenuously and appealed to the Chamber of Representatives to affirm the incompetence of the civil power to legislate in ecclesiastical matters. Rivadavia countered by requesting the removal of Medrano from his position as provisor. The Chamber approved the removal and notified the cathedral chapter, which took action in 1822. The chapter thereupon, with the approval of Rivadavia, elected Mariano Zavaleta as provisor of the diocese.[8]

Notwithstanding violent protests on the part of the *apostólicos*, the ecclesiastical reform was well received in Buenos Aires, even by the clergy. Dean Funes favored it and publicly refuted the arguments of Juan Muzi, who condemned the reform and national patronage.[9] Rivadavia's attack was not directed at religion in general, nor at the dogmas of the Catholic Church in particular, but only at the external control of that organization. He preferred a concordat which would convey to the government most of the authority that had been exercised in political affairs by the kings of Spain, but since an agreement with the pope was impossible at that time, he reiterated the intention of the government to retain the prerogatives of the Spanish monarchs and establish a national church. Thus, on September 3, 1821, Rivadavia declared that while the Holy See withheld recognition, and until a concordat should be concluded, the Argentinian government would deny to Rome any control over the Church in Argentina. The ecclesiastical policy of the great minister was, indeed, the only possible one, for since there existed in fact a national church, it was indispensable for the government legally to regularize its functions.[10] "Neither Rivadavia nor the clerics who assisted him

---

[8] Legón, *op. cit.*, pp. 473-475.

[9] For the attitude of Dean Funes on ecclesiastical polity see Silva, *Bolívar y Dean Funes*, p. 111.   [10] Ingenieros, *op. cit.*, I, 438.

in his reforms were Masons," said Rómulo Carbia, "nor was the reform, even in its most advanced stages, other than the consequence of a clear regalism, executed imprudently, with a well-defined object and a clear orientation. . . . In no case was the reform a Voltairean campaign against the Church."[11]

In 1826 the provinces of La Plata made another essay at union with a centralistic constitution and under the presidency of Bernardino Rivadavia. This constitution reproduced most of the provisions of the Law of 1819, regarding religion, but in spirit it tended to even greater tolerance. This spirit of tolerance was reflected in the treaty of amity and commerce with Great Britain, concluded in 1825. It guaranteed to British subjects perfect liberty of conscience and the right to worship inside their houses and churches. The first Protestant church was built in Buenos Aires in 1829. The Protestants were also given the right to maintain and control their own cemeteries. As in the earlier constitution, that of 1826 gave the president the right to nominate archbishops and bishops from triple lists prepared by the Senate. A new element of control was introduced by the provision which gave to the Supreme Court the power of exequatur with respect to all papal bulls and encyclicals, for it was to recommend to the president whether or not such documents should be admitted into the country.[12]

Mariano Medrano, secretly appointed apostolic delegate by Juan Muzi in 1825, did not dare, because of the circumstances of his appointment, to assert the prerogatives of his position while the government was under the control of Rivadavia. The resignation of that great statesman on June 27, 1827, did not improve conditions, for the "Jacobins," Dorrego and Manuel Moreno, were notorious "Federalists," and were antagonistic to the apostólicos. Even the infamous Lavalle, like his victim Dorrego, exercised to the full the patronal rights over the national Church. It was not until the ascendancy, in 1829, of Viamonte, a puppet of Juan Manuel de Rosas, who was already preparing the stage for

[11] Rómulo D. Carbia, "La Revolución de Mayo y la Iglesia," in *Anales de la Facultad de Derecho* (Buenos Aires, 1915), p. 271.

[12] Vedia, *op. cit.*, p. 100; L. S. Rowe, *The Federal System of the Argentine Republic* (Washington, 1921), p. 128.

his dictatorship, that the Conservatives came into their own and official relations with the Holy See entered a new phase. Until 1829 non-communication with Rome was virtually complete. Not since the unsuccessful mission of Valentín Gómez had a government in Buenos Aires attempted to negotiate with Rome, and, on the other hand, overtures by the pope, notably the Muzi mission, had been emphatically rejected. Yet it is true that, during this period, unofficial overtures were made by men like Friar Pacheco, and some priests of the interior provinces received bulls from Rome. Often these papal documents were sent in response to official provincial solicitation. For example, on December 22, 1825, Pope Leo XII, in answer to a petition of the government of San Juan, named Fray Justo Santa María de Oro, bishop *in partibus* and vicar apostolic of Cuyo.[13]

When Viamonte assumed control of the government, the *apostólica camarilla*, headed by Mariano Medrano, Gregorio Tagle, and Tomás Manuel de Anchorena, induced him to appeal to the pope for the nomination of a Bishop of Buenos Aires. On October 8, 1829, Governor Viamonte, through his minister Tomás Guido, wrote to the pope asking that he name a proprietary bishop, or one *in partibus*, for Buenos Aires, in order to provide for the spiritual necessities of the country, "so long as this should not be in contradiction of the existing laws of the land." This exception, referring to the laws of Rivadavia, indicates clearly that the right of national patronage had not been renounced, but, on the contrary, was reinforced by the government's presentation of the names of Diego Estanislao Zavaleta and Mariano Medrano for episcopal institution.[14] Over the protests of the Spanish ambassador, Labrador, Pope Pius VIII responded on March 13, 1830, that he had anticipated the Argentinian supplication by appointing, on October 7, 1829, Mariano Medrano as Bishop of Aulón, *in partibus* and Vicar Apostolic with authority to occupy

---

[13] In 1834 Pope Gregory XVI created the diocese of Cuyo and named Santa María de Oro the first bishop. The dismemberment of the Córdoban diocese, to which Cuyo belonged, created an irregular situation and a consequent serious ecclesiastical conflict which was finally settled by the government of the Confederation. (Legón, *op. cit.*, p. 492.)

[14] P. Leturia, "Alusiones en la Cámara Argentina al origen histórico del Patronato de Indias," in *Razón y Fé* (1927), Vol. 78, 334,

the vacant see.[15] Medrano, leaving his bull with the government for the exequatur, went to Rio de Janeiro in September, 1830, for his consecration. The *fiscal* Agrelo now entered the lists as a staunch champion of national patronage. His ecclesiastical policy, which was a middle position between ultramontane demands for an anti-regalistic concordat and Jacobin demands for separation of Church and State, was later embodied in the Constitution of 1853, and endures to the present time. He requested that the commission and instructions to the Vicar Apostolic, mentioned in the bull but not presented to the government, be submitted likewise for the exequatur. Medrano refused to accede, saying that they related to spiritual subjects. Fortunately for Medrano and the *apostólicos*, Tomás Manuel de Anchorena occupied the influential position of Minister of Cult. He contended that the exequatur did not apply to bulls and documents relating to spiritual matters. It would suffice, he declared, for Medrano to swear a solemn oath to observe and comply with the laws of the Province. This Medrano did on January 31, 1831.[16] The cathedral chapter, while recognizing Medrano as Vicar Apostolic, refused to concede that this title enabled him to assume control of the diocese. Consequently, on February 25, 1831, the chapter appealed to the government to restrain the Vicar Apostolic in his endeavors to assume jurisdiction. To end the controversy, Rosas signed a decree on March 23, 1831, to the effect that "it being absolutely necessary to end this controversy and avoid doubts and discussions that might cause disorders prejudicial to the ministers of the gospel, the government determines to recognize in all this province, Mariano Medrano, Bishop of Aulón, as Vicar Apostolic of this diocese of Buenos Aires with all and each of the rights with which he is authorized, and which a capitular vicar in a vacant episcopal see should enjoy." Due to Rosas' absence from the capital on a campaign, the chapter persisted in its opposition, and Medrano was unable to take possession of his see until August 3, 1831, when he was given governmental aid.[17]

---

[15] Ingenieros, *op. cit.,* II, 411. According to Ingenieros (*Ibid.,* II, 518) Medrano's appointment was conditioned by the pope on the understanding that it nullified the *regalías* of the Argentine nation.

[16] *Ibid.,* II, 420,   [17] Legón, *op. cit.,* pp. 493-494,

Anchorena, the *apostólico* minister who frankly questioned the validity of national patronage, was responsible for numerous acts of intolerance and religious persecution. For example, one of his decrees was aimed at the importation and reading of books "which manifestly tended to attack the moral teachings of the Gospels, the truth and sanctity of the religion of the State, and the divinity of Jesus Christ, its founder." Anchorena governed the Church and the clergy with such vigor that he was called Torquemada and his ministry, the Inquisition. "This epoch," said Ramos Mejía, "marked in the history of our moral life a phase of greatest danger because the liberty of conscience and thought was restricted." When Anchorena resigned on January 30, 1832, the increasing power of the *apostólicos* suffered a temporary decline.[18]

The controversy over the appointment of Mariano Medrano as vicar apostolic proved to be only a prelude to a more serious crisis resulting from his appointment as proprietary bishop. On July 2, 1832, Pope Gregory XVI, *motu proprio*, named Mariano Medrano Bishop of Buenos Aires. On the same day the Pope named Mariano Escalada, the provisor, Bishop of Aulón, *in partibus*, and Vicar Apostolic with authority to act as auxiliary of the diocese. Due to the fact that the government was at that time in the control of enemies of the *apostólicos*, Medrano and Escalada withheld presentation of their bulls, but finally, in August, 1833, they were forced to turn them over to the *fiscal*. Once more Agrelo rushed to the defense of Argentine patronage against the pretentions of the Roman Curia. Because of his objection to the use in the bull of the term *motu proprio*, which was interpreted to mean that the Pope disregarded the government's right of presentation, Medrano's bull was denied the *pase* or exequatur (December 19, 1833). The bull of Mariano Escalada was also retained by the government.[19]

To put an end to the ever-recurring disputes and disagreements over the nature and extent of national patronage, the government,

---

[18] Ingenieros, *op. cit.*, II, 425.

[19] Adolfo Saldías, *Historia de la Confederación Argentina* (Buenos Aires, 1911), V, 115-116.

acting on the proposal of Agrelo, appointed a special committee of thirty-nine theologians and jurists to pass judgment upon fourteen propositions, which, in the opinion of the government, ought to be accepted as basic principles of the *patronato nacional*. Some of these were as follows: (1) included in sovereignty, which is vested in the people, is the right of ecclesiastical patronage; (2) the nation has the right, under sovereignty, to grant or refuse the exequatur to all papal documents and communications; (3) the government has the right of presentation to ecclesiastical offices and benefices; (4) the government has the right to alter the limits of ecclesiastical jurisdictions; (5) the pope cannot reserve to himself the right to appoint to vacant sees or alter the territorial limits of dioceses; (6) the oath demanded of bishops should in no way operate to diminish their obligations to the State; (7) bishops should on taking oath, recognize the *patronato nacional* and swear fidelity and respect to the government; (8) all citizens should submit to the government for the exequatur any bull or communication of whatever description received from the Roman Curia; and (9) non-communication will continue until the papacy recognizes national rights in a concordat.[20]

The committee, with the exception of only two members, Anchorena and Felipe Arana, approved the fourteen propositions. These principles, together with the written opinions of the individual members of the committee, were published by Agrelo and became famous as the *Memorial Ajustado de 1834*. This document thereafter constituted a pattern for ecclesiastical policy in Argentina.

Agrelo, having the opinions of the members of the committee, consented, on March 24, 1834, to recognize Medrano as Bishop of Buenos Aires, since his name had in fact been presented to the pope in 1829. If there were no disposition to interpret the papal use of *motu proprio* too strictly, Medrano's appointment could be regarded as conforming to the national pretentions. Escalada, however, having never been nominated by the government, was refused recognition as bishop auxiliary. His bull was

---

[20] Chacaltana, *op. cit.*, pp. 115-118; Saldías, *op. cit.*, II, 197-199.

withheld until April 23, 1835, when Rosas, ten days after assuming dictatorial control over the government, ordered the exequatur.[21]

Under the dictatorship of Juan Manuel de Rosas (1835-1852) the Catholic Church was converted into a servile instrument of the tyranny. Although he was personally indifferent on religious matters, Rosas nevertheless understood that the Church could be used as a most efficacious instrument of his absolutism. His policy, therefore, was to protect the Church, even to the extent of being the persecutor of its political adversaries, but on condition that it should submit to his personal power. He cherished the *patronato*, but in the same spirit as he regarded his control of the civil government, i.e., he conceived it as being something personal, illimitable, and without legal checks. If the government were to function properly, no one should oppose his will. His aim was that of dual preëminence: pope and emperor.[22]

The Church allied itself with the tyranny at the start, and in the end was hopelessly subjected by it. Because Rosas was kindly disposed toward the ecclesiastical interests it was natural that, in the beginning, all elements adverse to the reforms of Rivadavia should adhere to his policy. For instance, many of the houses of the regulars, disestablished by Rivadavia, were restored and the Jesuits were allowed to return to the country. For obvious reasons the regulars supported the tyrant. But once enrolled in the service of the "Santa Causa de la Federación," and after the absolutism of the tyranny was converted into a regalistic absolutism of the worst kind, the clergy were unable to extricate themselves. Rosas began by assisting ecclesiastical interests and ended by persecuting the clergy. But Bishop Medrano, it appears, was a willing, abject supporter of Rosas; he was a sort of *mayordomo* to a feudal lord. "In the persons of Rosas and Medrano," says Ingenieros, "was realized the union of throne and altar."[23]

Rosas, realizing the necessity of discipline and morality in the

---

[21] Ingenieros, *op. cit.*, II, 519; Saldías, *op. cit.*, p. 117.

[22] Saldías (*op. cit.*, p. 115) defends Rosas as a good Catholic and a zealous protector of the patronage. He insists that Rosas did not promote antagonisms. His conclusions have not been accepted by the present writer.

[23] *Ibid.*, II, 520; Legón, *op. cit.*, p. 498.

lower clergy, was responsible for numerous decrees and orders which suspended, removed, or jailed priests for immoral conduct. He induced Medrano to consent to a diminution in the number of religious festival days. The ecclesiastical tribunals were also reformed. Theoretically appeals from the decisions of ecclesiastical courts in La Plata went to the archbishop of Chuquisaca. This, of course, was impracticable after the old Viceroyalty of La Plata had broken up into a number of independent states. Non-communication with Rome contributed to the difficulty of the problem since appeals to the Roman Curia were not allowed. Therefore it was provided by decree that cases in first instance should be heard by the provisor; in second instance by a member of the clergy named by the government on proposal of the bishop; and third, by the bishop and two members of the *Senado del Clero*, also named by the government on proposal of the bishop. In 1847 the Jesuits were expelled by order of Rosas on the charge of sedition.[24]

Rosas' insistence on the observance of the patronage was inflexible and brooked no violation. He declared that he would regard as invalid any bull, brief, or rescript which appeared to have emanated from the Roman Curia after May 25, 1810, and which had not received the exequatur of the Minister of Foreign Affairs. This invalidation was specifically extended to the bulls of bishops *in partibus infidelium*. Any violator of the decree was subject to punishment "as a disturber of the public order and an assailant of the sovereignty and independence of the republic."[25]

Of course the patronage was used abusively—outside of all civil and ecclesiastical limitations. The Church, unable to protect itself, was forced to depart from its spiritual mission and support some of the most ignominious acts of the terror. On December 7, 1836, a note was sent to Bishop Medrano commanding him to order the clergy, in all discourses of whatever nature, to counsel obedience to the Federal cause, and condemn that of the Unitarians. When the bull of the Bishop of Cuyo was granted the *pase* in October, 1839, the Bishop had to swear to defend and sustain,

---

[24] Sarsfield, *Relaciones del Estado con la Iglesia*, p. 147; Saldías, *op. cit.*, V, 117.

[25] Chacaltana, *op. cit.*, pp. 72-74; Saldías, *op. cit.*, V, 115.

in sermons, confessions, and conversations, the liberty and independence of the republic *under the Federal régime*. Thus, in place of an Argentine clergy, we have a Federal clergy. Indeed, the use of the Federal red in altar decorations was made compulsory and the faithful in Buenos Aires saw, on the very altars, the picture of Rosas the "Restorer of the Laws." Clerical humiliation and degradation reached their climax when, with Christ and the Virgin, the pictures and images of the heroes of the "Santa Causa de la Federación" were adored. Thus was established the cult of the tyrant and his political system.[26]

The overthrow of Rosas on the battlefield of Caseros by General Justo José de Urquiza and his Uruguayan and Brazilian allies necessitated a complete reorganization of the government of Argentina. With that end in view, Urquiza, who bore the title of "Provisional Director of the Argentine Confederation," convened a Constituent Assembly at Santa Fé in November, 1852. All the provinces, with the exception of Buenos Aires, were represented. Since the Convention drew heavily upon a notable treatise called "Bases and Suggestions for the Political Organization of the Argentine Republic," written for the guidance of the constituents by the distinguished publicist Juan Bautista Alberdi, it is appropriate to examine his suggestions regarding the proper legal relationship that should obtain between Church and State. According to Alberdi, solicitude for religion should be the first object of the fundamental law, for, he said, "it is for the complexion of peoples what pure blood is for the health of the individual." Yet, argued Alberdi, the ecclesiastical policy of Argentina should be dictated by reason, and even as the Spanish colonial religious system served political purposes, the logical policy for Argentina should be religious toleration. Immigrants must be attracted, not discouraged; as would certainly be the case if religious exclusion were adopted. "Religious liberty," he said, "is the means of populating the country." Alberdi's motto was: "To govern is to populate." Consequently, Article 3 of his project read: "The Confederation adopts and sustains the Catholic faith and guarantees liberty for all other faiths." With respect to the patronage he

---

[26] Ricardo Levene, *Lecciones de Historia Argentina* (Buenos Aires, 1919), II, 365; Ingenieros, *op. cit.*, II, 488 ff.

suggested that the president be given the power: (1) to select for archbishops, bishops, dignitaries, and prebends of cathedral churches, from triple lists of names prepared by the Senate; (2) to exercise the right of national patronage with respect to churches, benefices, and ecclesiastical persons; and (3) to grant or refuse the *pase* to bulls, briefs, and papal documents with the consent of the Senate, special legislation being required when they contained general or permanent dispositions.[27]

While accepting without question and little debate Alberdi's proposal on the patronage, some of the members of the Convention desired a less tolerant religious policy than he advocated. They wanted the constitution to declare that Catholicism was the religion of the State, and "the only true one." But this was opposed on the ground that the State represented the collectivity of people and it could not profess an intimate belief which was not that of all the inhabitants. Such a question, it was contended, was more proper for an ecclesiastical council than a political congress. Nevertheless, all accepted the proposition, "Catholicism is the dominant religion of the country"; i.e., it was the religion of the majority, and that gave the federal government the right to intervene in the cult. Therefore the final formula: the government supports the cult, but does not profess it, because conscience is outside its domain. That the suggestions of Alberdi, relating to religion, were adopted by the Convention of Santa Fé, can be evidenced by an examination of the Constitution of 1853. The principal religious clauses in that instrument were the following: (1) the federal government supports the Roman Catholic religion; (2) all inhabitants shall enjoy, subject to the laws regulating their exercise, the right freely to profess their religion; (3) aliens may practice freely their religion; (4) no member of the religious orders shall be elected to Congress; (5) Congress shall have the power: (a) to promote the conversion of the Indians on the frontiers; (b) to approve or reject concordats entered into with the Apostolic See, and to make rules for the exercise of the ecclesiastical patronage throughout the nation; (c) to admit into the territory of the nation religious orders in addition to those now existing; (6) the president, who

---

[27] Alberdi, *Bases y Puntos de Partida*, pp. 109-111, 285, 307, 308.

must be a Roman Catholic, is given the following powers: (a) he shall exercise the right of national ecclesiastical patronage by nominating bishops for cathedral churches, selected from the three names proposed to him by the Senate; (b) he shall, with the advice of the Supreme Court, grant or refuse passage to the decrees of councils, and bulls, briefs, and rescripts of the supreme pontiff of Rome, but said grant or refusal shall be made law whenever such ecclesiastical enactments contain provisions of a general or permanent character; and (c) he shall conclude and sign agreements with the pope.[28]

Unlike the earlier constitutions, that of 1853 did not declare Catholicism to be the faith of the State, but provided rather: "The federal government supports the Roman Catholic religion." This, it is contended, means that the Catholic religion is not the State religion in Argentina. It is impossible to accept such a conclusion, for the duty assumed by the State to "support" the Catholic cult is a vague, indeterminate obligation, subject to contradictory and antagonistic interpretations. Some see in it the *modus operandi* of a State-Church; others see in it the reverse. Some contend that "support" refers to financial aid, but they disagree greatly as to what should constitute a proper subsidy. It is argued by others that, if the framers of the Constitution wished to establish a State-Church they would have reproduced articles from earlier constitutions, instead of using the term "support," which only means "protect." Here is evidence, it is argued, that the Catholic religion is not the State religion.[29] But surely, if a faith is financially supported by the State, if some of its personnel is subject to governmental nomination, if the president of the republic must belong to that faith, if all religious ceremonies in which the State participates are conducted by that faith, and if pontifical documents issued for the governance of that faith are subject to governmental scrutiny, it is certainly the State religion quite as much as is the Established Church of England. In conclusion, the three fundamental principles of the Constitution relating to the ecclesi-

---

[28] Constitution of Argentina, Articles 2, 14, 20, 65, 67, 86; For the sessions of the Constituent Convention of 1853, see *Documentos relativos á la organización constitucional de la República Argentina* (Buenos Aires, 1911), III.

[29] Vedia, *op. cit.*, p. 42.

astical establishment are: (1) the national treasury defrays the expenses necessary for the maintenance of the Catholic Church; (2) the nation exercises the right of patronage; and (3) the government has the right to intervene in the organization of the Church, especially in all matters affecting the supreme interests of the social order.

In August, 1856, the Congress of the Confederation in enacting legislation for the organization of the ministries, incorporated Justice, Cult, and Public Instruction in one department. The jurisdiction of the division relating to Cult was defined as follows:

1. All that concerns the cult and the exercise of the national patronage.
2. All matters relating to the religious orders.
3. The issuance, according to the law, of the *pase,* or the retention of conciliar decrees, pontifical bulls, rescripts, and briefs of any ecclesiastical authority.
4. The examination of all appeals to the Holy See, or to any ecclesiastical authority outside of the territory of the Confederation.
5. Matters relating to the creation of dioceses, the territorial limits of same, and creation of parishes.
6. Establishment, direction, control, and support of ecclesiastical seminaries.
7. Matters relating to missions and the catechising of Indians.[30]

The national administration and control of matters relating to the Church remained in the Ministry of Justice, Cult, and Public Instruction until 1898 when the *Ministerio de Relaciones Exteriores y Culto* was organized.[31]

Not until 1860 did the Province of Buenos Aires become a member of the new federal union under the Constitution of 1853. The political schism in La Plata served to complicate the ecclesiastical problem, for in the capital city of Buenos Aires resided the prelate to whom was entrusted the pastoral cares of all the littoral which had entered the confederation. When the aged Bishop of Buenos Aires, Mariano Medrano, died, Auxiliary Bishop Mgr. Escalada, was presented for the vacancy by the government of the province

---

[30] *Colección Completa de Leyes Nacionales* (Buenos Aires, 1918), I, 233-234.
[31] *Recopilación de Leyes Usuales de la República Argentina* (Buenos Aires, 1927), p. 24.

19

in March, 1854. The pope preconized Esclada *motu proprio*, and thus when the bull of institution was presented to the governor for his *pase*, he was hesitant because he regarded the subject as of "a delicate nature." He therefore appointed a special committee to advise him on the matter. The committee, after due deliberation, recommended that, "since Escalada had been proposed by the government and had taken the oath," he should grant the exequatur. This was done on September 10, 1855. Immediately after assuming possession of the diocese, Escalada notified President Urquiza that he was to be regarded as ecclesiastical head of the littoral.[32]

President Urquiza, in the meantime, had taken steps to remedy the abnormal ecclesiastical situation by sending emissaries to Rome to negotiate the reëstablishment of religious relations. His first agent was Salvador Jiménez. Jiménez was instructed to petition for the creation of a littoral diocese free of Buenos Aires and to negotiate for a concordat. Very little is known about this mission, which was secretly conducted, other than that Jiménez was unable to accomplish anything, for the bases of a concordat suggested by the Cardinal-Secretary were incompatible with the Argentine Constitution.[33]

In 1855 the Congress of the Confederation, exercising its professed prerogative of national patronage, created a "Diocesis litoral" composed of the provinces of Santa Fé, Corrientes, and Entre Rios.[34] Since this action had to be confirmed by the pope, it was decided to send another emissary to Rome to point out the anomalous situation of dependent provinces of the see of Buenos Aires being separated politically from it, and to entreat the pope for a bull of erection. Juan B. Alberdi was chosen to represent Argentina before the Holy See. To him was recommended the subject of the creation of a bishopric of the littoral, and at the same time the provision of the vacant dioceses of Salta, Cór-

---

[32] Legón, *op. cit.*, pp. 507-508.   [33] *Ibid.*, p. 512.

[34] *Leyes Nacionales*, I, 176; For more legislation illustrative of the exercise of the patronage by the government of the Confederation, see *Leyes Nacionales*, I, 244 (scale of salaries for ecclesiastics); p. 274 (appropriation to defray the expenses from Europe of Capuchins to work in the missions); p. 343 (the President instructed to negotiate with pope for diminution in number of feast days); and pp. 352-353 (endowment of conciliar seminaries).

doba, and Cuyo. In exercising its right of patronage, the government presented names for the vacancies. Shortly after he initiated negotiations in Rome, Alberdi moved to Spain and the post at the Vatican was assumed by Benito Filippiani (1857). What Alberdi accomplished and the reason for his retirement are shrouded in mystery. It appears, however, that he opened negotiations for a concordat, for he said in a memorandum presented to the Holy See, "The Argentine government desires to celebrate a concordat with the Holy See. The Constitution (Article 27) authorizes it to enter into treaties with friendly nations; Rome is more than friendly to us; it is our spiritual capital." Then he said, "The erection of the new diocese will open the road to a concordat." President Urquiza did not attempt to conceal his desire to negotiate a concordat, for, in a message to Congress in 1857, he said, "In spite of the unquestionable legitimacy of the rights attaching to national patronage in our churches, I do not question that the conclusion of a concordat will remove all doubt and all reason for scruples of conscience, and for that reason I have resorted to the Supreme Pontiff to conclude one."[35]

Filippiani secured the canonical institution of the three bishops who had been presented for the vacancies in Salta, Córdoba, and Cuyo, and he was probably responsible for the appointment by Pius IX of Mgr. Marino Marini, Archbishop of Palmyra *in partibus*, as Apostolic Delegate to the Confederation. In September, 1858, Juan del Campillo replaced Filippiani as official representative at Rome. Del Campillo secured papal consent to a reduction in the number of religious holidays in Argentina and to the erection of a bishopric of the littoral. In July, 1859, Mgr. Segura was granted a bull of institution as bishop of the new diocese. But the negotiations over a concordat resulted in an impasse. Although the Cardinal-Secretary agreed to recognize national patronage as it related to presentation to archbishoprics and bishoprics, he positively refused to recognize the exercise of the exequatur with respect to all briefs and bulls. This was something that the papacy had never conceded to any country. Thus, the concordat, the principal object of Del Campillo's mission, was not concluded.[36]

[35] *Ibid.,* pp. 512-514.   [36] *Ibid.,* p. 516; Chacaltana, *op. cit.,* p. 291.

A curious incident cropped up in 1860 as a result of the treaty which Alberdi concluded with Spain. In that treaty the Spanish crown transferred its privileges of all kinds in La Plata to the Confederation. When he heard of this provision the nuncio in Madrid demanded a written statement that "these privileges" did not include patronage. Said Alberdi, "This resistance reveals the persuasion of the Holy See that the right of patronage is included among these things which the treaty confers on us, for on the other hand it would not have displayed such resistance."[37] Notwithstanding this apparent admission, the Vatican has never agreed that patronage is something which can be transferred as an element of sovereignty.

Technically all of the dioceses of Argentina were under the control of the Archbishop of Charcas. Such was the status on the eve of independence, and such it remained, in theory at least, after that event. Apostolic Delegate Marini, appreciating the need of freeing Argentina from dependence on a foreign archbishop, supported the movement to elevate the see of Buenos Aires into an archbishopric. After the reincorporation of Buenos Aires in the union, the solution of the problem was easy. In 1865 Buenos Aires was created a metropolitan see and Escalada was made the first archbishop.[38]

The government of the consolidated nation accentuated still more the regalism initiated or supported in Paraná, the capital of the Confederation. An incident which occurred shortly after the creation of the complete union evidences this marked regalistic attitude. When Bishop Segura of Paraná, diocese of the littoral, died, the ecclesiastical chapter proceeded to elect the dean, Miguel Vidal, as capitular vicar. This fact was communicated to the national government. The *fiscal*, Ferrería, characterized the action of the chapter as "very strange," and declared that it could not function without governmental approval. The election was patently illegal, declared the *fiscal*, but since the chapter did not act in a spirit of resistance to the government, nor refuse recognition of national patronage, he advised that the matter should be overlooked and the election confirmed. A circular was

---

[37] Legón, *op. cit.*, pp. 517-518.
[38] *Leyes Nacionales*, II, 213-214; Hernáez, *Colección de Bulas*, II, 309-315.

sent to all bishops acquainting them of the incident and recommending strict adherence to the laws in the future. Bishop Escalada of Buenos Aires, however, declared that he did not think it was the duty of the chapter to ask governmental permission to name a capitular vicar. He contended that, as long as the pope did not recognize the patronage, the prelates owed him obedience as the spiritual head. Ferrería countered with the statement that so long as no concordat was concluded the Constitution should be obeyed to the letter. When the Apostolic Delegate insisted on the right of the Church itself to provide for vacant dioceses, the *fiscal* proceeded to examine the credentials of the papal representative himself. Ferrería went so far as to issue a decree denying recognition of the title "apostolic delegate" since it was not recognized in public ecclesiastical law. Therefore, in spite of the fact that several years before, the government of Paraná had officially received the Apostolic Delegate, now, in 1863, his briefs were sent to the Supreme Court for study. In response to a protest by Marini, President Mitre intervened to assure him that whatever might be the decision of the Court, the government did not propose to alter the position which he occupied in the republic.[39]

Another, and much more serious controversy regarding the patronage was created when the capitular vicar of the diocese of Córdoba (*en sede vacante*) Dr. Jerónimo Clara declared in a pastoral on April 25, 1884, that no Catholic parent could legitimately send his daughters to a certain normal school for girls which was directed by Protestant women teachers. The government of Córdoba notified the national Minister of Cult, Eduardo Wilde, regarding the pastoral, and declared it to be subversive of the social order and opposed to the national authority. Wilde condemned the pastoral and ordered the cathedral chapter to take proper measures. The canons replied that they had no jurisdiction, and furthermore agreed with the Vicar that it was illicit for Catholic children to attend such schools. Since the chapter refused to act, the Vicar, Dr. Jerónimo Clara, was suspended from office. But neither he nor the chapter would recognize the validity of the government's action. On June 16th, the Vicar issued another pastoral in which he referred to "the pretended decree of destitu-

---

[39] Legón, *op. cit.*, pp. 522-524.

tion." He declared the decree to be null and void because it emanated from incompetent authority. In the national Parliament the pros and cons of the case were argued with great vehemence, but with opinion somewhat evenly divided as to the legal authority of the government to remove a prelate from office. Fortunately the government was not compelled to resort to force, for, at this juncture the new diocesan, Mgr. Tissera, took charge of the see and Clara was thus relieved of his authority.[40]

The controversy did not terminate by any means with the supplanting of the Vicar. On September 13, 1884, Bishop Buenaventura Risso Patrón published a pastoral on the subject of the schools of the diocese of Salta. He approved the stand of Vicar Clara and contended that what applied to Córdoba applied to Salta. Children could not be sent to schools directed by heretics, he said, without the parents incurring the penalty of being deprived of the sacraments. The vicars of Santiago del Estero and Jujuy joined Risso Patrón in defending Clara's stand. Since the national government regarded the tone of these declarations as being even more offensive than that of Clara himself, the three prelates were declared suspended by decree of November 3, 1884. The sudden death of Bishop Risso Patrón terminated his "case," but the question of the right of the government to remove the two vicars from office contributed to a bitter controversy in which once more there were repurcussions in the Parliament. The metropolitan and other bishops declared that the decree of November 3 was invalid for the authority to remove bishops and prelates belonged to the pope.[41]

Then the Apostolic Delegate, Mgr. Matera, became involved in the controversy. With or without justifiable foundation, it was popularly believed that the pontifical representative encouraged the opposition of the prelates. Consequently there was grave danger that his actions and words might be misconstrued; and this, in fact, proved to be the case. In September, 1884, Matera went to Córdoba, and while there he was privately interviewed by Miss Frances Armstrong, director of the normal school that had

[40] *Ibid.*, pp. 527-529.
[41] *Ibid.*, pp. 533-535.

been denounced by Clara. She evidently appealed to the Delegate to raise the anathema which hung over the school. Enemies of Matera charged that the Delegate consented to raise the ban on condition that the government accede to certain demands. Matera himself declared that he regarded his conversation with Miss Armstrong as a purely private and unofficial matter, and that he was thoroughly within his rights in advising her to announce that it was not her intention to proselyte in the school for the Protestant faith, and that, on the contrary, she would place no obstacle in the way of instruction in the Catholic catechism in the school. He particularly counseled her to direct her requests by petition to the government.

When Matera's conversation with Miss Armstrong was reported to the Minister of Cult, Eduardo Wilde, he became greatly aroused and declared that Matera was interfering in affairs over which he had no authority. The Minister of Foreign Relations requested the Apostolic Delegate to explain his conduct. Matera, in his reply, explained that the affair was no more than a private conversation and far from interfering he recommended that the legal course of petition be resorted to. But because of the peremptory demands of the government for an explanation, Matera lost control of his better reason and allowed certain damaging expressions to creep into his reply. The result was that, on October 14, the Apostolic Delegate was given his passports and allowed twenty-four hours to leave the country. The government of Argentina, although legally within its rights, was much too precipitate and harsh. It certainly should have been considerate enough to the the pope to allow him to recall his representative. Naturally, the Catholics protested the expulsion of the Delegate and from high and low places the incident was branded as a breach of diplomatic usage and a crowning national disgrace. The incident, at all events, emphasized the necessity of determining exactly the character and position of the papal representative. A doctrinal question which related to the rights of papal representatives in purely religious subjects was latent in the conflict. The attorney-general contended that neither prelates nor chapters had the right to enter into direct relations with the diplomatic representative of the pope. The pope's representative, said Vélez Sarsfield, ought to be considered only as envoy of the sovereign of the Papal States.[42]

President Roca, immediately after the expulsion of Matera, accredited Mariano Balcarce, Argentinian Minister to France, as envoy extraordinary and minister plenipotentiary on special mission to the Vatican, to explain to the pope why the conduct of the Delegate was unacceptable and to protest the loyalty and love of the Argentine Nation for the Holy See. Cardinal Jacobini, Secretary of State, far from reproving the acts of Matera, refused to censure him. He declared that Argentina's actions were contrary to all diplomatic practice. As long as Cardinal Jacobini was in charge of papal relations he refused to send a representative to Buenos Aires. When Cardinal Rampolla became Secretary of of State, Argentina decided to appeal to the Vatican once more. In 1887 the canon, Dr. Milciades Echague, was sent to Rome on special mission to arrange for a territorial division of the archbishopric and to secure a modification of the organization of the ecclesiastical tribunals. The mission was unsuccessful.

In 1892, shortly before relinquishing office, President Pellegrini despatched Vicente G. Quesada to Rome on special mission to heal the breach. He was instructed "to defend the right of patronage inherent in national sovereignty and to facilitate the regular procedure for its exercise in the provision of the first dignities of the Argentine Church." He was to refuse to consider a concordat, and the possible suggestion that a permanent nuncio be sent to Buenos Aires. According to Quesada it seemed that the instructions were entirely too rigid and severe and calculated to perpetuate the break. Nevertheless, he and Cardinal Rampolla negotiated in fine spirit and the preconization of Mgr. Pablo Padilla as Bishop of Salta was secured.

When Dr. Luís Saénz Peña became president, his foreign minister, Tomás Anchorena, instructed Quesada confidentially to terminate the negotiations as based on the instructions of the prior administration. They were ill-conceived, he felt, and any attempt to abide by them would, merely serve to perpetuate strained relations. "The Holy See," he said, "by celebrating a concordat, no doubt would recognize patronage in the national government or

---

[42] Sarsfield, *op. cit.*, pp. 133-134; Legón, *op. cit.*, pp. 536-539.

certain rights of patronage in ecclesiastical subjects such as are now more or less in vogue. But it will never recognize that patronage or those rights are inherent in sovereignty, for to no government, absolutely none, has it been conceded in that form."[43]

The opinion of Anchorena was sound and has been justified by subsequent history. Never has a concordat been concluded with Rome, but practically all that would have been guaranteed by a concordat has been secured by tacit agreement. The pope theoretically reserves the right to appoint bishops, but, actually, when a vacancy occurs, the federal Senate exercises the right of sending three names to the president who transmits one to the pontiff who has the choice of accepting or rejecting it. The pope's acquiescence in this procedure is a fact, but he has never ceased to argue that it is in no way to be regarded as a recognition of the inherence of patronage in sovereignty. Nor are the government's nominees always accepted as a matter of course, for very frequently, and as recently as 1923, the pope refused to confirm Mgr. de Andrea, the republic's nominee for the archiepiscopal see of Buenos Aires.[44] The government for some time refused to make another nomination, and thus for over two years during the Alvear administration the controversy between Argentina and the Vatican made the relations of Church and State an acute political problem. Throughout the controversy the government was very insistent that its patronal right should be protected to the limit. In his message to Congress the President said, "The Executive will admit no discussion over the right of patronage determined by the Constitution."[45] The Socialists, who stand for separation of Church and State, increased educational facilities for the poor, and a divorce law, as a complement to the existing civil marriage law, took advantage of the situation to renew their demands for a complete separation of the civil and ecclesiastical control. Finally, in the latter part of 1926, President Alvear suggested to the Vatican the appointment of Mgr. Fray Bottaro as

[43] *Ibid.*, p. 545.

[44] C. W. Gray, American Vice-Consul, to J. L. Mecham, Buenos Aires, January 3, 1928; *Ministerio de Relaciones Exteriores y Culto, Circular Informativa Mensual* (Buenos Aires, 1924), pp. 313-314.

[45] *Ministerio de Relaciones Exteriores y Culto, Circular Informativa Mensual* (Buenos Aires, 1925), pp. 1071-1072.

Archbishop of Buenos Aires. Papal confirmation was accorded and the crisis was passed.[46]

Unlike Peru, and unlike Chile up to 1925, the right of presentation in Argentina applies only to the first dignities of the Church, i.e., the archbishop and bishops. There is omission, in the Constitution, of the customary phrase that the government "exercises the powers of patronage respecting churches, benefices, and ecclesiastical persons." Thus it is presumable that the framers of the Constitution wished to leave the greatest liberty to the Church. The question as to whether or not the patronage applied to auxiliary bishops was settled in 1919 by the Supreme Court. The opinion of the Court was that the government had the right to nominate auxiliary bishops.[47] Yet the age-old question regarding the nature of the patronage is periodically argued in the Argentine press and in Parliament. *La Prensa* champions an extreme regalism, and, in the Parliament, Senator Leopoldo Melo has become the recognized leader of the regalists. Growing out of the controversy regarding the "provision" of the archbishop in 1925, Dr. Melo argued in the tribune and in print in the interest of a more extreme national control over the Church.[48] He was no more successful than the Socialists in Parliament, who presented a project in the Chamber declaring dissolved all religious communities, orders, and congregations; the expulsion from the country of all foreign members of the same who did not desire to enter lay activities, and the nationalization of their property.[49]

While the scope of the patronage is more restricted in Argentina than in many countries where the Catholic cult is the established religion, and notwithstanding the fact that there are no religious tests for exercising the suffrage or holding public office,[50] nevertheless the national government occupies an exceptional position in its relations to the Roman Catholic Church, as has already been

---

[46] *Current History*, December, 1926, pp. 439-440.

[47] José N. Matienzo, *Cuestiones de Derecho Público Argentino* (Buenos Aires, 1924), pp. 97-101.

[48] Leturia, *Origen del Patronato*, pp. 20-22.

[49] *La Prensa* (New York), September 2, 1927.

[50] The president and vice-president are the only officials of whom the Constitution demands a religious belief. Priests living in religious communities are not allowed the suffrage.

noted. Furthermore, the Holy See is represented at Buenos Aires by an apostolic nuncio, and the Argentine Nation has an accredited diplomatic representative at the Vatican. In 1927 this representative was raised to the rank of ambassador. In the Ministry of Foreign Affairs and Cult, there is a Subsecretary of Worship in charge of ecclesiastical matters as they relate to the government.

Although the clergy are allowed to communicate freely with Rome, a situation unknown under the *real patronato de Indias*, this does not apply to the admission of pontifical decrees. This right, argues Vedia, is a function of the State independent of cult and patronage.[51] It is interesting to note, however, that in those countries where the Church and State are separate the government does not undertake to pass upon the admission of papal documents. That being the case, it rarely happens that the right of the *pase* is not based on the patronage.

The relation of the provincial governments to the Roman Catholic Church calls for brief explanation. That there is no agreement on what is the legal relationship is evidenced by the fact that prominent constitutional authorities have given affirmative answers to each of the following questions: Does the province exercise the patronage of the Catholic Church within its territory to the extent permitted by the National Constitution? Does the province exercise the vice-patronage as agent of the federal power exclusively? Does not the patronage belong exclusively to the federal government which does not admit of any delegation of power whatever to the governors of the provinces?

The numerous political changes through which the provinces passed before a permanent Argentine Union was formed adds to the difficulty of arriving at a correct answer to the problem. When La Plata disintegrated in 1820, each province on assuming the plenitude of sovereignty, claimed that it inherited the exercise of the ecclesiastical patronage. In the Constitution of Corrientes of 1821, for example, the provincial governor was delegated all those powers relating to presentation, exequatur, and negotiation of a concordat, that had been given to the president of the defunct United Provinces by the Constitution of 1819. The same attitude toward the patronage was manifested in the succession of provin-

---

[51] Vedia, *op. cit.,* p. 439.

cial constitutions down to the perfection of the national union in 1860. Then the Constitution of Corrientes of 1864 provided that (1) the government was obliged to support the Catholic cult in those matters that properly belonged to it, and to promote its aggrandizement and progress; (2) the provincial legislature had the power to regulate the civil, judicial, and ecclesiastical division of the province, and to make rules for the exercise of the patronage in those matters not delegated to the president of the republic; and (3) the executive power had the right to exercise the patronage in those matters not delegated to the president.

Although the last two constitutions of Corrientes, dated 1889 and 1913, did not contain a word on the subject of patronage, it is contended that their silence does not mean a renunciation of the right. The province can still exercise the patronage regarding those matters not specifically granted to the central authority. It is to be noted that the constitutional delegation is not all-inclusive; for example, the president of the republic, says Article 86, Sec. 8, exercises the rights of national patronage in the presentation of bishops for cathedral churches, and by Sec. 9, he is conceded the right of exequatur. Outside of these rights, and the national support of the Catholic Church (Article 2), the province, which retains the powers not delegated (Article 104), has the right of patronage. Thus the provinces, by virtue of their residual patronal rights, can determine and regulate Church fees for marriages, baptisms, and other religious ceremonies. Also they can intervene in regulating the selection and tenure of parish priests. This in fact is the object of a decree of 1886, in Corrientes, which is still in force and constitutes the best guarantee the clergy of the province have for the undisturbed discharge of their parochial duties.[52]

Passing from matters relating to the political status of the Church, attention will be directed to its support, its property rights, and its relation to education, marriage, and the like. The support of the cult is regarded as an obligation based upon the enjoyment of the patronage. The government is required to make annual appropriations for the hierarchy, cathedral chapters, semi-

---

[52] Hernán F. Gómez, *Instituciones de la Provincia de Corrientes* (Buenos Aires, 1922), pp. 236-259.

naries, and Indian missions. This subvention is not large. The lower clergy of parochial churches and charitable institutions receive no aid from the State, but depend on fees and contributions of the faithful.[53] Only the priests attached to cathedrals are paid salaries, and consequently are regarded as government employees. Considerable revenue is derived by the Church from its properties. Since no restriction has ever been placed upon the ability of the Church to receive entailments and bequests, its real properties and other possessions are of great value. Church holdings have not been nationalized, with the exception of cathedrals. The other churches and buildings belong to their respective congregations. Cathedrals are exempt from taxation but other ecclesiastical edifices are assessed certain municipal imposts.[54]

The public schools in the Argentine Republic, as in the United States, are absolutely secular. The Church exercises no control over public education, and since 1884, no religious instruction can be given in public schools during regular hours. But the federal school law of 1888 provides that "after official hours, religious instruction [Catholic and otherwise] may be given to the children who voluntarily remain in the schools for the purpose of receiving it. This religious instruction in the public schools shall be given only by authorized ministers of the different persuasions, before or after school hours." A law of 1904 makes it a punishable offense to give religious instruction to children whose parents have not previously requested it. Ecclesiastics, male and female, are not prohibited from acting as instructors in public schools, but the practice is not general.[55] It is an interesting fact that Jewesses are rapidly increasing on the staffs of the public schools. They are well trained in the normal schools, and, of course, there is no sectarian test for teachers.[56]

About one-third of the educational institutions of the country depend on charitable and religious organizations for their support. The great majority of these are conducted by Catholic societies,

[53] *The Catholic World,* Vol. 116, p. 676.
[54] C. W. Gray to J. L. Mecham.
[55] Leyes Nacionales, VI, 34-35; Angel V. Andrada (ed.), *Leyes Nacionales, Decretos demas Resoluciones de la República Argentina* (Buenos Aires, 1927), II, 243-254.
[56] *River Plate Republics,* p. 29.

charitable organizations, and orders, for the Church itself does not maintain them. It is estimated that the Church controls about five per cent of the total school enrollment. The Catholics, in recent years, have spared no effort to strengthen their educational work. Their schools are generally housed in adequate, modern, and often impressive buildings, and the quality of instruction is excellent. Some of the largest secondary educational institutions are maintained by the Roman Church, and the grade of instruction rivals that of the government schools.[57] Protestant schools are not numerous, numbering perhaps less than two dozen. No religious school can operate without an official permit, and the courses of study must be the same as prescribed by the government for the public schools. In general, all private educational institutions are subject to such governmental supervision as will ensure a general uniformity of instruction throughout the republic in order that the status of the graduates of secondary public, private, and religious schools will be the same for the purpose of classification upon their application for entrance into the universities or other higher educational institutions. The Catholic schools generally charge no tuition fees. In some cases the national government and the respective municipalities contribute to their support. Diocesan seminaries are supported outright by annual federal appropriations.[58]

On November 2, 1888, a civil marriage law was passed and is still in force. This law grants validity only to marriages publicly solemnized in the office of the functionary in charge of the civil register[59] and before two witnesses. A concession is granted to contracting parties to have the ceremony performed in a private residence providing four witnesses are present. The registrar is forbidden to prevent the bride and groom from seeking to have their union blessed immediately after by a minister of their religion. Any priest who violates the law by performing the marriage ceremony before the civil act is subject to heavy penalty. The civil authorities charge a fee of ten paper pesos ($4.35); the

---

[57] *Christian Work in South America*, I, 241.

[58] *Ibid.; The Catholic World*, Vol. 116, p. 676.

[59] The law of the Civil Register was enacted October 31, 1884. (*Recop. de Leyes Usuales*, 1927, pp. 501-509.)

Church authorities have no fixed fee, this being left largely to individual priests or to the inclination of the celebrants. Divorce is not allowed in Argentina. Periodic attempts have been made to legalize divorce, but without success. There is legal separation, but separation does not permit of remarriage.[60]

Nor are all cemeteries controlled by the Church, as was the case under the Spanish régime and in the early days of independence. Catholics are allowed to maintain separate cemeteries, but they are subject, of course, as are those municipally controlled, to governmental supervision, sanitary control, and the like.[61] Thus, although Argentina is a Catholic country, and the Catholic Church is a State establishment, one encounters there lay primary education, civil marriage, and purely municipal cemeteries. The Church has been deprived of its traditional control of certain vital matters affecting the private lives of the inhabitants.

The intimate relation which exists between Church and State in Argentina does not indicate that freedom of religious worship is limited or menaced in any way. "It cannot be said," says Rowe, "that the material support given to the Catholic Church has strengthened its position. On the contrary the influence of the Church over the lives of the people is less in Argentina than in the United States. . . . Not only is religious liberty freely guaranteed in every section of Argentina, but also the problem of the relation between Church and State has been solved in a manner which has eliminated the question from the field of public discourse. The question for the time being at least, is considered as settled."[62]

Notwithstanding the privileged position of the Roman Catholic Church in the Argentine Republic its personnel is too deficient in numbers to minister adequately to the spiritual and social needs of its communicants. In a nation of approximately 9,000,000 people, there were only a few years ago only 1500 secular clergy and 500 regulars. These were supposed to care for 1019 churches and chapels.[63] It has been estimated that, if Argentina had in proportion to its total population as many clergymen as the State

---

[60] *The Argentine Civil Code* (F. L. Joanini, translator. Boston, 1917), Sec. II, Title I; *Leyes Nacionales,* VIII, 147.

[61] *Leyes Nacionales,* VI, 180.   [62] Rowe, *op. cit.,* p. 129.

[63] *Guía Eclesiástica* (Buenos Aires, 1915).

of New York, the number would be about 9,000. Moreover, Buenos Aires, a supposedly Catholic metropolis, has no more Catholic churches than has Philadelphia, a predominantly Protestant city of about equal size.[64] In an attempt to meet the scarcity of clergy, a large number of foreign priests have been introduced, particularly from Spain and Italy. It would seem that, since the Catholic Church is not taking advantage of its highly favored position to bring spiritual benefits to millions of Argentinians, the Protestants would find the great South American republic a fertile field to propagate their beliefs. Yet the favorable opportunity is neglected and outside of Buenos Aires practically no evangelical work is being done.[65]

No one expects that the present legal status of the Catholic Church in Argentina will last forever. The present arrangement will continue only until the Church and State come to feel that the most complete religious liberty is best for both. When the responsibilities and obligations become onerous to both parties, they will be glad to terminate the arrangement by mutual consent. The ideal status is, of course, a free Church in a free State, but the establishment of such a régime for many years after the winning of independence from Spain would have been a very unwise policy—as unwise as embarking immediately upon unrestrained democracy, after centuries of autocracy. The statesmen of Argentina displayed great acumen in avoiding a sudden and radical break with the religious past. They adopted, instead, the wise policy of disestablishing the Church gradually; of gradually releasing the bonds. When complete separation comes, it will find the State, the Church, and the people prepared for and willing to accept the change. Their mutual acquiescence will ensure the success of the new status.

---

[64] *Christian Work in South America,* I, 118-120.
[65] *Ibid.,* I, 118.

CHAPTER XI

THE CATHOLIC CHURCH IN BRAZIL AND URUGUAY

I

BRAZIL

Those who argue that it would be impolitic for Latin-American governments to bestow upon the Catholic Church free and unhampered control over its own organization stand refuted by the example of Brazil. The workability of the Brazilian policy of a free Church in a free State is an incontestable fact which should be invited to the attention of those anti-clerical reformers of Spanish-American republics who insist that the best safeguard against usurping clericalism is repression and surveillance.

In refreshing contrast to the tendency in so many of the Spanish-American republics, there has been manifested throughout the history of independent Brazil a fine spirit of toleration, existent in practice as well as in the letter of the law. Religion as a political issue has been a subject of very minor importance, and the country has been spared the political machinations and bloody encounters of the pro- and anti-clerical forces. For this reason the story of politico-religious relationships in Brazil can be told in a few words; but notwithstanding the brevity of the account, the object lesson is none the less forcible.

The transition of the Brazilian Church from patronal dependency on the Portuguese crown to patronal control exercised by an independent government was as gradual and free from violence as was the political metamorphosis of Brazil itself. The cutting of the political ties with the mother country was not, thanks to the establishment of a monarchy, regarded as so radical or revolutionary a step as the creation of republics on the ruins of the Spanish colonial empire. It was so much easier for the conservative elements, including the clergy, to stomach a Brazilian Empire, particularly since the hereditary emperor was a member of the

20

old Portuguese ruling house of Braganza. With a Braganza continuing at the head of the government in Brazil, the revolutionary movement assumed a very conservative aspect. The clergy, therefore, could and did support the independence cause.

Even in the abortive liberal republican revolt in Pernambuco, in 1817, so numerous and influential were the clerics that Oliveira Lima calls it "the revolution of the padres." The so-called spiritual precursor of this revolt was Bishop Azevedo Coutinho, founder of the Seminario de Olinda, and instructor of the "liberals of 1817." Although the hierarchy condemned the revolt as being an heretical enterprise, Dean Bernardo Ferreira Portugal did not hesitate to publish a pastoral "to disabuse scrupulous souls." The revolution, he declared, was not contrary to the Gospel. In illustration of the prominent rôle played by the clergy in this fruitless stroke at independence, fifty-seven priests, almost all of whom were affiliated with Masonry, were numbered among those pariots who were imprisoned after the suppression of the revolt.[1]

The great majority of the clerics who were favorable to the cause of independence were opposed to the republican form of government. It was fortunate for the independence movement that there was available in Brazil, in the person of Regent Pedro, the logical head of an independent monarchial State, for here was one who could command the support of the Church. When the Portuguese Cortes attempted to return Brazil to its old colonial status, the prelates joined the popular clamor that Pedro proclaim Brazilian independence.[2] And when the Regent declared independence at Ypiranga on September 7, 1822, he was attended by several clerics, and to one of these who cried "Viva o primerio rei do Brasil" belongs the honor of being the first to proclaim Pedro king of Brazil.[3]

A National Constituent Assembly, under the presidency of

---

[1] *Diccionario Historico, Geographico e Ethnographico do Brasil* (Rio de Janeiro, 1922), I, 1264-1265; Eugenio Vilhena de Moraes, "O Patriotismo e o Clero No Brasil," in *Revista do Instituto Historico e Geographico Brasileiro* (Rio de Janeiro, 1925), Tomo Especial, p. 126.

[2] "Representação do Bispo de S. Paulo, do 1° de Janeiro de 1822," in J. I. de Abreu e Lima, *Compendio da Historia do Brasil* (Rio de Janeiro, 1843), II, Appendix, pp. 24-25.

[3] *Dic. Hist. Geog.*, I, 1277.

José Caetano da Silva Coutinho, Bishop of Rio de Janeiro, met in Rio on April 17, 1823. In the Assembly were fifteen members of the clergy. A committee, headed by Antonio Carlos, and composed of José Bonifacio de Andrada and other leaders was entrusted with the task of drafting a project of a constitution. The draft as submitted by Antonio Carlos, and as adopted by the Assembly on August 30, 1823, contained the following religious clauses: (1) guarantee of religious liberty to all Christian communities; non-Christian religions to be tolerated, but their communicants to be excluded from the exercise of political rights; (2) the Roman Catholic religion to be that of the State above all others and the only one maintained by it; (3) the exercise of the patronage, as to the nomination for ecclesiastical benefices, vested in the emperor; (4) the right of conceding or denying the *pase* to pontifical documents vested in the emperor; and (5) grant to the bishops of the right of censorship, with government aid, of publications on dogma and morals. An effort on the part of the Masons in the constituent assembly to use in the preamble "Supreme Being" instead of "Holy Trinity" was defeated. With the exception that Protestants were not excluded from the exercise of political rights, the clergy could find very little to complain about in this constitution.[4]

The Emperor, however, was so dissatisfied with the "Constitution of 1823" that he arbitrarily dissolved the Assembly, set aside the Constitution, and selected a commission to frame a new fundamental law for the Empire. On March 25, 1824, an organic charter framed by Pedro's hand-picked committee, was proclaimed. Under this instrument, known as the "Imperial Constitution of 1824," Brazil was governed until 1889.

Few changes were made by Pedro in the religious provisions of the constitution of Antonio Carlos. "The Roman Catholic Apostolic religion," read the law, "will continue being the religion of the empire. All other religions will be permitted, with their domestic and private observance, in houses destined for that purpose, with-

---

[4] *Camara dos Deputados, Exposição Commemorativa do Centenario de Ia Constituinte do Brasil* (Rio de Janeiro, 1923); *Annaes do Parlamento Brasileiro, Assemblea Constituinte, 1823* (Rio de Janeiro 1876-1884), I, 46-48; Moraes, *op. cit.,* 138-142.

out any exterior form like a church."[5] The guarantee of the private exercise of other cults, even to Brazilians themselves, was a long step in advance of the contemporary Portuguese constitution, which allowed this only to foreigners, and forced Portuguese citizens to profess the religion of the State.[6] The plan of the constituents of 1823 to confer political rights only on Christians, was not adopted by Pedro, for the Constitution of 1824 conferred upon all naturalized foreigners, whatever their religion, the civil and political rights of Brazilian citizens. Yet in effect the full accord of political rights was restricted because of religious reasons. For example, members of the clergy and religious orders were denied the privilege of voting in parochial assemblies and non-Catholics were ineligible to election as deputies.[7] Religious toleration as guaranteed in Article 5 did not connote religious equality or even full religious liberty. With the Catholic Church established as the privileged faith there was a frank and legitimate disavowal of religious equality. Therefore it is senseless to contend, as have some critics, that the constitutional guarantee of religious liberty was contradicted in the Constitution itself.

It surely was not a serious derogation of religious liberty to require the emperor to "swear to maintain the Roman Catholic Apostolic religion," to prevent the external ceremonies of non-official religions or to prohibit non-Catholics from giving their meeting places the external appearance of a church. By judicial interpretation it was only a belfry and a bell which gave the building "the external appearance of a church."[8] There was no justification, however, for prohibiting the election of a non-Catholic as a deputy. This prohibition was particularly odious, since it applied only to deputies, and not, perhaps due to oversight, to senators, councillors, ministers, regents, and the monarch himself. In the last days of the Empire, however, naturalized Brazilians and non-

---

[5] Constitution of the Empire of Brazil, in H. G. James, *The Constitutional System of Brazil* (Washington, 1923), Appendix No. 2, Art. 5.

[6] Arosemena, *Estudios Constitucionales*, I, 55.

[7] *Constitution of the Empire*, Articles 6, 92, 95, 179.

[8] James C. Fletcher and D. P. Kidder, *Brazil and the Brazilians* (Boston, 1866), p. 140. In 1888 legislation was enacted suppressing the constitutional requirement that non-Catholic religious edifices should not have the external appearance of a church. (Benjamin Mossé, *Dom Pedro II*, Paris, 1889, p. 58.)

Catholics were eligible to election as senators and deputies. Considering the religious fanaticism of the peoples of Southern Europe, especially of the Iberian Peninsula, we must look upon Article 5 of the Imperial Constitution as a long step in the direction of tolerance. Finally, the emperor was given the right to appoint bishops and incumbents to ecclesiastical benefices, and to grant or withhold the exequatur to conciliar decrees, papal letters, and other ecclesiastical legislation.[9]

As a natural concomitant of the union of religion and politics in the Empire the clergy were supported out of the public treasury. This practice had colonial antecedents. The pope and the king of Portugal had entered into an agreement whereby the whole of the tithes was to go to the government on condition that the crown paid the clergy. The government therefore paid the ecclesiastics a regular stipend, which, during the last days of Portuguese rule in Brazil, was very meager. Consequently the clergy lived in a state of poverty. The imperial government continued to pay on an economical plan. Even the prelates were forced to live in moderation and simplicity. The economic status of the lay clergy furnished a marked contrast with that of the regulars who lived in opulence.[10] Also, in consequence of the Church-State union, public instruction was entrusted to the Catholic Church, and the cemeteries belonged to and were administered by the Church. Civil marriage was not recognized. A decree of November 3, 1827, provided for the effective observance of the dispositions of the Council of Trent on the subject of matrimony, and created a Tribunal of Ecclesiastical Relations at Bahia.[11] Although the external ceremonies of non-official cults were made dependent on the consent of the law, this consent was never given during the life of the empire. But notwithstanding the above the constitutional grant of religious toleration was fully tested and found to be a living letter.[12]

[9] *Constitution of the Empire,* Article 102; J. Burnichon, *Le Brésil d'aujourd 'hui* (Paris, 1910), p. 180.

[10] R. Walsh, *Notices of Brazil in 1828 and 1829* (Boston, 1831), I, 200-201.

[11] Basilio de Magalhães, "D. Pedro II e a Egreja," in *Rev. do Inst. Hist.,* Vol. 152, 386.

[12] Agenor de Roure, *A Constituinte Republicana* (Rio de Janeiro, 1920), p. 450.

There was a brief suspension of papal relations following the declaration of Brazilian independence. In August, 1824, the Emperor sent Francisco Correa Vidigal, a cleric, on special diplomatic mission to the Vatican to conclude a concordat and dispose of outstanding matters affecting the relations between Church and State. In particular he was instructed not to permit papal intervention in matters of State jurisdiction; to obtain an order to the effect that religious orders were no longer subject to superiors resident in Portugal, and to urge upon the pope the necessity of reforming the regular orders, of prohibiting the establishment of new convents, and of prohibiting the admission of foreign friars.[13] No immediate results were accomplished by Vidigal's mission, for the pope withheld recognition of Brazil until Portugal should recognize the Empire. But shortly after that event, the pope issued a bull, in 1827, which conceded to the crown the same rights which had formerly been exercised by the king of Portugal as secular patron and Grand Master of the Order of Christ. The attempt of the pope to concede to the Emperor prerogatives which the constitutional law had already conferred on him was repugnant. Consequently the exequatur was denied to the bull. On the ecclesiastical affairs committee of the Chamber of Deputies which recommended this drastic action were a number of priests who did not hesitate to characterize the pope's action as presumptive in the extreme. The controversy was settled in the following year (1828) by the inauguration of a *modus vivendi* by which the pope tolerated, but did not recognize, the right of patronage in the Brazilian government.[14] To free the Brazilian Church from dependence on Portuguese prelates the pope ordered, in 1828, the dioceses of Pará and Maranhão freed from the see of Lisbon and made suffragans of the archbishop of Bahia. The new bishoprics of Goyaz and Matto Grosso were also created. To provide for these changes in ecclesiastical jurisdiction the pope issued the necessary bulls which were granted the imperial exequatur.[15]

---

[13] Moraes, *op. cit.*, p. 146; Magalhães, *op. cit.*, pp. 386-387.

[14] Magalhães, *op. cit.*, pp. 386-387; P. A. Martin, "Causes of the Collapse of the Brazilian Empire," in *The Hispanic American Historical Review*, IV, 10; Claude I. Dawson, American Consul-General, to J. L. Mecham, Rio de Janeiro, December 6, 1927.

[15] Magalhães, *op. cit.*, p. 387.

As indicated by the above, regalism was dominant in Brazil in the early days of the Empire, and, in fact, it continued to be dominant throughout the imperial period. Since the time of Pombal, and due largely to the great influence of that minister, the Portuguese and Brazilian churches manifested pronounced Gallican tendencies. After independence in Brazil "the virus of Jansenist and Gallican heresy" persisted. If the Emperor and his imperial officials sought to make the State preponderant over the Church, they did not lack support from the Brazilian prelates and clergy. In the first legislative assembly (1826-1829) were twenty-two ecclesiastics openly committed to *regalismo*. Their concurrence in advising denial of the exequatur to the bull of 1827 has been noted. Furthermore the leading prelates were defenders of the prerogatives of the State against the direct pretentions of the Holy See. Among these were Romualdo Antonio de Seixas, Archbishop of Bahia, Marcos Antonio de Souza, Bishop of Maranhão, and José Caetano da Silva Coutinho, Bishop of Rio de Janeiro and Imperial Chaplain. Father Diogo Antonio Feijó, later regent of the Empire, was also a vigorous defender of regalism. The Church was under the tutelage of the State.[16] Numerous laws and decrees, many of them petty and vexatious, were issued providing for the constant intervention of the State in religous matters. Yet, despite the irritating supervision of State over Church, the clergy were so acquiescent that no serious opposition was aroused for over half a century.

Not only were the clergy of the early Empire essentially Gallican, but they were also marked by their liberalism. It is a matter of record that the clerics in the Constituent Assembly were more liberal than the laymen. Since most of them were Masons, this liberal attitude was partially due to Masonic influence.[17] Bishop José Caetano da Silva Coutinho, who presided over the Assembly, was a most enlightened individual, tolerant to every sect. He was Bishop of Rio de Janeiro when Lord Strangford negotiated a treaty, in 1810, which gave to the English the right to build a

---

[16] Magalhães, *op. cit.*, p. 386; Moraes, *op. cit.*, p. 145.

[17] *Assemblea Constituinte 1823*, I, 48; Moraes, *op. cit.*, p. 145; "A. Maçonaria e a Independencia," in *Documentos para a Historia da Independencia* (Rio de Janeiro, 1923), I, 394-399.

chapel for divine services, provided it was not erected as a public edifice, but as a private house, and did not use bells to assemble the congregation. The pope's nuncio protested this concession, but Bishop Silva Coutinho favored granting to the English the right to build a chapel. "The English," said he, "have really no religion; but they are a proud and obstinate people. If you oppose them, they will persist, and make it an affair of infinite importance; but if you concede to their wishes, the chapel will be built, and nobody will ever go near it." The bishop's prophesy proved to be true, for in 1828, the English church with a potential capacity of 600-700, was attended by a scant thirty or forty.[18]

As indicated by one of the subjects upon which Vidigal, special envoy to Rome, was particularly instructed, the regular orders were the objects of attack in Brazil. Not the government and people alone, but the lay clerics as well, were hostile to monastic institutions. The regulars were not numerous, but in comparison with the secular clergy, they were very wealthy. This disparity in economic status probably accounted in part for the opposition of the seculars. The regulars, moreover, were ultramontane in sympathy and foreign in composition and control. In short, they were branded as being anti-nationalist. Another cause of discontent with the regular orders was popular disapproval of the withdrawal from the worldly life, and reproduction, of so many males and females. It constituted an impediment in the way of populating a sparsely settled country. The secular clergy did not escape the same criticism. Senhor Feijó, a priest and member of the ecclesiastical committee of the Deputies proposed "that it would be proper to apply to the pope to relieve the clergy from the penalty annexed to marrying."[19] Abolition of ecclesiastical celibacy was also advocated as a measure of moral reform for a goodly number of priests kept concubines.

During the reign of Pedro I and under the Regency several acts were passed directed at the regular orders. The law of 1828 (1) prohibited entry and residence of foreign friars in the empire; (2) prohibited creation of new orders or religious associations of both sexes; and (3) expelled from the country friars

---

[18] Walsh, op. cit., I, 181-185, 205.
[19] Ibid., I, 201.

and congregations who obeyed superiors resident outside Brazil.[20] The Benedictines and Carmelites were prohibited from taking novices, a measure designed to bring about the total extinction of the orders. As congregations became extinct, their property was incorporated in the national patrimony.[21] To escape confiscation of their property, the orders resorted to alienation, but a law of December 9, 1830, declared null all alienations made by religious orders without governmental license.[22] In 1831, under the inspiration of Feijó, as Minister of Justice, the government undertook a reform of the religious orders in full accord with the papal internuncio at Rio de Janeiro. So bitter was the opposition to reform raised by the monks that a measure was introduced (1833) in the Parliament, providing for the secularization of all property of the regulars. It did not pass, but twenty years later it was again proposed by Nabuco de Araujo.[23] The suppression of numerous convents was not an unmixed blessing. Indispensable charitable work was performed by the orders. In all of the principal cities the convents were crowded with the lame, halt, and blind. In Rio, it was said, the whole mendicity was supported at the convents. The closing of some of the convents necessitated governmental assuming of control of the eleemosynary institutions or their transfer to the lay orders. This was attended by confusion and considerable hardship for the poor.[24]

In 1834 the question of abolition of ecclesiastical celibacy was again revived. The provincial council of São Paulo adopted the following resolution: (1) the bishops in the dioceses have the same rights as the pope over the Catholic Church; (2) the law of celibacy is simply disciplinary. In February, 1834, the Foreign Minister wrote a remarkable letter to the papal internuncio on the subject. He said that the imperial government believed that, in accordance with the São Paulo resolution, the matter of celibacy of curates was a matter of discipline which should be left to the sovereign determination of the State. Knowing that celibacy did

---

[20] Magalhães, *op. cit.*, p. 388.

[21] *Ibid.*, p. 388; Walsh, *op. cit.*, I, 201-208.

[22] Magalhães, *op. cit.*, 388.

[23] *Ibid.*, pp. 388-389.

[24] Walsh, *op. cit.*, I, 202.

not exist in fact, this situation made for great public immorality. The government desired, consequently, that energetic measures be adopted. He concluded by stating that he did not wish to have the opinion of the government made public.[25] Suffice it to say that ecclesiastical celibacy was not abolished, and that immorality among the clergy continued to be pronounced throughout the imperial period.

State supervision over the Church continued to develop and increase during the reign of Pedro II. The Emperor's attitude toward the Catholic faith has been greatly misunderstood. He has been charged with being a Voltairean, an evolutionist, and an atheist. As a matter of fact he ascribed to the dogmas of the Church, and, as one writer says, "Nothing said or written would have put him in the clutches of the Inquisition."[26] A liberal thinker, in matters of religion, he has been called, quite aptly "a *limited* Catholic." In sponsoring ecclesiastical reform, and in strengthening royal control over the Church, the Emperor was not actuated by anti-clerical motives. His campaign against the religious orders, inaugurated in 1854, had the full support of the papal internuncio and the bishops of Brazil. The need of reform of the decadent religious orders was recognized as being urgent and necessary by all good Catholics.[27] In 1854 the Emperor, in an *aviso*, declared that to him belonged the power of nominating to all benefices and dignities independent of the advice and counsel of the prelates, as was the custom before. This was carrying regalism to an extreme, and there was considerable truth in the allegation of the prelates, set forth in the *Pastoral Collectiva* of March 19, 1890, that their tutelage to the Empire was a form of servitude.[28] Yet the regalistic policy of the Emperor was not in any sense anti-religious.

A faithful and trustworthy description of religious conditions in Brazil in the first half of the reign of Pedro II has been left us by two Protestant missionaries, Rev. James C. Fletcher and Rev. D. P. Kidder. "It is my firm conviction," said Mr. Fletcher

---

[25] Magalhães, *op. cit.,* pp. 389-390.

[26] Magalhães de Azeredo, "Dom Pedro II, Traços da Sua Physionomia Moral," in *Rev. Do Inst. Hist. e Geog.,* Tomo Especial, 1925, p. 969.

[27] Magalhães, *op. cit.,* 393.

[28] *Ibid.,* p. 391; Padre Julio Maria, "A Religão," in *O Livro do Centenario* (Rio de Janeiro, 1901), I, 60.

in 1845, "that there is not a Roman Catholic country on the globe where there prevails a greater degree of toleration or a greater liberality of feeling toward Protestants. I will here state, that in all my residence and travels in Brazil in the character of a Protestant missionary, I never received the slightest opposition or indignity from the people. As might have been expected, a few of the priests made all the opposition they could; but the circumstance that these were unable to excite the people showed how little influence they possessed. On the other hand, perhaps quite as many of the clergy, and those of the most respectable in the empire, manifested toward us and our work both favor and friendship. From them, as well as from the intelligent laity, did we often hear the severest reprehension of abuses that were tolerated in the religious system and practices of the country, and sincere regrets that no more spirituality pervaded the public mind."[29]

In illustration of the spirit of tolerance might be mentioned the episode concerning the papal nuncio. In 1846 the papal nuncio in Brazil, Mgr. Bedini, visited Petropolis, a settlement in the mountains forty miles west of Rio de Janeiro. In that place were many German Protestants with their own chapels receiving governmental support. The regularly ordained pastors of these churches were legally authorized to officiate at nuptials, and indeed had performed several mixed marriage ceremonies. This practice scandalized the Nuncio, who declared that all Catholics so allied were living in concubinage, their marriages were void, and their children illegitimate. This declaration aroused a storm of protest and even a semi-official publication in Rio denounced Bedini. It insisted that it was the highest imprudence thus to kindle the fires of religious intolerance.[30]

In rather unpleasant contrast to the agreeable pictures of religious toleration described by Fletcher and Kidder, are their accusations of clerical corruption in imperial Brazil. The lives and practices of the priests were notoriously corrupt, contended the missionaries, and they cite several examples which fell under their personal observation. The messages of the Minister of Justice, it was argued, annually alluded to this state of affairs. Finally,

[29] Fletcher and Kidder, *op. cit.*, p. 143.
[30] *Ibid.*, pp. 142-143, 160.

a foreign naturalist who visited Brazil between the years 1836 and 1841, was quoted as follows: "The present clergy of Brazil are more debased and immoral than any other class of men." A consequence of the shameful immorality of the clergy was a loss of influence over the people. "Since independence," recites the missionary authors, "the priestly power has been broken and the potent hierarchy of Rome does not rule over the consciences and acts of men as in Chile or Mexico."[31]

Although Pedro II was criticised by the supporters of Mgr. Bedini for adopting a neutral attitude in the controversy in 1846, and not using his influence to prevent the spread of Protestant heresies, the Emperor continued to command the support of the clergy and the champions of clerical prerogatives. Yet it was inevitable that his lukewarm attitude on religion, his liberalism, and, above all, his fostering of an extreme *patronato nacional* would eventually arouse the opposition of the ultramontanists. The tranquil relations which had existed for so many years between Church and State were disturbed in 1873 by the so-called *questão religiosa*. This was a repercussion of the current ultramontane tendencies of the time, and it assumed the form in Brazil of an assault upon Freemasonry.

Since 1807, when the first lodge was founded in Bahia, Masonry had flourished in Brazil. In the last days of the colonial era the Masonic lodges were forces for the propagation of republican-democratic ideas. Their influence was felt in the Revolution of Pernambuco in 1817, and after the failure of that revolt the lodges continued to propagate liberal principles.[32] Under the Empire Masonry gathered into its membership numerous ecclesiastics. As has been noted above a great number of the clerical members of the Constituent Assembly of 1823 and of the first General Assembly were members of the clergy. High officials of the Empire including Pedro II and his prime minister, Baron Rio Branco, were Masons. On the other hand, in illustration of the harmonious relations which had existed between the Brazilian Church and Masonry, Masons were admitted freely into the

---

[31] *Ibid.,* pp. 140-142.

[32] Felisbello Freire, *Historia Constitucional da Republica dos Estados do Brasil* (Rio de Janeiro, 1893), I, 42-43.

irmandades or religious and benevolent associations. These brotherhoods, composed almost exclusively of laymen, were conducted under Church auspices and were supposed to be amenable to Church discipline. This liberal interrelationship between Church and Masonry continued in Brazil even after the publication of the *Syllabus* of Pius IX, which anathematized Masonry. The encyclical *quanta cura*, of which the *Syllabus* was an *addenda*, had never been approved by Pedro II. The government refused to accord the exequatur because it wished to avoid trouble, since so many good Catholics were members of Masonic lodges. The Emperor assumed the position that Brazilian Masonry was different from that of other lands. If the lodges were anti-Catholic elsewhere, they certainly were not in Brazil. The large number of clerics and other good Catholics in the lodges testified to that fact. Technically, therefore, the pope's opposition to Freemasonry had never been officially communicated to the Brazilian clergy.[33] Certain prelates, however, took it upon themselves to observe the commands of the Vatican and precipitated thereby the one serious religious conflict in the history of the Empire.

The initial event of the "religious question" was the act of Bishop Pedro Maria de Lacerda of Rio de Janeiro in ordering (March 3, 1872) the suspension of a priest who delivered a sermon in a Masonic lodge. The priest was ordered to abjure Masonry but refused.[34] The incident caused the smouldering fires of opposition between ultramontanists and Masonry to break into open flame. Under the presidency of Baron Rio Branco, Grand Master of the Masons, a great session was held in Rio de Janeiro on April 16, 1872. A resolution was adopted pledging the lodges to attack the episcopacy in the press and to invite all Masons of Brazil to take part in the battle against the Church. Although Masonry, in the early period of the Empire, manifested no antagonism toward the Church, such was no longer the case. Many hostile critics of Catholicism had been gathered into the membership of the lodges, and eventually they succeeded in identifying Masonry with their

---

[33] Magalhães, *op. cit.*, p. 397; Martin, *op. cit.*, p. 11.

[34] A. O. Viveiros de Castro, "Contribuiçoes Para A Biographia De D. Pedro II," in *Rev. do Inst. Hist. e Geog.*, Tomo Especial, 1925, pp. 477-479; Magalhães, *op. cit.*, p. 397.

own hostility to the Church. Whether the lodges sponsored this policy, as charged by the clergy, it is difficult to state. At any rate there were numerous recriminations and counter-recriminations. Suffice it to say that in 1872, prior to the action of Bishop Lacerda of Rio, Bishop Antonio de Macedo Costa of Pará was forced to publish a pastoral against the Masons because of the violent and scurrilous attack made upon him in the Masonic press.[35] It is not true, therefore, that the Masonic lodges were innocent of any responsibility for opening the religious question.

Bishop Lacerda was a timid soul, and became so frightened because of the furore he aroused that he hastened to reverse his position. The new Bishop of Olinda, on the contrary, determined with the reckless enthusiasm of youth, for he was but twenty-eight years of age, to seize the opportunity for initiating a reform designed to restore papal control over the Brazilian Church. On May 24, 1872, Vital Maria Gonçalves de Oliveira, a Capuchin and ardent ultramontanist, became bishop of the diocese of Olinda. He was considered by the Masons as a dangerous man and they did not delay putting him to the test. On June 27, 1872, the press announced that the Masonic lodge of Recife would commemorate the anniversary of its foundation by celebrating a mass. Bishop Vital ordered the clergy not to participate in any ceremony announced as Masonry, and all Catholic societies were ordered to expel such members as belonged to Masonic lodges. Interdicts were laid upon the churches that disobeyed the order.[36]

Lodges and brotherhoods appealed to the Emperor for relief. Before intervening officially the government adopted a conciliatory attitude. Shr. João Alfredo Corrêa de Oliveira, a Minister of State, wrote to Bishop Vital on February 15, 1873. He pointed out that the brotherhoods were not only religious but civil and under the latter capacity did not come under the authority of the Church. In attempting to control their membership the Bishop, consequently, was usurping the temporal prerogative. In his rejoinder the Bishop cited the papal allocution of September 25, 1865, which formally condemned Masonry. The government then sought the intervention of the papal internuncio. The internuncio

---

[35] *Dic. Hist. Geog.,* II, 229; Castro, *op. cit.,* pp. 477-478.

[36] Castro, *op. cit.,* pp. 479-480; Magalhães *op. cit.,* p. 398.

counseled the bishop against doing anything which would antagonize the government. Seeing that the papal representative would
do nothing for him, Vital wrote to the pope. In his reply, May 29,
1873, Pius IX praised the zeal of the Bishop and gave him full
power to work with all rigor against the Masonic brotherhoods.
Vital was ordered to convey this communication to all the bishops
of Brazil in order that they could do likewise in their dioceses.[37]
In attempting to enforce this papal order, which never received
the imperial exequatur, Bishop Vital made himself liable for violating the constitutional law.

Of the twelve prelates of the Empire, only one, Bishop Macedo
Costa of Pará joined Vital's crusade. The others observed a dis-
crete silence. On March 25, 1873, the Bishop of Pará issued a
pastoral combatting Masonry. He ordered all Masonic members of
irmandades to renounce Masonry or withdraw from the associations. Those that refused to expel their Masonic members were suspended.[38] As in Pernambuco churches and chapels were put under
the interdict in Pará.

In August, 1873, Pedro II sent the Baron de Penedo to the
Vatican on special mission to urge papal intervention in bringing
the recalcitrant prelates to reason. The mission was a complete
success, for Pope Pius IX, through his Secretary of State Cardinal Antonelli, wrote to the Bishop of Olinda on December 18,
1873, formally disapproving of his conduct and ordering the
restoration of the brotherhoods to their old status. The about face
in papal position was taken only after the Brazilian envoy assured
His Holiness that the government would not take drastic action
against the bishops. One of the greatest moot questions in Brazilian history is whether the pope really censured Bishop Vital.
Baron de Penedo claimed that the pope called Vital a "hot-head"
and that Cardinal Antonelli showed him the letter before it was
sent. A severe condemnation of the Bishop was said to be prefaced
with the words *Gesta tua non laudantum*. The letter received by
the prelate and as published by Bishop Costa a few years later
did not contain the passage. Did Penedo lie? Was the prelate

---

[37] Castro, *op. cit.*, pp. 485-490; Magalhães, *op. cit.*, p. 399.

[38] Castro, *op. cit.*, pp. 480-481; Magalhães, *op. cit.*, pp. 398-399; Martin,
op. cit., p. 13.

guilty of deleting the passage from the letter? Or did Cardinal Antonelli dupe Penedo and fail to send to the prelate the letter which was shown to the envoy? The present consensus of opinion in Brazil is that the last conjecture is correct. The measure of duplicity was evenly balanced. If Cardinal Antonelli wilfully misled Penedo, the envoy on the other hand was guilty of misinforming the pope.[39]

The government should have been satisfied with the pope's condemnation of the bishops, for it had won a complete victory, and, in the words of Bishop Macedo Costa, "Masonry was left all the honors of a triumph." But unfortunately, in a vengeful spirit, it decided to prosecute the prelates of Pará and Olinda. On the advice of the Council of State,[40] Pedro II ordered the bishops to withdraw the interdicts within fifteen days. Following their refusal to revoke the interdicts, their arrest was ordered on November 7, 1873.

In separate trials (February and June, 1874) before the Supreme Tribunal of Justice, the two bishops were convicted on the identical charges of violating Article 96 of the Criminal Code, to wit: "to seek to impede in any manner the will of the executive and moderative power, conforming to the constitution and the laws."[41] They were assessed the "intermediate" penalty of four years imprisonment at hard labor. The Emperor commuted the sentences to simple imprisonment. The two prelates were men of great scholarly attainments and virtue and enjoyed the affectionate regard of their flocks. To subject them to penal servitude, notwithstanding the seriousness of their offense, was impolitic because of the scandal and indignation this produced among the clergy and the faithful. Furthermore it was an act unworthy of the benevolent Emperor. Eventually, after the mischief was done, on

---

[39] Castro, *op. cit.*, pp. 508-512; Martin, *op. cit.*, p. 14; Padre Julio Maria, *op. cit.*, I, 91 ff.; Dr. Alexandre José Barboza Lima, "Um Grande Brasileiro, Frei Vital," in *Rev. do Inst. Hist. e Geog.*, LXXI, Parte II, 147; Magalhães, *op. cit.*, p. 400.

[40] Joaquin Nabuco opposed prosecution of the two bishops for, (1) it would affect the dignity and moral force of the episcopacy, and (2) imprisonment of the bishops would cause more trouble and stimulate a religious war. (Castro, *op. cit.*, pp. 496-497.)

[41] *Ibid.*, p. 506.

September 17, 1875, due to the intercession of the Princess Isabella, Pedro II granted the prelates amnesty.[42]

The religious conflict seriously weakened the prestige of the Empire. It proved, in the words of Oliveira Lima, that "the monarchy which acted in this fashion was not clerical." The bishops were regarded as martyrs and the clergy claimed that they were attacked in their essential liberties. The vigilant action of the State was an offense which the Church considered as an expression of despotism. There was no advantage in a pretended partnership of Church and State if they were not co-equals, and thus the clergy began to think seriously of the advantages of separation. The Bishop of Pará declared, "Give liberty to the Church of Jesus Christ. . . . Leave her to be governed according to her own laws."[43] Too late Pedro II realized that harmonious relations between Church and State can never be accomplished by forcing absolute submission of the former to the latter. It should be carefully noted, however, that the clergy, between the years 1870 and 1890, did not work for separation. If given a free choice between union and separation they undoubtedly would have selected the former. But so dissatisfied were they with even that status that they were unwilling, when the crisis came, to defend it with vigor. The papacy, however, stood firmly by the side of the monarchy to the end. In recognition of her emancipation of the slaves, the Princess Regent was given the Rose d'Or by Pope Leo XIII. On May 5, 1888, the pope sent a communication to the Brazilian bishops giving them sage advice to be passed on to the emancipated negroes. They should be urged, said the pontiff, to devote themselves as honest citizens for the advantage and good of the family and the State. They should respect their sovereign, obey the magistrates, and observe the laws.[44]

There were other elements in Brazil, however, that were campaigning for the dissolution of the Church-State connection. The most active of these were the Republicans, the Socialists, and the Positivists. They felt that, since the Church exercised a great

---

[42] *Ibid.,* pp. 505-506; *Dic. Hist. Geog.,* II, 229; Manuel Oliveira Lima, *Formation Historique de la Nationalité Brazilienne* (Paris, 1911), pp. 259-260.

[43] Oliveira Lima, *op. cit.,* p. 260.

[44] Mossé, *op. cit.,* p. 248.

21

influence in all matters relating to education and the social life of the people, no sweeping reform could be effected until its domination had been broken. The extreme liberalism of Pedro II invited the introduction and spread of radical political, social, and religious propaganda. This movement became so pronounced after about 1870 that that date is said to mark the intellectual emancipation of the country.[45] Since the various "isms," among them republicanism, socialism, Haeckelism, and Positivism, advocated a break with the past, necessarily the Catholic Church, the institution which was most closely associated with the past, was attacked with vigor. Above all, it must be made to relinquish its favored political position. An uninviting prospect, which tended to consolidate liberal opposition to the dynasty, was the ardent devotion to the Church of the heiress apparent, the Princess Isabella.[46] When Isabella acted as regent, during Pedro's absence in the United States and Europe, she showed herself to be swayed by Church influence in political questions. It was partly because of this fear of clericalism that the Empire was finally abolished.

Positivism, or the *Systema de Philosophia Positiva,* as it was known in Brazil, was propagated in that country by Benjamin Constant and Miguel Lemos.[47] The Positivists exercised an influence in the evolution of democracy in Brazil, far out of proportion to their restricted numbers. In defense of individual liberty they championed the abolition of negro slavery and the separation of the temporal from the spiritual authority. The divorce of religion from all political connection was regarded by the Positivists as

[45] Freire, *op. cit.,* I, 402, Oliveira Vianna, "A Queda Do Imperio," in *Rev. do Inst. Hist. e Geog.,* Tomo especial, 1925, pp. 838-839.

[46] The Princess was accused of being instrumental in bringing about the defeat, in the Deputies, of a bill to free Protestants from certain legal disabilities. (Martin, *op. cit.,* p. 23, n. 41.)

[47] Positivism as developed by August Comte is both a philosophical and a religious system. As a philosophy it denies the validity of metaphysical speculations, and maintains that sense experience is the only object and the supreme criterion of human knowledge. Abstractions are given collective notions. As a religious system Positivism denies the existence of a personal God and takes humanity, the Great Being, as the object of its veneration. Positivism has a cult, sacraments, and ceremonies. The Positivists erected a Temple of Humanity in Rio de Janeiro in 1891.

an essential of spiritual liberty. When a project to establish civil marriage was introduced in the Parliament, in 1884, Miguel Lemos said, "We do not fight for civil marriage as an expedient designed to favor immigration, but as a normal institution indispensable to good political organization, and as one of the most necessary conditions of spiritual liberty." In 1887 a project to secularize the cemeteries was introduced in the Senate. Shr. Teixeira Mendes, a Positivist leader, spoke publicly for the measure "as a necessity of our religious emancipation." In a letter written by the *Centro Positivista do Brasil* to the Bishop of Pará in 1888, an attempt was made to convince the prelate that all interests, including the clerical, would be best served by the overthrow of the Empire. The letter ended by predicting the fall of the Empire after the abolition of slavery.[48]

The prophesy of the *Centro Positivista* was correct; the abolition of slavery in Brazil was followed almost immediately by the overthrow of the Empire and the establishment of a federal republic. Since one of the demands of the anti-imperial forces was separation of Church and State, this reform was carried through with dispatch and thoroughness by the provisional government which exercised control from November 15, 1889 to February 25, 1891. By decree, dated January 7, 1890, Church and State were separated and the patronage was abolished. Freedom of worship was guaranteed and the federal and state authorities were prohibited from subsidizing any religion, or making any distinction between the inhabitants of the country based on religious or philosophical beliefs or opinions. Public officers were forbidden to interfere in any way with the formation of religious societies and it was declared to be unlawful to stir up religious dissension among the people. Religious corporations were granted juridic personality to acquire property and were recognized as valid owners of properties actually held by them. The salaries of those in the service of the Church were ordered to be discontinued at the expiration of a year. Thus, by the decree of separation the Catholic Church retained possession of its communicants, build-

---

[48] Freire, *op. cit.,* I, 410-411.

ings, lands, incomes, and hierarchical organization.[49]

Another decree of the provisional government, also dated January 7, 1890, abolished the existing religious holidays, except Sunday, and established nine new holidays commemorating secular events. On January 24, compulsory civil marriage was decreed, and, on January 26, Church nuptials, prior to the civil, were prohibited. On September 27, 1890, the existing cemeteries were secularized and put under the control of the municipalities. Religious bodies were allowed, in the future, to provide separate burial places, although always subject to the laws.[50]

The definitive status of the Roman Catholic Church in republican Brazil was worked out in the Constituent Congress which met in Rio de Janeiro on November 15, 1890. This body, composed of deputies elected by general ticket in each of the states, was not representative of the Brazilian nation, charged the spokesman of the clericals, Shr. Badaro. He said, "The provisional government opposed with a hand of iron the Catholic conscience of Brazil in the elections to the Convention."[51] It was true that the government manipulated the elections, but to what extent 'friends of the established Church were discriminated against it is impossible to say. The personnel of the Convention, as events proved, was above the average in liberality and forbearance.

When the Constituent Congress met, the provisional government sought to facilitate, and perhaps control, its deliberations by submitting to it a model constitution. The decrees of 1890 separating Church and State were incorporated into this draft. The following additional items were included. exclusion of the Jesuits, prohibition of the founding of new convents or monastic orders, denial of political rights to clerics, and imposing upon religious associations in their property rights the limits of the laws of mortmain.

The religious clauses of the project were subjected to careful scrutiny and extended debate in the Convention, which revealed

---

[49] *Constituição do Republica dos Estados Unidos do Brasil. Acompanhada das Leis Organicas Publicadas desde 15 de Novembra de 1889* (Rio de Janeiro, 1891), p. 49; James, *op. cit.*, p. 140.

[50] *Constituição do Republica . . . Acompanhada das Leis,* p. 50.

[51] Roure, *op. cit.,* p. 460.

itself as being less radical than the provisional government on the religious issues. Many members of the Assembly were of the same opinion as Shr. Coelho e Campos, who said that he favored Cavour's formula, "a free Church in a free State," and therefore he could not accept several of the religious provisions of the project. The exclusion of the Jesuits from the country aroused protests. More than one delegate defended the great work of the Society of Jesus in transplanting European civilization to the wilderness of Brazil, and they mentioned in particular the names of Fathers Nobrega and Anchieta. The majority being of the opinion that the exclusion of the Jesuits would not be worthy of a liberal constitution, voted to strike out of the project the clause relating to the order, but the prohibition of new convents and monastic orders was allowed to stand.[52]

The denial to clerics of all political rights also aroused opposition. This clause was amended to provide that no one could be declared incapable of holding office because he was a religious, excepting members of monastic orders subject to a vow of obedience. The reëstablishment of the laws of mortmain which had been enacted during the colonial period was also combatted successfully. Religious corporations were allowed to acquire property "according to the dispositions of the common law." A slight amendment to the provision legalizing civil marriage was also adopted by the Congress. To the words "The republic recognizes only civil marriage," were added, "which celebration is gratuitous."[53] At the present date, according to constitutional law, the civil marriage is free, but in reality revenue stamps amounting to a minimum of $5.00 are payable on the required documents. The fees charged by the Church are very considerable, amounting to $15.00 and up.[54] Since the constitutional project did not refer to divorce, but declared that civil marriage was indissoluble, certain members of the Congress attempted to have absolute divorce adopted. Their efforts ended in failure, as have all similar attempts to date.

Many Catholic partisans participated in the debates in the Constituent Congress. One of these, in defending the State-Church,

---

[52] *Ibid.*, pp. 472-473.
[53] *Ibid.*, p. 497.
[54] C. I. Dawson to J. L. Mecham.

said, "By a 'religious republic' we do not wish to say that the
republic is governed by the clergy, nor that there is subordination
to the Church; it signifies that the government recognizes the
fundamental principles of Christianity and does not expel God
from the constitutional charter as a myth and chimera." An unrestrained partisan, Shr. Badaro, precipitated a tumult in the
Assembly when he defended the Catholic religion. He condemned
the banishment of the Jesuits, obligatory civil marriage, secularization of cemeteries, and the laws of mortmain. All these were
manifestations, he said, of an irreligious spirit. A protest against
separation penned by the Bishop of Bahia, was read to the Congress. The prelate branded separation as "violent, radical, impossible, and gravely disturbing to the conscience of the nation."[55]

The clericals found an unexpected ally in the spokesman of the
Positivists, Shr. Demetrio Ribeiro. He opposed the laws of mortmain, the prohibition of new convents, the exclusion of the Jesuits,
and the political disabilities of the religious.Yet he was a staunch
advocate of the separation of the Church and State, for, on
January 7, 1891, on the anniversary of the decree of separation,
he made a motion that the Convention vote a resolution of "effective
solidarity on the political principle of complete separation of the
spiritual and temporal and their natural practical consequences."[56]

According to the Federal Republican Constitution promulgated
on February 24, 1891, the separation of Church and State in
Brazil is complete. Fortunate indeed is the Republic that the
majority of the members of the Constituent Congress were men
of forbearance and tolerance. There are no constitutional restrictions upon the liberty of conscience and religion; no tests for
exercising the suffrage or holding office. All political connections
between Church and State have been severed. Although the diplomatic corps at Rio de Janeiro enjoys the presence of a papal
nuncio as one of its members, and Brazil accredits an ambassador
to the Vatican, this adherence to tradition has no political significance. All pretentions to national patronage were abolished
in 1890. Today the government takes no part in the naming of
prelates, or in granting the *pase* to pontifical documents.

---

[55] Roure, *op. cit.,* pp. 456, 460, 466.

[56] *Ibid.,* p. 463.

A wise action of the fathers of the Republic was the bestowal on the Church of title to its properties. Nationalization of ecclesiastical holdings would have led inevitably to future conflicts between the temporal and spiritual organizations. All buildings used exclusively for religious purposes are exempt from taxation, but other realty owned by the Church is not. The government does not pay the salaries of those who entered the priesthood since the date of separation, nor does it contribute to the support of the Church in any other way, with the exception of making contributions to the missions which are regarded as an aid to national material progress.[57]

The disestablishment of the Church in Brazil also meant the breaking of the hold of the clergy upon the educational system of the country. Under the Constitution public instruction must be laical. Religious instruction may be given in the public schools but the government does not pay the teachers and the instruction must be after school hours. The Church, being deprived of its ancient control over public education, maintains a great number of elementary and secondary schools all over the country. The majority of the secondary schools are kept by the religious congregations, such as Jesuits, Benedictines, and the like. Female religious maintain all the best secondary schools for girls. The Catholic Church is also very active in Brazil in supporting hospitals and asylums. A *Misericordia* hospital is to be found in every part of the country. Also, *recolhimientos* for orphan girls are found in all the large cities.[58]

The separation of 1890 has not weakened the hold of the Catholic Church on the population of Brazil as a whole. Indeed, since that date, the Catholic Faith has flourished. Being removed from politics the Church has been able to concentrate its attention on the solution of its own internal problems. One of the most important of these tasks was the purification of the clergy, for it was realized that clerical immorality under the Empire undermined respect for the clergy and created a lukewarm attitude toward dissolution of the established Church. The remarkable increase of the population of Brazil by immigration since 1900 has been over-

[57] Mgr. Joaquin Nabuco, Archbishop of Rio de Janeiro, to J. L. Mecham, Rio de Janeiro, January 8, 1928.   [58] *Ibid.*

whelmingly Catholic. Therefore, whether or not the Church is subsidized by the State, the nation must continue Roman Catholic. At the present date the Brazilian Catholic Church is organized into sixteen archbishoprics.[59] In recognition of the importance of the Church in Brazil, the archbishop of Rio de Janeiro was created in 1905 the first cardinal in South America.

Although there is no great political party in Brazil with clerical affiliations, nevertheless the União Catholica Brasileira, founded in 1907, a great lay Catholic organization, has interested itself in political questions as they have affected the Church. Therefore, as a champion of Catholicism, it has combatted absolute divorce, non-teaching of religion in public schools, and the attempted suppression of the embassy at the Vatican. The União Catholica professes to be: "Defender and propagator of the Catholic religion; lover and aggrandizer of Brazil; protector of ecclesiastical authority; respecter of legitimate constitutional rights; antagonist of secret societies and sects condemned by the Church; champion of morality and foe of divorce; and, foe of immoral literature." The official publication of the União is the *Revista Social*.[60]

There has been considerable proselyting by several Protestant sects in Brazil, particularly the Methodist Episcopal, South, which was assigned the Brazilian missionary field. The foreign colonies, the German, English, and American, practise their own faiths freely in their own churches. The most numerous are, Methodists, Baptists, Lutherans, Anglicans, and Presbyterians. Most of the pastors are foreigners. Protestants have been particularly active in Brazil in fostering education. They maintain about one hundred schools, with two thousand pupils. This does not include about two hundred German Lutheran parochial schools in southern Brazil. The most notable Protestant school in South America is Mackenzie College of São Paulo, a Presbyterian institution. Another great Protestant college is the Isabella Hendrix, located in Bello Horizonte (capital of Minas Geraes). This college for girls is maintained by the Methodists of the United States.[61]

---

[59] *Annuario Catholico do Brasil* (Rio de Janeiro, 1928), pp. 191 ff.

[60] *Ibid.*, pp. 62-63.

[61] *Geographia do Brasil* (Sociedade de Geographia do Rio de Janeiro), X, 296.

Notwithstanding the praiseworthy efforts of the Protestants, their cult has not made any appreciable impression on the overwhelming Catholic character of the country. "For the simple, uneducated, rural population the symbolism of the Church and particularly its colorful festivals continue to make the old-time strong appeal."[62] The missionaries complain of the opposition of an intolerant Catholic clergy and the religious superstition of the masses. For example, agents of the American Bible Society said that the belief had been inculcated by the priests that the people had no right to read the Bible, even the Catholic version. The Bishop of Diamantina warned his flock against "false Bibles," and urged that the agents be not allowed to spread their propaganda.[63]

A well-known American missionary agent, Mr. S. G. Inman, reported in 1921, a great sweep of reaction and fanaticism in Brazil. The most successful reactionary movement of the Catholic Church, he contended, was in education. The object was to put all schools, both public and private, under a course of study that would effectually shut out foreign ideas and maintain the *status quo* of all instruction. To substantiate his claim that, in the name of patriotism, the clerics were fostering reactionary programs, Mr. Inman quotes from a pastoral of the Bishop of Marianna. Since this is illustrative of a particular type of clerical mind, certain extracts from the pastoral are herein reproduced:

If we desire a country truly free, mistress of her own destiny and governing herself by herself, with dependence on, or wardship from, no nation whatsoever, however friendly such an one may be proclaimed to be, we cannot favor, but rather oppose a tenacious and irreconcilable resistance to the Protestant propaganda, whose principal end in view is to establish the North American dominion in our Brazil. Of this, there is today no possible doubt, and the only one who will not confess it is the one who has some interest in dissimulating what is before the eyes of all. It is not the love of the truth that induces the American sects to spend in their Protestant propaganda sums so large that they mount up to millions of dollars. If it is the love of their neighbor and the love of God that brings

[62] Herman G. James, *Brazil After a Century of Independence* (New York, 1925), p. 527.

[63] Nevin O. Winter, *Brazil and her People of Today* (Boston, 1910), p. 298.

them to be missionaries to us, as with badly dissimulated feigning they affirm, why do they not make use of this charity in bringing to better terms the unfaithful who abound in the United States more than in any other country in the world that calls itself Christian? From the statistics of that Republic it is known that there are living there sixty millions of men without religion, without baptism, with no religious belief. There are more heathen there than in all the other American republics together. In Brazil we are all baptized, by the grace of God, and almost all believe in our Lord Jesus Christ, and profess the Catholic religion, in which we were born, and in which we want to die. Protestants know perfectly that we are saved in our religion, just as we know that for them salvation is impossible, unless it be that an invincible good faith may defend them at the divine judgment seat.[64]

It is inevitable that, in such an overwhelmingly Catholic country as Brazil, there should be popular suspicion, particularly among the ignorant masses, of dissident cults, and that the Catholic clergy should jealously guard their cherished tradition. Yet it is a notable fact that the Brazilian people, in their national and state legislation, have committed themselves in most emphatic terms in favor of religious liberty and toleration. "It is safe to say," writes an authority on Brazilian government, "that there is no other country in the world where the Roman Catholic faith is the traditional and prevailing faith of the inhabitants where there is a more complete separation of Church and State, or where there is greater freedom of conscience and worship. In theory there is even greater freedom guaranteed by the Brazilian constitution than by our own, for whereas there is nothing in the federal constitution of the United States that would prevent the individual states from establishing a religion or prohibiting the exercise thereof, nor anything to prevent the states from requiring a religious test as a qualification for public office, in Brazil the federal constitution explicitly forbids such action on the part of the states."[65]

---

[64] Inman, *South America Today*, pp. 65-67.
[65] James, *Const. System of Brazil*, pp. 140-141.

II

URUGUAY

Brazil's diminutive neighbor-state, the Oriental Republic of Uruguay, has also within recent years cut asunder the bonds which once tied the religious establishment to the political power. And, as in the vast Portuguese-American state, separation in Uruguay has been attended by satisfying and hopeful results. The progressive Spanish-American republic, which so often has been called the political and sociological laboratory of South America, dared to experiment in a new religious policy. The experiences of the past ten years tend to prove the success of the experiment.

In embarking upon an independent career Uruguay adopted as its religious policy that of its mentor and guardian, Argentina. The long-lived Constitution of 1830 (which was not supplanted until 1919), provided for the Catholic religion as that of the State, but it did not prohibit the exercise of dissident faiths. The guarantee of toleration of cults as early as 1830 was an exceptional feature of ecclesiastical policy in Latin America. But, in laying claim to the exercise of the ecclesiastical patronage, Uruguay merely adopted the practice of the other Latin-American states. Thus, the Constitution provided that the president should exercise the right of patronage; that he, with the advice of the Senate, should grant or refuse the exequatur to pontifical bulls.[66]

Prior to the establishment of Uruguayan independence, ecclesiastical jurisdiction in the Banda Oriental was subordinate to the diocesan of Buenos Aires. This situation which continued after the creation of the independent republic, was repugnant to the national sensibilities of Uruguayans. Consequently, Congress on July 17, 1830, ordered the president to petition the Holy See to create a separate diocese in the republic. The legislators went on record as being willing to defray the expenses of an episcopal see, but stipulated that the incumbent should be a citizen of the

---

[66] Constitution of 1830, in Arosemena, *op. cit.*, I, 213-234, Articles 5 and 81.

State.[67] The aspiration at the establishment of a national diocese was not satisfied for many years to come. Uruguay was constituted an apostolic vicarate, and not until 1878 was the diocese of Montevideo created.[68] Preliminary to the establishment of the diocese, the Apostolic Delegate to Argentina, Marino Marini, on February 24, 1863, conferred on the Vicar General of Uruguay the episcopal power of administering the sacrament of confirmation.[69]

Despite the fact that the Uruguayan Church continued to be under foreign ecclesiastical jurisdiction, the government exercised its constitutional right of ecclesiastical patronage. In the law of July 17, 1830, the Congress stipulated that the new bishop whenever created should be proposed as constitutionally required. In 1835, by act of Congress, the President was empowered to enter into an agreement with the apostolic vicar providing for the organizing of tribunals to hear ecclesiastical causes.[70] The government, also, was very jealous of its right over the *pase* required of pontifical documents. For example, the brief of Marino Marini mentioned above was refused publication in Uruguay until the consent of the Tribunal of Justice was secured.[71]

For nearly one hundred years, despite the perpetual political turmoil incident to the ups and downs of the factions known as *Blancos* and *Colorados*, the provisions in the Constitution of 1830 on the subject of religion were never altered. Yet, during these years the Church was subjected to attack, never as violent or devastating as that in Mexico, but nevertheless unremitting and effective. The result was that the privileged position of the Church was undermined and the so called union of Church and State became more fiction than fact. Under these circumstances, therefore, little opposition would be raised to absolute separation.

The bitter rivalry between the two traditional parties, the *Colorados* and the *Blancos*, has been a dominant factor in the history of the Uruguayan republic. But, as to professing distinctive policies, they differed very slightly, the principal aims of

---

[67] P. V. Goyena (ed.), *La Legislación Vigente de la República Oriental del Uruguay* (Montevideo, 1874), II, 464.

[68] *Cath. Ency.*, XV, 231.

[69] Goyena, *op. cit.*, II, 468.

[70] *Ibid.*, II, 491-492.

[71] *Ibid.*, II, 468.

both parties being to capture office and retain it; one represented the "ins" and the other the "outs." To a certain extent, however, the *Blancos* "were the partisans of absolutism, nationalists, and Catholics, and intolerant toward foreign cults. The *Colorados* were liberals and enemies of the Church."[72] But notwithstanding this difference, religion of itself has never been a contributing cause of civil war in Uruguay. This, however, has not prevented the *Colorados*, during their recurrent tenures of office, from enacting various ecclesiastical reform measures, which the *Blancos*, presumably because of their lack of interest, never attempted to revoke. The *Colorados*, as a general rule, have been mild and unaggressive anti-clericals, and the *Blancos* have been supine and lukewarm defenders of the State-Church. Under such a situation the power and prestige of the Church declined.

Although more far-reaching reform directed at the temporal prerogatives of the Church was not forthcoming until after 1880, certain incidents and acts occurring in the preceeding years may be mentioned to illustrate the unstable political status of the Church. In evidence of the liberal attitude of the government under President Fructuoso Rivera, provision was made in 1837 for the legalization of the civil marriage ceremony for the benefit of non-Catholics. According to existing law, the Catholic Church was given exclusive control over matrimony and no marriage was recognized by the law if not performed by a priest. This was a manifest injustice to non-Catholics, and thus the decree provided that non-Catholics were free to be married by the justices of the peace.[73] Foreign consuls retained the right until 1878 to perform the marriage ceremony for their nationals.[74]

In 1838 President Rivera suppressed the Franciscan convents and took their property for public use. "When there is not the required number of conventual inmates," read the presidential decree, "there should be no convents." There was considerable resentment in Uruguay, as in Brazil and other parts of Latin America, toward the too numerous religious of both sexes in a

---

[72] García Calderón, *Latin America,* pp. 131-132.

[73] Goyena, *op. cit.,* I, 369.

[74] *Leyes, Decretos y Reglamentos Vigentes en 1920* (Montevideo, 1920), p. 77.

young undeveloped land whose principal problem was population. It was regarded as manifestly unfair to the nation and economically unwise that able bodied men and women should abstain from their natural function of race reproduction. The opposition to the conventual life was not based, consequently, in anti-religious motives.[75]

In the late 1850's political elements somewhat antagonistic to the Church secured control of the government. The Jesuits who had been readmitted into the country a few years before were expelled in 1859. The vicissitudes suffered by the Company in other parts of Latin America were not escaped in the Oriental Republic. In 1861, public cemeteries were removed from ecclesiastical control and put under the direction and administration of *juntas económicas* of the respective departments. Soon, however, the political scales tipped to the other side, and in 1865, under President Venacio Flores, a *Colorado*, religious congregations dedicated to educational work were permitted reëntry into the country. By the terms of this decree the Jesuits returned to Uruguay.[76]

In the decade of the 1880's several important anti-clerical measures were adopted. Incidentally, it is interesting to note in this connection, that more anti-clerical legislation was adopted throughout Latin America in this decade than in any other equal space of time. By law of June 1, 1880, the *Registro del Estado Civil* was established. This act entrusted to the justices of the peace the exclusive right of registering vital statistics, a task hitherto monopolized by the clergy. By the terms of this law the Church was deprived of its one-time exclusive control over marriages, legitimization of births, and control of cemeteries.[77] A law of May 22, 1885, made the civil marriage compulsory and the only legal form. The civil ceremony was required to precede the religious and no ceremony should be regarded as binding in law which did not comply with the laws of the civil register. This

---

[75] Goyena, *op. cit.,* II, 469.

[76] *Ibid.,* II, 470.

[77] There is today only one cemetery in Montevideo not controlled by the government. This is the British cemetery which is non-sectarian. (C. Carrigan, American Consul-General in Charge, to J, L, Mecham, Montevideo, December 7, 1927.)

means that a child born of a Church marriage alone is regarded by the State as being illegitimate.[78] Although the religious ceremony satisfies no legal requirement, it is generally performed for Catholics after the celebration of the civil act. Approximately one-half of the civil ceremonies receive religious consecration.[79] The law of 1885 is in force today, substantially unchanged, with the exception that absolute divorce is permitted. Divorce is granted for the following causes: (a) adultery on the part of the woman under any circumstances; on the part of the husband when committed in the home, when committed publicly, or when the husband keeps a concubine; (b) attempt by either husband or wife against the life of the other, after the criminal sentence has been passed; (c) cruelty or serious injuries; (d) proposal of the husband to prostitute the wife; (e) attempt of husband or wife to prostitute their children; (f) continuous quarrels and disputes making life together insupportable; (g) penitentiary sentence for more than ten years; (h) voluntary desertion of the home for more than three years; (i) mutual consent; and (j) at the sole wish of the woman (*ad libitum*). Remarriage is permitted after a lapse of one year from the time of the granting of the decree. All cases relating to divorce, dissolution, or nullity of marriages are heard exclusively by the civil courts.[80] Since divorce has been made easy there has been a steady increase yearly.[81]

Governmental aid to the Catholic Church was constantly curtailed, until, in 1892, it amounted to only $19,712 per annum. The Church, therefore, as the State-Church, enjoyed little or no pecuniary advantage. The clergy and the various necessary ecclesiastical activities had to be supported by contributions of the faithful, bequests, fees, and income from real property. Separation, certainly, would impose no financial hardship upon the Church. It is important to note that the Catholic Church, as the State-Church, continued to enjoy, until 1919, when separation

---

[78] *Leyes, Decretos y Reglamentos Vigentes del Registro del Estado Civil* (Montevideo, 1921), Articles 83 and 91.

[79] In 1921, of 7,809 civil ceremonies, 3,873 received religious consecration. (*Anuario Estadístico de la República Oriental del Uruguay*, Montevideo, 1923, p. 23.)

[80] *Ibid.*, pp. 25, 38-39.

[81] *Anuario Estadístico*, 1923, p. 22.

occurred, a peculiar advantage with respect to education. Instruction in the Catholic faith was included in the general program of studies laid down for the schools operated by the State. Everything relating to the exercise of the national patronage and the religion of the State was entrusted to the *Departamento de Fomento, Cultos é Instrucción Público*. Of course the conduct of negotiations with the Holy See, with which official diplomatic relations were maintained until 1919, continued to be exercised by the Department of Foreign Relations.

The Church was disestablished in Uruguay when the republic adopted its present constitution on March 1, 1919. Considering the feeble ties which had joined Church and State, prior to the adoption of the Constitution of 1919, the act of separation cannot be regarded as a radical step. Nor, indeed, did the reform encounter serious opposition in any quarter. The opinion that absolute separation would be of mutual advantage to the temporal and spiritual orders seemed to be rather general. The severing of the traditional ties was accomplished, therefore, with a minimum of rancor and hard feeling.

In the Constitutional Convention (1916-1917) projects were introduced by the various parties and individual delegates for the guidance of the committee entrusted with the framing of a new constitution. In these projects appeared proposals for the separation of Church and State. With the exception of the project of the Unión Cívica, the Catholic party, all of the model constitutions provided for separation. Excepting the extreme Catholics, there seemed to be unanimity on separation, but considerable difference of opinion as to the disposal of Church property. But on this point, the moderate, and controlling elements of the two traditional parties agreed that the Catholic Church should be recognized as the legal owner of all edifices which had been constructed in whole or in part with funds from the national treasury. The agreement of the dominant parties on the issues of separation and disposition of Church buildings, really relegated the whole matter to a position of secondary importance in the Convention. It is true that extremists aired their views in considerable volume, but their proposals were refused by the Convention. Some of the counter-proposals were as follows: Dr. Juan B. Rocca, a Constitutional Nationalist, proposed that the government refuse recognition to the Church as owner of the property, but only as being in enjoyment of the usufruct. Doctors Emilio Frugoni and Celestino Mibelli, Socialists, suggested that ecclesiastical properties of national origin pass to the possession of the State to be devoted to public uses and no official subsidies be paid to any Church, congregation, or college which gave religious instruction. The proposal of the Unión Cívica was "the maintenance in all its integrity of the Constitution of 1830."[82]

The general committee appointed to draft a constitution reported, on August 10, 1917, the following article on the subject of religion: "All religious cults are free in Uruguay. The State does not recognize any religion. It recognizes in the Catholic Church ownership of all temples which have been, in whole or in part, constructed with funds from the national treasury, excepting only the chapels destined to the service of asylums, hospitals, jails, and other public establishments. It also declares exempt from all kinds of imposts, churches consecrated to the actual use of diverse cults.[83]

The introduction of the committee's recommendation was the occasion for general debate on the subject of separation. Señor Secco Illa, representing the Unión Cívica, attacked the report. Basing his argument primarily on the fact that Uruguay was sixty-one per cent Catholic, he advocated no change in the ecclesiastical policy of the Republic. Dr. Rocca, however, declared that religious sentiment would gain in prestige when the Catholic Church was freed absolutely from the influence of the State. The spirit of Article 5 of the Constitution of 1830 was profoundly altered during the years, he declared. For some time the State had no religion, and protection to the Roman Catholic Church was more nominal than effective, more apparent than real. Protection was offered in word, but denied in fact. Abolish this legal fiction, he demanded. The Socialists, Frugoni and Mibelli, were conspicuous during the debates as caustic interrogators of the spokesmen of

---

[82] *Diario de Sesiones de la H. Convención N. Constituyente de la República Oriental del Uruguay* (Montevideo, 1918), I, 181, 285-286, 460; Mariano de Vedia y Mitre, *El Gobierno del Uruguay* (Buenos Aires, 1919), p. 40.

[83] *Diario de la Convención,* IV, 11.

the Unión Cívica. The discussions on the whole, however, were remarkably good natured and were participated in by relatively few members. Quite evidently the Convention did not regard the question as being one of paramount importance. On August 30, 1917, the report of the committee was accepted without amendment.[84]

Under her new constitution, promulgated June 1, 1919, Uruguay enjoys complete separation of Church and State. The legal status of the Catholic Church and its members is little different from that of religious cults in the United States. Religious toleration is guaranteed by the Constitution. The State does not contribute to the support of any cult, nor is any religion discriminated against. The Catholic Church holds title to its property, which, acquired prior to 1919, is free from taxation. The Church is recognized in law as a juridic personality and there are no restrictions on its power to receive bequests of entailments.[85] The hierarchy is entirely free of governmental dictation and interference. Consequently the power to make ecclesiastical appointments is confined to the ecclesiastical prelates, and free and unimpeded communication is allowed between the Uruguayan clergy and the papacy. Diplomatic relations with the Holy See have been discontinued. In short, Uruguay has abandoned all pretentions to the control of ecclesiastical patronage. Public education has become entirely secular, for no longer can Catholic dogma be taught in schools supported by the government. Private schools of all grades are permitted and consequently the Catholic Church maintains a complete educational system in which religious instruction occupies an important position.[86]

The separation of the Church from the State in Uruguay has been a great success. As was predicted, the Church now has reassumed its legitimate position as a spiritual and social leader. There has been manifested a marked revival of loyalty to the dominant faith, which was given tangible evidence by the raising of

---

[84] *Ibid.*, I, 185-286, IV, 11 ff.

[85] *Constitución de la República Oriental del Uruguay* (Montevideo, 1919), Capitulo III; *Leyes, Decretos y Reglamentos de 1920*, p. 13.

[86] *Christian Work in South America*, I, 264-266; *Anuario Estadístico de 1923*, p. 115.

a popular endowment fund of $1,000,000 to compensate for the government support which was withdrawn in 1919.[87] Since the Roman Catholic organization in Uruguay is not extensive, its financial needs are not great. In 1924 there were in the Republic only eighty-five churches and chapels. There were 200 clergy regular and secular, and 150 nuns. The national episcopacy was comprised of one archbishop and two bishops. Although the population of Uruguay is slightly less than two millions, only approximately 500,000 are communicants of the Catholic faith.[88]

What is the secret of the success of separation in Uruguay? An exact answer is impossible to state, but undoubtedly the intelligence and tolerance of the Uruguayans themselves are important factors. The people of Uruguay are the most European, the most homogeneous, the best educated, and most progressive of Latin Americans. Because of their liberalism no restrictions were put upon the liberty of conscience and religion when the Republic was inaugurated, and also, because of this tolerance and progressivism ecclesiastical dependence on the political power was transformed long before 1919 into a mere fiction. Most emphatically was the spirit of tolerance and common sense displayed in the Constitutional Convention of 1917. The disestablishment act provided for *absolute* separation, and, unlike Mexico, for example, the Church was not put under supervision of the State. One of the greatest guarantees of the success of separation in Uruguay is the recognition of ownership by the Church of ecclesiastical properties. Confiscation would have aroused resentment and opposition. The nationalization of the properties and assignment to the Catholic Church for use would also have been an unwise move for it would have made the Church dependent on the government and subject to its dictation. It is undoubtedly true that the policy of Uruguay in releasing the ecclesiastical properties and in the observance of a minimum of surveillance over the Church has contributed to the peaceful and apparently successful solution of the religious problems. The Uruguayan method of handling the Church question is worthy of careful study by other Spanish-American republics.

---

[87] *Christian Work in South America,* I, 114.
[88] *Ibid.,* I, 114-115.

CHAPTER XII

CHURCH AND STATE IN THE REPUBLICS OF THE CARIBBEAN

I

HAITI

The island of Santo Domingo, originally called Española, was the first seat of Catholicism in America. From the seed planted by Father Boyl and the missionaries brought to America by Columbus and Ovando grew with amazing rapidity the towering and sheltering tree of Christianity. So rapid was the growth of the Catholic faith that Pope Julius II promulgated a bull in 1504, at the request of Queen Isabella, creating an archbishopric and two bishoprics in the island of Española. But since the rights of royal patronage were not recognized by the pope, King Ferdinand refused to consent to the creation of the sees. Finally the pope capitulated, and by the bull *universalis ecclesiae* (July 28, 1508) provided for the establishment of the archbishopric of Ayguacen, and the bishoprics of Maguen and Bayunen, all in the island of Española. Three sees, thus authorized, were never actually founded, for by 1510 the population of the island had declined so alarmingly as to make an elaborate ecclesiastical hierarchy superfluous. Ferdinand accordingly asked the pope to suppress the dioceses and create only one bishopric in Española and another in Porto Rico, both to be dependent on the archbishop of Seville. This was done by the bull *Romanus Pontifex*, August 8, 1511.[1] In 1547 the see of Santo Domingo was raised to the rank of an archbishopric.

When Spain lost to France (1697) her political control over the western part of the island, the *real patronato* over the Catholic Church in that region was terminated likewise. For over a hundred years the patronal control of the Catholic Church in

---

[1] *Supra.*

Haiti was exercised by the French crown with prerogatives not greatly dissimilar from, but by no means as comprehensive as, those possessed by the Spanish kings. In the meantime thousands of negro slaves were brought into the island, and eventually they outnumbered the whites several times to one.[2] Feeble efforts were exerted by the clergy, exclusively white, to convey the mysteries of Christianity to the blacks so recently wrested from the wilds of Africa. The clergy existed primarily for the service of the white population; the blacks were objects of secondary importance. Little wonder then that the slaves acquired only a very thin and impermanent veneer of Christianity. Furthermore, the French clergy in Haiti, it was charged, were inferior to those of the other French islands. Their character seems to have been consistently poor from the start. "A succession of bad and ignorant priests," wrote the Abbé Raynal in 1785, "has destroyed both respect for the cloth and the practice of religion in almost every parish of the colony. An atrocious greed has become the habitual vice of most of the parish priests."[3] The failure of the French clergy and missionaries to effect a permanent Christianization of the negro slaves is evidenced by the persistence to the present day of African religious rites called voodooism. Indeed, after the termination of the French domination, the practice of voodooism became almost universal, and the work of Christianization had to be undertaken anew in the nineteenth century.

From 1803, when the French withdrew from Haiti, until 1860, when a concordat was signed, the ecclesiastical system was in a semi-disorganized state, and the clergy were said to have been *sans foi ni loi.*[4] The Haitians, having none of their race trained for the priesthood, had perforce to rely on the white clergy for the administration of the sacraments and the government of the Catholic Church. The priests therefore were generally spared during the terrible massacre of the whites in 1805. An exception

---

[2] According to the 1788 census, there were in Haiti, 28,000 whites, 22,000 free colored, and 405,000 negro slaves. (Lathrop Stoddard, *The French Revolution in San Domingo,* New York, 1914, p. 9.)

[3] Venault de Charmilly, "Lettre a Bryan Edwards," quoted in Stoddard, *op. cit.,* pp. 22-23.

[4] "Hearings before a Select Committee on Haiti and Santo Domingo," United States Senate. Sen. Res. 112, 67 Cong. Washington, 1922, p. 1285.

to the usual rule of sparing the clergy was the massacre in Santiago on February 25th, of which we have a good description in a recent and authentic history of the Dominican Republic: "The Haitians, rendered jubilant by their easy victory, commenced an orgy of celebration by consuming the stores of tafia which they found in that city. They then turned their attention to rape, loot and murder, and when these pastimes palled, to the more refined pleasures afforded by torture. The greater part of the inhabitants had taken refuge in the church. All of these were slaughtered, and the priest officiating at the mass, Don José Vázquez, was burned alive, the sacred books and vestments furnishing the fuel. The church itself, piled high with the mutilated bodies of the dead, was then consumed by the flames."[5]

Although the first constitutions of the negro State, dating from that of 1801, recognized Catholicism as the State religion, the termination of French rule meant also a virtual cessation of relations with the papacy. The Holy See desired to control the Church in Haiti without any interference on the part of the temporal power, but the Haitian government, on the other hand, like the Spanish-American republics, advanced unacceptable pretentions to the exercise of the patronage. Under these conditions the clergy decreased in numbers and the influence of the Church waned. Had it not been for the Haitian annexation of Santo Domingo, the Spanish part of the island, in 1822, the prelacies in Haiti would have become extinct. As it was, the canonically instituted archbishop of Santo Domingo aided in continuing the recognized ecclesiastical succession in the island.

With few exceptions the Haitian rulers were harsh, if not oppressive, towards the Catholic Church. They considered the Church edifices as property of the State alone and religious services were continued only on sufferance of the government.[6]

The following description of religious and social conditions in the island in 1826 occurs in the report of the British Consul-General in Haiti: "The Government has appropriated all the Church prop-

---

[5] Sumner Welles, *Naboth's Vineyard, The Dominican Republic, 1844-1924* (New York, 1928), I, 35.

[6] Otto Schoenrich, *Santo Domingo* (New York, 1918), p. 187.

erty to its own use. The clergy rely wholly on the fees, two-thirds of which they are obliged to pay into the treasury. . . . It is not a subject of surprise that morality should be on as low a stage . . . marriage is scarcely thought of. . . ."[7] In 1828 there were in the island only about forty priests, and it was the professed determination of President Boyer not to increase this number, because the poverty-stricken government required the Church revenues for its own uses. Finally, in 1830, President Boyer expelled the archbishop of Santo Domingo and the bishop of Port-au-Prince, for political reasons. This act severed all connection with the papacy.[8]

In an effort to settle the dispute with Haiti, John England, Bishop of Charleston, was sent to Port-au-Prince, in 1834, in the capacity of a legate. Bishop England, being unable to reconcile the views of the pope and President Boyer, left Haiti, but he returned in 1836 to sign a concordat. He took this treaty with him to Rome hoping to have it ratified, but Gregory XII refused. Instead, Bishop England was sent back to Haiti with the title of "Vicar Apostolic, Administrator of the Church of Haiti." Boyer refused to receive him as the pope's agent in such a capacity. Thus, for a time, the diplomatic *pourparlers* were ended.[9]

In 1842 negotiations were resumed by Rome with the despatch of Joseph Rosati, Bishop of St. Louis (Missouri), to Port-au-Prince as papal legate. On February 17, 1842, Bishop Rosati signed a concordat with the Haitian government. This treaty which, by the way, was not ratified because of internal disturbances in Haiti, provided that: (1) the right to appoint archbishops and bishops vested in the president of Haiti, with the reservation to the pope of the right of granting canonical institution; (2) before prelates entered upon other duties of office, they were to take an oath of fealty and obedience to the govern-

---

[7] Quoted in Welles, *op. cit.*, I, 53.

[8] *Ibid.*, p. 186; James Franklin, *The Present State of Haiti* (London, 1822), pp. 393-394.

[9] J. N. Léger, *Haiti, Her History and Her Detractors* (New York, 1907), p. 187; Hernáez, *Colección de Bulas*, II, 30.

ment; and (3) bishops were empowered to appoint vicars-general, rectors, and parish vicars, reserving to the president the right to approve or reject these appointments.[10]

In 1860 President Geffrard reopened the parleys with the Vatican concerning the situation of the Catholic clergy in Haiti. When the Holy See abandoned its efforts to force on the negro republic high central control of the Church, the conclusion of a concordat was no longer a difficult matter. On March 28, 1860, a treaty which still regulates the relations of Haiti with the Holy See was signed at Rome by Cardinal Antonelli and M. Piérre Faubert for Haiti. This concordat secured full and special protection for the Roman Catholic Church in Haiti. "The Roman Catholic Apostolic religion," read Article 1, "which is the religion of the great majority of Haitians, will be specially protected, as well as its ministers, in the Republic of Haiti, and it will enjoy the rights and attributes which are proper to it." The Concordat insured the despatch to the island for the first time since independence, of a recognized and responsible priesthood. The Church undertook to establish parishes and missions, and, in the words of the Concordat, "those orders and institutions which are approved by the Catholic Church," including schools, hospitals, asylums, and orphanages. The instrument provided for the establishment of an archbishopric at Port-au-Prince, and dependent bishoprics elsewhere. The prelates, who were to be paid by the State, were to be nominated by the president of the Republic and approved by the pope. All were required to take an oath of fealty to the government. Provision was also made for the establishment and maintenance of cathedral chapters and seminaries. The priests were to be nominated by the bishops, but the nominations had to be approved by the government. In addition to the stipends which the clergy were to receive from the State, they were allowed to exact certain fees for the performance of special services like baptisms, marriages, and masses.[11] Two additional conventions entered into in 1861 and 1862 and a statute known as the *Loi des Fabriques*

---

[10] Léger, *op. cit.,* p. 187, note 5; Hernáez, *op. cit.,* II, 32.

[11] *Raccolta di Concordati,* pp. 929-934; Emily G. Balch (ed.), *Occupied Haiti* (New York, 1927), p. 5; Hernáez, *op. cit.,* II, 30.

provided for the carrying out of the terms of the concordat.[12]

The Concordat opened the way to the Vatican to establish an ecclesiastical organization in Haiti, and soon the Church was put on a regular footing which has ever since been maintained. In December, 1860, an apostolic delegate was sent to Haiti and on October 3, 1861, the hierarchy composed of an archdiocese and four dioceses was established. In conformity with an understanding between the papacy and the Haitian government French clerics and nuns were brought into the country in 1864 to assume the exclusive administration of the Church in its spiritual, charitable, and educational activities. They found religious conditions in a lamentable state. For example, with but one exception, every church building in Haiti has been constructed since 1860. The seminary of Saint Jacques in Quimper, France, was designated the particular one for the training of the Haitian priesthood. The Haitian government maintains twenty scholarships in this seminary.[13] At Port-au-Prince there is a seminary for the training of Haitian priests. In 1930 there were but eight native priests in the whole republic. The French priests, Brothers of Christian Instruction, and nuns, who number approximately seven hundred, are widely distributed over the country and are doing good work in charge of parishes, active mission work, education, and the charities. Indeed, they constitute the best informed foreign group in Haiti. During the World War the number of priests was somewhat reduced temporarily, for about forty were called to the French colors.[14]

Since 1860 the relations between the Catholic Church and the Haitian government have been most cordial. Barring a controversy in 1880, caused by clerical opposition to the civil marriage law, there has been little or no friction between the lay and ecclesiastical orders. Both parties have exhibited remarkable good faith in living up to the terms of the Concordat. In

---

[12] *Report of the President's Commission for the Study and Review of Conditions in the Republic of Haiti, March 26, 1930* (Washington, 1930), p. 15.

[13] *Livre Bleu D'Haiti* (Port-au-Prince, 1920), p. 141; Léger, *op. cit.*, p. 270.

[14] *Libre Bleu.* p. 141; *Report of President's Commission, 1930,* p. 16.

conformity with that convention, the Republic provides salaries for the archbishops, bishops, and priests. Each annual budget contains items for religious purposes, but not all of these appropriations are intended for the State-Church alone. Approximately ten per cent of the total amount is destined for the uses of the Protestant Churches, for the government aids and encourages the spread of the Christian religion of all denominations. Here is evidence of a marked spirit of tolerance, which has always been pronounced in Haiti. Full religious toleration has been recognized in the country since independence. The guarantee of freedom of conscience and religion is to be found in all of the Haitian constitutions.[15] The present instrument, which was promulgated in 1918, provides: "All cults are equally free. Each one has the right to profess his religion and freely exercise his cult, provided he does not disturb the public order."[16] This is the only statement contained in the Constitution on the subject of religion. The relationship existing between the Catholic Church and the government is based entirely upon the Concordat and legislation.

A large share of the burden of education in Haiti has been assumed by the Catholic Church. This state of affairs is not the consequence exactly of the existence of a privileged religion. Although the Roman Church receives governmental aid in supporting its schools, subsidies are also given Protestant educational enterprises. The commanding position of the Catholic Church in education is the result therefore, not of special privilege, but of the superiority of numbers enjoyed by that faith as the nominal faith of the great majority of the people.

Despite attempts of Haitian administrators to give more attention to public education, the Church continues to be the "right arm" of the Department of Public Instruction. The schools supported by public money, or receiving subventions, are the national "presbyterial," and "congregational" schools. In the national, or State schools, religious instruction is part of the curriculum. The presbyterial or priests' schools, and the

[15] *Catholic Encyclopedia,* VII, 114-115; Léger, *op. cit.,* p. 271.
[16] *Constitution de 1918 de La Republique D'Haiti* (Port-au-Prince, 1928), Art. 17.

congregational, or schools conducted by teaching orders, are of course, Catholic. There are 153 presbyterial schools with 10,623 pupils, and seventeen Brothers' schools with 6,731 students. The first-named schools are taught by lay teachers, generally women. The instructors in the Brothers', or congregational schools are about half Brothers and half laymen. It is generally conceded that these are the only ones which render an adequate return for money expended by the government. The teachers in the Catholic educational institutions are French men and women, members of religious orders. The most prominent male teaching order is the Brothers of Christian Instruction, while the Sisters of St. Joseph de Cluny and Les Filles de la Sagesse are the most important of the female orders. In 1930 there were thirty-six Sisters' schools in Haiti.[17]

Only a few natives are used as subordinate teachers in the schools. Some Haitians complain that the Church teaching does not give a sufficiently "patriotic" education and overemphasizes religion. Whatever might be the truth of this criticism there is little doubt that the type of instruction in the Church schools is vastly superior to that of the public schools. In addition to the Catholic educational work some teaching is being done by Protestant missionaries. A small government subsidy is enjoyed by certain Protestant educational undertakings.[18]

At the beginning of her national independence Haiti deprived the Church of its ancient control over marriage. The civil marriage was made the only legal form, but this did not prevent the religious ceremony from following the civil. The ministers of all creeds were forbidden to celebrate nuptials without requesting the presentation of the certificate of the civil marriage. After the conclusion of the Concordat the clergy were inclined to disregard this requirement and eventually they contended that they had the right to perform religious marriages without taking any notice of the civil ceremony. Because of the clerical opposition, the House of Representatives, in 1879, passed a resolution requesting the president to denounce the Concordat of

---

[17] *Report of the President's Commission, 1930,* pp. 16-17.

[18] Balch, *op. cit.,* pp. 96-98; *Livre Bleu,* pp. 141-143; *Senate Hearings,* p. 1349.

1860. When President Salomon prepared to carry out the wishes of the Congress the clergy decided that their opposition had gone too far, and consequently they promised to obey the civil marriage law. Since then there has been no friction over its observance. Unlike most of the countries where the Catholic Church is the State-Church, absolute divorce is legalized in Haiti. Divorce is granted for adultery and grave abuses, and when one of the parties is sentenced to *peines afflictives et infamantes*. Remarriage is allowed after the lapse of one year, but a divorced person is not allowed to remarry a former spouse.[19]

According to the foregoing it will be observed that the status of the Catholic Church in Haiti presents certain marked contrasts from that in other Latin-American countries where it enjoys the privileged position of a State establishment. In the first place, an alien clergy administers the Church in Haiti; the hierarchy and the lowly priests, the teaching brothers, and the nuns are foreigners. This situation arises from easily understood causes, but nevertheless it is interesting. A contrast is also found in rights of ownership in ecclesiastical property, for in Haiti, unlike other countries with a State-Church, the property is nationalized. Divorce is absolute, while in other countries it is conditional or prohibited. Finally, the Church, which is supported by the State, does not enjoy a monopoly of governmental subsidies for religious purposes.

What is the hold of Catholicism upon the inhabitants of Haiti today? Although generally regarded as a preponderatingly Catholic country, many doubt if this is true. In all but the highest circles the real religion of the people is of African origin, with a veneer of Christianity. These African rites are called generically voodooism; the different tribes had originally different religious ceremonies, but as no tribal distinctions have survived in Haiti, the result is a blend of the old superstitious practices. Voodooism is based upon fear; the propitiation of the deities being very important. Priests and teachers have tried for centuries to root out the superstitious practices, but they have scarcely made an impression. Several attempts have been made by the

---

[19] Civil Code of Haiti, Articles 213-219, 283-284; Léger, *op. cit.*, p. 283.

Haitian government to suppress voodooism, but it dares not be too stringent. Some of the presidents of Haiti, even, have been voodoo priests. It is contended that approximately ninety per cent of the Haitians are believers in voodoo and presumably good Catholics will attend the rites of the cult. Dr. Carl Kelsey tells that he approached a cabin where he witnessed a voodoo priest busy with rites over a deceased child. On being seen the priest shifted to the opposite side of the room where Christian emblems were displayed. The Christian celebrations, like Easter, have a strong African infusion. This situation is analogous to that of numerous Latin-American countries where pagan rites of the Indians persisted and became fused with Roman Catholicism. Catholic priests and Protestant missionaries are making a fine fight to eradicate paganism in Haiti—much has been accomplished, but much more remains to be done.[20] The Catholic Church as the State-Church of Haiti, is, therefore, above all else a great missionary enterprise.

II

THE DOMINICAN REPUBLIC

The Roman Catholic religion has been the State religion of the Dominican Republic since that country won its independence from Haiti in 1844. This is in recognition, according to the present constitution, of the fact that the majority of the Dominicans profess the Catholic religion.[21] Separation from the hateful Haitian domination had as one of its prime objects the reestablishment of the traditional religion of the Dominicans. The cry set up by the conspirators who inaugurated the revolt was "God, Country and Liberty,"[22] and when the independent republic was established the national motto became, "Diós, Patria, Libertad."

The ecclesiastical schism forced upon the Dominican people

[20] Balch, *op. cit.*, pp. 6, 97; *Senate Hearings,* pp. 1285-1286, 1386, 1781.

[21] "The relations of Church and State shall continue as at present, since the Roman Catholic Apostolic religion is that professed by a majority of the Dominicans." (Constitution of the Dominican Republic, 1925, Pan American Union, Washington, D. C., 1925, Art 92.)

[22] Welles, *op. cit.*, I, 59.

because of the actions of the Haitian government came to an end with the reëstablishment of the hierarchy by the pope in 1848.[23] Don Tomás de Portes é Infante was created archbishop of the ancient metropolitan see of Santo Domingo. Soon the Archbishop became involved in difficulties with President Santana (1853) because of his pro-Spanish sympathies and intervention in political matters. When the Spanish historian Don Mariano Torrente was sent to the Republic as special agent the chapter of the cathedral with the Archbishop at its head publicly welcomed him. Moreover, upon pointing out to the visitor the Spanish arms still fixed above the High Altar, the Archbishop said, "There we keep it as a reminder of better days and as a symbol of our hope for a happier and more tranquil future."[24] Santana accused the aged Archbishop of fostering dissatisfaction among the people and ordered him to take an oath of allegiance to the Constitution. Portes é Infante at first refused, but gave in at length and took the required oath. His troubles however caused him to lose his mind. Other prelates who refused to obey the orders of the President were exiled. By these summary methods Santana obtained a submissive clergy.[25]

The restoration of Spanish rule in Santo Domingo (1861) although welcomed by the clergy, did not prove to be an unmixed blessing. The new Spanish Archbishop, Don Bienvenido Monzón y Martín, aroused in the native clergy consternation and indignation by replacing Dominicans with Spanish priests in the most important posts, and by attempting to reform their lives, which, it must be admitted, were notoriously lax. But most resented of all was his action in forcing the native priests to abandon fees for their parochial services and content themselves with a meager monthly stipend.[26] The Dominican clergy, consequently, were not greatly exercised when Spain abandoned Santo Domingo in 1865.

From 1865 to the present date the history of the Church in the Dominican Republic has been devoid of important incident,

---

[23] Schoenrich, *op. cit.*, p. 186.

[24] Welles, *op. cit.*, I, 126.

[25] *Ibid.*, I, 131-132.

[26] *Ibid.*, I, 240-241.

excepting the elevation of two of the prelates to the position of president of the Republic. In 1880 Padre Fernando Arturo de Meriño, a man of extraordinary force of personality, eloquence, and presence, was elected president of the Dominican Republic. He was a complete success as an administrator, for, says Welles, "No more vigorous rule, no more decisive sway had ever previously been exercised by any Dominican President."[27] After his retirement from the presidency, Don Meriño won even greater fame as Archbishop of Santo Domingo.

In 1912, in an effort to ward off intervention by appeasing the United States, the Dominican Congress elected Adolfo A. Nouel, Archbishop of Santo Domingo, as Provisional President for a period of two years. Unlike his illustrious clerical predecessor in the presidency, Archbishop Nouel had neither the liking nor the talents for the Chief Magistracy of the Dominican Republic. He was glad therefore to relinquish his office before the expiration of the two year term. In 1922 another cleric, Canon Armando Lamarche Marchena failed of being elected to the presidency by a narrow margin.[28] The incidents mentioned are illustrative not only of the political activities of Dominican prelates and clerics, but also of the great confidence which they inspire, in a political manner, in the inhabitants of the island republic.

Although no concordat has ever been concluded between the Dominican Republic and the Vatican, friendly relations have always existed with the papacy. Diplomatic intercourse is cared for by the interchange of fully accredited representatives. In 1884 the Dominican government entered into a sort of working agreement with the Holy See, according to the terms of which the archbishop of Santo Domingo was to be appointed by the pope from a list of three names, native Dominicans or residents of the Republic, submitted by the Dominican Congress. The State agreed to pay the salaries of the archbishop and certain other ecclesiastical officials.[29] The government, although insistent on its right to present the *terna* for the election of the

---

[27] *Ibid.*, I, 439-441.
[28] *Ibid.*, II, 699-708, 873.
[29] Schoenrich, *op. cit.*, p. 186.

archbishop, has only made small appropriations for the support of the Church. The clergy, having no other sources of income, have been dependent upon contributions of the faithful.[30]

Ecclesiastical property, which is tax exempt, is administered by the Church, and presumably belongs to that organization. There is some dispute, however, as to whether the churches, which were built from public funds, are not the property of the State. After the establishment of independence, the Dominican government assumed an attitude similar to that of Haiti toward the ownership of church edifices and property. For example, by law of June 7, 1845, all mortgages and perpetual rents established in favor of the Church were declared abolished. And by a law of July 2 of the same year, all property, real and personal, formerly belonging to convents and orders no longer existing in the country, was formally appropriated by the State. But on the other hand, when a controversy arose in 1908 over the ownership of buildings and lands occupied by the Church, the government was forced to back down. This controversy was precipitated by the determination of the clerical authorities to erect a mausoleum in the cathedral for the remains of Archbishop Meriño. The government demanded that its permission be obtained first, but, when it was pointed out that the State officials had sought the permission of the Church to erect a mausoleum for Columbus in the cathedral, the government's protest was withdrawn.[31]

The Catholic Church exercises no control of an administrative nature over public education. Religious instruction may be given in the public schools at the request of the parents and members of the clergy may teach in them. The Church maintains numerous private schools of a primary and secondary character. These receive no aid from the government, although a Catholic seminary does receive an official subsidy. The Catholic and Protestant schools (there are only a few of the latter) must follow

---

[30] William B. Lawton, American Vice-Consul in Charge, to J. L. Mecham, Santo Domingo, October 17, 1927; Elias Brache Hijo, Secretario de Justicia é Instrucción Pública, to J. L. Mecham, Santo Domingo, May 17, 1928.

[31] Schoenrich, op. cit., pp. 186-187; Senate Hearings, p. 1321.

the general plan of instruction in public schools and are supervised by public inspectors.[32]

The Church is no longer in exclusive control of the institution of marriage in the Dominican Republic yet on the other hand marriages by priests can satisfy civil requirements. By the law of 1924 ecclesiastics are empowered to perform marriages having civil and religious force providing the act is inscribed in the civil register. The law therefore is similar to those of the United States. Legal separation is allowed, but not absolute divorce.[33]

There are no restrictions on liberty of conscience and religion in the Republic. Indeed, Dominican Catholicism is characterized by a marked tolerance for other sects. Yet, it is to be noted that Protestantism in the Republic is negligible, its churches are few and feeble. A number of denominations maintain missions and have about a dozen schools in the whole State. Most of the Protestants are negroes from the British West Indies and Virgin Islands. For these there are the Wesleyan Methodist Church of England and the African Methodist Church. Except as among the immigrants from Haiti, one finds no traces of the voodooism so dominant in the black republic.[34]

There are no religious tests for the exercise of the suffrage or for holding public office. The members of the clergy, on receiving the *beneplácito del prelado* (episcopal consent), can vote and be elected to public office. Accordingly, the clergy frequently participate in politics and often are office-holders. But they sit in Congress not as priests representing the Church, but as individuals representing their constituencies. Prelates have been elected to the highest office in the republic as has been noted. Notwithstanding the political activity of the clergy, their influence in the government is no more than in many countries where there is no union of Church and State.[35]

With the exception of a few friars brought over in recent years from France and Spain, the Dominican clergy is native,

---

[32] W. B. Lawton to J. L. Mecham.   [33] Elias Brache Hijo to J. L. Mecham.
[34] *Senate Hearings*, p. 1322; Schoenrich, *op. cit.*, p. 196.
[35] *Ibid.*, p. 195.

and has been trained in the seminary in Santo Domingo. The archbishop, by agreement with the Holy See, must be a native. The priests, as a body, are not respected by foreigners and educated natives, although they are held in superstitious veneration by the ignorant masses. The black sheep among the Dominican clergy are all too numerous; no inconsiderable number live openly with their women and drunkenness is frequent. The French priests of Haiti, models of moral rectitude, are disgusted with their fellow clerics in the eastern part of the island.[36]

Although the State-Church encounters practically no opposition in Protestantism and has the religious field to itself, it nevertheless is losing its hold upon a large number of the ninety per cent of the population counted as "Catholic." The Church is failing in its mission, but whether or not this is due to its union with the State is doubtful. The State is not a burden upon the Church and does not impose restrictions on its activities. On the other hand it is generous in according full political rights to clerics and in allowing religion to be taught in the schools.

With or without union, the Catholic Church, in the Dominican Republic could not prosper with its present clergy. It has been demonstrated that the native priests are incompetent and that the hierarchy is unwilling or unable to control them. A partial remedy for the ills of Catholicism in the Dominican Republic can certainly be found in the introduction of foreign priests to serve as models in elevating the general standards of the native clerics.

III

CUBA

When Cuba severed her political connection with Spain, she also terminated the ancient union of the civil and ecclesiastical orders. Since the Roman Catholic religion continued after independence to be virtually the only one of any standing in the island, the disestablishment of the Church was a phenomenon difficult for Americans to understand. Yet, the Catholic Church of Spanish Cuba was really a Spanish institution; all the bishops as well as most of the priests were appointed from Madrid. The

---

[36] *Ibid.,* pp. 188-190; *Senate Hearings,* pp. 1321-1322.

churchmen, therefore, during the rebellion, quite generally espoused the cause of Spain. The separation, consequently, was a national act of revenge in retaliation for the pro-Spanish activities of the clericals. Furthermore, it was felt that an institution which had been a bulwark of royalism and conservatism had to be deprived of political influence in the future, as a security measure for the republic. The opposition was to the Church as an institution quite apart from its dogma. This same kind of opposition is to be found throughout Latin America, but in it there is no encouragement for Protestantism.

When General John R. Brooke assumed authority, on January 1, 1899, as military governor of Cuba, he issued a proclamation declaring that the laws of the country were to continue in force and that they would be modified in the manner that necessity might advise. To aid him in consolidating peace, he named a Council of Secretaries, composed of natives. These Cuban secretaries immediately undertook to put through some measures against the Catholic Church. General Brooke was induced to enact a law establishing civil marriage as the only legally binding ceremony. A fee of one dollar was fixed by the measure. The Church objected to the law but without effect.[37]

When General Leonard Wood became Military Governor-General of Cuba, he was confronted with serious Church questions. The principal problems at issue were: (1) establishment of civil marriage; (2) confiscation of Church property, and (3) secularization of the cemeteries. In 1900 General Wood amended the civil marriage law so that a Church marriage, by any lawful sect, or a civil marriage should be equally valid. Divorce and nullification of marriages, however, were transferred from the ecclesiastical to the civil courts. In the interest of sanitary protection and equality of treatment, civil cemeteries were established. The Church was allowed to retain control over the cemeteries already in its possession, but they were subject to state regulation.[38]

---

[37] Eric F. Wood, *Leonard Wood* (New York, 1920), p. 159; Charles E. Chapman, *A History of the Cuban Republic* (New York, 1927), p. 119.

[38] Wood, *op. cit.*, pp. 159-160; John G. Holme, *The Life of Leonard Wood* (New York, 1920), p. 101.

The knotty question involving the Church property which had been confiscated was also brought to Governor Wood for settlement. The problem dated from 1837-1841, when Spain secularized a great portion of the property belonging to the religious orders. This act of seizure aroused protracted controversy with the Holy See and was not settled until the conclusion of the Concordat of 1861. By the terms of that instrument Spain agreed to pay to the Church an annual rental for the properties which had been put to secular uses by the government. This amounted to an allowance for the maintenance of worship. After the American intervention in Cuba the payments to the Church for the use of the properties ceased. The Church therefore demanded that the rent be paid or the properties returned. In finding a solution for this problem, as for other religious problems as well, Leonard Wood was guided by sound common sense and recognized fundamental principles of justice. Unhampered by prejudice he decided that the claims of the Church were just and reasonable, and so he agreed with the Bishop of Havana that the State should be granted an option to buy the property in question at an agreed valuation within five years from date. Until the date of purchase the State should pay an annual rental of five per cent of the accepted value.[39] In reporting on the settlement of the Church property controversy, General Wood said, "I consider this settlement of the question of the Church property as most important, and one which will remove from the coming Cuban government a great and fruitful source of annoyance."[40]

In the Constitutional Convention of 1900-1901 the Catholic Church was subjected to a vigorous attack. So radical were some of the members on the question of religion that one, Salvador Cisneros, former revolutionary president of Cuba, proposed to strike out of the preamble the phrase, "invoking the favor of God." After an animated debate over the religious

---

[39] Wood, *op. cit.*, pp. 161-162; Although President Estrada Palma called the attention of the Cuban Congress to the obligation to purchase the property, the Congress failed to act. The problem was not settled until the second American occupation. (Charles E. Magoon, *Republic of Cuba: Report of the Provisional Administration*, Havana, 1908, pp. 80-82.)

[40] Wood, *op. cit.*, p. 162.

article of the Constitution, the following was adopted: "The profession of all religions is free, as well as the exercise of all cults without limitation, except that they must respect Christian morality and public order. The Church will be separated from the State, and in no case will it subsidize any cult."[41]

"By definitely pronouncing for a separation of Church and State," says Professor Chapman, "the Cubans rid themselves of an issue that has disturbed the politics of their sister republics to the south."[42] On the other hand, it is very doubtful whether the subsequent harmonious relations between the Catholic Church and the State could have been possible had it not been for the restraining hand of General Wood. It was fortunate for the Church that an American, and a non-Catholic, had the authority to check a ruthless attack on the Church. To General Leonard Wood much credit is due for the successful solution of the religious question in Cuba. If the same wise restraint had been applied in other Latin-American countries, vexatious religious problems would never have arisen.

The legal status of the Catholic Church in Cuba is practically the same as in the United States. There are no restrictions on liberty of conscience and religion, and no religious tests for exercising suffrage or holding office. In an effort to be strictly non-partisan in religious matters, the government does not allow chapels in prisons. The Church is entirely independent of the State and no rights are enjoyed by the government in the election of ecclesiastical officers. Also, the government is enjoined by the Constitution from subsidizing any religion. An apostolic delegate for Cuba and Porto Rico resides at Havana, but he is not accredited to the Cuban government, and Cuba has no official representative at the Vatican. No concordat has ever been concluded between the Republic and the Holy See.[43]

Title to ecclesiastical property is vested in the Church. When Cuba threw off the Spanish yoke the Catholic Church narrowly

---

[41] *Constitución de la República de Cuba* (Havana, 1910), Art. 26; Howard B. Grose, *Advance in the Antilles* (New York, 1910), p. 43.

[42] Chapman, *op. cit.*, p. 134.

[43] John S. Mosher, American Vice-Consul, to J. L. Mecham, Havana, October 4, 1927; *Catholic Encyclopedia*, IV, 560-561.

escaped confiscation of its property by the State, thanks to the opposition of General Wood. Today the Church is the holder of extensive revenue producing properties. Upon these properties it must pay taxes, but edifices and places of worship are exempt. No restrictions are placed upon the ability of the Church to receive entailments. Wills and inheritances, as they affect the Church, are subject only to the civil law.[44]

Religion and religious sects are entirely divorced from public instruction in Cuba. No religious instruction is allowed in the public schools, and ecclesiastics cannot be employed in them. There are self-supporting Church schools, in which, of course, religious instruction is given. Nevertheless they are supervised by the Department of Public Instruction which requires them to conform to the public school laws. The children of the State schools receive religious instruction at the option of the parents, in what are known as *doctrinas*. These are classes conducted by the parish priests, on Church property, which meet on Saturdays. Most of the Catholic schools are for secondary and higher education. The Protestant schools in Cuba are not numerous.[45]

In 1899 the control of the institution of matrimony was wrested from the Church. At that time the civil ceremony was made the only legal form. The next year, however, as has been noted above, General Wood succeeded in having the law changed to make either the civil or the religious marriage legal and binding. Divorce was not recognized. But by the law of July 29, 1918, the civil ceremony was made once more the only legal form. The religious act is valid only when it complies with the requirements of the civil code. In other words, the religious marriage, no matter of what sect, has no legal force. The same law recognized absolute divorce. Remarriage is allowed one year after the granting of the divorce decree.[46]

With the exception of the debates on the marriage and divorce laws of 1918, the religious question has never been a subject of political discussion in the Cuban Republic. The status assigned the Catholic Church, and other religious sects, in the

---

[44] J. S. Mosher to J. L. Mecham.
[45] *Ibid.*
[46] *Ibid.*

Constitution of 1901, has proved to be eminently satisfactory to all concerned. In Cuba, as in Chile, Uruguay, and Brazil, the success of separation must be due in large measure to the wise decision to release the Church honorably and without restraint or government surveillance. It has been contended in several Latin-American countries that an absolutely free Church would be a political menace to the government. Such arguments were advanced in Cuba at the time of separation, but history has demonstrated that these fears are unfounded.

CHAPTER XIII

STATE CHURCH AND FREE CHURCH IN THE REPUBLICS OF CENTRAL AMERICA

I

THE FEDERATION OF CENTRAL AMERICA

Religion has been one of the most disturbing factors in the history of the republics of Central America. The Catholic Church in two of the republics, Guatemala and El Salvador, has undoubtedly suffered more vicissitudes in its fortunes than in other Latin-American countries, with the possible exception of Mexico and Ecuador. Yet, the aggravated nature of the problem was in no sense the result of exaggerated clerical abuses peculiar to Central America. Although it would be futile to deny the existence of clerical predominance in the spiritual, social, and even in the economic and political spheres of these countries, there was no marked difference in this respect from other parts of Spanish America. The bitter, devastating, politico-ecclesiastic conflicts were the result rather of attempts to enforce unwise policies, pro- and anti-clerical. The extremists among the clericals and anti-religionists alternated in control of the governments, and, with a vindictiveness common to bigots, insisted on forcing their remedies down the throats of their adversaries. There was no compromise on religious policy. The inevitable result was revolution and counter-revolution, repressive measures and retaliatory measures. With the exercise of common-sense, restraint, and tolerance, the issue would have been no more troublesome than it was in Brazil and Argentina.

When reports of the Mexican declaration of independence by the *Plan de Iguala* were received in Guatemala, the captain-general summoned an extraordinary council to decide upon a course of action. On September 15, 1821, the ecclesiastical and civil leaders met in a *Junta Consultativa*. The Archbishop of

Guatemala, D. Fray Ramón Casaus, and other ecclesiastics opposed an immediate declaration of independence and counseled delay until they should receive more news from Mexico. The majority of the *junta*, however, voted in favor of an immediate declaration of independence.[1] Article 10 of the manifesto of September 15, 1821, read as follows: "The Roman Catholic religion which we have professed in the past centuries and which we will profess in the future, will be preserved pure and unaltered, keeping alive the spirit of religion which has always distinguished Guatemala, respecting the ecclesiastical ministers secular and regular, protecting them in their persons and property."[2] The rights of religion were amply guaranteed by the *junta* which was controlled by the aristocratic class, reinforced by a liberal representation of the clergy. The action of the extraordinary council which met in Guatemala City was supposed to apply to the whole of the captaincy-general, yet the provinces were disposed to act individually. As a matter of fact, the province of Chiapas in a *cabildo abierto*, or town-meeting, at Ciudad Real, anticipated the action of Guatemala by declaring independence on September 3, 1821. On the same date Chiapas voted for annexation to the Mexican Empire of Iturbide. The clergy were prominently active in the secession movement in Chiapas, and the oaths of allegiance to the Empire were taken before the ecclesiastical authorities. The clergy, being hostile to the reforms of the liberal government in Spain respecting the Church, looked upon Iturbide as the savior of their ancient prerogatives and monopolies. He was called the "padre salvador de la religión y de la patria." On September 28, 1821, the province of Honduras declared independence of the motherland with the precise stipulation that the religion which all the inhabitants should recognize was the Roman Catholic Apostolic. On October 11, 1821, independence was declared

---

[1] Alejandro Marure, *Bosquejo Histórico de las Revoluciones de Centro-América* (Guatemala, 1877), p. 23; Floyd Cramer, *Our Neighbor Nicaragua* (New York, 1929), p. 45.

[2] Francisco Montero Barrantes, *Elementos de Historia de Costa Rica* (San José de Costa Rica, 1892), p. 174.

in León, Nicaragua, and on October 29, 1821, in Cartago, Costa Rica. In the *Junta Superior Gubernativa,* the provisional governing body in Costa Rica, four of the twelve members were clerics.[3]

All the provinces of Central America with the exception of El Salvador consented to annexation to Mexico. This action was sponsored by the Central American clergy because of the ascendancy enjoyed by the Church party in the Empire. In the short period that Central America was an appendage of the Empire of Iturbide, no change took place in the relations of Church and State. Consequently when the Central Americans, after the downfall of Augustín I, determined to establish their political independence under republican institutions, clerical opposition was encountered because the clergy felt that republics would be inimical to religion. One of the most inveterate opponents of republicanism was Bishop Nicolás García Jérez of León. He, a bitter enemy of liberal and free institutions since the days of the Granadine revolt of 1811,[4] influenced his clergy, after the fall of the Empire, to adopt a subversive attitude. Finally, on December 10, 1823, the Bishop submitted to the inevitable and swore an oath of recognition and submission to the republic. He probably believed, as did the majority of the clericals, that the Church would find protection in a Conservative control of the State. This belief was well-founded at that time, for the Conservatives controlled the National Constituent Assembly which met in Guatemala City on June 24, 1823. The president of the Assembly was José Matías Delgado, a cleric, of whom more later. On July 1, the Assembly proclaimed independence from Mexico and the establishment of a confederation of the provinces. In this proclamation the Catholic religion was declared to be that of the State. In the words of the proclamation it was "recog-

---

[3] *Ibid.,* p. 187; Félix Salgado, *Elementos de Historia de Honduras* (Tegucigalpa, 1927), p. 26.

[4] The rebellion in Granada in 1811, which aimed at independence, was put down with the aid of the Bishop of León. The Archbishop of Guatemala, Ramón Casaus, dispatched priests to the storm-center to preach against the insurgents. (Marure, *op. cit.,* p. 16.)

nized as a public duty, that the only religion of the Federation should be the Catholic Apostolic Roman."[5]

The withdrawal of the Mexican troops under General Filisola, on August 3, 1823, removed a considerable restraint upon the Liberals, and they were at greater liberty to carry out their plans. The membership of the Assembly was sharply divided into two groups. The Conservative or Moderate party, called contemptuously the "Serviles" by their opponents, was favorable to the centralistic form of government and protection to the Church in the retention of its *fueros*. The Liberals or Radicals, were federalists, and desired to see the abolition of unjust privileges. They were anxious for clerical reform. This party alignment, which appeared for the first time in the Constituent Assembly of 1823, was destined to perpetuation throughout the histories of the Central American republics. The Serviles, although in the majority in the Assembly, had to give way to the more aggressive, impetuous, and better organized Liberals. Thus the Serviles were not able to prevent the passage, in 1824, of certain anti-clerical laws. One of these subjected episcopal pastorals to the control and supervision of the government. In short, pastorals had to receive the *pase* like papal bulls. The immediate occasion for this law was the issuance of anti-republican pastorals by Archbishop Casaus. Another act provided that appointments of parish priests by the archbishop should be previously submitted for confirmation by the chief of state. A third law deprived the clergy of their privilege to import goods into the country free of duties.[6] On November 22, 1824, after seventeen months' deliberation, a constitution was finally proclaimed for the Federal Republic of Central America. Article 11 declared Roman Catholicism to be the religion of the State to the exclusion of the public exercise of any other. With the exception of the additional contradictory guarantee of toler-

---

[5] Barrantes, *op. cit.*, p. 204. Chiapas was not represented in the Assembly, since that province continued attached to Mexico. The Mexican Republic recognized the Federation of Central America on August 20, 1824.

[6] Marure, *op. cit.*, pp. 111, 160; H. H. Bancroft, *History of Central America* (San Francisco, 1887), III, 70-71, 628.

ation the Federal Constitution avoided the subject of religion. This omission contributed to subsequent acrimonious arguments as to whether the Federal or State governments controlled patronage. The clerics were by no means satisfied with the Constitution, because they felt that it did not accord them sufficient guarantees. Accordingly, many of them refused to swear an oath of allegiance to the Federation. The Franciscan friars of the Propaganda Fide in Guatemala were particularly obstinate in their refusal and precipitated riots (February, 1825). The State government of Guatemala displayed considerable energy in restoring order. In the end the clergy submitted and swore the necessary oaths of allegiance.[7]

The Constitutional Congress of the "Estados Federados de Centro América" was installed (February 6, 1825) under Liberal control. Mariano Gálvez, a Liberal leader and later the nemesis of the Catholic Church in Guatemala, was made president of the Congress. On April 21, 1825, the Congress chose Manuel José Arce, also presumed to be a Liberal, as the president of the Federation. Before being made president Arce had attacked clerical abuses, particularly in the regular orders. With the government in their control the Liberals decided that the time had arrived to do away with clerical privileges and bring the Church under the subjection of the civil authorities.

During the short-lived Liberal ascendancy, several laws were passed in 1826, against the Church. The tithes were reduced one-half; natural children were given the right to inherit *ab intestato*, and those of priests and nuns were placed in the same category; prelates of regular orders were forbidden to recognize obedience to or hold relations with their respective generals in Spain; and twenty-three years was established as the minimum age for entry into any convent. The anti-clerical laws of 1826 aroused the ire of the clergy and serious troubles ensued. The clericals, seizing this opportunity to destroy the opposition, gave utterance to most fanatical language and sowed alarm among the people. Even liberal-minded men, opposed to the too precipitate action of the extremists, took up the cause of the

[7] Augusto C. Coello, *El Digesto Constitucional de Honduras* (Tegucigalpa, 1923), p. 14; Marure, *op. cit.*, p. 120.

Church. By 1827 the Liberal control had been broken and once more the Conservatives were in the saddle.[8]

In the meantime, the States of the Federation were organizing governments under constitutions adopted in the following order: El Salvador, June 12, 1824; Costa Rica, January 21, 1825; Guatemala, October 11, 1825; Honduras, December 11, 1825, and Nicaragua, April 8, 1826. In these constitutions the Roman Catholic faith was declared to be the religion of the State. A serious and troublesome question over the control of ecclesiastical patronage confronted the government of the Federation immediately after its creation.

For many years, dating back into the Spanish colonial period, the people of Costa Rica and El Salvador had desired the establishment of separate and independent dioceses for the provinces, but their petitions were repulsed with exasperating regularity. When independence was won, the Salvadoreños, led by the independentist cleric D. Matios Delgado, who was ambitious to be the first bishop, endeavored to influence the National Constituent Assembly to establish a bishopric in El Salvador. But the Assembly decided (July 8, 1823) "that without prior and express accord with the papacy, no one could or ought to be presented for election to the prelacies." This did not balk Delgado, for he influenced the Constituent Congress of El Salvador ("less circumspect than the national representation") to erect a diocese in the State. The parish of San Salvador was converted into a diocese and Delgado was appointed the first bishop. The archbishop of Guatemala, D. Ramón Casaus, published an edict, June 21, 1824, declaring null and void the action of the Congress of Salvador. Delgado refused to resign and acted as bishop, though without papal confirmation, for about four years. El Salvador sent a representative to Rome to solicit the confirmation of Delgado by the pope. The pontiff refused to accede, and instead, on December 1, 1826, he issued a brief to the metropolitan of Guatemala declaring the acts of El Salvador illegitimate and contrary to the rights of the Holy See. All acts of Delgado were null and void and he was given fifty days to renounce his office under pain of being branded a schis-

---

[8] Bancroft, *op. cit.*, III, 628; Marure, *op. cit.*, p. 160.

matic. The Salvadorean government supported the pseudo-bishop and expelled many ecclesiastics from the territory because of their opposition to Delgado.[9]

The controversy concerning the diocese of San Salvador had a deep influence on the politics of all Central America. The Liberals supported Delgado, the Serviles supported the Archbishop of Guatemala. The National Constituent Assembly finally concerned itself with the question and appointed a committee to study the nature of patronage, particularly as it related to the establishment of dioceses. The patronage committee, or *Comisión de Negocios Eclesiásticos*, reported September 2, 1824, that (1) the Nation did not enjoy the right of patronage; (2) if it did, it would be simple patronage, or the right of presentation to a bishopric and not for the erection of an episcopal see; and (3) granted it acquired the patronage, it would be national in scope and could not be exercised by individual states. The committee also reported that El Salvador did not have the right to erect a bishopric because only the pope possessed this power.

The controversy over the new diocese was the immediate occasion for the writing and publication of numerous dissertations on the right of patronage. One of these, by D. Isidro Menéndez, published by the government of El Salvador, presents what might be called "the official governmental attitude." A portion of the argument was as follows: The Spanish kings enjoyed the right of absolute patronage and presentation over the Catholic Church in the Captaincy-General of Guatemala by virtue of its (patronage) being inherent in sovereignty, founded on ancient custom and prescription, possession of territory, foundation, dotation, and support of churches and benefices, and by concordats and privileges conceded by the pope. That the Spanish kings possessed the patronal right to create bishoprics is substantiated by reference to the Laws of the Indies. The patronage did not expire with the person of the king, but passed to his successors and to those who exercised the sovereign authority. Therefore it passed to republics after the termination

---

[9] Marure, *op. cit.*, pp. 129-135; Manuel Montúfar, *Memorias para la Historia de la Revolución de Centro-América* (Jalapa, 1832), p. 34.

of the Spanish control. The right of patronage, however, did not reside in the Confederation, but in each of the States, for this sovereign power was not conceded to the Federal government in the enumeration of powers delegated to it. This was certainly the case when, on August 25, 1823, a proposition was submitted to the Constituent Congress to add to Article 107 of the constitution, the following: "In the provision or nomination of prelacies, dignities, prebends, and other ecclesiastical benefices, the president of the republic shall exercise the intervention which in the concordats with the Holy See are reserved to the civil power of the republic." This proposition was sent to a committee and reported on October 7, 1823. The report of the committee was that it would be unwise to take these powers from the heads of the states. The article therefore was voted down by the Assembly and the Constitution consequently contained no mention of the right of patronage being vested in the federal government. If any consideration should be given to the intentions of the framers of the federal constitution, the case of El Salvador is strengthened thereby.[10]

The National Assembly accepted the report of the committee and declared, by decree of July 18, 1825, that the acts of the government of El Salvador were illegal. It was hoped that this action would calm the Archbishop. Then, to satisfy the populace, the Congress proceeded to create a bishopric for El Salvador. This pretended assumption of the right of patronage by the Federal Congress was distasteful to both the clergy and the people. The federal action, therefore, was generally ignored. Even the president refused to comply with the law.

The inhabitants of Costa Rica had also been desirous for many years to have a bishopric of their own, which should be independent of the episcopal see of León, Nicaragua. After the establishment of an independent State, the Assembly of Costa Rica was unwilling to remain dependent any longer on Nicaragua in ecclesiastical matters. Accordingly, on September 29, 1825, a decree was issued establishing the bishopric of San José

---

[10] *Exposición del Senador por el Estado de Nicaragua P. C. L. D. C. Isidro Menéndez . . . sobre el negocio de Obispado de S. Salvador* (San Salvador, 1825), pp. 9-11, 19-20.

with limits to be the same as those of the State. Fray Luís García was named bishop and the chapter of León was requested to delegate his functions to him. The chapter, regarding the action as uncanonical, appealed to the Assembly of Costa Rica to revoke the act in order to avoid a schism as in El Salvador. Fortunately Fray Luís García refused to accept the episcopal dignity and thus saved Costa Rica from serious consequences. The Costa Ricans were not so obdurate as the Salvadoreños and they decided to let the matter drop.[11]

Arce's election to the presidency, on April 21, 1825, was the result of a compromise between the parties. He pledged himself to remain neutral on certain matters, one of these being the question of the bishopric. He promised to leave the decision as to the creation of the see of San Salvador to the next Congress. But, as has been noted, its action was unsatisfactory to the President, espousing as he did the cause of the Serviles who wished to abolish the bishopric of El Salvador. The anti-clerical laws of 1826 were also displeasing to him, for he greatly desired not to alienate the Serviles. In the end, Arce, once a Liberal, became the head of the Serviles, and in league with the Archbishop, who had once preached against him, and with the friars who had called him a heretic, he supported the very opinions he had once combatted. But there was no hypocrisy or selfishness in the about-face made by Arce, for he acted on pure and upright motives. He did not accept the presidency as a partisan, but rather as the representative of all the people. Sincerely desirous of abolishing factionalism and establishing peace and harmony, he saw in the Liberal anti-clerical program disruptive factors which had to be curbed. In an *apologia*, Arce declared that it was his conviction that the Liberals of Guatemala were attempting to despoil the State of El Salvador of the tithes. This he would not sanction.[12] Here was a man who believed in

---

[11] *Revista de Costa Rica en el Siglo XIX* (San José de Costa Rica, 1902), pp. 309-311; Barrantes, *op. cit.*, p. 217.

[12] *Memoria de la Conducta Pública y Administrativa de Manuel José Arce* (Mexico, 1830), p. 15; Marure, *op. cit.*, p. 144.

moderation and compromise, but he suffered the all-too-common fate of moderators in Latin America.

For about two years (1827-1828) the Serviles were in the ascendancy. The reaction was carried to limits repugnant to Arce, but over which he had no control. Guatemala in particular was, in the opinion of a Liberal critic, under the domination of "the *togados* and *tonsurados,* who promulgated laws fit for the middle ages."[13] According to the same writer, who exaggerates somewhat, fanaticism was converted during this period of Servile control into a system of education, confession was a legal precept, the catechism of Ripalda[14] was the official textbook in the schools, the people were persecuted for liberal ideas, and the Church and State lived in close consort, with the archbishop as a god. Repression and reaction begot the inevitable—revolution. The Liberals took up arms and found an able leader in Francisco Morazán, a man of exceptional talents. Arce presented a weak opposition to the victorious march of the Liberals, perhaps because of his disgust with all extremists. At any rate, Morazán captured Guatemala City and Arce withdrew from the country. From April 13, 1829, when Morazán occupied the plaza of Guatemala City, until April 13, 1839, when General Carrera occupied it, the history of Central America was marked by an incessant struggle between the Serviles and the Liberals, with the latter in control of the government throughout this period.[15]

José Francisco Barrundia, senior senator of the Federal Congress, assumed the office of president of the Federation, but in reality he was only a puppet of Morazán, who was the real power. Morazán was elected to the presidency in his own right

---

[13] Raúl Aguero, *Guatemala, La Revolución Liberal de 1871* (San José de Costa Rica, 1914), p. 8.

[14] In the catechism of the Jesuit Ripalda appears the question, "Who is the Pope?" The answer is, "The Roman Pontiff whom all of us ought to obey."

[15] Mary W. Williams, "The Ecclesiastical Policy of Francisco Morazán and the Other Central American Liberals," in the *Hispanic American Historical Review,* May 1920, p. 128.

in May, 1832. After seizing control of the Federal government the Liberals instituted measures against their real or supposed enemies. The stage was thus set for the inauguration of an anti-clerical reform, the most drastic in all of Latin America up to that date.

The Liberals struck first at the Archbishop. Ramón Casaus y Torres, Spanish-born and a Dominican friar, had been nominated for the archiepiscopal see of Guatemala by the Spanish Council of the Regency on March 30, 1811. Shortly after he assumed office in July (although it is to be noted that the papal bull of his confirmation was not issued until 1815), he took a very active part in suppressing the independentist revolt in Granada. He published an edict declaring the rebels of 1811 to be monsters; the names "heretics" and "friends of independence" were synonymous to him. After the declaration of Central American independence, the Archbishop continued to be an inveterate enemy of republican and liberal institutions. It has been noted above that the government was forced, because of the anti-republican propaganda of the prelate, to restrict his activities by subjecting his pastorals to the rule of the *pase*. President Barrundia preferred a charge that the Archbishop was plotting against the government and ordered his expulsion from the country. Franciscans, Dominicans, and Recollet friars were also accused of plotting and their banishment was ordered. Those of the Order of Mercy and the Bethlehemite hospitallers were allowed to remain. On the night of July 10-11, 1829, armed forces, acting under orders of the president, seized the metropolitan and the friars, 289 in number, escorted them to the Atlantic Coast and embarked them for Havana. Numerous reports were circulated by the Serviles telling about the brutal treatment of the friars when being conducted to the coast, and while aboard ship en route to Cuba. There was evidently some basis for the accusations, but they were greatly exaggerated. Archbishop Casaus accepted a pension from the Spanish government in Cuba, and later was appointed administrator of the vacant see of Havana. He held this office until his death and persistently refused to return to Guatemala although a decree which declared him a traitor had been revoked in 1839.[16]

The banishment of the Archbishop and friars was by sole order of the president without congressional authorization. Therefore after the act had been accomplished, President Barrundia reported to the Congress, saying that he had acted without informing that body because he desired to maintain secrecy, and now wished to secure congressional approval. The desired vote of confidence was secured. In addition, on July 28, 1829, monastic orders were abolished and their property confiscated. On September 7, 1829, another law prohibited the entry into the Federation of members of any religious order. On June 13, 1830, the Congress confirmed the banishment of the Archbishop. He was formally charged with opposing independence, inciting rebellion, and receiving a subsidy from the Spanish king. As a consequence, he was declared a traitor and was permanently exiled. The see of Guatemala was declared vacant, and until it would be canonically filled, its income was to go to the national treasury. The chapter was to name, with the approval of the government, a vicar and governor.[17] The cathedral chapter named a vicar, but Casaus resisted the legality of this action and named a vicar on his own account. The whole situation remained in suspension until Pope Gregory XVI declared the capitular vicar to be the legal administrator.

On May 2, 1832, the Federal Congress proclaimed religious toleration. It decreed that all inhabitants of the Republic were free to adore God according to their beliefs, and that the national government protected the exercise of this liberty. Later, Congress declared marriage to be a civil contract, and the religious ceremony was not necessary for the satisfaction of legal requirements. Also, the right of appointing to ecclesiastical dignities belonged to the nation and was to be exercised by the president.[18]

The state governments were also under the control of the

---

[16] Bancroft, *op. cit.,* III, 30, 103-104, 628; Marure, *op. cit.,* p. 111; Montúfar, *Memorias,* p. 170; Williams, *Morazán,* pp. 129-133.

[17] Lorenzo Montúfar, *El General Francisco Morazán* (Guatemala, 1896), pp. 154-159.   [18] *Ibid.,* pp. 17-19; Bancroft, *op. cit.,* III, 629.

reformers during this period (1829-1839), and by state legislation the federal anti-clerical program was reinforced. The
jefe de estado, or governor, of the State of Guatemala was
Mariano Gálvez, the right-hand man of General Morazán.
Gálvez, in talents, temperament, and aspirations was not greatly unlike Valentín Gómez Farías of Mexico. He was called "the
regenerator" of Guatemala because of his reforms in the interest
of popular education. Gálvez also secularized the cemeteries,
reduced the number of Church holidays, allowed nuns to leave
convents and take their dowries, declared marriage a civil contract, and provided for absolute divorce. The marriage and
divorce laws were not favorably received by the people. Gálvez
had overstepped the bounds of prudence and provoked a revolt.
The Serviles and clerics fanned the flames of discontent by
branding him a heretic and a tyrant. The deadly ravages of a
cholera epidemic were used by the clerics to exploit the credulity
of the ignorant. In 1838 Gálvez fell, "a victim of the fanatics
and hypocrites," says an admirer. After the overthrow of the
reformer all his laws against the Church were suspended (July
26, 1838), the ecclesiastical *fueros* were restored, and the
Roman Catholic faith was reaffirmed as the religion of the State
of Guatemala.[19]

In Costa Rica, the *jefe de estado*, Braulio Carrillo, also reduced the number of religious feast days. He designated as days
of work all days except Sunday and a limited number of religious
and political holidays. He defended his action by saying that
the too numerous festivals were injurious to public morals and
the prosperity of the State. On March 31, 1835, the Assembly
of Costa Rica decreed the abolition of the tithes; "an ancient
and onerous impost," declared a critic, "which weighed upon
agriculture and property, sacrificing the people to the exigencies of the cult." The government's treasury assumed the obligations met in the past by the tithes. Their abolition resulted
in a rebellion in which many clerics were implicated. As a result,

---

[19] Rafael Aguirre Cinta, *Lecciones de Historia General de Guatemala*
(Guatemala, 1899), pp. 106-107; Montúfar, *Morazán*, pp. 15-17.

one was executed, several were banished, and many more were fined.[20]

The constitution of the State of Honduras, promulgated November 21, 1831, although recognizing the Roman Catholic faith as the State religion to the exclusion of the public exercise of any other, gave to the executive authority the right to approve titles for prelacies and other ecclesiastical benefices. An amendment, adopted in February, 1835, guaranteed religious toleration and "the maintenance of all cults in harmony with the laws." Other acts were passed affecting the clergy, among these being one legalizing the marriage of secular priests.

The ascendancy of Morazán, Gálvez, and the Liberals was terminated in 1839 when the forces of localism and religious fanaticism proved to be too strong for them. The immediate cause of the reactionary revolt was the belief of the fanatical Indians, encouraged by the priests, that the poisoning of the wells by the Liberals was the cause of the cholera scourge. The leader of the Indians was Rafael Carrera, a young, illiterate, mountaineer mestizo. A mere tool of the priests, Carrera declared a prime object of the Servile revolt to be the complete restoration to the clergy of their *fueros.* In March, 1839, Morazán was defeated and exiled and the Federation of Central America was dissolved.[21]

II

THE REPUBLICS OF CENTRAL AMERICA

(a) *Guatemala*

One of the first acts of the Constitutional Assembly of Guatemala, which was summoned by Carrera to frame a new constitution for the republic, was the abrogation of the reform laws of the Liberals and the restoration of the ecclesiastical *fueros.* The Serviles undid what their opponents had done. Once more the pendulum swung to the other extreme, and for many years,

---

[20] Barrantes, *op. cit.,* pp. 228-232.
[21] Coello, *op. cit.,* pp. 69, 85; Robertson, *Latin-American Nations,* p. 448; Williams, *Morazán,* p. 142.

particularly in Guatemala, the Serviles had their inning and made the most of it. From 1839 to 1865 General Rafael Carrera, dictator of Guatemala and recognized leader of the Serviles dominated nearly all of Central America. He was a tower of strength to the Catholic Church.

Not only were the *fueros* restored to the clergy of Guatemala, but the monastic orders were reëstablished and the exiled friars allowed to return. Guatemala was the only one of the Central American republics which revoked the ban against the regulars. Clerical exiles like Archbishop Casaus were invited to return, but since the metropolitan refused, Archbishop Coadjutor Francisco de Paula García Pelaez took charge of the see. In 1843 the Jesuits, who had been excluded since the expulsion of 1767, were allowed into the country. With the passage of the years the union of Church and State became more and more intimate. In the Constitution of 1851 the Church was granted representation in the Congress, the chapter being given two deputies. The next year, on October 7, 1852, the Cardinal-Secretary Antonelli and D. Fernando de Lorenzana for Guatemala, signed a concordat, which was ratified by President Carrera. By this agreement, which is notable as being the first concordat concluded with any Latin-American country, the republic recognized the Roman Catholic religion as the sole and exclusive religion of the State; promised to preserve the tithes and pay to the Church in addition a fixed sum from the national treasury; granted the clerics all kinds of privileges including that of control of education and the censorship of books. In return for these concessions the president of the republic received from the pope the right of the patronage, i.e., presentation.[22] The relations between Carrera and the Vatican, as can be imagined, were very close. In 1853, Carrera was decorated by the Holy Father with the Grand Cross of the Order of Saint Gregory the Great, of the military class. This was a reward for his encouragement of Catholicism, and truly he merited recognition as a staunch and uncompromising supporter of the faith.[23]

After the death of Carrera, in 1865, Vicente Cerna became

---

[22] *Raccolta di Concordati*, pp. 810-821.

[23] Cinta, *op. cit.*, pp. 121, 139-143.

president of Guatemala. Cerna, a Conservative, was also a warm friend of the Church. In fact, he was charged with being a too warm friend of the Jesuits. Although Cerna was reëlected to the presidency in 1869, the election was closely contested by the Liberals led by Miguel García Granados, a deputy. The rapid increase of Liberal strength, particularly in the middle classes of the towns and in the army, was an omen of impending change in the political situation. But true to tradition, the Liberals, now strong in the Congress, were unwilling to abide by the decision of the polls. In 1870, Granados headed an armed revolt. The uprising proved to be abortive and Granados sought safety in flight across the Mexican border. The overthrow of Dueñas, Servile dictator of El Salvador, by the Liberals of El Salvador and Honduras early in 1871, was a blow to conservatism throughout Central America, and revived the hopes of the Liberals of Guatemala. Granados organized a new expedition in Chiapas and invaded Guatemala. The final victory of the Liberals and the overthrow of Cerna were accomplished on June 29, 1871. Until a constitution could be framed and a regular government organized, García Granados governed as provisional president.[24]

The inevitable complement of Liberal political ascendancy was the institution of another anti-clerical reform more radical than any of the past. The first decree of the revolutionary government, dated May 24, 1871, expelled the Jesuits from the republic as obstacles to liberal ideas. The Society of Jesus had been permanently reëstablished in Guatemala by order of Carrera under pretext of alleged scarcity of competent priests for religious and educational work. Seventy-three Jesuits, most of them foreigners, were bundled aboard a steamer and shipped out of the country. They first went to El Salvador where they fared no better. On September 4, the property of the Jesuits was confiscated. On December 22, 1871, the tithes were suppressed and the government agreed to defray any deficit incurred in consequence by the diocese. The extinction of all male religious orders was next decreed. The native friars were permitted to remain in the country and were given monthly allowances for their sup-

---

[24] Bancroft, *op. cit.,* III, 415, 424-425.

port, but they were forbidden to show themselves in public with their clerical garbs. The property of the regulars was ordered confiscated. The State also absorbed properties held in mortmain. In the last months of the provisional presidency of García Granados the *fuero eclesiástico* in both civil and criminal causes was abolished, and the freedom of worship was decreed. These acts meant the destruction of the Concordat.[25]

According to Bancroft, when García Granados revolted, he had at first no intention of attacking the Church. He denied that his government had ever contemplated wounding the religious feelings of the nation. The resolve of the new régime "to cut loose of the ecclesiastical incubus, and to establish the supremacy of the civil authority in the State on a strong basis," was forced, says Bancroft, by "the priests who would not rest contented with the loss of their former high standing."[26] The statement is deficient in that it fails to acknowledge an uncompromising spirit on both sides. The Liberals were not inclined to tolerate the perpetuation of clerical privileges granted by Carrera, and, on the other hand, the clergy, very logically, were disposed to defend their rights. In October, 1871, Archbishop Piñol and Ortiz Urruela, Bishop of Teya *in partibus infidelium,* were ordered to leave the country because of their activities in promoting resistance to the reform. Papal relations were broken, and, since 1871, Guatemala has sent no diplomatic representative to the Vatican.

Justo R. Barrios succeeded García Granados to the presidency in June, 1873. Granados as an executive was not a success; he was unable to rule with the necessary firmness and as a result the reactionaries kept the country in turmoil. Barrios, on the contrary, ruled with a hand of iron; he tolerated no opposition. Under his dictatorship the forces of conservatism were well-nigh annihilated. Numerous acts of despotism and brutality have been attributed to him by his clerical enemies, and impartial judgment agrees that these stories were basically true. The anti-clerical policy adopted by Barrios has been compared with that of Morazán. He extended the prohibition of religious orders to

---

[25] *Ibid.,* III, 425-427; Cinta, *op. cit.,* pp. 196-201.
[26] Bancroft, *op. cit.,* III, 425.

the nunneries, confiscated their properties, and allowed each ex-nun a life pension of twelve dollars per month. All religious communities of either sex were forever forbidden in Guatemala. The disamortized capital was ordered to be devoted to the aid of commerce and agriculture. The Church buildings were used for educational purposes. Civil marriage was declared legal, cemeteries were secularized, and ecclesiastics were forbidden to appear outside of the churches with their frocks or other official insignia.[27] The anti-clerical reform measures of Granados and Barrios were given permanency by being incorporated into a new constitution. This document, adopted in December, 1879, and modified in 1887, is the instrument under which Guatemala is governed today. The anti-clerical régime is still in the ascendancy.

In 1884 the breach in Church and State relations was partially healed by the signing of a new concordat. By the terms of the new treaty Guatemala abandoned its rights to national patronage and the Papacy renounced claims to a privileged position for the Church in Guatemala. The principal provisions of the Concordat were as follows:

1. The Roman Pontiff was guaranteed the right of free communication with the prelates, clergy, and people of Guatemala.
2. The right of governing the clergy, the church, and maintaining discipline was vested in the ordinary.
3. The diocesan seminary of Guatemala was to be reëstablished and its administration and control were to vest in the diocesan prelate.
4. Occupants of the metropolitan see were to be appointed by the pope *motu proprio*.
5. When a vacancy should occur in the metropolitan see, the chapter should proceed freely to elect a capitular vicar.
6. The clergy were exempt from military service.
7. In compensation for properties of the Church which were confiscated by the State, the government of Guatemala assumed the obligation of paying to the Church annually 30,000 pesos.
8. The pope acquiesced in the confiscations, and agreed never to molest the holders of properties of which the Church had been deprived.[28]

---

[27] *Ibid.*, III, 427, 432-433; Cinta, *op. cit.*, p. 201.
[28] *Raccolta di Concordati*, pp. 1018-1020.

There is only theoretical separation of Church and State in Guatemala, for in fact, the Church is very much under temporal restraint. The government enjoys no right in the naming of priests; yet in the election and nomination of the archbishop it has always interfered, endeavoring in this way to enjoy the privilege of patronage without assuming its responsibilities.[29] There are no constitutional restrictions upon liberty of conscience with the exception that "the establishment of conventual congregations and all kinds of monastic institutions and associations is prohibited" (Article 25). The French Sisters of Charity are in the country by virtue of special treaty to direct the hospitals and government asylums. By very special privilege they have been allowed to direct the Asilo de Santa María and the Casa Central. There are no religious tests for the exercise of the suffrage. Yet, in a country where the great majority of the population is Roman Catholic, and where Jews and Protestants, English and French, are called "outsiders" and "judíos," one need not be surprised to hear a well-informed American official report, "*De jure* there are no religious tests for exercising the suffrage or holding office; *de facto* it's rather a long story."[30]

All ecclesiastical temporalities have been nationalized since 1871. The Church cannot hold title to any property, nor can it receive entailments and bequests. It is permitted to make use of the religious edifices and parochial residences.

By Article 18 of the Constitution instruction in the national institutes, colleges, and schools is entirely gratuitous and secular. Although there are no laws against ecclesiastics teaching in public schools, none have taught in them since 1871. Recently a notable exception to this rule was the employment of a priest to lecture on Spanish literature in the University of Guatemala. There are a few Catholic schools in Guatemala, giving instruction to about one thousand pupils, whereas before 1871 they were to be found in all the villages of the republic. Of late years some effort has been made to multiply the number of schools, but without success, since the introduction of the teaching orders

---

[29] H. Eric Trammell, American Vice Consul in Charge, to J. L. Mecham, Guatemala City, December 8, 1927.
[30] *Ibid.*

into the country is prohibited and it is impracticable to establish Church schools with paid lay teachers.[31]

Since 1879 civil marriage has been the only legal form in
Guatemala. A ceremony by a priest may follow the civil rites,
and generally does, but this does not satisfy civil requirements.
Although the only charge for the civil ceremony is the price of
the stamp-bearing documents, the rural magistrates are accustomed to levy exorbitant fees on the ignorant Indians. This
practice discourages marriage and is a reason for concubinage.
It is interesting to note that here the government is a responsible
cause of an unmoral practice for which the clergy is to blame in
some parts of Latin America. After one year of married life
absolute divorce is legal on application by mutual consent, or on
grounds of a determined cause.[32]

The Catholic Church has no cemeteries since it cannot own
property. The government owns all burial grounds, supervises
them, and collects all charges. The secularization of cemeteries
was decreed in November, 1879, as a sanitary measure, but the
real cause was the desire to deprive the Church of a powerful
means of exercising control over the populace.

The reforms of the decade of the 1870's are still a part of the
law of Guatemala. It is a most interesting phenomena, and unique,
too, in Latin America, that the anti-clerical laws should persist
for so long without change. Does it mean that the religious question has been settled in Guatemala? Or does it mean that the
Conservatives are only delayed in marshalling their forces for
the reaction? One thing is certain, and that is that the Church
is dissatisfied with a status which impairs its legitimate freedom
of action.

(b) El Salvador

Guatemala's little neighbor, El Salvador, experienced an almost
identical history of ecclesiastical relationships. This was the inevitable result of the all-too-common practice by the Central
American republics of interfering in the internal affairs of each
other. Yet, fortunate for the historian, this interrelationship made

---

[31] Ibid.; Ley Constitutiva de la República de Guatemala (Guatemala, 1912).
[32] Civil Code of Guatemala, Articles 123 and 182 (MS).

for a certain continuity and harmony of development in all of the republics.

After the overthrow of Morazán, the Conservatives in El Salvador set up an independent republic under a constitution (1841) which recognized only the Roman Catholic religion. Then Dr. Jorge Viteri y Ungo was sent to Rome to petition the pope to create a bishopric of San Salvador. The petition was granted. On September 28, 1842, Pope Gregory XVI signed a bull creating the episcopal see, and in October of the same year Viteri assumed the episcopal dignity as the first Bishop of San Salvador. Viteri's episcopal reign was short and stormy. Although he directed his clergy to refrain from interfering in political affairs, he forced the retirement of President Guzmán and established his puppet, Malespín, in the presidency (February, 1844). For a time the Bishop was dominant, but eventually his arrogance turned public opinion against him. In 1847 President Aguilar issued a decree to enforce the article of the penal code which condemned the practice of ecclesiastics making use of their spiritual offices to promote political disturbances. The Bishop was ordered out of Salvadorean territory and went to reside in Nicaragua. He was later transferred by the pope to the diocese of León.[33]

At the request of the government of El Salvador, the pope preconized Tomás Miguel Piñeda y Zaldana as administrator of the diocese with the right of succession. When Viteri was moved to the see of Nicaragua, Piñeda became the second bishop of San Salvador. But he also had his troubles with temporal authorities. The government, at that time in control of the Liberals, required the clergy to take an oath of allegiance. This they refused to do, and Bishop Piñeda and numerous clerics went to Guatemala, where they were kindly received by Carrera. When a change of government occurred in El Salvador, Bishop Piñeda returned and ruled until his death in 1875.[34] On June 10, 1862, President Barrios ratified a concordat which had been negotiated with Cardinal Antonelli by Fernando de Lorenzana. The

---

[33] *Revista de Costa Rica en Siglo XIX,* p. 312; Bancroft, *op. cit.,* III, 289-294; Hernáez, *Colección de Bulas,* II, 110.

[34] Bancroft, *op. cit.,* III, 303, 632.

terms of the instrument followed the same lines as those set down in 1852 in the concordats of Guatemala and Costa Rica.[35]

The Conservative president of El Salvador who welcomed the return of the exiled Bishop was Francisco Dueñas, an ardent defender of the clerical interests. Dueñas at one time had taken the vows as a Dominican, but when the convents were closed in 1829, he left the cloister and secured a papal dispensation. During the presidency of Dueñas (1863-1871) the clerical party was in the ascendancy and El Salvador experienced a far-reaching Conservative reaction. The privileged clerical status was constitutionalized in 1864.

The Conservative régime was terminated in 1871 by a combined attack upon Dueñas by the Liberals of Honduras and El Salvador. It was this victory which encouraged García Granados, then a refugee in Chiapas. From 1871 to the present date the histories of the ecclesiastical reform movements in El Salvador and Guatemala have been almost identical. Liberal governments established in both republics simultaneously instituted the same reforms, and then about the same time, gave permanence to these reforms in constitutions. Finally, these constitutions and clerical reforms proved to be permanent in both countries. Prior to the Liberal revolution of 1871 no other faith than the Catholic was tolerated in El Salvador. But as a result of the revolt, freedom of thought and religion was proclaimed, the cemeteries were removed from clerical control, civil marriage was legalized, education was made non-clerical, and monastic orders were abolished. All of these changes were embodied in the present Constitution which was promulgated on August 13, 1886.[36]

Church and State are separated in El Salvador. The government does not enjoy rights in the election of ecclesiastical officers, nor does it contribute in any way to the support of religion. The Constitution guarantees the free exercise of all faiths and

---

[35] *Raccolta di Concordati*, pp. 960-970.

[36] Bancroft, *op. cit.*, III, 392; Robertson, *op. cit.*, p. 452; International Bureau of American Republics, Bulletin No. 58, *The Republic of Salvador* (Washington, 1892), p. 33; *Constitución Política de la República de El Salvador* (San Salvador, 1914).

provides that no religious act shall serve to establish the civil status of persons. As in the Mexican Constitution of 1857, Article 15 of the Constitution of El Salvador reads: "No law can authorize any act or contract which has for its object the loss or irrevocable sacrifice of man's liberty, whether it be for labor, education, or religious vow." Monastic orders are therefore constitutionally prohibited. The Salvadoreños also drew upon the Mexican constitution in defining the property rights of the Church. All ecclesiastical corporations are prohibited from acquiring real estate, except for the actual services of the respective corporation. Title to its properties is vested in the Church. No restriction is placed upon its ability to receive bequests, providing they be not in real estate.

The position of the Church with reference to education is no different in El Salvador from that in Guatemala. Public education is divorced from all religious instruction. Nor are clerics allowed to teach in the public schools. About twenty per cent of the educational institutions in the Republic are Catholic. In them, of course, religious training is an important part of the curriculum. There are no Protestant schools in El Salvador.

Although El Salvador has not accredited a representative to the Holy See since 1868, and although, in addition, some bitterness was engendered because of the constitutional laws affecting religion, in recent years amicable relations have existed between El Salvador and the papacy. This has been evidenced by the elevation of the see of San Salvador to the archiepiscopal rank. When Alfonso Belloso y Sánchez, the present archbishop, was inaugurated on March 19, 1928, the solemn ceremony was attended by the president of the Republic, members of the cabinet, the diplomatic corps, and high functionaries of the civil, military, and ecclesiastical bodies.[37]

The anti-clerical attack in the Republic of El Salvador has been far-reaching, but in one notable respect it was not as radical as that of Guatemala. The Salvadoreños showed wise restraint in foregoing the nationalization of Church properties. Undoubtedly the relatively harmonious relations that have ex-

---

[37] *La Prensa* (New York), March 20, 1928.

isted between Church and State in the Republic are the result of the granting of free title to the Church of the buildings used for religious purposes. In interesting contrast to most of the Latin-American countries, the Catholic Church of El Salvador is greatly respected by the people and the attendance at masses is large and representative.

(c) *Honduras*

The fortunes of Catholicism in Honduras were closely linked with those of the faith in Guatemala. The ecclesiastical histories of Honduras and Guatemala dovetail in many places, but not to the remarkable extent noted as between El Salvador and Guatemala.

The Republic, after the dissolution of the Federation, was inaugurated under a Conservative régime. On January 11, 1840, the Congress was installed with ceremonies more religious than political. Forty-four *Te Deum* masses were sung on that day, and President Ferrera was "besmoked with incense in the cathedral." The next year the see of Honduras which had been vacant since 1819 was filled. At first the pope named the presbyter, Dr. José Trinidad Reyes for bishop, but the government was displeased with the nomination. The Vatican was notified that the bishop-elect had died, which was false. Gregory XVI then named Francisco de Paula Compoy, who had been recommended by the government.[38]

During the greater part of the period 1840 to 1880, administrations friendly to the clerical interests were in power. The constitutions of 1848, 1865, and 1873, established Roman Catholicism as the State religion to the exclusion of the public exercise of any other. Religious toleration was guaranteed in these words: "The high powers will protect it [the Roman Catholic Church] with wise laws, but neither these nor any other authority will intervene in the private exercise of any other cult that may be established in the country if these do not disturb public order." In 1861 a concordat was concluded with

---

[38] Bancroft, *op. cit.*, III, 310; Salgado, *op. cit.*, p. 39.

the papacy by President Guardiola. This agreement was almost identical, article for article, with the one negotiated with Guatemala in 1852.[39]

President Guardiola, a satellite of Carrera, and a staunch Servile, had the novel experience of being excommunicated. Miguel del Cid, capitular vicar of the vacant see of Honduras, opposed the granting of religious toleration to the inhabitants of the islands in the Bay of Bahía as provided by treaty with Great Britain. The vicar, angry because President Guardiola would not recommend him to the pope for the episcopal dignity, took the granting of religious toleration in the islands as a pretext to excommunicate the president whom he accused of persecuting the Church. The government forbade the publication of the decree and expelled the vicar. A special envoy secured papal approval of the conduct of President Guardiola. Pius IX ordered the excommunication raised and the vicar removed from his office.[40]

After the obstinate resistance of President Medina, leader of the reactionary elements, was broken down, a liberal anti-Church reform was instituted in Honduras contemporary with the reform in Guatemala and El Salvador. The Constitution of November 1, 1880, consolidated these reforms. Subsequent fundamental charters of government, promulgated in 1894, 1906, and 1924, extended even further the scope of the attack on the privileges and prerogatives of the Church.[41]

The separation of Church and State in Honduras dates from 1880 when President Marco Aurelio Soto revoked the Concordat. Since that date no diplomatic representative has been accredited to the Vatican. The Church is theoretically free and independent of the State. The government as a rule does not interfere in the filling of ecclesiastical vacancies or contribute to the support of the Church. Yet the State inspects and controls all creeds, according to the law and police regulations concerning their external ceremonies. The exercise of all religions not in opposition to the laws of the country is guaranteed by the

---

[39] Coello, *op. cit.*, pp. 100, 118.

[40] Salgado, *op. cit.*, pp. 50-51.

[41] For the constitutions of 1880, 1894, and 1906, see Coello, *op. cit.*

Constitution, yet the Catholic sympathies of the population react against all professors of dissident faiths. On the other hand, although the law says: "The civil status of persons shall not be submitted to a determined religious belief," we find, in another part of the Constitution: "The ministers of the several religions cannot fill public office." Furthermore, the establishment of monastic and conventual associations is prohibited. Since the abolition of the monastic orders by President Morazán, there have been no convents in Honduras.[42]

As in El Salvador, the Church in Honduras owns only its edifices and residences, upon which it does not pay taxes. About twenty years ago its real property was absorbed by the State. Having no revenue property and receiving no financial aid from the government (the tithes were abolished in 1871) the priests are very poor, depending entirely on fees and contributions for their support. Entailments and all endowments in favor of religious establishments are prohibited.[43]

On the subject of education the constitutional law reads: "Freedom of instruction is guaranteed. Instruction at the cost of public funds shall be laical." Thus religious teaching in the public schools is prohibited. Private schools are legalized, the government merely requiring that the study programs outlined in the Law of Public Instruction be followed in them. The Catholic Church maintains a considerable number in which religious subjects are taught. There are about half a dozen Protestant schools in Honduras.

The laws of Honduras establish the civil marriage ceremony as the only legal form. A Church marriage must not be performed prior to the civil. Divorce and separation are legalized. The cemeteries, as in El Salvador and Guatemala, have been secularized and are controlled entirely by the municipalities.[44]

The ecclesiastical reform in Honduras has followed almost the same course as in El Salvador. Similar salutary results, however, are not apparent. In Honduras there is a lamentable

---

[42] *Constitution of Honduras* (Washington, 1924), Articles 53, 54, 57, 64.
[43] *Ibid.*, Article 61; George P. Shaw, American Consul, to J. L. Mecham, Tegucigalpa, October 26, 1927.
[44] *Ibid.*

25

scarcity of priests. There is only one seminary in the whole country, and in 1927 it had an enrollment of only fourteen. The Church in Honduras is poverty-stricken and this prevents its entering the field of social action. Religion is at a low ebb. The people, although superstitious, pay little attention to the precepts of the Church. The preponderantly ignorant and unprogressive Indian and mestizo population, in striking contrast with the numerous white and literate population of El Salvador, constitutes the real problem in Honduras. There is great need of intelligent religious and educational work in the republic.[45]

(d) *Nicaragua*

The Catholic Church in Nicaragua has not suffered the vicissitudes it encountered in the republics of Guatemala, El Salvador, and Honduras. Also the Church enjoys a more favored legal status in Nicaragua today than it does in the other republics. In 1862 a Concordat was signed with the Vatican defining the relations between Church and State. Since then dissensions have occurred, but the controversies have been amicably settled. The principal features of the Concordat were the papal recognition of the national right of presentation and the government's assuming of the obligation to support the Church. The tithes were abolished in the same year.[46]

In witness of the strength of clericalism in Nicaragua, in 1871 when the rest of Central America was in revolt against the Church, the government gave shelter to the Jesuits who had been expelled from Guatemala. There was some slight opposition to this action, but it was easily overcome. But fears that the Jesuits would cause trouble were realized in May, 1881. A Spanish professor made a speech at the opening of the Instituto de Occidente, an educational institution under special government protection, in which he said that liberty of conscience and speech were necessary for the perfect education of free men. The Jesuits of León aroused the fanatical rabble by saying that the religion of their fathers was imperilled by the propaganda

---

[45] Dana G. Munro, *The Five Republics of Central America* (New York, 1918), p. 131; Edith M. Melick, *Seed Sowing in Honduras* (St. Louis, Mo., 1927), pp. 46-47.   [46] *Raccolta di Concordati,* pp. 948-959.

of the free-thinkers of the Instituto. They demanded prompt action on the part of Bishop Ulloa y Larrios, but the prelate refused to support them. Riots instigated by the Jesuits were suppressed by the government and the members of the order were expelled from Nicaraguan soil. This episode is not to be regarded as a counterpart of the Liberal movement in the neighboring republics, for the government which acted against the Jesuits was friendly to the Church, but obviously could not tolerate subversive acts.[47]

The delayed Liberal anti-clerical attack in Nicaragua occurred after 1894, during the dictatorial régime of Zelaya. Legislation violative of the Concordat terminated that agreement and really dissolved the union of Church and State. Because of his opposition, Bishop Ulloa y Larrios was banished to Panama. Until his death in 1908 his coadjutor, Bishop Simeone Pereira, succeeded him in the administration of the diocese of León. After the overthrow of Zelaya the Church found sympathetic support in the Conservative Party, which, with the aid of the United States, controlled Nicaragua until very recently.

Although Church and State are separated, the Catholic faith is still recognized as the State religion of Nicaragua. The religious clause of the constitution of 1911 reads, "The majority of the Nicaraguan people profess the Catholic, Apostolic, Roman religion. The State guarantees the free exercise of this cult; and also of all others so long as they do not oppose Christian morality and public order. The State is prohibited from issuing laws to protect or restrain particular cults."[48]

The Catholic Church occupies a privileged position in education in Nicaragua. Although it exercises no control over public education, the law requires that instruction in the Catholic religion be given in the public schools. The State pays the priests for this instruction.[49] In recognition of its inability to

---

[47] Bancroft, op. cit., III, 476, 484, 633-634.

[48] Constitución Política de la República de Nicaragua (Managua, 1911), Art. 5.

[49] Ministerio de Instrucción Pública to J. L. Mecham, Managua, December 17, 1927.

cope with the educational demands of the republic, the government of Nicaragua has adopted as a policy the solicitation of ecclesiastical coöperation in the meeting of the problem.

In a country preponderatingly Catholic, as is Nicaragua, and largely composed of ignorant and fanatical Indians and mestizos, the constitutional guarantee of religious toleration is very often only a theory. In the interior, removed from the capital and larger towns, Protestants are unwelcome rarities. Protestant missionaries have encountered serious opposition and been threatened with mob violence.[50] Nicaragua, however, is not exceptional in the intolerance of its masses. The same is true of the lower strata of all Central America, particularly those who reside in the interior regions. This is the result of centuries-old clerical instruction to look upon all foreigners as heretics and children of the devil.

(e) Costa Rica

Being further removed from the storm-center of Central America (Guatemala), Costa Rica was less influenced than her northern neighbors in the politico-ecclesiastical turmoils in that republic. In November, 1838, Costa Rica proclaimed her separation from the Federation of Central America. A Conservative régime, friendly to the Church, was set up under President Braulio Carrillo, but he proved to be so dictatorial that he was overthrown, and a Liberal government under Francisco Morazán, recently returned from exile in Peru, was established early in 1842. Morazán's tenure as president of Costa Rica was brief, for, in September, 1842, he was overthrown and executed by the Conservatives. The prospect of being ruled by the "anarchist" Morazán was revolting to the majority of Costa Ricans who were pronouncedly Conservative in opinion.[51]

From 1842 to 1883 very little occurred to disturb the placid waters of State-Church harmony. The several constitutions that were promulgated during this period were uniformly most friendly toward the Catholic Church which was declared to be the State-Church. The instruments of 1844, 1847, and 1859 declared that Roman Catholicism was the only religion to be

---

[50] Current History, September, 1925, p. 976. [51] Robertson, op. cit., p. 449.

tolerated. In 1860, however, a more liberal note was introduced into the constitutional law when it was provided that Roman Catholicism should be the State religion, but other denominations should be tolerated. The next constitution, that of 1871, which is still in force, continues the principle of religious toleration.[52]

The independent bishopric which the people of Costa Rica had solicited for nearly three centuries was finally created (February 28, 1850), by bull of Pope Pius IX. This freed the Church in Costa Rica from ecclesiastical control resident in another State, the Bishop of León in Nicaragua. Anselmo Llorente y Lafuente, a native of Cartago, was consecrated first Bishop of Costa Rica on November 7, 1851. After the creation of the bishopric, the people of Costa Rica wanted their own seminary, for candidates for the priesthood still had to go to León for training. A seminary was not founded in Costa Rica, however, until 1878.

In 1852 a concordat was negotiated with the papacy by Fernando de Lorenzana and was signed on the same date (October 7) as was the concordat with Guatemala. The terms differed but slightly from the Guatemalan concordat. By the terms of the Costa Rican instrument the jurisdiction previously exercised by the ecclesiastical authorities in litigations involving Church possessions or its temporal rights was transferred to the civil tribunals, but it was stipulated at the same time that, in courts of second and third instance, legal trial of criminal cases involving priests required the assistance of ecclesiastics nominated by the bishop, as judicial assessors. Today the jurisdiction of the Church court, or *Juzgado Eclesiástico*, extends over causes of discipline and moral conduct of the clergy, marriage as it refers to the sacraments, and causes of faith.[53]

Bishop Llorente, like the first Bishop of San Salvador, tasted the bitterness of exile. When he refused to pay, or allow his clergy to pay, an equitable tax decreed by Congress on September 29, 1858, for the support of the hospitals, he was expelled

---

[52] Barrantes, *op. cit.*, II, 93.

[53] *Raccolta di Concordati*, pp. 800-810; *Costa Rica en Siglo XIX*, pp. 297, 301, 316; Hernáez, *Colección de Bulas*, II, 114.

from Costa Rica by President Mora. The Bishop sought refuge in Nicaragua and remained there until August, 1859, when he returned to his see after the fall of his adversary. The overthrow of Mora, who, on the whole, had been friendly towards clerical interests, was due in no small degree to public indignation because of his banishment of the Bishop. One of the first acts of the new government was to recall Llorente, who ruled his diocese until his death in 1871. The government then proposed a successor who was not approved by the Roman Curia. Consequently a capitular vicar administered the diocese for almost ten years. Finally, in February, 1880, the pope confirmed the government's nominee, Bernard August Thiel.[54]

Bishop Thiel, like his predecessor, soon ran afoul of the government. In 1883 a decree was published forbidding the entry into the Republic of members of the Society of Jesus, although a few were allowed to remain in their college at Cartago. This act seemed to support the suspicion that President Fernández and his adherents were antagonistic to the Church. At least the Jesuits began to agitate and fanned the fires of intolerance and fanaticism in the ignorant masses. At first the Bishop refused to join in the attack on "the government which intended to destroy the religion of the majority," and he ordered his clergy to desist. But later he compromised himself, and, in July, 1884, suffered expulsion along with the Jesuits.[55] Fernández forthwith instituted anti-clerical measures. By decree the law of December 2, 1852, approving the Concordat, was derogated. Thus diplomatic relations with the papacy were broken. Then the cemeteries were secularized. Writes a partisan regarding this measure: "On that day came to an end the inhuman management of the cemeteries, by means of which the penalties of the Church persecuted human beings after death." Another decree prohibited the establishment of monastic orders or religious communities. Vicar Antonio Zamora who administered the diocese during the absence of Bishop

---

[54] *Costa Rica en Siglo* XIX, p. 350.

[55] The ban on the Jesuits is still in force. Recently a petition was presented to the National Congress asking that the law against the Jesuits be revoked. The president opposed saying the idea of readmitting the Jesuits horrified him. For this statement he was severely criticized. (*Chicago Tribune,* August 4, 1929.)

Thiel, was able to restore friendly relations with the government, so that, after the death of President Fernández, Thiel was allowed to return, upon promising to observe the laws and not interfere in political affairs. Since 1886 harmonious relations have prevailed between Church and State in Costa Rica.[56]

According to constitutional law the Catholic Church is the State-Church of Costa Rica. In recognition of this fact it receives subsidies from the government. On the other hand the national executive is entrusted with the exercise of the patronage. He also concedes or denies the *pase* to all pontifical documents and other dispatches of the ecclesiastical authority. The Congress is empowered to approve concordats. Since 1908 the Vatican and Costa Rica have exchanged diplomatic representatives. The papal internuncio accredited to Costa Rica is also the papal representative to the Church in the other Central American republics. Ecclesiastics do not suffer, in Costa Rica, the political disability, common to Latin America, of being ineligible to hold political office. At the present time several priests are members of Congress.

The politico-ecclesiastical relationships in Costa Rica have been the most intimate and harmonious of all the Central American republics. There have been occasional conflicts of jurisdiction between the lay and clerical officials, it is true, and Costa Rican prelates have suffered exile, but, fortunately for the interests of the Church, the State has displayed throughout a tolerant attitude. This policy, no doubt, is in recognition of the fact that the great majority of the population is very sympathetic towards the Catholic Church and wishes to accord it special privileges because of this fact.

(f) *Panama*

The Catholic Church in Panama, until the separation from Colombia, was united with the latter State. Thus the Concordat of 1886 regulated the status of the Church on the Isthmus, but when the independent Republic of Panama was established, Church and State were separated. This was due to the fact that liberal opinion which had insisted on separation for many years was

---

[56] Barrantes, *op. cit.*, II, 260-264, 300.

strong in Panama. The Constitution of 1904 recognizes the Roman Catholic religion as that of the majority of the Republic's inhabitants, but this bestows no special privilege on the Church. It is affirmation of a fact which could well have been omitted. Religious freedom is guaranteed and there are no religious tests for the enjoyment of political rights. The government has no privileges in the election of ecclesiastical officers, accredits no representative to the Vatican, and has no concordat with the papacy. Nor does the government contribute to the support of the Catholic Church, although it endows three scholarships in the seminary. Church property has not been nationalized, but title is vested in the particular corporations. There are no restrictions on the ability of the Church to receive entailments and bequests.[57]

Religious instruction may be given in the public schools and ecclesiastics are allowed to teach in them. The Catholic Church maintains primary pay schools for boys and girls; also some free schools. These are under governmental supervision as to sanitation and security. The Catholic schools are supported in part by subventions of the national government and the municipalities. They are rather numerous, bearing a ratio to the public schools of one to six.

Civil marriage has been legalized in Panama, but is not the only recognized form. The religious marriage is recognized as valid before the law for Catholics, providing they register with the *juez municipal*. Civil divorce also exists in Panama. Since 1910 the Church has been deprived of its administration of the cemeteries. Today the municipalities exercise this control.[58]

With only a few slight exceptions the political status of the Catholic Church in Panama is about the same as that in the United States. It is interesting to note that the two republics (Panama and Cuba) whose fortunes have been most closely linked with the United States have disposed of the religious question after the fashion of the Anglo-American Republic.

A survey of the political status of the Catholic Church in the

---

[57] Archbishop of Panama to J. L. Mecham, Panama, October 25, 1927; H. D. Myers, American Vice Consul in Charge, to J. L. Mecham, Panama, November 28, 1927.

[58] Archbishop of Panama to J. L. Mecham.

republics of Central America should not be concluded without
mention of the religious provisions in the constitutions of short-
lived Central American federations. In 1898, Honduras, Nicaragua, and El Salvador made an essay at union. The Constitution
of August 27, 1898, provided for (1) the guarantee of the free
exercise of all religions; (2) no religious act to serve to establish
the civil state of persons; and (3) public education to be laical,
and governmental financial support of private schools in which
religion is taught to be prohibited.[59] At that time (1898) the
three republics were in agreement on the above points relating
to religious policy. In 1921, Guatemala, El Salvador, and
Honduras adopted another federal constitution, also of brief
duration. This instrument contained the following provisions
touching on religion and the Church: (1) liberty of thought and
conscience guaranteed; (2) denial to the Federal Congress of
the right to legislate on religious matters; (3) instruction supported by the federal government to be laical; (4) no religious
act to serve to establish the civil state of persons; (5) prohibition
of all kinds of conventual congregations; and (6) prohibition of
entailments.[60] Like the Constitution of 1898, this most recent
instrument of government providing for a federal union in Central
America, contained in its religious clauses common ground for
all the republics to stand on in their relations to the Church.
Although adhering to an entirely different religious policy which
would make it impossible for her to accept the constitutions of
1898 and 1921, this was not the compelling factor which kept
Costa Rica out of the two federations.

In the republics of Central America one discovers in concentrated form all the divergences in ecclesiastical policy encountered in the other widely separated Latin-American countries.
Here in a limited geographical area is Panama with complete
separation of Church and State, Costa Rica with an established
Church, and Guatemala and El Salvador with the Church under
governmental control. Since these tiny republics differ but slightly one from another in their physical make-up and in their
fundamental problems, it is surprising that they should disagree

---

[59] Coello, *op. cit.*, p. 193.
[60] *Ibid.*, pp. 249-250.

so emphatically on the religious question. It would be futile to search in the historical background and in the economic, social, and racial conditions of the countries for an explanation of these inharmonious religious policies. It would seem, therefore, that the personal factor must be the controlling one, in some of the countries at least. The contradictory answers to the religious question have been submitted and their acceptance forced by individuals or groups more interested in the perpetuation and aggrandizement of their political authority than the welfare of their country.

CHAPTER XIV

CHURCH AND STATE CONFLICT
IN MEXICO: 1821-1854

The independence of Mexico, which the prelates of the Catholic Church had condemned as heresy, was finally achieved in 1821 under most exceptional circumstances. "It [independence] was the natural result," says Lucas Alamán, "of a simple change of front by the army, instigated by the higher clergy who were antagonistic to the Spanish Cortes. . . . Independence was achieved by the very ones who had opposed it."[1] The restoration of the Spanish liberal Constitution of 1812, the confiscation of part of the Church's property, the abolition of the Inquisition, the establishment of a free press, and the seizure of the tithes of the clergy, produced greater discontent in Mexico than in Spain, for, again quoting Alamán, "In Mexico those offended by the measures were the most influential and the most elevated." The menace of the extension to Mexico of the restrictions on clerical privileges, as well as the actual property losses (for there part of the Church's wealth had been seized arbitrarily by Spanish officials to combat revolt), forced the clergy to the conclusion that absolute separation from Spain and its radicalism was necessary. Priests declared from their pulpits that the preservation of Catholicism demanded freedom from Spain. "The clergy of Mexico," says a recent writer, "preferred to sacrifice the allegiance they owed to their king, from whom they had received preferments, rather than run the risk of losing their privileges."[2] It is undoubtedly true that anxiety over the preservation of their civil and political rights was the compelling factor in causing the clergy to cast their lot for independence, but it should also be recorded, in justice to the numerous less selfishly-minded clerics, that they conscientiously interpreted the acts of the Spanish

---

[1] Riva Palacio, *México á Través de Los Siglos*, III, 657.

[2] Callcott, *Church and State in Mexico*, p. 35.

Cortes as an attack on dogmatic religion itself. The course of revolution tended to atheism; such was the lesson of the French Revolution.

Having decided on independence, a meeting of conservative leaders, prominent among whom were several clerics, was held in the oratorio of the church of San Felipe Neri in Mexico City. It was decided to compromise with the rebels who were in the field continuing the struggle initiated by Hidalgo, and, when control should be established over the independence movement, to create a monarchy with a Spanish *infante* at the head. The conspirators were careful not to mention constitutional institutions.[3] The plans of the conservative rebels were translated into acts without the slightest hitch. On February 24, 1821, Agustín de Iturbide, leader of the royalist forces and co-conspirator, and Vicente Guerrero, leader of the liberal rebels, proclaimed the famous *Plan de Iguala*. "The *Plan* provided a scheme whereby all the inhabitants of New Spain could unite, on the basis of mutual toleration, in establishing the political independence of the country."[4] Its principal provisions were: (1) the preservation of the Roman Catholic religion and clerical privileges; (2) independence; and (3) equality of creoles and Europeans in the government. So universal was the appeal of the *Plan* to all classes that nothing could stop the triumphant march of Iturbide and the Army of the Three Guarantees. On September 27, "El Libertador," as the mestizo turn-coat was called by an adoring populace, occupied Mexico City. The definitive separation of Mexico had been accomplished under terms satisfactory to the ecclesiastics. Only the Roman Catholic religion was to be tolerated and the members of the regular and secular clergy were to be protected in all their rights and properties. In other words the ecclesiastical *fueros* were guaranteed.

It was necessary, however, to incorporate these guarantees into constitutional law and establish a capable government will-

---

[3] Riva Palacio, *op. cit.*, III, 662-663; Tiburio Catalán to Gen. Vicente Guerrero, Chilapa, April 8, 1822. Riva Palacio Papers in the García Collection, University of Texas Library.

[4] Priestley, *The Mexican Nation*, p. 247; Gamboa, *Leyes Constitucionales*, pp. 282-285.

ing to insure their observance. The first provisional government organized after the signing of the Treaty of Córdoba (August 24, 1821), was a *Junta Gubernativa*. After the *Junta* was installed, the members went to the cathedral and took an oath to fulfill faithfully the *Plan de Iguala* and the Treaty of Córdoba. After this act they proceeded to the chapter room and unamimously elected Iturbide president of the *Junta*. A *Te Deum* processional march in the church and a *misa de gracia* followed. The first government of independent Mexico was inaugurated under clerical auspices. Shortly after, when a Regency was organized, Iturbide became its president. The Bishop of Puebla, Antonio Joaquín Pérez, succeeded to the presidency of the *Junta*. A vacancy in the Regency, created by the death of O'Donojú on October 8, was filled by the appointment of the Bishop of Puebla. Archbishop Fonte was then offered the presidency of the *Junta*, but refused for fear of compromising himself. On February 4, 1822, a Constituent Congress in which the clergy were well represented, was convoked. Before organizing for business the deputies, accompanied by the *Junta* and the Regency, went to the cathedral and heard mass. There all took an oath to support the Roman Catholic religion to the exclusion of all others. "This religious ceremony," says a Mexican historian, "indicates the supremacy of the clergy, without whose intervention in matters of policy, acts would have been illegal and all authority would have been insecure and weak."[5]

For nine months the Constituent Congress, divided into irreconcilable monarchist and republican groups, sat without doing anything constructive on the constitution. Finally Iturbide, ambitious and baited beyond endurance by the constituents, took matters into his own hands and forced the Congress to choose him as emperor. Since the clericals feared that the majority of the deputies were inclining toward a republic, the very idea of which was repulsive to them, they hastened to the support of Iturbide and the Empire. On July 25, 1822, Agustín I was crowned as Emperor in a stately ceremony in which several ecclesiastical prelates officiated. "The Mexicans, struggling for a

[5] Riva Palacio, *op. cit.*, IV, 16, 18, 54-55; *Colección de los Decretos y Ordenes del Soberano Congreso Mexicano* (Mexico, 1825), p. 39.

liberal independence, had been tricked into a conservative one by Iturbide and the Church."[6]

Augustín I desired to appear as the recognized champion of the Church and earnestly protested to that effect. The religious guarantees of the *Plan de Iguala* were ardently reaffirmed. He declared that the faith of his Empire should be Catholic, Apostolic, and Roman, without toleration of any other; and that the secular and regular clergy should be protected in their *fueros* and preëminences. The "Spanish priests," who had held themselves aloof at the time of Iturbide's elevation, for they wanted a Bourbon on the throne, gradually accommodated themselves to the new régime. But not so Archbishop Fonte. A peninsular, he regarded independence as treason and abandoned his metropolitan see after the creation of the Empire and returned to Spain. When the Mexican government wished to declare the see vacant it received a rebuff from the pope. Bishops Bergosa of Oaxaca and Cabañas of Guadalajara were also seriously compromised because of their vehement polemics against independence.[7]

Despite clerical support, the Empire was overthrown within a year after its creation. The elements of opposition to Iturbide have been cleverly tabulated by an American historian as "The cheated absolutists, disappointed borbonistas, cajoled insurgents, distanced comrades, eclipsed leaders and unsuccessful claimants, the patriots, indignant that a cruel royalist should be the heir to the revolution, the republicans, few in number but increasingly influential, the friends of those he had massacred, and behind all the Scottish Rite Freemasons, who were liberals yet partisans of Spain."[8] It was not true that the Empire was attacked because of the clerical domination. Despite the fact that there was a rising opposition to the ecclesiastical *fuero*, Iturbide was dethroned not because of the nature of his following, but because of his political blunders. Indeed, these very mistakes weakened his clerical support, and when the crisis arrived the clergy were not willing to assume a determined stand on his behalf. In other words, opposition to the Church was a minor factor in contributing to the downfall of the Empire.

[6] Priestley, *op. cit.*, p. 261.   [7] Riva Palacio, *op. cit.*, III, 356.
[8] Justin H. Smith, *The War with Mexico* (New York, 1919), I, 34.

Although the clerics had not been backward in assuming management of governmental affairs, they refused to concede to the State any control over the Church. They revealed the goal of their ambitions in the discussions relating to the patronage. On October 19, 1821, Iturbide, as president of the Regency, requested Archbishop Fonte to state what policy the government should pursue in the matter of filling the ever-increasing ecclesiastical vacancies. Since "the cure of souls" did not admit of delay, said Iturbide, the Archbishop should hazard an opinion as to what should be done in order that the right of patronage might be preserved until an agreement on this matter could be concluded with the pope. Fonte did not care to assume personally the responsibility of an answer, therefore he consulted his chapter and a *junta* of bishops. The prelates announced as their opinion that (1) with the winning of independence the patronage which had been conceded by the pope to the kings of Spain, came to an end; (2) to exercise the patronage, it was necessary for the Mexican government to receive the same concession from the pope; and (3) in the meantime the provision of ecclesiastical places belonged by right of devolution in each diocese to the respective ordinary acting with the canons.[9] The report of the *junta* of prelates, as communicated to the Regency by Archbishop Fonte, seemed to support the charge that the Mexican clergy felt that the hour had arrived to liberate themselves from dependence on the civil power.

The Regency transmitted the report of the *junta* of bishops to the Minister of Justice and Ecclesiastical Affairs, who, on April 17, 1822, rendered a contradictory opinion. He declared that the Mexican State, as the successor to the sovereign rights of the Spanish kings in New Spain, inherited the exercise of the patronage which was inherent in sovereignty. The patronage committees of the Congress also failed to agree with the *junta* of bishops. The first committee reported on June 21, 1823, that patronage was based on sovereignty, and not on a transitory government. Therefore the Mexican patronage resided in the nation. According to this report: "The patronage is to be

---

[9] *Dictamen de la Comisión de Patronato, June 21, 1823* (Mexico, 1823), pp. 3-5; *Colección Eclesiástica Mejicana* (Mexico, 1834), I, 10-14.

exercised immediately, excepting the nomination of bishops, if it is regarded as being essential to the good of the Church to await a declaration by the pope." A second congressional committee reported on March 8, 1824, that the right of the patronage belonged to the nation and that the lesser ecclesiastical vacancies could be filled by nomination on the part of the government. However, it was advised, the providing of vacant archbishoprics and bishoprics should be postponed until a concordat could be concluded.[10]

The advisability of negotiating an agreement with the Vatican was generally recognized in Mexico soon after separation from the motherland. Due to clerical pressure, the Congress authorized the Regency to send an envoy to Rome and advised that the prelates be consulted beforehand in the preparation of the instructions. The departure of the envoy was indefinitely postponed for various reasons. On April 17, 1823, the government was again instructed by the Congress to send "an agent to the court of Rome to manifest to His Holiness that the Catholic religion is the only one of the State, and to pay to him in consequence the respect due to the head of the Church."[11] Finally, after a long delay, Francisco Pablo Vázquez went to Europe as the Mexican envoy to the pope.

After the overthrow of Iturbide a call was issued for a Constituent Congress to take up once more the task of framing a fundamental charter. The Congress met on November 7, 1823. The republicans enjoyed an overwhelming majority, but they were divided into factions favoring either the centralist or the federalist form of government. The clerics, discomfited by the imperial *débàcle*, were tardy in adopting a policy to meet the new situation, with the result that the Congress was remarkably free of Church influence. Yet, numerous religious were included in the membership of the Congress, and two of these, Miguel Ramos Arizpe and Servando Mier, were the leaders, respectively, of the Federalist and Centralist groups.

Since it was imperative that a permanent government be estab-

---

[10] *Dictamen de Patronato,* pp. 5-6, 11-18.

[11] Juan A. Mateos, *Historia Parlamentaria de los Congresos Mexicanos de 1821 á 1857* (Mexico, 1877), I, 404; II, 269-273.

lished with the least possible delay, the Congress promulgated the *Acta Constitutiva* (January 31, 1824) which was to serve as the constitution until a detailed federal republican instrument could be framed. The *Acta*, for which Ramos Arizpe was principally responsible, provided in Article 4 that: "The religion of the Mexican nation is and shall be perpetually the Roman Catholic Apostolic. The nation will protect it by wise and just laws and prohibits the exercise of any other." In the debates on the *Acta*, Article 4 was approved without much opposition.[12]

In May, 1823, Stephen F. Austin, a close friend of Arizpe, gave to the famous Mexican Federalist a brief summary of a federal constitution. Austin based his draft on the Constitution of the United States, but departed from the American model in providing for the union of Church and State in Mexico. Ramos Arizpe disagreed with some of the articles which tended to minimize the independence and influence of the Church.[13]

In the Federal Constitution which was finally adopted on October 4, 1824, Article 4 of the *Acta* was retained without change, but there were numerous additions defining the status of the State-Church. The most important of these were the power of the State to conclude concordats, grant or refuse the exequatur to all pontifical documents, and make rules for the exercise of the patronage. Although archbishops, bishops, provisors, and vicars general were declared ineligible to election as senators or deputies, nevertheless full political rights were guaranteed to all other members of the clergy. And, most important of all, the preservation of the ecclesiastical *fueros* was guaranteed.[14] The disposition of the religious question by the Congress of 1824 was significant for at least two reasons. In the first place, the constituents took a definite stand in favor of national patronage. There was almost unanimous agreement that the Church was not to be freed from all governmental control. Secondly, it was demonstrated that the Mexican nation approved the retention

---

[12] *Ibid.,* II, 610-612; José M. Gamboa, *Leyes Constitucionales de México durante El Siglo XIX* (Mexico, 1901), p. 303.

[13] William A. Whatley, *The Formation of the Mexican Constitution of 1824* (M. A. Thesis, University of Texas, 1921), pp. 69 ff.

[14] Mateos, *op. cit.,* II, 806-814, 855-877; Gamboa, *op. cit.,* 237-283.

of Catholicism as the State religion and opposed toleration toward other sects. It was not necessary for the Church to fight aggressively for a privileged spiritual position. That status was freely recognized by a populace which firmly believed as a principle of faith in the spiritual supremacy of the Church.

There should be no occasion for mystification then, that immediately after the Catholic Church was established by unanimous consent as the State-Church, it was subjected to attack. The cause of complaint was not the exclusive privileges enjoyed by the Church in the purely religious sphere (very little was thought about religious freedom in Mexico in 1824), but rather its economic domination. In spite of minor confiscations of property, it has been estimated that, whereas before the Revolution Church property values amounted to 65,000,000 *pesos*, after the Revolution they totaled 179,000,000 *pesos*. During the same period the number of clergy actually declined by one-third. About one-fourth of the nation's wealth belonged to the Church. "Due to the decline in the number of ecclesiastics while the quantity of Church property was increasing, there developed a condition of absentee landlordism or the latifundia evil."[15] Independence under creole leadership only served to aggrandize the Church in wealth and prestige. During the next thirty years its strength and riches continued to increase until it became the most powerful institutionalized force in the country.

The revolutionary hero Guadalupe Victoria was elected first president of Mexico under the Constitution of 1824. Like Washington, he attempted to remain neutral in political matters and selected his advisers from the rival political parties. This ill-advised policy is described by a contemporary historian: "The irrational attempt to unite repellent elements passed from the Congress to the government, from Don Miguel Ramos Arizpe to President Victoria. The first tried to unite in a single body of

---

[15] Callcott, *op. cit.*, p. 66. Father Mariano Cuevas, on checking over Dr. Callcott's references, especially Mariano Otero, *Ensayo sobre la Cuestión Social* (Mexico, 1842), pointed out to the writer certain indisputable exaggerations in Callcott's figures. It is practically impossible to arrive at the exact sums, nor is it necessary for the purposes of this study, for, as any fair-minded historian of Mexico would admit, the Church in Mexico was very wealthy, and that situation constituted a problem.

laws liberty of thought and of the press with religious intolerance, legal equality with the *fueros* of the privileged class, the clergy and the military; the second established as a rule of government a division into equal parts of the ministry between the two great parties that contended for possession of the power. What resulted from such a state of things? A system of sterility and weakness which can be maintained for a short time, but which cannot be permanent."[16]

The so-called political parties which Victoria tried unsuccessfully to reconcile were the Conservatives and the Liberals. The former recruited most of their members from the landed aristocracy, the military, and the clergy. These were the classes which zealously guarded their privileges or *fueros*. Most of the old adherents of monarchy and centralism supported this party. The Liberals were largely creole and mestizo professional people and intellectuals, who were without special privilege; consequently they were democrats, for to them democracy meant equality of all peoples. They also supported federalism, which was understood to guarantee individual freedom. The most important groups within the two parties were the two branches of Masonry —the *Escoceses* or Scottish Rite Masons, in the Conservative party, and the *Yorkinos*, or the York Rite Masons, in the Liberal party.

The *Escoceses* had long been active in the political life of Mexico. As ardent partisans of Spain they had opposed Iturbide and contributed materially to the accomplishment of his overthrow. Although a Federal Republic was established on the ruins of the Empire, the *Escoceses* continued to champion the principle of centralism, and the more reactionary members supported monarchism, or even a restoration of Spanish authority under a liberal constitution. The York Rite lodge was not organized in Mexico until after the establishment of the Republic. The idea of organizing the Masonic branch to counteract the centralistic and anti-republican propaganda of the *Escoceses* was conceived by two curates, José María Alpuche and Ramos Arizpe. After five lodges had been formed, the American Minister Joel Poinsett

---

[16] José María Luís Mora, *Obras Sueltas* (Paris, 1847), I, viii.

was asked to secure in the United States letters patent to install the grand lodge. This was Poinsett's only activity in the organization of the *Yorkinos*.[17] He was criticised, however, as acting with deliberate purpose to destroy the Conservative influence in the country, particularly the ecclesiastical. Yet the division of contending political aspirants into Centralists and Federalists, Scottish and York Rite Masons, is deceptive. "These were ephemeral alignments," says Gruening, "for a massed assault on the treasury." There was no loyalty to any other idea. "The political history of Mexico from 1825 to 1850," says the same writer, "is primarily the history of the army which noisily occupied the foreground; the Church filled the background and pulled the strings of its marionettes."[18]

When the *Yorkinos* were in charge of the administration, liberal reforms were attempted, as was to be expected. "Slowly the work of reform continued against the group of clerical privileges. The law of February 7, 1828, gave to the State of Chihuahua the buildings of the College of Jesuits which was located in its territory. On April 18 of the same year the *Desierto de los Carmelitas* was given to San Bartolo, Santa Rosa, and San Bernabé, towns of the Federal District. On May 10, 1829, the sale of the temporalities (*bienes de temporalidades*) was ordered. This, together with the property of monastic orders, the Hospitallers, Jesuits, and the Inquisition, which had been declared the property of the nation, ascended to 8,880,604 *pesos*."[19] Thus the first republican assault upon the Church was confined almost exclusively to its temporalities. Since the army was also attacked because of its *fueros* and participation in political disturbances, the two privileged orders tended to draw together into a league of mutual protection.

Several attempts were made in the administration of President Victoria to establish relations with the papacy. After his election to the presidency Guadalupe Victoria wrote to Leo XII, naïvely expecting that he would be recognized by a simple notification.

---

[17] Callcott, *op. cit.*, p. 56.

[18] Gruening, *Mexico and Its Heritage*, p. 51.

[19] Francisco Bulnes, *Juárez y las Revoluciones de Ayutla y de la Reforma* (Mexico, 1905), pp. 83-84.

But recognition was not forthcoming. Instead, the pope sent an encyclical to the American clergy urging them to aid the king of Spain. The publication of the encyclical created intense indignation among all classes in Mexico; chapters and prelates joined in the national protest against the papal proposal that allegiance to the detested Ferdinand be restored. Ramos Arizpe, Minister of Justice and Ecclesiastical Affairs, instructed Francisco Vázquez, recently dispatched to Rome as the Mexican representative, to register a protest against the encyclical "which seemed so foreign to the head of the Church." From Brussels Vázquez wrote the Cardinal-Secretary. Assuming that the pope's ill-advised action was the result of misinformation, Vázquez attempted to present a true account of Mexico's loyalty to the Church and the impossibility of a restoration of Spanish rule. Cardinal Somaglia responded almost immediately requesting that Vázquez proceed to Rome. The Cardinal, however, discretely avoided any mention of the encyclical and referred to the President of Mexico as "Sua Eccellenza il Signore Comandante Generale, Dr. Guadalupe Vittoria."[20]

Since the Constitution of 1824 provided for the national exercise of the patronage, the Republic was anxious that it should receive papal approval without delay because of the imperative need of filling ecclesiastical vacancies, for after 1821 the number of clerics had diminished considerably. It is said that by 1830 the total had been reduced by one-third. The reasons for the marked decrease were natural death, flight, and difficulty of ordination due to the lack of bishops. The last-named cause was the principal one. Some of the bishops, like Abad y Queipo, left the country even before the consummation of independence. Others like Archbishop Fonte left later. At the end of 1821 there were five bishops in Mexico, but in 1827 not a single one remained.[21] Despite the imperative need of remedying the distressing scarcity of prelates and clergy, the Congress was not disposed to secure the filling of the vacancies by sacrificing national claims

---

[20] Joaquín Ramírez Cabañas (ed.), *Las Relaciones entre México y el Vaticano* (Mexico, 1928), pp. 14-27.

[21] Col. Vázquez Medía to Guadalupe Victoria, Cempoala, July 16, 1828. Riva Palacio Papers.

to the patronage. The deputies were willing, however, to waste much valuable time in discussing its nature. "It was a very singular thing," said Zavala in an ironical vein, "to see the Council of Ministers occupying itself with the provision and nomination of ecclesiastical prelates while the government was threatened by a faction and the republic was on the verge of a civil war."[22]

After years of fruitless discussion the Congress finally agreed, October 13, 1827, on a set of instructions to guide the negotiations of the Mexican agent to the pope. Vázquez, it will be recalled, had been in Brussels for over two years awaiting these orders. Numerous members of the Mexican clergy expressed considerable alarm because the instructions contained a demand that the pope authorize in the Mexican nation the exercise of the patronage. A great number of books and pamphlets were written attacking this right. The most important of these were collected, in 1834, into a four volume publication called *Colección Eclesiástica Mejicana*. The clergy were very unwilling, it was evident, to abandon their efforts to be free of temporal control. As for the history of Vázquez's mission after he was conveyed the long-delayed instructions, a discussion is unnecessary here, since the details were narrated elsewhere.[23]

The presidential candidates to succeed Guadalupe Victoria were Manuel Gómez Pedraza, a conservative *Yorkino* who enjoyed the support of Ramos Arizpe and Victoria, and Vicente Guerrero, grand master of the Yorkinos. Guerrero was supported by Alpuche, Zavala, and Poinsett. In this election, as in that of 1823, the clergy were unorganized and exerted little influence. Although Gómez Pedraza was the undoubted legal victor at the polls in the presidential election of 1829, Guerrero possessed himself of the presidency by resorting to arms. The Congress confirmed his "election," and named Anastasio Bustamante as vice president. But Guerrero's tenure in the office of the chief executive was short-lived. A new Conservative party made up of the clergy, army, *hacendados* (or property holders), and the remnants of the *Escoceses* and better born Yorkinos, coöperated under the leader-

[22] Lorenzo de Zavala, *Ensayo Histórico de las Revoluciones de México* (Paris, 1831-32), II, 199.

[23] Supra, pp. 102-103.

ship of Vice-President Bustamante to overthrow Guerrero. Bustamante then "succeeded" to the presidency (February, 1830).[24]

The conservative administration of Anastasio Bustamante was very friendly to the Catholic Church and aided in restoring to that organization its former influence. Liberal and heretical ideas were vigorously stamped out, and tolerance was condemned as being conducive to the promotion of schism. The ultramontane sympathies of Bustamante and his Foreign Minister, Lucas Alamán, were shown by their willingness to abandon the right of patronal presentation. With congressional authorization Alamán sent to Vázquez for submission to the pope the names of candidates selected by the ecclesiastical chapters for appointment to the vacant benefices. The pope was asked to institute, not on the presentation of a civil sovereign, but simply *de motu proprio*. There was to be no mention of any government, republic, or state, said Zavala, but the question was to be submitted solely as one relating to "some regions called Mexican."[25] But for reasons noted elsewhere the pope was not ready to nominate the individuals whose names were given to him by the Mexican agent. The pointiff's offer to name apostolic vicars or bishops *in partibus* was refused by Vázquez. But when Gregory XVI became pope, Vázquez secured the desired nominations of bishops for the vacant sees. In the Consistory of 1831, Gregory XVI preconized *motu proprio* proprietary bishops for the sees of Puebla, Chiapas, Linares, Guadalajara, Durango, and Michoacán. Having abandoned the right of presentation to bishoprics, the government of Bustamante enacted a law, May 16, 1831, granting to the clergy the free election of canons. These acts clearly implied abandonment of all pretention to the patronage. It was a great triumph for clericalism.[26]

The harmony established between the clergy and the government was rudely destroyed two years later when an ephemeral Liberal government was established. When Iturbide was over-

---

[24] Callcott, *op. cit.*, pp. 68-69.

[25] Zavala, *op. cit.*, II, 230-231.

[26] Zubieta, *Misiones Diplomáticas de Colombia*, 589; Riva Palacio, *op. cit.*, IV, 284.

thrown a partisan of the Empire prophesied that the civil government would no longer enforce the payment of the tithes, that Church property would not be safe, that the regular orders would be destroyed, that education would be secularized, and that the whole Church system would be weakened. The prophesy was fulfilled in 1833.

To understand the "Reform of 1833" it is necessary to analyse its causes. On this subject writers have advanced the widest possible variety of explanations. In the opinion of Bancroft, Gómez Farías "labored to crush the politico-theocratic power, and thus save democratic principles and institutions on the basis of an absolute independence between the civil and ecclesiastical jurisdictions."[27] According to this historian, the political activities of the Church were thought to be an obstacle to the development of Mexican democracy. It would be well if he had explained the meaning of "democracy" as understood by the Liberals. Lorenzo de Zavala, caustic critic of the Catholic Church, and an actor in the drama he describes, was of the opinion that the overwhelming wealth and power of the Church made it a menace to the State. He wrote, "The ecclesiastical hierarchy, with its rents, its *fueros*, and its power, is of such a nature that it is not possible to preserve it in a popular government without destroying at the same time the public peace and the principle of equality. He who sanctions its existence sanctions perpetual discord."[28] Many writers are inclined to see pronounced social abuses, in addition to the political and economic, as causes of the Liberal reaction of 1833. The winning of independence resulted in the "degradation of the masses and the elevation of the men of power," writes a recent Mexican historian. He continues, "The high public functionaries, the *mitrados* (prelates), the university doctors, the clergy, the nobility, and the rich proprietors were disposed to annihilate the people who were demanding their rights. . . . And the middle classes, terrorized and fearful of losing their interests, reinforced the aristocratic phalanx in opposition to the popular classes."[29] In the opinion of this historian, and his theory is shared by most

---

[27] H. H. Bancroft, *History of Mexico* (San Francisco, 1888), VI, 583.

[28] Zavala, *op. cit.,* II, 237.

[29] Alfonso Toro, *La Iglesia y El Estado en México* (Mexico, 1927), p. 100.

writers who are not pro-clericals, Gómez Farías assaulted the privileged orders because he was the champion of the rights of the masses.

Ecclesiastical historians, on the other hand, refuse to admit the existence of any abuses in the Church in the years immediately following independence. They deny that Gómez Farías and the Liberals were actuated by deep-seated political, social, and economic motives. To them the whole affair can be simply explained as an atheistic movement aimed at religion itself. Gómez Farías and his followers were all disciples of the devil. Father Mariano Cuevas, in his recent history of the Church in Mexico, attempts to prove that the *Yorkinos* with Poinsett as the directive evil genius, were responsible for the anti-clerical attack. He insinuates that Poinsett bribed Farías, once a faithful Catholic, to join the enemies of the Church. This Jesuit historian achieves the height of absurdity when he asserts that American influence was responsible for the suppression of the University of Mexico because it was painful to Americans to see a Mexican institution so much older than their own universities.[30]

It is the opinion of the present writer that the actual causes of the Reform of 1833 are to be found somewhere between the extreme statements mentioned above. Gómez Farías did not attack Catholicism as a religion. He was no Luther with a program of dogmatic reform, nor was he a Voltaire impatient of all dogma, for he wrote concerning the education of his children, "Keep the Sabbath holy, hear mass on appointed days in church, and observe Christian practices."[31] An analysis of his reform measures fails to reveal any indication of an organized assault on the tenets of Catholicism. On the other hand, another examination of the reform laws fails to prove the existence of a class movement. The "Liberals of 1833," politicians, intellectuals, and professional people, have been unwarrantedly credited with championing the rights of the downtrodden masses. If so, why was not legislation

---

[30] Cuevas, *La Iglesia in México,* V, 196. It is to be hoped that it was not because of statements such as the above that the University of Louvain recently conferred the honorary doctorate on Father Cuevas.

[31] "Reglas que deberán observar mis hijos." Undated MS, Gómez Farías Papers. García Collection.

enacted to benefit the lowest classes? If it was a social movement, why the absence of social legislation? If it is contended
that the Liberals did not have time to enact this legislation,
one might query if they displayed any hesitation in plunging the
country into reform. The truth is that the "masses" were entirely outside the picture and were of little concern to either
party. Bancroft came the closest to the truth when he said that
Gómez Farías "labored to crush the politico-theocratic power."
The political alliance of the clergy and the other elements compos-
ing the Conservative party had to be broken up by destroying
the ecclesiastical *fueros*. And why the attack? It was in order
that the Liberals might seize control of the government and force
the adoption of their *political* program which was intended to
make Mexico safe for democracy, that is, for the Liberals.

Following the overthrow of the Conservative régime of
Bustamante, a new president and vice president were elected.
The victorious candidates were Antonio López de Santa Anna
and Gómez Farías. If Santa Anna belonged to any party, which
was doubtful, he was, like his vice president, a Liberal. At least
he had been fairly consistent up to 1833 in supporting liberal
principles. A new Congress was also elected when the Liberal flood
was at its crest. The result was "the reddest Congress Mexico
had had up to that time." The radical deputies were not inclined to forget the indignities and injuries they had suffered
at the hands of the Conservatives, particularly in the States
where there had been numerous bitter struggles for the possession
of local government.[32] Thus the Congress convened in an atmosphere charged with a spirit of intolerance and vengeance.

From April 1, 1833, to April 24, 1834, with only a few
short interruptions, Santa Anna allowed Gómez Farías to exercise the executive control. The reason for this peculiar procedure
on the part of the President has been the cause of considerable
bewilderment to historians. Some explain that Santa Anna was
never in earnest as a Liberal, but simply wished to use Gómez
Farías as a foil to test public sentiment on a progressive program. Others explain that Santa Anna was really sincere when

---

[32] Riva Palacio, *op. cit.*, IV, 306.

he declared that ill-health kept him on his estate, "Manga de Clavo."[33] "It would seem," says Callcott, "that he was just about neutral in the whole matter, and was carefully watching the signs of the times."[34]

With the alacrity of an impractical idealist and a novice in government, Farías seized the opportunity afforded him by the wily Santa Anna to plunge Mexico into an orgy of reform. Since the Congress worked hand in glove with the Vice President and was thoroughly in accord with his program, it should be understood that the "Reform of 1833" was a coöperative affair. Therefore, when referring to these acts as the work of Gómez Farías it is intended that the Congress should also be included.

Immediately after the deputies had assembled rumors began to circulate that a law was passed in a secret session which declared that the patronage of the Mexican Church resided in national sovereignty, and that ordinances would be issued regulating its exercise. Although the rumored law was not actually adopted until several months later, the clergy charged that the government was irreligious and preached a crusade against it. The Minister of Justice and Ecclesiastical Affairs was finally obliged to issue a circular (June 6, 1833) advising the clergy not to deal with political matters from the pulpit and to restrict their discourses to religious affairs. During the year several more circulars were issued ordering the religious not to mix in political affairs.[35]

The opening gun of the Liberal attack was aimed at the ecclesiastical temporalities. The objectives of the assault were two-fold, that is, it was hoped that by depriving the Church of its wealth not only would it be rendered politically impotent, but the financial straits of the government would be relieved. The opulence of the Church contrasted with the empty public treasury and more than once the authorities were moved to tap the clerical coffers. The Liberals, not being under the restraint of their

---

[33] In a letter to Gómez Farías, dated Manga de Clavo, March 16, 1833, Santa Anna explained that ill-health made it impossible for him to go to the Capital. Gómez Farías Papers.   [34] Callcott, *op. cit.*, p. 100.

[35] Manuel Dublán y José María Lozano (eds.), *Legislación Mexicana* (Mexico, 1876-1904), II, 531-532, 533, 535, 578.

Conservative predecessors, zealously initiated the attack on the ecclesiastical temporalities. On August 17, Congress secularized the missions of Alta and Baja California. The rule of the mission fathers, dating from the days of Junípero Serra, was terminated by the establishment, in the erstwhile mission districts, of parishes with secular clergy. Fifteen hundred *pesos* annually were assigned to meet the expenses of each parish. The mission lands and buildings were confiscated and divided among the settlers and natives. Unfortunately the Indians were defrauded of their lands and the greater part of the old mission estates fell into the hands of political grafters. To defray the expenses assumed in supporting the Church in the Californias, the government drew upon the pious fund of the California missions which had also been confiscated.[36] Father Cuevas asserts that the California missions were secularized because of American influence, for this step would facilitate the separation of California from Mexico. This is just another of the numerous ridiculous assertions contained in his *Historia de la Iglesia en México*. The California missions were selected as the first object of Liberal attack for economic and political reasons. The pious fund and the rich mission lands tempted the impecunious Liberals who were sadly in need of funds to prosecute their program. In addition, it was felt that the mission control of California savored too much of a theocracy which stifled colonization and should therefore be abolished. Later the hospitals, real estate, and other property belonging to the Philippines missions were confiscated. This was in line with the policy to nationalize all pious funds whose revenue went out of the country. On April 16, 1834, all the missions of the republic were ordered secularized and their properties nationalized. The governors of the states were empowered to determine the parish limits in the old mission districts.[37] But, since the economic situation of the government continued to be most precarious, Lorenzo de Zavala presented a proposition in the Chamber of Deputies for the settlement of the public debt. He suggested as the only possible solution of the national financial problem the confiscation of all properties held in mortmain. He

[36] *Ibid.,* II, 603.
[37] *Ibid.,* II, 689.

estimated that the ecclesiastical resources were sufficient to pay off the national debt and support the Church if the latter were under government control.[38] His plan was not adopted, but it was an unmistakable harbinger of future disaster for the clericals. Therefore, many of the religious orders, to defend themselves against impending confiscation, either sold or transferred their properties. These subterfuges were halted by act of Congress which declared the illegality of sale or alienation in any manner of property and capital held in mortmain.[39]

The ecclesiastical monopoly of public education was also attacked because the reformers felt that the Church was using the schools to inculcate its political propaganda in the minds of the tender youths of the country. In the schools the clergy enjoyed an invaluable aid to the perpetuation of their supremacy. No other act of Gómez Farías and the Liberals more exactly illustrates their lack of practical sense than their promulgation of a law which completely secularized public education. That the government was totally unprepared to assume this burden seemed to be an inconsequential detail. Better that the children of Mexico should be without schools of any description, thought the Liberal reformers, than that the public Catholic schools should be allowed to train future champions of the clerical cause. Even the venerable old University of Mexico was suppressed because its faculty was composed of priests. The suppression was announced to the nation thus: "The public is notified that this aristocratic institution, purely a glittering ornament which performs no public educational service, has been abolished." The property of the University and of the College of Santa María de Todos Santos, which was also extinguished, was ordered applied to the support of public education. A committee known as the *Dirección General de Instrucción Pública* was organized to regulate education in all the public institutions of learning supported by the nation in the Federal District and in the territories.[40]

The Liberals were moving inevitably toward the separation of Church and State. The next step taken in that direction was

[38] Bulnes, *op. cit.,* p. 90.

[39] Riva Palacio, *op. cit.,* IV, 334-335.

[40] *Ibid.,* IV, 332; Dublán y Lozano, *op. cit.,* II, 563-566, 574-575.

the passage of a decree (October 27) which freed the citizens of the civil responsibliity of paying the tithes. Prior to this it had been the custom, dating from colonial times, for the government to enforce payment. According to this law the individual was restored complete freedom to act according to the dictates of his conscience. Although the income from the tithes had decreased greatly, and during the five year period from 1829 to 1833 only 5,211,628 *pesos* had been collected, nevertheless the clergy strenuously opposed in principle the withdrawal of State compulsion. They correctly interpreted this act to be a preliminary to the complete withdrawal of governmental support of the Church.[41] So pronounced did clerical opposition become that it was necessary for the Minister of Justice, Ándres Quintana Roo, to issue a circular to the state authorities recommending that they prevent priests from discussing political questions from the pulpits. He declared that the priests should be made to understand that they were subjects of the temporal authority, and that "the president has [had] taken as an invariable rule of conduct the separation of interests of religion from those of the government."[42]

The clerical conscience was scandalized by the passage of another law (November 6) which repealed all laws imposing any kind of compulsion, direct or indirect, on the fulfillment of monastic vows. The religious of both sexes were accorded absolute freedom to forswear their vows and reënter secular life. "This was a blow at the very heart of the Church system," says Callcott. "For a young girl who had taken vows as a 'bride of Christ' to forswear those vows and enter into family life as a wife and mother was not only indecent; it was repulsive and sacrilegious in the extreme."[43]

The recently won independence of the Church, acquired by Bustamante's renunciation of the national patronage, was terminated when the government assumed, as repository of the exercise of sovereignty, the appointment of the officers of the Church. On November 3 Quintana Roo issued a decree revoking the law

---

[41] *Ibid.*, II, 577-578; Victor Quintamilla to Manuel López Escudero, Mexico, February 12, 1834. Riva Palacio Papers.   [42] Riva Palacio, *op. cit.*, IV, 333.
[43] Callcott, *op. cit.*, pp. 92-93; Dublán y Lozano, *op. cit.*, II, 580.

of May 16, 1831, which gave to the clergy the free election of canons. This law was declared to be "a work of violence, an attack on the rights of the nation, and consequently null." On December 17 the government commanded that vacant curacies be filled as provided by the laws of the Indies. The president of the republic and the governors of the states were to exercise the patronal powers formerly possessed by the viceroys, presidents of audiencias, and governors. The restoration of the national patronage, with its implication of the subordination of the Church to the State, was so repugnant to the prelates that they resolved to suffer martyrdom even before obeying the law of December 17. Bishop Vázquez of Puebla called it "a sacrilegious pronouncement against the divine authority of the pope." The Bishop of Monterey declared that the government had invaded the spiritual domain and therefore he could not obey the law. The metropolitan chapter of Mexico protested to Gómez Farías that it could not take an oath to obey a law which, because of its very nature, should be decided by a national council, "or at least by a respectable ecclesiastical *junta* like the one summoned by Iturbide in 1821." On April 22, 1834, the prelates were granted a thirty-day extension, under penalty of exile, to fulfill the law of December 17. Several preferred exile to submission.[44]

The religious reform had been carried forward too far and too rapidly. A general outcry was raised against the Liberal idealists who had thought it easy to reform society profoundly by laws and decrees. Their fallacious reasoning was revealed by the overwhelming opposition which they aroused and the suddenness with which they were ousted from control. A simultaneous attack on the military *fueros* caused the militarists to ally themselves with the clericals under the *Plan de Cuernavaca* to destroy all principles of the Reform and restore the *fueros* in all their purity. Their battle-cry became, "Religión y Fueros." The fanatical masses were easily rallied to the support of the Church for it was not difficult for the clergy to convince the people that their sacred religion was being attacked. The Liberals should have realized the nature of the opposition and proceeded slowly. But

---

[44] Riva Palacio, *op. cit.*, IV, 334-337.

reformers in general, and Latin-American in particular, have decidedly one-tracked minds, and refuse to recognize other more moderate courses leading to the same goal.

Valentín Gómez Farías was not a man who, having gained power, would be willing to temporize merely to retain control, for power was to him only a more efficacious means of expediting the Reform. "He loved his country," said Bulnes, "like the biblical patriarch Abraham loved his son, with dagger upraised over his heart, ready to kill if liberty, the god of his tabernacle, so willed it."[45]

When Santa Anna had definitely decided in which direction the opinion of the influential tended, he determined to abandon his retreat in his hacienda and assume the leadership of the Conservative reaction—whatever might have been his opinions in the past. He revealed himself, thereby, to be an astute politician who follows public opinion and not a statesman who moulds it. Santa Anna returned to the capital, says Alamán, "as the supporter of the discontented and the hope of the persecuted and the plaintful." The aristrocrats and the high officers of the Church who had looked upon him with disdain, now appealed to him to save them from the reformists.[46]

The trust of the clericals was not misplaced, for Santa Anna proved to be the savior of the Church. He immediately dissolved the Congress and issued a series of executive decrees suspending the various anti-religious laws, "until a general Congress should meet." Needless to say he was in no hurry about convoking another Congress. To satisfy the clergy he named as Minister of Justice and Ecclesiastical Affairs, Bishop Juan Cayetano Portugal of Michoacán. *Te Deums* were sung in praise of Santa Anna, "El Salvador." The clergy were commanded by the metropolitan chapter to say prayers for "the great and virtuous chief Don Antonio López de Santa Anna, restorer of the liberty of the Church."[47] "Viva la Religión y el ilustre Santa Anna," shouted the masses. The Liberals were denounced as heretics and dangerous citizens, and Gómez Farías had to bear the brunt of

[45] Bulnes, *Júarez y las Revoluciones de Ayutla*, p. 87.
[46] Riva Palacio, *op. cit.*, IV, 338.
[47] *Ibid.*, IV, 345-346.

the attack. He was finally forced to leave the country amid cries of "arch-fiend" and "Judas."

The delayed election of a new Congress was held in December, 1834. As was to be expected, the military-clerical coalition emerged victorious. On January 4, 1835, the Congress assembled in Mexico City, determined to translate the *Plan de Cuernavaca* into legal action. This meant the abrogation of the various reforms of the Liberal régime (for they had only been suspended by Santa Anna), and the substitution for the federal system, of the centralistic form of government.

One of the first acts of the reactionary Congress was to declare the office of the vice presidency legally vacant. Gómez Farías had been living in exile for nearly six months. The University of Mexico was reëstablished and a committee was organized to formulate a plan of public instruction. This action constituted recognition, by the Conservatives, that the old school system as controlled by the Church was defective and needed reform. Other measures of the Liberals which were revoked were the secularization of the California missions and the depriving of the religious communities of the free right to dispose of their properties.[48]

When Santa Anna betrayed a tendency to vacillate in his support of the *Plan de Cuernavaca*, which Dr. Arrillaga, clerical leader, said the nation supported for no other reason than because of the attack on religion, he was subjected to such severe criticism and opposition that he preferred to retire to his hacienda. On January 28, 1835, General Miguel Barragán was named president *ad interim*. It seemed impossible now that anything could disturb the triumph of the clericals. Yet trouble started almost immediately when the Minister of Justice and Ecclesiastical Affairs, Joaquín de Iturbide,[49] incorporated in his departmental report a defence of national patronage. This statement created a furore among the clergy, who rushed to the capital in great numbers to fight personally for the abrogation

---

[48] Dublán y Lozano, *op. cit.*, III, 39-40, 96.

[49] Bishop Portugal had resigned from the Ministry of State as a protest against Santa Anna's inclination to favor national patronage. (Toro, *op. cit.*, p. 120.)

27

of the laws. In this they were temporarily successful for the various laws that established national patronage were revoked.

The old privileged status of the Catholic Church having been restored, the Assembly turned to the fulfillment of another pledge of the *Plan de Cuernavaca*, that is, the establishment of a centralistic government. By decree of October 3, 1835, centralism was proclaimed, and on December 30, 1836, a centralistic constitution was promulgated. This constitution, known as *Las Siete Leyes*, contained substantially the same provisions regarding the Church as the Constitution of 1824. But this was very displeasing to the clergy, for they hoped to establish their complete independence of the temporal authorities. The incorporation into the fundamental charter of clauses providing for the *pase* for all pontifical communications, and the assuming by the government, until the conclusion of a concordat, of the right of presentation, were vigorously opposed by the clergy but to no effect. Although there was dissatisfaction because of certain features of the centralistic constitution, the religious wisely recognized the inestimable value of its guarantees and hastened to swear oaths of allegiance to it.[50]

Notwithstanding the failure of the clergy to force upon the Assembly all of the constitutional guarantees they wished, they were able, after the promulgation of that instrument, to remain in the political ascendancy for quite a time. In illustration of the extent of the clerical reaction: when the pope issued a brief (1836) authorizing a reduction in the number of religious feast days, the Chamber of Deputies which was made up of priests and their partisans, refused admission to the brief because of the injury this would cause the clergy, who derived financial profit from the fiestas. Little consideration was given to the economic advantage to the country at large that would result from a decrease in the number of days of idleness. It would appear, then, that the Mexican Conservatives were more clerical than the pope. It was not until 1839 that the *pase* was granted to the brief of Gregory XVI.[51]

Since ecclesiastical affairs were so satisfactorily settled for

---

[50] Riva Palacio, *op. cit.*, IV, 386.

[51] Toro, *op. cit.*, p. 126.

the Church, it was but natural that the pope should accord political recognition to the Mexican Republic. In November, 1836, Manuel Díaz de Bonilla was received as the official Mexican representative and the pope dispatched an internuncio to Mexico. Since papal funds were low it was agreed that the internuncio was to be supported by the Mexican government. This illustrates the extent of the reaction under President Anastacio Bustamante, who, under clerical auspices, had assumed the presidency in 1837. Bishop Vázquez of Puebla received a papal commission to institute canonical processes for the filling of vacant bishoprics. Accordingly several sees were filled, including that of Mexico which had become vacant when Archbishop Fonte died after living for many years in exile. By brief of April 25, 1837, the diocese of Chiapas was detached from the archdiocese of Guatemala, and united to that of Mexico. The Holy See, however, displayed reluctance to negotiate a concordat with Mexico. Minister Bonilla was told by the Cardinal-Secretary that a concordat was inadvisable, but that a project could be negotiated concerning the problems of the tithes and appointments.[52] The pope evidently was unwilling, as were the Mexican prelates, to recognize national patronage.

President Bustamante, champion of the Church though he was, again aroused clerical opposition. The perennial financial embarrassments of the government necessitated numerous plans to raise money, none of which availed. Since no one but the clergy had money, the popular demand was that Church properties should be mortgaged. Bustamante, seeing no other escape, invited the clericals to make a loan. The metropolitan chapter acceded, but limited the loan to 750,000 *pesos*. Fears that this was but a prelude to a wholesale confiscation of Church properties and wealth, caused the clericals to withdraw their support from Bustamante. The Liberals, witnessing this division in the ranks of their enemies, took courage, and labored for a return to power.

A revolt against Bustamante occurred in 1840, but the time for the reëstablishment of Liberalism had not arrived. Instead,

---

[52] Cabañas, *op. cit.*, pp. LXX-LXXII.

as a result of bewildering military plots and counterplots, the irrepressible Santa Anna was restored to supremacy with a program of "personalistic centralism." Santa Anna was felicitated by the clergy on the triumph of the revolution, but not so enthusiastically as in 1834. Before long it became alarmingly apparent to the clergy that they had erred grievously in deserting Bustamante for the wily lord of Manga del Clavo. The latter was more aggressive than his predecessor in reminding the ecclesiastics of their duty as citizens to contribute to the common expenses of the government. He commenced by demanding that the chapter of Mexico cover the unpaid part of the loan demanded by the preceding administration. The pious fund of the California missions was again nationalized, silver plate deposited in the cathedral of Puebla was confiscated, religious orders were forced to make contributions, and the Archbishop of Mexico was obliged to accept drafts up to 170,000 *pesos*. To prevent the sale of ecclesiastical property to escape the burden placed upon it by the government, civil permits for all bills of sale were required. Later the government issued orders prohibiting the sale of Church jewels. The guilty parties were to be treated as robbers. Santa Anna was not unfriendly or antagonistic toward the Church, for witness his decree allowing the Jesuits and members of monastic orders to reënter the country. He merely refused to countenance the clerical habit of looking upon all governments as if they were the servants of the Church, and, on the other hand, of never wishing to spend a cent for their support.[53]

The Congress, assembled on June 10, 1842, to produce a new constitution, in accordance with the *Plan de Tacubaya*, proved to be liberal and federalistic. Since the deputies would not acquiesce in the wishes of Santa Anna, who wanted centralism with himself as the center, he retired in a huff to his hacienda and left the constituents to draft a liberal, federal, instrument of government. The new project, while still in the embryonic stage, was criticised by the reactionary press as an attack on the Catholic faith and the honor and dignity of the army. One

---

[53] Dublán y Lozano, *op. cit.*, IV, 111, 301-302, 363; Toro, *op. cit.*, pp. 134, 141-142.

diatribe is worthy of being quoted. It read:

When the nation was declared united in 1821 its first desire was that of conserving the religion of our fathers without contact with or tolerance of any other; that was the first of the articles of the *Plan de Iguala;* that was repeated in the *Acta Constitutiva* of January 31, 1824; the same was said in the federal constitution of October 4 of the same year, and in the particular constitutions of all the states, and in the constitutional laws of 1836. In vain did some attempt to prevent that religion from being professed exclusively; that religion which is the one divine, true, and only one which can save man. In spite of this, there now come some young Protestant apprentices, saying in Article 31 of the constitutional project, "The Nation professes the Roman Catholic Apostolic religion, and does not permit the public exercise of any other." Then its authors pretend that it admits the private exercise of other cults, and no inhabitant of the republic can be persecuted who erects a chapel or oratory, not public, in which he, his family and his servants can worship. . . . But still in Article 13 we read: "Private instruction is free." Thus Protestants, atheists, and deists can establish private schools and teach their beliefs. Could a committee of atheists do more?[54]

Santa Anna's henchmen easily accomplished the dissolution of the federalist Congress, and a "safe" *Junta* of Notables was convened to produce a "satisfactory" fundamental charter. On June 13, 1843, the *Bases Orgánicas*, the third of Mexico's national constitutions, was adopted. This instrument declared that the nation professed and protected the Roman Catholic religion to the exclusion of any other. Also, the military and ecclesiastical *fueros* were recognized. In this constitution were to be found the customary features regarding the negotiation of concordats and the admission of pontifical communications.[55]

From the middle of June, 1834, to the early part of 1846, says Father Cuevas, the Mexican Church enjoyed a period of relative tranquillity. By this he probably means that, during this period, no serious attack was made on Church property, which indeed was the case. His explanation of this favorable state of affairs is that the *Yorkinos* did not have their customary Amer-

---

[54] Riva Palacio, *op. cit.,* IV, 491.
[55] For the *Leyes Bases Orgánicas de 1843,* see Gamboa, *op. cit.,* pp. 428-482.

ican aid. Cuevas attributes all the vicissitudes of the Church and of the Mexican nation to the insidious influence of the Masons and the Yankees.[56] But the greatly increased financial burden placed on the State, because of the American war, caused the government to turn once more to the clergy for financial succor. The Church was powerful in official councils at the beginning of the war with the United States. In January, 1846, General Paredes, at the head of a coalition of ecclesiastical, military, and monarchial groups, seized control of the government. This general, who had shamefully diverted his army which had been organized at great national sacrifice to oppose the impending invasion by the United States, was "elected" president of the Republic by a *Junta* presided over by Archbishop Posada. Paredes was entirely clerical and ultramontane in his sympathies. He chose the Bishop of Chiapas as his Minister of Justice and Ecclesiastical Affairs, and in his summons for an extraordinary Congress he assigned twenty of the seats to the ecclesiastical prelates.[57]

Paredes, however, needed money to prosecute the war. In April he called on the Church to contribute 200,000 *pesos* per month for the support of the government. The clergy protested and the Archbishop declared that the share assigned to the archiepiscopal see, 98,000 *pesos*, was more than its total revenue. Paredes' tenure of power was of short duration, for in August, 1846, he was overthrown by Santa Anna and Gómez Farías, the former now posing as a federalist and champion of the Constitution of 1824. General Salas, puppet of Santa Anna, acted as provisional president while his master assumed control of the army. To aid Santa Anna in organizing the military resources, General Salas ordered all property owners, civilian and ecclesiastical, to pay to the government a sum equal to one month's rent. This contribution was to be paid in four parts distributed over a period of four months. Since this expedient was a failure, the provisional president ordered the issuance of letters of credit up to 2,000,000 *pesos* charged to the secular and regular clergy. This sum was to be guaranteed by designated Church proper-

---

[56] Cuevas, *op. cit.*, p. 234.

[57] Dublán y Lozano, *op. cit.*, V, 105-120.

ties, and in order that there should be no evasion, the clergy were prohibited from alienating property.[58]

Late in December Santa Anna and Gómez Farías were elected president and vice-president respectively. Once more Santa Anna refrained from assuming the executive control, but instead, led an army against the invading Americans, and left Gómez Farías at the capital in control of the government. The Vice President was no longer a zealous reformer, for years spent in exile had cooled his idealistic ardor. There was no danger, then, of a renewal of his old reform program, but necessity compelled him to seek clerical aid to finance the war. The condition of the public finances was distressing; the treasury was completely exhausted, and the Congress was at its wit's end to meet the urgent pleas of Santa Anna for food, clothing, and munitions for his troops. With affairs in this critical state, Santa Anna wrote Gómez Farías confidentially suggesting that he have the Congress authorize a loan secured by a mortgage of Church property. The bill was passed after a stormy session at 10 a.m. on January 10, 1847. By 12 noon the archiepiscopal chapter of Mexico had filed a protest, declaring that the law was contrary to an act of the Council of Trent and that the Church would not observe it. Furthermore, anyone who should attempt to enforce the law would be excommunicated. Despite the clerical protest Gómez Farías issued an executive decree providing that the government should raise 15,000,000 *pesos* by mortgaging or selling ecclesiastical property held in mortmain, excepting that of educational and charitable institutions.[59]

The clergy complained bitterly and many churches were closed in protest; but the government ordered them reopened. Although Santa Anna had written Gómez Farías congratulating him on the passage of the law, he unexpectedly altered his attitude and deserted his vice president. On March 29, 1847, he issued a decree revoking the law of January 10, in return for a cash payment of $2,000,000 by the clergy. In short, he accepted a bribe to restrain the attack on the clerical temporalities. A second time Gómez Farías was disgraced and forced out of office be-

---

[58] *Ibid.*, V, 211-217; Riva Palacio, *op. cit.*, IV, 592, 598.

[59] *Ibid.*, IV, 589-608; Dublán y Lozano, V, 246-248.

cause of his crafty, treacherous colleague. Since Gómez Farías would not resign the Congress proceeded to abolish the office of the vice presidency. Once more the Church had successfully withstood a determined effort to destroy its temporalities.

Under President José Joaquín Herrera (1848-1851), who enjoyed the distinction of being the first president since Guadalupe Victoria to serve out his full term of office, the Church gained in wealth and influence. It became the dominant factor in Mexican politico-economic affairs. In evidence of Mexico's loyalty to Catholicism and to the head of the Church, President Herrera invited Pope Pius IX, at that time beset with political difficulties, to move the papal see to Mexico. The Congress, no less Catholic than the president, voted a gift of 25,000 *pesos* to the pope.[60]

Because of his desire to see the great number of ecclesiastical vacancies in Mexico filled, President Herrera secured the passage of a temporary law providing for appointments until a concordat should be concluded. This law required the chapters of vacant sees to present to the government a list of at least three names from which one was to be selected to be presented to the pope. The clergy opposed the law because of their desire to be free of all dependence on the civil power. Nevertheless they acquiesced and submitted the lists. The names of those selected by the government for the vacancies were then sent to the pope by a special envoy who was instructed to request that, in the bulls of institution the clause *motu proprio* be omitted. The pope consented and preconized those presented by the Mexican government.[61]

After the retirement of Herrera, a feeble and corrupt Liberal régime was terminated in short order by a Conservative revolt initiated under the *Plan de Hospicio* (July 1852). There had been many *pronunciamientos* of the military in Mexico, but this was the first proclaimed by the clericals. The plan was formulated in the cathedral chapter of Guadalajara. The revolt resulted eventually in the recall of Santa Anna from his most recent "perpetual exile" to run as the Conservative candidate

---

[60] Riva Palacio, *op. cit.*, IV, 638-639.
[61] Cuevas, *op. cit.*, V, 269-270.

for the presidency. Santa Anna, while in exile, had been in correspondence with Lucas Alamán, spokesman of the Conservatives, and he returned with the understanding that he would be supported if he agreed to a program of cessation of political activity against the Church and security for the holders of large propertied interests. Alamán told Santa Anna, "It is absolutely necessary to support the Catholic religion . . . for we consider it to be the only common link which ties all Mexicans."[62]

On March 17, 1853, Santa Anna was elected president, and Lucas Alamán was made his Minister of Foreign Relations. The staunch old clerical and monarchial champion died in June, but the president, not unmindful of his obligations to the clericals, made an effort to continue the policies initiated by Alamán. The Mexican minister at Rome was ordered to reopen the subject of a concordat. By 1854 the negotiations had proceeded to the working out of details, but the Revolution of Ayutla broke them off. Santa Anna also adopted, with clerical support, Alamán's plan to secure a European sovereign for a Mexican throne. It is doubtful if he was a sincere monarchist. He probably hoped to manipulate the movement, as Iturbide had done, for his own advancement. The Jesuits were reintroduced into Mexico to assist in the education of the poorer classes and much of their property was restored to them. Also, he revoked the decree of November 6, 1833, which denied protection of the laws for the fulfillment of monastic vows. But, notwithstanding his acts favorable to the Church, Santa Anna did not intend to relinquish control to the clergy. This was made apparent by a decree which provided that the *fueros* were not to be effective in crimes of conspiracy.

Popular fear of the over-ambitious dictator, whose full official title was "Benmérito de la patria, General de División, Gran Maestre de la Nacional y distinguida Orden de Guadalupe, Gran Cruz de la Real y distinguida Orden española de Carlos III, y Presidente de la República Mexicana," finally accomplished his overthrow. "The discovery of the monarchist intrigue, the sale of La Mesilla, the declaration of the perpetual dictator-

[62] Toro, *op. cit.*, pp. 205, 209.

ship, the despoiliations of the *camarilla* of Santa Anna, which caused a deficit of more than 20,000,000 *pesos* annually, the hateful, ridiculous, and ruinous contributions that were invented to cover it, killed the patience of the people, and provoked a real revolution, the most sanguinary that had been seen in Mexico since the wars for independence."[63] The Liberal *Plan de Ayutla* (March 1, 1854) not only initiated a revolt which accomplished the definitive extrusion of Santa Anna from the political stage of Mexico, but inaugurated the most bitter and devastating attack which the Catholic Church had ever experienced in the land of the Aztecs.

---

[63] *Ibid.,* p. 231.

CHAPTER XV

CHURCH AND STATE CONFLICT
IN MEXICO: 1855-1874

In its inception the Revolution of Ayutla was hardly more than a national protest against a man who, consumed by ambition, aspired to the establishment of absolutism. Santa Anna taxed to the limit the patience of civilized society, says Bulnes, and therefore he was rejected by "a formidable and tacit coalition of all the sensible political elements of the nation."[1] All factions, the Liberals, Moderates, and Conservatives were represented in the movement which accomplished the overthrow of the dictator. After the flight of Santa Anna, however, each faction tried to perpetuate its interests and make the revolution its own. The reactionaries were determined to establish guarantees for the clerical and military privileges and secure the ascendancy of the great landlords. They hoped to turn back the clock to the good old colonial times of special privilege. Modernism should not be tolerated in Mexico. The Liberal group, composed of class-conscious mestizos and Indians, and a few creoles, "aimed at the emancipation of the country from ecclesiastical domination, and at the release of the government from military adventurers who dominated through identity of interest with the Church."[2] They proposed to make the revolution a real one and create a society based on modern principles. This conflict of economic, racial, and social interests made for civil war, which in turn opened the way for the first serious effort in Mexican history to create a democratic and constitutional government. Unlike the innumerable praetorian revolts which had distraught Mexico during the first quarter-century of her independence, the conflict which raged after the overthrow of Santa Anna was

---

[1] Bulnes, *Juárez y Las Revoluciones de Ayutla y de Reforma*, p. 117.
[2] Priestley, *The Mexican Nation*, p. 317.

Mexico's first really popular revolution—and for that reason it triumphed.

A Liberal revolutionary *junta* which met in Cuernavaca on October 4, 1855, and which was presided over by the old Liberal reformer Valentín Gómez Farías, elected Juan Álvarez provisional president of Mexico. Álvarez appointed as his ministers Ignacio Comonfort (War), Melchor Ocampo (State), Guillermo Prieto (Treasury), Benito Juárez (Justice and Ecclesiastical Affairs), and Miguel Lerdo de Tejada (Public Works). Álvarez and Juárez were full-blooded Indians, a clear indication that a new class was coming to the front in Mexico. All members of the cabinet were Masons, and, with the possible exception of Comonfort, they were anti-clericals, a situation which boded ill for the Catholic Church.[3]

On November 23, 1855, the Minister of Justice and Ecclesiastical Affairs led the initial assault on the breastworks of intrenched privilege when he issued a decree which popularly bears his name, *Ley Juárez*. This decree suppressed all special courts except the military and the ecclesiastical; and, as for these, they were deprived of all jurisdiction in civil suits. The military courts were to have jurisdiction only in cases arising from military crimes. The ecclesiastical tribunals were to hear common crimes of the members of their *fuero*, but it was provided that even the *fuero eclesiástico* was renunciable in common crimes. An accused religious could choose a civil or ecclesiastical court at will.[4]

The abolition of the special tribunals was a desirable and necessary measure, for the doctrine of equality before the law opposed the *fueros*. The principles of the *Ley Juárez* were sound and logical, but, like Gómez Farías in 1833, Benito Juárez displayed little tact in initiating the reform. The time was not propitious for embarking upon an anti-clerical program, for not only were the clergy violently opposed to reform, but the Moderates were gravely distrustful, and in the mestizos and Indians there still lingered a fear of the privileged orders. In addition,

---

[3] Callcott, *Church and State in Mexico,* pp. 235-236; Cuevas, *La Iglesia en México,* V, 285.

[4] Dublán y Lozano, *Legislación Mexicana,* VII, 598.

division was appearing in the ranks of the Liberals; there was a tendency to divide into antagonistic groups of Radicals and Moderates. With the political situation such as it was, and with public opinion divided on the advisability of religious reform, tact would have dictated a cautious period of preparation before issuing a law so fraught with potential dissension as the *Ley Juárez*. But Benito Juárez was another born reformer who did not know the meaning of temporization.

As was to be expected immediate and vehement clerical opposition was aroused by the decree which reorganized the judicial administration. On November 27, 1855, the Archbishop of Mexico wrote Juárez a protest. He declared that the ecclesiastical privilege of special courts had been generally recognized since the establishment of the Church in New Spain; that it was in fact an essential and inherent element of the Church, and that the only legitimate and canonical procedure for modifying it was through appeal to the pope. Juárez replied that the measure did not touch religion in any way, and that the sole purpose of promulgating the decree was to establish social equality.[5] Clerical opponents of the *Ley Juárez* claimed that the dignity of the Church and the maintenance of a respected priesthood required separate trials for the clergy. The granting to the accused of the privilege of renouncing the ecclesiastical *fuero*, was condemned as conducing to the defeat of justice by placing the courts at the disposition of the criminal, and not the criminal at the disposition of the courts. The clergy were ordered not to renounce their *fueros* under pain of drastic ecclesiastical penalties.

Since the *Ley Juárez* also struck at the privileges of the military, once more the Church and army united in defense of their *fueros*. Again the battle-cry was: *Religión y Fueros!* In evidence of this union can be cited the Conservative-clerical conspiracy headed by Padre Francisco Javier Miranda and General José Uraga. Their plan embodied the following three main points: (1) deposition of President Álvarez; (2) respect for and defense of Church property and prohibition of publi-

---

[5] Fortino Hipólito Vera (ed.), *Colección de Documentos Eclesiásticos de México* (Amecameca, 1887), II, 91; Dublán y Lozano, *op. cit.*, VII, 614.

cations in criticism of the clergy; and (3) restoration of the Constitution of 1824.[6] The opposition to the government, both from without and within, forced Álvarez to relinquish the presidency to Comonfort (December 12, 1855). This political shift signified a temporary swing of influence to the side of the Moderates.

Ignacio Comonfort, a semi-Conservative and "friend at court for the clergy,"[7] selected for his cabinet men of only moderately liberal ideas, and there was not a Mason among them. It is not to be presumed, however, that Comonfort was a tool of the clericals. His suppression of the Puebla rebellion proves the contrary. Opposition to the *Ley Juárez* was so pronounced in Puebla, a clerical stronghold, that an armed insurrection was incited and financed by the clergy. Comonfort vigorously suppressed the revolt, but at considerable expense to the public treasury. He then issued a decree (March 31, 1856), ordering the sequestration of property of the diocese of Puebla in sufficient amount to reimburse the government for the expenses incurred in quelling the uprising. The governor of the State was given dictatorial power to put the decree into effect, and an office was established for the handling of the confiscated property.[8] This drastic measure was designed to serve as a warning to the clergy that further resistance would be met by the confiscation of their temporalities. The ecclesiastics, with their accustomed stubbornness, refused to take heed.

In the meantime, the Constituent Congress, which had been called by President Álvarez, as provided by the *Plan de Ayutla*, was formally convened on February 18, 1856. The session was opened with cries of "Viva el Congreso Constituyente! Viva Comonfort! Viva la libertad! Mueran los reaccionarios!" The delegates had been elected by a complicated, indirect method, and no ecclesiastic was allowed to vote or be voted for. There was frank and deliberate design on the part of the Liberals to secure complete control of the Congress. The great Conservative leaders, and naturally the clerics, were not present and even

---

[6] Riva Palacio, *México á Través de Los Siglos,* V, 87.

[7] Callcott, *op. cit.,* p. 237.

[8] Dublán y Lozano, VIII, 143-144.

the moderates were only partially represented. If the Constituent Congresses of 1856 and 1916 had been really popular, representative bodies, the Constitutions of 1857 and 1917 would have been more generally acceptable. A constitution which is a party or factional pronouncement cannot be enduring. The great majority of the constituents of 1856 were lawyers. The rest were militarists and employees of the Federal and State governments. The industrial, commercial, and laboring elements were not represented in the personnel of the Convention; the majority of the delegates were political theorists more interested in theory than in economic matters. Says Bulnes, "The constituents represented a country which did not eat, or drink, or sleep, or work. . . . The country of the constituents was occupied only by two groups of incorporeal choirists, without any other function than to intone theocratic or demagogic hymns."[9] Such was the personnel of the Convention, which, in open session, set itself to the task of formulating a new democratic constitution for Mexico. A committee composed of seven members was appointed on February 21 to prepare the draft of a constitution. The committee's project was not reported to the Convention until June 16. After that date it was debated article by article. Until the Congress should conclude its labors, Comonfort promulgated a temporary plan of government known as the *Estatuto Orgánico Provisional*. By this instrument the clergy were denied the right of citizenship.[10]

Since the *Ley Juárez* was only an executive decree of the provisional government, although it enjoyed the force of a regular legislative act, it was deemed advisable to secure its ratification by the Constituent Congress. This action would not only give the decree a more "popular" character, but would commit the Congress to the abolition of the *fueros*. Therefore the *Ley Juárez* was submitted for the approval of the Congress, and, after a two days' debate, it was adopted by a vote of 82 to 1. A few of the delegates, although approving the measure in principle, expressed some doubt as to the legitimacy and advisability of

---

[9] Bulnes, *op. cit.*, pp. 214-215.

[10] Francisco Zarco, *Historia del Congreso Estraordinario Constituyente de 1856 y 1857* (Mexico, 1857), I, 61, 306-326, 467-487.

passing upon it at that time. The subject belonged to the constitution, they felt, and should not be discussed until after the constitutional project had been submitted by the committee. Zarco,
the historian of the Convention, after recording the passage of
the law, writes with enthusiasm: "No more *fueros!* No more
privileges! No more exceptions! Equality for all citizens! Perfect sovereignty of the temporal power! Justice for all!"[11]

On June 25, 1856, the second notable anti-clerical reform
measure was promulgated. This decree, named the *Ley Lerdo*
from its author Lerdo de Tejada, Minister of the Treasury,
provided that no corporation, civil or ecclesiastical, would be
permitted to acquire or own real property, except that which
was directly used for the purposes of worship. The properties
then owned by such corporations would be sold at a price which
at six per cent would yield the rent actually being charged.
Tenants were to be given first choice to purchase, but if they
did not take proper steps to secure their rights within three
months, the property would be offered for public sale at the
same price. Properties not rented or leased would be sold at
public auction. All sales were subject to the payment of the
alcabala, or sales tax, at five per cent. The law did not confiscate property; it decreed the necessity of alienating Church
realty held in mortmain and turning back the proceeds to the
Church.

The purpose of the *Ley Lerdo* was explained in a circular
which accompanied the decree. The object of the measure, according to Lerdo de Tejada, was to make all large property-
holders disgorge and sell to the middle and poor classes, thereby
making real property more mobile and conducing to its improvement and development. It would tend to equalize the taxation of
all real estate and increase the revenue of the government by
the receipts from the *alcabala* and other forms of taxation.[12]
It is to be noted that Lerdo de Tejada emphasized only the economic advantages of the measure. He remained silent on the
political aspects of the law which were extremely important,
for it was hoped that the disamortization of Church properties

---

[11] *Ibid.,* I, 166-182.   [12] Dublán y Lozano, VIII, 197-201.

would destroy the political influence of the Church.

The decree of disamortization was submitted to the Congress for its approval on June 28, 1856. Rules of procedure were set aside and all efforts of the opposition to block the measure were futile. After a short debate, the decree was approved on the same day by a vote of 84 to 8. Francisco Zarco defended the *Ley Lerdo* as a moderate measure. He said that the Reforms of 1833 and 1847 had failed because they were too radical. The law of disamortization, on the other hand, did not confiscate, it merely changed the form of property and reimbursed the owner. The right of ecclesiastical corporations to perform all economic functions except that of owning real property was not questioned. Convents, churches, clerical residences, and educational and charitable institutions were not disturbed.[13]

The *Ley Lerdo*, an act that would be deserving of the severest condemnation in a modern, progressive country, was a legitimate measure in the Mexico of 1856. On the eve of the Reform the Church was said to own over one-third of the land in Mexico. It is not possible, nor indeed is it necessary, to give in exact figures the amount of clerical capital, for there is little disagreement that the Church was unbelievably rich, controlling all agricultural activity by means of heavy mortgages and enjoying an enormous revenue. This concentration of wealth, for obvious reasons, was economically bad, but it was made doubly so since it was used to control public opinion for the support of the reactionary clerical program. Since the political aim of the Mexican Church was a reversion to the medieval theocratic State, it was best for Mexico that the reaction be halted at any cost—even at the expense of depriving the Church of its temporalities. If the disamortization law was drastic, the clergy themselves were to blame because of their refusal to recognize the existence of a modern world.

The economic results of the *Ley Lerdo*, for the eighteen months when it was in force, were disappointing to the Mexican government. The law did not fulfill its object of creating a new class of small landholders. Instead it made a few rich men richer

---

[13] *Ibid.*, VIII, 202; Zarco, *op. cit.*, I, 593-605.

and concentrated the land in large holdings. The poor, whom
the law was intended to benefit, did not buy the land, either
because they did not have sufficient money to pay the registry
fees, or because they were unwilling to run the risk of clerical
maledictions. The Indians and mestizos remained as innocent of
private land ownership as before. The Church now had large
sums of money to reinvest, and consequently its economic influence was not diminished. It even managed to hold property
by proxy, for many of the tenants of clerical lands had the
property adjudicated to them to keep in trust.[14]

The promulgation of the disamortization law stirred up a
veritable hornet's nest of clerical and Conservative opposition.
The attack on its property was regarded as a sword's thrust
at the very heart of the Church. Archbishop Garza immediately
(July 7, 1856) penned a vigorous protest to the government.
He declared that, although not personally opposed, as a prelate
he was forced to fight, for the government had no jurisdiction
over the Church, even as to its property rights. He said he would
defend the position of the Church until the Holy See had approved the law.[15] Bishop Labastida of Puebla was so violent in
his protests that President Comonfort was forced to exile him.
Bishops Clemente de Jesús Munguía called the *Ley Lerdo ciso-
mática, anárquica, impolítica y estéril.* All tenants of clerical
lands were threatened with dire consequences if they dared to
denounce the properties occupied by them. Because they purchased the residences in which they lived, the dean and two
canons of the cathedral chapter of Mexico were suspended by
the Archbishop.

In a papal allocution, date December 15, 1856, Pope Pius IX
condemned the reform legislation: "In order that the faithful
who live there [Mexico] may know and the Catholic world may
understand that we energetically reprove all that the Mexican
government has done against the Catholic religion, against the
Church and its sacred ministers and pastors, against its laws,
rights, and properties, as well as against the authority of this
Holy See, we lift our pontifical voice with apostolic freedom,

---

[14] Phipps, *The Agrarian Question in Mexico,* pp. 79-80.
[15] Vera, *op. cit.,* III, 201 ff.

in this full assembly to condemn, reprove, and declare null and void the said decrees, and whatever else the civil authority has put into effect with such contempt of ecclesiastical authority and this Apostolic See."[16] Numerous seditious pamphlets were published by the clergy. One of them read, in part, as follows: "Attention, Mexicans! Alarm! Observe with fear how the government of the tyrant Comonfort has calumniated the innocent priests of San Francisco,[17] only to seize the silver of the Church, and [how he has] begun to destroy our religion, and to profane those holy places that Martin Luther and Peter (sic) Calvin would respect. Do not permit that! Death before the destruction of religion! Eternal hate to the tyrants! The curse of God fall upon those men of nefarious memory; upon these sacrilegious robbers. . . . Viva the immunity of the Church!"[18]

The envenomed fierceness with which the clergy resisted provoked new reform measures, some of which really did assault the purely spiritual dominion of the Church. Decrees were issued allowing those who had taken religious vows to forswear them and once more the Jesuits, who had been readmitted into Mexico by Santa Anna, were expelled from the country. The University of Mexico was closed on the charge that it was a source of pernicious doctrine and a center of clerical propaganda. The control of the cemeteries which had been wholly vested in the Church was taken from it and given to the Department of Public Hygiene. The clerics had been too prone in the past to refuse burial because the families of the deceased did not have the means to meet the exorbitant burial charges. Another law provided for the civil registration of vital statistics.[19]

On April 11, 1857, Comonfort signed a decree of Minister Iglesias (hence the name of the law: *Ley Iglesias*), which pro-

---

[16] *Ibid.,* I, 585-589.

[17] The friars of the convent of San Francisco in Mexico City were caught red-handed fomenting a revolt. President Comonfort, thereupon, ordered the suppression of the convent, the nationalization of its property, and the opening of a street through the premises of the convent. (Dublán y Lozano, *op. cit.,* VIII, 244-245.)

[18] Toro, *La Iglesia y El Estado en México,* p. 308.

[19] Dublán y Lozano, *op. cit.,* VII, 266-267; VIII, 154; Riva Palacio, *op. cit.,* V, 770.

hibited coaction of the government in the collection of parochial subventions and limited the fees for the performance of religious ceremonies. If the recipient of the religious service was not earning a living wage, the clergy were required to perform their duties for charity. Although this law was very clearly of a retaliatory, as well as of a reformist nature, clerical abuses legitimized its promulgation. The fees were numerous and heavy and often the priests were heartless in squeezing the *centavos* from their poverty-stricken parishioners. In commenting on the exorbitant fees for marriages, H. G. Ward, first British minister to Mexico wrote: "In states where the daily wages of the labourer do not exceed two *reales* and where a cottage can be built for four dollars, its unfortunate inhabitants are forced to pay twenty-two dollars for their marriage fees; a sum which exceeds half their yearly earnings, in a country where Feast and Fast days reduce the number of *días útiles* (on which labour is permitted) to about one hundred and seventy-five. The consequence is, that the Indian either cohabits with his future wife until she becomes pregnant (when the priest is compelled to marry them with or without fees), or, if more religiously disposed, contracts debts and even commits thefts, rather than not satisfy the demands of the ministers of that religion, the spirit of which appears to be so little understood."[20]

The Constitution of 1857 embodied the religious policy of the Liberals. Thus, public education was declared to be free (Article 3). This article was put into the Constitution despite arguments of its opponents who contended that freedom of education would give complete license for charlatans to prey upon the public. Article 5 nullified the compulsory observance of religious vows. Although this provision did not abolish the monastic orders, it contained the germ of their suppression. It struck at the very foundation of the Church, claimed the ecclesiastics, "for if religious vows were not supported by the government, the regular clergy of both sexes would leave their institutions and enter into a state of matrimony, thus bringing scandal upon their organizations and undoing much of the work accomplished

[20] H. G. Ward, *Mexico in 1827* (London, 1828), I, 336.

at so great a cost."[21] The *Ley Juárez* was constitutionalized as Article 13, which prohibited *fueros*, or special tribunals. Likewise, Article 27, which prohibited religious corporations from acquiring and administering real estate except that destined immediately and directly for the purposes of worship, was in reality the *Ley Lerdo*. This article was regarded by the clergy as being the most drastic of all, for, it has been remarked, "If the Constitution provided the cause of the Three Years War, it was because it included Article 27—the law of June 25."[22]

In order to circumvent more effectively the political activities of the clergy, the Constitution provided (Articles 56 and 77) that they were ineligible to election as president of the Republic or as national representatives. The right of the suffrage, however, was restored to the ecclesiastics. The Federal government (Article 123) was given the right to intervene "in matters of religious worship and outward ecclesiastical forms" only as the laws might designate. The nature and extent of governmental intervention was not defined and could only be determined by actual practice. There was no reference in the Constitution to ecclesiastical patronage, nor indeed was there any mention of the Roman Catholic religion as the religion of the State. This omission, says Father Cuevas, amounted to national apostasy. The Constitution was also silent on the subject of religious liberty. The project submitted to the Convention by the committee contained the following article on religion (Article 15): "The exercise of any religious cult shall not be prohibited or impeded by any law or order. But since the Roman Catholic religion has been the exclusive religion of the Mexican people, the Congress of the Union will protect it by just and wise laws."[23] Religious freedom, among the various questions considered by the Convention, seemed to command the greatest interest, as evidenced by the extended and lively debates and the crowded galleries. The debates on this article extended from July 29 to August 5.

---

[21] Callcott, *op. cit.*, p. 285. For the Constitution of 1857, see Gamboa, *op. cit.*, pp. 528-589.

[22] Andrés Molina Enríquez, *La Reforma y Juárez* (Mexico, 1906), p. 71.

[23] Zarco, *op. cit.*, I, 469.

Delegate José Mata, in defending freedom of worship said, "The Hispanic race is the only one which presents today to the civilized world the shameful spectacle of embracing in its bosom men who desire to tyrannize over the human conscience; the only people in whose midst is still discussed the right to worship God according to one's own conscience." A champion of the clerical cause, Deputy Castañeda, asked, "In a people where there is religious unity, can the public authorities introduce the tolerance of cults?" Religions were mutually exclusive, he contended, and to introduce others into Mexico was deliberately to ask for trouble. Since tolerance was contrary to the national will, said Señor Castañeda, the representatives of an essentially religious nation should not attack a vital and favorite principle of the people. The weight of Comonfort's government was then thrown into the fight against the article, because it was regarded as being premature and inadvisable. Three of his ministers ascended the tribune and argued against the measure. Minister of Justice Montes said, "It [Article 15] will be contrary to the will of the absolute majority of the nation." Minister of Foreign Relations de la Rosa opposed the article as a dangerous innovation, and declared that when he saw the moral effects of tolerance in the United States he did not desire it for Mexico.[24]

After a week's debate on Article 15 the question was referred back to the committee where it continued to repose until the end of the session. Although the sentiment of the majority of the constituents was undeniably in favor of religious freedom, they were timorous—afraid to face the issue squarely and proceed to the logical limits of their reform program. Thus the Constitution was drafted with no definite religious items in its bill of rights. Some people professed to believe that the defeat of Article 15 of the constitutional project left the Roman Catholic religion the State faith to the exclusion of any other. This was not the case, for, according to Article 6, the "expression of ideas," or the liberty of conscience was guaranteed, and the liberty of cults was no more than a particular kind of liberty of conscience.[25] Furthermore the absolute guarantees of freedom of speech, the

---

[24] *Ibid.*, I, 674, 771-876. [25] Bulnes, *op. cit.*, p. 229.

press, and education made it quite clear that freedom of religious worship would also be guaranteed.

Such were the religious clauses of the Constitution of 1857. A small and unrepresentative group of revolutionaries had resolved to free the nation forcibly and somewhat against its will from clerical domination. To accomplish this end an attempt was made to shatter the material power of the Church. These visionaries thought that a people profoundly submerged in Catholicism for three hundred years and fondly attached to the ecclesiastical authority, could be forced to repudiate the past by a decree. That this was not possible, the subsequent history of the religious question in Mexico bears emphatic testimony.

The new Constitution was published on February 12, 1857, and a decree was issued by Comonfort ordering all public officials to swear an oath of allegiance to it. But the clergy forbade government officials on pain of deprivation of the sacraments to take the oath of allegiance or to purchase property in mortmain. They even went to the extent of denying burial to those who had sworn to observe the Constitution.[26] Archbishop Garza addressed a circular to all the bishops declaring that no faithful Catholic could swear allegiance to it. Bishop Munguía of Michoacán declared that he was opposed to the constitutional articles which provided for liberty of instruction, thought, press, and association; those that prohibited religious vows, titles of nobility, and honorary titles; and those abolishing the *fueros* and prohibiting the acquisition by religious corporations of real property. He also protested against the articles which defined obligations of citizenship, created a national guard, and declared that sovereignty resided in the people. The clergy wrote an infinite number of pamphlets and volumes on the question of the relations of Church and State. One of these by Bishop Munguía, containing nearly a thousand pages, urged rebellion and disobedience to the government. On the other hand the Bishop of Oaxaca was conspicious among the prelates because of his acceptance of the Constitution. He ordered a *Te Deum* mass sung in its honor. Many priests, also, refused to obey the strict

---

[26] Vera, *op. cit.*, I, 21.

orders of the hierarchy regarding the non-observance of the Constitution.[27]

The Constitution of 1857 was inaugurated under unsympathetic auspices. Comonfort, elected constitutional president, was of the opinion that the new "Magna Charta" was too radical and that it was not representative of the majority public opinion. Furthermore he was timorous of clerical opposition. He therefore was an advocate of thoroughgoing amendment. Of the 155 deputies elected to the National Federal Congress only twenty-one had served in the Constituent Congress. Bulnes professed to see in this meager representation of ex-constituents disapproval of the Constitution and repudiation of the reformists.[28] On December 19, 1857, the military-clerical alliance under the leadership of General Félix Zuloaga declared war upon the Constitution. Their *plan*, issued in Tacubaya, called for: (1) inviolability of Church property and revenues and reëstablishment of former exactions; (2) reëstablishment of the *fueros*; (3) censorship of the press; (4) the Roman Catholic religion as the sole and exclusive religion of Mexico; (5) immigrants to come only from Catholic countries; (6) overthrow of the Constitution of 1857 and use of a dictatorship subservient to Church only; (7) a monarchy to be established if possible, and if not, a European protectorate; and (8) high tariff, internal duties, and use of monopolies.[29] In short, the Conservatives offered the people of Mexico militarism and religion of the middle ages.

Comonfort accepted the *Plan de Tacubaya* and made a faltering attempt to assume leadership of the reaction, but his vacillation caused his repudiation by all parties. After his ignominious flight from the country, the reactionary army took Mexico City and General Zuloaga was proclaimed president. "The Conservative forces gave the provisional presidency to General D. Félix Zuloaga with as much right or more than the Liberals had three years before when they enthroned the traitor Álvarez," says Father Cuevas.[30] To Mexican partisans, legality is a relative

---

[27] Toro, *op. cit.*, pp. 258-260; Vicente Riva Palacio to Mariano Riva Palacio, Mexico, January 29, 1857. Riva Palacio Papers.

[28] Bulnes, *op. cit.*, pp. 247-248.

[29] Callcott, *op. cit.*, p. 315.   [30] Cuevas, *op. cit.*, V, 317.

matter depending on which side of a question one finds himself. Comonfort's betrayed Liberal colleagues rushed to arms in defense of the Constitution, and Benito Juárez, legal successor to the presidency, was proclaimed constitutional president of Mexico. The Liberals set up a government in Vera Cruz, whereas the Conservatives retained possession of the capital. Thus was initiated a war to the death between the military-clerical alliance and the defenders of liberal ideas. The War of the Reform was essentially a religious conflict, and for that reason, perhaps, it was characterized by excessive plunder, rapine, brutal reprisals, and a general spirit of extermination. Prisoners were slaughtered in cold blood, doctors and nurses were killed, and churches were sacked. The clergy made it a holy war. They supported it financially, and the Conservative soldiers carried crosses, rosaries, and pictures of saints. "On the liberal side it was a struggle for freedom of thought and speech, for the extinction of clerical participation in affairs of state, for the nationalization of great areas of land held by the Church, for the normal participation of laymen in government, for complete equality of all citizens before the law, for intellectual progress and modernity. On the conservative side the ideal was Church and Army control, with a foreign constitutional monarchy in the background. All the old Spanish abuses based on the colonial conception of political society were to be perpetuated: special privileges, absence of liberty of conscience, class domination."[31]

After the triumph of the praetorian movement which accomplished the extrusion of Comonfort, General Zuloaga annulled the Liberal reform legislation, and restored the special privileges to the army and clergy. His program, according to Bulnes, was that of intimate union of Church and State—an intolerant Church privileged as it was in the eleventh century, opulent as an Asiatic monarchy over black social misery; and science on its knees before theology, with *fueros* as justice.[32]

Shortly after his assuming of the presidency Zuloaga wrote to Pius IX assuring him of the piety and devotion of the Mexican

---

[31] Priestley, *op. cit.*, p. 337.   [32] Bulnes, *op. cit.*, p. 330.

nation. The Pope replied immediately expressing great satisfaction because of the happy turn of Mexican affairs. By decree of March 1, 1858, much of the Church property was ordered restored to it. But when Zuloaga tried to restore ecclesiastical lands alienated under the *Ley Lerdo* he came into conflict with foreign nations whose citizens had bought these lands. His attempt to impose forced loans on aliens also involved him in foreign complications. The incapacity of Zuloaga finally necessitated his being pushed aside and General Miramón, who had been the real prop of the Conservative government, assumed the presidency on December 30, 1858. Miramón offered to preserve the independence and prerogatives of the clergy and the *fueros* of the army. Although he recognized the necessity of certain ecclesiastical reforms, he preferred to undertake them in coöperation with the prelates.[33]

From his temporary capital in Vera Cruz President Juárez issued a manifesto declaring his intention to make war measures of the reform legislation. The government was disposed, he said, to maintain the Constitution and to abolish despotism, hypocrisy, immorality, and disorder. To accomplish this it was necessary to end the fratricidal war initiated by the clergy and to deprive them of all the means of further resistance. To bring this about, declared Juárez, it was necessary to carry the Reform to its logical conclusion, i.e., separation of Church and State, suppression of convents, extinction of all religious congregations, liberty of conscience, and nationalization of Church property. In fulfillment of his promise, Juárez, during the course of the War of the Reform released an avalanche of anti-clerical laws upon the Church. These laws, as was frankly confessed, were military measures designed rather for moral effect than practical execution; as a challenge rather than a definite piece of legislation; for they were promulgated when the Liberals controlled only a part of Mexico. These laws, which constituted an undisguised attack on the spiritual domain of the Catholic Church, seemed

---

[33] Gen. Miguel Miramón to Gen. Manuel María Calvo, San Luís Potosí, July 16, 1858. Comonfort Papers, García Collection; Riva Palacio, *op. cit.*, V, 281-282.

to aim at the destruction of the Church itself. They are comparable, as war measures, to Lincoln's Emancipation Proclamation.

The ecclesiastical temporalities were made the first object of special Liberal attention, because it was felt that if the civil war were to be ended, it could only be by depriving the Church of its revenues. On November 3, 1858, President Juárez decreed the illegality of the clerical practice of procuring money on the security of Church real estate. On December 7, 1858, a loan of 2,500,000 *pesos* was imposed on the clergy. This exaction was described as an "equivalent" of the loan made a short time before to the Conservative government. On July 12, 1859, Juárez issued an executive decree nationalizing ecclesiastical holdings. All property of the regular and secular clergy, whether rural or urban, real estate, stocks, or shares, was declared as coming under the dominion of the nation. Such Church buildings and residences of the secular clergy as should be designated by the state governors to be adequate for public worship were to be excepted from the nationalization law. A decree known as the "Reglamento para el Cumplimiento de la Ley de Nacionalización" was promulgated on the following day. Its object was to stipulate the manner in which nationalization should take place. Special offices were to be established to take the inventories and sell the property at public auction; extremely liberal terms were offered to prospective purchasers and rewards were offered to induce people to denounce property concealed by the clerics.[34]

The nationalization law was actual confiscation of Church properties and not a purchase. It was an extreme measure and under ordinary conditions could never have been condoned. The clergy, however, were in open rebellion against the constitutional government and were devoting the funds of the faithful to war purposes. It was therefore a proper war measure to deprive the Conservative enemy of its principal source of income. It was indeed unfortunate that the Mexican Church should have been deprived of income adequate to carry on necessary ecclesiastical

---

[34] Dublán y Lozano, *op. cit.*, VIII, 657-661, 675-688; W. H. Callcott, *Liberalism in Mexico, 1857-1929* (Stanford University, 1931), pp. 22-23.

activities, but such was the consequence of stubborn resistance to inevitable reform.

The law of July 12, the most important of the so-called "Laws of the Reform," also provided for separation of Church and State; the free performance of religious services by priests; suppression of all *cofradías* and of religious communities for men, and the transfer of antiques, works of art, and books from the suppressed convents to the national museums and libraries. The law also provided for a partial suppression of nunneries. Novitiates were closed and nuns were encouraged to leave the cloisters. Other laws which followed in rapid succession proclaimed religious toleration, reduced the number of religious feast days, secularized cemeteries, and established the civil register for vital statistics. Marriage was made a civil contract, and although legal separation was recognized, absolute divorce was prohibited. This law was necessitated, explained a circular issued by the Minister of Justice, because matrimony as a sacrament had been used by the clergy as one of the most efficacious means of securing disobedience to the laws. Because Article 3 of the law of July 12 established "perfect independence of Church and State," the Mexican legation in Rome was withdrawn. On December 4, 1860, another law was passed containing several provisions to make effective the separation of Church and State. These were: (1) protection by law of all religious beliefs on a plane of perfect equality; (2) independence of all cults in purely spiritual matters; (3) abolition of the religious oath and substitution of the simple promise to tell the truth; (4) no religious ceremonies outside of churches; (5) use of church bells subject to police regulation; (6) abolition of the right of asylum; (7) pontifical communications of a spiritual nature no longer subject to the exequatur; and (8) public officials prohibited from aiding or officiating in acts of religion. All of these measures were promulgated in the name of "God, Liberty, and Reform."[35]

Following the final constitutionalist victory at the battle of Calpulalpam, the Liberal army entered Mexico City on December 27, 1860. Juárez lost no time in wreaking vengeance upon

---

[35] Dublán y Lozano, *op. cit.*, VIII, 688-695, 705, 762-766; Toro, *op. cit.*, pp. 280-286.

his defeated clerical adversaries and in carrying on to even more extreme limits the anti-clerical reform. Because of the alliance of the prelates with the erstwhile Conservative government, Juárez ordered the expulsion from the Republic of the apostolic delegate, Archbishop Garza, and four of the bishops. All Cathedral chapters were suppressed with the exception of that of Guadalajara, which had protested against the French intervention. The number of churches open to the cult was reduced. For example, in the Federal District twenty-five were closed, but surely this did not work a hardship on the church-goers since thirty-five remained open.[36]

The decree of nationalization of Church properties was promptly put into effect after the occupation of the capital city. Those properties that had enjoyed the protection of Zuloaga and Miramón now fell into the control of the constitutional government. Furthermore hospitals and charitable institutions that had been administered by the ecclesiastics were secularized. Finally all nuns were excloistered, their dowries were returned, and their properties were confiscated. "The number of landholders must have increased by many thousands," says McBride, "the fruits of the nationalization of Church lands falling mainly into the hands of the mestizos."[37] Forty thousand transfers of property are said to have taken place. Yet the attempt to replenish the bankrupt national treasury by expropriation and nationalization ended in failure. Although it is claimed that the nationalizing operations produced for the treasury from two to six million dollars, it was necessary for Juárez to declare a moratorium, which in turn brought about the allied intervention.

The clergy were the real authors of the French intervention. Having been conquered completely on the field of battle by the constitutionalist forces, they turned to intrigue and worked for the founding of a monarchy under European protection. To preserve their privileges the Mexican clergy had renounced their legitimate sovereign in 1821; to save the Church from serious injury at the hands of the Liberal reformers, the clericals were

---

[36] Dublán y Lozano, *op. cit.*, IX, 12-13, 524-525, 321-322.

[37] George McCutchen McBride, *The Land Systems of Mexico* (New York, 1923), p. 71.

willing, in 1861, to compromise the independence of their country. Mexican history shows that, on the part of the ecclesiastics, sentiments of national fealty were secondary to loyalty to the Church. Notwithstanding the naïve protestation of the Mexican prelates at the time of the Intervention that they did not interfere in political matters, the apostolic nuncio informed the Empress Carlota that "the clergy had made the empire."[38] And Father Cuevas, whose narrow prejudice in favor of the clerical cause admits of no question, proudly confesses, "To their honor, the conservatives and the Mexican bishops wished and procured a liberating intervention and a Mexican Empire." In justification of this action, he adds, "To call an auxiliary army when it is absolutely necessary to save the national dignity and independence is laudable and in all times admitted in the rights and practices of nations. This army promised to respect all our sovereignty and territory and promised to retire when its mission was completed."[39] The willingness of Juárez to accept an American protectorate by the McLean-Ocampo Treaty, which, fortunately for Mexico, was repudiated by the United States Senate, was condemned by the Conservatives as the basest treachery. And indeed, the willingness of Juárez to purchase a Liberal victory at the cost of national independence is an indelible blot upon the reputation of the "Hero of the Reform." Yet the Conservatives and their apologists actually condoned the French intervention and the undeniable violation of Mexican sovereignty.

The invading French, who were received with *Te Deum* masses along the line of march to Mexico City, forced Juárez to evacuate the capital in May, 1863. General Forey, the French commander, thereupon set up a Regency, composed of Mexican monarchists and clericals, to act as a temporary governing body. The president of the Regency was General Juan Almonte, recently returned from the court of Napoleon III where he had earnestly advocated the establishment of monarchy in Mexico under French protection. Another member of the Regency was the recently exiled Archbishop Labastida. The clergy, who fondly hoped that

---

[38] Infra, p. 450.
[39] Cuevas, *op. cit.*, V, 340.

their every wish would be granted by the French, received a rude awakening immediately after General Forey's arrival in Mexico City. In pursuance of Napoleon's orders his general issued a proclamation announcing that the proprietors of nationalized ecclesiastical property which had been regularly and legally adjudicated to them would not be disturbed in their peaceful possession, and only fraudulent sales would be subject to revision. "The Catholic religion," he announced, "will be protected and the bishops will be placed anew in their dioceses. I believe it is possible to add that the Emperor will view with pleasure the proclamation of liberty of cults by the government." Since the Regency wished to initiate a real clerical reaction, a breach with the French began to appear at a very early date. Forey wrote Napoleon, "I believe in honoring religion and its ministers, although these in this country are not always very honorable; but it is to be feared that they are going far to put the country at the feet of the clergy."[40]

Archbishop Labastida, "scheming and unprincipled churchman," was so uncompromising in his demands for a restoration of all clerical properties that Marshal Bazaine, successor to General Forey, removed him from the Regency.[41] It became abundantly evident, even in the early days of the Intervention, that the clergy would be satisfied with nothing less than a complete restoration of their old-time status. The Mexican clergy, like the Bourbons, "learned nothing and forgot nothing."

In July, 1863, an "Assembly of Notables," carefully selected by the French, proclaimed the establishment of a monarchy under a moderate, hereditary, Catholic prince with the title of Emperor of Mexico. The imperial crown was to be offered to Archduke Maximilian of Austria, and, in the event of his refusal, Napoleon III was to be asked to choose another Catholic prince for Mexico. But it was not necessary to call upon Napoleon for additional aid, since the young Archduke and particularly his brilliant and

---

[40] Toro, *op. cit.*, pp. 308-312; F. Boquet to Marshal Bazaine, Paris, July 18, 1862, in *Archivo Bazaine*, I, 6.

[41] Percy F. Martin, *Maximilian in Mexico* (New York, 1914), p. 133; Riva Palacio, *op. cit.*, V, 623.

ambitious wife Carlota, were willing to undertake the Mexican adventure. When Maximilian accepted the Mexican throne he went to Rome to see the pope, for he somewhat faintly recognized the importance of finding a solution for the religious problem in the Aztec State. When the pope said that though the rights of nations were great and must be satisfied, but those of the Church were greater, Maximilian should have gained an intimation of what the future had in store for him. Unfortunately he failed to come to a clear understanding with the pope. All he did was to request that a papal nuncio be sent to Mexico where everything could be settled later. Napoleon himself had advised Maximilian to settle all complications affecting Church affairs before accepting the Mexican throne. The failure of the prince to come to an understanding before leaving Europe was a blunder for which he paid with his life.[42]

On the very day that Emperor Maximilian and the Empress Carlota entered Mexico City (June 12, 1864), a pastoral was published by the Mexican prelates. They declared that they, in fulfillment of their sacred ministry, had remained aloof from political questions and strife of parties, and that the revolution was the result of sin. The faithful were exhorted to observe their religious duties and masses were ordered celebrated *pro electo Imperatore.* This pastoral was a covert threat that the very existence of the imperial government depended on what solution the Emperor would give to the problem of the Church.

Maximilian, essentially a liberal, was determined not to head a blind reaction. He was convinced that it was impossible and impracticable to initiate a counter-revolution and restore to the clergy all of their old privileges and particularly their property. He thought, in his innocence, not knowing the Mexican clergy, that the Church question could be settled in an entirely Catholic and equitable manner through the celebration of a concordat. The Emperor therefore impatiently awaited the arrival of the nuncio, but months passed before Pius IX fulfilled his promise. Maximilian repeatedly urged the pope, through the Mexican agent in Rome, to hasten the departure of his representative and

---

[42] Egan Caesar Count Corti, *Maximilian and Charlotte of Mexico* (New York, 1928), II, 409-410; Martin, *op. cit.,* p. 257.

to instruct him not to support the extravagant demands of the Mexican clergy.[43]

The pope's ambassador, Mgr. Meglia, finally arrived in Mexico on December 10, 1864. That the Holy Father refused to acquiesce in Maximilian's request that he do not support the extravagant pretentions of the Mexican clergy was clearly evidenced by a letter which the nuncio conveyed to Maximilian from the pope. The cardinal principles upon which an agreement was to be based, said Pius IX, were: (1) annulment of all the reform laws; (2) establishment of the Catholic faith to the exclusion of all other creeds; (3) entire freedom of the bishops in the exercise of their ecclesiastical functions; (4) restoration of the religious orders; (5) placing of both public and private instruction under clerical supervision; and (6) removal of all restrictions which kept the Church in dependence upon the State.[44]

Although Maximilian was stunned by the uncompromising nature of the papal demands, he communicated to the Nuncio a counter-proposal of nine points which constituted his idea of a fair and equitable understanding. The liberal and enlightened Emperor proposed as the basis of a concordat: (1) toleration for all cults, but protection for the Roman Catholic religion as the religion of the State; (2) support of the Catholic cult and its ministers from the public treasury; (3) performance of all religious services by priests to be gratuitous; (4) cession to the Mexican government of all rights respecting the ecclesiastical properties which had been nationalized; (5) the emperor to have the same rights over the Church as were once possessed by the kings of Spain; (6) reëstablishment, by agreement between the pope and the emperor, of *some* of the religious orders; (7) *fueros* (agreement to be worked out); (8) the civil register to be entrusted, wherever convenient, to parish priests to perform the duties of the civil functionaries; and (9) cemeteries (agreement to be worked out).[45]

---

[43] Toro, *op. cit.*, pp. 323-325.

[44] E. Léfèvre, *Historia de la Intervención Francesa en Méjico* (Brussels and London, 1869), II, 17; Bazaine to the Minister of War (France), December 10, 1864, in *Archivo Bazaine*, XI, 2045.

[45] Toro, *op. cit.*, p. 326.

The Nuncio, after being delivered Maximilian's counter-proposals, went into conference with Archbishop Labastida and other prelates. The decision was that the Emperor's proposals were unacceptable. The Nuncio then announced that his instructions did not allow him to negotiate on the basis of the Emperor's demands. This was a blow to Maximilian for he realized then that the pope had abandoned him, and his hopes for a satisfactory settlement of the Church question were doomed. The Empress asked for a conference with Mgr. Meglia, and it was on that occasion that he told her it was the clergy who had made the Empire. It was quite evident to all that Archbishop Labastida had poisoned the ear of the Nuncio, for immediately after his arrival in Mexico he had given every indication of being willing to compromise. "It is evident enough," wrote Carlota to Empress Eugenie, "that behind all the doings of the nuncio, who is a mere puppet, is concealed the figure of Mgr. Labastida, whose bad Italian I know so well that I can recognize it in every line."[46] When the Nuncio's obstinacy exasperated beyond endurance, Carlota suggested to Bazaine that he should be thrown from the window. The mission of Mgr. Meglia came to an unfortunate end in April, 1865, when he left Mexico suddenly and in great rage because of a rebuff he had received from the Minister of Foreign Affairs. This was induced because of an insulting letter addressed to the Emperor after the promulgation of a decree which recognized the legal rights of purchasers of nationalized ecclesiastical property. "Maximilian, citizen and member of the Christian Church," wrote the Foreign Minister, "bows in subservience to the spiritual authority of the Father of the Faithful; but Maximilian, Emperor and representative of Mexican sovereignty, recognizes no power upon earth superior to his own."[47]

Since negotiations with the Nuncio had failed, Maximilian sent a commission to Rome to appeal directly to Pius IX. However, they were told that the pope would never consent to a diminution of the rights of the clergy. When notified that the

---

[46] Corti, *op. cit.*, II, 456; Bazaine to the Minister of War (France), December 27, 1864, in *Archivo Bazaine*, XI, 2078.

[47] Martin, *op. cit.*, p. 261.

pontiff had branded his government as being anti-Catholic, Maximilian declared that the Mexican archbishop and bishops did not understand the modern age or real Catholicism; they lacked Christian hearts. If the pope excommunicated him, he said, he would be the fourth archduke of Austria who had been excommunicated.[48]

As can be surmised from the above, the Emperor and Empress entertained very poor opinions of the Mexican clergy. Maximilian wrote to Gutiérrez Estrada, Mexican monarchical agent in Paris, "There are three classes which are the worst thing I have found in the country so far; the judicial functionaries, the army officers, and the greater part of the clergy. None of them know their duties and they live for money alone. The judges are corrupt, the officers have no sense of honor, and the clergy are lacking in Christian charity and morality."[49] In an address to the Mexican prelates, Maximilian said, "You claim that the Mexican Church has never taken part in political revolutions. I would to God it were so, but sad testimony proves that the very dignitaries of the Church have fomented revolutions, and a part of the clergy have opposed a very active resistance to the State. Admit, my estimable prelates, that the Mexican Church, with a lamentable fatality, has mixed too much in politics and temporal matters, neglecting by this activity the Catholic instruction of their flocks. Yes, the Mexican people are good and pious, but in great part they are not Catholic in the real sense of the Gospel, and this is not their fault. It is necessary that they should be instructed and administered the sacraments, freely."[50] In commenting on the insistence of the prelates that they should be restored their properties in their entirety, Empress Carlota said, "It is not a question of the property of the clergy to be exact, but of the bishops, who were swimming in abundance, while the mere priests were dying of hunger." Carlota wrote to Empress Eugenie, "Here, on the contrary, I am sorry to state, that contrary to what M. Gutiérrez Estrada and his companions affirm, Catholicism in this country is of a very mediocre grade. The

---

[48] Toro, *op. cit.*, p. 342.

[49] Corti, *op. cit.*, II, 438.

[50] Toro, *op. cit.*, pp. 342-343.

pseudo-Catholicism established by the conquest, with a mixture of Indian religion, has died with the clerical property, its principal base. Now, since all people need a religion, many persons are inclined to Protestantism as the most convenient, and above all as the least expensive, because the sacraments cost so much." The poor opinion of the Mexican clergy entertained by the sovereigns was shared by members of their household, all supposedly good Catholics in Europe. Abbot Domenech said that Mexican Catholicism, due to the lack of instruction in the dogmas of religion, had assumed an idolatrous character. The cult of the saints and of the virgins left little time, he said, for thoughts of God himself.[51]

Maximilian, thoroughly disgusted with the Mexican prelates, the nuncio, and the pope, threatened to ratify the laws of Juárez. He ordered the Minister of Justice (December 27, 1864) to confirm all legitimate acquisitions of clerical property by the law of amortization. A special office was created to review titles of property previously expropriated. By the same decree it was provided that all clerics were to be paid salaries by the State. This decree aroused a storm of protest and caused an open breach between the Emperor and the clericals. Putting the clergy on a salary basis was condemned as a measure designed to deprive them of their independence. "A salary from the State," said the Empress, "would never bring them in so much, and while we are struggling here to establish the Church's position, it is their ideal to live in Europe on their money." Other decrees of a reformist nature guaranteed religious toleration, opened the cemeteries to persons of all creeds, enforced the law of Juárez suppressing ecclesiastical *fueros*, and provided for the imperial exequatur of all pontifical communications.[52] The decrees of Maximilian affecting the Church justified the reforms of Juárez and the Liberals. It is contended that Maximilian supported some of the reformist measures of Juárez in an effort to win the good-will of the Liberals. This was true, but, notwithstanding, the Emperor's actions were based in sincere and conscientious conviction.

---

[51] *Ibid.*, pp. 329, 335.
[52] *Ibid.*, pp. 339-340; Corti, *op. cit.*, II, 469.

The plan of Maximilian to reconcile the conflicting factions by a partial recognition of the Juárez program failed to secure the adherence of the Liberals and served to alienate the churchmen. When the clergy saw that their monarchial choice would not be their docile instrument, and that their position under the monarchy was no better than it had been under the republic, they turned on Maximilian with incredible venom. The very expectation that the Emperor would be a placid and amenable tool in the hands of the clerics was what caused them to work so persistently for a monarchial government. The awakening therefore was a severe blow.

The withdrawal of the French and the callous indifference of Pius IX to Maximilian and his cause sealed the fate of the unfortunate monarch. Retribution was at hand because of his failure to study the ecclesiastical question thoroughly before leaving Europe. A more critical and less trusting individual would have discerned the hidden dangers which imperiled the monarchial enterprise from the beginning.

After the unfortunate and impolitic execution of Maximilian, which act constitutes another indelible stain upon the reputation of Juárez, the Liberals were given an opportunity to require general enforcement and observance of the Reform Laws. The clerical party was completely shattered, and the Church was required to give absolute obedience to the existing laws. The restored Liberal government issued a circular to the governors of the states (July 20, 1868) urging upon them the enforcement of the Reform Laws. The preface to the circular read, "Since the law of July 12, 1859, declared that there existed a perfect independence between the Church and State, the government has been careful not to intervene in any of the purely ecclesiastical subjects, guaranteeing to the clergy the most ample liberty in the exercise of their spiritual functions."[53] This statement, as an example of ingenuous denial of the actual situation, deserves to be classed with the declaration of the prelates that they did not interfere in politics.

In an effort to facilitate the liquidation of Church properties, Juárez established the "Administration of Nationalized Prop-

---

[53] Dublán y Lozano, op. cit., X, 396.

erty," and offered liberal rewards to those who would consent to denounce property concealed by the clericals. Between the years 1869 and 1879 a considerable amount of Church holdings was liquidated. The actual proceeds to the government were slightly less than $2,500,000. The net financial result of the whole process of expropriation until 1892, when nationalized ecclesiastical property was declared free from further claims by the treasury, was that $100,000,000 of Church property was acquired by private owners and the government realized a few millions in revenue. The principal purpose of the Reform, the destruction of the economic power of the clergy, was not completely achieved, since much of the Church's property was still held for it by proxies and large sums were paid to the clergy by the new proprietors in return for declarations that the Church renounced all rights of ownership of the particular property.[54]

After the death of Juárez (1872) the clergy began to agitate anew for the abrogation of the Reform Laws. They hoped that President Lerdo de Tejada would be more favorable; but they were disappointed. After assuming the presidency Lerdo issued a manifesto declaring his intention to insist on a strict observance of the Laws of the Reform. Indeed, the President facilitated the incorporation of the Reform Laws into the Constitution. On October 5, 1873, certain "additions and reforms of the Federal Constitution" were promulgated. Those Laws of the Reform which were constitutionalized were: (1) the separation of Church and State; (2) civil marriage; (3) prohibition to religious institutions of the right to acquire real estate or imposts on it; (4) substitution of a simple promise to tell the truth in place of the religious oath; and (5) illegality of monastic vows.[55]

On December 14, 1874, enabling legislation was passed by the Congress to facilitate the operation of the recently constitutionalized Laws of the Reform. Into this law was gathered much of the radical legislation of the previous twenty years. For example, under the subject of separation of Church and State, it was provided that no religious instruction was to be given in any

---

[54] Phipps, *op. cit.*, pp. 90-93.

[55] Dublán y Lozano, *op. cit.*, XII, 502-504; Callcott, *Liberalism in Mexico*, pp. 92-93.

public institution, no religious act could be performed outside of churches, clerics could not wear distinctive garbs outside of ecclesiastical premises, and church bells were to be used only as a summons to religious services. Infractions of the sections relating to the separation of Church and State, the acquisition of real estate, and prohibition of monastic orders, were declared to be federal offenses and subject to trial in the federal courts. Cases arising under violation of the legal provisions relating to the simple promise to tell the truth and civil matrimony were placed under the jurisdiction of the local courts.[56]

The constitutionalizing of the Laws of the Reform marked the end of an epoch in the ecclesiastical history of Mexico. Henceforth there was to be no open attempt of the clergy to dominate politics. Church and State were definitively separated. The Reform had been won at last, for notwithstanding its disregard during the subsequent Díaz period its existence as constitutional law was a constant deterrent to extravagant clerical pretentions. No longer did the clergy dare to campaign for the establishment of a medieval theocracy. They declared themselves as being eminently satisfied if accorded the guarantees of a free Church in a free State.

---

[56] *Ibid.*, XII, 683-688.

CHAPTER XVI

CHURCH AND STATE CONFLICT IN MEXICO: 1875-1933

The anti-Church reform movement initiated by Gómez Farías and resumed by Benito Juárez had seemingly attained its goal by 1874. The victory, however, proved to be illusory and temporary, for during the long dictatorship of Porfirio Díaz, who began as a liberal and became a conservative, a policy of "conciliation," i.e., ignoring the Reform, was adopted. Without abrogation of any of them, he allowed the laws to fall into disuse. Thus, with the tacit consent of Díaz there was a rebirth of ecclesiastical influence which provided fuel for the flames of revolt which broke out in 1910.

In seeking relief from the radicalism of Juárez and Lerdo de Tejada the clericals aided Díaz in his several attempts to seize control of the government. It is asserted that the clergy gave considerable financial support to the furtherance of the final successful *coup* of 1876. It is also charged that "the hero of Puebla" agreed in return for clerical support to make a concordat with the pope and derogate the Laws of Reform. Whatever may have been the truth of these charges, it is nevertheless a fact that "Porfirio Díaz attached the clerical party to his triumphal chariot with promises which he amply fulfilled."[1]

Díaz was quite aware of the continued power of the clergy in Catholic Mexico, notwithstanding the recent attacks. He aimed therefore, as a matter of policy, and despite the fact that he was a grand master of Freemasonry, to consolidate and perpetuate his authority by obtaining first the sympathy and confidence and later the frank and active coöperation of the ecclesiastics. He conciliated the wishes of the bishops.

Although Porfirio Díaz made no attempt to have the Laws of Reform removed from the statute books, for it is thought he

---

[1] Edmundo González-Blanco, *Carranza y la Revolución de México* (Madrid, 1916), p. 339; Francisco Bulnes, *El Verdadero Díaz* (Mexico, 1920), p. 90.

wished to have the written law serve as a potential menace should the clergy get out of hand, he nevertheless left the discretional application of the laws to the officials of each locality. The degree of enforcement, for this reason, varied greatly in different parts of Mexico. This accounts, then, for the contradictory assertions of writers that the Reform Laws were or were not enforced during the Díaz régime.

In circulars issued by the Ministry of Interior on April 12, 1881, March 27, 1885, and September 11, 1889, one can detect relaxation on the part of the state authorities in the enforcement of the religious laws. The Minister charged that, in violation of the Constitution, priests were wearing distinctive garbs in the streets, religious processions and services were being performed outside of the churches, priests were discoursing in the pulpits on political subjects, and monastic orders were known to exist clandestinely. The governors were urged to see that the laws were enforced.[2]

Thanks to *la política de conciliación*, the Church recovered much of its lost fortune. In addition to sums saved from the ruin wrought by the Reform, and the conservation of property through the acts of intermediaries in agreement with the clergy, the Church received handsome gifts and bequests, for it was impossible to distinguish between gifts for current expenses and gifts that would render the parishes wealthy. Even the tithes were surreptitiously reëstablished, for almoners went soliciting from house to house, and those who refused to pay were ostracized. "The economic recovery of the Church progressed so far under Díaz that it was charged as late as 1916 that ten per cent of the capital of the country belonged to the clergy, who loaned money in the name of European bankers."[3] It is estimated that, from 1874 to 1910, the value of ecclesiastical property increased from 50,000,000 *pesos* to double that amount. Priests once more became landlords, money lenders, and business men. Many church edifices that had been retired from the cult were restored and many new churches were constructed. In 1907 there were

---

[2] Dublán y Lozano, *Legislación Mexicana*, XIV, 738-739, XVII, 151-152, XIX, 550-551.

[3] Phipps, *The Agrarian Question in Mexico*, pp. 94-95.

over 8,765 churches and chapels in Mexico and 1,350 vicarages. A foreign observer wrote at that time: "The hold which the Church has upon the affections of the common people is in no way shaken, and there are probably more places of religious worship in the Republic of Mexico than in any Roman Catholic country in the world, not excepting either Spain or Italy."[4]

In education also the prime position of the Church was re-established. Under Díaz very little was done by the government for general education, and the burden which was once more put upon the clergy, was taken up with alacrity. A number of new Catholic colleges were opened and a new system of elementary schools was built up. In 1885 there were 276 Catholic schools in Mexico and in 1905 there were 593. During these "years of reconstruction," as Cuevas calls the Díaz period, new convents were clandestinely founded in agreement with the authorities, and many of the religious orders were restored. To replace in the hospitals the 450 expelled *Hermanas de Caridad*, the order of the *Hermanas Mexicanas Guadalupanas* was founded by Antonio Placarte y Labastida. Another Mexican female order, *La Congregación de las Siervas del S. Corazón*, began in 1888 to care for orphan girls. The country again abounded with convents, for monks and nuns founded under pretext of being schools and charitable institutions. The black *soutanos* of the clergy again became a familiar sight in the streets. Public religious acts also became common. Sumptuous *fiestas* like the Coronation of the Virgin of Guadalupe and other celebrated images, Eucharistic congresses, and golden anniversaries of prelates were celebrated in public.[5]

Such was the remarkable development and prosperity of the Church during the Díaz dictatorship that five new archbishoprics (Durango, Linares, Oaxaca, Puebla, and Yucatán) and eight new bishoprics (Cuernavaca, Chihuahua, Saltillo, Tepic, Tehuantepec, Aguascalientes, Tabasco, and Campeche) were

---

[4] Martin, *Mexico of the Twentieth Century*, I, 93.

[5] Cuevas, *La Iglesia en México*, V, 409; Rodolfo Menéndez Mena, *The Work of the Clergy and the Religious Persecution in Mexico* (New York, 1916), p. 18; Carleton Beals, *Porfirio Díaz* (Philadelphia and London, 1932), pp. 341-342.

created. More dioceses were erected during the Díaz period, says Cuevas, than in the time of Philip II.

For several years the Dictator acted covertly and cautiously in the execution of his policy toward the Church, for he realized the danger of attempting a too sudden and public renunciation of the anti-clerical laws. It was not until after 1890 that his "policy of conciliation" became sufficiently noticeable to be discussed in the press. By that time, however, his dictatorship had been firmly established and most of the old Liberal warriors of the Reform had passed from the stage of Mexican politics. Therefore, there was less need for dissimulation. In 1904 the pope sent a special delegate, Mgr. Serafini, Archbishop of Spoleto, to see if it were possible to renew the old associations of Church and State, and reëstablish diplomatic relations with Mexico. But Serafini, like other papal emissaries to Mexico, failed. Even the attempted bribe of creating a Mexican cardinal would not budge the President from his determination not to restore Mexican representation at the Vatican.[6] In reality, however, Díaz maintained almost official relations with the resident apostolic delegates. He even intervened to suggest to the Vatican who should be named as bishops. "It was public and notorious besides," writes an historian of this period, "that the Mexican consul in Rome, an Italian named Angelini, was a real confidential diplomatic agent of the Mexican government to the Holy See."[7]

In view of the many favors received from the Dictator, the Mexican clergy, essentially partners of the Díaz system, had little occasion to exhibit their former rebelliousness. There was consequently a cessation of clerical intrigues and political machinations. Although there was realization that the existence of the Reform Laws was a sword of Damocles which constantly menaced the extra-legal position of the Church, it was feared that agitation for an amendment of the Constitution would stir up a latent, but powerful opposition. In addition, it did not conform to "Porfirian policy" to release clerical dependence by the reëstablishment of ecclesiastical privileges. Thus, since the "understanding" between Díaz and the clergy depended on cir-

---

[6] Martin, op. cit., I, 93-94.

[7] Toro, La Iglesia y el Estado en México, p. 359.

cumstance, i.e., the continuance of the dictatorship, he had in the Church his most faithful ally. It should be no occasion for surprise, therefore, that the ecclesiastics opposed the Madero movement.

When the Revolution of 1910 broke out the clergy in all the pulpits of the land combatted it; Madero's motives were decried and his policy was censured. Although Madero's *Plan de San Luís Potosí* contained no allusion to religious reform, there nevertheless was much in the program which alarmed the clericals. The promise of agrarian reform alarmed because it was feared that the despoiling of the great estates would affect the holdings which had been acquired or retained clandestinely. Furthermore, the promise of educational reform caused the clericals to fear for the educational facilities which they had established throughout Mexico with the acquiescence of the Díaz administration. Consequently, a "National Catholic Party" was organized under the patronage of the prelates for the ostensible purpose of combatting the impending social and economic reform.[8] In the campaign which preceded the elections held in October, 1911, the clerical partisans worked energetically for the defeat of Madero and the capture of the government. Ambassador Henry Lane Wilson reported to the Secretary of State on July 11, 1911, "The Roman Catholic Church and the party which takes its name have become violently antagonistic to Madero, and are busily engaged throughout the Republic in aspersing his motives, decrying his policies, and censuring the weakness and vacillation which is supposed to characterize his direction of affairs."[9] An historian of the period, one very unfriendly to the clergy, describes the clerical opposition to Madero:

"All [of the clergy] from the highest to the lowest, availed themselves of religious offices, the confessional, the pulpit, doctrine, dogma, faith, superstition, and all the instruments at hand to gain proselytes. They worked on the consciences of the people, their friends and their servants, using the formidable argument of eternal salvation, and when the ballot boxes were

---

[8] Pérez Lugo, *La Cuestión Religiosa en México*, p. 32; Pedro González-Blanco, *De Porfirio Díaz á Carranza* (Madrid, 1916), p. 340.

[9] Quoted in Gruening, *Mexico and Its Heritage*, p. 212, note 2.

installed they placed about them standards bearing significant legends. On many of them, for example, were inscribed the words: 'Here you vote for God.' The Catholic Church thus attempted in this way to convert itself into a temporal power in rivalry to the State; it endeavored to reëstablish the theocratic régime of the middle ages."[10] Notwithstanding the violent clerical opposition, Francisco I. Madero was nearly unanimously elected in what has been declared to have been the only real election that Mexico had had up to that time.[11] The clerical attempt to halt the Revolution failed.

Although Francisco Madero initiated no policy of an anti-clerical nature, his overthrow by Victoriano Huerta was hailed with delight by the ecclesiastics, for it was hoped that Huerta, professed champion of the "Porfirian system," would also support the Díaz ecclesiastical policy of conciliation. In the Church of Soledad, in Oaxaca, four days after the murder of Madero, a solemn mass of thanksgiving was celebrated for the salvation of the Republic. The clergy are even charged with having loaned Huerta $10,000,000, exacting in exchange for the loan the right to designate certain clerical partisans for appointment to the Ministry of State. The reëntry of the Church into the political arena was most ill-advised. For says Gruening, "When the clergy, as of old, supported the coup d'état against the elected government and its survivors gathering to recapture control, it sowed the wind. When Huerta, despite his ruthless butchery of political opponents, was overthrown, it reaped the whirlwind."[12]

The leader of the revolt against the Huerta-Catholic-Aristo-cratic reaction was Venustiano Carranza, Governor of the State of Coahuila. The revolution was prefaced with the customary "plan," this one being known as the *Plan de Guadalupe* (March 26, 1913). The *pronunciamiento* was brief; it announced refusal of its signatories to recognize Victoriano Huerta as constitu-

---

[10] Jorge Vera-Estañol, *Carranza and His Bolshevik Régime* (Los Angeles, Cal., 1920), pp. 24-25.

[11] Byron G. Skelton, *Electoral Theories and Practices in Mexico* (M. A. Thesis, University of Texas, 1928), p. 168.

[12] Gruening, *op. cit.*, p. 213.

tional president of Mexico. Carranza was proclaimed First Chief of the Constitutionalist Army, and it was provided that he should, after the occupation of Mexico City, exercise the Executive Power until a general election should be convoked.[13] The immediate object of the revolution was purely political, i.e., restoration of constitutional government. But as the civil war was protracted and it became necessary to conciliate or punish factions, social and economic reform was incorporated into the Constitutionalists' program. Thus it happened that, because of clerical support of Huerta, the Church was once more subjected to an embittered assault. But clerical opposition to the success of liberalism, as represented by the Constitutionalist forces, was not the sole cause of the anti-Church attack. The revolutionaries also feared, not the actual but the potential, and somewhat imaginary, opposition of the clergy to the adoption of a comprehensive reform program. Memory of the Church as the traditional arch-opponent of democracy and liberalism persisted in their minds, and it became very necessary, therefore, to anticipate the inevitable clerical reaction. In short, anti-clericalism had become a tradition in liberalism. It can hardly be denied, furthermore, that the Church and its clergy were assaulted because a goodly number of the so-called "Constitutionalists" had repudiated the tenets of Catholicism. Those who attacked the Catholic clergy because of their political activities, marched side by side in the Constitutionalist Army with the opponents of Catholicism as a religion. But, although it is undeniable that atheism was partly responsible for the anti-clerical attack which was initiated by Carranza and continues to the present day, there seems to be no reason to reject the protestations of Mexican officials that the reform was not aimed at the Church in its spiritual sphere, but at the clergy in their temporal activities.

The outrages committed on the clergy and the Church during the struggle against Huerta and after his overthrow were revolting. They were made to pay dearly for their support of the reaction. In explanation of the wanton desecration of churches and holy objects, one of the Constitutionalist generals, Salvador

---

[13] *Codificación de los Decretos del C. Venustiano Carranza* (Mexico, 1915), p. 7.

Alvarado said: "It was for the deliberate purpose of showing the Indians that the lightning would not strike—that the Constitutionalists were not the enemies of God as the priests had told them, that generals rode their horses into churches and publicly smashed the statues of the venerated saints."[14] It can hardly be doubted that these generals had little respect for the faith, quite aside from their lack of respect for the clergy.

Father Francis Clement Kelley, author of *The Book of Red and Yellow*, published in 1915, described in lurid detail the alleged crimes perpetrated upon the servitors of the faith. Except that the atrocities were more localized and not general throughout Mexico, Father Kelly's accounts are substantially correct. They present a fair picture of actual conditions, despite the efforts of revolutionary apologists from the time of Carranza to the present day to brand the work as a book of lies. Some partisans, although admitting the occurrence of acts of violence, seek to exonerate Carranza and the "respectable revolutionaries" by charging that the worst crimes were committed by Francisco Villa and his followers, "who exaggerated the just resentment of the Constitutionalist party against the members of the Catholic clergy."[15] But that the First Chief was in accord with Pancho Villa in sanctioning the outrages admits of little doubt. On July 8, 1914, the two leaders defined the objects of the Revolution in a formal agreement:

The present conflict being a struggle of the impecunious against the abuses of the powerful, and understanding that the causes of the evils that bear down the country spring from pretorianism, plutocracy, and clericalism, the Divisions of the North and of the Northeast, solemnly pledge themselves to fight until complete banishment of the ex-Federal army, which shall be superseded by the Constitutional Army, to set up democratic institutions in our country, to bring welfare to labor, financial emancipation to the peasant by an equitable apportionment of land, and other means tending to solve the agrarian question, to correct, chastise, and hold to their responsibilities such members of the Roman Catholic clergy as may have lent moral or physical support to the usurper, Victoriano Huerta.[16]

[14] Guening, *op. cit.*, p. 214.

[15] González-Blanco, *De Porfirio Díaz á Carranza*, p. 135.

[16] Gruening, *op. cit.*, p. 98.

It can be readily appreciated that the clergy who lent their "moral support" could by a broad definition of the term be made to comprehend well-nigh the entire ecclesiastical body.

On July 29, 1914, General Villa telegraphed General Villareal, Governor of Nuevo León, who had restricted the exercise of the Catholic cult and even prohibited the confession:

I sincerely and enthusiastically felicitate you on the decree which you have just published imposing restrictions on the clergy in the State which you govern with such dignity. I also am inclined to follow your wise example because I, like you, think the greatest enemy to our progress and liberty is the corrupting clergy, who for so long have dominated our country. (Signed) Francisco Villa.[17]

After his break with Carranza, Villa, in making a bid for conservative support, publicly charged Carranza with violating the guarantee of liberty of conscience by permitting the governors to take vengeance on the clergy for their support of the conservatives. He also accused Don Venustiano "of having profoundly offended the religious sentiments of the people by acts condemned by civilization and natural law." The First Chief replied, "General Villa who now seeks a reconciliation with the clergy, showing himself so respectful to religion and its practices, expelled the clerics, closed the churches, and prohibited all kinds of religious acts in the places occupied during the campaign."[18] There appears to be little doubt that Villa was insincere in his religious policy. This undoubted lack of sincerity on the part of so many of the revolutionary leaders increases the difficulty of analyzing and evaluating motives and causes.

As early as October 17, 1913, it was clear that Venustiano Carranza contemplated enforcement of the Laws of Reform. In a decree published on that date which provided for the organization of the provisional national administration, he created eight secretariats, and to one of these, the Ministry of Interior, was entrusted "Liberty of cults and supervision of this branch." There was evidently intention here to enforce strictly the laws

---

[17] González-Blanco, *Carranza y la Revolución*, pp. 345-346.
[18] González-Blanco, *De Porfirio Díaz á Carranza*, p. 135.

relating to religious liberty and its corollary, the separation of Church and State. There was no occasion for surprise, therefore, particularly in view of the acts of violence committed by the Constitutionalists upon the clergy, that Carranza's declaration of Constitutional aims, published in Vera Cruz on December 12, 1914, contained a guarantee of strict enforcement of the Laws of Reform. He also promised an amendment to the laws relating to marriage and the civil state of persons. In fulfillment of his promise to change the marriage laws, the First Chief decreed on December 29, 1914, the amendment of the law of December 14, 1874, to legalize divorce after three years of marriage, by mutual consent or because of serious cause. Remarriage after divorce was legalized. On January 29, 1915, the civil code of the Federal District and of the territories was amended to provide for absolute divorce.[19]

On June 11, 1915, Carranza announced the reform program of the Constitutionalists in the most comprehensive statement issued up to that date. On religious policy he said: "The constitutional laws of Mexico known under the name of Laws of Reform, which establish the separation of the Church and State and which guarantee to the individual the the right of worship in accordance with his own conscience and without offending public order, shall be strictly observed; therefore, no one shall suffer in his life, freedom, and property because of his religious beliefs. Temples shall continue to be the property of the nation according to the laws in force, and the Constitutionalist Government shall again cede for the purposes of worship those which may be necessary."[20] This statement was probably designed, in part to gain the support and quiet the fears of Catholics in view of the various crimes committed against them. But Carranza's promise of fair treatment under the law was insufficient, for the clericals could be satisfied with nothing less than a revocation or suspension of the Laws of Reform. That the policy and activities of the First Chief amounted to a denial of religious liberty was the interpretation of the American Government. President Wilson

---

[19] *Decretos de Carranza*, pp. 29, 136, 147, 168.
[20] *Ibid.*, p. 220.

demanded as one of his conditions of recognition that religious freedom be guaranteed—not only for Americans, but for Mexicans as well.[21]

In pursuance of the declaration that the churches were the property of the nation, and that the government would turn over for the purposes of worship those edifices deemed necessary, a law was passed (August 22, 1916) creating machinery to make the status effective. The law read:

I.   So long as churches are open to the services of any creed, they remain assimilated to the properties destined to a public service, and subject to the oversight of the Department of Interior, so far as concerns the exercise of the creed; and to the Department of Treasury respecting matters relating to their use, preservation, and improvement.

II.   The First Chieftaincy, through the Department of Interior, is the sole authority which can order the closing of churches in order to retire them from religious service and to consolidate their property. Consequently the local and municipal authorities must refrain from making decision on this matter.

III.   Right of use of the said properties being consolidated with direct control by the nation, the possession, preservation, and administration of the same shall be in charge of the Department of Treasury.

IV.   The person in charge of the Executive Power must designate the churches devoted to a public service, and of what the public service to which they are designated consists, in accordance with a previous favorable opinion from the Department of Treasury.

V.   When a church is legally withdrawn from the creed, the Departments of Treasury and Interior shall order a survey of the church and shall proceed to inventory what it contains, transmitting to the head under whose jurisdiction the church was when closed, the ornaments, vestments, and other movable goods devoted to religious services, with the exception of those acquired earlier than the law of nationalization of July 12, 1859; objects of artistic or historic interest must be placed at the disposition of the Secretary of the Department of Public Instruction and Fine Arts to be turned over to museums, lyceums, libraries, and other educational establishments.[22]

The above law removed any doubt, if indeed any existed, that it

[21] Gruening, *op. cit.*, p. 587.
[22] *Diario Oficial* (Mexico City), September 9, 1916.

was Carranza's intention to subordinate the Church to the strictest governmental control. By the time the Constitutionalists had achieved victory and were ready to convene in a constituent convention they were rampantly anti-clerical and anxious to increase the severity of the Laws of Reform.

In fulfillment of the oft-repeated assurance that when order should be established a properly elected constituent congress would be convoked to elevate to constitutional status the numerous reform-decrees published during the course of the civil war, Carranza issued a call for the election in September, 1916. The delegates were to be "popularly" elected, subject to their taking an oath of loyalty to the *Plan de Guadalupe.* In other words only Constitutionalists were eligible to election as delegates; those who supported in any way the governments or factions hostile to the Constitutionalist cause were barred from the polls. The elections resulted then, in a Constitutionalist party convention, and it was this body which proceeded to give the Mexican nation an instrument of government "representative of the popular will." That the Constitutionalists did not represent the Mexican majority was readily admitted by delegate Machorro Narváez. He said in the Convention: "The present Revolution is not yet popular in Mexico. The greater part of the Mexican people is still against the Revolution; the upper class, some of the old intellectual element, a part of the middle class, and some of the laboring class, are against the Revolution. Clerks and office employees, who are the mainstay of the middle class, are against the Revolution. We are still a minority."[23] The deputies were divided into two major groups, one extremely radical, the other moderately radical. The first group which found its principal support on the outside in General Álvaro Obregón, has been called the "Jacobinos Obregonistas." They, counting forty-five generals in their number, constituted the majority. The second group less radically inclined, supported Carranza's program which was surprisingly moderate. They have been called the "Liberales Carrancistas."[24]

---

[23] *Diario de los Debates del Congreso Constituyente* (Mexico, 1917), I, 71; L. Melgarejo Randolf y J. Fernández Rojas, *El Congreso Constituyente de 1917* (Mexico, 1917), pp. 124, 749.   [24] *Ibid.,* pp. 749-750.

The inaugural session of the Constituent Congress was held in the Teatro Iturbide, in Querétaro, on December 1, 1916. Venustiano Carranza presided at the opening session and presented to the Convention a model constitution which was to serve as the basis of its discussions. The proposed constitution proved to be more conservative than that of 1857. It contained no labor code or provision for the nationalization of land or subsoil. The religious clauses likewise were mild when compared with the provisions eventually adopted.[25] It should be noted, however, that Carranza accepted the Constitution of 1917 without protest. His failure therefore to include in his project certain articles which were adopted, did not necessarily mean that he was opposed to them. So, with respect to the religious articles. Although some of the most radical features of the present constitution were not suggested by Carranza, there is no reason to doubt that they were acceptable to him.

The relation of the Church to education elicited greater interest and discussion than perhaps any other subject before the Convention. This was due, not only to the recognized importance of education in itself, but since this was the first subject introduced to the Convention affecting the status of the Church, the opportunity was seized on that occasion to debate the religious question in general. Later there was little or no debate on any of the other religious articles. On the subject of education the Constitution of 1857 (Article 3) read: "Instruction is free." Carranza suggested as an amendment to this article: "There will be complete liberty of instruction; but that given in official educational institutions will be laical, and primary, elementary, and superior instruction in the said establishments will be free."[26]

The committee on the constitution, reported unfavorably on Article 3 of Carranza's project and suggested as a substitute: "There will be liberty of education, but that given in official educational institutions will be laical, the same as in the private primary, elementary, and superior schools. No religious corpo-

---

[25] For the project, see *Diario de Debates,* I, 260-270.

[26] *Ibid.,* I, 341. Article 4 of the Laws of Reform prohibited religious education in public schools.

ration, minister of any cult or person belonging to any similar association can establish or direct schools of primary grade, nor instruct personally in any college. The private primary schools can only be established subject to governmental vigilance. Primary instruction is obligatory for all Mexicans and instruction will be free in all official establishments." Thus the committee went considerably farther than Carranza and suggested that all education of a primary and secondary nature, public and private, be purged of religious instruction, and that religious schools of a primary nature be abolished.

Deputy Múgica, chairman of the committee on the constitution, in defending the report said: "It is just to restrain a natural right when its free exercise affects the security of society or prevents its development. . . . The clergy is alone responsible for the plots which have been hatched here and in foreign countries against the constitutional government; the clergy is the eternal enemy which is never conquered, but which is disposed to struggle to the end."[27] All primary Church schools should be abolished, he urged, as a national security measure.

Deputy Chapa, a "Liberal Carrancista" said: "If each article of the constitution is approved with the spirit, tendencies, and significance of Article 3 as proposed by the committee, we will have made a constitution of rabid jacobinism. . . . We have come here not to change the liberal principles of '57, but to adopt in the same spirit the necessary additions proposed by the First Chief as being immediately necessary for the Mexican people." Another deputy, Señor Cravioto, attacked the committee's report by presenting figures to prove that there was no menace in the religious schools. In 1907, when school attendance was at its greatest, there were 9,620 public schools and 586 clerical schools. The actual attendance of the public schools was 343,981, and of the clerical schools, 23,605. Since the educational needs of Mexico were so great, he opposed the destruction of the Catholic schools. "The real liberal triumph over religious instruction," he said, "is to combat it on its own ground, by multiplying our schools."[28]

[27] *Ibid.,* I, 366-367; Randolf y Rojas, *op. cit.,* p. 395.
[28] *Diario de Debates,* I, 471, 448-450.

On December 16, 1916, by a vote of 99 to 54, the committee's report on Article 3 was accepted with only one amendment. The introductory words, "There will be liberty of education," were stricken from the article, thereby evidencing frank confession on the part of the constituents that they were not guaranteeing educational liberty in Mexico. The announcement of the vote on the article was greeted by cries of "Viva la Revolución! Viva el C. Primer Jefe! La Patria se ha salvado!"[29] The vote on this, the first religious article submitted for the consideration of the Convention, showed clearly that the "Jacobins" or extreme radicals, were in control and that the religious clauses of the new constitution would be the most drastic in the entire history of the Republic.

Carranza's proposal that the establishment of monastic orders be prohibited, as provided in the old constitution, was approved by the Convention (Article 5). Likewise, the proposal of the First Chief that religious liberty be guaranteed was approved and incorporated in Article 24, which read:

> Every one is free to embrace the religion of his choice and to practice all ceremonies, devotions, or observances of his respective creed, either in places of public worship or at home, provided they do not constitute an offense punishable by law.
>
> Every religious act of public worship shall be performed strictly within the places of public worship, which shall be at all times under governmental supervision.

These were drawn largely from the Leyes de Reforma of December 14, 1874.

With respect to the property rights of religious institutions, the First Chief proposed substantially the adoption of Article 27 of the Constitution of 1857. According to this Article, as amended May 14, 1901, no religious institution had the legal capacity to acquire or administer real property other than the buildings immediately and directly destined to the services of the cult. Nor did they have the legal capacity to acquire loans or administer loans made on such real property. In addition, Carranza proposed that charitable institutions belonging to or administered by religious corporations be denied the right to ac-

---

[29] *Ibid.*, I, 530; Randolf y Rojas, *op. cit.*, p. 445.

quire real estate except that destined for the direct and immediate use of these institutions. It is indeed surprising that Carranza, in view of prior acts and declarations should have excepted church buildings necessary for the cult from the nationalization edict, but such was the case.

The Convention, however, went beyond Carranza's proposal and declared that even the church buildings required for the immediate uses of the cult belonged to the nation, and all religious charitable enterprises were abolished. The religious sections of Article 27, into which these provisions were incorporated, read as follows:

II. The religious institutions known as Churches, irrespective of creed, shall in no case have legal capacity to acquire, hold, or administer real property or loans made on such real property; all such real property or loans as may be at present held by the said religious institutions, either on their own behalf or through third parties, shall vest in the Nation, and any one shall have the right to denounce property so held. Presumptive proof shall be sufficient to declare the denunciation well-founded. Places of public worship are the property of the Nation as represented by the Federal government, which shall determine which of them may continue to be devoted to their present purposes. Episcopal residences, rectories, seminaries, orphan asylums or collegiate establishments of religious institutions, convents or any other buildings, built or designed for the administration, propaganda, or teaching of the tenets of any religious creed shall forthwith vest, as of full right, directly in the Nation, to be used exclusively for the public services of the Federation or of the States, within their respective jurisdiction. All places of public worship which shall later be erected shall be the property of the Nation.

III. Public and private charitable institutions for the sick and needy, for scientific research, or for the diffusion of knowledge, mutual aid societies or organizations formed for any lawful purpose shall in no case acquire, hold or administer loans made on real property, unless the mortgage terms do not exceed ten years. In no case shall institutions of this character be under the patronage, direction, administration, charge or supervision of religious corporations or institutions, nor of ministers of any religious creed or of their dependents, even though either the former or the latter shall not be in active service.[30]

---

[30] Randolf y Rojas, *op. cit.*, p. 301. Clauses II and III of the 1917 text are partly taken from the Laws of Reform.

The excluding of the Church from any participation in the administration of charitable and eleemosynary institutions was a most radical action, particularly in a country like Mexico which depended so greatly upon the religious hospitals and orphanages. So insistent and stubbornly determined were the "Jacobin reformers" that activities of the Catholic clergy should be restricted solely to the administration of the sacraments and conduct of religious services, that they felt it justifiable to impose sacrifices upon orphans and the sick. Too engrossed were they in the reform to consider the consequences.

Most of the religious innovations, constitutionally speaking, were incorporated in Article 130. This article, although it included, as suggested by Carranza, provisions prohibiting to Congress the power to enact any law establishing or forbidding any religion; establishing marriage as a civil contract; and prohibiting the religious oath, went far beyond any proposal made by the First Chief. The principal additional features are: (1) the law recognizes no juridic personality in religious institutions known as churches, and ministers of creeds shall be considered as persons exercising a profession; (2) the state legislatures shall have the exclusive power of determining the maximum number of ministers of religious creeds according to the needs of each locality; (3) only Mexicans by birth may be ministers of any religious creed in Mexico; (4) no minister shall either publicly or privately (either in public or private meetings or in acts of worship) criticise the fundamental laws of the country, or the authorities; (5) members of the clergy shall have no vote, nor be eligible to office, nor be allowed to assemble for political purposes; (6) new temples shall not be dedicated without the permission of the Department of Interior; (7) every place of worship shall have a caretaker who shall be legally responsible for the faithful performance of the laws within the said place of worship, and for all the objects used for purposes of worship; (8) the municipal authorities, under penalty of fine and dismissal, shall keep a register of the churches and of their caretakers, and shall report to the Department of Interior through the State governor, any permission to open to the public use a new place of worship, as well as any change in the caretakers; (9) studies carried on in ecclesiastical seminaries shall not be accredited in any official institution; (10) no periodical publication of a religious nature shall comment upon political affairs of the nation, nor give any information regarding the acts of officials or of private individuals in so far as the latter have to do with public affairs; (11) political associations, bearing any indication by their name to any religious belief are prohibited; (12) no assemblies of any political character shall be held within places of worship; (13) no ministers shall inherit, either personally or indirectly, any real property possessed by a religious association, or any property of other ministers of the same creed, or private individuals to whom he is not related by blood within the fourth degree; and (14), no trial by jury shall ever be granted for the infraction of any of the preceding provisions.

Some of the provisions of Article 130 were taken from the constitutional amendment of 1873 (Article 123) and the Laws of Reform (1874). Most of them, however, were original with the constituents and exceeded in severity all prior legislation on ecclesiastical matters. The denial of juridic personality to the church, the prohibition of foreign clergy of all creeds, the limitation on the number of ministers, and additional limitations on the political and property rights of individual members of the clergy were the "Jacobin" contribution to the body of Mexican anti-clerical legislation. The denial of the right of trial by jury to violators of the religious clauses of the Constitution was recognition by the constituents of the unpopular nature of their reforms. Yet this measure does not appear to be so drastic when one considers that jury trial is not regarded with the same respect in Latin America as in Anglo-America, and that the jury system was abolished in the Mexican Federal District and territories in December, 1929.

Barring the debates on Article 3, the other religious clauses of the Constitution were adopted with little or no discussion. The vote of December 16 was accepted as meaning that the extreme radicals were to have their way and thereafter no attempt was made to block them. Very often votes on separate articles were dispensed with and they were accepted *en masse*.

For example, Article 5, having to do with monastic vows, was unanimously approved in combination with the labor article.[31] Article 27 did not come before the Convention until the final days of the session, and then evidently the members were anxious to adjourn, for the measure was adopted hurriedly and with no attention devoted to its religious clauses. The Constituent Convention closed its session on January 31, 1917, and on February 5, the result of its labors was promulgated by Carranza. The Constitution became effective on May 1, 1917.

The evident intention of the "Jacobins of Querétaro" was to drive the Church out of politics, to destroy its social influence, and to confine it strictly to the field of religion. To accomplish this they contradicted the guarantee of religious freedom and put the Church under the domination of the State. The Constitution of 1917 went far beyond that of 1857 in its curtailment of clerical power—indeed, if strictly executed, the very existence of the Church would have been threatened.

The religious clauses, however, were not enforced, either by Carranza or by Obregón. Because of their desire to consolidate their political positions they refrained from stirring up additional opposition by seeking a strict enforcement of Article 130. For nearly eight years, so far as interference with the Church was concerned the new Constitution might as well have been non-existent. Although ecclesiastical primary schools were forbidden a great number continued to be operated with governmental consent. In commenting on this tolerance toward religious schools, President Obregón said, "We are not unaware of the menace of these Catholic schools whose aim is to inculcate anti-government and anti-revolutionary propaganda. But at present there is not money enough nor facilities for the government to teach all Mexican children. It is preferable that they

---

[31] *Diario de Debates,* I, 553. Some radical proposals made by the Yucatanese delegation, which fortunately were not accepted by the Convention, were: (1) abolition of auricular confession; (2) denial to priests of the right to hold real estate; (3) the Church to pay rent for the use of edifices; (4) official commissioners to administer the donations of the faithful; and (5) no priest to be less than fifty years old.

receive any instruction rather than grow illiterate."[32]

The constitutional prohibition of religious orders, male and female, was also disregarded. The nuns particularly were active in hospital and other charitable work. The foreign clergy too, had not been bothered. Also the law against public religious ceremonials and demonstrations were violated with impunity. During the presidency of Obregón numerous "coronations" of the Virgin were celebrated in various parts of Mexico. These ceremonies in which a concourse of prelates officiated were generally accompanied by processions or other manifestations outside of the churches. When the first bishop of Tacambaro was instituted (July, 1921), several acts of a religious character were performed outside of the churches.

Notwithstanding the uneasiness of the clergy because of the menace of "reglamentation" and enforcement of the Constitution, the Church prospered during the Obregón administration. New dioceses were created, other dioceses forcibly abandoned during the Revolution were reoccupied, and Church councils and Eucharistic congresses were held. The remarkable progress made by the clergy in restoring the prestige of the Church was undoubtedly responsible for the "Cubilete" episode. On January 11, 1923, on the summit of Cubilete Mountain in Guanajuato, and in the presence of a vast gathering of people and eleven prelates, Apostolic Delegate Mgr. Philippi, placed the first stone on the monument to "Christ the King." The ceremony, undoubtedly religious, and described as solemn and imposing, evoked governmental action. On January 13, Obregón announced the expulsion of the Apostolic Delegate because of his participation in an illegal public religious ceremony. The pope requested the government to suspend the expulsion of Mgr. Philippi, but he was not heeded, and the Delegate left Mexico. The Mexican prelates who participated in the affair were not bothered, yet it was undoubtedly the intention of Obregón that they should take warning and he chose to issue it in a dramatic manner.[33]

---

[32] Gruening, *op. cit.,* p. 220.

[33] Luís C. Balderrama, *El Clero y el Gobierno de México* (Mexico, 1927), I, 156-159.

Although the Federal government was remiss in the matter of enforcing the religious clauses of the Constitution, some of the State legislatures proceeded to exercise in an intolerant manner rights vested in them by the Federal Constitution. In Yucatan sixteen was established as the maximum number of ministers of each religious creed for the whole State. The legislature of Durango in May, 1923, provided that only twenty-five priests could function in the State. In Chihuahua tumults and riots were caused (July, 1923) because of a decree which limited the number of priests in the State to seventy-five. All of these laws were revoked soon after their passage. The injustice of the attempts to limit the Catholic priesthood to such small numbers in the Mexican states can admit of little argument. The enemies of the clergy, in the enthusiasm of the attack, proceeded too far to the other extreme. Years before there undoubtedly had been too many priests, monks, and nuns in Mexico, but that situation no longer existed. It cannot be said that Mexico was priest-ridden after the days of the Reform. In illustration further of official radicalism in the states may be cited the decree issued in October, 1925, in the State of Tabasco, which required priests of all creeds to marry in order to exercise the duties of their office. Several priests were arrested within a month after the issuance of the decree because of their refusal to marry.[34]

In his attempt to decrease the power and influence of the Catholic Church in Mexico, Benito Juárez encouraged the development of Protestantism. But his efforts were attended by scant success. In recent years another Mexican government pursued an analogous policy by encouraging the development of a "National" Catholic Church. "La Iglesia Ortodoxa Católica Apostólica Mexicana," or the Schismatic Church, as it was more popularly known, was formally founded on February 18, 1925. The government turned over to the new cult some churches which had once belonged to the Roman Catholic organization. The church of Corpus Christi in Mexico City was the head church of the National faith, and the seat of the "patriarch," José

---

[34] *Ibid.*, I, 159-160; *Current History*, December, 1925, p. 412.

Joaquín Pérez. On August 1, 1925, "La Restauración," official organ of the new sect was published. The schismatics were also very active in printing and distributing anti-Roman Catholic and anti-papal literature. Typical of these were broadsides urging Mexicans to "cease enriching the greatest enemy of Mexico —the pope!" To advertise the fact that the National Church exacted no fees for the performance of special services, a circular was distributed containing the great number of charges made by the Catholic Church for the performance of services and for special dispensations. The fundamental bases of the schismatic cult were announced as:

I. Our Church does not constitute a sect but it is based on the real religion which was founded by our Divine Master and Redeemer.

II. The Holy Scripture of the Old and New Testaments are the headstone of our church, and they can be freely interpreted by the members, as can also tradition and the liturgy.

III. The purity of the most Blessed Virgin Mary, Our Mother and Mistress, is an article of faith with us and no one can belong to the real religion without this belief. The saints also ought to be venerated.

IV. The power of ruling and governing the Catholic Apostolic Mexican Church resides in its primate or patriarch, independent of Rome, the Pope, or authority of the Vatican, and it has no relation to it. The Mexican Patriarch is the only one who will have power to order the ministers and confer on them the power to administer the Holy Sacraments.

V. The Holy Sacraments ought to be administered without any charge in order to end the practice of simony which exists in the Church of Rome, and only for the intention or application of the Holy Sacrifice of the Mass can alms be received, and then they must be freely given by the one who makes the request; the members of the Church are not required to pay tithes or primacies.

VI. The priest of the Mexican Church ought to be a useful member of society, obedient to the laws and institutions of our Fatherland, and not a person who is supported by the labor of someone else.

VII. Ecclesiastical celibacy is abolished as immoral and unnatural; the priest ought to make a home and by respecting it learn to respect that of others.

VIII. All the services and liturgical books ought to be in the Castilian language.

IX. The clergy of the Mexican Church do not pretend to exercise temporal or spiritual dominion over those adhering to it.

X. Our God is a perfect Being without anger or vengeance, thus He does not condemn for all eternity man made in his image and likeness. Punishment for sin is in direct proportion to the act, and its duration is determined by the degree of culpability."[35]

The Schismatic Church, notwithstanding governmental encouragement, was predestined to failure from the beginning. The populace regarded it with scorn and indifference, and its converts were few. The inability of Protestantism to make headway in Mexico, and the dismal failure of the "National" church are additional proof of the well-known fact that there is no substitute for Roman Catholicism in Latin America—it is a case of the Catholic faith or none at all.

Although some of the State governments enacted anti-clerical legislation, the National government itself, during the administrations of Carranza and Obregón, made little or no attempt to enforce the constitutional articles defining the status of religious sects. It was not until President Plutarco Elías Calles assumed control of the Mexican government nearly nine years after the promulgation of the Constitution of 1917, that those articles were converted into a living reality. The intention of the Calles administration to enforce the religious provisions of the Constitution was first made known on February 11, 1926. On that date was published the first of a series of increasingly drastic laws and regulations, which culminated in a few months in the suspension of all religious exercises in the Catholic churches in Mexico.

What caused the sword of Damocles to descend upon the heads of the Mexican clergy? The immediate cause, asserted President Calles in an interview which was printed in the *New York Herald Tribune*, on February 24, 1926, was the public display of disobedience on the part of the Catholic organizations, the Mexican Episcopacy, and even the head of the Mexican Catholic Church. On February 4, 1926, there appeared in "El Universal," one of the leading newspapers in Mexico, an interview with Archbishop Mora y del Río. The article read in part as follows:

---

[35] The writer is indebted to Professor Herbert Gambrell of Southern Methodist University, Dallas, for publications of the Schismatic Church.

The most illustrious Señor Archbishop of Mexico was pleased to give to our reporter Señor Ignacio Monroy, the following statement dictated by him: "The doctrine of the Church is unvariable, because it is the divinely revealed truth. The protest which we Mexican prelates formulated against the Constitution of 1917 respecting the articles which are opposed to religious liberty and dogmas is maintained firmly. It has not been modified but strengthened because it is derived from the doctrine of the Church. The information which "El Universal" published on January 27 to the effect that there would be inaugurated a campaign against the laws, unjust and contrary to natural right, is perfectly true. The Episcopacy, clergy, and Catholics do not recognize and combat Articles 3, 5, 27, and 130 of the existing constitution. This decision we cannot by any motive alter without being traitors to our faith and our religion.

The Secretary of Interior, Adalberto Tejeda, took immediate cognizance of the statement of the Archbishop, which he regarded as being seditious. "The State permits to the Catholic Church," he said, "the exercise of its functions up to a point where it does not constitute an obstacle to progress and the development of the people; but it cannot, nor ought not to tolerate [a declaration] that the constitutional laws are not recognized and are combatted, as was declared in the mentioned statement." Since the government's duty is to see that the laws are respected, said Señor Tejeda, he was presenting the facts, fully documented, to the Attorney General. The Archbishop asked for an immediate hearing, and was accommodated. The reporter insisted that his account was correct, for, he contended, Archbishop Mora read it to him from a prepared copy. The attorney for the Archbishop, however, denied that the prelate was correctly quoted. Since this, whether it were true or not meant retraction by the prelate, the government was willing to dismiss the charge.[36]

The League for the Defense of Religious Liberty, the Union of Catholic Women, the Knights of Columbus, and other Catholic associations applauded Archbishop Mora y del Río, and showed clearly their hostility to the government. On February 8, 1926, the Mexican Episcopacy endorsed the attitude of the Primate by publishing "La Protesta Colectiva del Episcopado."

---

[36] Balderrama, *op. cit.*, I, 39, 42; *Excelsior*, February 5, 1926.

This document, signed by Mora y del Río and all the archbishops and bishops proclaimed the principles of the Constitution to be contrary to the most sacred rights of the Church, Mexican society, and Christians. "It tears up by the roots," declared the prelates, "the few rights which the Constitution of 1857 (admitted *in its essential principles,* as the fundamental law by all Mexicans) guarantees to the Church as a society and to Catholics as individuals. . . . Not intending to meddle in political questions, but to defend in a manner which is possible to us, religious liberty of Christian people in view of the rude attack which had been made on religion, we limit ourselves to protest against the attempt energetically and decorously." Disclaiming any seditious motives, but a duty to defend the rights of the Church, the prelates enumerated those parts of the Constitution which they opposed and which made religious liberty illusory.[37]

What caused the Mexican Episcopacy to invite disaster by publicly repudiating the Constitution? The National government had not, up to February, 1926, taken any steps to enforce the religious clauses. Yet it was generally understood that President Calles was intent on enforcing the Constitution as a whole and to the letter. He, unlike his predecessor in the presidential office, was a man with an essentially one-track mind; tenacious, stubborn, uncompromising, once he embarked upon a given course, nothing could swerve him. Having determined to enforce the constitutional law the President would let no consideration deter him, and whatever might be the consequences he insisted that the commands of the fundamental charter be observed. "Even if the recent public display of disobedience and opposition to the fundamental laws of the country by the head of the Mexican Catholic Church had not been made," said President Calles in his interview with the reporter of the *New York Herald-Tribune,* on February 24, "this government in complying with its duty to observe and cause to be observed the Constitution of the country would have proceeded in the manner it has." In obedience to presidential request the Congress was already considering legislation relating to the hitherto neglected articles

[37] *El Universal,* February 8, 1926; Toro, *op. cit.,* p. 464.

27 and 123, concerning the rights of foreigners in land and the rights of labor respectively. Legislation for the enforcement of the other neglected article (130) it was feared would come next. Furthermore, legislation in the states was becoming so oppressive as to warrant clerical protest on its own account.

It has been suggested that the Episcopacy, seeking to take advantage of Mexico's embarrassment, published the protest when relations between the Calles and Coolidge governments over oil and land appeared to be leading to war. Conclusive proof, however, cannot be found to support this thesis. Another allegation, that the prelates were encouraged in their opposition by the pope himself, appears to have better substantiation. Following the return from Rome of Archbishop González of Durango and Bishop Mora of San Luís Potosí, an assembly of the National Episcopacy was held in which it was agreed to combat articles 3, 5, 24, 27, and 130 of the Constitution. The prelates of Durango and San Luís delivered to the assembly a letter (dated February 2) from the pope which undoubtedly influenced the action of the prelates. This letter, which was not released for publication until April 19, denounced in strong, bitter terms the Mexican government, the statute laws, and the Constitution. It said:

It is scarcely necessary for us to tell you how wicked are the regulations and laws invoked against the Catholic citizens of Mexico which have been sanctioned by officials hostile to the Church, and which by their enforcement long have oppressed you. You are fully aware that these laws are far from being reasonable laws, nor are they useful and necessary for the common good as assuredly all laws should be. On the contrary, they do not seem to merit the name of laws. Indeed, we are moved all the more insistently to utter this public protest and condemnation of such laws, seeing that day after day the warfare against the Catholic religion is being waged more bitterly by the rulers of the Republic.

A significant part of the letter advised and commanded the bishops to develop "united Catholic action." Although admonishing the clergy against violation of the Constitution by becoming members of any political party, the pope counseled that "they ought in keeping with their priestly office, and safeguard-

31

ing the sacredness of their ministry, to promote the welfare of their country by diligent and religious exercise of their civil rights and duties, and by setting a good example which the faithful can follow so that each one of them will studiously comply with their public obligations as the laws of God and the Church demand."[38]

Whatever may have decided the Mexican Episcopacy to voice public repudiation of the obnoxious religious articles there is no doubt that it was this call to the faithful to disobey the law which caused President Calles to make effective at once the constitutional prescriptions which up to that time had been latent. On February 11, 1926, the Attorney General announced that all Church property not already in the possession of the nation had been nationalized, and that orders had been issued for the arrest and deportation of all foreign priests. On the next day another order was issued for the closing of all schools, asylums, and convents where religious instruction was given. On February 13, the Minister of Interior telegraphed all the state governors calling their attention to the necessity of enforcing articles 3, 5, and 130 of the Federal Constitution. They were urged to introduce these subjects, with the least possible delay, to the State legislatures.[39]

The arrest of foreign priests for the purpose of deportation was begun without warning on the night of February 10. By September, 183 foreign-born clericals had been expelled. The great majority of these were Spaniards. Considerable protest and some violence attended the expulsion of the foreign priests. In explanation of his action President Calles said, "The measure which was taken prohibiting foreign ministers to act had a reason, but you [Anglo-Americans] cannot appreciate it since you do not have it in your country. But in Latin America the foreign priests have always signified a calamity, particularly the Roman Catholic priests, because all the waste of Rome and of all Europe was sent to our countries, and there have been thousands of curates who have come to 'fanaticize' our people and submerge them in ignorance, and take away from here all

---

[38] Balderrama, *op. cit.*, I, 38; *New York Times*, April 20, 1926.
[39] *Current History*, April, 1926, p. 116; Balderrama, *op. cit.*, I, 49.

that they were able." As for foreign Protestant ministers they also were not allowed to function, for, said President Calles, "The law clearly states that all priests of all cults must be of Mexican nationality. Actually the Protestant ministers are working in Mexico without harming anyone for they have always adjusted themselves to the law."[40] Minister Tejeda issued a warning statement (May 22) that all foreign Protestant ministers who failed to comply with the law would be deported.

According to a statement of the Minister of Interior (February 18) investigation had disclosed that many convents existed under pretext of being Catholic colleges. Against these the government proceeded, but "with the greatest moderation." By September, 73 convents, 129 schools attached to convents, and 118 orphan asylums under religious control had been closed.[41] In some instances the closing was attended by rioting. French and Spanish nuns engaged in teaching in such institutions were deported.

On February 26 the Secretary of Public Instruction directed all private schools to register with the Ministry of Public Instruction within sixty days or be closed. Private primary schools were forbidden to teach religious subjects, or to have any connection with churches or ecclesiastical corporations. Ministers of any creed and members of religious orders were forbidden to serve as teachers. On April 24 new rules were issued by the Ministry of Public Instruction for private schools. They were prohibited from using pictures, paintings, or anything that would indicate religious ideas. The mere mention of anything religious, including the names of saints was interdicted, and the schools were to have no communication with any buildings dedicated to religious purposes.[42]

The request of President Calles that the state governments proceed to an immediate "reglamentation" of the religious laws

[40] *Excelsior* (Mexico City), August 10, 1926; Toro, *op. cit.*, pp. 425, 454.

[41] *Memoria de la Secretaría de Gobernación, 1925 á 1926,* in Toro, *op. cit.*, pp. 455-458.

[42] *El Universal,* February 26 and April 24, 1926; J. M. Puig Casauranc, *La cuestión religiosa en relación con la educación pública en México* (Mexico, 1928), pp. 10-26.

met with a ready response, at least with respect to the determination of the number of priests who could legally function. By September, 1926, the following quotas had been established.[43]

Aguascalientes	One minister for each 5,000 inhabitants.
Tamaulipas	Twelve ministers for all the state.
Nayarit	Forty for all the state.
Colima	One for each 5,000 inhabitants in the capital and one for each municipality.
Coahuila	Twelve for Saltillo, five for Torreón, and three each for the following municipalities: Piedras Negras, Monclova, Parras, and San Pedro de las Colonias; two for Matamoros, and one for each of the remaining settlements in the state.
San Luís Potosí	One for each municipality, two for Matehuala, Rio Verde, and Santa María del Río, and ten for the capital.
Michoacán	Ten for Morelia, four for Patzcuaro and five more municipalities, three in Zinapecuaro and seven more municipalties, two in Indaparapeo and seventeen more municipalities, and one each in the remaining municipalities.
Sonora	One for each 10,000 inhabitants.
Durango	Twenty-five for each cult in all the state.
Chihuahua	One for each 9,000 inhabitants.
Yucatán	Forty for all the state.
Jalisco	Two hundred and fifty for all the state.
Puebla	One for each 4,000 inhabitants.
Tabasco	Six for all the state.
Vera Cruz	One for 10,000 inhabitants; two for 30,000, four for 60,000, and beyond that number, six for each cult.
Campeche	Five for all the state.

Restriction of the Catholic clergy as in the State of Campeche to five priests, and, as in the State of Sonora, to one priest to each 10,000 inhabitants, the majority of whom are Catholics, was oppressive, intolerant, and violative of the principle of religious liberty. Of this there can be little argument. The restrictions also were discriminatory in that non-Catholic cults, despite

---

[43] *Memoria de Secretaría de Gobernación, 1925 á 1926*, pp. 459-460.

their meager numbers, were often given the same number of ministers as were allowed the Catholic Church. The enemies of Catholicism were legislating it out of existence in Mexico.

The offensive of the Federal and State governments against the Catholic Church aroused a storm of protests and indignation in Mexico and in foreign countries, particularly in the United States. On March 9, Ambassador Sheffield presented a note to the Foreign Minister expressing the hope that American citizens would not be obliged to undergo actual hardship or injury in Mexico because of their religious beliefs and practices. This was as far as the government of the United States was willing to proceed in spite of the urgent demands of American Catholic prelates and laymen. Not even the expulsion in May, of Mgr. George Caruana, Bishop of Porto Rico, and an American citizen, who went to Mexico as papal delegate, would cause President Coolidge or Secretary Kellogg to alter their attitude.[44]

So vehement and injudicious were the protests of some of the Mexican prelates against the intolerable legislation that they soon found themselves in the toils of the law. Bishop Zarate of Huejutla, State of Durango, was ordered to appear for trial on a charge of violating the law that "no minister of religious creeds shall criticise the fundamental laws of the country, the authorities in particular, or the government in general." The Bishop refused to appear, saying that the civil magistrates had no authority over purely ecclesiastical subjects. Therefore he was arrested on May 13. He appeared before the civil judge in all his ecclesiastical regalia and it was necessary to remove them forcibly. He was subsequently released on bond. The Bishop of Tacambaro, State of Michoacán, was ordered (April 21) to present himself in court to answer charges of having issued a pastoral libeling the government. Bishop Herrar y Piña of Monterey was also cited for urging his priests and parishioners to offer passive resistance to the efforts of the government. Bishop Zarafe of Pachuca, having been found guilty of inciting to re-

[44] *Current History*, July, 1926, p. 615; Callcott, *Liberalism in Mexico*, pp. 370-372.

bellion was sentenced to confinement in jail. The Bishop of Tamaulipas was also arrested (June 17) and churches in his diocese were closed, because of his refusal to order the registration of priests. The Bishop of Vera Cruz, more circumspect, counseled his parishioners to be prudent and to avoid irresponsible actions. He declared that it was his desire "to establish a new era of harmony between the civil government and the Church, each one complying with its duties and obligations." When Archbishop Mora y del Río, in a letter to President Calles attempted to justify the actions of the rebellious clerics, the President declared that the religious laws would be maintained and any act of rebellion or lack of respect would be punished. "I wish you to understand now and always," he said, "that agitation within and without this country will not alter the purpose of this government."[45]

On July 21, 1926, President Calles issued a decree to become effective August 1, providing for the reform of the penal code in the Federal District and the territories in matters relating to religious offenses. A detailed scale of fines and punishments was worked out to cover every possible infringement of the religious clauses of the Constitution. But beyond the provision for the registration of all ministers of any religious creed before the civil authorities, this decree was merely a recapitulation of the various constitutional clauses and existing statutes relating to religion and education. Specific instructions were given to municipal officials who were charged with putting the decree into effect and penalties were prescribed for those failing to do so.[46] On July 23, President Calles issued supplementary regulations giving effect more specifically to the constitutional prohibition of religious teaching in private schools. By these regulations no minister of any religious cult could act as the director or teacher in such schools. No private educational institution might have chapels, oratories, or other places of public worship, or have on their premises pictures, statues, images, or objects of a religious nature. The schools were given one month in which

---

[45] Balderrama, *op. cit.*, I, 51-53; *Current History*, August, 1926, p. 783.
[46] "Reformas al Código Penal," in Pérez Lugo, *op. cit.*, pp. 258-263.

to file with the Secretariat of Public Instruction detailed information concerning their ownership, sources of revenue, and religious affiliation, if any.[47]

The answer of the National League for the Defense of Religious Liberty in Mexico to the decree of July 21, was the announcement that, as a measure of defense against the government's persecution of the Catholic Church, there would be launched on July 31 a nation-wide boycott. The plan was for all Catholics to refrain from purchasing anything but the necessities of life. "The purpose of this campaign," announced a circular of the League, "is to create in the nation a state of intense economic crisis which will oblige the government to bring to an end the situation of legal oppression under which the Catholic Church exists in this country." Archbishop Mora y del Río and Bishop Pascual Díaz, Secretary of the Episcopate, called upon all Catholics to coöperate in the boycott. The pope, however, refused to countenance such a plan of action. He recommended instead public prayers and the seeking of peaceful means to settle the difficulty. August 1, a day commemorative of St. Peter-in-Chains, was designated by the Holy Father as the date for special prayers throughout the world for the cessation of the Mexican government's persecution of the Catholics.[48]

Since the Catholic prelates of Mexico felt that it was impossible to practice their sacred ministry under the conditions imposed by Calles' decree, particularly the requirement that all priests be registered, they agreed, with papal approval, to withdraw the priests from all the churches in the Republic. The momentous decision to suspend all religious services was made public on July 25 in a pastoral letter signed by eight archbishops and twenty-nine bishops. "We order that," read the pastoral, "after July 31 until we order otherwise all religious services requiring the intervention of priests shall be suspended in all the churches of the country." The edifices were not to be closed but were to be entrusted to the care of the worshippers. Denying that their conduct constituted rebellion the prelates declared

---

[47] *Excelsior*, July 24, 1926.

[48] *Memoria de Secretaría de Gobernación*, p. 470; Balderrama, *op. cit.*, I, 64.

that they were employing "the only way open to manifest non-conformance with the anti-religious laws of the Constitution."[49]

The government would not countenance the proposal of the Episcopate that the abandoned churches be turned over to committees or individuals named by the priests but insisted that the civil authorities should assume immediate control. The municipal authorities were then to appoint committees of honorable residents who should be responsible for the churches, and keep them open for public use.[50] President Calles refused to grant that he had added in any way to the severity of the religious clauses of the Constitution. This in fact was true, with the exception of the registration requirement. The object of the register, said the President, was to enable the government to know who were entrusted with the churches and who were responsible for what went on inside of them. The Catholic hierarchy alleged, however, that registration would give the State unlimited control over the clergy and would enable it to license a priest who had not been designated by his bishop.[51]

The final religious services were held on July 30. On the following day the priests made inventories of the contents of the churches and removed their personal belongings before the formal delivery to the civil committees on August 1. The withdrawal of the priests from the churches, denoting as it did the suspension of the administration of the sacraments in a country composed of approximately eighty to ninety per cent Catholics, was a drastic action which was confidently expected in many quarters to create serious disturbances in Mexico. However, the transfer of the churches to the government was accomplished without serious disorder. In summing up the developments of July 31 to August 3, Minister Tejeda said:

The delivery of the churches to the citizens' committees, in accordance with Constitutional Article 130, is proceeding satisfactorily, according to notices received from the States. Unfortunate but slight disorders occurred in Cuidad Guzmán, Torreón and Irapuato, but

[49] *El Universal*, July 25, 1926.
[50] *Ibid.*, July 29, 1926.
[51] *Excelsior*, August 10, 1926.

in each place they were easily suppressed by the police. All of them, as well as those which occurred in this capital, were provoked by small groups of women. Up to the present time order has been preserved throughout the country and there is no reason to believe that it will be disturbed. The Catholics continue as formerly to attend their churches.[52]

The drastic and unprecedented action on the part of the Mexican Catholic prelates in ordering the suspension of all religious exercises attracted once more the eyes of the Catholic world to the Mexican situation. Pastorals condemning the Mexican rulers were issued in the United States by Cardinals Mundelein and Hayes, and in Latin America by the archbishops of Caracas, Rio de Janeiro, Santiago de Chile, and Santa Fé de Bogotá. "L'Osservatore Romano," official Vatican publication, attacked President Calles with considerable fury. "La Tribuna," semi-official paper of Mussolini, accused international Masonry as being the inspirer of the Mexican laws.[53] These Roman periodicals, like the Mexican clergy themselves, failed to concede that the Church contributed in any way to its misfortunes.

On August 3 President Leguía of Peru telegraphed President Calles urging him "to use his powerful influence in reëstablishing harmonious relations with the Church." President Calles, in his reply of August 4, told the dictator of Peru that he was willing to regard the message as merely a personal expression and in no wise official. "The Constitution of Mexico is not a special law," he explained to President Leguía, "but a general and fundamental code which I am obliged and am decided to enforce without fear of interdicts or supernatural punishment."[54]

The appeal of the Knights of Columbus to Secretary Kellogg to intervene in the religious conflict was met with the usual refusal. The policy of the Coolidge government was that unless American lives and property rights were placed in jeopardy the Church-State conflict was an internal problem of the Republic

---

[52] *Current History*, September, 1926, p. 837.

[53] Balderrama, *op. cit.*, I, 110-114.

[54] *Ibid.*, I, 222-223.

of Mexico. Efforts in and out of Mexico to bring about American intervention were disapproved by the pope. He saw in this a great danger to Catholics of Mexico, for it presented them as anti-patriots and it excited resentment against them and against the United States.[55]

On the other hand the Mexican government was not without words of encouragement and approval. Thousands of messages of support were sent to President Calles from deputies, senators, political associations, and workers' organizations. Ex-President Obregón's message was of inestimable value because it meant that the armed forces, over which Obregón exercised dominant control, were behind the government and made resistance impossible. The Regional Confederation of Mexican Workers, called the *Crom,* stood solidly behind the President throughout the crisis. On Sunday, August 1, a parade of approximately 50,000 men and women, organized by the *Crom,* filed past President Calles in testimony of loyalty to the government. The Federation of Syndicated Workers of the Federal District conducted public debates on the religious issue in the Teatro Isis in Mexico City. These discussions conducted in a partisan manner by the anti-clerical forces failed to clarify the beclouded issues.[56]

On August 19, Archbishop Leopoldo Ruíz and Bishop Pascual Díaz, acting for the Episcopacy, and invoking their constitutional guarantee of the right of petition, solicited of President Calles the following liberties: conscience, thought, religion, instruction, association, and the press. The President, after acknowledging the propriety of the action of the Episcopate in petitioning him as one of the authorities vested with the power of initiating legislation, replied that, since his philosophical and political convictions rendered him thoroughly in accord with the legislation in question, he found himself unable to acquiesce in their requests. Furthermore, he pointed out, although quite unconvincingly, that there was no denial of liberty of conscience, thought, religion, instruction, association, and the press, for these very rights were guaranteed by articles 3, 6, 7, 9 and 24

---

[55] *Ibid.,* I, 123.　　　　　　　[56] *Ibid.,* I, 78-79; 146-147.

of the Constitution. Since these articles guaranteed everything the prelates demanded, the President felt that their request was unnecessary.[57]

President Calles' denial that his measures voided religious liberty was in line with his oft-repeated declaration that his government was engaged in no conflict with the Church and that the problem did not relate to dogma. If the Episcopacy suspended services on its own account, he said, then the government had no interest in seeing their renewal, "because it did not interfere in the liberty of beliefs." Minister Estreda backed up his Chief by declaring that the laws did not contain any prohibition in the matter of creeds. Aarón Sáenz, Minister of Foreign Relations, said, "The Mexican government not only tolerates, but it respects as well, as does any other country, all religious creeds. To say that the Mexican government persecutes any determined religion is a malicious falsehood." It was indeed true that no direct attempt had been made to alter dogma and articles of faith, but hierarchial control was destroyed, no longer could effective discipline be maintained, and the conduct of the faith was put under governmental supervision. Surely this was denial of religious freedom and official persecution. If not, then interference with dogma, and that alone, constitutes violation of the right of religious liberty.[58]

Having been refused succor by President Calles, the Episcopate turned next to the Congress. On September 7, 1926, a petition was presented asking for modifications in the religious legislation. "There is no tyranny worse than that of bad laws," read the petition. "It is the strict duty of the Catholics to procure the abrogation of the bad laws before they annihilate religious liberty in Mexico. . . . What is it that we ask? Neither tolerance, nor complacency, much less prerogatives or laws. We demand liberty. We do not demand anything except liberty and for all religions."[59] Conditions had indeed changed in Mexico. The Catholic clergy were now earnestly begging for mere tolerance which they a hundred years before had been unwilling to

[57] Pérez Lugo, op. cit., pp. 404–408; Balderrama, op. cit., I, 81.
[58] Balderrama, op. cit., I, 181, II, 29; El Universal, August 12, 1926.
[59] Toro, op. cit., pp. 434–440.

accord to other sects. The petition received short shrift in the Chamber of Deputies, for, on September 23, 1926, a resolution was adopted by vote of 171 to 1, declaring that, since petitions could only be presented by citizens, and since by their public declarations not to observe the Constitution the heads of the Catholic Church had lost their citizenship, therefore the Chamber of Deputies could not legally listen to the petition.[60]

It is not necessary to examine the legal or moral justification of this ingenious maneuver on the part of Congress, nor to stress the fact that the President and the Deputies interpreted the right of petition in different lights. The attitude of the legislators was such that, even had the petition been received, they would have refused to amend the legislation in any way. In reply to the adverse action of the Chamber, the Episcopate issued a long statement urging the Catholics not to give up the fight for amendment of the laws.

The stern intent of the Mexican government not to abate its policy was evidenced by the publication on October 16, of a presidential regulation limiting the number of Catholic priests and ministers of every denomination to 90 for each in the Federal District, 18 in the Territory of Lower California, and 3 in the Territory of Quintana Roo. Prior to the suspension of services there were 136 churches in the Federal District, cared for by 289 priests. The presidential regulation required every priest to register with the president of the municipality. On November 25, a new bill of religious regulations, based on Article 130 of the Constitution, was passed by the Congress. This bill proposed to make more rigid in many respects the prior presidential regulations. Its declared intention was to seal every loophole making evasion possible and to prepare the way for complete and absolute enforcement. In addition to the reënactment of former regulations, but with greater vigor, the bill provided that foreign colonies should be allowed to have foreign ministers for six years, during which time native Mexicans must be trained to take their places, and services by laymen and the holding of private masses were declared illegal.[61]

[60] Balderrama, op. cit., I, 196-197.

[61] Ibid., II, 145-147; Current History, December, 1926, pp. 410, 437.

Since the boycott which went into effect on July 31 proved to be a total failure, the League for the Defense of Religious Liberty, and other Catholic organizations and individuals, even including some priests, resorted to armed violence. The principal scenes of revolutionary movements were the states of Jalisco, Guerrero, Michoacán, Colima, Guanajuato, Querétaro, Puebla, and Vera Cruz. The "Cristero" revolt continued in the State of Jalisco until July, 1929. An announcement of the League after the resumption of religious services, admitted that it had supported the religious rebels in their resort to arms against the government since 1926. It denied, however, that the Mexican Episcopate or the Vatican had supported the armed conflict in any way.[62] The government, however, confident that the clergy were responsible for the revolutionary movements, issued an order, January 30, 1927, requiring all Catholic priests in Mexico to report to the Minister of Interior before February 10, under penalty of being declared outlaws. Later a regulation required priests and prelates to appear daily at the Ministry of Interior to sign the register. Bishop Pascual Díaz, spokesman of the Episcopate, was deported on January 12 on the charge of being the intellectual leader of the Catholic rebellion.[63]

The increasing violence of the revolt culminated, on April 21, 1927, in the arraignment before Minister Tejeda of several of the leading prelates on the charge of inciting to revolt. In refuting the charge Archbishop Mora y del Río told Minister Tejeda: "We have aided no revolution. We have plotted no revolution, but we do claim that the Catholics of Mexico have the right to fight for their rights by peaceful means first and with arms in an extremity." Because of this statement the Archbishop and five other prelates were ordered deported from Mexico immediately. They entered the United States at Laredo, Texas, on April 23. The deportation of other prelates followed.[64]

In explaining the status of the religious situation, President

---

[62] *Current History*, September, 1929, p. 1137; Callcott, *Liberalism in Mexico*, pp. 367-368, 379-380.

[63] *Memoria de la Secretaría de Gobernación* (Mexico, 1927), Sec. *Cultos*.

[64] *El Universal*, April 22 and 23.

Calles reported in his message to Congress on September 1, 1927: "The religious law has been strictly enforced, and it can be said that the religious conflict caused by the rebellious clergy now has practically concluded for the laws have been complied with despite the futile resistance of the clergy. The Mexican people have shown themselves indifferent to the suspension of services. Some church edifices have been dedicated by the government to public uses. Priests who have shown willingness to obey the laws have been permitted to exercise their ministry."[65] It should be noted, however, that very few priests consented without the permission of their superiors to register. Those who registered were regarded as schismatics.

Due to the efforts of Ambassador Morrow, who was working for a settlement of the Church-State controversy, a secret meeting occurred in Vera Cruz, April 4, 1928, between Father J. J. Burke, C.S.P., General Secretary of the Catholic Welfare Conference and President Calles. The meeting resulted in a tentative understanding substantially the same as the one adopted in June, 1929.[66]

It was reported in June, 1928, that the pope had submitted to the Congregation on Extraordinary Ecclesiastical Affairs the determination of the conditions under which the Mexican clergy should return to the churches and it was hoped that some adjustment might be effected. At this juncture President-elect Obregón was assassinated on July 17, 1928. Notwithstanding Obregón's pre-election declaration that there would be no change in the governmental attitude on the Catholic question, it had been persistently reported that he was anxious to end the conflict. President Calles' statement that Obregón was the victim of "direct clerical action" was premature, untrue, ill-considered, and seriously retarded a rapprochement with the papacy. The murder was the work of a religious fanatic instigated by a nun who acted independently of the Catholic clergy or organizations.[67]

[65] *Excelsior*, September 2, 1927.

[66] Walter Lippmann, "Church and State in Mexico; The American Mediation," in *Foreign Affairs*, VIII, No. 2. (January, 1930), p. 186.

[67] *Current History*, September, 1928, pp. 1026-1027; Callcott, *Liberalism in Mexico*, p. 377.

It is interesting to note that during the religious crisis, when political revolutions occurred in Mexico the Catholics resolutely refused to be identified with these movements, notwithstanding repeated bids made for their support. Generals Gómez and Serrano, in revolting against the Calles-Obregón machine in October, 1927, invoked Catholic aid in vain. In March, 1929, during his rebellion against the Federal government, General Escobar proclaimed religious liberty and the abrogation of the anti-religious laws. Again the Catholics refused to take the bait. Perhaps they recalled that this same Escobar, two years before, in enforcing the Calles' decrees had directed the arrest of thousands of Catholics and had executed priests. Escobar's about-face on religious policy was very reminiscent of Pancho Villa's action.[68]

A partial settlement of the religious difficulty and the resumption of services in the Catholic Churches of Mexico followed soon upon the heels of the inauguration of President Emilio Portes Gil. In outlining his religious policy, the new President said on May 1, 1929: "No religion will be persecuted, nor is the government guilty of any persecution of any sect. Liberty of conscience will be respected as heretofore. The Catholic clergy, when they wish, may renew the exercise of their rites with only one obligation, that they respect the laws of the land as the ministers of other denominations are doing."[69]

Archbishop Ruíz y Flores, senior prelate of Mexico, then in the United States, detected a tone of conciliation in the President's statement and said that the Catholic Church and its ministers were prepared to coöperate with the Mexican government in every proper and moral effort for the benefit of the Mexican people. Portes Gil thereupon expressed his willingness to discuss the problem with the Archbishop. Having received permission from the pope to undertake negotiations, Archbishop Ruíz and Bishop Pascual Díaz returned to Mexico. Several conferences occurred between the Mexican President and the prelates. Ambassador Morrow of the United States has been credited with contributing to the successful outcome of the conferences. On

[68] Lippmann, *op. cit.*, p. 203.
[69] *New York Times*, May 2, 1929.

June 17 the basis for a settlement was approved, and on June 21 the pope signified his acceptance.

The understanding between President Portes Gil and the Mexican prelates was not a formal, signed contract or treaty, but merely a verbal "gentleman's agreement." The only authentic, published statement on the nature of the agreement was the signed statement of the President which was given to the press on June 21, 1926. He said:

> I take advantage of this opportunity to declare publicity and with all clarity that it is not the spirit of the Constitution, nor of the laws, nor of the government of the Republic to destroy the identity of the Catholic Church, nor of any other cult, nor to intervene in any manner in its spiritual functions. According to the oath which I took when I assumed the Provisional Government of Mexico to obey and cause to be obeyed the Constitution of the Republic and its laws, my purpose has been at all times to comply honestly with this oath and to see that the laws are applied without sectarian tendency and without injury to anyone. . . . With reference to certain articles of the law which have not been clearly understood, I take advantage of this opportunity to declare:
>
> I. The provision of the law which required the registration of ministers does not mean that the government can register those who have not been named by a hierarchial superior of the religious creed in question or in accordance with its regulations.
>
> II. With regard to religious instruction, the constitution and laws in force definitely prohibit it in primary or higher schools, whether public or private, but this does not prevent ministers of any religion from imparting its doctrines within the church confines to adults and their children, who may attend for that purpose.
>
> III. The Constitution as well as the laws of the country guarantee to all residents of the republic the right of petition, and therefore the members of any church may apply to the appropriate authorities for amendment, repeal or passage of any law.[70]

Superficially it would appear that the Church received little or no concession from the State, and that the agreement marked a complete backdown on the part of the former. Such in fact was not the case, for the agreement in the matter of registration of ministers was all-important. There was tacit acknowledgment of the right of the hierarchy to designate priests who were to

---

[70] *New York Times,* June 22, 1929; *Excelsior,* June 22, 1929.

register. This amounted to a virtual acknowledgment of the corporate rights of the Church and the authority of the bishop of the diocese, the constitutional denial of juridic personality to religious institutions to the contrary notwithstanding. Thus the means of fortifying the principle of authority for which the Mexican clergy had contended and in defense of which they suspended religious exercises was recognized and guaranteed by the State. This was a real victory for the clergy.

The declaration of Portes Gil that it was not the purpose of the State to interfere in any way with the spiritual functions of the Catholic Church, was interpreted by Archbishop Ruíz to mean that "the laws will not be applied in a spirit of passion and sectarianism, but, on the contrary, in a spirit compatible with the existence of the Church's liberty." In other words there was guaranteed assurance that the government would put aside the utterly ruthless and vindictive methods of the Calles administration. In pursuance of this guarantee the central government, to curb extreme local anti-clerical legislation, ordered all governors, state legislatures, and municipal authorities to recognize the Federal government's supremacy and authority in questions relating to religious worship, and its exclusive right to allocate churches. The Church was assured immunity against local radicalism.[71] This again was a clerical victory—yet, a precarious victory, for the observance of the agreement depended on the state of mind of relatively few men.

It is interesting and significant to note that President Portes Gil in reporting to the Mexican Congress on the settlement of the religious issue did not state that any concession had been made to the Catholic prelates. He said:

In declarations published in the American press in the month of May, the Señor Archbishop of the Roman Catholic Cult, Leopoldo Ruíz y Flores, expressed the intention of the clergy to reopen the Catholic cult in the Republic, and as a consequence of these declarations, he who speaks (the President) announced that as concerned the government there was no opposition to the said reopening of the Roman Catholic Church, always and when the priests of that creed submitted to the existing laws of the Republic in matters of the cult. . . .

---

[71] *Ibid.*, June 23 and September 2, 1929.

The *Secretaría de Gobernación* has sent special circulars to the governors of the states relative to the observance of the constitutional dispositions: Articles 24, 27, and 130, the amending dispositions of the Penal Code in the matter of cults, and the regulatory law of the constitutional article cited above.[72]

The President, for obvious reasons, did not undertake to tell the Congress that the Catholic clergy reassumed their spiritual duties in Mexico on receiving official assurance that the government recognized the corporate rights of the Church—a status denied by the Constitution. The compromise-agreement, let it be repeated, was a strictly executive matter.

On June 27, 1929, masses were celebrated in Mexico for the first time since July 30, 1926. On September 17, 1929, Mgr. Pascual Díaz was formally installed as Archbishop of Mexico in the Basilica of Guadalupe. The return of the priests to the ministration of their flocks was attended by great rejoicing and the voicing of fervent prayers of public thanksgiving. The report was widely circulated that the religious question in Mexico had been "settled."

Yet, the National League for the Defense of Religious Liberty, quite correctly, as later events proved, branded the accord of June 21 as merely "a sort of armistice." A warning was issued that much remained to be settled apart from the resumption of Catholic services in Mexico. The extremists were not averse to the use of arms to recover "the legitimate rights of the Church." The opponents of the agreement became so menacing that Mgr. Ruíz y Flores, Apostolic Delegate, and Archbishop Díaz rushed to the press in its defense. They denied that the Church had accepted the religious laws of the Calles régime. The accord was merely the basis for reaching a more complete understanding. It was not the time, said the Apostolic Delegate, to discuss, but to obey. This was counseled by the Pope himself. There is little doubt that the prelates were sincerely laboring in support of a policy of conciliation and coöperation.[73]

---

[72] Informe rendido por El C. Lic. Emilio Portes Gil, Presidente Provisional de los Estados Unidos Mexicanos ante el H. Congreso de la Unión el día 1° de Septiembre de 1929 (Mexico, 1929), pp. 14-15.

[73] Abbe Alphonse Lugan, "Church and State in Mexico," in *Current History*, February, 1931, pp. 672-675.

Those in Mexico and the outside world who had allowed themselves to be lulled into the belief that the religious question in
Mexico had been settled were rudely awakened in June, 1931.
In the State of Vera Cruz, always radical, a law was put into
effect on June 18 restricting the number of priests to one for
each 100,000 inhabitants. This would permit only eleven priests
to function in the state.[74] This law, which was sponsored by
Governor Adalberto Tejeda, ex-Minister of Gobernación and a
fanatical anti-clerical, was a manifest attempt to destroy the
Catholic Church in Vera Cruz and still remain within the confines of "constitutionality." The Federal Constitution gives to
the states "the exclusive power to determine the maximum number of ministers of religious creeds according to the needs of
each locality" (Art. 130). It is obvious, however, to any rational
being that a solitary priest is not capable of ministering to the
spiritual needs of the Catholics numbered among 100,000 Vera
Crucians.

President Ortiz Rubio was besieged with petitions protesting
against the alleged unconstitutionality of the Vera Cruz law.
The President, however, did not see fit to act, declaring that he
was unable to interfere with the sovereignty of a state. A meri-
torious policy if faithfully applied by the Executive in Mexico.
Yet such is not the case, for on August 7, the Governor of
Durango was removed for permitting violations of the state religious laws. It was contended that, whereas the state laws permitted only twenty-seven priests, the Governor permitted about
two hundred.

The Vera Cruz law seems to have given an impetus to a renewal of the anti-clerical campaign, particularly in the direction
of imposing greater restrictions on the number of clergy.
Chiapas, with a population of 350,000, restricted the clergy to
nine; Yucatán, with 400,000, to nine. Tabasco went the limit by
prohibiting any priest from officiating in religious ceremonies.
These actions were taken in the fall of 1931.

Blind as always, the Mexican clergy scorned caution and celebrated (Dec. 1, 1931) the 400th anniversary of the appearance

---

[74] *New York Times,* June 19, 1931.

of the Virgin of Guadalupe with unexampled pomp and ceremony. The Guadalupe celebration aroused anti-clerical sentiment which almost immediately found expression in legislation.
On December 30 a law went into effect restricting the number
of clergy for the Federal District and for the Territory of
Lower California to one for each 50,000 population. This meant
that the priests of Mexico City were reduced from 90 to 24.
Since January 1932 more restrictive limitations have been applied in several of the states: Chihuahua, 1 to 9,000; Guanajuato, 1 to 25,000; Durango, 25 for the state; Chiapas, 4 for
the state; Mexico, 34 for the state. Eventually, in some of the
states, e.g. Vera Cruz and Chiapas, religious services were suspended altogether. Illustrative of the fanaticism with which the
anti-clerical campaign has proceeded, the Legislature of Querétaro (Dec. 4, 1932) requested the Federal Congress to expro-
priate all Catholic churches throughout the country and convert them into schools and recreational centers. Incidental to
this most recent anti-Church outburst many of the prelates have
again gone into exile. In October, 1932, Archbishop Ruíz y
Flores, the Apostolic Delegate, was deported as an "undesirable
alien." Although a native of Mexico he was declared a foreigner
because he "owed allegiance to a foreign sovereign"—the pope.[75]

The religious question in Mexico is still, most emphatically,
an open question. Moreover it will not be settled so long as the
regulations, and statutory and constitutional laws which deny
to the Catholic clergy legitimate control over their own ecclesiastical organization remain in force. Extraordinary governmental control and supervision must be abandoned. It is conceded that this was not possible in the past because of the refusal of the clergy to confine their efforts exclusively to the field
of spiritual endeavor. There is good reason to believe, however,
that the Catholic clergy of Mexico have learned their lesson, and
that they will gladly consent to leave politics alone. That they
will be very careful in the future not to violate the constitutional
prohibition of clerical-political activity can be read in a state-

---

[75] The above summary of recent events is based on the *Memorias de la
Secretaría de Gobernación* (1930, 1931, 1932, 3 vols.) and the files of *El Universal* and *The New York Times*.

ment published by Archbishop Ruíz y Flores. He said that while Catholic laymen have the right as citizens to participate in politics and support any candidate to the presidency which they care to, the Mexican Episcopacy and clergy should remain absolutely neutral on any political issue.[76]

The Mexican clergy are on trial. Their ability and willingness to remain within the confines of their spiritual domain is being tested. If it is demonstrated after a few years that the State, and particularly "The Revolution," have nothing to fear from a free Church, it can be confidently expected that the present drastic and illiberal laws will be revoked. On that date it will be safe to say that the religious question in Mexico has been settled.

---

[76] *Excelsior,* June 26, 1929.

CHAPTER XVII

CONCLUSION

The ecclesiastical policies of the various Latin-American nations, as described in the preceding chapters, present marked divergencies. In some countries, like Argentina, Colombia, and Peru, the old Church-State relationship that existed in the colonial period has been perpetuated, but with certain modifications. In other nations, such as Brazil, Chile, Cuba, Panama, and Uruguay, the connection between Church and State has been dissolved, and a situation rather similar to that which exists in the United States obtains. In still other countries, of which Mexico is the best example, the Church has not only been disestablished, but has been put under strict State surveillance. That a predominantly Roman Catholic populace, which lived for centuries under a common politico-religious régime, should, after independent governments had been organized, apply such diverse remedies for the solution of the religious problem, is both interesting and perplexing.

When embarking upon their independent careers the nations of Latin America adhered for a time to uniformity in religious policy, i.e., Catholicism continued to be the State religion. Indeed, with the sole exception of Argentina (then called the United Provinces of La Plata) religious toleration to the extent of allowing the public exercise of dissident faiths was not among the guarantees of the first national constitutions. Thus, when the youthful nations of Latin America undertook the direction of their own destinies, they were faithful to the religious policy of the Motherland.

Yet, in a short time opposition to the favored cult appeared and it began to be shorn of its old time privileges. In the decades of the 1820's and 1830's the Catholic Church was subjected to attack in many of the republics, particularly in Argentina, Chile, Mexico, and the Federation of Central America.

What was the cause of this radical change in ecclesiastical policy?

The basis of this early opposition to the Roman Catholic organization—not the Roman Catholic religion—was largely political. The abolition of tithes, suppression of religious orders, confiscation of ecclesiastical property, and like measures, were as a rule acts of vengeance wreaked upon the clergy by their political opponents. As was explained in the first chapter, the Spanish crown leaned heavily upon the members of the ecclesiastical organization for the governance of the Indies. Prelates and clerics held official positions high and low; they were a component part of the political organization. If it is not charitable to criticise too severely the failure of Latin Americans to govern successfully under representative political institutions, considering their tutelage for centuries under an absolute monarch, it is likewise unfair to expect the clergy to abandon immediately their ancient practice of participating in governmental affairs. It was inconceivable that this habit should be changed forthwith when independence was established. On the contrary, the ecclesiastics plunged into politics with greater zeal than before, for they felt, quite correctly, that their rights would be endangered in representative republics.

But those who engaged in Latin-American politics, particularly as they were played in the early days of independence, ought to have been prepared for the consequences of defeat. The opposition, let it be known, was hardly ever "honorable," but was regarded as an enemy of the State and was generally meted the punishment of traitors. Since the clergy who adhered to colonial tradition and chose to take part in political questions were often so unfortunate as to be on the losing side, they frequently suffered the fate of the defeated opposition. Their rights and prerogatives were curtailed in order to nullify their ability to exercise political influence in the future.

These early anti-clericals were not reformers in the proper sense of the term. Their opposition was not based on spiritual, social, or economic causes. The "reformers," recruited almost exclusively from the creoles, had no complaint to find with Catholic dogmas and tenets; representatives of a privileged social class, they manifested little interest in the welfare of the lower classes; and if they regarded clerical wealth as an evil, it was because this wealth made the Church powerful politically. The pose of the anti-clericals as champions of representative government, the rights of the masses, and purity of faith was often insincere and untrue. Usually their sole object was to acquire control of the government and make it impossible to oust them. It is conceded that there were sincere reformers like Gómez Farías, but such men were exceptional, and unfortunately they were impractical idealists who by unwise and precipitate action caused much more harm than good.

With the passing of the mid-nineteenth century, the position of the Catholic Church in Latin America became increasingly unstable. In Mexico, Colombia, Venezuela, Chile, Ecuador, and Central America, severe anti-clerical laws were put into force, and in several of the republics Church and State were separated. The first republic to proclaim separation was Colombia in 1853. This status proved to be temporary, however. The first republic permanently to disestablish the Church was Mexico, but that State, as we have seen, was unwilling to release the Church and continued to exercise an oppressive supervision over it. Soon after Mexico, some of the Central American republics disestablished the Church, but intolerantly burdened it with strict State control. In 1890, in Brazil, the alliance of Church and State inherited by the Empire from Portugal was dissolved. In the twentieth century the trend toward separation has continued. Cuba and Panama, states which came into existence under the tutelage of the United States at the beginning of the century, provided in their constitutions for complete separation. In Ecuador only a quarter of a century after the most extreme clerical reaction in all the history of Latin America, ecclesiastical policy was carried to the other extreme and the official ties between the spiritual and temporal orders were severed. In 1917 Uruguay dissolved the old connection, formed in 1830. The most recent and one of the most serious losses sustained by the pope was the separation of Church and State in Chile.

The revolutionary step of disestablishing the Church was accomplished peacefully in Brazil, Uruguay, and Chile. In these three important countries the Church was allowed to retain its property unconditionally, and to go its own way without governmental interference. Apparently the policy of releasing the Church properties and observing a minimum of surveillance contributed to the peaceful and seemingly successful transition. In Mexico, however, a contrary policy was adopted with most unfortunate consequences. Since the position occupied by the Catholic Church in that republic was not appreciably different than in other Latin-American countries, it does not necessarily follow that the bestowal of complete independence upon the Mexican Church would have been followed by the same happy results. The activities of the clergy during the Maximilian period certainly proved that the time had not arrived to establish an independent Church. Since that time, however, the Mexican clergy have evidently learned their lesson, and at the present date it would probably be safe to allow the Catholic Church the same rights it enjoys in Brazil and Chile.

Citizens of the United States unacquainted with the facts have been too prone to regard Mexico as the only rebellious member of the Catholic flock in Latin America. That this is not true has been conclusively demonstrated in the preceding chapters. In Venezuela, Colombia, Ecuador, and Chile, the Church was attacked, sometimes with considerable animosity. In several of the lesser countries too, like Guatemala, El Salvador, and Honduras, the same vicissitudes were suffered. Although the attacks in Mexico were more bitter and the results more disastrous, to say that the Mexican remedies were more severe because the abuses were more glaring would not be absolutely true. In other countries the Church was quite as wealthy, relatively speaking, and as much of a political factor.

A significant feature of the religious conflicts has been the uncompromising attitude of the opposing factions. The difficulty intrinsically is not insuperable, as is evidenced by its satisfactory settlement in several of the countries through the application of a policy of mutual respect and fair play. But in many of the nations of Central and South America the intolerance of clericals and anti-clericals alike makes a solution well nigh impossible. Neither side is willing to concede any errors in its own program or virtues in that of the opposition. Consequently, as history reveals, there has been a constant ebb and flow of clerical and anti-clerical oppression.

It would not be correct to contend that the anti-clerical assault of the last three quarters of a century continued to be retaliatory vengeance for clerical political activities, although this is still one of the major causes. New classes and leaders primarily interested in social and economic reform began to emerge. They attacked the Church, a conservative institution always identified with privilege and vested interests, because it was regarded as an obstacle to social and economic progress. There was new appreciation that the ecclesiastical situation and Church-State relationships were antiquated, reactionary, and out of tune with modern conditions. Well-founded principles, and not merely partisan prejudice underlay the new anti-clerical assault. Leaders like Juárez in Mexico, and Balmaceda in Chile formulated programs and inspired followings. In later days, therefore, anti-clericalism in Latin America became, to a certain degree, a political philosophy and plan of action pointing the way to the modern world as the goal.

Americans are often puzzled to find the Church in admittedly Catholic countries subjected to more restrictive legislation than even in Protestant lands. The questions arise: Why is it necessary to hedge the Church by such restrictions? and, Why do the Catholics who constitute the majority tolerate such measures? The first question has already been answered. But, to repeat, the habit of the clergy of meddling in politics and assuming an inordinate supervision over the lives of their parishioners make restriction necessary. The clergy of Latin America are totally different from the priesthood in the United States. This fact must be born in mind if the Latin-American religious situation is to be understood.

As for the second question, it is indeed astonishing that an overwhelmingly Catholic populace should tolerate religious oppression. There were many prophesies in 1926, when the drastic anti-clerical legislation was enforced in Mexico, that there would be a popular uprising. It is true that isolated revolts took place but a general uprising failed to materialize. One could reasonably expect that if the Latin Americans are as devoted to the faith as they are supposed to be, the anti-religious laws would be impossible of enforcement. The writer takes no stock in the argument that the people do not revolt since they understand that the reforms are directed at the Church in its temporal aspects and not at the Church as a religion. Undeveloped intellects are incapable of appreciating such fine distinctions. The most loyal Catholics are to be numbered among the women and the members of the lowest classes—those least capable of offering opposition to the government's edicts.[1] Most of the men of the higher classes are "nominal" Catholics, that is, they abstain from contact with the sacraments until the time for the ministration of extreme unction. These men would not fight to the death for the faith. It should be noted furthermore, that the lowest classes, principally Indians, entertain a profound respect for authority; obedience to superior will has been taught them for centuries, and therefore they would not be apt to oppose the will of the officials—particularly when they are backed by the power of the army. Thus it comes about that in Catholic countries the religion of the majority can be persecuted.

Several of the Latin-American countries have, by adhering to wise and tolerant action, attained in separation a satisfactory solution of the vexing religious question. But in other nations the people are not prepared for the radical change, and therefore they must not be hurried. Their rulers must exercise restraint and make the transition as gradual as possible. On the other hand the Catholic Church should put no obstacle in the way of this change. It should recognize that the modern world is committed to the idea that the ideal ecclesiastical status is a free Church in a free State. Adherence to the old pretentions will lead to bitter disputes with inevitable anti-clerical attacks and consequent weakening of the hold of the clergy upon the faithful. Recognition of the new order and accommodation to the changed world by a complete severance of Church-State rela-

---

[1] One of the principal reasons why the women are not given the suffrage in Latin America is the fear that their votes will be influenced by the clergy.

tions, will lead to an active and prosperous Church, which can enjoy the confidence and love of its communicants.[2]

---

[2] Several of these concluding remarks have been taken from the writer's article, "Latin America's Fight Against Clerical Domination," published in *Current History,* January, 1929, pp. 565-570.

BIBLIOGRAPHY

A. PRIMARY SOURCES

I. MANUSCRIPTS

Archivo Bazaine: Correspondencia de Achille Francois Bazaine, 1862-1867. 26 vols. An invaluable collection of some 60,000 pages on the French Intervention in Mexico. Contains numerous allusions to the reactionary policy of the Mexican clergy.

Gómez Farías Papers. Letters and papers, official and private, of the Gómez Farías family, covering the period 1820 to 1857. The collection yielded items relating to politico-ecclesiastical relations, particularly for the premature reform régime of 1834.

Riva Palacio Papers. The private correspondence of a notable Mexican publicist and historian. Contains information relating to the religious question in the Revolution of Ayutla and the Wars of the Reform.

(Note: The above documents are to be found in the Genaro García Collection in the Library of the University of Texas. This manuscript collection which once belonged to the notable Mexican historian and collector, contains a wealth of materials on the religious question beyond the needs of the present study.)

II. OFFICIAL DOCUMENTS AND OTHER PRINTED SOURCES

Alarcón, Federico, comp. *Código Penal Boliviano.* La Paz, 1902.

Andrada, Ángel V., comp. *Leyes Nacionales, decretos y demas resoluciones que se refieren á la administración y gobierno de la capital federal y territorios nacionales de la República Argentina.* Buenos Aires, 1927. 2 vols.

Anguita, Ricardo, comp. *Leyes promulgadas en Chile desde 1810 hasta el 1° de Junio de 1912.* Santiago, 1912-1913. 4 vols.

Annaes do Parliamento Brasileiro, Assembléa Constituinte, 1823. Rio de Janeiro, 1876-1884. 6 vols.

Anuario Estadístico de la República Oriental del Uruguay. Montevideo, 1923.

Arancel Eclesiástico de la Diócesis de La Paz. La Paz, 1927. An interesting schedule of fees for various religious services.

Archivo Santander. Bogotá, 1924-1925. 4 vols. Correspondence of General Santander. Throws new light on his policies with respect to the Church.

Arosemena, Justo. *Estudios Constitucionales sobre los gobiernos de la América Latina.* Paris, 1888. 2 vols. A collection of the constitutions in force at the time of date of publication.

Balderrama, Luís C. *El Clero y el Gobierno de México.* Mexico, 1927. 2 vols. Collection of documents (Vol. 2) of a varied nature, to explain the religious crisis of 1926. A government propaganda publication.

Bolivia, Constitución Política del Estado y Reglamentos de Debates del Senado y de la Cámara de Diputados. La Paz, 1926.

Branch, H. N., trans. *The Mexican Constitution of 1917 compared with the Constitution of 1857.* Supplement to *Annals of the American Academy of Political and Social Science,* 1917. Constitutional articles arranged in parallel columns. Enables one to ascertain easily the additions made in 1917 to the religious clauses of 1857.

Cabañas, Joaquín Ramírez, ed. *Las Relaciones entre México y el Vaticano.* Mexico, 1928. Number 27 of the *Archivo Histórico Diplomático Mexicano.*

Camara dos Deputados, Exposição Commemorativa do Centenario da 1ª Constituinte do Brasil. Rio de Janeiro, 1923. The religious question in the first Brazilian constitutional convention.

Carranza, Adolfo P., ed. *El Clero Argentino de 1810 á 1830.* Buenos Aires, 1907. 2 vols. A collection of patriotic orations, allocutions, and panegyrics by La Platan clerics.

Christian Work in South America; The Montevideo Congress, 1925. New York, 1925. 2 vols. Official Report of the Congress on Christian Work in South America. Contains considerable valuable information on contemporary religious conditions.

Cleven, N. A. N. *Readings in Hispanic American History.* New York, 1927. Contains important bulls and decrees relating to the Church in Colonial Spanish America.

Codificación de los Decretos del C. Venustiano Carranza. Mexico, 1915. In the "Pre-Constitutional" decrees of the First Chief, herein contained, are detected the germs of the anti-clerical provisions of the Constitution of 1917.

Coello, Augusto C. *El Digesto Constitucional de Honduras.* Tegucigalpa, 1923.

Colección Completa de Leyes Nacionales Sancionadas por el Honorable Congreso durante los Años 1852 á 1917. Buenos Aires, 1918.

Colección de los Decretos y Ordenes del Soberano Congreso Mexicano. Mexico, 1825.

Colección Eclesiástica Mejicana. Mexico, 1834. 4 vols.

Constitução do Republica dos Estados Unidos do Brasil Acompanhada das Leis Organicas Publicadas desde 15 de Novembra de 1889. Rio de Janeiro, 1891.

Constitución de la República de Cuba. Havana, 1910.

Constitución de la República Oriental del Uruguay. Montevideo, 1919.

Constitution de 1918 de La Republique D' Haiti. Port-au-Prince, 1928.

Constitución de los Estados Unidos de Venezuela Sancionada por El Congreso Nacional en 1925. Caracas, 1925.

Constitución Política de la República de El Salvador. San Salvador, 1914.

Constitución Política de la República del Ecuador. Quito, 1929.

Constitución Política de la República de Nicaragua. Managua, 1911.

Constitución y Leyes Políticas de la República de Chile Vigente en 1881. Santiago, 1881.

Constitution of Chile. Pan-American Union, Washington, 1925.

Constitution of Honduras. Pan-American Union, Washington, 1924.

Constitution of the Dominican Republic, 1925. Pan-American Union, Washington, 1925.

Diario de los Debates del Congreso Constituyente. Mexico, 1916-1917. 2 vols. The debates in the Querétaro Convention show the anti-clerical temper of the Constituents. It was an extremely prejudiced body.

Diario de Sesiones de la H. Convención N. Constituyente de la República Oriental del Uruguay. Montevideo, 1918. Contains the debates on separation of Church and State.

Dictamen de la Comisión de Patronato. Mexico, 1823. Report of the first committee on the patronage. It upheld national rights.

Dictamen sobre Provisión de Benefices Eclesiásticos. Mexico, 1824. Report of the committee on the patronage to the Mexican Constituent Congress. It was regalistic in nature.

Documentos para a Historia da Independencia. Rio de Janeiro, 1923. Contains information on the participation of the clergy and the Masons in the independence movement.

Documentos relativos á la organización constitucional de la República Argentina. Buenos Aires, 1911. 3 vols. The documents cover the period 1851-1883. Vol. 3 contains exclusively documents relating to the general constituent congress of 1853.

Dublán, Manuel y Lozano, José María, eds. *Legislación Mexicana ó Colección completa de las Disposicionas legislativas expedidas desde la Independencia de la República*. Mexico, 1876-1890. 19 vols.

El Informe de Peñalver y Vergara, in Leturia, *La acción diplomática* (see below), pp. 294-295. Letter in original Latin, written to the pope by the Colombian envoys from London, March 27, 1820.

El Libro Amarillo de los Estados Unidos de Venezuela presentado al Congreso Nacional en sus sesiones de 1930 por el Ministro de

Relaciones Exteriores. Caracas, 1930. Contains report of official relations with the Vatican for the preceding year.

Encinas, Diego de. *Provisiones, Cédulas, Capítulos de Ordenanzas . . . tocantes al buen gobierno de las Indias.* Madrid, 1596. 4 vols. Contains *cédulas* and other documents emanating from the Council of the Indies not found in the *Recopilación de Leyes de los Reynos de las Indias.*

Exposición del Senador por el Estado de Nicaragua P. C. L. D. C. Isidro Menéndez . . . sobre el negocio do Obispado de S. Salvador. San Salvador, 1825.

Gamboa, José M. *Leyes Constitucionales de México Durante el siglo XIX.* Mexico, 1901. Contains not only all the National Constitutions with their amendments, but the Constitution of Cádiz, the Constitution of Apatzingan, and the *Plan de Iguala.*

García, Genaro, ed. *El Clero de México durante la Dominación Española, según el Archivo Inédito Archiepiscopal Metropolitano.* Mexico, 1906.

————*El Clero de México y la Guerra de Independencia.* Mexico, 1906. Published by García in an effort to refute the claim that the clergy supported the Revolution.

————*La Inquisición de México.* Mexico, 1906. Collection of documents on the Inquisition in New Spain. This is Vol. 5 of the *Documentos Inéditos ó Muy Raros.* (36 vols. 1906-1913).

García Calderón, Eduardo, ed. *Constitución, Códigos, y Leyes del Peru.* Lima, 1923.

Goyena, Pablo V., comp. *La Legislación Vigente de la República Oriental del Uruguay.* Montevideo, 1874-1876. 2 vols.

"Hearings before a Select Committee on Haiti and Santo Domingo," United States Senate. Sen. Res. 112, 67 Cong., Washington, 1922. Contains information on the religious and educational situations in the two republics.

Hernáez, Francisco Javier. *Colección de Bulas, Breves, y Otros Documentos relativos á la Iglesia de América y Filipinas.* Brussels, 1879. 2 vols. An invaluable work for the ecclesiastical history of the Americas. Contains all bulls for the colonial and republican periods to the date of publication.

Hernandez y Dávalos, J. E., ed. *Colección de Documentos para la Historia de la Guerra de Independencia de México de 1808 á 1821.* Mexico, 1877-1882. 6 vols.

Informe Rendido por El C. Lic. Emilio Portes Gil, Presidente Provisional de los Estados Unidos Mexicanos ante el H. Congreso de la Unión el día 1° de Septiembre de 1929. Mexico, 1929. The Provisional President reports the religious settlement of June, 1929.

Instrucciones Reservadas que los Virreyes de Nueva España Dejaron á sus Sucesores. Mexico, 1867. The state of the Church and ecclesiastical business always occupied a prominent position in the instructions of the viceroys to their successors.

Instrucción Pública en Venezuela. Caracas, 1922.

Investigation of Mexican Affairs. Hearing before a subcommittee of the Committee on Foreign Relations, United States Senate, Sixty-sixth Congress, first session, pursuant to S. Res. 106 directing the Committee on Foreign Relations to investigate the matter of outrages on citizens of the United States in Mexico. Washington, 1919. 3 vols. The famous Fall Report.

Joanini, F. L., trans. *The Argentine Civil Code.* Boston, 1917.

La Encíclica "Etsi longissimo" de 30 de enero de 1816, in Leturia, *La acción diplomática,* pp. 281-282. Pope Pius VII to the prelates and clergy of Spanish America in support of Ferdinand VII.

La Nueva Ensenañza. Asunción, November, 1927.

La primera carta oficial del Vicepresidente Santander á Pío VII. 18 Julio 1822, in Leturia, *La acción diplomática,* pp. 301-302.

Lecuna, Vicente, ed. *Cartas del Libertador.* Caracas, 1929-1930. 10 vols. A remarkably well edited work and contains an excellent index (Vol. 10). Bolívar's attitude toward the Church and religion, during his last years, shown in a new light, according to these letters.

Lecuna, Vicente, ed. *Documentos Referentes á la Creación de Bolivia.* Caracas, 1924. 2 vols.

Léfèvre, Eugène. *Historia de la Intervención Francesa en Méjico.* Brussels and London, 1869. 2 vols. Official documents from the private secretariat of Maximilian. Published by order of President Juárez.

Ley Constitutiva de la República de Guatemala decretada por la Asamblea Nacional Constituyente en 11 de diciembre de 1879. Guatemala, 1912.

Leyes, Decretos y Reglamentos Vigentes del Registro del Estado Civil. Montevideo, 1921.

Leyes, Decretos y Reglamentos Vigentes en 1920. Montevideo, 1920.

Livre Bleu D'Haiti. Port-au-Prince, 1920. An official publication containing descriptive data of a varied nature; some on religion and education.

Magoon, Charles E. *Republic of Cuba: Report of the Provisional Administration.* Havana, 1908. Used for report on the status of the confiscated Church properties agreement.

Mateos, Juan A. *Historia Parliamentaria de los Congresos Mexicanos de 1821 á 1857.* Mexico, 1877-1912. 25 vols.

Melgarejo Randolf, L. y Fernandez Rojas, J., eds. *El Congreso Constituyente de 1916 y 1917. Reseña histórico de los debates á que dieron las reformas de la constitución de 1857.* Mexico, 1917. For the religious question in the Convention.

Memorandum del General Guzmán Blanco. Caracas, 1876. Letters written by Guzmán Blanco while on campaign during the years 1870-1873. There are frequent references to clerical opposition.

Memoria de la Conducta Pública y Administrativa de Manuel José Arce. Mexico, 1830. Arce's defence of his administration as president of the Confederation of Central America.

Memorias de la Secretaría de Gobernación. Mexico, 1926-1932. 7 vols. Contains reports of federal and state legislation concerning the Church.

Memoria que Presente el Ministro de Relaciones Interiores al Congreso Nacional en 1909. Caracas, 1909. Contains a discussion of a controversy relating to the delimitation of ecclesiastical jurisdiction. Illustrates the *Patronato Nacional.*

Mensaje Leido por S. E. el Presidente de la República. Santiago, June 1, 1923. President Arturo Alessandri proposes separation of Church and State in Chile.

Mensaje Leido por S. E. el Vicepresidente de la República en la Apertura del Congreso Nacional el 21 de Mayo de 1927. Santiago, 1927. Vice President Carlos Ibañez, on concessions made to Church schools.

Mensaje de Presidente de la República de Colombia al Congreso Nacional en las Sesiones de 1926. Bogotá, 1926. References to ecclesiastical relations.

Mensaje Presidencial al Congreso Nacional en las Sesiones Ordinarias de 1929. Bogotá, 1929. References to ecclesiastical business.

Mery, Eulojio Rojas, ed. *Códigos de Chile.* Santiago, 1893.

Ministerio del Interior, Actas Oficiales de las Sesiones celebradas por la Comisión y Subcomisiones encargadas del estudio del Proyecto de Nueva Constitución Política de la República. Santiago, 1925.

Ministerio de Relaciones Exteriores y Culto, Circular Informativa Mensual. Buenos Aires, 1924. Contains discussion of the recent controversy over the appointment to the Archiepiscopal see of Buenos Aires.

Ministerio de Relaciones Exteriores y Culto, Circular Informativa Mensual. Buenos Aires, 1925.

Nueva Recopilación. Madrid, 1775. 2 vols. Both an abridgment and continuation of the *Recopilación de Leyes de los Reynos de las Indias.*

Olaechea, Guillermo, ed. *La Constitución del Peru.* Lima, 1922.

Olivo, Juan F. *Constituciones del Peru, 1821-1919.* Lima, 1922.

Páez, José Antonio. *Autobiografía de General José Antonio Páez.* New York, 1867-1869. 2 vols.

Peña y Reyes, Antonio de la. *León XII y 'Los Paises Hispano-Americanos.* Mexico, 1924. Vol. IX of the *Archivo Histórico Diplomático Mexicano.*

Pérez Lugo, J., ed. *La Cuestión Religiosa en México. Recopilación de Leyes Disposiciones Legales y Documentos para el Estudio de este Problema Político.* Mexico, 1927. A carefully selected, but essentially impartial, set of source materials to aid in explaining the religious crisis of 1926. Is best for the period 1857-1876. Contains a brief introduction of a rather marked anti-clerical tone. Was published as government propaganda.

Pombo, Manuel Antonio, y Guerra, José Joaquín. *Constituciones de Colombia.* Bogotá, 1911. 2 vols. A useful collection of all the national and state constitutions.

Proyecto de Constitución para la República de Bolivia y Discurso del Libertador. Buenos Aires, 1826. The argument of the Liberator in support of his model constitution for the new state of Bolivia, contains some remarkable observations regarding religious toleration and separation of Church and State.

Pruvonena, P., ed. *Memorias y Documentos para la Historia de la Independencia del Peru.* Paris, 1858.

Raccolta di Concordati su Materie Ecclesiastiche Tra la Santa Sede e Le Autorita Civil. Rome, 1919. A collection of all the concordats entered into by the Papacy to the time of publication. Invaluable for a history of politico-ecclesiastical relations.

Ramírez Cabañas, Joaquín, ed. *Las Relaciones entre México y el Vaticano.* Mexico, 1928. No. 27, *Archivo Histórico Diplomático Mexicano.* A useful collection of documents illustrative of Mexican relations with the Papacy from 1822 to 1861.

Recopilación de Leyes, Usuales de la República Argentina. Buenos Aires, 1927.

Recopilación de Leyes de los Reynos de las Indias. Madrid, 1756, 2 ed. 2 vols. In the Laws of the Indies can be seen the intimate relations which existed between Church and State in the Spanish colonies. An indispensable source for the history of the *Real Patronato de las Indias.* For a history of this work together with an analysis of its contents, see H. H. Bancroft, *History of Central America,* I, 285-288.

Relazione stesa da Mgr. Mazio per la Coñgne dei 18 Aprili 1823, in Leturia, *La acción diplomática,* pp. 282-293. Report, prepared by the secretary of the Congregation on Extraordinary Ecclesiastical Business, on the deliberations of the Congregation concerning the Church in La Plata. A document of exceptional importance in the Vatican archives. Contains the proposal of Friar Pacheco to the Congregation.

Report of the President's Commission for the Study and Review of Conditions in the Republic of Haiti, March 26, 1930. Washington, 1930. Contains an informative statement on the status of the Catholic Church in Haiti.

Rodríguez, J. I. *American Constitutions.* Washington, 1906. 2 vols. A collection of Latin American constitutions, in original languages and in translation.

Roure, Agenor de. *A Constituinte Republicana.* Rio de Janeiro, 1920. The religious question and separation of Church and State in the Republican Constitutional Convention of 1890.

Salazár, Francisco Ignacio. *Actas de la Convención Nacional del Ecuador, Año de 1835.* Quito, 1891.

Sanjinés, Jenaro. *Las Constituciones de Bolivia.* La Paz, 1906.

Uribe, Antonio José, ed. *Anales Diplomáticos y Consulares de Colombia.* Bogotá, 1920. Volume VI of Public Treaty Series contains the concordat of 1887, and supplementary conventions.

Vera, Fortino Hipólito, ed. *Colección de Documentos Eclesiásticos dc Méxioo.* Amecameca, 1887. 3 vols. Laws and regulations of the Mexican hierarchy for both the colonial and republican periods.

Zarco, Francisco. *Historia del Congreso Estraordinario Constituyente de 1856 y 1857.* Mexico, 1857. 2 vols. A very useful work for the attitude of the constituents toward the religious question. An index to the above is Basilio Pérez Gallardo, *Guía para consultar la Historia del Congreso Constituyente de 1857.* Mexico, 1878.

III. CORRESPONDENCE (COMMUNICATIONS TO THE AUTHOR)

Ackerman, Ralph H. American Commercial Attaché, Santiago, Chile, December 3, 1927.

Beers, LeRoy E. American Vice-Consul in Charge, San Salvador, El Salvador, October 14, 1927.

Brache, Elías, hijo. Secretario de Estado de Justicia é Instrucción Pública, República Dominicana, Santo Domingo, 17 de Mayo de 1928.

Brioschi, Pedro Adán. Arzobispo de Cartagena, Cartagena, 7 de Noviembre de 1927.

Carrigan, C. American Consul-General in Charge, Montevideo, December 7, 1927.

Clum, Harold D. American Consul in Charge, Guayaquil, Ecuador, November 11, 1927.

Consulado-General de Chile, Nueva York, 21 de Mayo de 1927.

Dawson, Claude I. American Consul-General, Rio de Janeiro, December 6, 1927.

El Secretario, Ministerio de Hacienda y Crédito Público, República de Colombia, Bogotá, Noviembre 17 de 1927.

El Secretario, Ministerio de Relaciones Exteriores, República de Colombia, Bogotá, Noviembre 5 de 1927.

Feliú, Luís E., hijo. Consul-General of Chile, New York, August 10, 1931.

Gonzalo Salas, J. A. Director Administrativo del Ministerio de Relaciones Interiores, República de Venezuela, Caracas, 17 de Octubre de 1927.

Gray, C. W. American Vice-Consul, Buenos Aires, January 3, 1928.

Guillermo, Arzobispo de Panamá, Panamá, 25 de Octubre de 1927.

Lawton, William B. American Vice-Consul in Charge, Santo Domingo, Dominican Republic, October 17, 1927.

León, Camille S. Secretairerie D'Etat des Cultes, République d'Haiti, Port-au-Prince, le 20 Octobre, 1927.

Lissón, Dn. Emilio. Arzobispo de la Arquidiócesis, Lima, 24 de Noviembre de 1927.

Lissón, Dn. Emilio. Arzobispo de Lima, Lima, Diciembre 23 de 1927.

Loayza, Luís Aurelio. Jefe de la Sección de Culto y Beneficencia, Ministerio de Justicia, Instrucción, Culto y Beneficencia, República de Peru, Lima, 24 de Noviembre de 1927.

McGurk, J. F. American Consul, La Paz, Bolivia, October 6, 1927.

Makinson, George A. American Consul in Charge, Callao-Lima, Peru, January 13, 1928.

Mangabeira, Octavio. Ministro das Relações Exteriores, Estados Unidos do Brasil, Rio de Janeiro, 22 de dezembro de 1927.

Mena, Luís A. de. Arz. Coad., Arzobispado de Santo Domingo, Santo Domingo, 26 de Septiembre de 1927.

Mosher, John S. American Vice-Consul, Havana, October 4, 1927.

Myers, H. D. American Vice-Consul in Charge, Panama, November 28, 1927.

Nabuco, Rev. Ft. Joaquin. Cancilleria Archiepiscopal, Rio de Janeiro, January 8, 1928.

Pierini, Mons. Francisco. Arzobispo de La Plata—Sucre (Bolivia), Sucre, 17 de Noviembre de 1927.

Pierini, Mons. Francisco. Arzobispo de La Plata—Sucre (Bolivia), Sucre, 22 de Noviembre de 1927.

Reñas, Francisco S. Ministro de Instrucción Pública, República de Nicaragua, Managua, 17 de Diciembre de 1927.

Schurman, Dr. O. H. Canciller, El Secretario del Señor Arzobispo, Tegucigalpa, Honduras, 8 de Febrero de 1928.

Shaw, George P. American Consul, Tegucigalpa, October 26, 1927.

Sieffert, Mons. Augusto. Obispo de La Paz, Bolivia, 29 de Diciembre de 1927.

Trammell, H. Eric. American Vice Consul in Charge, Guatemala City, December 8, 1927.

Vélez, Jorge. Ministro de Gobierno, República de Colombia, Bogotá, 12 de Diciembre de 1927.

Wolcott, H. M. American Consul, Caracas, November 22, 1927.

IV. PERIODICALS AND NEWSPAPERS

(Key: N—Newspapers; G—Government Publication; M—Magazine.)

Anales de la Facultad de Derecho. Buenos Aires, 1915. (M)

Annuario Catholico do Brasil. Rio de Janeiro, 1928. (M)

The Catholic Historical Review. Washington, 1928. (M)

The Chicago Tribune, Chicago. August 24, 1929. (N)

Christian Science Monitor. Boston, 1918-1933. (N)

The Commonweal. New York, March 25 and April 1, 1931. (M)

Current History Magazine. New York, 1920-1933. (M)

Diario Oficial. Bogotá, January 19, 1928. (G)

Diario Oficial. Mexico, 1916, 1920-1933. (G)

Excelsior. Mexico, 1917-1933. (N)

Gaceta Oficial. Caracas, June 17, 1924. (G)

The Hispanic American Historical Review. Durham, N. C., 1921, 1927, 1933. (M)

La Nación. Santiago de Chile, 1920-1930. (N)

The New York Herald Tribune. New York, Feb. 24, 1926. (N)

The New York Times. New York, 1910-1933. (N)

La Prensa. Buenos Aires, 1923-1928. (N)

La Prensa. New York, 1927-1929. (N)

Razón y Fé. Madrid, 1927. (M)

Revista de Instrucción Pública. Caracas, February, 1910. (G)

*Revista do Instituto Historico e Geographico Brasileiro. Rio de Janeiro, 1838———. (M)

The San Antonio Express. San Antonio, Texas, 1926-1933. (N)

El Universal. Mexico, 1926-1933. (N)

B. SECONDARY REFERENCES

Abad y Queipo, Manuel. *Breve Exposición sobre el Real Patronato.* Madrid, 1820.

Abreu e Lima, José Ignacio de. *Compendio da Historia do Brasil.* Rio de Janeiro, 1843. 2 vols.

Agüero, Raúl. *Guatemala, La Revolución Liberal de 1871 y las Administraciones del Lcdo don Manuel Estrada Cabrera.* San José de Costa Rica, 1914. Exaggerated praise of the liberal cause and its leaders.

Aguirre, Joaquín. *Curso de Disciplina Eclesiástica General*. Madrid, 1871. 4 vols. Used for the origins and early history of the patronage.

Akers, Charles E. A *History of South America, 1854-1904*. London, 1912.

Alamán, Lucas. *Historia de Méjico*. Mexico, 1849-1850. 5 vols. Since Alamán was a conservative supporter of the Church, his data on the wealth of the colonial Church and frank confession of corruption in clerical ranks can be accepted as the truth.

Alberdi, Juan B. *Bases y Puntos de Partida para la Organización de la República Argentina*. Buenos Aires, 1914. This was the famous model used by the Convention of Santa Fé in 1853 in framing the present constitution of the Argentine Republic. Alberdi presents an able argument in favor of religious toleration.

Alessandri, Arturo. *Reformas Constitucionales*. Santiago, 1925. President Alessandri defends separation of Church and State in Chile.

Altamira y Crevea, Rafael. *Historia de España y de la Civilización Española*. Barcelona, 1900-1914. 4 vols. Useful for the origins and early history of the Patronato Español.

Alvarado, Lisandro. *Historia de la Revolución Federal en Venezuela*. Caracas, 1909.

Amunátegui, Miguel Luís. *Los Precursores de la Independencia de Chile*. Santiago, 1870. 3 vols. As one of the contributing causes of the Wars for Independence, the abuses of the ecclesiastical governments of the colonies are discussed. Some of the observations appear to be radical and are not accepted by Galdames.

Arboleda, Gustavo. *Historia Contemporanea de Colombia desde la disolución de la antigua república hasta la época presente*. Bogotá, 1918.

Arguedas, Alcides. *Historia General de Bolivia*. La Paz, 1922. The best modern history of Bolivia.

Arosemena, Justo. *Estudios Constitucionales sobre los gobiernos de la América Latina*. Paris, 1888. 2 vols. Commentaries on the existing (1888) Latin-American constitutions with observations on the religious clauses. Is particularly useful for discussions of the constitutional development of each country.

Artaud de Montor, Alexis Francois. *Histoire du Pape León XII*. Paris, 1873.

Auyso, T. "El Privilegio de los reyes de España en la presentación de obispos," in *Razón y Fé*. Madrid, 1904, II.

Ayarragaray, Lucas. *La Iglesia en América y la Dominación Española*. Buenos Aires, 1920. A scholarly and valuable work. Is one of the first studies of the kind based on materials in the Vatican archives.

Azeredo, Magalhães de. "Dom Pedro II. Traços da sua Physionomia Moral," in *Revista do Instituto Historico e Geographico Brasileiro*. Tomo Especial, 1925.

Balch, Emily G., ed. *Occupied Haiti*. New York, 1927. Report of a committee of six (Women's International League for Peace and Freedom) on conditions in Haiti. Contains some information on the religious and educational situation.

Balderrama, Luís C. *El Clero y el Gobierno de México*. Mexico, 1927. 2 vols. Volume one, "Apuntes Para La Historia de La Crisis en 1926," contains a vigorous pro-government discussion of the recent religious issue.

Bancroft, Hubert Howe. *History of Central America*. San Francisco, 1882-1887. 3 vols. This is the most adequate and accurate history of Central America up to the date of publication. References to the ecclesiastical subjects are rather scattered.

——*History of Mexico*. San Francisco, 1883-1887. 5 vols. Claimed to be the best history of Mexico in any language.

Baralt, Rafael María y Díaz, Ramón. *Resumen de la Historia de Venezuela*. Curazao, 1887. 3 vols. Comprehends the period 1797 to 1837.

Barboza Lima, Alexandre José. "Um Grande Brasileiro, Frei Vital," in *Rev. do Inst. Hist. e Geog.*, LXXI, Pt. II, pp. 145-152. A eulogy of the Bishop of Olinda, major figure in the religious crisis of 1873.

Barrantes, Francisco Montero. *Elementos de Historia de Costa Rica*. San José de Costa Rica, 1892.

Beals, Carleton. *Porfirio Díaz*. Philadelphia and London, 1932. Not as much attention as one might properly expect is devoted to Díaz's religious policy.

Berthe, A. *García Moreno, President de L'Equateur*. Paris, 1887. The "Catholic President" of Ecuador is glorified by his clerical biographer. The work is extravagantly eulogistic and strongly ultramontane.

Brainerd, Heloise. *Public Instruction in Paraguay*. Pan American Union, Washington, 1928. *Bulletin* No. 10. Education Series.

Bravo, Joaquín Rodríguez. *Estudios Constitucionales*. Santiago de Chile, 1888. A commentary on the constitution of 1833. Contains certain useful observations on the patronage.

Browning, Webster E. *The River Plate Republics*. London, 1928. A leading Evangelical Missionary describes religious conditions in Argentina, Paraguay, and Uruguay. Is characterized by considerable sympathetic understanding and tolerance.

Browning, W. E., Ritchie, John, and Grubb, K. G. *The West Coast Republics of South America*. London, 1930. The status of Catholicism and the progress of Protestantism in Peru, Bolivia, and Chile is discussed by Evangelical Missionaries. Severe critics of the Church, their conclusions can be accepted with only minor reservations.

Bulnes, Francisco. *El Verdadero Díaz y la revolución*. Mexico, 1920. An attack on Díaz; a companion work of the author's *Juárez*.

————*Juárez y las Revoluciones de Ayutla y de Reforma*. Mexico, 1905. A scathing attack on Juárez and the Liberals of 1857. A valuable work in that it has helped to tone down the eulogisms of Juárez.

Burnichon, Joseph. *Le Bresil d'ajourd'hui*. Paris, 1910.

Cabrera, Luís. *The Religious Question in Mexico*. New York, 1915. Cabrera, a member of the Catholic Party, discusses clerical political action under Madero and Huerta. Is prejudiced and must be used with caution.

Callcott, Wilfred Hardy. *Church and State in Mexico, 1822-1857*. Durham, 1926. A useful and trustworthy work. There are serious omissions, however: for example, there is no reference to the patronage problem or to papal relations.

————*Liberalism in Mexico, 1857-1929*. Stanford University, 1931. This is a continuation of the author's *Church and State in Mexico, 1822-1857*. Although politico-ecclesiastical relations are not emphasized to the extent that they were in the first volume, these matters are always devoted prime consideration. Chapter XV, "The Church—The Future" is a discussion of the recent conflict.

Camacho, José María. *Compendio de la Historia de Bolivia*. La Paz, 1927.

Cárcano, Ramón J. *Primeras Luchas entre La Iglesia y El Estado en la Gobernación de Tucumán, Siglo XVI*. Buenos Aires, 1929. Vol. IV of the series, *Biblioteca de Historia Argentina y Americana*. Illustrative of the actual relations between the civil and ecclesiastical powers in a frontier Spanish colony in South America.

Cevallos, Pedro Fermín. *Resumen de la Historia del Ecuador desde su origin hasta 1845*. Guayaquil, 1886-1889. 6 vols. The first five volumes comprise the period of the title. Volume VI is a political geography of Ecuador in 1887.

Chacaltana, Cesáreo. *Patronato Nacional Argentino*. Buenos Aires, 1885. A defence of the national prerogatives as against the pretentions of the ultra-clericals. The immediate occasion for this study was the controversy concerning Señor Clara, vicar of Córdoba.

Chapman, Charles E. *A History of the Cuban Republic.* New York, 1927. A scholarly work in which the facts are fearlessly told. Contains a brief statement concerning the religious issue at the time of the establishment of the republic.

Cinta, Rafael Aguirre. *Lecciones de Historia General de Guatemala.* Guatemala, 1899.

Corti, Count Egon Caesar. *Maximilian and Charlotte of Mexico.* New York, 1928. 2 vols. (Catherine Alison Phillips, translator). This is undoubtedly the foremost work on the Emperor Maximilian. His relations with the Mexican clergy are treated in a most adequate manner.

Cramer, Floyd. *Our Neighbor Nicaragua.* New York, 1929.

Crivelli, Camilo. *Los Protestantes y la América Latina.* Rome, 1931. The author a Jesuit, is obsessed with the idea that the United States is using Protestant missionary enterprise to prepare the way for the absorption of Latin America.

Cuevas, Mariano. *Historia de la Iglesia en México.* Mexico, El Paso, 1921-1928. 5 vols. A work representative of considerable industry and not without value. The first four volumes, on colonial New Spain, are more accurate and trustworthy than Volume 5 which was written when Father Cuevas was an exile in the United States and embittered toward the Mexican Government.

Cunningham Graham, R. B. *A Vanished Arcadia.* New York, 1901. A sympathetic treatment of the Jesuit Republic of Paraguay.

Curtis, William E. *Venezuela.* New York, 1896. Used for the Church-State conflict during the régime of Guzmán Blanco. Contains many inaccuracies, but useful nevertheless.

Dávalos y Lissón, Pedro. *La Primera Centuria; Causas geográficas, políticas y económicas que han detenido el progreso moral y material del Peru en el primer siglo de su vida independiente.* Lima, 1919-1926. 4 vols. This work is sincere and accurate. It contains a searching criticism of religious conditions in Peru.

Dellhora, Guillermo. *La Iglesia Católica ante la Crítica en el Pensamiento y en el Arte.* Mexico, 1929. Excerpts of anti-clerical thought culled from the works of the masters in arts, letters, and sciences. Venomously antagonistic toward the church and particularly the pope. A government publication.

Díaz Lemos, Ángel M. *Compendio de Geografía de la República de Colombia.* Barcelona, 1907.

Diccionario Historico, Geographico e Ethnographico do Brasil. Rio de Janeiro, 1922. 2 vols. Commemorative of the first centenary of independence. Published by Instituto Historico e Geographico Brasileiro.

Enock, C. R. *Ecuador*. London, 1914.

Enríquez, Andrés. *La Reforma y Juárez*. Mexico, 1906.

Espinosa, Julio Bañados. *Balmaceda, su Gobierno, y la Revolución de 1891*. Paris, 1894. Contains a very good discussion of the anti-clerical legislation of the 1880's.

Estrada, José Manuel de. *La Iglesia y el Estado y otros Ensayos Políticos y de Crítica Literaria*. Buenos Aires, 1929. Volume XXVII of the series, *Grandes Escritores Argentinos*. A defense of the State-Church system in Argentina, somewhat ultramontane in view.

Fabié, Antonio María. *Ensayo Histórico de la Legislación Española*. Madrid, 1896. Used for a study of the origins of *Real Patronato de las Indias*.

Fermandoiz, José Luís. *El Conflicto Eclesiástico de Tacna*. Santiago, 1923. A full, and fair, discussion of the difficult and delicate problem of ecclesiastical jurisdiction in Tacna and Arica after the War of the Pacific.

Fisher, Lillian Estelle. *Viceregal Administration in the Spanish-American Colonies*. Berkeley, 1926. An excellent and informative section of this book is devoted to the Viceroy as Vice-patron.

Fletcher, James C., and Kidder, D. O. *Brazil and the Brazilians*. Boston, 1866. The authors were Protestant missionaries in Brazil in the 1840's. Their criticism of religious conditions in the Empire is remarkably fair and temperate.

Franklin, James. *The Present State of Haiti*. London, 1822.

Frasso, Pedro. *De Regio Patronato*. Madrid, 1677. Frasso was one of the foremost lay defenders of *regalismo* during the colonial period.

Freire, Felisbello. *Historia Constitucional da Republica dos Estados do Brasil*. Rio de Janeiro, 1894. 3 v. in 2.

García Calderón, Francisco. *Latin America, Its Rise and Progress*. London, 1913. An informing interpretative discussion of Latin American history by a brilliant Peruvian litterateur.

——*Le Pérou Contemporain*. Paris, 1907.

——*Les démocraties latines de l'Amérique*. Paris, 1912.

Galdames, Luís. *Estudio de la Historia de Chile*. Santiago, 1911. The best short history of Chile. In matters relating to the Church is tolerant.

——*Historia de Chile: La Evolución Constitucional 1810-1925*. Santiago, 1926. Vol. I. Volume I, the only volume of the projected work published to date, covers the period 1810-1833.

In so far as the Church and religious problems are discussed, these are treated sympathetically.

Geographia do Brasil. Sociedade de Geographia do Rio de Janeiro, 1923, Vol. X.

Gil Fortoul, José. *Historia Constitucional de Venezuela.* Berlin, 1907-1909. 2 vols. A superior political history of Venezuela to about 1870. For the most part is accurate and trustworthy. Is an invaluable reference for the history of Great Colombia.

Gómez, Hernán F. *Instituciones de la Provincia de Corrientes.* Buenos Aires, 1922. This work proved to be valuable for the study of the relation of the Church to the provincial governments.

González Blanco, Edmundo. *Carranza y La Revolución de México.* Madrid, 1916. "An examination of the Mexican Revolution from the economic and political point of view." A defence before the Spanish people of the Constitutional cause.

Gonzáles Blanco, Pedro. *De Porfirio Díaz á Carranza.* Madrid, 1916. Lectures delivered in the Ateneo (Madrid) "explaining" the Mexican Revolution. Contains interesting material on clerical persecution by the Constitutionalists.

Groot, José Manuel. *Historia Eclesiástica y Civil de Nueva Granada.* Bogotá, 1889-1893. 4 vols. Originally intended to be an ecclesiastical history, but resolved into a political work (to 1830) as well. Written designedly to "correct" contemporary anti-clerical histories.

Grose, Howard B. *Advance in the Antilles.* New York, 1910. A very prejudiced (anti-Catholic) discussion of missionary problems in Cuba and Porto Rico.

Gruening, Ernest. *Mexico and Its Heritage.* New York, 1928. The chapters on the Catholic Church which manifest a pronounced anti-Church bias are the least satisfactory part of an otherwise useful book.

Guerra, José Guillermo. *La Constitución de 1925.* Santiago, 1929. Señor Guerra, a member of the Constituent Convention, discusses the new Constitution and incidentally the act of separation which he supported.

Guía Eclesiástica. Buenos Aires, 1915.

Guinán, Francisco González. *Historia del Gobierno de la Aclamación.* Caracas, 1899. A history of Guzmán Blanco's final tenure of power.

Hackett, Charles Wilson. *The Mexican Revolution and the United States, 1910-1926.* World Peace Foundation, Vol. IX (1926), No. 5. An historical note on Mexico's attitude toward religious organization, written by Denys P. Myers, is appended to Professor Hackett's study.

Henao, Jesús María y Arrubla, Gerardo. *Historia de Colombia*. Bogotá, 1912. 2 vols. The best short modern history of Colombia.

Holme, John G. *The Life of Leonard Wood*. New York, 1920. Contains a discussion of Wood's handling of religious problems in Cuba.

Humboldt, Alexander von. *Ensayo Político sobre el Reyno de la Nueva España*. Madrid, 1811. 2 vols. Translated from the original French. A valuable reference for the economic status of the Church and the clergy in New Spain on the eve of independence.

Huneeus y Gana, Dr. Jorge. *Obras de Don Jorge Huneeus*. Santiago, 1890. 2 vols. A noted commentator on the Chilean constitution. He makes interesting observations (Vol. I) on the religious article (Article 5).

Icazbalceta, Joaquín García. *Biografía de don Fr. Juan de Zumárraga*. Mexico, 1881. For the early political status of the Church in New Spain.

Ingenieros, José. *La Evolución de las Ideas Argentinas*. Buenos Aires, 1918. A scholarly work which contains much valuable information regarding the early relations of the Church and State in Argentina.

Inman, Samuel Guy. *South America Today*. New York, 1921. A discussion of the religious outlook in South America by the Secretary of the Committee on Coöperation in Latin America (An Evangelical Missionary organization).

James, Herman G. *Brazil After a Century of Independence*. New York, 1925.

――――*The Constitutional System of Brazil*. Washington, 1923. A scholarly study. Contains copies of both the imperial and the republican constitutions.

Koebel, W. H. *Paraguay*. London, 1917.

Lea, H. C. *The Inquisition in the Spanish Dependencies*. New York, 1908. A classic treatment of the subject.

Lee, John. *Religious Liberty in South America*. New York, 1907. Useful for religious legislation in Ecuador under President Eloy Alfaro.

Léger, J. N. *Haiti, Her History and Her Detractors*. New York, 1907. Written by the Haitian minister to the United States in an effort to present "the facts" to the American people. Somewhat colored by prejudice, but as a whole is a very acceptable work.

Legón, Faustino J. *Doctrina y Ejercicio del Patronato Nacional*. Buenos Aires, 1920. According to Father Leturia (*La acción diplomática*, p. 42, n. 25) this is "a book of solid doctrine (ultramontane), exact historical method, and based on a great quantity of materials, printed and unprinted, although the latter are only from the Buenos Aires archives." The book, says the Jesuit historian, is somewhat deficient because of failure to use the Vatican archives.

Leturia, P. Pedro. "Alusiones en la Cámara Argentina al Origen Histórico del Patronato de Indias," in *Razón y Fé*, 1927, Vol. 78, pp. 326-335.

———"El Origen Histórico del Patronato de Indias," in *Razón y Fé*, 1927, Vol. 78, pp. 20-36.

———*La Acción Diplomática de Bolívar ante Pío VII, 1820-1823.* Madrid, 1925. An excellent work of research based almost exclusively on materials in the Vatican archives.

———"La Célebre Encíclica de León XII sobre la independencia de la América española en 21 de septiembre de 1824," in *Razón y Fé*, May, 1925.

Levene, Ricardo. *Lecciones de Historia Argentina.* Buenos Aires, 1919. 2 vols. Regarded as the best short history of Argentina. Contains only a summary discussion of the Church in Argentina.

Lippmann, Walter. "Church and State in Mexico. The American Mediation," in *Foreign Affairs.* VIII. No. 2 (January, 1930), pp. 186-208. An account of the mediation of Ambassador Morrow in the Church-State conflict in Mexico.

Lleras Acosta, Carlos Alberto. *Instrucción Cívica.* Bogotá, 1926.

Lorente, Sebastián. *Historia del Peru bajo los Borbones.* Lima, 1871. Contains statements on ecclesiastical conditions in the viceroyalty of Peru on the eve of independence.

Lugan, Abbe Alphonse. "Church and State in Mexico," in *Current History,* February, 1931, pp. 672-676. An exposition of the *modus vivendi* of 1929.

McBride, George McCutchen. *The Land Systems of Mexico.* New York, 1923. The agrarian problem as it affected the Church and vice versa, are somewhat neglected in this work.

Magalhães, Basilio de. "D. Pedro II e a Egreja," in *Revista do Instituto Historico e Geographico Brasileiro,* Vol. 152 (1928), pp. 385-409.

Maria, Padre Julio. "A Religão," in *O Livro do Centenario.* Rio de Janeiro, 1901.

Marsh, Margaret A. *The Bankers in Bolivia.* New York, 1928.

Martin, P. A. "Causes of the Collapse of the Brazilian Empire," in *The Hispanic American Historical Review,* IV (1921), pp. 4-48.

Martin, Percy F. *Mexico of the Twentieth Century.* London, 1907.

———*Maximilian in Mexico.* New York, 1914. Useful for religious policies and relations during the Second Empire.

——Peru in the Twentieth Century. London, 1911.

Marure, Alejandro. Bosquejo Histórico de las Revoluciones de Centro-América desde 1811 hasta 1834. Guatemala, 1877-1878. 2 vols. A Liberal, and partisan, history written by order of President Mariano Gálvez of Guatemala.

Matienzo, José N. Cuestiones de Derecho Público Argentino. Buenos Aires, 1924. One of the "cases" discussed in this work is that of the patronage.

Mecham, J. Lloyd. "Latin America's Fight Against Clerical Domination," in Current History, January, 1929, pp. 565-570.

——"The Origins of Real Patronato de Indias," in The Catholic Historical Review, July, 1928, pp. 205-228.

——"The Papacy and Spanish-American Independence," in The Hispanic American Historical Review, May, 1929, pp. 154-175.

Medina, José Toribio. Historia del Tribunal del Santo Oficio de la Inquisición en México. Santiago, 1905. A master work on the Inquisition.

Melick, Edith M. Seed Sowing in Honduras. St. Louis, Mo., 1927.

Menéndez Mena, Rodolfo. The Work of the Clergy and the Religious Persecution in Mexico. New York, 1916. Revelations of anti-clerical outrages by the Constitutionalists.

Monsalve, José D. El Ideal Político del Libertador Simón Bolívar. Madrid, 1917. 2 vols. The final chapter in this original work (II, Chap. 26) is devoted to Bolívar's religious ideals. Bolívar, according to Monsalve, was a sincere Catholic, and were it not for this he would never have been Liberator.

Montalvo, Juan. Las Catilinarias. Paris, 1925. 2 vols. Ecuador under General Vientemilla and the régime which followed García Moreno.

Montúfar, Lorenzo. El General Francisco Morazán. Guatemala, 1896. The life and career of the great Liberal written in a partisan manner by a notable Liberal historian.

——Reseña Histórica de Centro-América. Guatemala, 1878-1881. A Liberal history. Designed to supplement the work of Marure. A violently anti-clerical work. Extends to about 1850.

Montúfar, Manuel. Memorias para la Historia de la Revolución de Centro-América. Jalapa, 1832.

Mora, José María Luís. Obras Sueltas. Paris, 1847. 2 vols. Essays on government and politics. Useful for the period following the establishment of the first federal republic in Mexico.

Moraes, Eugenio Vilhena de. "O Patriotismo e o Clero no Brasil," in Revista do Instituto Historico e Geographico Brasileiro. Rio de Janeiro, 1925. Tomo 99. Vol. 153, pp. 113-168.

Moses, Bernard. *Spain's Declining Power in South America.* Berkeley, 1919. Allusions to the ecclesiastical state of South America in the middle of the eighteenth century.

———*The Spanish Dependencies in South America.* New York, 1914. 2 vols. "The Church in Relation to the Civil Government" (Chap. XII, Vol. II) is one of the best short discussions of the *real patronato.*

———*The Intellectual Background of the Revolution in South America, 1810-1824.* New York, 1926.

Mossé, Benjamin. *Dom Pedro II.* Paris, 1889.

Munro, Dana G. *The Five Republics of Central America.* New York, 1918. After Bancroft this is the most acceptable history of Central America. The discussions of the religious issues, however, are inadequate.

Núñez, Rafael. *La Reforma Política en Colombia.* Bogotá, 1886. The famous Colombian President reveals somewhat incidentally his ideas on religious policy.

O'Leary, Daniel F. *Bolívar y la Emancipación de Sud-América.* Madrid, 1915. 2 vols. *Memorias* of General O'Leary, comrade of the Liberator. Translated from English by his son Simón B. O'Leary.

Oliveira Lima, Manuel. *Formation Historique de la Nationalité Brazilienne.* Paris, 1911.

Otero, Mariano. *Ensayo sobre la Cuestión Social.* Mexico, 1842. An acceptable discussion, with statistical data, of the religious situation in Mexico after the establishment of the Republic.

Pastoral Letter of the Catholic Episcopate of the United States on the Religious Situation in Mexico. New York, December, 1926. A defence of the Mexican clergy whom it was charged the Mexican Government wished to enslave. Issued for propaganda purposes in the United States.

Phipps, Helen. *Some Aspects of the Agrarian Question in Mexico.* University of Texas *Bulletin,* No. 2515. Austin, 1925. A very useful study of the land problem in Mexico during the colonial and republican periods. Since the extensive ecclesiastical holdings was a major issue, considerable attention is devoted to agrarian legislation as it affected the Church.

Piaggio, Agustín. *La Influencia del Clero en la Independencia Argentina, 1810-1820.* Barcelona, 1912. An exposition of the contribution of the clergy of La Plata to the winning of independence.

Pineda, E. R. "Church and State in Mexico," in *The Commonweal,* New York, March 25, and April 1, 1931.

Puig Casauranc, José Manuel. *La Cuestión religiosa en relación con la educación pública en México.* Mexico, 1928.

Rebello, Annibal Velloso. "García Moreno," in *Revista do Instituto Historico e Geographico Brasileiro,* Rio de Janeiro, 1920, CXLI, pp. 75-214.

Renan, Ernest. *Histoire des Origines du Christianisme.* Paris, 1863-1899. 7 vols. Renan describes (VI, 93 ff.) early episcopal elections.

Republic of Salvador, The. International Bureau of American Republics, Washington, 1892. *Bulletin* No. 58.

Restrepo, José Manuel. *Historia de la Revolución de la República de Colombia.* Besançon, 1858. 4 vols. An excellent history of the Revolution to the breakup of Great Colombia.

Restrepo, Juan Pablo. *La Iglesia y el Estado en Colombia.* London, 1881. The status of the Church in its relation to the State is fully discussed from every angle. This is one of the most comprehensive and scholarly treatments the writer has seen.

Revista de Costa Rica en el Siglo XIX. San José de Costa Rica, 1902.

Ribadeneyra, Antonio Joaquín de. *Manuel Compendio de el Regio Patronato Indiano.* Madrid, 1755. Ribadeneyra was the outstanding exponent of regalism during the colonial period. His study was "official."

Riva Palacio, Vicente, ed. *México á Través de Los Siglos.* Mexico, Barcelona, 1888-89. 5 vols. This is the best history of Mexico with the possible exception of Bancroft's *History of Mexico.* The extensive reproduction of sources makes it to a large extent a collection of source materials. This work is conspicious among Mexican histories for its balanced judgment.

Robertson, William Spence. *History of the Latin-American Nations.* New York, 1925.

———*Rise of the Spanish-American Republics.* New York, 1918.

Roldán, Alcibiades. *Elementos de Derecho Constitucional de Chile.* Santiago, 1917. Commentaries on the Chilean Constitution. A useful reference for the political status of the established cult. Contains interesting observations on the patronage.

Rowe, Leo S. *The Federal System of the Argentine Republic.* Washington, 1921.

Saldías, Adolfo. *Historia de la Confederación Argentina, Rosas y su Época.* Buenos Aires, 1911. 5 vols. Used particularly for a study of the Church under the Rosas dictatorship. The author is remarkably sympathetic toward Rosas, and seeks to defend his religious policy.

Salgado, Félix. *Elementos de Historia de Honduras.* Tegucigalpa, 1927.

Sallusti, José. *Historia de las Misiones Apostólicas de Monseñor Juan Muzi en el Estado de Chile.* Santiago, 1906. A full account of the famous mission of Apostolic Delegate Muzi to Chile in 1823.

Sarsfield, Dalmacio Vélez. *Relaciones del Estado con la Iglesia en la Antigua América Española*. Buenos Aires, 1889. A vigorous defence of *patronato nacional* by one of Argentina's leading Constitutional lawyers.

Schoenrich, Otto. *Santo Domingo*. New York, 1918.

Shea, J. J. *The Life of Pope Pius IX*. New York, 1877.

Silva, J. Francisco V. *El Libertador Bolívar y el Deán Funes en la Política Argentina*. Madrid, 1918. This work, devoted to the support of Bolívar's plan of Spanish-American unity by the famous dean, contains some information on the ecclesiastical policy in La Plata.

Skelton, Byron G. *Electoral Theories and Practices in Mexico*. University of Texas, 1928. M. A. Thesis.

Smith, Justin H. *The War with Mexico*. New York, 1919. 2 vols.

Solórzano y Pereyra, Juan de. *Política Indiana*. Madrid, 1776. 2 vols. This was the foremost commentary on the Laws of the Indies. Solórzano, like Ribadeneyra, defended *regalismo*.

Stanger, Francis Merriman. "Church and State in Peru," in *The Hispanic American Historical Review*, November, 1927, pp. 410-437.

Stoddard, Lathrop. *The French Revolution in San Domingo*. New York, 1914.

Stuart, Graham H. *The Governmental System of Peru*. Washington, 1925. This is an excellent discussion not only of the present Constitution, but also of the preceding Constitutions of Peru.

Toro, Alfonso. *La Iglesia y El Estado en México*. Mexico, 1927. A publication of the *Archivo General de la Nación, Secretaría de Gobernación*. A survey of the conflicts between the Catholic clergy and the Mexican governments from independence to 1926. A very cursory treatment of the events since 1901. This work was one of the numerous "official" studies published in defense of the anti-clerical program of the Calles administration.

Uroz, Antonio. *La Cuestión Religiosa en México*. Mexico, 1926. A defense of the policy of President Calles in the crisis of 1926.

Vedia, Agustín de. *Constitución Argentina*. Buenos Aires, 1907. An able commentary.

Vedia y Mitre, Mariano de. *De Rivadavia á Rosas*. Buenos Aires, 1930. Volume V of the series, *Biblioteca de Historia Argentina y Americana,* presents a brief discussion of the reforms of Rivadavia.

————*El Gobierno del Uruguay: Estudio Constitucional de la Reforma de 1917*. Buenos Aires, 1919.

Veloz Goiticoa, N. *Venezuela. Caracas*, 1905.

Vera-Estañol, Jorge. *Carranza and His Bolshevik Régime*. Los Angeles, Cal., 1920. A severe attack on Carranza's policies, including his anti-religious measures.

Vergara, Francisco V. *Historia de Chile*. Valparaiso, 1898.

Vianna, Oliveira. "A Queda do Imperio," in *Rev. do Inst. Hist. e Geog.* Tomo Especial, 1925. pp. 787-887.

Villanueva, Carlos A. *La Santa Alianza*. Paris, 1912.

Villarán, L. F. *La Constitución Peruana*. Lima, 1899. A commentary on the Constitution of 1860.

Viveiros de Castro, A. O. "Contribuições para a Biographia de D. Pedro II," in *Rev. do Inst. Hist. e Geog.* Tomo Especial, 1925. pp. 477-534.

Walle, Paul. *Bolivia*. London, 1914.

Walsh, R. *Notices of Brazil in 1828 and 1829*. Boston, 1831. 2 vols.

Ward, H. G. *Mexico in 1827*. London, 1828. 2 vols. Britain's first minister to Mexico does not neglect brief mention in his well-known book of the religious situation in Mexico.

Warden, David B. *Histoire de L' Empire du Brezil depues sa Découverte jusqua nos jours*. Paris, 1832-1833. 2 vols.

Washburn, Charles A. *A History of Paraguay*. Boston, 1871. 2 vols.

Watters, Mary. "The Present Status of the Church in Venezuela," in the *Hispanic American Historical Review*, XIII (February, 1933), pp. 23-45.

Welles, Sumner. *Naboth's Vineyard, The Dominican Republic, 1844-1924*. New York, 1928. 2 vols. The most recent and the best history of the Dominican Republic. There are scattered references to the Church and the clergy.

Whatley, William A. *The Formation of the Mexican Constitution of 1824*. University of Texas, 1921. M. A. Thesis.

Wheeler, W. R. and Browning, W. E. *Modern Missions on the Spanish Main*. Philadelphia, 1925. A discussion of Protestant missionary enterprise in Colombia and Venezuela. A searching, and sometimes too severe criticism of the deficiencies of Roman Catholicism in the two republics.

Williams, Mary W. "The Ecclesiastical Policy of Francisco Morazán and Other Central American Liberals," in *The Hispanic American Historical Review*, May, 1920, pp. 119-143.

————*The People and Politics of Latin America*. Boston, 1930.

Winter, Nevin O. *Brazil and her People of Today*. Boston, 1910.

Wood, Eric F. *Leonard Wood*. New York, 1920. There is a brief discussion in this work of Wood's able management of Church problems in Cuba.

Zamora, Matías Gómez. *Regio Patronato Español é Indiano*. Madrid,

1897. A very scholarly study of patronato. Is perhaps the leading work written from the ultramontane viewpoint.

Zavala, Lorenzo de. *Ensayo Histórico de las Revoluciones de México desde 1808 hasta 1830.* Mexico, 1845. 2 vols. Zavala's anti-clerical bias often leads him to extravagant and ludicrous limits. Is a useful work for factual information but one must be on guard against the conclusions.

Ziegler, Aloysius K. *Church and State in Visigothic Spain.* Washington, D. C., 1930.

Zubieta, Pedro A. *Apuntaciones sobre las Primeras Misiones Diplomáticas de Colombia.* Bogotá, 1924. This work contains in Chapter XXX an excellent discussion of Colombian relations with the papacy until the time of papal recognition.

INDEX

Abad y Queipo, Manuel, Bishop-elect of Michoacán, opposes confiscation, 48; excommunicates Hidalgo, 62-63; removed from see, 64; leaves Mexico, 405
Acta Constitutiva (Mexico), religious clauses in, 401
Adrian VI, pope, concession to Spanish Crown, 11
Agrelo, *fiscal*, champion of patronage (Argentina), 281, 282
Aguascalientes, bishopric of, 458
Aguilar, President of Salvador, 380
Aguirre y Texada, Dr. Juan Luís de, report on patronage, 57
Akers, C. E., quoted, 167-168
Alamán, Lucas, on wealth of Colonial Church, 46; quoted, 51, 64, 65, 395; ultramontane, 407; manages return of Santa Anna, death of, 425
Alberdi, Juan Bautista, religion in constitutional project of, 286; represents Argentina at Rome, 290-291; on patronage, 292
Alberti, Manuel, clerical supporter of independence, 60
Alessandri, Arturo, President of Chile, sponsors separation, 268; quoted on separation, 270
Alexander II, pope, concedes right of presentation, 8
Alexander VI, pope, grants of to Catholic Kings, 11; famous bulls of, 13; grants request of Catholic Kings, 14; Aragonese, issues bull, 15; contributions of to *real patronato de Indias*, 20-21
Alfaro, Eloy, President of Ecuador, anti-clerical policy of, 188; new constitution of, separation of Church and State by, 189
Alfonso X, King of Castile, claims control over episcopal elections, 9
Almonte, General Juan, President of Regency (Mexico), 446
Alpuche, José María, organizes Masonic branch, 403
Alto Peru, *see* Bolivia
Alvarado, Salvador, Constitutionalist general, quoted, 462-463
Álvarez, Juan, provisional president of Mexico, 428; ousted, 430

Alvear, President of Argentina, 297
Anchorena, Tomás Manuel de, member of *apostólicos*, 280; Minister of Cult (Argentina), 281; doubts validity of patronage, 282, 283, 296
Ancón, Treaty of, religious problem contributed by, 265
Andrada, José Bonifacio de, drafts Brazilian constitution, 307
Andre y Guerrero, patriot bishop, 69
Angelini, Mexican confidential agent in Rome, 459
Antonelli, Jacobo, Cardinal Secretary of State, negotiates concordat, 176; involvement in Brazilian religious question, 319; signs concordat with Haiti, 344, with Guatemala, 374, with Salvador, 380
Aparicio, Spanish *chargé* at Rome, 83; opposes Friar Pacheco, 87; objects to Chilean delegation, 89
Arana, Felipe, disapproves patronage (Argentina), 283
Arancel Eclesiástico, schedule of fees in La Paz, 226
Araujo, Nabuco de, proposes reform of regulars in Brazil, 313
Arce, Manuel José, President of the Central American Federation, short-lived anti-clerical reform, 364-365; abandons anti-clericalism, 368-369; reaction disgusts, retires, 369
Ardreú, Rafael, bishop *in partibus*, Córdova, 68
Arequipa, Bishop of, in Tacna-Arica religious controversy, 265-266
Argentina, *Estatuto Provisional*, Constitution of 1819, 55; patronage claimed by *Junta*, patronal problem concerning see of Córdova, 57; patronal pretentions, 58; clerical support of independence, 59-60; clerical opposition to independence, 68-69; early attempts to negotiate with Rome, 77; Pacheco negotiates for in Rome, 86; Muzi in, 90-91; appointment of titular bishops for, 104; religion in Constitution of 1819, 275-276; reforms of Rivadavia, 276-277; opposition and acceptance of Rivadavia's reforms, 277-278; tolerance in, 279; assertion and defence of patronal powers, 279-281; dis-

35

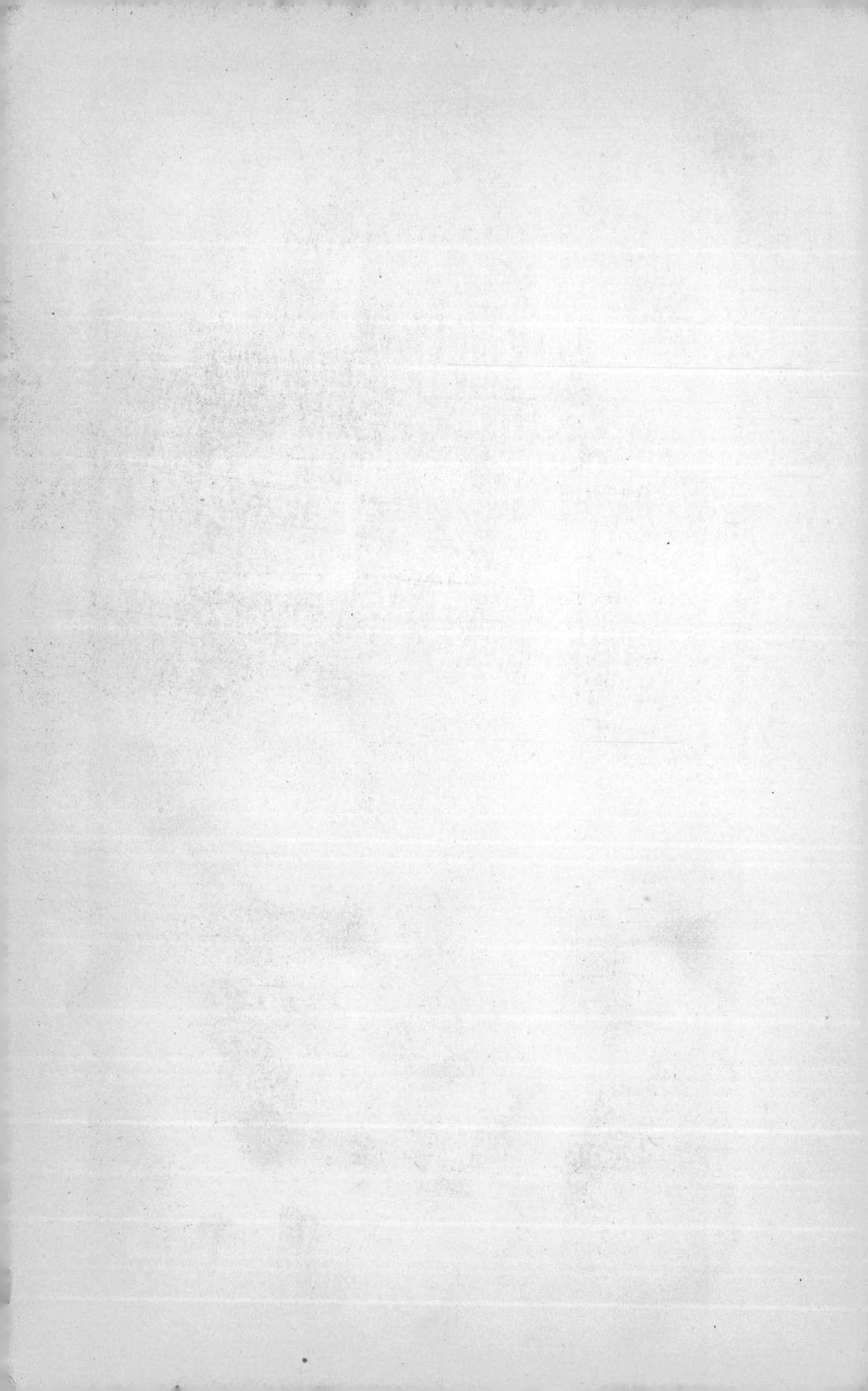